Welcoming Students Who Are Deaf-Blind into Typical Classrooms

Welcoming Students Who Are Deaf-Blind into Typical Classrooms

Facilitating School Participation, Learning, and Friendships

Edited by

Norris G. Haring, Ed.D.
Professor Emeritus
College of Education
Office of Special Education
University of Washington, Seattle

and

Lyle T. Romer, Ph.D.
Project Coordinator
College of Education
Office of Special Education
University of Washington, Seattle

·P·A·U·L·H·
BROOKES
PUBLISHING CO

Baltimore • London • Toronto • Sydney

Paul H. Brookes Publishing Co.
Post Office Box 10624
Baltimore, Maryland 21285-0624

Copyright © 1995 by Paul H. Brookes Publishing Co., Inc.
All rights reserved.

Typeset by Brushwood Graphics, Inc., Baltimore, Maryland.
Manufactured in the United States of America by
The Maple Press Co., York, Pennsylvania.

Library of Congress Cataloging-in-Publication Data

Welcoming students who are deaf-blind into typical classrooms :
    facilitating school participation, learning, and friendships /
    edited by Norris G. Haring and Lyle T. Romer.
        p.   cm.
    Includes bibliographical references and index.
    ISBN 1-55766-144-8
    1. Blind-deaf children—Education—United States.
    2. Mainstreaming in education—United States.   I. Haring, Norris
    G., 1923–   .   II. Romer, Lyle T.
    HV1597.2.W45   1995
    371.1′1′0973—dc20   94-44799
                                                                    CIP

British Library Cataloguing-in-Publication data are available from the British Library.

Contents

Contributors

Felix F. Billingsley, Ph.D.
Professor
College of Education
Office of Special Education
University of Washington
Experimental Education Unit, WJ-10
Seattle, Washington 98195

Catherine Breen, Ph.D.
Coordinator of Special Education Support
  Services
Santa Barbara County Education Office
4400 Cathedral Oaks Road
Santa Barbara, California 93160-6307

Andrew R. Byrne, M.S.
Certified Mental Health Counselor and
  Consultant
A.R. Bryne & Associates
946 East Hemmi Road
Everson, Washington 98247

Philippa H. Campbell, Ph.D.
Center for Research in Human Development
  and Education
Temple University
9th Floor, Ritter Hall Annex
13th & Cecil B. Moore Avenue
Philadelphia, Pennsylvania 19122

Joyce Ford
Parent
4640 Seymour Drive
Boise, Idaho 83704

Bud Fredericks, Ed.D.
Research Professor
Teaching Research Division
Western Oregon State College
345 Monmouth Avenue
Monmouth, Oregon 97361

Charles W. Freeman, M.Ed.
Office of Special Education Programs
U.S. Department of Education
400 Maryland Avenue
Washington, D.C. 20202

Kathleen Gee, Ph.D.
Assistant Professor
Department of Special Education
University of Kansas
3001 Dole Building
Lawrence, Kansas 66045

Lori Goetz, Ph.D.
Department of Special Education
San Francisco State University
California Research Institute
612 Font Boulevard
San Francisco, California 94132

Norris G. Haring, Ed.D.
Professor Emeritus
College of Education
Office of Special Education
University of Washington
103 Miller Hall, DQ-12
Seattle, Washington 98195

Thomas Haring, Ph.D. (deceased)

Joan Houghton, MS.Ed.
Program Associate
Helen Keller National Center—
    Technical Assistance Center
4330 Shawnee Mission Parkway, #108
Shawnee Mission, Kansas 66205-2522

Robert Huven, M.Ed.
Consultant
Washington Programs for Children with
    Deaf-Blindness
Puget Sound Educational Service District
400 S.W. 152nd Street
Burien, Washington 98166-2209

Kathleen Liberty, Ph.D.
Senior Lecturer in Education
University of Canterbury
Private Bag 4800
Christchurch
NEW ZEALAND

Bonnie McBride, M.S.
Project Coordinator
Inclusive Education Research Group
University of Washington
Experimental Education Unit, WJ-10
Seattle, Washington 98195

Barbara A.B. McLetchie, Ph.D.
Coordinator
Teacher Preparation in Deaf-Blindness
Boston College
Campion Hall—CASE
Chestnut Hill, Massachusetts 02167-3813

Rona L. Pogrund, Ph.D.
Consultant, Visual Impairments
10042 Circleview Drive
Austin, Texas 78733

Jeanne Glidden Prickett, Ed.D.
Coordinator of Materials Development
AFB Deaf-Blind Project
c/o Mississippi School for the Deaf
Superintendent Residence
1253 Eastover Drive
Jackson, Mississippi 39211

Lyle T. Romer, Ph.D.
Project Coordinator
College of Education
Office of Special Education
University of Washington
103 Miller Hall, DQ-12
Seattle, Washington 98195

Mary A. Romer
Project Director
Residential Technical Assistance Project
Catholic Community Services
1932 1st Avenue, Suite 905
Seattle, Washington 98101

Richard Rosenberg, Ph.D.
Vocational Coordinator
Whittier Union High School District
9401 South Painter Avenue
Whittier, California 90605

Richard Schutz, Ph.D.
Associate Professor
Child and Family Studies
Florida Mental Health Institute
University of South Florida
Tampa, Florida 33620

Ilene S. Schwartz, Ph.D.
Assistant Professor
College of Education
Office of Special Education
103 Miller Hall, DQ-12
Seattle, Washington 98195

Shepherd Siegel, Ph.D.
Director, King County Vocational/
    Special Education Coooperative
Director, Career Ladder Program
Puget Sound Educational Service District
400 S.W. 152nd Street
Burien, Washington 98166-2209

Kathleen Stremel, M.A.
Principal Investigator
Department of Special Education
University of Southern Mississippi
Box 5115
Hattiesburg, Mississippi 39406-5115

R. Paul Thompson, M.A.
Former Deputy Director
Division of Education Services
Office of Special Education Programs
U.S. Department of Education
4007-D Bridgeport Way West
Tacoma, Washington 98464

Therese Rafalowski Welch, M.Ed.
Coordinator of Consortium Activities
AFB Deaf-Blind Project
P.O. Box 183
Webster, New York 14580

Jennifer White
Technical Assistance Coordinator
Friends for Life Project
Puget Sound Educational Service District
400 S.W. 152nd Street
Burien, Washington 98166-2209

Foreword

From Miracle Workers to Teachers: Where We Have Been and Where We Are Going

Since the mid-1970s, special education has gradually moved from a medically driven, diagnostic-prescriptive approach designed to remediate deficits toward an outcomes-driven orientation designed to produce valued and connected lifestyles. Once viewed by many as a place, special education is emerging as an instructional support and active partner in creating classrooms and schools where both adults and children work together to support the active learning and membership of all students. Although teachers were once expected to be "the experts" who imparted wisdom and directed learning, they are increasingly becoming members of collaborative teams. Collaboration involves teachers working with parents and other school personnel to plan, adapt, implement, problem solve, and provide supports for the meaningful involvement of students in social and academic activities. As part of systemic educational reform initiatives, classrooms across the nation are being restructured to meet multiple instructional needs.

As I read the contents of this book, I was reminded of how the trends and evolution of special education are reflected in our personal and professional experiences. Nearly 20 years ago I was forced to examine my beliefs about disability and pedagogy as a graduate student in the "multihandicapped hearing impaired" teacher training program at Gallaudet University. I came to this program equipped with both classroom teaching and residential program experience involving a broad range of individuals with diverse abilities (and disability labels). I had teaching credentials in elementary and special education (i.e., categorical certification in "blind and partially sighted," "all classes of the mentally retarded," and "orthopedic and physical handicaps"). In addition, I had grown up among people who were deaf and others who had cognitive disabilities; I believed that I viewed deafness and other disabilities as part of the human condition.

However, this belief was challenged during a meeting to plan coursework when my adviser asked me about the types of students I wanted to work with and the schools I was interested in for practicum experience. I am embarrassed to admit that I responded, "Anyone, anyplace will be fine, but, please, *not* deaf-blind students!" Despite numerous positive experiences with people who were deaf and people who were blind, I had wholeheartedly bought into the concept that in deaf-blind individuals, the deafness and blindness were not additive but resulted in a dramatically different (and devastating) disability. My perception of "deaf-blindness" was one of overwhelming darkness, silence, and isolation that required teachers to be "miracle workers." Frankly, I did not think I was up to this seemingly insurmountable challenge.

Fortunately, my adviser did not honor my request and instead scheduled me to work with students labeled as deaf-blind at several school sites! As I became increasingly involved with students who were deaf-blind (some due to maternal rubella, others due to Usher syndrome), I learned that despite their shared label, each individual student possessed a unique personality with diverse interests, abilities, and challenges. I discovered that in spite of our differences—or maybe because of them—people are united by the common need to be connected to and valued by others.

Around the time of the passage of the Education for All Handicapped Children Act of 1975 (PL 94-142), I remember speaking with many parents of children with disabilities who were grateful to have people willing to work with their children, appreciative that their children could now attend public schools, and thankful for someone to recognize that their children had skills and not just deficits and labels. I also recall being told how special and how patient we "special ed types" were: special people, doing special things, with special children, slowly and patiently. For me, such "professional preciousness" was correlated to a "wonderful facility syndrome," in which I believed there had to be a critical mass of highly trained specialists with special equipment to work with kids with low-incidence disabilities. "Bring them to us!" It took me an inordinately long time to understand that perhaps the reference to a "normal rhythm of the day for a school-age child" meant that the child was actually considered a valued member of his or her neighborhood school community. I began questioning the effectiveness of a service delivery system that separated students from their families, schools, and communities.

After feeling entirely too "special" for too long, I began to question whether I had been too willing to buy into an ethic that was as egocentric as it was patronizing and stigmatizing. Such questioning led to the process of letting go of professional preciousness while striving for interactions that were respectful and did not stigmatize disability, yet still acknowledged and addressed the multifaceted issues involved with providing supports to produce valued lifestyles.

While clarifying one's beliefs is critical, our values must be wedded to instructional technology—just as process needs to be married to outcomes. The complex support needs of students who are deaf-blind (e.g., language and communication, orientation and mobility, adaptation of sensory information) must be addressed while ensuring delivery of appropriate instructional/academic content, attainment of functional life skills, and development of social relationships and social networks. Achieving valued student outcomes requires us to work together as team members to solve problems and to celebrate successes. Teachers can no longer be "the experts," nor is this desirable. We cannot do it alone; rather we must listen to and learn from parents and the students themselves as well as specialists and other educators. However, establishing and maintaining a collaborative ethic can be as challenging as it is rewarding!

Since working at the U.S. Department of Education's Office of Special Education Programs, I have had the opportunity to work with talented people from across the nation who are committed to producing meaningful and valued outcomes for students in inclusive school programs. Some of what I have learned follows:

- There is no one strategy to promote inclusive school environments and bottom-up change. Context is critical.
- Resistance to inclusion must be dealt with by respecting and acknowledging people's concerns, creating a vision, and providing resources to enable teachers to implement effective integrated educational services. Coercion is not an effective strategy to install durable systemic reform and improvement.
- The notion of inclusion is slippery, depending for its meaning not just on a description of events or conditions, but also on the meaning it holds for those involved in the experience. Although students with disabilities may be physically integrated, they may remain socially and programmatically isolated in school classes (even in classes working to be inclusive).
- The concept of "school membership" is one way in which to view student inclusion in the school community. The structure of the school day (e.g., class scheduling, how students move through the schedule) and how instructional content is delivered are factors that may define membership across different school contexts. How these factors contribute to whether students are identified as "visitors" rather than "members" of a class are issues to be considered.
- "School membership status" may be easier to achieve in high schools because every student can be viewed as a "visitor." High school classes are 1) periodic, 2) limited in duration, 3) composed of different students, and 4) taught by multiple teachers. All students follow an individualized, multiclass schedule, and, in a sense, all students can be viewed as "visitors" who move from class to class. This individual scheduling and student movement in the school allows students with disabilities to move to and from general education classes, into community-based instruction, and back into school without creating a disruption in the instructional sequence or social fabric of the high school environment.
- In contrast to the high school environment, elementary school classes tend to 1) stay in the same classroom setting, 2) move within the school as a unit, 3) have stable student composition throughout the school day, and 4) be taught by one teacher. Rather than having an individualized schedule, students tend to function as part of large or small groups. Having a student with disabilities move in and out of the general education elementary classroom may disrupt the programmatic and social milieu of the class and contributes to the child being viewed as a "visitor" rather than as a "school/class member."
- The presence of an adult can sometimes be a stimulus to set the student with disabilities apart from classmates. The issue of providing support is complex and everchanging. For example, teaching assistants may feel they need to provide individualized instruction to students who are deaf-blind in order to "do their job" in inclusive settings. When this occurs, the teaching assistant may become a "paid barrier" in the physical, social, and academic inclusion of students. Among the challenges for adults (e.g., teacher, interpreter/tutor, intervenor, teaching assistant) are 1) ensuring that students are actively involved and have access to adequate contextual informaion and 2) knowing when to

fade supports so that the adult is not a paid barrier who obstructs membership and participation in inclusive school contexts.

- Sometimes architectural and communication barriers appear insurmountable to students, families, and school personnel and contribute to attitudinal barriers in household, school, and community environments. There is often minimal use of adaptations and accommodations to increase participation and inclusion; many parents and professionals may erroneously conclude that the student does not fit into the activity and thus maybe the student doesn't need to be there. This happens more frequently than most people would care to recognize.

- Collaborative team members must remain vigilant to ensure that they use and refine strategies that result in student inclusion physically, socially, and programmatically.

Recently a parent telephoned me to share an experience she had with her daughter's school. During a meeting she asked questions about the school's transition from a self-contained classroom model that provided some integration to a full inclusion program. The special ed director told her, "Trust me, I know what's best for your child." Rather than viewing this parent as a team member, the implementers of this "inclusive school program" dismissed her issues and concerns; she was excluded from the ongoing process of designing inclusive school contexts for her child. What is wrong with this picture? Was this an example of professionals clinging to "miracle worker" status? Did school personnel have the world view that they, rather than the student and his or her family, are the critical element? What about empowerment, developing a shared vision, and designing strategies via collaborative problem solving? Are our actions and words consistent with our beliefs and values?

The contents of this book, *Welcoming Students Who Are Deaf-Blind into Typical Classrooms: Facilitating School Participation, Learning, and Friendships*, provides a comprehensive picture of inclusive educational practices that are now occurring across the United States. This information reflects the simultaneous expansion of the field's knowledge base as well as the experiential base of parents and professionals. The authors describe, respect, and acknowledge the complex instructional support needs of students who are deaf-blind. As the contents illustrate, there is no one strategy to promote inclusive school environments. I hope this book will help to bridge the gap between our rhetoric and our actions so that we create schools that have the capacity to provide meaningful participation and inclusion of all students, including students who are deaf-blind.

Anne Smith, Ed.D.
Education Research Analyst
Office of Special Education Programs
U.S. Department of Education

Preface

As we began to offer a methods of instruction course for general and special education teachers of students with deaf-blindness, we searched for a comprehensive textbook. The volume we had chosen for the past several years, *Innovative Program Design for Individuals with Dual Sensory Impairments* (Goetz, Guess, & Stremel-Campbell, 1987), is now out of print. We wanted to provide a text that would focus on ensuring students with deaf-blindness the social advantages of inclusive education while at the same time providing the very systematic, specialized instructional procedures necessary for them to gain essential skills for functioning in general education and other integrated settings.

At the outset of nearly 10 years of research into the considerations and variables related to improving the educational experiences of students with deaf-blindness, we investigated the perceived barriers to providing inclusive educational opportunities as they were voiced by professionals and family members. We found that the lack of essential programmatic supports and training (tactile communication, orientation and mobility, fluent signing environments, braille instruction, etc.) posed some notable barriers; however, the most common barriers identified were attitudinal. Students with deaf-blindness were held back from many opportunities to interact with their peers without disabilities largely because of fear, stereotypes, and invalid assumptions. Furthermore, because training and support in communication, braille, language interpretation, and orientation and mobility need to be provided regardless of setting, we felt that a book that addresses such attitudinal issues while providing practical suggestions on how to adapt and modify instruction for inclusive settings would best serve to improve the educational opportunities of students who are deaf-blind.

Collaborative training models have several important elements, including: 1) a common purpose, 2) a dispersed leadership, and 3) mutual control among members. This differs from coordinated models in which authority rests with individual team members. The shared commitment of several experts working in true collaboration with family members strengthens effectiveness. Unless we can effectively provide special services designed specifically for students with deaf-blindness in inclusive settings, it is likely that ineffective practices will be-

---

In the educational milieu, we often refer to *students who are deaf-blind* or *students with deaf-blindness*. However, in the adult deaf-blind community, cultural advocates reinforce their positive self-identities by using the phrases *deaf-blind person*, *deaf-blind people*, and *deaf-blind community*. Most adults, service providers, and family members have strong feelings about one or more of these labels. The book uses all five terms out of respect to the individuals being described.

come commonplace in education. In keeping with these beliefs, many of the chapters in this book stress the crucial role played by collaborative teams.

We designed this textbook to include a range of information that is traditionally divided into two volumes: one volume that provides an introduction to the field of deaf-blindness and broad coverage of the services necessary for instruction and a second volume that offers instructional strategies and procedures. The present volume combines some introductory materials, a historical perspective of services for students with deaf-blindness, and a selection of strategies for preparing teachers and students without disabilities to include students with deaf-blindness. Procedures for building social and communicative skills are discussed as well as broad guidelines for implementing behavioral support strategies, adapting environments, and providing instruction in natural settings. Current issues relevant to inclusion are considered and essential values are highlighted that serve as the fundamental basis for bringing all students into the classrooms and communities where they reside.

The book is divided into four sections. Section I, Including Students with Deaf-Blindness in Typical Education Settings, includes Chapters 1–4. Chapter 1 presents a comprehensive introduction to the concept of inclusion. Chapter 2 discusses the role of legislative support in the field of education for students with deaf-blindness from the mid-1960s to the present. The chapter illustrates how critical this support has been to the growth of programs of research, development, and services for these students. Chapter 3 provides a vision of inclusion from the viewpoint of one parent who worked tirelessly for the inclusion of her son who has deaf-blindness and other severe disabilities in his neighborhood school. The chapter also raises some of the concerns regarding inclusion expressed by other parents of children with deaf-blindness. Chapter 4 concludes Section I with an examination of the results of a series of studies on the process of inclusion involving 22 students with deaf-blindness in 15 school districts. The chapter examines strategies for reversing exclusionary attitudes while moving toward including students with deaf-blindness in typical education settings.

Section II, Preparing to Welcome Students Who Are Deaf-Blind into Your Classroom, includes Chapters 5–9. Chapter 5 identifies current issues that complicate the professional preparation of teachers in the field of deaf-blindness. Comprehensive suggestions are offered to prepare teachers to work collaboratively with family members and students, general educators, and other professionals to fulfill the vision of inclusion in the school and the community. Chapter 6 identifies and discusses the influence of numerous factors affecting the content and methodologies of education programs for students with deaf-blindness. The authors stress the necessity of bringing the student, family, friends, and other community members into the planning and decision-making process to develop valued lifestyle plans for these students. Chapter 7 discusses the value of using social validity assessments to elicit feedback on educational goals and interventions to achieve meaningful outcomes for each individual student. Chapter 8 describes national trends in education throughout the past decade, which have leaned toward providing a variety of services through the more comprehensive efforts of the collaborative team. Data from an applied research project is presented to illustrate how collaborative team efforts benefit students with deaf-blindness, their parents, their peers, the school, and the community. Chapter 9 concludes this section with a wealth of valuable strategies for making adaptations that will accommodate the successful inclusion of students with deaf-blindness in typically encountered environments. Physical as well as social adaptations are discussed and a logical process for evaluating the need for adaptations and their impact on student performance is presented.

Section III, School Dynamics: Facilitating Communication and Friendships, includes Chapters 10 and 11. Chapter 10 offers strategies for considering the social and physical environments of a student with deaf-blindness, as well as the typical routines and activities carried out in those environments, to develop a functional, interactive communication system for that student. Chapter 11 discusses the processes involved in developing friendships and other social interactions among students with deaf-blindness and their peers.

The final section of the book, Support Strategies, includes Chapters 12–18. Chapter 12 offers a concise analysis of the elements of behavioral support along with practical suggestions for the application of behavioral principles to help some students with deaf-blindness. Chapter 13 stresses the use of activities and therapeutic routines as a way of supporting students with deaf-blindness in natural settings through integrated programming. The chapter also provides descriptions of additional disabilities that students with deaf-blindness may have and how these disabilities can be supported to improve skill performance. Chapter 14 discusses the critical issue of orientation and mobility. The authors provide significant detail concerning how to teach people with deaf-blindness to develop the skills necessary to move and orient independently in a functional variety of settings. Chapter 15 describes the elements of early intervention education programs for young children who are deaf-blind. The authors fully discuss the values that should govern such programs and relate the issues of developmentally appropriate programming to children who are deaf-blind. Chapter 16 provides the reader with a highly practical set of procedures for including students with deaf-blindness in general education settings. The chapter includes helpful forms, charts, and other decision-making tools for use by both professionals and families. Chapter 17 offers a view of the essential considerations involved in helping a student with deaf-blindness to move into new and challenging community environments.

The final chapter in the book, Chapter 18, highlights some of the issues that will affect the future of inclusive educational opportunities for students with deaf-blindness, including the need for greater focus on the effects of education on the lifestyles of students and their families. We believe that educators must face their fear of fallibility and learn to teach the value of inclusion not through rhetoric, but, more importantly, through an open and enthusiastic welcome of all who are interested in improving the lifestyles of students with deaf-blindness.

It would be detrimental to the lifestyles of these students to assume that there are any easy, complete, and final answers to the questions that surround the issue of inclusion. Rather, the meaning of inclusion for students who are deaf-blind must continue to be defined over time. Deaf-blindness has often been described as an isolating disability, one that increases the distances between people. We believe that such distances are what make us all unique individuals and that these distances can eventually be overcome. To quote Carter Heyward:

> We touch this strength, our power, who we are in the world, when we are most fully in touch with one another and with the world. There is no doubt in my mind that, in so doing, we are participants in ongoing incarnation, bringing god to life in the world. For god is nothing more than the eternally creative source of our relational power, our common strength. . . . (Heyward, 1984, p. 124)

REFERENCES

Heyward, C. (1984). *Our passion for justice: Images of power, sexuality, and liberation.* Cleveland: Pilgrim Press.
Goetz, L., Guess, D., & Stremel-Campbell, K. (Eds.). (1987). *Innovative program design for individuals with dual sensory impairments.* Baltimore: Paul H. Brookes Publishing Co.

Acknowledgments

Lyle wanted to acknowledge several members of his family who have provided personal inspiration and support, so we concluded that separate acknowledgments would be appropriate. However, I want to strongly endorse the acknowledgments made in Lyle's version, including the parents, students, and professional staff who have been working with me in many instances since 1987.

As editors, it is important to reflect on the superior performance of each of the authors who contributed to this volume. I feel that without exception they represent the highest quality of authorship and the greatest range of professional expertise available. Three of our authors have provided me with an extra measure of inspiration.

One of these is Therese Rafalowski Welch. In 1987, she was the Washington State coordinator of programs for students who are deaf-blind. At the annual Project Directors meeting in Washington, D.C., Therese drew me aside and said, "We must strengthen our efforts for students who are deaf-blind in the state of Washington, and you must do your part." I was somewhat amazed at her boldness, but later I decided she was absolutely right. That was the beginning of our collaborative research and demonstration efforts. Throughout these 7 years, we have had strong continuous commitment from the Office of the Superintendent of Public Instruction and Dr. Betty Hyde and from Marcia Fankhauser of the Puget Sound Educational Service District.

Second, Joyce Ford has also been a source of inspiration. Her national efforts on behalf of the parents of children who are deaf-blind exemplify her facile approach to communicating with other parents and professionals. I am convinced that her efforts have made a significant difference in the lives of persons who are deaf-blind.

Finally, I want to acknowledge Anne Smith of the Office of Special Education Programs for her many contributions to and support for our projects. She has provided the most knowledgeable, continuous monitoring and interaction I have ever encountered in my 34 years of experience with federal project support. In addition, her regular calls expressing concern for me and my son Tom's family during his grave illness were an important source of comfort.

Norris G. Haring

One of the more difficult tasks associated with writing, or in this case editing, a book is sitting down to acknowledge all of the less visible, although no less important, people who have had a hand in shaping the messages contained in the book. I offer my apologies to anyone who is not mentioned specifically. I am no less indebted to you, and it is entirely my error that any omissions have been made.

I often facilitate groups of people that form, or hopefully will form, circles of support for people with deaf-blindness and other developmental disabilities. This has afforded me numerous occasions to reflect upon my own circles of support and how much they mean to me. At the innermost circle of my life are my wife, Mary, my son, Justin, and my daughter-in-law, Nicole. They are such a pervasive and integral part of my thinking, beliefs, and values that my life would be incomprehensible without them. Also very close in my circle is the influence of my mother, Helen Romer, who provided the foundation upon which the lessons of my later teachers could take hold. I also have many friends who have been in supportive roles in my life, and I thank them for their patience, their understanding, and the opportunities to enjoy their companionship.

I consider myself very fortunate to have had many fine teachers. I doubt I would have continued to work with people with developmental disabilities if not for the example of Bud Fredericks, the man who gave Mary and me our first position as houseparents in a group home for eight women in 1973. Bud's influence continues to this day, as does the influence of a dear friend and teacher, Mary Heyer. I have also had the good fortune to work with Rob Horner who taught me a great deal about being creative, working hard, and maintaining my focus on the lifestyles of people with disabilities. More recently I have had my thinking challenged through personal contact with and through the writings of John O'Brien, Connie Lyle-O'Brien, Pat Puckett, Beth Mount, and Herb Lovett.

I have met many interesting and stimulating people during my career, none more so than the people with disabilities whose lives I entered and who became a part of mine. I think of Treba, Carol, Lillian, Sharon, Sue, Helena, Linda, and Mary, the women whose home I shared for 2½ years in the early 1970s. I know we were all pretty scared of each other at times and of what might happen to us in our daily journeys. I now remember with great fondness the extent to which they contributed to my quality of life.

Most recently I have had the pleasure of working with a wonderful special education teacher, Carolyn Weakly. Carolyn and her family, particularly her son, Dan, have been a tremendous source of inspiration to me. Physical education teacher Jeanette Charboneau has been an exemplar of commitment to inclusive education for all students. Bob Huven, Jennifer White, and Kay Adamson have taught me so much I can never imagine balancing the ledger with them. Through them I have met several members of the deaf-blind community of Seattle—Patrick Cave, Leslie Peterson, Mark Landreneau, and Janie Neal—who are now esteemed colleagues and collaborators.

Many families have become a part of our projects at the University of Washington, and through this involvement have also become major sources of inspiration and learning for Norris and myself. Margie Griffith, Chuck and Phylis Pyle, Donna Gloede, Joanne Brown, Kathy Hayes, and Marianne Robinson have been especially important to our work. We would also like to offer our sincere appreciation to Marcia Fankhauser, Mick Moore, and Terry Lindquist, administrators at Puget Sound Educational Service District who have offered us a collaborative environment and important support for our projects. Chris Nemeth, Ericka Rado, and Connie Mace, all former staff of projects at the University of Washington, taught us much about working with students with deaf-blindness.

I would also like to thank Susan Graham, who turned reams of ramblings into coherent drafts of manuscripts, and Victoria Thulman of Paul H. Brookes Publishing Co. for her consistency, her creativity, her belief in the project, and her frequent reminders of due dates. It was a pleasure to work with an editor who displayed such dedication to her craft and who knew the literature better than many who claim membership in our profession.

Finally, I would like to acknowledge the influence of two people I have not met, but who have nonetheless affected me through their writings. Wendell Berry's novels, essays, and poems have helped me clarify my own thinking about community and how people and places are so intertwined as to be inextricable. What Wendell Berry has helped me think, Raymond Carver, through his poetry, has helped me feel. If this book has the impact he describes as "words that linger as deeds," then let those deeds be a positive influence on the lifestyles of people with deaf-blindness.

Lyle T. Romer

Welcoming Students Who Are Deaf-Blind into Typical Classrooms

INCLUDING STUDENTS WITH DEAF-BLINDNESS IN TYPICAL EDUCATION SETTINGS

Chapter 1

Inclusion of Students Who Are Deaf-Blind

What Does the Future Hold?

Lori Goetz

Full inclusion occurs when students with disabilities are full-time members of age-appropriate, typical classrooms in their home schools (whatever school they would attend if they did not have disabilities) and receive any supports necessary to participate in both the academic and social communities of their peers. Inclusive education continues to emerge as a promising educational practice for teaching students with severe disabilities, and in conjunction with the widespread restructuring efforts that are now sweeping the nation's schools, inclusive schooling may hold the potential for improved educational outcomes for all students, not just those with disabilities (National Association of School Boards, 1993; Sailor, Gee, & Karasoff, 1993; Sailor, Gerry, & Wilson, 1991). For students with severe and multiple disabilities, a small but growing data base documents positive outcomes associated with inclusive schooling (Hunt & Farron-Davis, 1993; Hunt,

Farron-Davis, Beckstead, Curtis, & Goetz, 1994); a growing technology concerning administrative, logistical, and curricular practices for accomplishing full inclusion is now available (cf. Stainback & Stainback, 1990, 1992); and a clear mandate exists to offer these students the same opportunities for friendship and social participation that are available to their peers without disabilities (Strully & Strully, 1989).

What about students who are deaf-blind? These students present unique educational needs to any service delivery system in terms of communication (Jensema, 1979; Rowland & Schweigert, 1990), mobility (Welch, 1993), and sensory functioning (Langley & DuBose, 1980; Niswander, 1987). The heterogeneous nature of these students in terms of cognitive and functional capacities (Fredericks & Baldwin, 1987; Riggio, 1992) adds complexity to the design and delivery of effective education programs. Despite reports

Preparation of this manuscript was supported in part by grants from the United States Department of Education, Office of Special Education & Rehabilitative Services/Special Education Program (Grant Nos. H086G00003 and H025D30013). No official endorsement is intended or should be inferred.

of successful participation of students who are deaf-blind in inclusive programs (Dennis, Edelman, & Cloninger, 1992), recent evaluations of current service delivery for this population suggest that many students who are deaf-blind are not being well-served at the local level (Collins, 1992). Within this context, the current volume represents the emerging knowledge base on serving students who are deaf-blind within general (though not necessarily inclusive) education. Although much has been learned and demonstrated a great deal remains for implementation and investigation. If fully inclusive programs are indeed intended to support *all* students with disabilities successfully, the unique support needs of students who are deaf-blind must be addressed, and outcomes for all students must be evaluated.

WHAT IS INCLUSION?

When students with disabilities are fully included as members of age-appropriate education classrooms in their home schools, the meaning of the term *special education* is transformed. Special education becomes not a *placement*, but a *service*, that is provided to students in the context of typical classrooms, schools, and communities. As presented in Table 1, Neary and Halvorsen (1994) have specified 15 markers indicative of fully inclusive programs developed by the PEERS Project, the federally funded systems change grant of the California State Department of Education. As indicated by these markers, there is zero exclusion in a fully inclusive school; students participate in core curriculum and activities that provide the context for meeting individualized education program (IEP) objectives. Students receive supplementary and special education services through regularly planned, collaborative teaming by special and general educators, related ser-

vice professionals, paraprofessionals, parents, peers, and administrators. There is no "special day class" (SDC) at the site, but the staff-to-student ratio for an itinerant special educator (support facilitator) is equivalent to an SDC ratio. Any services provided by paraprofessional staff are regularly supervised and monitored by certificated staff. Finally, effective inclusion programs are closely tied to general education methods reflective of curricular and instructional practices, such as cooperative learning and activity-based instruction, associated with restructured schools (cf. Sailor, Gerry, et al., 1991).

Provocative data exist that suggest a potential relationship between educational practices and multiple positive outcomes for students with severe disabilities. For example, Hunt and Farron-Davis (1993) report differences in the quality of IEP objectives, with higher scores for IEPs written when students were full-time members of general education classrooms. Hunt, Farron-Davis, et al. (1994) analyzed the outcomes for two groups of students with severe disabilities who were placed either in general education or integrated special education classes and found that students with severe cognitive disabilities who were members of general education classes were more *actively engaged* in the activities of the school day than students with cognitive disabilities in special education programs. In addition, the results of the study indicated that the students participated in a greater number of academic activities if they were members of general education classrooms. The educational objectives on their IEPs, however, did not reflect a significant increase in academic objectives or a decrease in basic communication, social, and sensory-motor objectives. Hunt, Staub, Alwell, and Goetz (1994) also demonstrated that three elementary-age students with severe, multiple disabilities acquired basic communica-

Table 1. Inclusive education/supported education

The following characteristics are indicators of fully inclusive programs for students with disabilities. They are meant as guidelines in planning for inclusion and also as a means for maintaining the integrity of the term, "Inclusive" or "Supported Education."

1. Students are members of chronologically age-appropriate general education classrooms in their normal schools of attendance, or in magnet schools or public schools of choice when these options exist for students without disabilities.
2. Students move with peers to subsequent grades in school.
3. No special class exists except as a place for enrichment activities for all students.
4. Disability type or severity of disability does not preclude involvement in full inclusion programs.
5. The special education and general education teachers collaborate to ensure:
   a. The student's natural participation as a regular member of the class
   b. The systematic instruction of the student's IEP objectives
   c. The adaptation of core curriculum and/or materials to facilitate student participation and learning
6. Effective instructional strategies (e.g., cooperative learning, activity-based instruction, whole language) are supported and encouraged in the general education classroom. Classrooms promote student responsibility for learning through strategies such as student-led conferences, student involvement in IEPs and planning meetings, etc.
7. The staff-to-student ratio for an itinerant special education teacher and aides is equivalent to the special class ratio and funding support is at least the level it would be for a special class.
8. Supplemental instructional services (e.g., communication, mobility, adapted P.E.) are provided to students in classrooms and community settings through a transdisciplinary team approach.
9. Regularly scheduled collaborative planning meetings are held with general education staff, special education staff, parents, and related-service staff in attendance as indicated, in order to support initial and ongoing program development and monitoring.
10. There is always a certificated employee (special education teacher, resource specialist, or other) assigned to supervise and assist any classified staff (e.g., paraprofessional) working with specific students in general education classrooms.
11. Special education students who are fully included are considered a part of the total class count for class size purposes. In other words, even when a student is not counted for general education ADA, she or he is not an "extra" student above the contractual class size.
12. General ability awareness is provided to staff, students, and parents at the school site through formal or informal means, on an individualized basis. This is most effective when ability awareness is incorporated within the general education curriculum.
13. Plans exist for transition of students to next classes and schools of attendance in inclusive situations.
14. Districts and SELPAs (special education local planning agencies) obtain any necessary waivers of the Education Code to implement supported education.
15. Supported education efforts are coordinated with school restructuring at the district and site level, and a clear commitment to an inclusive option is demonstrated by the Board of Education and Superintendent.
16. There is adequate training/staff development provided for all involved.

In summary, all students are members of the general education classroom, with some students requiring varying levels of support from special education. Hence, the term "Supported Education." This term, although synonymous with "Full Inclusion," is explicit in acknowledging the importance of providing support services within the regular classroom, when necessary, to ensure a quality educational program.

From Neary, T., & Halvorsen, A. (1994). *Inclusive education guidelines.* Sacramento: PEERS Project, California State Department of Education.

tion and motor objectives within cooperative learning activities conducted in their general education classroom.

In relation to social inclusion, Evans, Salisbury, Palombaro, Berryman, and Hollowood (1992) reported outcomes of measures of social competence (Meyer, Cole, McQuarter, & Reichle, 1990), sociometric analyses, and time-sampled classroom observation codes for eight students with severe disabilities and a gender-matched sample of students without disabilities, all of whom were in general education classrooms. Opportunities for interaction and social acceptance were not uniquely associated with status as a student with disabilities. This suggests that other factors (such as the general standards held by the students without disabilities) may play an important role in social inclusion for any student.

Taken together, these findings suggest that inclusive schooling may dramatically influence outcomes for students with severe disabilities. However, many questions remain unanswered. The small samples involved in the available data sets and variability in the definition of the independent variable (full inclusion) limit the inferences that can be drawn from these findings. Of equal importance to the discussion presented here, the samples of students did not include students who are deaf-blind.

INCLUSION OF STUDENTS WHO ARE DEAF-BLIND

Students who are deaf-blind represent a heterogeneous group in terms of cognitive and functional capacities (cf. Baldwin & Bullis, 1993; Riggio, 1992; Smithdas, 1995). The unique support needs of these students include specialized communication and mobility instruction (cf. Huebner, Welch, & Prickett, 1993), the ongoing adaptation of sensory information (cf. Rikhye, Gothelf, & Appell, 1989), and the provision of experiential learning opportunities in the context of safe, but responsive, environments (cf. Welch, 1993). Collins (1992) has suggested that the specific condition of deaf-blindness requires that, in addition to functional curricula that is age-appropriate, at least the following be part of the student's IEP:

- Language goals reflecting the student's most useful modality
- Sensory development activities
- Teaching strategies that consider the student's preferred learning styles

- Mobility training
- Cognitive skill expansion through adaptation of sensory input
- Increased opportunities for social interaction
- Instruction in reading and writing, if appropriate

The IEPs of students who are deaf-blind highlight an ongoing theme woven throughout the national discussion on inclusive schooling: balancing the "academic" outcomes of schooling, that is, learning the skills and concepts associated with mastery of a discrete content area (e.g., algebra or braille) with the "social participation" outcomes of schooling (e.g., going to a school prom or developing a lifelong friendship).

Achieving an effective balance between these areas of curricular emphasis requires shared understanding and consensus among families, consumers, and educators as to desired outcomes of schooling. Data concerning traditional program outcome measures, including graduation rates, learning rates (as measured by standardized tests), postsecondary schooling, and employment for special education students are sporadic (Lipsky & Gartner, 1989). For the population of students who are deaf-blind, available outcome data as they transition out of school are similarly incomplete (cf. Everson & McNulty, 1995). What few data there are reveal a discouraging picture in terms of traditional outcomes such as employment and postsecondary schooling (Wagner, 1989). In Chapter 3 of this volume, Ford and Fredericks review the available data concerning parental perspectives and raise the issue of curricular emphasis (academic learning vs. social participation vs. life skills and community-based training). Determination of the desired outcomes sought by parents, educators, and participants alike is a necessary first step; investigation of the relationship between these outcomes and specific schooling practices (cf. Wang, 1989) would then enable educational decision making based upon both values and data.

Such data do not yet exist. In their absence, analysis of the indicators that mark a quality program from the perspective of professionals (Collins, 1992) as well as parents (Giangreco, Cloninger, Mueller, Yuan, & Ashworth, 1991) suggests that both improved academic skills, including skills learned through provision of specialized services such as braille or sign language and social skills learned through participation in social activities, are valued outcomes that full inclusion programs must address. Promising practices, based upon evidence from learners who are deaf-blind and/or learners with severe and multiple disabilities, demonstrate how both these outcomes might be facilitated.

Curriculum Development

Inclusion in typical classrooms of students who are deaf-blind and who themselves represent a wide variety of abilities and needs presents major questions regarding the development of appropriate curricula and instructional strategies. Concerns arise about successful adaptation of both content and teaching methodologies in general education for learners who do not gather and access ongoing information in a traditional manner (see Downing & Eichinger, 1990; Maxon, Tedder, Marmion, & Lamb, 1993). The student must be an active participant in the class in ways that are individualized to reflect his or her particular learning needs and IEP goals. Several of the chapters in the current volume offer models of curriculum development responsive to these concerns (see, e.g., chaps. 15 and 16, this volume).

Gee (see chap. 14, this volume); Gee, Alwell, Graham, and Goetz (1994); and Gee, Graham, Oshima, Yoshioka, and Goetz (1991) have extended the principles of dis-

crepancy analysis and partial participation (Baumgart et al., 1982; Ferguson & Baumgart, 1991) and the practices of chain interruption (Alwell, Hunt, Goetz, & Sailor, 1989; Hunt, Goetz, Alwell, & Sailor, 1986) and discrepant moments (Van Dijk, 1965, 1986; Van Dijk & Janssen, 1989) to develop instructional procedures that both enhance the stimuli of the ongoing context and capitalize upon motivation to produce or initiate behavior. Through an analysis of the social and environmental variables in ongoing typical classroom activities, along with observation of the student within that context, routine behaviors and the environmental cues most salient to the learner for interpretation of the routine are identified. Adaptations are used as needed to bring the routine to the student. Once cues have been identified, the type of participation or partial participation recommended (cf. Ferguson & Baumgart, 1991) is individually determined. The instructional strategies then used may incorporate time delay (Touchette, 1971), prompt fading, or chain interruption (Hunt et al., 1986), all of which have been successful with students who are deaf-blind and who have multiple disabilities (cf. Gee et al., 1991).

Contextual analysis and instruction offer empirically validated teaching strategies (Gee, 1993; Gee et al., 1991) to ensure that students with deaf-blindness and multiple disabilities are not merely present in the typical classroom, but are participating in individually determined ways that can enhance both skill acquisition and social participation. Resolution of questions concerning how much time is spent in academic instruction, functional life skills instruction, and experiential learning may also rest, in part, in curricular strategies such as contextual analysis. Such curricular strategies have multiple outcomes: students can acquire discrete skills (such as activating a microswitch through a head turn) in complex social and academic contexts (such as a unit on cooking and measuring) through a paradigm that captures experiential learning dimensions.

Billingsley, Huven, and Romer (see chap. 12, this volume) provide another example of how students who are deaf-blind can be well-served educationally in the typical classroom in the curricular area of challenging behavior. The development of functional, adaptive behaviors through simultaneous use of multiple intervention strategies, while respecting and preserving the dignity of the individual, reflects a significant shift in perspective from earlier emphases upon behavior reduction and teacher control. Positive behavioral support (cf. Horner et al., 1990) seeks to understand the function that a challenging behavior serves for the individual exhibiting it (cf. O'Neill, Horner, Albin, Storey, & Sprague, 1990) and promotes alternative responses that achieve the same result and are adaptive to the context. An array of data-based interventions are available from which the behavioral support team can draw in developing strategies to prevent, teach alternatives, and react in response to challenging behaviors (Janney, Black, & Ferlo, 1989). As Billingsley et al. note in Chapter 12 of this volume, the wider range of naturally occurring cues and consequences inherent in the ongoing events of the general education classroom can function both to promote generalization and maintenance of adaptive behaviors and to decrease teacher-imposed control.

Neary and Halvorsen (1994) have specified that a fully inclusive program should emphasize "the student's natural participation as a member of the class . . . and systematic instruction of the student's IEP objectives." Reports from Gee et al. (1991) and Billingsley et al. (chap. 12, this volume) offer at least two empirically validated curricular development strategies to promote this goal. These strategies, along with other strategies presented in this volume, also underline a fundamental premise: acquisition of new skills, behaviors, and concepts occurs *within* the ongoing social context of the typical classroom.

Specialized Services

Students who are deaf-blind must have available a variety of specialized services, ranging from braille, to sign language, to interpreters with skills specific to deaf-blindness (cf. Curry, 1989; Petronio, 1988). Provision of these specialized services, which are essential to the outcomes of academic achievement and meaningful social participation, remains one of the serious challenges facing inclusive education. The fact that the need for these services may in itself be fluid, due in part to potential variability in sensory functioning even within one individual who is deaf-blind, complicates this challenge; the shortage of trained personnel, as articulated by McLetchie (see chap. 5, this volume) adds further complexity. Although the role of the teacher of students who are deaf-blind may change and redefine itself as full inclusion programs emerge, the need for persons trained in the fundamental knowledge base of deaf-blindness remains constant.

Collaborative Teaming

Collaborative teaming (see chap. 8, this volume) offers a potential means of addressing the provision of specialized services. Transdisciplinary teaming has long been an established practice for students with multiple diverse needs (cf. Campbell, 1987; Giangreco, 1990; Orelove & Sobsey, 1991). A variety of professionals and related service personnel have been involved in the IEP team of an individual who is deaf-blind. This team includes speech-language specialists; audiologists; vision specialists; occupational and physical therapists; and often medical personnel, in addition to parents (or other primary care providers) and the focus student himself or herself.

Inclusive schooling changes the composition of this team. In addition to parents, specialized service personnel, and the student's general education teacher, the team must include the following:

- The student's primary support teacher (a special education teacher with training specific to students who are deaf or hearing impaired, blind or visually impaired, or deaf-blind or training specific to cognitive or learning disabilities),
- Paraprofessional support staff
- The student's general education peers
- Any other persons chosen to advocate for the student (e.g., a disability-specific mentor)

One unresolved question concerns determination of the student's primary support teacher (Gee & Goetz, 1993). The heterogeneity of the population dictates that this role may best be filled by a variety of personnel. For students with deaf-blindness who are at grade level, and who do not have cognitive disabilities, the general education teacher may, in fact, be the primary support teacher, with additional support, for example, from specialists in braille, interpreters, and speech-language therapists (cf. Sternberg-White & Johnson, 1992). For other students, who are deaf-blind, assistance from a support teacher trained in the area of severe multiple disabilities may be more appropriate (cf. Alwell & Triulzi, 1993).

In addition to changing the composition of the team, full inclusion also requires that the teaming process be a collaborative one, in which team members share a common vision and goal that is the outcome of the services that are provided (cf. Bruner, 1991; Rainforth, York, & Macdonald, 1992). Transdisciplinary and coordinated service delivery models emphasize role release and joint ac-

tivities, but differ from collaborative teaming models in terms of several essential elements, including mission, authority and accountability, and resources and rewards (Wilder Foundation, 1992). For example, collaborative teaming requires the creation of a common vision, whereas coordinated teaming simply reviews the goals of each individual member for compatibility. Collaborative models utilize dispersed leadership and mutual control among members, whereas in coordinated team models, authority rests with individual team members. Thus, effective collaborative teams rely upon consensus building and problem-solving strategies that utilize the discipline-specific knowledge that each team member brings to the collaborative process.

Collaborative teams address the issue of specialized service delivery in several ways. In order to provide disability-specific expertise, teachers trained in deaf-blindness may function as primary support teachers for deaf-blind students served in inclusive programs. As addressed by Neary and Halvorsen (1994), the staff-to-student ratio should be no less than it would be if these students were served in a self-contained special class. However, the low incidence of deaf-blindness may result in a support teacher whose responsibilities lie across several schools or even districts. Initial data suggest that such a model has multiple positive outcomes when applied to programs for students with severe disabilities (Hunt, Farron-Davis, et al., 1994). Resolving specific issues in the delivery of specialized services by utilizing the expertise of all team members to solve problems collaboratively is another way in which teams may contribute to achieving specialized service delivery. While sounding, perhaps, too "pat," genuinely collaborative teamwork has resolved issues in service delivery that, on appearances, seemed insurmountable (cf. Salisbury, Palombaro, & Evans, 1993).

The development of effective collaborative teams is also consistent with emerging trends in service delivery to families, including school-based health clinics (Certo, 1993) and integrated service delivery models (Karasoff & Wilson, 1992). These trends reflect a growing recognition of both the increasing diversity of all of the students (general and special education) served in our schools and the need for service delivery systems that effectively and efficiently utilize discipline-specific expertise in the educational process.

Social Inclusion

Contextual curriculum design and the development of effective collaborative teams are validated strategies designed to achieve positive learning outcomes for students with deaf blindness. However, another hallmark of inclusive schooling is the greatly expanded potential for increased social interactions. Collins (1992) has identified increased opportunity for interaction as a necessary feature of an educational program. While opportunity is clearly necessary, it is not sufficient to achieve the outcome of being a valued member in the social context (cf. Sacks & Wolffe, 1990). Successful supported schooling must also provide strategies for using increased social interaction opportunities to achieve meaningful social relationships, ranging from relationships among peers with and without disabilities to experiences in the context of disability-specific culture (cf. Lipton, 1993).

Goetz and Hunt (1992) have reviewed the available experimental data evaluating outcomes in full inclusion programs for students with severe and multiple disabilities and conclude that several factors in full inclusion settings may collectively contribute to achieving positive social outcomes for both the student with disabilities and his or her peers. Some degree of third-party facilitation, such as provision of information that enables respectful interactions appears to be a critical factor. Provision of a discrete medium for interaction, be it a conversation book (Hunt, Alwell, & Goetz, 1991), a small-group math lesson (Graham, 1992), or a cooperative learning group (Hunt, Staub, et al., 1994) also appears to be an essential element. Finally, although not analyzed experimentally, there is a provocative possibility that the context of naturally occurring interactions among students with disabilities and their schoolmates through the development of "circles of support" (Forest & Lusthaus, 1989) may also contribute to positive outcomes. Circles of support are small groups of students who come together regularly to share and to problem solve. In all of the classrooms that participated in the studies reviewed by Goetz and Hunt (1992), circles of support for students with disabilities were ongoing and were facilitated through both formal (see, e.g., *Circles of Friends*, Forest & Lusthaus, 1989) and/or informal means (see, e.g., *Partners at Lunch*, Breen & Lovinger, 1992).

Alwell, Graham, and Gee (1993) have identified several facilitation strategies of particular value in providing information to peers. The role of the instructional staff in modeling and facilitating natural, normalized, and respectful interactions between the student with disabilities and all adults and peers is clearly identified. For students who are deaf-blind, interpretation for peers and staff of the focus student's communicative and other behaviors and interpretation of social information for the focus student are ways to facilitate respectful interactions. For example, in response to a peer's question, the teacher might respond, "Bill always stops for several minutes before he comes through the door from recess because changes in the texture of the ground bother him." Or the teacher might remind a peer to tell the focus student, "Everyone's laughing because Tony secretly moved the garbage can away from Ms. Triulzi's desk, and now she keeps throwing her garbage on the floor without knowing it."

Even with peers participating as team members and staff facilitating natural peer interactions through provision of social information, some students who are deaf-blind (as well as other students) may need more formalized support to make friends. The *Circles of Friends* Program (Forest & Lusthaus, 1989) has been evaluated from both a qualitative perspective (cf. Ferguson, Jeanchild, & Carter, 1991; Perske, 1988) and from a quantitative perspective (Hirose, 1993), and has demonstrated promising outcomes for the quality of life (cf. Dennis, Williams, Giangreco, & Cloninger, 1993) and the social inclusion of students with disabilities. In this program, a core group of peers meets regularly with the focus student to share his or her successes and challenges and to make new commitments to activities that will include and support him or her. Extension of these strategies to students who are deaf-blind, with attention to the focus student as a valued participant both in and out of school, is a logical next step.

FUTURE DIRECTIONS FOR RESEARCH

Downing and Eichinger (1990) review traditional programs for students who are deaf-blind and suggest that application of particular best practices for students with severe disabilities, rather than development of completely unique and separate program strategies, may yield positive student outcomes. A small body of research also suggests that practices developed for students with severe disabilities may, in fact, also lead to positive outcomes for students who are deaf-blind. Supported employment (Gaylord-Ross, Lee, Casey, Rosenberg, & Goetz, 1991; Goetz, Lee, Casey, & Gaylord-Ross, 1991; Griffin & Lowry, 1989), basic skill instruction in the context of integrated school and community environments (Gee, Graham, Sailor, & Goetz, 1995), use of time delay and chain interruption to teach communication skills and reciprocal interactions between students who are deaf-blind and their peers without disabilities (Gee et al., 1991; Graham, 1992), and person-centered planning processes (Perlroth, Pumpian, Hesche, & Campbell, 1993) are all practices initially developed for students with severe disabilities that have been successfully extended to students who are deaf-blind. Based upon evidence from this growing body of literature, innovative practices such as contextual curriculum development, collaborative teaming, and support circles appear to hold promise in developing inclusive educational programs that meet the unique needs of students who are deaf-blind.

The data base evaluating these practices, however, must continue to be enlarged. Both academic content learning and the growth of meaningful social relationships are valued educational outcomes for all students. When a student who is deaf-blind is a full-time member of the typical classroom, what are the academic achievement outcomes for the student and for his or her peers? What are the friendship outcomes for the student and his or her peers? Answers to these questions will require ongoing research and evaluation as well as, perhaps, a reconceptualization of how successful schooling outcomes are defined. Goetz and Hunt (1992), for example, review the available data concerning inclusion outcomes and the perspectives of families and peers, and they hypothesize that a new role is emerging for peers with and without disabilities in fully inclusive settings: that of interactive partners, in which initiator and respondent roles are freely interchanged among peers, and diverse support functions for all participants (cf. Furman & Robbins, 1985) are accomplished. Rather than the purely didactic role of a peer tutor (Haring, Breen, Pitts-Conway, Lee, & Gaylord-Ross, 1987) or the purely social role of a "special friend" (Voeltz et al., 1983), mutually supportive behaviors that encompass both social and task-related content areas characterize this peer relationship.

Documentation of interactive partnership outcomes associated with inclusive schooling, as well as more traditional achievement and social interaction outcomes, is a critical step in evaluating full inclusion for all students. Inclusion of students with disability-specific specialized support needs may require new definitions of "success" and "schooling." Sailor (1991) has argued that students with disabilities can facilitate school restructuring by bringing additional resources to the school site. In addition to this resource infusion, inclusion of students who are deaf-blind provides the opportunity for a new understanding of what it means for any student to be a classmate.

REFERENCES

Alwell, M., Graham, N., & Gee, K. (1993). *Creating community*. In K. Gee & L. Goetz (Eds.), *Active interactions: Program manual*. San Francisco State University, Department of Special Education, Active Interactions Project.

Alwell, M., Hunt, P., Goetz, L., & Sailor, W. (1989). Teaching generalized communicative behaviors within interrupted behavior chain contexts. *Journal of The Association for Persons with Severe Handicaps, 14*, 91–100.

Alwell, M., & Triulzi, L. (1993, April 30). *Serving students with multiple severe disabilities in inclusive programs*. Paper presented at CAL-TASH Conference, Burbank, CA.

Baldwin, V., & Bullis, M. (1993). Census of the population. In D. Watson & M. Taff-Watson (Eds.), *A model service delivery system for persons who are deaf-blind* (pp. 19–30). Little Rock: University of Arkansas Rehabilitation Research & Training Center for Persons Who Are Deaf or Hard of Hearing.

Baumgart, D., Brown, L., Pumpian, I., Nisbet, J., Ford, A., Sweet, M., Messina, R., & Schroeder, J. (1982). Principle of partial participation and individualized adaptations in educational programs for severely handicapped students. *Journal of The Association for Persons with Severe Handicaps, 7*, 17–27.

Breen, C., & Lovinger, C. (1992). PAL (Partners at Lunch Club): Evaluation of a program to support social relations in a junior high school. In C. Breen, C. Kennedy, & T. Haring (Eds.), *Social context research project* (pp. 106–128). Santa Barbara: University of California.

Bruner, C. (1991). *Thinking collaboratively: Ten questions and answers to help policy makers improve children's services*. Washington, DC: Education and Human Services Consortium.

Campbell, P. (1987). The integrated programming team: An approach for coordinating professionals of various disciplines in programs for students with severe and multiple handicaps. *Journal of The Association for Persons with Severe Handicaps, 12*(2), 107–116.

Certo, N. (1993). *California Adolescent School-Based Clinics Project*. (Interagency Agreement No. 91-13608 between the California Department of Health Services, Maternal & Child Health Branch, and San Francisco State University, Department of Special Education). San Francisco: California Department of Health Services, Maternal & Child Health Branch.

Collins, M.T. (1992, March). Plenary Address: Reflections and future directions. *Proceedings of the National Conference on Deaf-Blindness: Deaf-blind services in the 90's* (PR. 46–58). Sponsored by Hilton/Perkins National Program, Washington, DC.

Curry, S. (1989). *Low incidence disability program quality study*. Sacramento: California State Department of Education.

Dennis, R.E., Edelman, S., & Cloninger, C. (1992). *I've counted Jon: Transformational experiences of general education teachers educating students with dual sensory impairments. Deaf Blind Services in the 90s*. Washington, DC: Hilton Perkins National Program.

Dennis, R.E., Williams, W., Giangreco, M.F., & Cloninger, C.J. (1993). Quality of life as context for planning and evaluation of services for people with disabilities. *Exceptional Children, 59*(6), 499–512.

Downing, J., & Eichinger, J. (1990). Instructional strategies for learners with dual sensory impairments in integrated settings. *Journal of The Association for Persons with Severe Handicaps, 15*(2), 98–105.

Evans, I., Salisbury, C., Palombaro, M., Berryman, J., & Hollowood, T. (1992). Peer interactions and social acceptance of elementary-age children with severe disabilities in an inclusive school. *Journal of The Association for Persons with Severe Handicaps, 17*(4), 205–212.

Everson, J.L., & McNulty, J. (1995). What happens when children with deaf-blindness grow up? An overview of transitional services. In J. Everson (Ed.), *Supporting young adults who are deaf-blind in their communities: A transition planning guide for service providers, families, and friends.* Baltimore: Paul H. Brookes Publishing Co.

Ferguson, D., & Baumgart, D. (1991). Partial participation revisited. *Journal of The Association for Persons with Severe Handicaps, 16*(4), 218–227.

Ferguson, D., Jeanchild, L., & Carter, P. (1991). *The best tadpoles are in Room 8: Report on a school that's changing itself.* Eugene: Specialized Training Program, University of Oregon.

Forest, M., & Lusthaus, E. (1989). Promoting educational equity for all students: Circles and maps. In S. Stainback, W. Stainback, & M. Forest (Eds.), *Educating all students in the mainstream of regular education* (pp. 43–57). Baltimore: Paul H. Brookes Publishing Co.

Fredericks, H.D., & Baldwin, V.L. (1987). Individuals with dual sensory impairments: Who are they? How are they educated? In L. Goetz, D. Guess, & K. Stremel-Campbell (Eds.), *Innovative program design for individuals with dual sensory impairments* (pp. 3–14). Baltimore: Paul H. Brookes Publishing Co.

Furman, W., & Robbins, P. (1985). What's the point?: Issues in the selection of treatment objectives. In B. Schneider, K. Rubin, & J. Ledingham (Eds.), *Children's peer relations: Issues in assessment and intervention* (pp. 41–54). New York: Springer-Verlag.

Gaylord-Ross, R., Lee, M., Casey, S., Rosenberg, B., & Goetz, L. (1991). Supported employment for deaf-blind youth in transition. *Career Development for Exceptional Individuals, 14*, 77–89.

Gee, K. (1993, May). *An experimental and qualitative investigation into the motivation and competence of peer interactions involving students with severe, multiple disabilities in middle school classrooms.* Unpublished doctoral dissertation, San Francisco State University-University of California, Berkeley, Joint Doctoral Program.

Gee, K., Alwell, M., Graham, N., & Goetz, L. (1994). *Inclusive instructional design: Facilitating informed and active learning for students who are deaf-blind in inclusive schools.* San Francisco: The California Research Institute.

Gee, K., & Goetz, L. (Eds.). (1993). *Active interactions: Project manual.* San Francisco State University, Department of Special Education, Active Interactions Project (OSERS/SEP Grant #H086G00003).

Gee, K., Graham, N., Oshima, G., Yoshioka, K., & Goetz, L. (1991). Teaching students to request the continuation of routine activities by using time delay and increasing physical assistance in the context of chain interruption. *Journal of The Association for Persons with Severe Handicaps, 16*, 154–167.

Gee, K., Graham, N., Sailor, W., & Goetz, L. (1995). Use of integrated, general education and community settings as primary contexts for skill instruction of students with severe, multiple disabilities. *Behavior Modification, 19*(1).

Giangreco, M.F. (1990). Making related service decisions for students with severe disabilities: Roles, criteria, and authority. *Journal of The Association for Persons with Severe Handicaps, 15*(1), 22–31.

Giangreco, M., Cloninger, C., Mueller, P., Yuan, S., & Ashworth, S. (1991). Perspectives of parents whose children have dual sensory impairments. *Journal of The Association for Persons with Severe Handicaps, 16*(1), 14–24.

Giangreco, M., Dennis, R., Cloninger, C., Edelman, S., & Schattman, R. (1992). *I've counted Jon: Transformational experiences of teachers educating students with disabilities.* Burlington, VT: Center for Developmental Disabilities.

Giangreco, M.F., Edelman, S., & Dennis, R. (1991). Common professional practices that interfere with the integrated delivery of related services. *Remedial and Special Education, 12*(1), 16–24.

Goetz, G., & Hunt, P. (1992). *Development of optimal learning and social environments in full inclusion settings.* United States Department of Education. (OSERS Grant #H086D30001). San Francisco State University, California Research Institute.

Goetz, L., Lee, M., Casey, S., & Gaylord-Ross, R. (1991). Integrated work for persons with dual sensory impairments: Strategies for inclusion.

Journal of The Association for Persons with Severe Handicaps, 16, 154–167.

Graham, N. (1992). *Use of time delay to increase reciprocal interactions between students with dual sensory impairments and their nondisabled peers in inclusive settings.* Unpublished master's thesis, San Francisco State University.

Griffin, S.L., & Lowry, J. (1989). Supported employment for persons with deaf-blindness and mental retardation. *Journal of Visual Impairment and Blindness, 83*(10), 495–499.

Haring, T., Breen, C., Pitts-Conway, V., Lee, M., & Gaylord-Ross, R. (1987). Adolescent peer tutoring and special friend experiences. *Journal of The Association for Persons with Severe Handicaps, 12,* 280–286.

Hirose, A. (1993). *Evaluating circles of support.* Unpublished master's thesis, California State University at Hayward.

Horner, R., Dunlap, G., Koegel, R., Carr, E.G., Sailor, W., Anderson, J., Albin, R.W., & O'Neill, R.E. (1990). Toward a technology of "nonaversive" behavioral support. *Journal of The Association for Persons with Severe Handicaps, 15,* 125–132.

Huebner, K., Welch, T., & Prickett, J. (1993). *Deaf-blind learners: A self-study curriculum in communication and mobility.* New York: American Foundation for the Blind Consortium.

Hunt, P., Alwell, M., & Goetz, L. (1991). Establishing conversational exchanges with family and friends: Moving from training to meaningful communication. *The Journal of Special Education, 25*(3), 305–319.

Hunt, P., & Farron-Davis, F. (1993). A preliminary investigation of IEP quality and content associated with placement in general education versus special education classes. *Journal of The Association for Persons with Severe Handicaps, 17*(4), 247–253.

Hunt, P., Farron-Davis, F., Beckstead, S., Curtis, D., & Goetz, L. (1994). Evaluating the effects of placement of students with severe disabilities in regular education versus special classes, *Journal of The Association for Persons with Severe Handicaps, 19*(3), 200–214.

Hunt, P., Goetz, L., Alwell, M., & Sailor, W. (1986). Using an interrupted behavior chain strategy to teach generalized communication skills to students with severe disabilities. *Journal of The Association for Persons with Severe Handicaps, 11*(3), 196–204.

Hunt, P., Staub, D., Alwell, M., & Goetz, L. (1994). Achievement by all students within the context of cooperative learning groups. *Journal of The Association for Persons with Severe Handicaps, 19*(4).

Janney, R., Black, J., & Ferlo, M. (1989). *A problem-solving approach to challenging behaviors: Strategies for parents and educators of people with developmental disabilities & challenging behaviors.* Syracuse, NY: Syracuse University, Child-Centered Inservice Training and Technical Assistance Network.

Jensema, C. (1979). A review of communication systems used by deaf-blind people: Part I. *American Annals of the Deaf, 124*(6), 720–725.

Karasoff, P., & Wilson, W.C. (1992). *Integrated services specialist training.* (OSERS/Personnel Preparation Grant #H029C20053). San Francisco State University, Department of Special Education.

Langley, B., & DuBose, R. (1980). *Functional vision inventory for the multiply and severely handicapped.* Chicago: Stoelting.

Lipsky, D.K., & Gartner, A. (1989). The current situation. In D.K. Lipsky & A. Gartner (Eds.), *Beyond separate education: Quality education for all* (pp. 3–24). Baltimore: Paul H. Brookes Publishing Co.

Lipton, D. (1993, May 1). *Inclusion in the 90s: Advocacy, family, and curriculum issues.* Keynote address, CAL-TASH Conference, Burbank, CA.

Maxon, B.J., Tedder, N.E., Marmion, S., & Lamb, S. (1993). The education of youths who are deaf-blind: Learning tasks and teaching methods. *Journal of Visual Impairment & Blindness, 87*(7), 259–262.

Meyer, L., Cole, D., McQuarter, R., & Reichle, J. (1990). Validation of the Assessment of Social Competence [ASC] for children and young adults with developmental disabilities. *Journal of The Association for Persons with Severe Handicaps, 15,* 57–68.

National Association of School Boards. (1993). *Winners all: A call for inclusive schools* (Monograph). Alexandria, VA: Author.

Neary, T., & Halvorsen, A. (1994). *Inclusive education guidelines.* Sacramento: PEERS Project, California State Department of Education.

Niswander, P. (1987). Audiometric assessment and management. In L. Goetz, D. Guess, & K. Stremel-Campbell (Eds.), *Innovative program design for individuals with dual sensory impairments.* Baltimore: Paul H. Brookes Publishing Co.

O'Neill, R.E., Horner, R.H., Albin, R.W., Storey, K., & Sprague, J.R. (1990). *Functional analysis of problem behavior: A practical assessment guide.* Sycamore, IL: Sycamore.

Orelove, F.P., & Sobsey, D. (1991). *Educating children with multiple disabilities: A transdisciplinary approach.* Baltimore: Paul H. Brookes Publishing Co.

Perlroth, P., Pumpian, I., Hesche, S., & Campbell, C. (1993, Winter). Transition planning for individuals who are deaf and blind: A person-centered approach. *OSERS News in Print,* 24–30.

Perske, R. (1988). *Circles of friends.* Nashville: Abingdon Press.

Petronio, K. (1988). Interpreting for deaf-blind students: Factors to consider. *American Annals of the Deaf, 133*(3), 226–229.

Rainforth, B., York, J., & McDonald, C. (1992). *Collaborative teams for students with severe disabilities: Integrating therapy and educational services.* Baltimore: Paul H. Brookes Publishing Co.

Riggio, M. (1992). A changing population of children and youth with deaf-blindness: A changing role of the deaf-blind specialist/teacher (Reaction paper). *Proceedings of the National Conference on Deaf-Blindness: Deaf-blind services in the 90's–Revitalization and future directions* (pp. 20–27). Sponsored by Hilton/Perkins National Program, Washington, DC.

Rikhye, C., Gothelf, C., & Appell, M. (1989). A classroom environment checklist for students with dual sensory impairments. *Teaching Exceptional Children, 22*(1), 44–46.

Rowland, C., & Schweigert, P. (1990). *Tangible symbol systems: Symbolic communication for individuals with multisensory impairments.* Tucson, AZ: Communication Skill Builders.

Sacks, S., & Wolffe, K. (1990). *The importance of social skills in the transition process for students who are visually impaired.* Paper supported by the National Institute on Disability & Rehabilitation Research, United States Department of Education; The American Foundation for the Blind; and the University of Texas at Austin.

Sailor, W. (1991). Special education in the restructured school. *Remedial and Special Education, 12*(6), 8–22.

Sailor, W., Gee, K., & Karasoff, P. (1993). Full inclusion and school restructuring. In M. Snell (Ed.), *Instruction of students with severe disabilities* (4th ed.) (pp. 1–30). New York: Merrill/Macmillan.

Sailor, W., Gerry, M., & Wilson, W.C. (1991). Policy implications of emergent full inclusion models for the education of students with severe disabilities. In M. Wang, H. Walberg, & M. Reynolds (Eds.), *The handbook of special education* (Vol. IVF). Oxford, England: Pergamon.

Salisbury, C.L., Palombaro, M.M., & Evans, I. (1993). *Collaborative problem solving: Instructor's manual.* Binghamton: State University of New York at Binghamton.

Smithdas, J. (1995). Foreword. In J. Everson (Ed.), *Supporting young adults who are deaf-blind in their communities: A transition planning guide for service providers, families, and friends.* Baltimore: Paul H. Brookes Publishing Co.

Stainback, S., & Stainback, W. (Eds.). (1992). *Curriculum considerations in inclusive classrooms: Facilitating learning for all students.* Baltimore: Paul H. Brookes Publishing Co.

Stainback, W., & Stainback, S. (Eds.). (1990). *Support networks for inclusive schooling: Interdependent integrated education.* Baltimore: Paul H. Brookes Publishing Co.

Sternberg-White, L., & Johnson, S. (1992). *TEAM Training: A 622-C demonstration proposal.* Sacramento: California State Department of Special Education.

Strully, J., & Strully, C. (1989). Friendships as an educational goal. In W. Stainback, S. Stainback, & M. Forest (Eds.), *Educating all students in the mainstream of regular education* (pp. 59–68). Baltimore: Paul H. Brookes Publishing Co.

Touchette, P. (1971). Transfer of stimulus control: Measuring the moment of transfer. *Journal of Experimental Analysis of Behavior, 15,* 347–354.

Van Dijk, J. (1965). The first steps of the deaf-blind child toward language. *Proceedings of the Conference on the Deaf-Blind* (pp. 47–50). Boston: Perkins School for the Blind.

Van Dijk, J. (1986). An educational curriculum for deaf-blind multihandicapped persons. In D. Ellis (Ed.), *Sensory impairments in mentally handicapped people* (pp. 375–382). London: Croom Helm.

Van Dijk, M., & Janssen, M. (1989). *An educational program for deaf blind students.* Paper presented at the Washington State Department of Educational Annual Summer Institute, Seattle.

Voeltz, L.M., Hemphill, N., Brown, S., Kishi, G., Klein, R., Fruehing, F.R., Collie, J., Levy, G., & Kuke, C. (1983). *The special friends program: A trainer's manual for integrated school settings* (rev. ed.). Honolulu: University of Hawaii, Department of Special Education, Hawaii Integration Project.

Wagner, M. (1989). *The transition experiences of youth with disabilities: A report from the National*

Longitudinal Transition Study. Menlo Park, CA: Stanford Research Institute.

Wang, M. (1989). Adaptive instruction: An alternative for accommodating student diversity through the curriculum. In D.K. Lipsky & A. Gartner (Eds.), *Beyond separate education: Quality education for all* (pp. 99–119). Baltimore: Paul H. Brookes Publishing Co.

Welch, T. (1993). Learning and concept development. In K. Huebner, T. Welch, & J. Prickett (Eds.), *Deaf-blind learners: A self-study curriculum in communication and mobility.* New York: American Foundation for the Blind Consortium.

Wilder Foundation. (1992). *Collaboration: What makes it work. A review of research literature on factors influencing successful collaboration.* Minneapolis: Author.

Chapter 2

A History of Federal Support for Students with Deaf-Blindness

R. Paul Thompson
and Charles W. Freeman

Prior to 1933, no formal education programs existed for people with deaf-blindness. In fact, in 1928, the Bureau of the Census reported that there were only 169 people with deaf-blindness in the United States (a figure likely to be more reflective of an error in measurement than of the actual number of people). From the 1930s to the 1950s, several states instituted programs in the form of residential schools for students with deaf-blindness. However, it remained for the emergence of federal support to spur the growth of such programs to other states, the initiation of research and demonstration projects to improve the quality of educational services, and the widespread availability of technical assistance to assist states and programs in serving students with deaf-blindness. This chapter traces the evolution of this federal support and illustrates how the partnership of federal, state, university, and school district programs have fostered the continual growth and refinement of services to individuals with deaf-blindness from the early 1950s to the early 1990s. Table 1 summarizes U.S. legislation discussed in this chapter.

EARLY DEVELOPMENTAL PERIOD OF FEDERAL SUPPORT: 1950–1969

Throughout the 1950s and 1960s, most educational programs for children with deaf-blindness were provided at state residential schools for children who were either blind or deaf. These programs were few in number and scattered widely across the United States. Additionally, the few programs available typically limited their enrollment to those children who were perceived to be of average or above-average intelligence.

The general reluctance to enroll children with deaf-blindness who also had other serious disabilities can be appreciated when considering the complex challenges in providing educational services to these children. Waterhouse (1977) observed that in deaf-blindness, the resulting compound disability is different from, and greater than, the sum of the component disabilities. Schein (1978) further emphasized that "the presence of a second handicapping condition does not add to the handicapped person's problems, it *multiplies* them" (p. 4). Conlon (1991) noted

Table 1. U.S. legislation supporting educational services for children with deaf-blindness

Public law (PL)	Title	U.S. code	Year	Principal provisions relating to children with deaf-blindness
PL 89-10	Elementary and Secondary Education Act of 1965	20 U.S.C. §241 et seq.	1965	• Provided grants to States to assist local school districts to meet special educational needs of educationally-deprived children in low income areas. (Children with disabilities in low income areas also eligible.)
PL 89-313	Amendments to the Elementary and Secondary Education Act of 1966	20 U.S.C. §843	1966	• Provided grants to State agencies on behalf of children with disabilities in state-operated and state-supported schools.
PL 89-750	Elementary and Secondary Education Amendments of 1966	20 U.S.C. §873 et seq.	1966	• Established the Bureau of Education for the Handicapped and assigned it responsibility to carry out programs of education and training for children with disabilities. • Grants to states to support services to children who are migratory, neglected and delinquent.
PL 90-247	Elementary and Secondary Education Amendments of 1967	20 U.S.C. §877b	1967	• Established the Centers and Services for Deaf-Blind Children Program, including provision of diagnostic services for and programs for the adjustment, orientation, and education of children with deaf-blindness and consultative services to their parents and other service providers. • Authorized research, development or demonstration, training of personnel, and dissemination of materials.
PL 91-230	Reauthorization of Elementary and Secondary Education Programs	20 U.S.C. §1401 et seq.	1970	• Established Bureau of Education of the Handicapped within the Office of Education. • Established Part C, to include: regional resource centers, centers and services for deaf-blind children, and early education for handicapped children and applied authority for each of these programs to conduct research, development and demonstration, training of personnel, and dissemination activities.
PL 94-142	Education for All Handicapped Children Act of 1975	20 U.S.C. §1411	1975	• Established Part B as Assistance for Education of All Handicapped Children; mandated provision by States of a free appropriate public education for children with disabilities (children with deaf-blindness meeting the criteria).

PL 98-199	Education of the Handicapped Act Amendments of 1983	20 U.S.C. §1402	1983	• Established Office of Special Education with Office of Special Education and Rehabilitative Services, with responsibility to administer programs for children with disabilities. • Established a National Advisory Committee on the Education of Handicapped Children and Youth. • Established provision regarding architectural barriers. • Authorized a grant to provide technical assistance to all state and multi-state projects for children with deaf-blindness and a grant to provide technical assistance to states to facilitate the transition of individuals with deaf-blindness from education to employment and other postsecondary options.
PL 99-457	Education of the Handicapped Act Amendments of 1986	20 U.S.C. §1422	1986	• Established Handicapped Infants and Toddlers Program; amended Preschool Grants Program; amended provision of services to Native American children with disabilities; added responsibility for evaluation of programs to the Secretary. • Authorized issuance of awards for extended school year projects in Centers and Services for Deaf-Blind Children Program. • Expanded authority under Centers and Services for Deaf-Blind Children Program to support research, development and demonstration, training, and dissemination activities for children with other severe disabilities.
PL 101-476	Education of the Handicapped Act Amendments of 1990 (IDEA)	20 U.S.C. §1422	1990	• Added definition of deaf-blindness. • Authorized award of a national clearinghouse on deaf-blindness and award of "pilot projects." • Clarified that program services could be extended to infants and toddlers. • Deleted program authority to award extended school year, Statewide Systems Change projects, and projects serving children with disabilities other than deaf-blindness. • Added more flexibility in provision of services to facilitate transition from educational to other services by making "adolescents" and "young adults," as opposed to only "youth," upon age twenty-two," eligible for services.

that during this period, children born with deaf-blindness entered "a world ill-equipped to provide for them. They were born into families that had not known persons with such disabilities. They were living in communities where appropriate medical assistance and immediate, appropriate interventions were not available" (p. 42).

School-age children with deaf-blindness who functioned below-average intellectually were most often placed in residential schools or "asylums" where they were typically provided only custodial and life-sustaining services. Many of the schools serving these children were physically located in remote areas or at isolated sites in cities where the students (often termed "inmates") could be obscured from the view of the general public. During this period, personnel trained to instruct children with deaf-blindness were few in number, and opportunities for personnel in-service training and acquaintance with new methodology and teaching materials were very limited. The nation's teacher training programs for addressing the learning needs of children with disabilities were just being developed, as were standards for teacher certification.

Elementary and Secondary Education Act (ESEA) of 1965: PL 89-10

In the early 1960s, the U.S. Congress enacted the Elementary and Secondary Education Act (ESEA) of 1965. This act was created in response to a growing public demand for federal assistance to support education programs for children with special needs. This landmark legislation authorized the awarding of funds to assist state and local school districts in meeting the special academic needs of educationally deprived children in low income areas. Although not so specified in the legislation, children with disabilities, including those with deaf-blindness, who lived in low income areas were considered to be "educationally deprived" and consequently were eligible for services under this program.

ESEA Amendments of 1966 and 1967

Despite its general application to national education programs, a significant number of children with disabilities participating in state-operated and state-supported schools did not fall within the purview of the new ESEA statute. Congress corrected this oversight with the passage of PL 89-313 on November 1, 1966, which established eligibility for state agencies that are "directly responsible for providing, on a non-school-district basis, free public education for handicapped children" to receive annual appropriations based on the numbers of such children served (PL 89-313, §16[a][5]).

Congress further amended ESEA with PL 89-750. Enacted November 1, 1966, this legislation established Title VI—Education of Handicapped Children—"for the purpose of assisting the States in the initiation, expansion, and improvement of programs and projects . . . for the education of handicapped children . . . at the preschool, elementary and secondary school levels" (ESEA, Title VI, §601). Section 609 of PL 89-750 provided for the establishment of the Bureau of Education for the Handicapped "for administering and carrying out programs and projects relating to the education and training of the handicapped, including programs and projects for the training of teachers of the handicapped and for research in such education and training" (PL 89-750, §609).

Section 103(a) of this law authorized federal support to state education agencies for establishing or improving programs for children of migratory agricultural workers, while Section 104(a)(c) authorized federal payments based on the number of children in the school districts ages 5–17 who were living in the community with their families, living in institutions for children who are neglected or delinquent, or children being supported in foster homes with public funds. Early records indicate that a few children with deaf-blindness who also met the criteria of being migratory, neglected, or delinquent were served by funds under this amendment.

On April 3, 1967, Congress reauthorized ESEA with an amendment that established regional resource centers, promoted the recruitment of personnel through the dissemination of information concerning educational opportunities for people with disabilities, and created Title VI of the Elementary and Secondary Education Act of 1965, designating this title as the *Education of the Handicapped Act*.

Results of ESEA and Its Early Amendments

Reflecting on the 1968–1969 accomplishments of these newly authorized federal programs, the U.S. Office of Education reported on activities supported under ESEA (as amended) and under PL 89-313 in three documents: 1) *Resumes of Projects for Handicapped Children Funded under the PL 89-313 Amendment to Title I, ESEA—Fiscal Year 1968*, which described the nature of the children served and the types of services provided in PL 89-313–funded projects; 2) *Selected Projects for Handicapped Children* under PL 89-313 and Title VI-A, ESEA-Fiscal Year 1968, with similar information on 164 Title VI-A and 66 PL 89-313 projects; and 3) a summary document of educational accomplishments of children served under both programs, *Better Education for Handicapped Children* (1968). Although the actual number of children with deaf-blindness who participated in these projects was not reported, a limited number of such children participated in early programs at the Alabama Institute for the Deaf and Blind, Perkins School for the Blind in Watertown, Massachusetts, and the state Schools for the Blind in Michigan and California.

Centers and Services for Deaf-Blind Children Program: PL 90-247

In spite of significant national interest throughout the later 1960s in the needs of children with disabilities, the unique needs of children with deaf-blindness remained largely unrecognized during this period. Dantona (1977) observed that:

> It took the devastating and catastrophic force of the rubella epidemic that swept across the United States in 1964 and 1965 to bring about an acknowledgement of the neglect and indifference that had for so long characterized public attitudes toward deaf-blind and other severely handicapped children. (p. 172)

Thus, while the ESEA amendments were under consideration by Congress, the disastrous results of the 1964 and 1965 rubella epidemic gained national attention. This epidemic left in its wake approximately 2,500 children with deaf-blindness who would be in need of extensive, special educational services beginning by school year 1969. Theodore Ellenbogen, then Assistant General Counsel, Division of Legislation for the U.S. Department of Health, Education, and Welfare (HEW), forwarded a first draft of the Centers and Services for Deaf-Blind Children program to be inserted in Senate Bill 1125 (H.R. 7819) of the Elementary and Secondary Education Amendments of 1967. The draft proposed the establishment of centers for children with deaf-blindness that would provide for their adjustment, orientation, and education by integrating all professional and allied services. The program also stipulated support for the development or demonstration of new or improved methods, approaches, or techniques contributing to the adjustment of these children.

James M. Frey, Acting Assistant Director for Legislative Reference, Budget Bureau, expressed serious doubts as to the need for and desirability of the proposed amendment, suggesting that any special program for such children should be an integral part of the regional resource centers program (J.M. Frey, departmental memorandum, October 2, 1967). The HEW countered Frey's rejection of their proposal and continued with strong support for the proposed services.

Considerations by Congress The growing public support at this time for programs serving children with deaf-blindness soon found an audience with congressional committees. Committee members in discussions for the proposed new Centers and Services for Deaf-Blind Children Program observed that the majority of the nation's children with deaf-blindness were receiving no special education and training services and, furthermore, that many were thought to be remaining at home without any education or intervention (U.S. Senate, Committee on Labor and Public Welfare, Report No. 726, November 6, 1967.) The Senate passed a bill on December 11, 1967, essentially endorsing a bill approved by the House (H.R. 7819), that added a new Part C, Centers and Services for Deaf-Blind Children, to the ESEA. Through a limited number of model centers for children with deaf-blindness, the bill provided

> a program designed to develop and bring to bear upon such children, beginning as early as feasible in life, those specialized, intensive professional and allied services, methods, and aids that are found to be most effective to enable them to achieve their full potential for communication with and adjustment to the world around them, for useful and meaningful participation in society, and for self-fulfillment. (U.S. House of Representatives, House Resolution 7819, Part C, §609, December 11, 1967)

The bill authorized the Secretary "to make grants to or contracts with public or nonprofit private agencies, organizations, or institutions to pay all or part of the cost of establishment (including, when necessary, construction) or operation, or both, of centers for deaf-blind children (House Resolu-

tion 7819, Part C, 609[b]). The centers to be funded under this bill were to provide: 1) comprehensive diagnostic and evaluative services for children with deaf-blindness; 2) a program for the adjustment, orientation, and education of children with deaf-blindness; and 3) effective consultative services for parents, teachers, and others who play a direct role in the lives of these children. The HEW Secretary was authorized to support costs of:

1. Research to identify and meet the full range of special needs of children with deaf-blindness
2. Development or demonstration of new, or improvements in existing, methods, approaches, or techniques
3. Training (either directly or otherwise) of professional and allied personnel engaged or preparing to engage in programs specifically designed for children with deaf-blindness
4. Dissemination of materials and information about practices found effective in working with children with deaf-blindness

Adoption of Legislation The legislation resulting from this extended congressional action was signed by President Johnson on January 2, 1968, as PL 90-247. With the passage of this legislation, the Centers and Services for Deaf-Blind Children Program finally became a reality. Originally, eight centers were funded with 1 million dollars, with the number of centers being increased shortly thereafter to 10. These regional centers were located in Alabama, California, Colorado, Massachusetts, Michigan, Minnesota, New York, North Carolina, Texas, and Washington. The centers began by identifying existing services and determining what additional services were needed. As mandated by the law, these services included comprehensive diagnostic and evaluative services; a program of adjustment, orientation, and education; and consultative services for parents, teachers, and relevant others. The program's regional structure in these early years proved to be effective in the delivery of early direct services and technical assistance to children with deaf-blindness. However, few state education agencies recognized at first their individual responsibilities for assuring strong, independent state services delivery systems.

FEDERAL EDUCATIONAL SUPPORT FOR CHILDREN WITH DISABILITIES: 1970–1985

Education of the Handicapped Act of 1970: PL 91-230

The ESEA was further modified by PL 91-230, enacted April 13, 1970. This significant law amended ESEA to include a new Title VI-Education of the Handicapped Act (EHA). It defined "handicapped children" as children who are "mentally retarded, hard of hearing, deaf, speech impaired, visually handicapped, seriously emotionally disturbed, crippled, or other health impaired children who by reason thereof require special education and related services" (20 U.S.C., §1401). The act established the Bureau for Education of the Handicapped within the Office of Education and assigned to the Bureau the responsibility for administration of programs relating to the handicapped (20 U.S.C. §1402).

Part C of this legislation became the repository for several EHA programs providing benefits and services to persons with disabilities, including Section 621—Regional Resource Centers, Section 622—Centers and Services for Deaf-Blind Children, and Section 623—Early Education for Handicapped Children. Section 624 of this legislation extended benefits across each of the programs under Part C, by authorizing support for research, innovation, personnel preparation, and dissemination of program information and findings. Part D of this act provided support for the training of personnel for the education of people with disabilities, Part E addressed research and demonstration projects, Part F supported instructional media for people with disabilities, and Part G addressed special programs for children with specific learning disabilities (20 U.S.C. §1411 et seq.).

Modifications to the EHA

With the inclusion of the program of services for children with deaf-blindness as a component under Part C of EHA, an overlap of project funding eligibility for programs serving children with deaf-blindness under EHA provisions and the deaf-blind centers program became evident. This overlap issue was not immediately addressed by the Congress in its legislation or by the HEW in its regulations.

Regulations responding to changes affected by PL 91-230 were published in the *Federal Register* as a notice of proposed rule making on October 11, 1973 (Vol. 38, no. 196, pp. 28230–28247). Final regulations for the program were incorporated as Part 121c of Title 45—Public Welfare of the Code of Federal Regulations, and were published in the February 20, 1975 issue of the *Register* (Vol. 40, no. 35, p. 7414).

Included in the revised regulations was a definition of children with deaf-blindness as:

> children who have auditory and visual handicaps, the combination of which causes such severe communication and other developmental and educational problems that they cannot properly be accommodated in special education programs solely for the hearing handicapped child or for the visually handicapped child. (U.S. Code of Federal Regulations, Title 45, 121c.37)

Education for All Handicapped Children Act of 1975: PL 94-142

Congress completed another major educational action with the passage of the strongly worded PL 94-142, entitled The Education for All Handicapped Children Act (EHA) of 1975. (*Note*: the acronym "EHA" has been officially used to designate both the Education of the Handicapped Act and the Education for All Handicapped Children Act, which amended the original EHA.) Part B of this legislation, Assistance for Education of All Handicapped Children, mandated the provision by the states of a free, appropriate public education to children with disabilities as a condition for receipt of federal funding. Over the next few years, states were to come into compliance with the Part B mandate, extending the age of children eligible to receive Part B, EHA services, down toward birth and upward toward age 21. The gradual assumption of mandated responsibility by states to provide educational services for more and more of their children with disabilities brought increased awareness of the overlap of funding programs serving children with deaf-blindness, from both the Part B, EHA and the Centers and Services for Deaf-Blind Children Program.

Amendments to EHA

As the states began their phase-in of services mandated under Part B, EHA, Congress and the U.S. Department of Education directed attention to legislative changes needed in the discretionary programs of EHA, including the Services to Deaf-Blind Children and Youth Program. Concerns regarding this program centered on an anticipated increase in the number of children with deaf-blindness, as well as a recognition of the complexity of their needs.

Estimates on the incidence of these children varied. A National Communicable Dis-ease Center (CDC) report of 1969 indicated that as a result of the national rubella epidemic of 1964–1965 (which resulted in 12,500,000 cases of rubella), approximately 3,580 children now had both visual and hearing impairments. A 1971 survey by the National Center for Health Statistics reported that there were 9,596,000 persons with visual impairments and 14,491,000 persons with hearing impairments at all age levels living in the United States, with 2,559,000 of these (10.6%) having both vision and hearing impairments. A 1976–1977 survey by the Office of Demographic Studies, Gallaudet College, indicated that there were 4,247 students who were deaf with concomitant visual impairments enrolled in 14 different types of programs. Furthermore, the October 6, 1982 House Report (No. 98-410) referenced an unpublished study by Dr. Chelimsky of the Institute for Program Evaluation, U.S. General Accounting Office, which affirmed that there was an absence of information on the exact number of children with deaf-blindness in the nation, the number of such children being served, and the impact of the services being provided. Chelimsky also reported that the extent and nature of services available to these children after they reach the age of 22 years was unclear.

Concerning the complexity of needs, a special study directed by Hanley (1981), Executive Director, Mountain Plains Regional Center for Deaf-Blind children, was presented as testimony before the Subcommittee on the Handicapped on May 21 and 23, 1983. Hanley reported that a majority of the nation's population with deaf-blindness also had severe and multiple disabilities and thus required even more specialized services than was previously recognized. The House Committee, responding to this information, stated that its intent was that the program should emphasize provision of technical assistance to those serving children and youth with deaf-blindness, along with preservice or in-service personnel training in the replication of exemplary practices and enhancement of parental involvement in services provided by the program (U.S. House of Representatives, House Report 3435). In its hearings, the Senate Committee emphasized that its intent was that children with deaf-blindness "be educated with their non-handicapped peers to the greatest extent possible while still receiving special education and related services according to their unique needs" (Senate Report No. 98-191, p. 16).

Education of the Handicapped Act Amendments of 1983: PL 98-199

PL 98-199 was signed into law on December 2, 1983. This legislation authorized support for two technical assistance awards: one to provide technical assistance to state agencies in building their capacity to assure that children and youth with deaf-blindness received a free, appropriate public education, as had been mandated under the companion Part B-EHA legislation, and the second award to promote the capacity of states to facilitate the transition of youth with deaf-blindness who have reached the age of 21, from school to postschool and adult living and working environments.

Revision of Program Regulations

Proposed program regulations, published in the *Federal Register* on April 30, 1984 (Vol. 49, no. 84, pp. 18418–18423) and followed by final regulations published in the *Federal Register* on July 11, 1984 (Vol. 49, no. 134, p. 28160) responded to Congressional committee recommendations and suggestions from service providers across the country, including representatives from six regional deaf-blind centers, six state departments of special education, and three universities. The revisions established two top priorities for use of program funds: 1) the provision of

services to children and youth with deaf-blindness and 2) the provision of technical assistance to states to build their capacity to expand services to children with deaf-blindness. Additionally, the regulations established geographical regions for the conduct of projects, specified types of technical assistance to be made available by the two newly authorized technical assistance providers, described the dissemination activities authorized under the program, and authorized the collection and analysis of data on the number and nature of children served by the program and their service providers. The regulations shifted the program emphasis from provision of direct services to children with deaf-blindness, to provision of technical assistance to develop state education agency capacity to serve children and youth with deaf-blindness; authorized awards to states to operate programs independently from a regional center; and authorized award of research and demonstration projects to improve practices and techniques in educating children and youth with deaf-blindness.

New program trends emerged as a result of the revised regulations and included

1. Focus on provision of technical assistance with a reduction of direct services
2. Withdrawal of many states from the former so-called "regional centers" projects to become individual, single state projects
3. Increased emphasis on funding demonstration and research projects promoting effective program practices

The Association for Persons with Severe Handicaps (TASH) was the successful grantee to provide technical assistance in building state capacity to provide services to school-age children, while the Helen Keller National Center (HKNC) was the successful grantee to address the needs of youth transitioning into postschool settings. A third special award was granted in 1984 to the Gallaudet University in support of a nationwide project for the dissemination of information concerning the nature, needs, educational programming practices, and other service delivery project information.

Impact of Legislation

The legislative period of 1970–1985 is one of contrasts. It began with educational practices principally formed on an individual, teacher-intuitive basis. It bridged to a time of sharing, with service providers exchanging information on best practices verified for effectiveness. Blea and Overbeck (1977) described the beginning picture as one where "empirical research focusing specifically upon the development and education of the deaf-blind child, per se, [was] practically nil" (p. 256). Wolf, Delk, and Schein (1982), in conducting a needs assessment of services to individuals with deaf-blindness, concurred with this observation and summarized that the "two most critical areas, aside from employment, [were]: communication and transportation" (p. 71).

This period was distinguished by the initiation in 1978 of program support for innovation. Three exploratory, model projects designed to develop improved, effective services were funded. These projects included

1. Teaching Research of Monmouth, Oregon, which demonstrated that students with deaf-blindness, ages 13–21, could be educated in a typical general education classroom
2. The Frederic Burk Foundation, San Francisco State University, which documented success in providing nonsegregated services to children with deaf-blindness ages 5–12
3. Deafness Research and Training Center, New York University, which developed procedures for providing comprehensive

assessment and educational services to children with deaf-blindness, ages 3–18, either in their homes or in custodial institutions

The period of 1970–1985 was also marked with increased interest in providing services to children with multiple disabilities, including deaf-blindness. In response to this interest, the Bureau of Education for the Handicapped (BEH) organized a task force to consider the educational needs of these children, charging the committee to propose strategies implementing

> a new Bureau-wide objective in the 1974–1978 Five Year Plan: to enable the most severely handicapped children and youth to become as independent as possible, thereby reducing their requirements for institutional care and providing opportunities for self-development. (Thompson, Wilcox, & York, 1980, p. 1)

In an effort to promote a greater exchange of information in the fields of deaf-blindness and other severe disabilities, BEH convened a national conference in 1978: *Innovation in Education for Deaf-Blind Children and Youth*. Dr. Ed Martin, Commissioner of Education, addressing the convened educators and directors of projects from these two significant fields, stated the following:

> This is a marvelous and dignified kind of work that has attracted you and we are glad that the federal government has been of help in behalf of some of the most vulnerable people in our society. In 1969, when the first centers were funded, less than 100 children were served by six or seven programs. Today there are nearly 300 programs throughout all the states and territories, serving 5872 deaf-blind children, and probably 5000 people, including parents, teachers, and medical personnel, have lent their skills to providing these services.
>
> Of these 5872 children, nearly 2300 are served entirely with non VI-C monies, and the remainder receive services through Title VI-C and other federal, state, and local funds. Today's budget of $16 million represents $3 of other money for each VI-C dollar, and this

funding pattern has been established without a mandate that states must match the federal contribution. (Department of Health, Education, and Welfare, 1978, p. 1)

ENHANCEMENT AND EXPANSION PERIOD: 1986–1992

By the mid-1980s, programs addressing the needs of children with disabilities had markedly expanded both in number and comprehensiveness. Refinements in methodology, an increase in the variety and extent of resources to meet instructional needs, and the numbers of trained personnel had also improved. With this expansion, however, the nation became aware of even greater needs of this population, including infants and toddlers at risk of developmental delays and disabilities, preschool children evidencing complex problems resulting from parental drug addiction and alcohol abuse, secondary and postsecondary children and youth failing to transition effectively into changing community living and working environments.

Education of the Handicapped Act Amendments of 1986: PL 99-457

Public Law 99-457 was legislated in response to the growing need for services. It established a new Handicapped Infants and Toddlers Program and amended the Preschool Grants Program. Specific to the Centers and Services for Deaf-Blind Children Program, PL 99-457 authorized extended school–year demonstration programs for children and youth with severe disabilities, including children and youth with deaf-blindness, and expanded the range of disabilities of children eligible to be included in research, development, or demonstration projects, as authorized under the Program for Severely Handicapped Children. PL 99-457, however, disregarded a recommendation of the Budget Office of the U.S. Department of Educa-

tion that the Centers program be merged with the Program for Severely Handicapped Children.

Regulatory Revisions to PL 99-457

The development of revised program regulations complementing PL 99-457 extended over a 24-month period. Proposed regulations were published in the *Federal Register* in November of 1988 (Vol. 53, no. 225, pp. 47406–47410, 1988); final regulations followed 5 months later (Vol. 54, no. 72, pp. 15308–15313, 1989). In the revisions, the Department of Education addressed the funding inequity for the state awards by specifying four factors to be used in establishing award levels:

1. The number of children and youth with disabilities in the state
2. The number of children and youth with deaf-blindness in the state
3. The relative cost of providing services authorized under the program to children and youth with deaf-blindness in the state
4. The quality of the application submitted

The use of child-count data in the award determination for the state and multi-state projects improved reporting of children with deaf-blindness. Attempts in previous years to "centrally collect information about the deaf-blind population was done on a voluntary basis and resulted in a general undercounting of the population nationwide" (Baldwin, 1991, p. 2). Under PL 99-457, applicants for the program were required to submit an annual report of the number of children with deaf-blindness being served. Based on a study by Baldwin (1991), who estimated an incidence ratio of approximately 2 students with deaf-blindness per 1,000 students with disabilities, it could be further estimated that there were from 7,214 to 10,958 children with deaf-blindness in the nation as of 1989. Responding to the new evaluation criteria, applications submitted for state and multi-state projects, as well as for demonstration projects, evidenced marked improvement in the comprehensiveness and overall quality of project activities.

1990 Reauthorization of EHA

In 1990, considering the reauthorization of the Education of the Handicapped Act, the Department of Education once again proposed to congressional committees that the Services for Deaf-Blind Children Program be merged with the Program for Severely Handicapped Children. The department's view reflected recommendations of certain professional educators advocating for educational services based on behavior and learning similarities between children with deaf-blindness and those with other serious disabilities. This proposed merger of the two programs generated a prompt response, both enthusiastic and negative, from the field. Representing opposition to such a merger, Collins and Marshall (1989) testified before Congressional committees on behalf of the National Coalition on Deaf-Blindness. They proposed that

1. A definition of deaf-blindness be included in the regulations
2. Seventy percent (70%) of the program funds be used to support single and multistate centers for children with deaf-blindness
3. Authority authorizing the use of 622 (Services for Deaf-Blind Children) funds for 624(a) (Program for Children with Severe Disabilities) activities be deleted
4. Eligibility of children for services under the program be restricted to only those children with deaf-blindness

The deletion of authority to include children with severe disabilities from projects supported by the program became a major concern for other national interest groups and individuals. These organizations also appealed to Congress. They contended for the educational advantages offered by projects including children with deaf-blindness to also be made available to those with other severe disabilities.

Education of the Handicapped Act Amendments of 1990: PL 101-476

House bill H.R. 1013, and Senate bill S. 1824 reflected Congressional response to the input received from the various interest groups concerning reauthorization of the EHA. However, because of significant differences between these two bills, a conference committee was convened to seek a mutually acceptable resolution. The resulting legislation, the Education of the Handicapped Act Amendments of 1990 (PL 101-476) was signed by President George Bush on October 30, 1990.

These amendments reauthorized the discretionary programs under Parts C through G of the EHA and made certain changes to Parts A, B, and H. This law renamed the EHA as The Individuals with Disabilities Education Act. It changed the term *handicapped children* to *children with disabilities*, added two new categories of disability: *autism* and *traumatic brain injury*, defined *transition services*, created the Program for Children and Youth with Serious Emotional Disturbance, and authorized provision of services in most discretionary programs to include infants and toddlers with disabilities.

Changes affecting the Services for Children with Deaf-Blindness Program responded to many of the recommendations of the National Coalition and other organizations serving this population. Among these changes, the new legislation

1. Added local education agencies (LEAs) and Part H lead agencies to state edu-

cation agencies (SEAs) as program beneficiaries

2. Included infants and toddlers and early intervention services to the scope of the program
3. Provided services to facilitate transition from educational to other services by allowing adolescents and young adults (as opposed to the previous restriction of only "youth, upon attaining age 22") to become eligible for such services
4. Provided a definition of children with deaf-blindness, including in that definition infants and toddlers identified as having deaf-blindness
5. Authorized support for pilot supplementary services by single and multistate projects as well as a national clearinghouse for children with deaf-blindness
6. Authorized funding for pilot, research, development or demonstration, or replication projects, preservice and inservice training, and parental involvement activities; children with severe disabilities other than deaf-blindness became ineligible for project participation

Impact of Legislative Changes Resulting From PL 99-457 and PL 101-476

The impact of legislative changes resulting from PL 99-457 and PL 101-476 was substantive and pronounced. Funding competitions during this period demonstrate the impact of these laws. The competitions were characterized by formulation of and research pertaining to innovative educational approaches. Specifically, they addressed development of social skills, skills related to the transition to differing education programs and to community living environments, inservice training of personnel, supported employment, and utilization and validation of innovations. Evidence of the success of these projects included a proliferation of professional publications reporting project activi-

ties and achievements and presentations of project findings and research results in national and international conferences.

Several particularly significant projects were funded following the enactment of this legislation. In 1990, the American Foundation for the Blind, in a consortium effort with other national service providers, was awarded a 4-year project to develop, evaluate, and disseminate new or improved curricula and materials for the inservice training and self-study use of special education personnel to deliver educational services that meet the unique needs of children and youth with multiple disabilities, including those with deaf-blindness. This project focused specifically on communication and mobility skills. Teaching Research Division was awarded a national clearinghouse for children with deaf-blindness project and a second award to conduct the National Symposium on Provision of Educational and Related Services to Children with Deaf-Blindness. St. Luke's/Roosevelt Hospital Center and the University of Oregon were awarded research projects addressing the social relationships of children and adolescents with deaf-blindness. However, despite these accomplishments, there is still concern that not enough is being done. Collins (1992), in addressing the March 1992 National Conference on Deaf-Blindness, cautioned that the current era is one in which funding is less than adequate and more difficult to obtain.

AN OVERVIEW OF SERVICES FOR CHILDREN WITH DEAF-BLINDNESS

In March 1887, Anne Sullivan, a graduate of the Perkins School for the Blind, began to teach a 6-year-old with deaf-blindness named Helen Keller. The young Helen frequently demonstrated violent tantrums, but even with the tantrums, she responded to Anne's efforts to teach her the names of familiar objects. At first Helen considered this process to be simply an interesting game. It was not until April 5, 1887, that she first sensed the relationship between objects and language. Spelling "w-a-t-e-r" as it gushed forth from the water pump onto Helen's hand, Anne had penetrated a void in learning. Anne described this unique experience:

> The word coming so close upon the sensation of cold water rushing over her hand seemed to startle her. She dropped the mug and stood transfixed. A new light came into her face. She spelled "water" several times. Then she dropped to the ground and asked for its name. She pointed to the pump and the trellis, and suddenly turning around, she asked for my name. I spelled "teacher." (Braddy, 1933, p. 126)

Helen Keller went on to become the first person with deaf-blindness to receive a bachelor's degree from Radcliffe College. Her exceptional life of humanitarian service in speaking out across the globe as to the dignity of people with disabilities and their rights to full citizenship privileges clearly demonstrates the extended benefits to society of teaching individuals with deaf-blindness. From the spelling of "w-a-t-e-r" in the hand of a wondering Helen Keller first sensing a relationship between words and her world, to the awareness of a nation of parents, siblings, and a vast array of other persons seeking to bring about a similar awakening in others, programs and services for children with deaf-blindness have come a long way.

Prior to 1965, programs for these children were few in number, scattered across the face of the nation, and limited in their enrollment only to those students who clearly indicated promise of academic achievement. The fortunate few were taught following traditional procedures that their teachers had found successful when instructing children without disabilities. Intuition and initiative were their craft, waged with anxiousness and anticipation. Their teaching methods were rarely shared with others in a similar pursuit.

Meeting the educational needs of this population was demanding. Hicks and Pfau (1979) observed

> It is impossible to plan an effective educational or rehabilitative program for multihandicapped persons simply by understanding the nature of the isolated handicaps and then attempting to extricate the handicaps one from the other. . . . Multiple handicaps become so intertwined and interlaced that they synergistically complicate and compound the problem. (p. 76)

The rubella epidemic of 1964–1965 greatly increased national awareness of the paucity of academic programs for children with multiple disabilities. Many children were emerging from the epidemic with both deafness and blindness to confront an ill-prepared and understaffed resource of trained service providers. Fortunately, the time for realization of this problem was ripe. With the enactment of the Elementary and Secondary Education Act of 1965 (PL 89-10), America had just begun to direct certain of its federal treasury to support programs for the educationally deprived.

The Centers and Services for Deaf-Blind Children Program began in 1969 with funding of 1 million dollars. By 1976, the federal coffers offered their peak release of 16 million in appropriated funds. The number of students served by funded programs increased from approximately 150 to more than 5,000 before the 1970s had passed into history.

In 1974, with the establishment of the program for children with severe disabilities, a new profession of educators emerged: a limited, but expanding, battery of professionals determined to address the issue of equal rights to education for these children. Following closely in 1976, the Centers and Services for Deaf-Blind Children Program initiated awards to support development, demonstration, training, and dissemination activities to address the needs of children with additional, complex disabilities. The federal dollar had demonstrated that children with deaf-blindness could learn and achieve success. Federal funding was being used to prime new developments, take educational risks and validate their effectiveness, and leverage the generation of state and local funds to meet the rising costs for improved services.

In this arena of change, teaching guides and products produced in isolated settings were being reexamined and reevaluated. Traditional procedures were being challenged by evidence of greater promise in alternative practices. National meetings and symposiums were convened to assess the "state of the art" and to define directions for the future. But with all these signs of progress, still too little attention was being given to the compelling needs for counseling and the sustaining of dedicated efforts on the part of parents and families of children with deaf-blindness. Trained teachers were dropping out of service, "burned out" through an overtaxing and overextending of their patient efforts. The training of replacements to the educational force was lagging desperately behind need.

With the passage in 1975 of the Education of All Handicapped Children Act (PL 94-142), a new national dedication to meeting the needs of persons with disabilities, their parents, and service providers was declared. Spawning from this significant legislation were the amendments of 1983 and 1986 that brought with their implementation in local schools across the country important improvements in the federal programs serving individuals with deaf-blindness. States began accepting and acting upon a greater recognition of their responsibility for these children, while federal dollars were being directed toward carving out new techniques for teaching, researching cause and effect, conducting project assessments, and disseminating and demonstrating strategies for achieving better results. Figure 1 indicates

the number and types of services provided to children with deaf-blindness under federal funding from the years 1978 to 1992.

It remained for the enactment of the Individuals with Disabilities Education Act (1990) to bring about the present vista of federal support. The Part H program for infants and toddlers and the ESEA Section 619 Preschool Program for children ages 3–5 combine objectives with the far-reaching Part B Education of the Handicapped program to set new standards of excellence in service for children with disabilities of all ages.

It is upon the strength of these sister programs, refining themselves through application to the realities of ever-increasing need, that the Services for Children with Deaf-Blindness Program, significantly amended by this act, has in like manner moved ahead. A program that began in the 1960s in isolated residential schools has emerged into a program as varied and exciting as the students it was determined to serve. It is now typically located in inclusive programs in neighborhood schools. There has been a reexamination, review, adjustment, adaptation, and modification motivated by a sense of urgency by a program struggling to achieve its mission. Table 2 shows the number of children with deaf-blindness benefiting, numbers and types of activities, and amount of funding provided as a result of the legislation covered in this chapter.

Meyer's (1991) perceptions of changes in educational programming for children with severe disabilities can be as keenly observed in similar services for children with deaf-blindness:

> The major shifts in curriculum from a developmental to an environmental reference and in vocational training from a transition service to a supported employment model both represent examples of how professional practices have acknowledged the fundamental flaw in approaches focusing upon the remediation of individual deficits. . . . The emphasis has unequivocally shifted to support models: the

SERVICES FOR CHILDREN WITH DEAF-BLINDNESS PROGRAM
TYPES OF DEMONSTRATION, RESEARCH,
AND IN-SERVICE TRAINING PROJECTS FUNDED - 1978-1992

Model Projects	1978	1979	1980	1981	1982	1983	1984	1985	1986	1987	1988	1989	1990	1991	1992
Model Projects--Children	2	2	2												
Model Projects--Youth	1	1	1												
Deaf-Blind Conference	1		1												
Innov. Vocational--Youth			3	3	3										
Innov. Educ. Practices			3	3	3	1	1								
Deinstitution/Integration			2	2	2	1	1								
Integrated Educ. Services				1	1	1									
Innovative Voc.Practices				1	1	1									
Total Life Planning					2	4	4	3	3	3					
Vocational Educ. Training					2	3	3								
Institutes-Integration					2*	2*	2*	2*	2*						
Institutes-Generalization					2*	2*	2*	2*	2*						
Ident. Child. At-Risk					1	2	2								
Adaptive Curriculum					1	2	2	1							
Statewide System Change					5*	8*	8*	9*	7*	8*	3*	7*			
Supported Employ. Skills					2	2	10	5							
Innovative Model					2	5	5	10	11	11	8	4			
Deaf-Blind Study (Count)					1										
Communication Skills					1	1	1	1	4	3	3				
Social Skills								3	3						
Transition Skills										4	4	4			
In-service Training										6	8	8	2		
Supported Employment										1	1	1			
Dissemin. of Information										1	1	1			
Extended School Year											1	1	1		
Contextual Innovations												1	1	4	3
Utilization of Innovations												4	7	8	4

Figure 1.   Number and types of demonstration, research, and inservice training projects funded under the Services for Children with Deaf-Blindness Program: 1978–1992.

Figure 1. (continued)

Model Projects	1978	1979	1980	1981	1982	1983	1984	1985	1986	1987	1988	1989	1990	1991	1992
Validation of Innovations												6	8	8	2
Training of Educators													1	1	1
Symposium--Deaf-Blind														1	
Research--Deaf-Blind															2
Clearinghouse--D-Blind															1

* Projects supported jointly with Program for Children with Severe Disabilities funds.

Table 2. Services for children with deaf-blindness program expenditures: 1969–1992[a]

Fiscal year	Children with deaf-blindness benefitting	State, multi-state, technical assistance and dissemination projects		Demonstration, research, training, system change projects		Evaluation studies, field readers, etc.[b]		Totals	
		No.	Amount	No.	Amount	No.	Amount	No.	Amount
1969	4,050	8	1,000	0	0		0	8	1,000
1970	4,100	10	2,000	0	0		0	10	2,000
1971	4,200	10	4,500	0	0		0	10	4,500
1972	4,270	10	7,500	0	0		0	10	7,500
1973	4,310	10	10,000	0	0		0	10	10,000
1974	4,330	10	14,055	0	0		0	10	14,055
1975	4,350	10	12,000	0	0		0	10	12,000
1976	4,600	10	16,000	0	0		0	10	16,000
1977	4,820	10	16,000	0	0		0	10	16,000
1978	5,270	10	15,000	4	1,000		0	14	16,000
1979	5,467	10	14,500	3	1,500		0	13	16,000
1980	5,223	10	14,350	12	1,650		0	22	16,000
1981	5,362	10	14,250	10	1,750		0	20	16,000
1982	5,155	15	13,352	25	1,993		15	40	15,360
1983	3,714	15	10,800	33	4,500		60	48	15,360
1984	4,351	26	11,993	33	2,181	2	826	61	15,000
1985	4,227	33	9,154	36	5,239	4	607	73	15,000
1986	4,613	38	8,251	33	5,681	2	423	73	14,355
1987	5,247	44	8,586	38	6,397	3	17	85	15,000
1988	5,442	45	8,185	32	6,044	3	132	80	14,361
1989	5,956	46	8,146	38	6,008	2	107	86	14,261
1990	6,656	52	8,965	15	5,580	3	10	70	14,555
1991	7,297	51	9,075	22	3,326	2	448	75	12,849
1992	7,839	52	11,008	13	1,698	2	294	67	13,000
TOTAL			248,670		54,547		2,939		306,156

[a]Funds are expressed in $1,000. Count of Children served FY 1969–1977 are estimates.
[b]Includes unobligated funds remaining after award of all grants/contracts.

individual is indeed taught as many new (useful) skills as possible, but the system must also be designed to "fill in" for the absence of any critical skills through support models. (p. 633)

Making these significant changes possible over time in an effort to meet the needs of a comparatively small population of children with deaf-blindness has been the combined success of thousands of parents and service providers whose patient but persistent pursuit of their objective was not to be thwarted. While much effort was volunteered as a freewill offering of service, present results could not have been achieved without the expenditure of millions of dollars carved out of strained state and local resources. Undergirding these resources has been a significant federal financial contribution building on the present and reaching out to future fields

of accomplishment. It was particularly insightful that Wolf et al. (1982) observed a decade ago that "a continued federal presence is desirable in the education of deaf-blind children and youth" (p. 77).

Today's Services for Children with Deaf-Blindness Program is a strong, vital program, critically looking at itself with both caution and optimism: cautious that what appears to be progress today will be so proven in time; optimistic that the benefits will yet appear. Thousands are now within our circle that were once without, in a world of their own. It is with some savory, yet restrained, satisfaction in the success of these programs, that those who have given much, have gained much. It is in the hope for such success in others yet to benefit that each future effort promises its reward.

REFERENCES

Baldwin, V. (1991). Understanding the deaf-blind population. *Traces, 1*(2), 2.

Blea, W.A., & Overbeck, D. (1977). Research needs in the area of the deaf-blind. In E. Lowe & C. Rouin (Eds.), *State of the art: Perspectives on Serving Deaf-Blind Children.* Sacramento: California State Department of Education.

Braddy, N. (1933). *Anne Sullivan Macy: The story behind Helen Keller.* New York: Doubleday.

Collins, M.T. (1992, March). Plenary address: Reflections and future directions. *Proceedings of the National Conference on Deaf-Blindness: Deaf-blind services in the 90's* (pp. 46–58). Sponsored by Hilton/Perkins National Program, Washington, DC.

Collins, M., & Marshall, S. (1989). *Deaf-blind services in 1989—A briefing paper regarding reauthorization of the Education of the Handicapped Act, Title VI, Part C-Centers and Services for Deaf-Blind Children.* Washington, DC: National Coalition on Deaf-Blindness.

Conlon, S. (1991). The federal government's role in educating people with dual sensory impairment. *ASHA Journal, 33*(11), 42.

Dantona, R. (1977). Services for deaf-blind children. *Exceptional Children, 43*(3), 172.

Demographic Studies. (1977). Gallaudet College. Washington, DC: Gallaudet College, Office of Demographic Studies, Division of Research.

Department of Health, Education, and Welfare. Office of Education; Bureau of Education for the Handicapped. (1978, December). *National conference on innovation in education for deaf-blind children and youth.* Washington, DC: Author.

Elementary and Secondary Education Act of 1965, PL 89-10. Title 20, U.S.C. §241 et seq.

Elementary and Secondary Education Act Amendments of 1966, PL 89-313. Title 20, U.S.C. §843.

Elementary and Secondary Education Amendments of 1966, PL 89-750. Title 20, U.S.C. §873 et seq.

Elementary and Secondary Education Amendments of 1967, PL 90-247. Title 20, U.S.C. §877b.

Education for All Handicapped Children Act of 1975, PL 94-142. (August 23, 1977). Title 20, U.S.C. 1401 et seq: *U.S. Statutes at Large, 89,* 773–796.

Education of the Handicapped Act of 1970 (EHA), PL 91-230. (April 13, 1970). Title 20, U.S.C. 1400 et seq: *U.S. Statutes at Large, 84,* 121–195.

Education of the Handicapped Act Amendments of 1983, PL 98-199. Title 20, U.S.C. 101 et seq: *U.S. Statutes at Large, 97,* 1357–1375.

Education of the Handicapped Act Amendments of 1986, PL 99-457. (October 8, 1986). Title 20, U.S.C. 1400 et seq: *U.S. Statutes at Large, 100,* 1145–1177.

Education of the Handicapped Act Amendments of 1990, PL 101-476. Title 20, U.S.C. §1422.

Federal Register, vol. 38, no. 196, pp. 28230–28247 (1973).

Federal Register, vol. 40, no. 35, p. 7414 (1975).

Federal Register, vol. 49, no. 84, pp. 18418–18423 (1984).

Federal Register, vol. 49, no. 134, p. 28160 (1984).

Federal Register, vol. 53, no. 225, pp. 47406–47410 (1988).

Federal Register, vol. 54, no. 72, pp. 15308–15313 (1989).

Hanley, D. (1981). *Centers and services for deaf-blind children—Forum report.* Washington, DC: U.S. Department of Education.

Hicks, W.M., & Pfau, G.S. (1979, April). Deaf-visually impaired persons: incidence and services. *American Annals of the Deaf,* p. 76.

Individuals with Disabilities Education Act of 1990 (IDEA), PL 101-476. (October 30, 1990). Title 20, U.S.C. 1400 et seq: *U.S. Statutes at Large, 104,* 1103–1151.

Meyer, L.H. (1991). Advocacy, research, and typical practices—A call for the reduction of discrepancies between what is and what ought to be and how to get there. In L.H. Meyer, C.A. Peck, & L. Brown (Eds.), *Critical issues in the lives of people with severe disabilities* (pp. 629–649). Baltimore: Paul H. Brookes Publishing Co.

National Center for Health Statistics Report of 1971. (1971). Washington, DC: U.S. Department of Health and Human Services, Office of Health Research, Statistics, and Technology of the Public Health.

National Communicable Disease Center (CDC) Report of 1969. (1969). Washington, DC: U.S. Department of Health and Human Services, Office of Health Research, Statistics, and Technology of the Public Health.

Office of Education, Bureau of Education for the Handicapped. (1968). *Better education for handicapped children.* Washington, DC: U.S. Government Printing Office.

Office of Education, Bureau of Education for the Handicapped. (1968). *Resumés of Projects for Handicapped Children Funded under the P.L. 89-313 Amendment to Title I, ESEA-Fiscal Year 1968.* Washington, DC: U.S. Government Printing Office.

Office of Education, Bureau of Education for the Handicapped. (1969). *Selected projects for handicapped children under PL 89-313 and title VI-A, ESEA-fiscal year 1968.* Washington, DC: U.S. Government Printing Office.

Schein, J.D. (1978, September). *Simultaneous deafness and blindness.* Paper presented at the Workshop on Education and Rehabilitation of Persons Who Are Both Deaf and Blind, St. Thomas, Virgin Islands.

Stewart, D. (1812). *Some accounts of a boy born blind and deaf.* Transactions of the Royal Society of Edinburgh.

Thompson, R.P., Wilcox, B., & York, R. (1980). The federal program for the severely handicapped—historical perspective, analysis, and overview. In B. Wilcox & R. York (Eds.), *Quality education for the severely handicapped—The federal investment.* Washington, DC: U.S. Department of Education.

U.S. Code of Federal Regulations, Title 45, 121.c.37.

U.S. House of Representatives, House Report No. 3435 on Senate Bill No. 98-191, 1983.

U.S. House of Representatives, House Resolution No. 7819, part C, §609, December 11, 1967.

U.S. Senate, Committee on Labor and Public Welfare, *Report No. 726,* November 6, 1967.

U.S. Senate, *Senate Report No. 98-191* (p. 16), 1983.

Waterhouse, E.J. (1977). Education of the deaf-blind in the United States of America—1837–1967. In E.L. Lowell & C.C. Rouin (Eds.), *State of the art: Perspectives on serving deaf-blind children* (pp. 5–17). Sacramento: California State Department of Education.

Wolf, E.G., Delk, M.T., & Schein, J.D. (1982). *Needs Assessment of Services to Deaf-Blind Individuals.* Silver Spring, MD: REDEX (Rehabilitation and Education Experts).

Chapter 3

Perceptions of Inclusion by Parents of Children Who Are Deaf-Blind

*Joyce Ford
and Bud Fredericks*

This chapter presents the perceptions of parents of children and youth who are deaf-blind regarding the inclusion of their children in neighborhood schools and typical education classrooms. It cites in detail the experiences of one author as she worked for the inclusion of her child. The chapter also presents concerns about inclusion as expressed by other parents of children who are deaf-blind. These concerns raise important issues and indicate directions for professional research. Finally, the authors, both parents of children with disabilities, present a series of recommendations regarding the inclusion of children and youth who are deaf-blind.

The perceptions of parents of children who are deaf-blind have not been greatly studied by the professional community. Giangreco, Cloninger, Mueller, Yuan, and Ashworth (1991) conducted a survey of 28 parents of school-age children in Vermont who are deaf-blind. Parents indicated no preferences for inclusion or segregation but did indicate an aversion to change. Whether inclusive or segregated, a parent's satisfaction with his or her child's educational placement correlated with the degree to which teachers and staff demonstrated a genuine concern for the child by working hard to make his or her school experience positive and meaningful. Wolf (1982), in a survey of 44 parents of children who are deaf-blind, concluded that parents' main apprehensions concerned the future of their children once they reach adulthood. In 1983, Vadasy and Fewell (1986) surveyed mothers of children affected by rubella who were served by the Deaf-Blind Treatment and Evaluation Center at George Peabody College for Teachers between 1970 and 1978. Forty-one mothers responded whose children were adolescents at the time of the study. Although this was one of the more comprehensive surveys ever conducted of parents of children and youth who are deaf-blind and covered such subjects as living situations, children's income and vocational experiences, marital status of the parents, employment and socioeconomic status of the parents, and supports for the mothers, no information was gathered about the education programs in which the youth had been placed.

When these mothers were asked to identify the supports that they desired to make it easier for them to care for their child, 11 mothers (27%) specified more family support, 5 (12%) wanted supplemental income, and 4 (10%) desired a daytime activity for their child and more parent training. Special education was selected as the second (n = 7 [17%]) and the third (n = 8 [20%]) most needed support. It is also interesting to note that the major concern of these parents was for the future of their children and the paucity of adult residential and vocational services.

Since the implementation of Public Law 94-142 (Education for All Handicapped Children Act of 1975), only one study (Giangreco et al., 1991) has focused on the perceptions of parents of children who are deaf-blind regarding school inclusion. Only 28 parents were surveyed, and all respondents were located in a state that has espoused inclusion. With the recent increased emphasis on inclusion of children in neighborhood schools and typical education classrooms, it seems imperative that more information be gathered from parents concerning what is most needed to support their children. We hope that this chapter adds to that process.

EVERY PERSON HAS A RIGHT TO DIGNITY, VALUE, AND SELF-ESTEEM

We, the parents who are writing this chapter, believe that children who are deaf-blind will achieve their fullest potential when they have both the opportunity and the necessary supports to be included with their peers without disabilities across all educational settings. We believe this to be true based on our experi-

ences with our own children; upon the experiences of children and adults who have been with our children; and upon the similar experiences of other people, both parents and professionals. We hold this philosophy to be true for all children and for all people.

We believe that every person has a right to dignity, value, and self-esteem and that those qualities are only fully realized when a person is part of a larger community of people who share similar personal values. We believe that acceptance of differences can be learned, and it is this learning that allows people to feel comfortable with each other when differences are present. These values are developed during childhood, and the educational community plays a fundamental role in the formation of these values.

We believe that the development of relationships within families, between friends, and among community members is an inherent need for all individuals, including those individuals with severe disabilities such as deaf-blindness. Learning how to form these relationships begins in childhood and is therefore an important outcome of education. We believe that our values as a society are reflected in the way we respond to those who are most often denied opportunities to achieve the very components of personal fulfillment that are accepted as normal and often taken for granted. An inclusive education plan can and should address all of these beliefs, and, when it does, society as a whole will benefit.

MY SON RILEY

In September of 1983, my son Riley was born during the 27th week of my pregnancy, approximately 3 months prematurely. The diagnosis of his disabilities came sporadically, beginning when he was 3 months old and continuing over a period of 2 years. This meant that the delivery of intervention services also began without our full knowledge of the extent or impact of his disabilities. While services for Riley continued to be delivered following full diagnosis, I felt that the manner in which these services were being delivered would change as we learned more about him. As the extent of his disabilities became evident, I was at times overwhelmed by the response of professionals and educators; not all parents and children receive such a response. I feel very fortunate to have been the recipient of many positive responses, but not all of the responses have been so. Riley's inclusive education program, then, has been a collective result of these positive and negative experiences. It has involved continual modification, flexibility, and creativity on the part of many people, whether directly or indirectly involved, who have helped or continue to help Riley to achieve his educational goals. For this reason, I will present my experiences in chronological fashion to reflect that evolution, and to allow the reader an opportunity to draw his or her own conclusions.

Riley's First Two Years

Riley was hospitalized in a neonatal intensive care unit (NICU) following his birth. He began life weighing 1 pound, 13 ounces, and we were told that he would need to weigh at least 5 pounds before he would be able to come home. However, it was the complications with Riley's lungs that ultimately determined the length of his stay. During the third month of his hospitalization we were informed that Riley's retinas had completely detached and that he was totally blind. We were told that he would need intervention as soon as possible following discharge. We continued to wait for that day.

After 4½ months, Riley was finally strong enough to come home. He was still quite frail and required constant oxygen. He had difficulty keeping formula down and was con-

fined to the house to limit his exposure to respiratory infections. He did not sleep at night and would pull the taped oxygen canula from his face, often ripping his delicate skin. It was a time of exhaustion that seemed to be unending. Trips to the doctor and hospital became a frequent routine. It was not the homecoming I had anticipated.

Early intervention also began during this first year. Initial assessment at a development center that served only children and adults with disabilities indicated that Riley had increased muscle tone in some areas, had decreased muscle tone in others, and was tactile defensive. Riley was scheduled for half-hour occupational therapy visits twice a week. The therapy sessions seldom lasted longer than a few minutes. Although Riley had been diagnosed as blind prior to the intervention, there was little offered to accommodate that. After his clothing was removed, he was plunged into styrofoam chips. A footbath of vibrating beans was next followed by rolling on a large therapy ball. I called it "therapy 'til you puke." It meant that Riley was so unprepared, overstimulated, and frustrated that his body physically could not tolerate the therapy. He would cry until his body was rigid and trembling; vomiting consistently ended each session. At this point I did not know that Riley was unprepared, overstimulated, or frustrated. I only knew that this was not helping him. I began making excuses not to go to the therapy sessions.

Cerebral palsy (CP) was the next diagnosis to surface. This came when Riley was about 10 months old, and, to my best recollection, I cannot say that this diagnosis had any impact on the way services were delivered. Riley continued his uncontrollable crying and vomiting, and I continued to withdraw from the professionals. We were now only keeping perhaps one appointment a month. By the end of the first year, I discontinued therapies altogether. My only professional support was Riley's pediatrician and a consultant from the School for the Blind who brought me dish mops, sponges, flashlights, and a list of things to do. I felt extremely guilty for not being able to bring myself to put Riley through the ordeal of the therapy when these two supports continually insisted that it was necessary. Looking at this scenario from an educated perspective, it is very easy to say, "This parent needed to advocate for better and more appropriate services." Without a doubt I needed to do that. Yet, consider these questions: Who would tell me that? How was I to know what the better services were? How was I to judge what was appropriate and what was inappropriate? I did not know of any other children like Riley, nor did anyone with whom I had contact. I did not possess the knowledge or experience, and everyone I was depending upon to guide me was telling me I was going in the wrong direction. To follow their direction violated every maternal instinct I had. I was labeled as unresponsive and overprotective.

At the age of 2, Riley was diagnosed as severely-to-profoundly deaf. I was told that his CP involvement was such that he would never walk, and, given the circumstances of all of his disabilities, it was unlikely that he would be able to learn. The recommendation was that we should "call the people who take care of such untidy matters and get on with your lives."

I was both unwilling and unable to follow that advice. I decided to rethink my response to earlier recommendations for therapy. I applied for those services to begin again. They did, and, while Riley was better able to tolerate the therapies, I did not see any particularly notable results in the year that followed. I couldn't understand why the therapist wanted Riley to operate a "visual" toy when she knew that Riley was totally blind, or why she wanted him to lift his head to a ringing bell

when, as near as I could tell, neither she, I, nor anyone else would be expected to look toward a sound when vision and hearing were the problems. It was suggested that these questions could be the result of my grief and denial, and, since the therapists were genuinely kind and caring people, they thought it could be beneficial if I were connected to other families of children with similar needs. My label of unresponsive and overprotective had now grown to include grieving and impractical. Something had to be done with me!

Connecting with Other Families and Developing a Support System

When Riley was 3 years old, a family retreat was held in the Seattle area, sponsored by the coordinator of deaf-blind services for Washington State. I agreed to attend. We did not realize at the time what an important connection this would ultimately become. I learned that there were other families who were facing similar difficulties. I realized that there were other children like Riley and that there were specific educational techniques that were helpful in working with these children. Communication techniques primarily captured my attention, as I recognized that these were basic, fundamental, and essential for my son. Still, I had no idea where to begin or how to convince others of this need. Fortunately, I was now connected to people who had the ability to help me bring those techniques to the people who were working with him.

This began what was to evolve into a very unique support system for Riley, a support system centered around communication. At 3, we would work to build an appropriate preschool program for him. By the age of 4, and until he was 5, he would have his own intervenor to continually feed him information through sign language. We would surround him with communication through objects, symbols, textures, smells, and language. It was very slow. We wanted to see tangible results immediately, but they came in microdoses often weeks apart, or longer. Riley taught us to be consistent and patient, and, when we were, his progress would display itself. We celebrated his success and ours as well.

Transition to Public School

In the fall of his fifth year, Riley moved to public school. This was the first transition we encountered. Public school was a new world for Riley and me. As it turned out, it was a new world for school staff as well. This was the first year that this particular elementary school would house self-contained classrooms for children with disabilities. Riley would be the first child who is deaf-blind to be a member of one of those classrooms, as well as the first child who is deaf-blind to enroll in this public school district. This, however, did not appear to be of any major concern to anyone other than my husband and myself. We were told that we had much to learn about the system; there was the individualized education program (IEP), the child study team, a special education teacher, a teacher's aide, and 10 other children with disabilities, roughly twice as many as there had been at the development center. The ideas were different. They spoke of integration as a requirement of law. (Note: it was called *integration*, as opposed to *inclusion*, at that time. That is *what* they called it!) They spoke of services as a requirement of law. They spoke of the IEP as a requirement of law. They spoke very little about Riley, his needs, or our desires. They felt the intervenor concept was actually inhibiting Riley and limiting his interaction with others. They knew that overprotective parents, such as myself, always wanted one-to-one aides, but that was not an option now. They had a program and Riley would need to fit into it. I

desperately wanted to be off to an agreeable start, to work with the system, and to work through our differences. I also didn't feel I had any other reasonable options or alternatives, and so the school year began on their terms.

Integration had been established as a standard at the time that Riley entered into public school. There was a place on the IEP form that indicated how much time Riley would spend in integrated environments. Theoretically it appeared appropriate, but in actuality it translated into eating lunch at a separate table in the lunchroom and having recess at the same time of day as the typical education classrooms, but at a separate location on the playground. To me, it was just the establishment of segregation within integrated settings, and it made very little sense. Still, it met the guidelines for integration. Because moving play equipment was not permitted on the playground, Riley was allowed to relax by standing at the tether ball pole. This was the one, of course, that did not have a ball attached to it. Needless to say, neither he nor any of his peers without disabilities found this activity inviting.

As slow as progress had been before, it now appeared to have come to a stop. Measures to provide appropriate communication programs all but ceased. Riley lost the few expressive signs he had been using at home. I believed that we were backsliding, but I was assured that Riley was just experiencing plateaus as many children with disabilities do. However, this was not the worst of the matter. He was severely bitten by another student with disabilities during recess: five times on the face, neck, and ear. His arm was bitten three times in another incident during rest time. A third instance on a bus left an injury on his hand. As difficult as it was to find anything positive about this situation, these injuries made it possible for us finally to reduce the size of the classroom and to acquire

the one-to-one aide we had asked for originally. Unfortunately, Riley no longer wanted
to go to school. It hurt to go to school. He
began displaying self-abusive behaviors, and
his actions against himself became consistently more aggressive. He was uncooperative and cried most of the day. I was repeatedly called to the school to bring him home.

My suggestions to utilize the resources and
knowledge of the development center were
not welcomed. I was informed that the staff
members there were not certified teachers,
and therefore their instruction on techniques
would not be solicited. Keep in mind that
these techniques had been brought to the
center by credible authorities in deaf-blind
education, such as Kat Stremel, Debra Chen,
and Terry Rafalowski Welch. This was not a
haphazardly constructed program. Still, the
administration and staff members at the
public school were not enticed. They did
agree to allow the speech therapist from the
center to come to Riley's class and make
some suggestions for working with him, yet
few suggestions were implemented.

I was angry, frustrated, and lost. I turned
back to the people who helped to bring services to Riley's program in the beginning.
They were anxious to help, but encountered
similar resistance. During a technical assistance needs assessment, the classroom
teacher ordered the TRACES[1] consultant out
of her classroom. It was obvious to me that in
order for Riley to receive appropriate services, I was going to need to fight. We were
clearly at war. I was afraid that Riley, now
5 years old, would become the casualty. I
knew that we would have to be creative and
very, very careful. I knew that I was now
considered an adversary of the system. In
retrospect, it is rather sad to think that I was
considered such when my entire energy had
been directed toward acquiring educational

services—services that I believed the education system was mandated to deliver. At this
point, integration was very low on my priority
list and inclusion was not even remotely a
dream. How could it be, when appropriate
services were this difficult to attain?

An "IEP" for the School System

The second year began differently. My husband and I had drawn up a contract that
stated that communication was the primary
objective across all of Riley's services, and
based on that principle he would need to
have an intervenor, or an interpreter/tutor as
the position would now be called. Seven
other requirements were listed. It was, I sup-
pose, an IEP for the system. It listed what
was expected of them—team meetings, in-
service training, communication systems,
meaningful functional programs, and trained
personnel—so that Riley's IEP could, in fact,
be carried out. This was a prerequisite to
Riley's IEP, and, without the support and sig-
nature of the entire child study team, the IEP
was to be considered null and void. It caused
quite an uproar. There had never been such a
document before. No one wanted to sign it. It
took nearly a month, but we finally met and
signed the IEP and the school began to follow the terms we had prescribed.

Riley had a new teacher now. She was not
only new to him, but to teaching as well. He
also had the first ever interpreter/tutor, who
was also new to the education field. (Riley
had an intervenor before, but this was a first
for the school district.) Neither of them had
experience with students who are deaf-blind.
Still, they were dedicated and interested in
delivering appropriate educational services
to Riley. This turned out to be one of the
most important ingredients for success. With
assistance from the Idaho Project Coordinator for Students Who Are Deaf-Blind,

---

[1]The national technical assistance agency at Teaching Research for Children and Youth Who Are Deaf-Blind.

TRACES, and a consulting teacher from Oregon, the in-service training began. The pre-IEP contract indicated the need for quarterly in-service training. While the training was organized through the project coordinator and school administration, the topics, frequency, and requests for financial assistance through TRACES were generally left to my direction. It took considerable prodding of both school staff and administration to meet the quarterly agreement. It was this essential training that sustained positive program changes and team building and ultimately led to inclusion.

Integration was approached both similarly and differently during this second year. "Reverse integration" was introduced, bringing students without disabilities into the self-contained classroom for small periods of time. Although these students were not the same age, there were specific activities that the children participated in together, and it was obvious to any observer that mutual pleasure was the outcome. In-service training on communication was also utilized; calendar boxes and thermoforms emerged.

Once again we began to see growth—both in Riley and within the team. Without abandoning my desires for Riley, I moved my focus to the team. It was apparent that this was the foundation for consistent service delivery. We needed to become stronger and more closely aligned in our direction. The teacher committed herself to the action plans developed during the in-service training. She accepted the role as team leader and actively shared the new knowledge acquired with the other team members. She looked for ways to implement the strategies and to build upon Riley's strengths. She spent a good deal of time instructing Riley's interpreter/tutor on the delivery of programs and the collection of data.

The interpreter/tutor also strived to increase her knowledge and implement the new teaching strategies. Consistency in communication became a primary focus, and, since she was able to accompany Riley throughout his daily activities, that consistency was shared with each team member who interacted with him. I felt fortunate that Riley was placed with the same teacher and interpreter/tutor the following year. Only a couple of the team members changed.

Riley was now 7 years old, and the teacher became an advocate for the children within the classroom. The principal supported her request for adaptive playground equipment and approached the parent-teacher organization for financial assistance. This new equipment allowed children, both with and without disabilities, to play together with minimal adult assistance. We were getting closer to what I believed integration for Riley should look like, although admittedly I never truly had a clear picture of it. Communication skills were developing much better now than they had in the past 2 years, and Riley was generally much happier. While he was using very little expressive language, it was apparent that he understood much of what was being communicated to him in various forms, including sign language. I was anxious to see his development in the next year, now that a solid foundation had been built. I was disappointed to learn that Riley's teacher would be leaving special education at the end of that year. She called it "burn out." I didn't understand. She had only been teaching for 2 years. She told me that I was not the only "difficult" parent she had. Yet another label to add to my ever growing list!

The consistency of the interpreter/tutor helped us to ease into a different special education classroom the following year. The teacher of this classroom appeared open and interested, in spite of my reputation and her self-admitted lack of knowledge about deaf-blindness. The training continued. We focused on communication, mobility, and team development. We altered the structure of services and reduced the "pull-out" time. We strived to incorporate the services within the context of naturally occurring events throughout the day. Still, I was not content with the segregated/integrated lunch situation. I insisted that Riley be removed from the lunchroom and that functional eating skills be worked upon intensely within the classroom so that Riley could be more integrated during lunchtime. At 8, he was still throwing food off of his lunch tray at school for others to retrieve. He did not play this game at home. Our springer spaniel saw to that. If food left the tray at home, it was gone forever. I understood this; Riley understood this; the dog understood this. No one at school understood this. It took confining Riley to his classroom, and making him retrieve the food he had thrown, to put an end to the game. Now, it seemed, everyone was content with Riley's program. It was suggested that we watch a couple of videos in lieu of another formal in-service. This did not happen.

Inclusion in the General Classroom

I wanted more integration. This picture still wasn't clear. When was Riley going to have friends? When was he really going to be a member of the school? We were talking about functional activities and community-based services, but in all honesty I was having a difficult time visualizing where and when these two components would meet the rest of the world. Who was I going to "reverse integrate" when Riley was 23? I expressed my concerns openly.

The next in-service would change the course of Riley's placement. By March of 1992, he would move into a typical third grade classroom. Integration was no longer the subject; inclusion was. This inclusion would be facilitated by his interpreter/tutor, with support from the other members of the team. I knew that Riley needed to be supported with com-

munication above all other aspects. I believed with certainty that meaningful relationships would not form without significant supports for him and for the other children in the classroom as well. It was to our advantage that the position of the interpreter/tutor had been in place for several years.

Still, I felt anxious and uncomfortable. We were moving so quickly, and I wished that I knew more about how to do this, what to look for, and what to expect. I didn't have a model to look at; for that matter, none of us did. We were all very uncertain as to how we would make inclusion work. We knew that most of what we were trying to accomplish would be "trial-and-error," and I wondered if in the long run this would be detrimental for Riley. I questioned my own values and reasons. I had seen another student in another state who had been included. Her frail medical condition added to the difficulty in accomplishing this goal. Occasionally one of her classmates would approach her and wipe the saliva from her chin. It was the only type of interaction I witnessed in the entire time that we observed the classroom. I knew that I wanted inclusion to be more than a transference of caregiving for Riley. I believed that special education was not a place, but rather a set of services. Likewise, I came to know that inclusion is not the removal of special education supports and services because a student's placement has changed. Nevertheless, none of us had prior experience in doing this, and so it was very difficult to translate our visions and dreams for Riley into daily activities. My greatest concern, however, was that someone would try to sabotage the inclusion attempt. I knew about old-school thinking and resistance to change. I knew that almost everyone would feel more comfortable in keeping Riley in the "capsule" of self-containment. No one admitted to these feelings. Outwardly they displayed an enthusiasm to make the inclusion successful.

I worried that friendships would be "staged" or "assigned." I believed in the concept that friends choose each other; they are not appointed by the oldest person in the room. Still, my underlying fear was that no one would choose Riley. What if I was wrong about this? How would this affect future services? It took a while for me to realize how much my own fears of rejection and failure were influencing the establishment of a valid social structure. Beneath my fears, I really did believe that friendships and relationships would occur naturally among the children, regardless of disabilities. I especially believed that this would occur if both Riley and the other children were given the opportunity and the means to cross the barriers and be seen for their abilities. I wanted Riley to appear capable and competent, even if it meant partial participation, or in his case, "fractional" participation. I hoped that we could help the other children to understand this, but I had no idea how we would attempt to explain this concept to them.

Others around me were questioning the validity and value of inclusion. Why would I remove Riley from a system that was just beginning to serve his needs and place him in one that had never been tried? They understood what my concerns were on a social level, but they felt obligated to remind me that children do not acquire their educational goals through osmosis. Had I forgotten that Riley had a lot of time to make up? Some were even so bold as to suggest that Riley's inclusion could in fact be detrimental to the other students in the classroom. What was I trying to prove? These were not the educators who questioned me. These were my friends and family members.

It seemed that the grown-ups had already made up their minds. I knew then that what we were attempting was against all odds. Once again I felt isolated. To one close friend and professional in this field, I described it "as though I was jumping off of a cliff with no idea where the bottom was." I found myself repeatedly defending the very values that we hold sacred for all children. The wisdom of the 8-year-olds would lead us.

It was astounding to witness the reception Riley received from his new classmates. The problem was not if he would have friends; rather it was how we would make the numbers of them more manageable for him. The children were literally fighting over who would get to be with him at any specific time. I thought he would be the child isolated on the playground during recess. Instead, he was at the core of 10 or more children. We invited the students to help us solve the numbers problem and then implemented their plan and praised them for their ideas. They were eager to include Riley in their activities. They wanted him to be capable and competent, not to simply appear that way. They translated this into expectations. It was a quality we had not been able to capture within the self-contained classroom. It was more than I had ever imagined. My hopes for success soared. They fell sharply when his interpreter/tutor resigned without warning 2 weeks later.

Riley returned to the self-contained classroom for about half of his school day. There was no one experienced in tactile sign to step in. Substitute aides worked with him and the search began for a permanent replacement. Communication and consistency dropped. I realized how central a support the interpreter/tutor was to Riley and to his program delivery as well. There were not many applicants, and it took about 3 weeks before the position was filled.

During this same time, I read an article that had been distributed to educators statewide through a university publication. Although the publication was primarily focused on the positive aspects of inclusion, this particular article clearly presented a

negative viewpoint toward including children with severe disabilities in typical educational settings. I felt terribly betrayed when I
realized that the article had been authored
by a key administrator of Riley's team, someone who had led me to believe he was backing this effort. It affirmed all the fears I had
held—the lack of support, deception, differences in philosophy, rejection, and a projec-
tion of failure. I had to wonder how much
this attitude had influenced the resignation
of the interpreter/tutor. I cannot think of
anything that threatened the very existence
of Riley's inclusion more than this. It was difficult to look beyond the attitude and reach
out to the beneficial opportunities that these
circumstances presented. I am not sure that I
would have been able to do that without the
continued support from professionals outside of the local school system.

As with anything, you find that which you
are willing to create. This was an opportunity to redefine our vision for Riley; take
charge of our direction; strengthen the composition of the team; set forth by example the
values we believed in; and attain the support
of higher, more influential administrators.
We resolved the questions, concerns, and
necessity of the interpreter/tutor position.
We added a facilitator to the team who would
serve as anchor to the team and work to ensure that team meetings, in-service training,
and communication among the team members and between the team and school administration were consistent. She did not replace the teacher as case manager, nor my
parental role in the direction of services. She
was to facilitate the function of the team and
to ensure that the inclusion policy of the
school district was met. We discussed both
immediate and long-range issues around
transition and extended school year programs. We began again. This time, however,
it was from a new viewpoint—one that had

Riley, his needs, and our desires and expectations at the center.

Due to the late start, and the complications
we encountered, the team decided that Riley
had not been given a fair shot at third grade.
We elected to have him remain in that grade
for another year. We all felt that there was a
considerable change in academic programming between the third and fourth grades,
and we needed to be better at our inclusion
skills before we moved on.

At the time of this writing, Riley's old classmates are in fourth grade. They are feeling
somewhat left out but are working through
it. Some of the fourth grade girls are teaching
the third graders how to sign with Riley. The
boys are involved as well. I recently spent an
afternoon with Riley's new classmates. We
"played deaf-blind" as an exercise in sensitivity. I wanted them to *feel* what was needed,
without having to be *told*. The kids understood. That same day Riley received 14 spontaneous invitations to do "regular" things,
like "regular" kids. One little boy summarized our efforts eloquently with the question,
"Do you think that Riley could come to my
house to play with me?"

Do I think that inclusion is difficult? I
think we're making it harder than it needs to
be. It takes effort, support, and dedication.
Do I think it's worth it? Absolutely. How else
will the grown-ups ever understand?

PARENTAL ISSUES AND CONCERNS

Both of the authors of this chapter have insisted on their children being included in
neighborhood schools, or as an intermediary
step, in general education programs in other
schools in the district, and being mainstreamed to the maximum extent possible.
As you have just read, the experiences of one
of the authors have been successful up to
now, albeit not without difficulties. The sec-

ond author had fewer difficulties but was equally successful. Both authors are advocates for inclusion. Yet we recognize that many other parents have not been as successful; in fact, many oppose inclusion. We recognize that we cannot speak for all parents; however, we attempt in this section of the chapter to present perspectives of parents with whom we have had contact. The situations and perspectives presented are not unique; they represent the views of many parents and should be recognized by professionals as valid. Giangreco et al. (1991) found concerns similar to those that we cite. We suggest that professionals must be prepared to discuss these issues with parents. In some cases, research may be necessary to obtain adequate responses to the issues being raised.

Inclusion and the Educational Curriculum

Perhaps the most oft-recited litany of parental concerns about inclusion focuses on the educational curriculum. There are a variety of issues embedded in this area. Many parents recognize that, if their child is to function in the world of people without disabilities, they must be taught how to do so. They also recognize that this learning can best occur through exposure to their peers without disabilities. The potential benefits of such exposure and interaction are manifold: the child will learn how to interact with individuals without disabilities, acquire social skills, feel comfortable in typical environments, and have greater opportunities to establish new relationships and a good quality of life.

Yet many families have concerns about the academic side of the child's education: Will my child be able to learn as much in a typical classroom as she will in a special education environment? Are there any data that say that children who are included and spend their time in typical classrooms learn as efficiently as they might in a classroom where their program is totally individualized and their pace of learning is geared to their abilities? These parents' concerns spring from the fact that most speakers, writers, and videotapes have focused on the social advantages of inclusion and have not sufficiently addressed the other types of learning that can occur within an inclusive situation.

Related to concerns about academic learning is the concern often expressed that the general classroom teacher will not be able to individualize the curriculum for the child. Parents recognize that typical educational environments do not generally individualize curricula for general education students and thus pace learning based on the average student's abilities. Therefore, why should parents believe that, because their child has a disability, the typical classroom teacher will be able to individualize curricula for their child?

Some parents, especially those of older children, raise a different type of curricular issue. Because they want their child upon graduation to have the necessary skills to function as effectively as possible, they insist that the child be schooled in a functional or life skills curriculum. They also insist that the child receive community-based vocational training during the high school years. Most of these parents recognize that this type of curriculum is not usually taught within the general education program. Therefore, they insist that it be provided in a special environment with teachers qualified to instruct these specific kinds of skills.

Parental Time, Commitment, and Knowledge

Both authors devoted a great deal of personal time to ensure high-quality integrated experiences for their children. Both authors also had opportunities to acquire much knowledge about quality inclusion and how it could be accomplished. The majority of parents do not have the time to advocate for their children's programs except in the annual IEP meeting and also do not have the time or opportunity to observe in the school or to learn from reading or from others about the education of their children.

We speak here of concerned parents, those who want the best education for their child, but because of economic conditions, job requirements, marital arrangements, and other personal situations are unable to devote the time to advocate for their child. The single mother or father who rushes to get the children ready for school and him- or herself ready for work; who has to arrange for babysitting or child care after school; who comes home in the evening after a day's work, cooks for the children and tries to provide them some quality time, and then must get ready for the next day's work, has little time for the IEP and much less time to observe in the school, seek training, and advocate for appropriate programs. The same may be true for the family with two working adults who need the two incomes to survive.

These families do not have time to work with the schools to achieve inclusion. If the school that their child with disabilities attends is not the neighborhood school or does not believe in inclusion, these parents, although they may verbally espouse inclusion, do not have time to change their child's situation or learn about what the professionals are saying, and they will accept whatever the school delivers.

Professionals often denigrate parents for not being stronger advocates for their children. Many parents would like to have the luxury of time to do so, but they are unable. Professionals might strive to understand the economic and marital situations that create a seeming lack of parental commitment.

Communication Skills Training

Communication is the keystone for all educational considerations of children and youth who are deaf-blind. Almost all parents of these children learn very quickly that this is so. Parents also perceive that many teachers who have not been trained to teach students who are deaf-blind do not have an appreciation of the importance of communication practice. Therefore, parents become concerned about inclusion: Who is going to ensure that my child will have adequate communication skills training? Who is qualified to provide that training within the inclusive environment?

It is important to understand that this parental concern is pervasive. The majority of children and youth who are deaf-blind and who attend public schools are currently being supported or taught by special education teachers who have not been trained in the field of deaf-blindness. No formal surveys have been completed but, while conducting technical assistance throughout the United States, TRACES staff have observed that the majority of children and youth who are deaf-blind in public schools are being supported or taught by teachers who have been trained as teachers of children with other severe disabilities. Although they have some training regarding the importance of communication, their knowledge of the needs of children who are deaf-blind is generally inadequate.

This situation is further exacerbated by the fact that most speech clinicians who are supporting children with deaf-blindness in public schools also have little training regarding the communication needs of these students. Although special assistance may be available through the coordinator of deaf-blind services within the state and through national technical assistance efforts, the parent frequently is not aware of these services, and school districts neglect to request them. Thus, parents are frustrated by the failure of the education system to recognize the communication needs of their children and validly question the wisdom of inclusion. If the special education programs are unable to provide adequate communication training for my child, they wonder, why should I believe that an inclusive program will do any better?

Vulnerability to Other Children

Parents of children with disabilities are generally more protective of these children than they are of their children without disabilities. They remember teasing and childhood cruelty that occurred during their own school years, and they frequently question whether their child with disabilities will be abused or teased by the other children in an inclusive environment.

Perceived Attitudes of School Administrators

Many parents tend to gravitate toward the special education teacher as their main support in the public school. Yet most professionals realize that it is the school principal who makes or breaks a program of inclusion. Professionals also realize that it is the school superintendent who establishes a policy that facilitates inclusion at the school level. Some parents view the principal or superintendent as unapproachable, someone to whom they go only as a last resort and then with trepidation. Other parents fail to make the connection between successful inclusionary programs and the attitude of the principal. Still others see the principal as one who erects the barriers to inclusion and who always presents the economic or administrative reasons why it cannot be done. Some perceive the principal as paying "lip service" to the concept of inclusion and then sabotaging it through the erection of subtle barriers. Other administrators are seen as doing all they can to avoid interactions with parents.

Whether these parents' perceptions are accurate for any given situation would be argued by both parents and administrators. Suffice it to say that these perceptions do exist. They exist because of significant breakdowns in communication between administrators and parents and, perhaps, between administrators and teachers.

The Fear of Community Backlash

The majority of school districts within the United States today face difficult economic decisions, shrinking budgets, higher demands for services, and overloaded staff. Many parents of children with disabilities worry that because it costs more to educate a child who is deaf-blind than it does to educate children with other disabilities or children without disabilities, there will be a backlash within the community in protest of these higher costs. They envision that this backlash will produce one or more of the following scenarios: 1) service to their children will be significantly cut, 2) both subtle and overt discrimination will occur in school toward their children, and 3) there will be a public outcry against such costs that will cause their families to be the focus of public outrage. This anxiety about a backlash causes some parents to be apologetic about requesting services, thus weakening their advocacy. Because they fail to express their anxiety about backlash, school staff do not accurately perceive the parents' and their children's needs and desires.

Transition to Adulthood

Parents of children with disabilities generally establish formal and informal support networks within their communities with whom they share experiences about their children and provide support for one another. When parents of adults who are deaf-blind share their experiences with parents of school-age children, some concerns are raised about the basic assumptions regarding inclusion. Parents of adults who are deaf-blind report that generally their son or daughter has few friends who do not have a disability. If he or she has a service provider, staff members within the facility are frequently looked upon as friends. But generally, friends are other people with disabilities with whom most leisure activities are shared.

Parents of adults who are deaf-blind also report that friends without disabilities who were present during the school years drift away after graduation. They go to college, get married, and develop new relationships. The individual with disabilities who was once their friend as a child loses contact. The adult with disabilities has extreme difficulties developing new friends without disabilities. There are acquaintances and support networks, but few friends. In one community in Oregon where the second author examined a sample of 25 individual support plans of adults with moderate and severe disabilities (not deaf-blindness) who were receiving community-based services through state resources, only three listed "significant others" (friend or relative) who were not ex-staff or intimate family and who did not have a disability. This was in a community that had practiced quality school integration and inclusion for the previous 15 years.

Faced with this information, some parents of school-age children begin to question one of the basic assumptions of inclusion: Will my child be able to build a network of friends without disabilities that will survive over time? Would it not be better for my child's social life to be focused around others with disabilities in school if these are to be his or her principal lifelong friends?

Anxiety About Lifelong Support

A concern that most parents begin to have at some point is anxiety about what will hap-

pen to their child once the parent(s) is (are) no longer around. As the child grows older, this concern is more apt to be expressed. This generalized anxiety may cause parents to make certain decisions regarding the educational or residential placements of their children. We suggest that professionals might be sensitive to this concern and its implications.

RECOMMENDATIONS

As we wrote this section, we recognized that we were presenting only one point of view— that of the parent. We know that there are many irritating things that we parents do that make life difficult for school professionals. Some of our decisions and concerns may seem illogical and impractical. We do believe, however, that if school professionals are able to recognize and understand some of our concerns, our communications could improve significantly, as could inclusive practices.

As we cited this litany, we could imagine the responses of some professionals. We recognize that many of these perceptions are held by parents because of the local situations in which they find themselves. If a parent has not had the opportunity to see a good inclusive program at work, then some of the above concerns will be expressed. We also recognize that many local school administrators have not been previously exposed to inclusive programs and, because they know of no alternatives, do not offer any to parents.

Some of what we mentioned, for example, the lack of friends without disabilities at adulthood, seems to challenge strongly held values and positions. Such a challenge is not our purpose. Perhaps a challenge of another sort is. Better information, based upon sound research, is essential. In the remaining section, we list questions that we do not think have been adequately answered by the professional and parent advocates for inclusion. We also list a series of actions that we think are necessary to improve parent–professional partnerships and opportunities for quality inclusion.

Our own experiences, coupled with the information that we receive from other parents about their reluctance to include their child in a typical education program, have generated a number of thoughts about inclusion and its value for children and youth who are deaf-blind. In turn, those thoughts have generated a number of recommendations that we offer to professionals in the following pages.

There is a need to ascertain in a scientific manner the perceptions of parents of students who are deaf-blind. Specifically, there is a need to record and understand parents' perceptions about inclusion. What we have presented in this chapter is not scientific; it merely represents what we two parents have heard over the years from other parents. How well we have represented other parents' views is questionable. Certainly, it would seem that the opinions of parents of consumers of education have value for the professional community, and, in fact, may well dictate how some services are offered. We could locate no studies that asked parents of students who are deaf-blind their opinions about integration and inclusion or attempted to learn from them what was needed to achieve successful inclusion.

Values should drive research. If we value inclusion, it is time to do studies that answer some of the questions posed by parents:

- What are the best ways to ensure that communication needs are consistently addressed and met in inclusive settings for the student who is deaf-blind?
- Does a student in an inclusive situation

learn as much academically as a student in a segregated environment?
- Does the inclusive situation offer valid opportunities to establish friendships, and can those friendships be maintained after graduation?
- Can a functional curriculum be taught in a typical educational environment better than in a special educational environment as measured by student learning?
- At what age or point of service delivery should we begin to address inclusion for a student?
- How will the inclusive setting better prepare students who are deaf-blind to meet the transitions that occur during the school years?

We believe that research regarding inclusion of students who are deaf-blind needs to be programmatic in nature and not merely a series of isolated studies. Moreover, the program of research must cover the range of disability variations among people who are deaf-blind to include students who also have developmental disabilities.

We know that people generally respond to more complex issues once basic needs are met. People will not step to a higher rung on the ladder until they have successfully reached the rung below. We cannot expect people to concentrate their efforts on the dynamics of interpersonal relationships when they have no food for their family or money with which to buy it. Similarly, we cannot expect parents of students who are deaf-blind to move toward inclusion when basic appropriate educational needs are going unmet.

We must recognize that challenging a system to acquire basic appropriate educational services or to provide inclusion creates anxiety for parents. We cannot ignore this anxiety or the equally pervasive anxiety parents perceive about community backlash. Professionals need to recognize these anxieties, as parents will often hesitate to express their concerns as a means of self-preservation and self-protection. After all, in "against-all-odds" situations of any sort, the least attractive option is to display a weakness.

This may mean that there is no single solution to this issue and that some solutions may in fact be in conflict with what professionals want. It is reasonable to say, then, that the first solution may be to accept that the direction of services must come from the individual who is deaf-blind and from his or her parents. This would represent a step toward meeting basic needs and generating responses to more complex issues such as inclusion. It would also be a step toward reducing parental fears of bureaucracy and sabotage.

We believe that the cornerstone of inclusion for students who are deaf-blind is the opportunity to practice communication skills. Communication needs cross all environments and ages and must be carefully considered and consistently met. This communication must flow to the student as well as from the student to others. Special education services are often perceived by parents of children who are deaf-blind as disheartening because these environments do not recognize communication as the primary need—the "mother of all services." We openly talk about a student's behavior problems, motivation, problems, comprehension problems, never recognizing that in many instances we are not communicating to the student or responding to the student's communication. We cannot begin to realize the potential that inclusion holds, or for that matter impose judgment on its value, until we recognize the manner in which we consistently address the communication needs of the student. Part of meeting the communication needs of students who are

deaf-blind is teaching students without disabilities how to communicate with those who have disabilities. Moreover, there is a requirement, if we are to educate people to accept diversity, to assist them to be sensitive to the needs of those with disabilities and to recognize individual value and worth regardless of ability.

Parents should not have to spend countless hours advocating for appropriate services and inclusion for their children. Nor should they have to educate the professional community. Some parents become tired of advocating and would welcome professionals within school districts to take the lead in recommending inclusion, advocating for it, and facilitating the supports necessary for it to succeed. We recognize that there are some school professionals who do what we recommend, but our perception is that they are in the minority.

There is a need to recognize that parents' visions and dreams for their children are influenced by what is available. Can parents be expected to know what to ask for if they are unable to see a model? Person-centered services that incorporate family desires through education expand the visions that parents have for their children and that educators have for their students. Using this avenue as a catalyst for service enhancement is advantageous to the student, the parents, and the system. We believe that it will also improve the likelihood of successful parent–professional relationships and the establishment of effective educational teams, two components that are vital in achieving inclusion.

Therefore, a fundamental need exists to establish models of inclusion through demonstration grants. These models should incorporate parental perceptions attained through research and be publicized throughout the professional community that provides services and supports to students who are deaf-blind. Likewise, we need to make these models accessible to parents. Models help parents and school systems to look beyond the present and to generate new ideas and energy for the future. This energy in turn feeds the system, and educators, students, parents, siblings, and society as a whole will begin to move toward the next rung on the ladder. It is this upward progression that is the essence of inclusion.

REFERENCES

Giangreco, M.F., Cloninger, C.J., Mueller, P.H., Yuan, S., & Ashworth, S. (1991). Perspectives of parents whose children have dual sensory impairments. *Journal of The Association For Persons With Severe Handicaps, 16,* 14–24.

Wolf, E.G. (1982). *Needs assessment of services to deaf-blind individuals. Final Report.* Silver Spring, MD: REDEX.

Vadasy, P.F., & Fewell, R.R. (1986). Mothers of deaf-blind children. In R.R. Fewell & P.F. Vadasy (Eds.), *Families of handicapped children* (pp. 121–148). Austin: PRO-ED.

Chapter 4

Establishing Inclusive School Communities

Kathleen Liberty
and Norris Haring

Since the mid-1970s, persons with disabilities, parents, advocates, educators, and others have together developed and demonstrated significant progress in normalizing home, school, work, and community life. Participation of students with severe and multiple disabilities in a multitude of integrated environments is also emerging, and comparable progress with students who have deaf-blindness is underway (Goetz, Guess, & Stremel-Campbell, 1987; Goetz, Lee, Johnston, & Gaylord-Ross, 1991; Haring & Liberty, 1991). However, what needs to be achieved is inclusion. Biklen (1990) explains

> Inclusion communicates something more than "integration." It means people participating in families, schools (and classrooms), in work places, and in community life. "Inclusion" implies that people are welcomed, that each person reaches out to include another person. Inclusion is different from "letting in" or "adding on." Inclusion conveys the idea that we appreciate each other, that we see each other's gifts, that we value being together. Inclusion speaks to the importance of relationships. Other as-

pects of our work, for example, our learning and teaching skills, abilities, and techniques, are not ends in themselves, but merely avenues to inclusion. (p. 1)

The inclusion of students with deaf-blindness in general education who may also have medically fragile conditions and other disabilities poses a challenge to parents, educators, and school systems (Giangreco, Cloninger, Mueller, Yuan, & Ashworth, 1991; Izen & Brown, 1991). Parents whose children have not experienced inclusion may be challenged by the prospect, fearing that their child would "regress, be neglected or overlooked, be exposed to undesirable behaviors, not receive enough appropriate stimulation, miss his/her classmates, lack challenging learning opportunities, and that the change would be disruptive" (Giangreco et al., 1991, p. 20). Parents might also fear for their child's health and the effects of stress on both their child and themselves (Giangreco et al., 1991; McDonald, 1985). General education teachers and school systems are challenged by the

This activity was supported in part by the U.S. Department of Education (Grant No. G008730410; CFDA 86.086H; Project No. 086HH70001). However, the content expressed herein does not necessarily reflect the position or policy of the U.S. Department of Education, and no official endorsement by the Department should be inferred.

discrepancies assumed to exist between the perceived needs of the student and the resources available (Schalock & Jenson, 1986).

Teachers of persons with deaf-blindness and multiple disabilities may also be challenged by inclusion (Brown et al., 1979; Sailor et al., 1986). Izen and Brown (1991) surveyed teachers of students with multiple disabilities. They found that some did not teach integration skills or use integration strategies for community living and employment. There are still many students for whom inclusion is a dream yet to be realized. In this chapter, the authors discuss the foundations of exclusion and strategies for overcoming challenges to full inclusion.

THE OBSTACLES AND STRATEGIES FOR INCLUSION PROJECT

As a basis for an examination of the challenges to inclusion, the authors present rationales for exclusion revealed in a project that studied the nature of exclusion and then developed strategies for inclusion of students with deaf-blindness. This study was carried out by the authors over a 5-year period and involved different school systems in the metropolitan Everett-Seattle-Tacoma area of Washington state. The 22 students in the project ranged from 6 to 21 years old, and about two thirds of them lived in a residential institution. They were classified as having the most severe disabilities among the citizens of Washington state. Almost all of the students had deaf-blindness, seizure disorders, and cerebral palsy. Some were very ill, and two students died during the project's first 2 years.

Most of those who lived at the institution began residing there when they became too heavy for their families to lift, and their teachers had been unable to teach them independent mobility. The students went to eight different classrooms maintained by

public school systems; six classrooms were situated in five different public schools, and two classrooms were located at the residential institution. Of the six public school classrooms, total segregation was maintained in five; that is, the students with disabilities arrived and departed on different buses, at different times of day, and used different entrances and exits from the other students. They ate lunch in their classrooms and were generally taken outside when other students were not. General education students occasionally came in to "work with" a student with disabilities; however, this was not monitored, the students were not taught how to interact with each other, and usually nothing that seemed very meaningful for either participant occurred. The students with disabilities almost never entered general education classrooms. Gartner and Lipsky attribute the exclusion of pupils with disabilities from general education settings almost entirely to the "attitudinal milieu [in which] persons with disabilities are neither treated like nor viewed as 'normal people'" (Gartner & Lipsky, 1987, p. 380).

In working with the school district and the institution to expand the inclusive experiences available to pupils with deaf-blindness and multiple disabilities, the authors interviewed 72 professionals and 26 parents. All of the participants were given copies of the interview questions in advance. During the interviews, the professionals and parents were asked to identify potential inclusive settings and experiences for the student with deaf-blindness. An average of seven people were interviewed for each student in the project.

Initially, the special education personnel involved were able to identify inclusive activities for only about 20% of the students. They identified more than 180 reasons why inclusion was inappropriate or impossible. About 39% of these reasons were associated with perceived student characteristics and included the following:

1. Health problems (e.g., too fragile to travel in a vehicle) (22%)
2. Student behaviors that were considered inappropriate (e.g., masturbation) (9%)
3. Skills students did not have that were considered prerequisite (e.g., play skills to participate in recess, skills to communicate with peers without disabilities) (8%)

At least one challenge from each of these categories was identified for 21 of the 22 students (Haring & Liberty, 1991). About 52% of the reasons why inclusion was considered inappropriate or impossible were identified as structures in the service delivery system. They included insufficient or untrained staff, lack of equipment, lack of support services, and costs and availability of transportation. The other 9% of reasons identified were overt expressions of attitudes about inclusion, such as "Christine's cognitive level is too low [for her] to benefit," and "Frank's parents will never let him," or "Elizabeth's teacher will never permit that."

When professionals were asked to explain why a particular student was not already included in an activity they had recommended or why no integrated activities were suggested for a particular student, the authors were met with a barrage of reasons. The difficulty that staff had in even identifying inclusive situations and the volume of reasons given for why inclusion was not possible provided evidence that Gartner and Lipsky's (1987) "attitudinal milieu" was operating to prevent inclusion of students with deaf-blindness.

SOCIAL PROCESSES OF EXCLUSION

The "attitudinal milieu" that makes exclusion possible is embedded in social processes.

Those who are recognized members of a community are protected within the scope of the justice and value systems of their community (Gould, 1981; Opotow, 1990a). Persons who are not perceived to be a part of a community are excluded, and thus community values and rules are not applied to them as they are to people within the community. In some cases, values and fairness might be ignored completely. As Opotow (1990a) writes, "People who are slaves, children, women, aged, Black, Jewish, mentally retarded, physically handicapped, and insane constitute a partial list of beings whose rights have been abrogated or eliminated because of their exclusion from the scope of justice" (p. 3).

Fine (1990) points out that public schools constitute communities where

political negotiations, although typically unacknowledged, determine who shall enter, remain in, and become excluded from these communities. Policies and practices in schools regularly monitor the following: Who gets what? Who is entitled to receive special resources? How can fair allocations of tax resources be determined and sustained? (p. 107)

There is virtually no argument against the fact that students with deaf-blindness and multiple disabilities experience schooling differently from students without disabilities (Gartner & Lipsky, 1987). A few years ago, both a national survey and a United States Department of Education report indicated that roughly half of the students with deaf-blindness surveyed were being excluded from general education classrooms (Biklen, 1988; Bullis & Otos, 1988). Once students with disabilities gained their legitimate access to the education community, "the issue of social justice has shifted to the process of exclusion, that is, students' differential *experiences* and *outcomes* once inside these communities" (Fine, 1990, p. 108).

The exclusion of students with deaf-blindness and multiple disabilities from general education schooling is deeply embedded in the social process of exclusion (Opotow, 1990b). Bus and Kruizenga (1989) and Mehan (1987) present detailed analyses of statements made during placement meetings, indicating that inconsistent placement decisions are made for students with similar disabilities and that many decisions are based on funding and program availability, not on the needs of the students being placed.

It is very important to detect exclusion in operation because it may be the key to successful inclusion. As Opotow wrote, "The rationalizations and justifications that support moral exclusion render it difficult to detect. Therefore, it is important to be able to recognize its characteristic symptoms, and this ability may also offer opportunities to arrest its advance" (Opotow, 1990a, p. 9).

Exclusionary policies and processes can be identified at all levels of the student placement and educational planning process. In our own study, the authors found little difference in the rationalizations offered by administrators, teachers, aides, therapists, nurses, physicians, or parents. Snell and Eichner (1989) state the "primary reason" that inclusion has not been widely adopted is "because those people who are charged with effecting the federal requirements on a statewide and local level have at best passively resisted, and at worst, actively fought implementation of it" (p. 122). It is important to recognize that while the overt manifestations of resistance may vary, they are all similarly rooted in an exclusionary philosophy.

Rationalizations may be categorized according to exclusionary processes identified by Opotow (1990a). Many of these processes provide a facade of normality and caring for exclusionists who use a wide variety of "reasons" to justify their behavior. The variety of rationalizations, excuses, and justifications made to the authors in the interviews conducted during their study provide a guide to the symptoms of exclusion listed in Table 1.

Comparative Processes

The first category of symptoms of exclusion are justifications based on the comparisons of students without disabilities and students with deaf-blindness. These processes include: 1) prejudice (e.g., "You can't expect these children to learn like normal kids."), 2) dehumanization (e.g., "Kathy doesn't notice what's going on around her, no way."), 3) condescension (e.g., "I know she's 17 but she's got a mental age of 3 months."), 4) the use of euphemisms (e.g., "The *special* class is the right placement."), and 5) expressions of fear of contamination ("We can't jeopardize the education of the regular kids by putting her in there."). Izen and Brown (1991) provide a description of comparative processes in teachers who did not provide integration experiences because "they did not think this approach would benefit their students" (p. 98). In these teachers' perceptions, the students' disabilities somehow made them clearly different from, and less deserving than, other students who presumably benefit from inclusion.

Conditional Processes

Conditional processes, the second set of symptoms, include rationalizations based on the conditions under which a student may enter the community of the inclusive school. These range from establishing prerequisite standards (e.g., "He can't go there until he stops masturbating."), to providing resources needed by learners with disabilities only in segregated settings (e.g., "But there isn't anyone there who can feed him."). The particular irony of providing resources to students with disabilities in segregated settings and then using the lack of resources in inclusive settings to justify continued placement in segregated settings is discussed in detail by Taylor (1988). It is critical to identify this rationale as a symptom of exclusion because those same school districts find it

Table 1. Processes in the exclusion of students with disabilities from general education

Process	Manifestation in exclusion of children with disabilities
Comparative processes	
Prejudicial comparisons	Believing that a child without disabilities is superior to a child with disabilities
Denigrating comparisons	Disparaging children with disabilities as idiots and imbeciles (e.g., "too handicapped to learn," "functioning at an infantile level")
Dehumanizing comparisons	Believing that children with disabilities do not feel or notice what happens to them; attitude that children with deaf-blindness are not aware of their surroundings, or do not mind doing dull, repetitive tasks
Self-righteous comparisons	Justifying separate classes because they are an improvement over earlier programs or somehow "better" than programs in other countries
Condescending comparisons	Treating and teaching individuals with disabilities as though they were children or in some way younger than their actual age; using a "mental age" or "developmental level" as a descriptor
Euphemistic language	Using terms that mask or misrepresent exclusion (e.g., special education, resource room, exceptional child center)
Fear of contamination	Perceiving learners with disabilities as a threat to typical classroom organization and the achievement of typical students
Reduction of standards	Perceiving one's belief in exclusion as proper; replacing standards that restrain exclusion (e.g., least restric' environment [LRE] mandate in PL 94-142) with less stringent standards that condone exclusion (e.g., perceiv:ng LRE as a continuum that accepts total segregation and separate classes as acceptable options)
Technical orientation	Concentrating on techniques and details as efficient means while ignoring outcomes (e.g., in IEP planning, directing attention to systematic instruction and deceleration of inappropriate behavior while ignoring segregation, exclusion, lack of instruction in social skills, community living, and employment
Psychological distance	Ceasing to perceive individuals with disabilities as people; talking about persons with disabilities in their presence, but as if they were not present or could not "understand," referring to children as "the BDs" or "the trainables," and so forth
Conditional processes	
Double standards	Having rules to include some students in certain classrooms and school events and a different set of rules and procedures to exclude students with disabilities from those same classrooms and events
	Providing resources for some students with disabilities in segregated environments and then using the fact that those resources are in segregated environments to justify exclusion from inclusive settings
	Providing resources for some students (e.g., music instruction, remedial reading) in inclusive settings, but not providing resources for students with deaf-blindness in inclusive settings
Conditional entry, prerequisite standards	Requiring that students with disabilities meet certain standards of health, behavior, and skills as prerequisites for inclusion
Groupthink	Refusing to accept evidence, data, research, and opinion about the practicality, success, benefits, and so forth of inclusion while accepting evidence, data, research, and opinion about the problems, challenges, and advantages of exclusion

(continued)

Table 1. *(continued)*

Process	Manifestation in exclusion of children with disabilities
Group processes	
Transcendent ideologies	Believing that oneself or one's group is possessed of better judgment, wisdom, and experience, which justifies segregation as necessary for the student's own best interests
Moral engulfment	Accepting segregation because colleagues oppose inclusion
Displacement	Going along with exclusionary policies because a higher authority (e.g., principal, school district) assumes responsibility for the consequences
Spreading the blame	Distributing responsibility for exclusion among group members, colleagues, and "the system"
Denial processes	
Concealment	Rejecting, disparaging, concealing, misrepresenting, resisting, or ignoring effects of exclusion on students with disabilities
Blaming the victim	Blaming the student with disabilities for not learning certain skills or for engaging in behaviors not considered "appropriate" and using those behaviors or skill needs to justify exclusion
Desecration	Denial of the person with a disability; refusing to teach needed skills or supply prosthetics, such as glasses and hearing aids, on the grounds of money or severity of disability
Temporal justification	Believing one's acceptance of exclusion is an exception—"just this once" or "just for this learner"
Glorifying exclusion	Perceiving exclusion as a legitimate form of education
Normalizing exclusion	Accepting exclusion as usual or ordinary because of years of exclusionary practices and acceptance of it by educators and society

Adapted from Opotow (1990a).

unquestionably simple to provide resources for students without disabilities in general education settings (e.g., music instruction, athletic training, enrichment programs, yearbooks, dances).

Another manifestation of this process is identifying a resource as needed in the inclusive environment that is not even available in the segregated setting (e.g., "He needs constant individual attention."). Teachers of learners with multiple disabilities report they excluded their students from integration strategies because of insufficient administrative support and insufficient resources (Izen & Brown, 1991). It is easier to perceive the exclusionary basis of these reasons if they are turned around (e.g., "Administrative support is available for segregation," and "Resources are only available in special settings."). In the authors' study, the fact that staffing and resources in integrated settings were inadequate comprised slightly more than half of the justifications for exclusion (Haring & Liberty, 1991).

Group Processes and Denial

Exclusion is also symptomatic in group processes. These rationalizations range from transcendent ideologies (e.g., "All of the people on the IEP team feel the same way.") to displacement of responsibility for exclusion (e.g., "This district just isn't ready for this—especially the other teachers."). Finally, those who engage in exclusion often deny their own culpability. Symptoms of these denial processes include blaming the learner for exclusion (e.g., "Mark is just too medically fragile to attend a regular school.") to glorification of exclusion (e.g., "These special classes provide the best possible education for these kinds of students.").

Misconceptions Regarding Deaf-Blindness and Learning

The authors found at the beginning of their project that some staff did not seem to consider how the pupils' deaf-blindness, as distinct from their other disabilities, might affect their learning. Only the four students perceived to be the "highest functioning" had any vision or hearing aids; aids for the rest were not recommended by physicians who felt that there was "no benefit" and not advocated by teachers, who apparently concurred with the physicians' determination that students had to "earn" aids through some demonstration of intelligence. The notion that the aids themselves could have permitted the expression of "intelligence" was apparently not considered. These actions are also symptoms of exclusion.

Inappropriate Instructional Strategies Instructional strategies appropriate to students with deaf-blindness were not always provided. For example, several students had IEP objectives that included following a verbal instruction to pick up an object. Performance of the skill as set out in the objective required that the pupil have adequate vision and hearing. Alternative, appropriate strategies for teaching reaching and grasping to students with deaf-blindness were apparently not considered. Similar objectives continued to be established year after year. A learner's failure to "pass" such objectives was attributed to "mental retardation" rather than to the failure to adapt objectives and instruction to the challenges of the individual learner. As Ellis (1986) points out, this is one of the most terrible of tragedies for persons with deaf-blindness because perceptions of severe intellectual disability are so ultimately damaging to the opportunities made available to the individual so diagnosed. Rather than look for causes of instructional failure in their own teaching, exclusionists used a "blame the victim" rationalization for exclusion. About 40% of the justifications for exclusion heard by the authors involved student characteristics, including skills, behavior, and health (Haring & Liberty, 1991). That is, the exclusionist used the characteristics of the learners to justify excluding them.

Biologically Based Rationales for Exclusion
Biologically based rationalizations and justifications for exclusion remain all too frequent. Haring and Liberty (1991) found that half of the inclusive environments proposed for children and teens with deaf-blindness and multiple disabilities were initially rejected by IEP team members on the grounds that the pupil's health and disabilities made inclusion impossible, and that the pupil would never learn the skills thought to be prerequisite to "benefit" from inclusion (e.g., communication with peers without disabilities). "Skill deficits are a consequence of her disabilities and will not be affected by any type of instruction, so there is no point in providing it!" (Haring & Liberty, 1991, p. 30). Thus, the pupil is not only excluded from inclusive activities by virtue of his or her disability, he or she is further excluded from instruction in the very skills that are "required" for inclusion.

Of the many rationalizations and justifications presented in Table 1, one of the most superficially compelling is that the exclusion of learners with deaf-blindness and multiple disabilities is a direct, inevitable, and characteristic outcome of the severity of their disabilities. As other rationalizations and justifications used for excluding learners with perceived "milder" disabilities fail under close scrutiny, the biological/medical justifications used to exclude children with multiple disabilities apparently increase in frequency. As Meyerson (1988) points out:

> In disability, there is a salient *biological* component and a resulting belief by some that the problems of this group arise as much or more from inherent biological inadequacies as from social forces. Similar beliefs of biological inferiority in blacks, women, and certain ethnic groups were common not many years ago, but they are rarely heard today. (p. 179)

Dussault (1989) provides a historical perspective on the statutes in education that legally justified exclusion based on the severity of disability. Although the more overtly discriminatory statutes have been replaced in recent years, it has not been as simple to erase hundreds of years of exclusionary educational policies that are woven into societal processes (Meyerson, 1988; Sailor, Gee, Goetz, & Graham, 1988).

Lack of Teacher Preparation   During the project, it became evident that some team members were not trained in the teaching skills appropriate to their pupils. Most staff were not aware of the newest advances in instruction and technology that support learning by persons with multiple disabilities and deaf-blindness. This may be attributed to deficits in personnel preparation programs (Damerell, 1985) or in state certification procedures (Geiger & Justen, 1983; "Opposite trends," 1988), or in how personnel are assigned within a school district (Hilton & Liberty, 1986). Whatever the combination of factors that result in a teacher being assigned to teach pupils whom she or he is not prepared to teach, the end results are likely to be horrific for both the teacher and the student.

When a teacher tries to teach students without suitable preparation, it is likely that even his or her best efforts will be unsuccessful, and pupils will not learn. The teacher consequently fails to receive the natural reinforcers for teaching: the joys of seeing students learn. If this situation is repeated over a long period of time, and with many students, behavioral principles suggest that the teacher's teaching behaviors will gradually decrease. In such classrooms, the teacher's time is spent in noninstructional activities, such as caretaking, paperwork, and "fun" activities (e.g., parties, videos, and field trips); little time is spent in direct instruction. Like anyone in an avoidance paradigm, the teacher will avoid performing a response (i.e., teaching) that is unlikely to be reinforced (i.e., by student learning). Given human nature, the teacher is also likely to defend himself or herself and others with a socially acceptable explanation such as "these students are just too disabled to learn." Thompson and Guess (1989) quoted a teacher's observation that "I see no programming going on for many of these students because people think there isn't much you can do" (p. 12).

Lipsky and Gartner (1987) suggest that this very attitude about student learning must be changed before education will really be effective for students with disabilities. Atherton and Atherton (1987) concur: "We began to realize that our daughter's biggest handicap was society itself with its preconceived ideas and assumptions about people with disabilities" (p. 2). According to Lipsky and Gartner, overcoming this handicap would mean

> First and foremost, children would be considered more alike than different. And it would be recognized that all children are different in intellectual, physical, and psychological characteristics. Thus, every child would be considered able to learn in most environments. This is not to ignore that students, not just those labeled as handicapped, have distinctive needs, possess various strengths and weaknesses, and often require individual attention. Of course, they do. Rather it is both to recognize the reality of that situation and to be aware that school and classroom organization, as well as instructional programs, are available which can address student differences in integrated settings. . . . Further, the teaching skills inherent in the concept of quality education are ones which are required by both general and special education teachers. (p. 71)

IDENTIFYING STRATEGIES TO SUPPORT INCLUSION

There have been several notable case studies on changing public school systems from segregated to inclusive for students with severe disabilities. Meyer and Kishi (1985) described a process of integrating students with severe disabilities in public schools in Honolulu that incorporated the following steps:

1. Legislative and litigated consent degrees involving the schools' provision of appropriate education to children with disabilities
2. Elimination of alternative services for students with disabilities ("forced choice")
3. Elimination of "entry" criteria (e.g., requirement that students be toilet trained)
4. Elimination of architectural barriers
5. Identification of funds for transportation costs
6. Establishment of "credibility of integrated model" (Meyer & Kishi, 1985, p. 237)
7. Convincing administrators that integration is the correct approach
8. Reassurance of parents about quality of programs available in integrated settings
9. Training of general education personnel
10. Use of local expertise and professionals to implement the program, rather than outside consultants

McDonnell and Hardman (1989) also describe steps for systemwide change for integration:

1. Develop an overall strategy for change, not just physical proximity.
2. Obtain top-level administrative support.
3. Involve parents, community leaders, advocacy groups, and professionals in planning.
4. Place students in their own neighborhood schools to minimize resistance and to provide an efficient means of meeting inservice training, transportation, and related service provision needs.

5. Maintain or improve service quality with flexibility regarding how services are provided.

6. Build in feedback and evaluation to determine the extent of inclusion.

Snell and Eichner (1989) reviewed several case studies of integration, and concluded

> There is no single approach for attaining integration for students with profound disabilities. . . . [However] there is an underlying principle that is relevant to any such analysis: the move to an integrated service delivery model should be understood as being nothing less than effecting social change. . . . Thus, the process and context of the debate is essentially a political one. The extent to which advocates for integration are successful will depend upon whether those persons can effectively marshal the political forces within that community. (p. 124)

In suggesting strategies to achieve integration, Snell and Eichner (1989) began with the need to obtain organizational support through a political process: "Without some positive beliefs and attitudes about integration at the administrator's and principal's level, the change process stops (Snell & Eichner, 1989, p. 127). The steps they suggest to achieve integration include

1. Determination of existing authority hierarchy of school system
2. Assessment of needs of students to be integrated and integration sites, attitudes, and potential problems
3. Creation of integration planning committee or task force
4. Development of an appropriate service delivery model
5. Selection of initial implementation sites and staff to provide a successful model
6. Implementation of a responsive staff development program
7. Fostering a positive attitude toward integration in the school community and with parents through joint planning and other strategies

All of the steps described by McDonnell and Hardman (1989), Meyer and Kishi (1985), and Snell and Eichner (1989) suggest different approaches to solving what is essentially the only challenge to inclusion. All of the rationalizations justifying exclusion are symptoms of a whole philosophy of exclusion. It is clear that, to achieve successful inclusion, it is this philosophy that must be overcome.

Addressing Exclusionary Attitudes

Changing the attitudes of exclusion held by all possible participants in the school community is required for successful inclusion. As long as attitudes of exclusion persist, it is likely that the inclusion of children with disabilities will be only a pro forma compliance (Haring & Liberty, 1991). This can result in the types of situations described by Ferguson and Baumgart (1991), where the student with disabilities is merely placed in proximity to students without disabilities, or in scenarios where students with disabilities are moved to general education classrooms, but the resources available to them in segregated settings do not move (Taylor, 1988). Both of these examples illustrate how pro forma situations superficially appear to be inclusive, but in actuality, have been so poorly planned that failure is inevitable. Thus, the failure itself can then be used to justify exclusion ("We tried, but it didn't work").

In order to change exclusion to inclusion, it is necessary to understand the conditions under which exclusion develops and is maintained. "Moral exclusion emerges when *group differences* (or 'we–they' distinctions) are salient and when difficult life conditions (such as harsh social circumstances, destructive conflict or threat) exist" (Opotow, 1990b, p. 174). Certainly the "we–they" distinctions in the education of individuals with deaf-blindness and other disabilities have been predominant. From the establishment of separate institutions to the establishment of separate classes, the history of treatment and education is one that rests almost completely on such a division. The "we–they" division, based on "perceived conflicts of interest, give[s] rise to group categorizations; conflict of interest and categorisation (sic) contribute to moral justifications for unjust procedures, which can themselves be injurious and which permit other harmful outcomes to ensue" (Opotow, 1990b, p. 174). The first step in the elimination of exclusion must be to break down the "we–they" distinction.

Exclusionists are most motivated by the need to see themselves favorably (Jussim, 1990). They will seek out information and experiences that strengthen their sense of self and avoid information and experiences that threaten their self-concepts. Change to a new self is threatening, and thus exclusionists are more motivated to maintain their beliefs than to change them. Jussim (1990) reviewed research on how stereotyped attitudes about "them" can be modified, and concludes that

> Stereotype-based expectancies are highly responsive to disconfirming evidence. Although people sometimes interpret *ambiguous* information in ways consistent with their expectations, even small amounts of information inconsistent with the stereotype may lead to the revision of the perceivers' impression of a *particular* person. (p. 14, second emphasis added)

While discussion of successes in other programs may help participants decide to try inclusion, it will be success on their "home ground" that will provoke the first subtle change in attitude. Snell and Eichner (1989) state that "positive attitude changes are dependent primarily upon having one's concerns about integration addressed and having adequate information concerning students with severe and profound disabilities" (p. 132). The implication of Jussim's idea is

that as exclusionists are presented with evidence about the successful inclusion of students they know personally, the "evidence" gradually disconfirms the basis of their attitudes. It is necessary to structure initial inclusion so that exclusionists are unable to avoid the evidence and implications of successful inclusive situations. People with exclusionary attitudes might be cognitively rigid (Jussim, 1990), which means that it might take many exemplars of successful inclusion of students they know before attitudes begin to change (Cook, 1990). Larson and Lakin (1991) also provide evidence of the power of disconfirming evidence on the attitudes of parents following community placement of their children.

Start-Points for Change

It should be clear that the purpose of engaging in strategies for change is to change the attitudes of educational personnel. Inclusion of the students is theirs by right, moral and legal, and not something that has to be "earned" by meeting prerequisite criteria. Attitude change within an organization can be structured from the "top down" or from the "bottom up," or simultaneously, as suggested by Snell and Eichner (1989).

Top-Down Approach Whenever change is structured from the top of the authority hierarchy down, resistance to the change can be expected to expand with each step down the chain, unless the people affecting the change at each level are able to project the changes in terms of attitudes, rather than just additional administrative requirements. In the worst possible scenario, when coercion is used, inclusion will only be accepted grudgingly as a way for administrators to avoid hassles with attorneys, hearing officers, parents, evaluators, and inspectors, and as a way for teachers to avoid hassles with administrators and parents. Sansone and Zigmond (1986) described "mainstreaming" programs that affect barely 5% of children with mild and moderate disabilities, and which are administered from "the top" by school district officials in such a way as to reinforce the rationalizations that participating students do not benefit.

Jussim (1990) described a model of change in terms of attitudes about race and gender. This model can be applied to inclusive situations for students with deaf-blindness when change is directed from the "top" of an administrative structure as follows:

1. The inclusion program should be introduced at a meeting by the principal and the program manager directly to the teachers and people personally involved, rather than through announcement, circulars, and so on.
2. The presentation should include explicit information and expectations about staff behavior:
   a. the social justice and morality of inclusion (cf. each student is morally entitled to be included regardless of disability) should be emphasized
   b. the symptoms of exclusion should be explained (cf. see Table 1)
   c. the expectation for behavior on the part of the school staff should be explicitly stated
3. The principal/manager must explicitly convey high expectations for the success of inclusion for all of the students and not discuss problems or appear hesitant or apologetic.
4. The principal/manager must provide background information about past exclusion and the often subtle effects of stereotypes and exclusionary attitudes. If teachers can be made aware of past injustices, they may act more sympathetically and supportively—intentionally reducing their own prejudices.
5. The principal/manager must personally demonstrate information that discon-

firms the attitudes of exclusion by referring to specific students and situations in which inclusion has been successful, even if these instances are from other districts.

Bottom-Up Approach "Bottom-up" has been the traditional change model in public schools. An extraordinary number of changes have come from advocates who are not part of the system, and parents and their children who are typically seen at the "bottom" of school hierarchies (e.g., the impetus for PL 94-142 came from parents and legislators, not from schools). Such a struggle is difficult and time consuming. It also is likely to result in the alienation of administrators who are likely to resist change suggested by those they view as lower in status than themselves.

Simultaneous Change Approach A third alternative is to address change across the system simultaneously (Thousand & Villa, 1989). Piuma, Halvorsen, Murray, Beckstead, and Sailor (1983) found communication between staff at the same level of decision-making in the school system hierarchy to be a key to effective change. Cook (1990) discussed using cooperative intergroup efforts to achieve change. Within most school systems, a small group of people are responsible for planning an individualized education program (IEP) for each student with special needs. Usually this group would include the student; the student's teachers and parents; an administrator; and sometimes specialists, such as language specialists, occupational therapists, and so on. Each student's education is planned by a group comprised of different people from other students' groups. However, each teacher, specialist, and administrator is likely to be a member of several students' IEP groups. This is a natural group with which to begin the change process.

Wray and Wieck (1985) also think that the IEP planning group, which takes an individual approach to students, is a good place to begin to work for inclusion. Change at this level in the school structure begins with a peer group with a similar aim, working to achieve similar goals with the same individual student. Successful planning and implementation of inclusion by the IEP group will result in the "personalized" disconfirming evidence required to change any exclusionist attitudes held by members of the group. A similar starting point for change can be achieved by creating small teams to plan for inclusion. A group of about four people, including the student, parent, and teachers, is probably large enough to allow for a range of ideas and small enough to find regular meeting times.

Selecting Student Exemplars

The next step is to select which student's IEP or small planning group will be among the first instances of inclusion. The success of the first exemplars is critical to changing exclusionary attitudes. If a number of the first exemplars are failures, attitudes of exclusion will be reinforced.

It would *appear* most logical to select learners with the highest probability of a smooth transition to a successful inclusive experience. However, there are several reasons for questioning this approach. First, it is simply not possible to predict which learners will have success. Thirty years ago, Stevens inaccurately predicted that "the profoundly retarded individual is considered, on the basis of current knowledge and practices, incapable of profiting from any type of training or education" (Stevens, 1964, p. 4). (Studies proving that he was wrong in this assumption were already underway [e.g., Hollis & Gorton, 1967].) It is similarly impossible to say that some learners will be successfully included while others will not be. Haring and Liberty (1991) found that all of the students with deaf-blindness and multiple disabilities in their study demonstrated positive

changes as a result of inclusion. Therefore our best prediction is that *any* learner will be able to provide the disconfirming evidence of successful inclusion that is required for attitude change.

As any student can be successfully included, it is better *not* to have a procedure for selecting students to participate in the first instances of school inclusion. It is likely that any process used to select exemplars will be transparent to others, and thus the value of the exemplar as disconfirming evidence will be reduced (e.g., "Well, they picked the easiest kid. It won't work with Sally."). Fundamentally, *any* criteria used to select exemplars are likely to be inherently exclusionary and so contravene inclusive behavior at the outset. An inclusive community cannot be built by beginning with an exclusionary process of selecting students to be included.

Instead, begin inclusion with every student's IEP group. This approach has several advantages. First, everyone is simultaneously involved in change, reducing the possibility of mutual reinforcement of exclusionary attitudes. Second, any possible failure of inclusion by a group will be offset by the majority of successful outcomes. Third, the multiple successful exemplars will provide a large body of disconfirming evidence. Fourth, group cohesion will be increased if the members perceive that all are working to fulfill similar expectancies of successful inclusion for a particular student. Fifth, peer comparison between groups can be used as situational influences to facilitate changing attitudes if required (Cook, 1990).

The other component of the exemplar is the inclusive situation. How is the situation most likely to provide disconfirming evidence to be selected? Again, it must be emphasized that this cannot be predicted on the information known at the outset of any case. The most reliable predictor for success is the quality, nature, and speed with which attitude change is effected, and the methods for predicting *that* are simply not available. The desired outcome is that the attitudes of exclusion are replaced with inclusive attitudes and behaviors, so that eventually every learner is unquestionably accepted as a citizen of the community. The first step in this process must be that the group make its own choice of the situation where inclusion begins.

Practical Steps Toward Achieving Change

The first step toward achieving change is for administrators to inform groups about the value and need for inclusion and to communicate expectations for success. After this, administrators at the top will serve as facilitators of the planning groups, which are responsible for all decisions about inclusion. The groups may start meeting separately to plan and accomplish inclusion for a particular student. Discussion should not dwell on relative merits of inclusion per se, nor about the problems of other learners or situations, but only about how the aim is to be achieved with this particular student. Remember: the purpose of the meeting is to achieve attitude change—the students do not have to "earn" inclusion. One primary indicator of the group's progress is the acceptance of the attendance and participation of the learner at every meeting. The group should attempt to adhere to the following sequence of steps and strategies in their discussions:

1. *Establish ground rules:* First, the group must decide in advance a set time for meeting duration and determine a permanent meeting schedule. It is likely to be more conducive to good attendance to have frequent, regularly scheduled meetings of, for example, 30 minutes in duration every Tuesday at lunch time. The longer the meetings become, the more likely members will avoid them, and if they do attend, adverse reac-

tions to meeting for inclusion may develop. If the group is unable to determine a mutually satisfactory schedule, then all of the student planning groups should be reformed to accommodate scheduling needs.

Second, the group should decide on a rotation method for the meeting chairperson. Each team member should participate as a group leader to increase cohesion, prevent one person from dominating, avoid festering disagreements, and ensure that if one staff member leaves, the group itself will not be destroyed. Leadership role sharing will help change exclusionist attitudes. The leader role will mean that the goals of inclusion must be put forth and supported by the person in the leadership role. Exclusionists would be put in the situation of advocating for inclusion counter to their existing attitudes. Role playing a counter attitude may be necessary for attitude change (Cook, 1990).

Third, the group should plan for a rotating record keeper for each meeting, as it will be necessary to have a written record to forestall future arguments about decisions already made at an earlier meeting. The note taker should be rotated, so that each person engages in writing content that may be challenging to their own exclusionary attitudes.

Finally, the group should agree to follow rules or procedures for controlling discussions, and enforcement of these procedures will be the responsibility of the chairperson at each meeting. These items may require several meetings before they are resolved, but they are crucial to establishing effective change (Phillips & McCullough, 1990).

2. *Nominate possible inclusive situations:* The group should nominate several possible inclusive settings. The McGill Action Planning System (MAPS) (Vandercook, York, & Forest, 1989) provides a procedure to help group members work through the nomination process within a structure that develops advocacy and understanding within the

group. The process focuses on the development of a consensual written plan involving public statements by participants to answer the following questions:

a. What is the student's history?
b. What is your dream for her or him?
c. What is your nightmare?
d. What words can you use to describe him or her?
e. What are his or her strengths, gifts, and abilities?
f. What are her or his needs?
g. What would her or his ideal school day look like, and what must be accomplished so that this is achieved?

This process will help identify symptoms of exclusion in a systematic fashion while at the same time create a positive climate for attitude change (e.g., see Vandercook et al., 1989). (See also chap. 6, this volume, for a fuller description of MAPs and lifestyle planning.)

Alternate structures may also be used. Liberty, Haring, Moran, and Fisher (1989) developed a checklist (see Figure 1) for use by inclusion planning group members to initiate naming inclusive settings and to identify potential problems associated by group members with nominated settings. The chairperson should set the tone by accepting each nominated situation as a possibility to be considered later. If this tolerance for different ideas can be achieved by the chairperson, the other group members will become increasingly confident about presenting alternatives and accepting intergroup differences. These behaviors are evidence of the first step toward attitude change.

3. *Prioritize nominated inclusive situations:* Once all possibilities within a situation category have been identified, the next step is to rank order the nominations. Any criteria the group decides to use is acceptable. Achieving a ranking will give the group

a sense of cohesion without the necessity of confronting the exclusionary attitudes; working together will be reinforced.

4. *Develop detailed description of desired inclusion:* Once a ranking of situations has been achieved, an attempt should be made to define the details of the desired inclusion, such as the types of interpersonal interactions sought, the activities that will be engaged in, and so on. The checklist (Figure 1) provides a structure that may be used to guide this discussion.

5. *Identify challenges to inclusion:* Once details of the desired inclusive situation are clear, specific barriers or challenges to achieving it should be identified. The checklist provides a list of potential problem categories that may help stimulate this discussion as well. It is during this time that the first overt symptoms of exclusion are likely to be observed. The chairperson should strive to see that each challenge or barrier to inclusion is included in the list. However, the contributor of each challenge must explain explicitly how it relates to the specific situation under discussion. This process will create a list that can be identified as "problems looking for solutions."

6. *Repeat the steps for each inclusive situation:* Work through another desired situation, defining its details and challenges. In this fashion, the group will be alternating between statements about inclusion and opportunities to express attitudes of exclusion, creating repeated exposure to the conflict and awareness of the problems. Working through the entire checklist should assist in identifying the most obvious objections and challenges to inclusion.

7. *Select the inclusive situation to be achieved first:* Construct a list of the "top-ranked" inclusive situations. These must be sequenced by the group in the order in which they are to be addressed. That is, the situation that is the first priority will be the

Checklist for Inclusion of

Student _____ Age _____ Date _____
School _____ District _____
Participants: _____

What is an inclusive situation? "Inclusion communicates something more than 'integration.' It means people participating in families, schools (and classrooms), in workplaces, and in community life. 'Inclusion' implies that people are welcomed, that each person reaches out to include another person. Inclusion is different from 'letting in' or 'adding on.' Inclusion conveys the idea that we appreciate each other, that we see each other's gifts, that we value being together. Inclusion speaks to the importance of relationships. Other aspects of our work, for example, our learning and teaching skills, abilities, and techniques, are not ends in themselves, but merely avenues to inclusion" (Biklen, 1990, p. 1).

What is the Checklist? The Checklist is to be used to guide thought and discussion about students with disabilities, to identify inclusive situations, to identify challenging issues that prevent a student from being included.

How can the Checklist be used? Most of the time, as soon as we begin to think about inclusion, all of the reasons why it cannot work for a particular student crowd our thoughts. For example, "If only Jack didn't make so much noise, and if only I had more staff, and if only the principal was more supportive, then Jack could attend school assemblies." Listing all the challenging issues first is intimidating and discouraging. The Checklist is designed to make the process positive.

The Checklist is useful to parents and professionals in planning for elementary and secondary students with disabilities. During the process of completing the Checklist, you should: 1) identify potential inclusive situations in six different categories, 2) pick the highest priority in each, 3) detail the situation, 4) describe the challenges that are preventing participation, and finally, you will 5) prioritize the six situations you have identified. Identifying and gaining access to new situations should be a part of the ongoing educational process. Inclusive situations in the current school setting (e.g., eating in the cafeteria) and situations in the future (e.g., employment) should be identified.

No matter what the student's age, it is not too soon to start this process. For students who are near graduation age, it is imperative that specific work and living situations be identified as soon as possible. We all know of students who have left school without jobs or without the skills to get a job. We know students who could live in an apartment, but are placed on waiting lists with no hope of moving for several years.

For younger students, inclusion can result in participation in a broader range of school activities and a higher quality of school life. Identification of living and work situations is important for these students as well because they may need to access certain situations now in order to be ready for their future independence. There may be challenges that can be overcome if preparations are started early (e.g., raising funds to make a group home accessible to wheelchairs or expanding community placements in supported employment).

I. School Settings

Step 1. Select settings.

Check and then rank order

Current	Future		Current	Future	
_____	_____	P.E.	_____	_____	Assemblies
_____	_____	Art	_____	_____	Music
_____	_____	Recess	_____	_____	Math
_____	_____	Reading	_____	_____	Science
_____	_____	Tutor	_____	_____	Be tutored
_____	_____	Library	_____	_____	Cafeteria
_____	_____	School job (hall monitor, class aide, note courier)			
_____	_____	Other: _____			

Figure 1.   Checklist for planning for inclusion. (Adapted from Liberty, Haring, Moran, & Fisher [1989].).

Step 2: Identify the top priority situation.   Identify the top priority situation in the section by marking a #1 next to it and then identify the activity, location, peer group, time of day, and so forth as specifically as you can. For example: "P.E. with Mr. Butler's class, 9:15–9:45, M, W, F in south gym"; "Pep assemblies, Fridays before home games, 2:15 in gym"; or "Northgate Mall, 105th and Northgate Way, Saturday mornings with his brother." If you cannot specify the information, then at least one of the challenging issues is identified, for example: "Location is a problem because I don't know of a P.E. class he can join," or "Staffing is an issue because I don't know whom he will go to the games with, and he can't go alone because he is not independently mobile." Determine the level of participation that best describes the desired inclusion. All activities should include interactions and interpersonal experiences among all individuals.

Participate in typical activities: The student will participate in typical activities, without special help or adaptations. Examples of participation in typical activities include hanging out at the mall, playing volleyball, attending a football game, dancing at a school dance, eating lunch in the school cafeteria, and going to a movie. The activity can be defined according to the way in which students without disabilities participate in the activity.

Special adaptations: The student will participate in the typical activity with special adaptations, such as use of an interpreter, calculators, or specialized equipment.

Partial participation: The student performs some of the typical activities, with or without special adaptations. For example: the student joins a reading group in the first grade, but does not read aloud. Or, the student joins a basketball game and keeps score, but does not play. In exercise class, the student does only upper-body exercises.

Parallel activity: The student participates in an activity that is similar, but not identical, to those of the others in the situation and that is also appropriate to the situation. For example: the student lifts weights in gym while other students play volleyball.

Fill in the blanks
Inclusion will involve (activity) with (other pupils) in the (location) at (times).

Step 3: Identify and explain challenges to inclusion.   Examples: Transportation is a barrier because "there is no bus to the swimming pool (and no money for a bus)"; skill level is a barrier because "he doesn't know how to play any of the games"; behavior is a barrier because "he masturbates in front of the girls"; equipment is a barrier because "there is no wheelchair swing on the playground"; staffing is a barrier because "there is no one to feed him lunch in the cafeteria."

Describe the challenges

Skill level is a challenge because: _____

Behavior is a challenge because: _____

Health/medical problems are challenges because: _____

Staffing is a challenge because: _____
Materials, equipment, and/or supplies are challenges because: _____

Services are a challenge because: _____

Transportation is a challenge because: _____

Other challenges are: _____

(continued)

Figure 1. (*continued*)

II. School-Based Recreation

Step 1: Select settings.

Check and then rank order

Current	Future		Current	Future	
_____	_____ Swimming program		_____	_____ Field trips	
_____	_____ School dance (attend)		_____	_____ Dance committee	
_____	_____ School club		_____	_____ Extracurricular activity	
_____	_____ Athletic events (attend)		_____	_____ Sports teams or clubs	
_____	_____ Yearbook (participate)		_____	_____ Fundraising events	
_____	_____ School play (participate)				
_____	_____ Other				

Steps 2 and 3: Repeat Steps 2 and 3 from Part I.

III. Community-Based Recreation

Step 1: Identify situations.

Check and number in order of priority

Current	Future		Current	Future	
_____	_____ Use park facilities		_____	_____ Visit zoo	
_____	_____ Go to aquarium		_____	_____ Visit museum	
_____	_____ Go to Science Center		_____	_____ Visit gallery	
_____	_____ Eat at restaurant		_____	_____ Shop at store	
_____	_____ Use fitness center		_____	_____ Attend sports event	
_____	_____ Attend cultural events		_____	_____ Go to movies	
_____	_____ Hang out at the mall		_____	_____ Go bowling	
_____	_____ Play a musical instrument		_____	_____ Play golf	
_____	_____ Visit a neighbor or friend		_____	_____ Go fishing	
_____	_____ Take a vacation		_____	_____ Go boating	
_____	_____ Ride public bus		_____	_____ Go camping	
_____	_____ Go horseback riding		_____	_____ Go to the beach	
_____	_____ Church/synagogue activities		_____	_____ Use YWCA/YMCA	
_____	_____ Choose/operate radio/tv/video				
_____	_____ Join Girl Scouts, Boy Scouts, Campfire, etc.				
_____	_____ Go to the store or minimart with friends after school				
_____	_____ Other _____				

Steps 2 and 3: Repeat Steps 2 and 3 from Part I.

Figure 1. (*continued*)

IV. Class Placement

Step 1: Identify current and more desirable situation.

Mark "C" for current or "F" for future.
___ Part time
___ Full time
___ with students of same chronological age
   ___ in classroom ($+/-$ 2 years) and ___ in school building ($+/-$ 5 years)
   ___ in community setting ($+/-$ 20 years)
___ inclusion with students without disabilities
   ___ in classroom
   ___ in school
   ___ in community setting ($+/-$ 20 years)
___ at home
___ more than one classroom or location (describe)

Full time: An educational placement is full time if a student spends all of his or her school day in this placement.

Part time: An educational placement is part time if a student spends his or her school day in two or more placements *or* is in two or more placements during the week.

Homebound: Homebound instruction refers to instruction for a student in his or her home. It includes a teacher or therapist going to the student's home to provide instruction or providing instruction through telecommunications. Homebound also includes students who live in a state institution and attend school on their living unit.

Inclusion: An inclusive class or school is one in which students with and without disabilities are placed.

Age appropriate: A placement is age appropriate if the students are within about 30 months in age of each other. Three years younger, and no more than 3 years older, than your student is considered age appropriate except in community situations, or vocational preparation situations, where a wide range of ages is typical.

Step 2: Identify school/location of future placement OR explain why no change is identified.

Fill in the blanks
Inclusion placement will be with (other pupils) in the (location) at (times).

Step 3. Repeat Step 3 from Part I.

V. Living Situations

Step 1: Identify current and more desirable situation.

Mark "C" for current or "F" for future.

___ Live with parents/friends	___ Live with spouse
___ Foster home	___ Family-style group home
___ Staffed group home	___ Intensive tenant support
___ Supported apartment living	___ Independent living
___ Other	

(*continued*)

Figure 1.   *(continued)*

Family-style group home: House "parents" live in the home. Learning in a family atmosphere is emphasized where members of the "family" take responsibility for keeping the family and the home functioning well.
Staffed group home: A staffed group home provides in-home training and support for a group of people living in a single dwelling. Staff do not live in the group home.
Intensive tenant support: Intensive tenant support includes 24-hour training and supervision for people living in their own home or apartment.
Supported apartment living: Supported apartment living provides in-home training and support for people living in their own home or apartment.
Independent living: Independent living refers to living in one's own home or apartment without supervision or agency support.

Step 2: Identify location of situation OR explain why no change is identified.

Fill in the blanks
Inclusive living situation will be with (describe living companions) at (location) at (address).

Step 3. Repeat Step 3 from Part I.

VI. Postschool Employment

Step 1: Identify most desired situation.

Check and rank order
_____ Employment training
_____ Supported employment
_____ Competitive employment
_____ Enclave/group supported employment
_____ Other

_____ Sheltered workshop
_____ Individual employment
_____ Self-employment

Sheltered workshop: Sheltered workshop is defined as a segregated work/training environment where all workers have a disability and work for less than minimum wage.
Supported employment: Supported employment includes training in skills and provision of support to an individual at the job site.
Enclave/group supported employment: Enclave/group supported employment is defined as training in skills and provision of support to a group of eight or fewer individuals with disabilities employed in an enclave or on a crew.
Individual employment: Individual employment is placement into job training at the job site and follow-along to help maintain the person in the job.
Competitive employment: Competitive employment is employment in a business with no external support other than that typically provided for all employees.

Step 2:   Record the names of suggested work places.

Fill in the blanks
Inclusion employment will be (describe what the job is) with (describe work mates) at (location) at (address).

Figure 1. *(continued)*

Step 3: Identify where the student will receive vocational training in preparation for employment.

Fill in the blanks
Employment training will be (describe what the job is) with (describe work mates) at (location) at (address).

Type: check one
_____ Work-study program   _____ Vocational education class
_____ Employment training program   _____ Other: _____

Work-study: Work-study refers to an approach to education at the high school level that combines classwork and employment as part of a student's program.
Vocational education class: Vocational education classes include classes that provide specific vocational training (e.g., auto mechanics, wood shop).

Step 4: Repeat Step 3 from Part I.

VII. Summary

Step 1: List priority situation from each domain.

Copy from Parts I–VI
School Settings _____
School-Based Recreation _____
Community-Based Recreation _____
Class Placement _____
Living Situations _____
PostSchool Employment _____

Step 2: Identify one priority situation from above and place a ☆ next to it.

Step 3: Specify IEP objectives. As a final check to the suitability of the situation for the pupil's education, please specify below the IEP objectives to be achieved, taught, and maintained in the priority situation.

IEP objectives:

Step 4: List the criteria by which inclusion will be evaluated.

Evaluation criteria:

Step 5: For each challenge identified for the priority situation, start brainstorming strategies to overcome it. Begin here:

one to which the group will address its initial efforts, resources, and commitment. The group should agree to delay trying to achieve all of the inclusive activities at once because it is unlikely from a practical viewpoint that sufficient time and energy are available to ensure success, and second, because a go-slow, step-by-step process is more conducive to changing exclusionary attitudes. Finally, a slower process that is successful will produce more meaningful attitude change than a faster process that might bruise feelings or be otherwise unsuccessful.

8. *Review group membership:* At this point, it is likely that it will be necessary to expand the group by determining key personnel who are perhaps involved in the target situation, but are not currently involved in the group. For example, if one target situation is inclusion in the school cafeteria, the cafeteria supervisor should now be included in the group. The group itself should plan how to get key persons involved, and then execute the plan. If key personnel cannot become a part of the team, the group should consider moving to the next-ranked situation or to an alternative strategy for getting key persons involved. Once a key person is involved, that person should also add to the list of barriers the things he or she perceives as challenges to inclusion. If the learner has not been attending and participating in the team meetings up until this point, the chairperson should suggest that this is actually required, morally, as well as legally.

9. *Identify strategies to confront challenges:* Next, for the target situation, the group should identify strategies for each obstacle. Strategies may be identified by looking at barriers as challenges; brainstorming within the group; soliciting suggestions from professionals in other groups, specialists, agencies listed in the telephone directory, from individuals at colleges, universities, and other public service agencies; or reviewing books and journals available at libraries.

Each challenge should be addressed separately, and a number of alternative methods for overcoming them should be discussed. Only one challenge should be addressed at each meeting. If this policy results in a 5-minute meeting, so much the better—the "extra" time will be a reinforcer for solving a particular problem. Attitudes will be changed faster if team members feel positive about the meetings, but not if members are pressured into meeting some artificial deadline. If questions remain at the end of the meeting, individual group members may be given a small task to complete, such as telephoning for information, finding a book, talking to an agency representative, and so on. When the group has agreed on how a challenge may be overcome, the next challenge should be addressed at the following meeting.

10. *Implement strategies, achieve inclusion, and evaluate:* A timeline should be created to ensure that strategies for overcoming challenges are completed in the sequence necessary for achieving inclusion. Although excessive pressure will be counterproductive, the group should set a target date by which strategies must be in place and inclusion initiated. The group should also develop an evaluation plan based on their description of what desirable inclusion will look like.

Evaluation is the critical step to ensuring that exclusionists face the disconfirming evidence. The evaluation procedures should be determined at the time of implementation and should involve each team member in collecting objective information about inclusion. Procedures should preclude, insofar as is possible, subjective interpretations of impact in preference of objectively written records of actual events. It is essential that team members collect the "evidence" that disconfirms their own expectations and attitudes, that this information be shared, and the implications faced before planning for another student. An evaluation model appropriate for assessing the inclusion of students with deaf-blindness is described by Meyer and Eichinger (1987).

Scaffolding Challenges and Strategies

As strategies are identified and implemented, new problems, heretofore unvoiced, can be expected. In our project, as soon as some challenges were evidently overcome, new barriers were erected, and the real roots of exclusion were eventually exposed (Haring & Liberty, 1991). Strategies for achieving inclusion blossomed to encompass tangles of policies, people, events, perceptions, skills, resources, equipment, and so forth.

For example, as staffing problems were initially confronted, it became apparent that it was automatically assumed that a one-to-one ratio was required because some group members never expected the student to be able to learn to perform more competently. For example, staffing was a problem in making the school cafeteria accessible for Julia (a student in our project with deaf-blindness, cerebral palsy, and epilepsy) because someone had to accompany her to and from the cafeteria as well as feed her. The concept that Julia could be taught to get to the cafeteria on her own and feed herself was simply not ever considered by her group. In their perception, "the skills that the student doesn't have, she will never have. Skill deficits are a consequence of her disabilities and will not be affected by any type of instruction. So there is no point in providing it." To justify their attitudes, some group members produced evidence that Julia had learned very little in all her years in school.

Rather than seeing such depressing data as indicating a long-term need for better instructional programs, some members saw this as a justification for exclusion. When Julia did begin to learn to feed herself during instruction developed from the "Green Bean" program (see Inman & Black, 1987) and from basic procedures for acquisition of new

skills (Liberty, Haring, & Martin, 1981)—disconfirming evidence of the truest sort—members raised new objections, including that the school couldn't afford a janitor to "clean up" after her. This new "challenge" resulted in the exploration of the idea that the janitor cleaned up after all the students and that the criteria for "neat" eating was not applied to other students. Finally, it was seen that Julia's eating skills did not produce any greater mess than other students who spilled food or left paper litter. Once discussions get down to specific details, strategies for overcoming all challenges can be identified. This is another step in confronting exclusionists with disconfirming evidence. The following case study illustrates how the inclusion planning process works.

CASE STUDY: INCLUSION OF MARK

Mark was almost 19 years old when inclusion was first considered. He was living in a residential institution at the time, and he attended school in a classroom just a few rooms away from his sleeping area. His records indicated that he had a 65-decibel loss to his hearing and a scanning nystagmus vision disorder. Specialists had been unable to determine how well he was able to see, although they felt his pupils did respond to light. He also had a seizure disorder. As is typical for individuals with multiple disabilities (Aman, Paxton, Field, & Foote, 1986), he was medicated daily with Valium (2 mg), Tegretol (1400 mg), Zarontin (1000 mg), and phenobarbital (90 mg). Research indicates the serious problems of combining medications for seizures as well as the inhibiting effects of seizure control medication on alertness and learning (Gadow, 1986a, 1986b; Spooner & Dykes, 1982). (Mark's medication was eventually reduced and changed.) Staff difficulties in teaching and managing Mark's feeding, nutrition, and health had resulted in Mark being fed through a gastrostomy system with an open incision to his upper intestine. Mark rarely went outside because it was thought that his health was too fragile. He had not been taught to walk and had difficulty sitting because of his scoliosis. He scored in the lowest category of independence on the *Inventory for Client and Agency Planning* (Bruininks, Hill, Wetherman, & Woodcock, 1986), and his school programs had been unsuccessful in teaching him how to manipulate objects in his environment or to care for his own needs. It is not known if his medication regimen was considered to be the source of his health, nutrition, and learning difficulties. The team members depended primarily on interpreting Mark's facial expressions for his expressive communication.

Mark's Inclusion Planning Team

The team that worked toward inclusion for Mark included his teacher, a teacher's aide, an adaptive physical education specialist, a speech and language specialist, an occupational therapist, a school administrator, and his mother. They identified inclusive situations including a new school placement (attending full time with a group of students his age in a high school serving students with and without disabilities); a supported living situation; and trips to go swimming and to other places in the community, such as parks and shops.

Challenges to inclusion in a new school setting were identified as difficulty in transportation due to Mark's 24-hour drip-system feeding equipment, the need to train the teachers and other personnel at the new school to keep Mark's equipment and medication balanced and safe, and permission from Mark's physician for him to travel and attend school with others who might be ill. For swimming and other activities in the community, these same challenges were identified. For a new living situation, the challenges addressed were the scarcity of options and opposition from current residential staff. When supported living was first proposed, it was also suggested that Mark's mother would object. But she hastened to correct that misattribution.

The group discussed how to prioritize the inclusive situations. The ease with which members felt that inclusion might be achieved probably contributed more to the ranking of the situation than to the desirability of the various settings for Mark. Situations were prioritized as follows: 1) new school, 2) community settings, 3) swimming, and 4) supported living. At this point in the planning, Mark's prospective teacher in the new school joined the team.

Inclusion in the New School

In order to plan for inclusion in the new school, strategies were identified and tasks accepted by various team members. Mark's medical problems were discussed with his physician by one of the team members. It was determined that as other individuals with similar disabilities were already being transported, Mark could be safely transported with them.

The second barrier was approached by determining, with the physician's assistance, which medical needs had to be met at the new school. The medical management of individuals with multiple health issues is complex, and when a student dies, the implications and ramifications of the death affect not only his or her family, friends, and caregivers, but also the service agencies with which he or she is involved. It is not surprising, in a litigious society, that schools, sometimes perceived as being "deep pockets" for a civil suit, are wary about moving a student with complex health needs from a relatively known environment to a relatively unknown environment away from his home. The largest association of special educators, the Council for Exceptional Children, has adopted a policy that "urges state and local education and health agencies to implement procedures for jointly serving students who challenge life or health support" that will support inclusion of students with profound challenges ("CEC advocates," 1988).

The strategies to overcome challenges to Mark's inclusion involved training someone to respond to the pump alarm on the gastrostomy feeding system, install batteries for one part of the system, and ensure that the system was properly connected to an electrical outlet. It was also necessary to train an individual to provide medication and treatment for any significant change in Mark's health, to respond to any tonic clonic seizures, and to know when to call for medical assistance. These problems were addressed by discussing the strategies with the school nurse, who was willing to be trained in procedures involving gastrostomy feeding and other emergency problems. She also joined the inclusion team. Next the team determined that the medical staff who were currently responsible for responding to emergency problems were willing to train the school nurse without charge. Emergency procedures were discussed with Mark's physician and with the director of medical services for the institution where he lived, and the nurse was trained in these as well.

The school district administrator responsible for both the class at the institution and the high school program agreed with the new school placement. As it was then the end of the school year, a target date for inclusion for the beginning of the next school year was established. At this time, all the necessary training and new procedures would be completed.

Inclusion in the Community

Strategies for inclusion in community situations began with challenging the traditional idea of "field trips." Conventional special ed-

ucation programs often incorporated visits to community settings during the school day. Usually these occasions consisted of a group of students from special education visiting, as a group, a shop, grocery store, movie theater, skating rink, mall, or other community setting. Transportation to and from the setting was accomplished as a group, usually in a school bus or van. Teachers supervised the students.

Exclusion is at the center of the traditional "field-trip" approach because: 1) students with disabilities are grouped together while students without disabilities are excluded, 2) there are no possibilities for interaction with same-age peers because they are in school, and 3) shopping or other activities in large groups with a teacher is a stigmatizing experience not shared by peers without disabilities (Snell, 1983). Instead, community inclusion was structured as a joint excursion by Mark and a peer or a friend/teacher with a specific purpose in mind, such as going for a swim. The activity would be scheduled at a time of day when same-age peers also engaged in the activity. Because many peers of the same age had finished high school, some times in the day, such as lunchtime, were possible times for same-age interaction. People who considered themselves Mark's friend included a peer, a noncertified teacher, a school aide, related services staff, and his teacher (cf. Baumgart & VanWalleghem, 1986). Because of Mark's health needs and because of desire by the team not to request more funds, it was decided that someone who was already trained would accompany him. Scheduling problems were resolved by setting the duration in advance.

Transportation issues were approached by listing several different types of community activities (e.g., going to a park, shopping in a grocery store) of varying distances from Mark's home and then finding the modes of transportation available (i.e., public bus with wheelchair lift, walking, cabulance, taxi, school bus, private auto, school auto) and the costs associated with each. Next, sources of funds for those transportation modes that did have a fee were identified, including Mark's SSI (supplemental security income) allowance, school field trip funds, donations, and fundraising. Insurance issues relating to the use of private cars for transportation were also addressed.

Next, the team developed a permission form with the help of Mark's physician. This was similar to the permission form used by students in general education and was to be mailed to the physician 24 hours before a visit. Thus, the physician had the ability to cancel if he felt that Mark's health was at risk.

For swimming, because transportation and staffing problems/solutions were interwoven with the location problem, the group first identified five community pools, including a commercial hot tub salon and one pool at another local high school. They also suggested installing small pools or hot tubs in Mark's new school, including strategies for raising the funds for such a venture. At this point, the team began to function proactively for other students at the school as well, indicating some progress in changing attitudes of exclusion.

Transportation challenges were determined for other community situations, and sources for funds for entrance fees to pools were located. The group found a trainer to train staff or peers to swim with Mark as well as an appropriate water program. Procedures for selecting and scheduling staff and/or peers to travel to the pool with him were arranged. A similar physician's permission procedure was developed.

Supported Living

For the supported living situation, the team was unable to find a residential support agency that would place Mark on their waiting list. This same challenge was faced by numerous inclusion teams. As strategy discussions continued, some additional challenges were identified. Some team members were affiliated with a union and had, upon joining the union, signed a loyalty oath in which they promised not to advocate for "off residential grounds" services or placements. Some of these individuals feared losing their jobs or other repercussions if they advocated for community living, and discussions with them also included involvement with the state division of developmental disabilities. About this time, the residential institution in which Mark lived began working with parents to design and build residential support programs in the community. Several team members became involved in this effort.

Outcomes

Although Mark deserved to have always been included in the life of his community, he had spent virtually his entire life in the exiled state of the excluded. The gradual work of his team finally resulted in Mark's access to part of what he should always have had. The inclusive school placement did not occur as planned. At the end of the school year, the team discovered that Mark's placement could not be changed because funding patterns for students with disabilities in his district were tied to staff ratios for separate classrooms serving children with profound disabilities and deaf-blindness. The funding would *not* follow the student into the inclusive setting, unless 10 or so students were "included" in the same setting, which was not desirable. Also, if Mark did move to an inclusive setting, a teacher would lose her position because the staff ratio in the room he moved from would fall below the magic number. In this way, the funding policy acted as a disincentive to inclusion. Team members discussed possible strategies for changing such policies over the long term. However, Mark turned 21 and became ineligible for public school programs during this period. He also remained on the institution's waiting list for consideration for supported living.

Mark did begin going into the community to parks and shops and going swimming with another young adult about his own age within the time frame selected by the team. During these inclusive situations, Mark was much more engaged in what was going on around him, more communicative, and smiled and laughed a great deal more than in his separate classroom (see Figure 2).

EVALUATING CHANGE

In the authors' study, 72 professionals and 26 parents participated on inclusion teams. At the beginning of the project, *every* participant identified challenges to inclusion that could be classified as symptomatic of exclusion. Of the 22 situations in which team-generated strategies were implemented, 20 situations achieved inclusion successfully (Haring & Liberty, 1991). The success of inclusion from the student's point of view was determined by looking for changes in behavior and biobehavioral states suggested by team members and from a literature review (i.e., Evans & Scotti, 1989; Guess et al., 1988; Sternberg, Pegnatore, & Hill, 1983). Behaviors that were quantitatively assessed included determining whether the student was more engaged in the inclusive situation than in a segregated situation, whether the number of social interactions increased, and whether he or she communicated more frequently in the inclusive situation.

In evaluating inclusion, most students were much more fully engaged with their peers in inclusive settings, although three students were always attentive and participating in both inclusive and segregated situations. Students were consistently more commu-

nicative, both initiating and responding to contacts while they were being included. Overall, entering a new situation resulted in positive changes for all of the students involved, providing disconfirming evidence to those group members who initially opposed inclusion for reasons and rationalizations that fit into the schema of exclusion.

The process of discussing specifics of each setting and challenges to inclusion meant that all of the team members eventually provided to each other most of the disconfirming evidence needed for attitude change. When the concept of inclusion was first broached, possible settings were often rejected as soon as they were mentioned. This seemed to occur when the individual felt that the number and complexity of the challenges were so overwhelming that even a discussion of possible situations seemed a waste of time. However, the process of confronting each challenge on an individual basis, and then brainstorming strategies for overcoming each before tackling the next one, proved to be a "one step at a time" approach that gradually built confidence and contributed to a change in attitudes. The success of these inclusive situations provided the first set of disconfirming evidence to the exclusionists.

This approach also forced individualization of inclusion plans, avoiding situations where insensitivity to the unique challenges of each exceptional pupil has led to inappropriate placements and raised the ires of administrators and the community. The Council for Exceptional Children, the National Education Association, the American Association of School Administrators, and the National Association of Elementary School Principals have endorsed a statement calling for individualization of these decisions on a case-by-case choice of the best placements ("Educators warn," 1987). The strategies discussed provide a means of achieving this

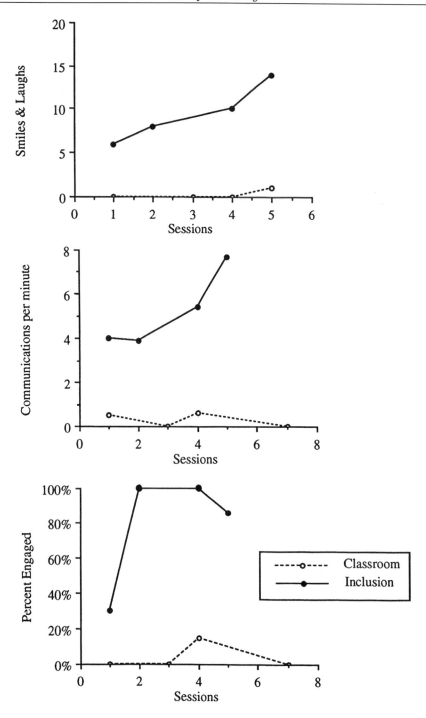

Figure 2.   Mark's engagement in an inclusive situation compared with his engagement in his separate classroom.

goal. Our results also support Wyant and Bell's (1981) suggestion that problem solving on an individual basis is most likely to be effective and planning from the individual student up through the team instead of from the administration down is most likely to identify these strategies.

ATTITUDES OF INCLUSION

Meyerson (1988) describes changes over the last 40 years in the field of disability and points out that a major shift in the perception of disability as a flaw in the individual to its perception as rooted in societal attitudes is now occurring. There are at least three overt signs that can be used to determine if attitudes of exclusion are being replaced with attitudes of inclusion (Opotow, 1990a). One indicator is that the consideration of fairness will apply to learners with disabilities. Thus, statements like, "He's just too medically fragile," would be replaced with statements like "Students in the typical classroom don't have to prove they're healthy."

Another indicator would be a willingness to share resources. Thus, instead of hearing, "We just can't afford to have an aide to work with these disabled kids," we would hear, "Maybe instead of new football uniforms this year, we can get an aide for kids with disabilities." Another indicator would be a willingness to sacrifice to facilitate the well-being of a child with disabilities. For example, instead of, "I couldn't possibly handle a kid like that, since I don't know anything about them," it might be offered, "Can you give me some information so I can learn about kids with those needs?"

In our project, all of the professionals involved except one teacher and his aide changed in observable ways, including attending inservice training sessions to learn new instructional skills, acting as a facilitator when a student first entered an inclusion set-

ting, advocating for change in how placement decisions were made, encouraging more residential options, and/or advocating for appropriate hearing and vision aids. As McDonnell and Hardman (1989) point out, "A willingness to learn new patterns for providing services to students will be required by specialists as they apply their expertise in new organizational models" (p. 72). Thus, the procedures used in the project did produce the initial evidence of a change in attitudes.

When inclusion is firmly established, it is likely that all three indicators will be obviously present (Opotow, 1990a). This is supported by Gans' (1987) finding that the more contact a general educator has with a wide range of student abilities, the more willing she or he was to include students with disabilities. For the teachers in Gans' study, the disconfirming evidence had likely reached the point at which attitude change had occurred. When similar attitude shifts occur for the majority of teachers and professionals, Lipsky and Gartner (1987) will no longer have to wonder "What would education for those with handicapping conditions be like if we thought of them as full-fledged human beings, capable of achievement and worthy of respect?" because they will automatically be included as the "full-fledged human beings" that they are (p. 70).

Attitude change programs are required until all indicators have been repeatedly observed (Opotow, 1990a). As long as attitudes of exclusion prevail, students with disabilities and their families will face the same old battles for inclusion with school personnel. The most important challenge facing us is to change attitudes of exclusion to attitudes of inclusion. As Hamre-Nietupski and colleagues (1988) discovered in a 4-year effort, continual goal setting and movement by the agents of change produced change only gradually, for a few children at a time. How-

ever, once attitudes of exclusion can be overcome, the rationalizations and justifications
used to block inclusion each time it is suggested will disappear, replaced by an attitude
of "Can-do!" for *all* the members of our
communities.

REFERENCES

Aman, M., Paxton, J., Field, C., & Foote, S. (1986). Prevalence of toxic anticonvulsant drug concentrations in mentally retarded persons with epilepsy. *American Journal of Mental Deficiency, 90*(6), 643–650.

Atherton, L., & Atherton, B. (1987, December). The good news. *Newsletter of The Association for Persons with Severe Handicaps, 13*(120), 2–3.

Baumgart, D., & VanWalleghem, J. (1986). Staffing strategies for implementing community-based instruction. *Journal of The Association for Persons with Severe Handicaps, 11*(2), 92–102.

Biklen, D. (1988). The myth of clinical judgment. *Journal of Social Issues, 44*(1), 127–140.

Biklen, D. (1990). Action for inclusion. *Newsletter of The Association for Persons with Severe Handicaps, 16*(6), 1.

Brown, L., Branston, M.B., Hamre-Nietupski, S., Pumpian, I., Certo, N., & Gruenewald, L.A. (1979). A strategy for developing chronological age appropriate and functional curricular content for severely handicapped adolescents and young adults. *Journal of Special Education, 13,* 81–90.

Bruininks, R.H., Hill, B.K., Wetherman, R.F., & Woodcock, R.W. (1986). *Inventory for client and agency planning.* Allen, TX: DLM Teaching Resources.

Bullis, M., & Otos, M. (1988). Characteristics of programs for children with deaf-blindness: Results of a national survey. *Journal of The Association for Persons with Severe Handicaps, 13*(2), 110–115.

Bus, A., & Kruizenga, T. (1989). Diagnostic problem-solving behavior of expert practitioners in the field of learning disabilities. *Journal of School Psychology, 27,* 277–287.

CEC advocates services for children needing medical support. (1988, April 13). *Education of the Handicapped,* 7–8.

Cook, S. (1990). Toward a psychology of improving justice: Research on extending the equality principle to victims of social injustice. *Journal of Social Issues, 46*(1), 147–161.

Damerell, R. (1985). *Education's smoking gun: How teachers' colleges have destroyed education in America.* New York: Freundlich Books.

Dussault, W.L.E. (1989). Is a policy of exclusion based upon severity of disability legally defensible? In F. Brown & D.H. Lehr (Eds.), *Persons with profound disabilities: Issues and practices* (pp. 43–59). Baltimore: Paul H. Brookes Publishing Co.

Educators warn of "growing insensitivity" to handicapped students. (1987, June 10). *Education of the Handicapped,* 7–8.

Ellis, D. (1986). The epidemiology of visual impairment in people with a mental handicap. In D. Ellis (Ed.), *Sensory impairments in mentally handicapped people* (pp. 3–34). London: Croom Helm.

Evans, I., & Scotti, J. (1989). Defining meaningful outcomes for persons with profound disabilities. In F. Brown & D.H. Lehr (Eds.), *Persons with profound disabilities: Issues and practices* (pp. 83–108). Baltimore: Paul H. Brookes Publishing Co.

Ferguson, D.L., & Baumgart, D. (1991). Partial participation revisited. *Journal of The Association for Persons with Severe Handicaps, 16*(4), 218–227.

Fine, M. (1990). "The Public" in public schools: The social construction/constriction of moral communities. *Journal of Social Issues, 46*(1), 107–119.

Gadow, K.D. (1986a). *Children on medication, Vol. 1: Hyperactivity, learning disabilities and mental retardation.* San Diego: College-Hill Press.

Gadow, K.D. (1986b). *Children on medication, Vol. 2: Epilepsy, emotional disturbance and adolescent disorders.* San Diego: College-Hill Press.

Gans, K. (1987). Willingness of regular and special educators to teach students with handicaps. *Exceptional Children, 54*(1), 41–45.

Gartner, A., & Lipsky, D.K. (1987). Beyond special education: Toward a quality system for all students. *Harvard Educational Review, 57*(4), 367–395.

Geiger, W., & Justen, J. (1983). Definitions of severely handicapped and requirements for teacher certification. A survey of state departments of education. *Journal of The Association for the Severely Handicapped, 8*(1), 25–29.

Giangreco, M., Cloninger, C., Mueller, P., Yuan, S., & Ashworth, S. (1991). Perspectives of parents whose children have dual sensory impairments. *Journal of The Association for Persons with Severe Handicaps, 16*(1), 14–24.

Goetz, L., Guess, D., & Stremel-Campbell, K. (Eds.). (1987). *Innovative program design for individuals with dual sensory impairments.* Baltimore: Paul H. Brookes Publishing Co.

Goetz, L., Lee, M., Johnston, S., & Gaylord-Ross, R. (1991). Employment of persons with dual sensory impairments: Strategies for inclusion. *Journal of The Association for Persons with Severe Handicaps, 16*(3), 131–139.

Gould, S.J. (1981). *The mismeasure of man.* New York: W.W. Norton.

Guess, D., Mulligan-Ault, M., Roberts, S., Struth, J., Siegel-Causey, E., Thompson, B., Bronicki, G., & Guy, B. (1988). Implications of biobehavioral states for the education and treatment of students with the most profoundly handicapping conditions. *Journal of The Association for Persons with Severe Handicaps, 13*(3), 163–174.

Hamre-Nietupski, S., Krajewski, L., Nietupski, J., Ostercamp, D., Sensor, K., & Opheim, B. (1988). Parent/professional partnerships in advocacy: Developing integrated options within resistive systems. *Journal of The Association for Persons with Severe Handicaps, 13*(4), 251–259.

Haring, N., & Liberty, K.A. (1991). *Investigation of obstacles and strategies for less restrictive education of deaf-blind children and youth: Final Report.* Seattle: University of Washington, College of Education.

Hilton, A., & Liberty, K. (1986, November). *Analysis of progress of integrated secondary students with profound mental retardation.* Paper presented at the International Conference of The Association for Persons with Severe Handicaps, San Francisco, CA.

Hollis, J.H., & Gorton, C. (1967). Training severely and profoundly developmentally retarded children. *Mental Retardation, 5*(4), 20–24.

Inman, D., & Black, C. (1987). *The green bean program: Self-feeding curriculum for students who are deaf and blind.* Unpublished manuscript, Oregon Research Institute, Eugene.

Izen, C., & Brown, F. (1991). Education and treatment needs of students with profound, multiply handicapping, and medically fragile conditions: A survey of teachers' perceptions. *Journal of The Association for Persons with Severe Handicaps, 16*(2), 94–103.

Jussim, L. (1990). Social reality and social problems: The role of expectancies. *Journal of Social Issues, 46*(2), 9–34.

Larson, S., & Lakin, K.C. (1991). Parent attitudes about residential placement before and after deinstitutionalization: A research synthesis. *Journal of The Association for Persons with Severe Handicaps, 16*(1), 25–38.

Liberty, K.A., Haring, N.G., & Martin, M. (1981). Teaching new skills to the severely handicapped. *Journal of The Association for Persons with Severe Handicaps, 6*(1), 5–13.

Liberty, K., Haring, N., Moran, D., & Fisher, M. (1989). *Inclusive situations: Access targets and challenges.* Seattle: University of Washington, College of Education.

Lipsky, D.K., & Gartner, A. (1987). Capable of achievement and worthy of respect: Education for handicapped students as if they were full-fledged human beings. *Exceptional Children, 54*(1), 69–74.

Macdonald, E.P. (1985). Medical needs of severely developmentally disabled persons residing in the community. *American Journal of Mental Deficiency, 90*(2), 171–176.

McDonnell, A.P., & Hardman, M.L. (1989). The desegregation of America's special schools: Strategies for change. *Journal of The Association for Persons with Severe Handicaps, 14*(1), 68–74.

Mehan, H. (1987). Language and schooling. In G. Spindler & L. Spindler (Eds.), *Interpretive ethnography of education: At home and abroad.* Hillsdale, NJ: L. Erlbaum.

Meyer, L., & Eichinger, J. (1987). Program evaluation in support of program development: Needs, strategies, and future directions. In L. Goetz, D. Guess, & K. Stremel-Campbell (Eds.), *Innovative program design for individuals with dual sensory impairments* (pp. 313–346). Baltimore: Paul H. Brookes Publishing Co.

Meyer, L.H., & Kishi, G.S. (1985). School integration strategies. In K.C. Lakin & R.H. Bruininks (Eds.), *Strategies for achieving community integration of developmentally disabled citizens* (pp. 231–252). Baltimore: Paul H. Brookes Publishing Co.

Meyerson, L. (1988). The social psychology of physical disability: 1948 and 1988. *Journal of Social Issues, 44*(1), 173–188.

Opotow, S. (1990a). Moral exclusion and injustice: An introduction. *Journal of Social Issues, 46*(1), 1–20.

Opotow, S. (1990b). Deterring moral exclusion. *Journal of Social Issues, 46*(1), 173–182.

"Opposite trends in teaching standards." (1988, April 13). *Education of the Handicapped,* p. 8.

Phillips, V., & McCullough, L. (1990). Consultation-based programming: Instituting the collaborative ethic in schools. *Exceptional Children, 56*(4), 291–304.

Piuma, C., Halvorsen, A., Murray, C., Beckstead, S., & Sailor, W. (1983). *Project REACH administrator's manual.* San Francisco: San Francisco State University and San Francisco Unified School District, Project REACH.

Sailor, W., Gee, K., Goetz, L., & Graham, N. (1988). Progress in educating students with the most severe disabilities: Is there any? *Journal of The Association for Persons with Severe Handicaps, 13*(2), 87–99.

Sailor, W., Halvorsen, A., Anderson, J., Goetz, L., Gee, K., Doering, K., & Hunt, P. (1986). Community intensive instruction. In R.H. Horner, L.H. Meyer, & H.D. Fredericks (Eds.), *Education of learners with severe handicaps: Exemplary service strategies* (pp. 251–288). Baltimore: Paul H. Brookes Publishing Co.

Sansone, J., & Zigmond, N. (1986). Evaluating mainstreaming through an analysis of students' schedules. *Exceptional Children, 52,* 452–458.

Schalock, R.L., & Jensen, C.M. (1986). Assessing the goodness-of-fit between persons and their environments. *Journal of The Association for Persons with Severe Handicaps, 11*(2), 103–109.

Snell, M. (1983). Field trips and public image. *Newsletter of The Association for Persons with Severe Handicaps, 9*(2), 1–2.

Snell, M.E., & Eichner, S.J. (1989). Integration for students with profound disabilities. In F. Brown & D.H. Lehr (Eds.), *Persons with profound disabilities: issues and practices* (pp. 109–138). Baltimore: Paul H. Brookes Publishing Co.

Spooner, F., & Dykes, M. (1982). Epilepsy: Impact upon severely and profoundly handicapped persons. *Journal of The Association for Persons with Severe Handicaps, 7*(3), 87–96.

Sternberg, L., Pegnatore, L., & Hill, C. (1983). Establishing interactive communication behaviors with profoundly mentally handicapped students. *Journal of The Association for the Severely Handicapped, 8*(2), 39–46.

Stevens, H. (1964). Overview. In H. Stevens and R. Heber (Eds.), *Mental retardation: A review of research* (pp. 1–15). Chicago: The University of Chicago Press.

Taylor, S.J. (1988). Caught in the continuum: A critical analysis of the principle of the least restrictive environment. *Journal of The Association for Persons with Severe Handicaps, 13*(1), 41–53.

Thompson, B., & Guess, D. (1989). Students who experience the most profound disabilities: Teacher perspectives. In F. Brown & D.H. Lehr (Eds.), *Persons with profound disabilities: Issues and practices* (pp. 3–42). Baltimore: Paul H. Brookes Publishing Co.

Thousand, J., & Villa, R. (1989). Enhancing success in heterogeneous schools. In S. Stainback, W. Stainback, & M. Forest (Eds.), *Educating all students in the mainstream of regular education* (pp. 89–104). Baltimore: Paul H. Brookes Publishing Co.

Vandercook, T., York, J., & Forest, M. (1989). The McGill Action Planning System (MAPS): A strategy for building the vision. *Journal of The Association for Persons with Severe Handicaps, 14*(3), 205–215.

Wray, L., & Wieck, C. (1985). Moving persons with developmental disabilities toward less restrictive environments through case management. In K.C. Lakin & R.H. Bruininks (Eds.), *Strategies for achieving community integration of developmentally disabled citizens* (pp. 219–230). Baltimore: Paul H. Brookes Publishing Co.

Wyant, S., & Bell, W. (1981). Diagnosing and dealing with barriers to change. In M. Gassholt (Ed.), *Organizing for change: Inservice and staff development in special education.* Seattle: Program Development Assistance System, College of Education, University of Washington.

PREPARING TO WELCOME STUDENTS WHO ARE DEAF-BLIND INTO YOUR CLASSROOM

Chapter 5

Teacher Preparation

Barbara A.B. McLetchie

There is a strong national interest in providing education to students with disabilities, including those who are deaf-blind, in regular schools and in community-based settings. Given that "the purpose of schooling is to enable all students to actively participate in their communities" (Ferguson, Meyer, Jeanchild, Juniper, & Zingo, 1992, p. 226), a look at general teacher education is a logical starting point for this chapter on teacher preparation in the field of deaf-blindness. Without question, preparing qualified men and women to become teachers of children with and without disabilities is vital to our society. Teachers play major roles that shape children's destinies. Despite the importance of teacher education, the teaching profession has been viewed negatively by university administrators and society, and teachers are held to inadequate standards by the teaching profession itself (Brandt, 1991).

There are issues in teacher education that create debate, even heated arguments. These issues involve crucial questions for which there are no simple answers: Should teacher preparation exist at all? How much should preservice teachers be trained in pedagogy as opposed to liberal arts? Should teachers be trained at the graduate or undergraduate level (Holmes Group, 1986)? Should society hold the teaching profession to the same high standards it expects from other professions such as law or medicine (Goodlad & Keating, 1990)? Is field-based experience valuable? Do teachers learn what they need to know to deal with the real problems of today's schools? Should general education merge with special education (Stainback & Stainback, 1989)? Should all teachers be prepared to teach all children (Lilly, 1988; Pugach, 1987; Stainback & Stainback, 1989)?

Professionals, paraprofessionals, individuals who are deaf-blind, and their families must continually ask these critical questions and pursue the answers. This chapter is based upon the following assumptions that address some of these questions:

1. Teachers can be prepared. Teacher education that includes field-based experience makes a positive difference.
2. Special education teacher preparation should continue to exist. This is one of the foundations of special education that has existed for a century (Kauffman, 1989). However, special education must

The author acknowledges the assistance of Dr. Sherrill Butterfield and Dr. Richard Jackson in the preparation of this manuscript.

work cooperatively with general education preparation efforts. Both need to influence each other and solve common problems together in both service delivery and personnel preparation.

3. Teacher preparation in deaf-blindness requires specialized training. To assume otherwise is to trivialize the extensive and synergistic effects of combined vision and hearing loss upon all aspects of human development. The teacher of students who are deaf-blind is an ongoing learner who creatively integrates and adapts knowledge and experience from regular education, from special studies in blindness and visual impairments, deafness and hearing impairments, severe disabilities, and deaf-blindness to meet the needs of individual learners. This textbook serves as a training tool that provides specialized preparation in deaf-blindness.

This chapter first sketches the history of educating individuals who are deaf-blind. Then, current issues in preparing personnel to work with infants, children, and youth who are deaf-blind are discussed. These issues include the critical shortage of qualified personnel, the geographic dispersion of the deaf-blind population, the need for standards, and the roles of teachers. These roles continually evolve to meet the new challenges imposed by societal changes and the needs of people who are deaf-blind. The chapter concludes with a vision of the future in the preparation of personnel who will have the tremendous responsibility of including learners who are deaf-blind as participants in their homes, schools, and communities. This vision requires a redesign of personnel preparation at the university level, including effective links with general education. The future will demand that teacher preparation programs in deaf-blindness col-

laborate with one another, with practitioners in the field, with families, and with deaf-blind adults.

TEACHERS OF INDIVIDUALS WHO ARE DEAF-BLIND: HISTORICAL BACKGROUND

Although documented educational intervention with people who are deaf-blind dates back to the late 18th century, there was no formalized teacher preparation in deaf-blind education until the 20th century. Among the early teachers in deaf-blind education in the late 1700s and the 1800s were a priest, an individual's family members, an illiterate man, a physician, and a young woman who only had a high school diploma. The records of those teachers' intervention with their students, the publicizing of the educational results, and the recognition of the need for teachers with specialized preparation in deaf-blindness provide the backdrop for a discussion of current issues and future directions in the 1990s.

Records indicate that education of individuals who are deaf-blind began in France. Victorine Morriseau (1789–1832), who lost her hearing at a very young age and became blind at 12, was taught at the Institution for the Deaf in Paris in the late 1700s. The curriculum her teacher, Abbé Perier, followed was based on religion. Although the methodology is not clear, Victorine learned to read by methods similar to those used at the time for people who were blind. Victorine spent her life in the institution (Waterhouse, 1975).

In the late 1700s and early 1800s in Scotland, teaching individuals who were deaf-blind was of interest to the philosopher Dugald Stewart. Stewart commented on the lack of information concerning people who were deaf-blind and related the story of James Mitchell, born in 1795, who was the son of a minister. James was born with cataracts and deafness. He learned to communicate with gestures and could identify people. It appears that James's teachers were his family members, mostly his sister. There is no documentation about James's adult life or when he died (Lane, 1984; Waterhouse, 1975).

Laura Bridgman was the first person who was deaf-blind to be educated in the United States for whom there are written records. Laura was born on a farm outside Hanover, New Hampshire, in 1829. She lost her sight and hearing at 2 years of age. A neighbor, Asa Tenney, who was considered to be illiterate, taught Laura to explore her environment and to comprehend the functional use of objects. Dr. Samuel Gridley Howe, a medical doctor and the first Director of Perkins School for the Blind, heard about Laura through a colleague at Dartmouth College, Medical Department. Dr. Howe convinced the Bridgmans to send Laura to Perkins where she was enrolled in 1837 with the Director as her teacher. Although Laura had invented several gestures for people and things in her home environment, Dr. Howe began his intervention by labeling objects with raised print. The goals were to match the labels to the correct object, then to sequence the letters of each object name appropriately. She was also taught the manual alphabet (26 different hand configurations, each of which represents a letter of the alphabet). Laura attempted to return home to New Hampshire twice. In both cases she was reported to be depressed and was isolated because few people could communicate with her. She lived at Perkins until she died in 1889 (Lane, 1984; Waterhouse, 1975).

Today one should question the functionality of Dr. Howe's approach (key and spoon were among the first objects taught to Laura out of context in the classroom). Teachers might also ask why Dr. Howe did not use the gestures Laura had used effectively at home as a starting point for beginning communication intervention. However, Dr. Howe documented his interventions scrupulously and publicized his success and the accomplishments of his pupil. Perkins became known for its commitment to educating students who were deaf-blind. This commitment continues to the present day.

So famous was Laura Bridgman that Charles Dickens (1868) wrote about her in his *American Notes* which were read by Helen Keller's parents. Michael Anagnos, son-in-law to Samuel Gridley Howe, was the Director of Perkins when the Kellers wrote asking for a teacher for Helen. He immediately thought of his recent graduate from Perkins, Anne Sullivan. Anne Sullivan prepared herself to work with Helen by reading Dr. Howe's writings. She also knew Laura Bridgman well because Anne herself had been at Perkins as a student for 6 years. Laura provided Anne Sullivan with an excellent internship experience with a deaf-blind adult. Laura taught Anne tactile communication and fingerspelling. Anne Sullivan used Dr. Howe's work as her textbook for teaching Helen.

Anne arrived at the Keller home in Tuscumbia, Alabama, in 1887. Helen was 6 years old, having lost her vision and hearing at 19 months (Lash, 1980). Anne Sullivan was an ongoing learner who was always in the process of learning how to teach Helen more effectively. She wrote several letters to friends asking advice. Soon after arriving in Alabama, Anne felt overwhelmed with her responsibility. However, Anne was determined to talk into Helen's hands with her fingers, spelling the way a mother talks into a baby's ears (Braddy, 1933). After making the initial connection between a word spelled into her hand, and its referent, water, Helen's progress was rapid in receptive and expressive language. Teaching occurred in natural environments that were meaningful and age appropriate. Vocabulary was determined by the child's interests and motivation. Anne Sullivan's methods would today be considered best practices.

Where Should Students Who Are Deaf-Blind Be Educated?

As the education of students who were deaf-blind continued into the 20th century, questions arose as to whether schools for the deaf or schools for the blind were more appropriate. Some of these students attended schools for the deaf, while others went to schools for the blind; the New York Institution for the Instruction of the Deaf, the American Asylum for the Deaf in Connecticut, Perkins School for the Blind in Massachusetts, and Overbrook School for the Blind in Pennsylvania are examples. There is documentation that one student, Helen Schultz, who was deaf-blind, went to regular school for part of her education and became a very typical adult (Waterhouse, 1975). However, the question of placement of students who were deaf-blind in general education settings did not seem to be an issue worth debating. Helen Keller's success at attending Radcliffe College with adequate interpreter support and the fact that Helen was fully included in the college community was applauded by all, but not considered an option or a model for other students. Best practices continued to be placement in either schools for the deaf or schools for the blind.

Nearly a century ago, Helen Keller and Anne Sullivan both advocated establishing teacher training in deaf-blindness. This idea was not supported by Mr. William Wade (1904) in his monograph on people who were deaf-blind in the United States. Mr. Wade happened to be a financial supporter of Helen's education and the education of other students who were deaf-blind (Waterhouse, 1975), and, therefore, his opinion

influenced many other people. The preparation of teachers of children who were deaf-blind during the first part of this century depended highly upon each teacher's initiative and commitment and the knowledge they gained from colleagues at either schools for the deaf or schools for the blind. Many teachers contacted Perkins for advice in teaching their students who were deaf-blind. Some practitioners sought what would now be termed technical assistance from Perkins School for The Blind, which began to formalize teacher education in the 1930s. Teachers from other parts of the country came to Perkins to learn. During this time, enrollment in the Deaf-Blind Unit was approximately 18 students. Personnel preparation included training paraprofessionals, who were responsible for students who were deaf-blind in their residences. It is also reported that teachers from Perkins went to other schools to provide assistance (Farrell, 1956; Waterhouse, 1975).

The Tadoma Method Inis Hall used the Tadoma Method of instructing students at Perkins during the 1930s. This method taught the student who was deaf-blind to learn to speechread and to speak by placing his or her hands upon the speaker's face and throat to feel the vibrations of speech and the placement of the lips. This method, a tactile variation of the oral method still used with deaf students, was used successfully with many students who were adventitiously deaf and blind. Although Ms. Hall left Perkins, the Tadoma Method continued to be used and was considered by many to be the best method of educational intervention until the 1960s. This meant that teachers who came to Perkins from all over the world were trained in the Tadoma Method, driven by the philosophy that individuals who were deaf-blind should learn to speak in order to survive in the hearing world. Students who were deaf-blind learned fingerspelling, but the use of signs was not permitted. Needless to say there were few, if any, students with multiple disabilities and deaf-blindness being educated during this time, and the views of the deaf community were not yet advocated with adequate power.

Expanding Educational Services for Children Who Were Deaf-Blind In 1953, a conference was held supported by the American Foundation for the Blind, Perkins School for The Blind, and several other organizations (Waterhouse, 1975). A key agenda item was expanding educational services for children who were deaf-blind. This conference signaled the need for teachers if services were to be increased. Applicants to Perkins who were deaf-blind were being rejected because of the shortage of teachers (Waterhouse, 1975). In 1956, in response to the need for trained teachers, Perkins established university affiliations with Harvard University, Boston University, and then Boston College, which has prepared teachers of the deaf-blind for over a quarter of a century. In that same year (1956), Helen Keller dedicated a school building at Perkins in her and Anne Sullivan's names. The building symbolized three goals: 1) to educate children who were deaf-blind, 2) to train teachers of children who were deaf-blind, and 3) to do research. It is interesting to note that these goals are often incorporated into present-day requests for proposals in personnel preparation from the Office of Special Education and Rehabilitation Services.

The Rubella Epidemic: 1963–1965

As a result of the rubella epidemic (1963–1965), many students who were deaf-blind now had additional disabilities, and there was a pressing need to prepare teachers to serve 6,000 school-age children who were deaf-blind as a result of rubella, as opposed to the approximately 500 students who were deaf-blind who were enrolled in programs in the early 1960s (Conlon, 1991). Teacher preparation in deaf-blindness was a national emergency. In 1966, in the wake of the rubella epidemic, the 100th anniversary of Anne Sullivan's birth was celebrated. The Anne Sullivan Centennial coupled with the critical need for teachers of rubella children who would soon be school age were two powerful catalysts that led to the federal government's establishment of 10 regional centers for children who were deaf-blind.

The challenges presented by many of the children with congenital rubella meant that methodologies had to be changed or modified. For example, the Tadoma Method often could not be used successfully with students who were deaf-blind and had additional disabilities. Methods of educational intervention became individualized, which meant that teachers in deaf-blind education had to be prepared to serve a heterogeneous population of learners. The active involvement of parents, especially those of preschool children who were deaf-blind, became more crucial during the late 1960s. However, teachers during this time were mostly trained to serve students in special schools and classes.

The historical foundations upon which formalized teacher preparation in deaf-blindness were established set the stage for current issues in preparing teachers to work with infants, children, and youth who are deaf-blind and with students' families. The next section addresses some of these issues.

CURRENT ISSUES IN DEAF-BLIND EDUCATION

Chapter 2 of this volume chronicles the role of the federal government in services to school-age children who are deaf-blind. A retrospective view of the 1970s and 1980s shows that the changing levels of the federal government's involvement in teacher preparation in deaf-blindness, along with new philosophical directions, created some of the critical issues in teacher preparation in deaf-blindness. Current issues are the need for teachers, the level of teaching standards, and the roles of teachers in educating students who are deaf-blind.

Need for Teachers

In the 1970s, there were several university programs training teachers to serve school-age children who were deaf-blind. These federally supported programs, which dotted the country, graduated over 100 teachers per year who assumed teaching jobs and administrative positions of leadership (Collins, 1992). The 1980s witnessed less federal involvement in all aspects of education. The effects in special education teacher preparation at the university level were dwindling numbers of faculty and an erosion or obliteration of programs, especially those in low-incidence disabilities, with programs for teacher preparation in deaf-blindness often the first to be eliminated. Simultaneously, there was a change of philosophy accompanied by federal legislation and state responses, which targeted inclusive educational settings as philosophically desirable. This shift is illustrated in the following example. In states served by the New England Center for Deaf-Blind Services (Maine, New Hampshire, Massachusetts, and Connecticut) "215 deaf-blind children in 1982 were served in 29 school buildings. In 1992, 267 children were located in 218 different programs or sites. This same phenomenon repeats itself in every state and region of the nation" (Collins, 1992, p. 49).

The need for trained teachers is as critical today as it was when children who were deaf-blind as a result of congenital rubella were school age. A survey of Section 622 (now 307.11) coordinators (persons responsible for federally funded services to learners who are deaf-blind) (McLetchie, 1993) high-

lights the shortage of teachers. Respondents from 45 states, the Virgin Islands, and Puerto Rico reported a total of 6,741 students who were deaf-blind ages birth to 22 years. These students were being served by approximately 3,668 teachers. State coordinators for deaf-blind services estimated that only six percent (6%) of those teachers had personnel preparation in deaf-blindness. Additionally, although the rubella population are now adults, the number of children ages birth to 22 who are deaf-blind has not fallen (Baldwin, 1991). In 1992, approximately 36 teachers were graduated nationally with teacher preparation in deaf-blindness (McLetchie, 1992).

The convergence of historical events, the lower level of federal support in the last decade specifically targeted for teacher preparation in deaf-blind education, the change in placement philosophy, and the ongoing incidence of deaf-blindness have created a major challenge. There are now too few teachers, for too many children, too widely dispersed throughout the country.

Teacher Standards

The issue of standards, or lack thereof, also plagues general education. Goodlad and Keating's (1990) comments about standards in general education also apply to the education of students who are deaf-blind. Standards are waived when there is a shortage of teachers. This practice would not occur in other professions such as law or medicine. Teacher preparation requires redesign and renewal. Teachers are being graduated without the competencies needed to manage complex problems. Goodlad stated in a recent interview "there is a lack of connectedness between the schooling enterprise and the preparation of those who staff it" (Brandt, 1991, p. 5).

Standards for teachers in deaf-blind education that are developed in concert with standards evolving in general education can help assure that students who are deaf-blind will have quality education. Standards can also be a force for professional identity. Although standards are not the only solution to the multitude of problems faced by teachers today, standards are the vital foundations from which best practices emanate. Strong standards can also serve as self-evaluation tools for teachers so that they can become ongoing learners by pursuing study in areas in which their knowledge and skills are weak. Standards, therefore, address the issue of the competency of existing personnel. Reith (1990) makes the point that the field of severe disabilities grew so rapidly that practitioners hired may not have been adequately prepared to implement best practices. Reith's assumption also applies to students who are deaf-blind because it is not atypical for these students to be in classes with students with other severe disabilities. Standards should not be teacher-centered; rather they should focus upon the relationships between teacher and child, teacher and other personnel, and the teacher and the student's family. Standards can be conceptualized by examining the roles of teachers.

Teachers' Roles and Responsibilities

It is the responsibility of teacher educators to expose aspiring teachers in deaf-blind education to the expanding roles and responsibilities of teachers of students who are deaf-blind. Each aspiring teacher should have coursework and field-based experience related to the range of abilities in the very heterogeneous population of individuals who are deaf-blind. Teacher educators also have a responsibility to help aspiring teachers evaluate their own strengths and weaknesses so they can seek further education and actual experience in a specific area or choose jobs in subspecialties in the field of deaf-blind education, in which they have the greatest strength and motivation. For example, work-

ing with an individual who has Usher's Syndrome (associated with congenital hearing loss and progressive loss of vision in adolescence or young adulthood) is very different than working with a child who is deaf-blind and who also has cognitive and physical disabilities and requires special medical care. Teachers admittedly have different skill levels and interests, but with appropriate education linked with field-based experiences, most should be able to assume the major roles addressed in the following sections.

Assessor and Translator   The teacher is an *assessor* of the learner's abilities across all environments and *translator* of the assessment information for the development of appropriate teaching strategies. Assessment is the starting point for all meaningful intervention and an ongoing process to assure that strategies continually evolve to meet the ever-changing needs of the learner who is deaf-blind. Teachers must be trained in state-of-the-art formal and informal assessment procedures. Most learners who are deaf-blind have some residual hearing and vision, therefore, strengths in these areas are important to assess because the majority of students who are deaf-blind can benefit from hearing aids and glasses. Functional hearing and vision are addressed specifically because learners who are deaf-blind, especially those who have other disabilities, may have been considered by other professionals without experience in deaf-blindness to be unable to benefit from amplification and/or glasses.

Assessment information should be gathered from a variety of sources and must emphasize the abilities of the learner. A deficit description or model that focuses upon disabilities and negative aspects of the person, may discourage others from accepting the challenge of including the learner who is deaf-blind in normalized environments (Mount, 1992). The teacher translates assessment information regarding a student to develop strategies; the translation process also involves first describing the individual as a whole and unique person.

Provider of Orientation and Mobility Opportunities The teacher is a provider of opportunities for the learner who is deaf-blind to move effectively and purposefully in a variety of environments. Students who are deaf-blind have goals in orientation and mobility, the ultimate one being to enter an environment and function as safely and as independently as possible (Hill & Ponder, 1976). The teacher must be prepared in the basic concepts of orientation and mobility and be able to work with an orientation and mobility specialist to create opportunities that will encourage independent travel skills. Children who are deaf-blind and physically challenged should also be considered capable of orientation and mobility activities that could include a strategy as simple as letting the child trail the wall when his or her wheel chair is pushed or stopping at designated places and giving the child an opportunity to recognize his or her location.

This major teaching role also relates to developing communication through a movement-based approach. All human communication requires some form of movement, ranging from extending a glass to request a drink to the intricate movements of the speech mechanism required to say "drink." van Dijk's (1967) philosophy, which began with his work with children who were deaf-blind as a result of rubella, stresses the importance of the child's expanding knowledge of the environment through moving and interacting with another person. The increased awareness of one's self and other human beings and the enjoyment of moving and acting together with other people provide the basis for developing communication skills and meaningful relationships (van Dijk, 1967; Writer,

1987). (See chap. 14, this volume, for further information on the issue of orientation and mobility.)

Communication Partner and Facilitator The teacher is a communication partner and an interpreter of life's events for the learner who has combined vision and hearing loss and a facilitator in developing effective communication partnerships between the learner who is deaf-blind and others. This role is the heart and core of all intervention with learners who are deaf-blind. The ability to teach a child who is deaf-blind to communicate effectively is critical. This role requires specialized coursework and experience so the teacher can learn to adapt to the child's current communication abilities and challenge the child to go to his or her highest possible level of communication. The teacher's role is to connect the child with people and events in meaningful, accessible forms and to be an interpreter so that others can understand the communication messages sent by the learner who is deaf-blind. For some students, this requires using nonsymbolic forms, while others may understand symbolic communication.

Despite the fact that early foundations of nonsymbolic communication are the essential roots of language development, teachers often lack preparation in this area (Siegel-Causey, 1989). Teacher preparation in communication should include skills to teach peer partners in general education settings how to read and expand upon both nonsymbolic and symbolic forms of communication. This is especially important because many learners who are deaf-blind are at nonsymbolic levels (Siegel-Causey & Downing, 1987). If peer partners in the school and community cannot effectively use and respond to nonsymbolic forms of communication, the learner who is deaf-blind is isolated, not integrated or included. Through the use of communication partners, learners gain control. For example, a communication partner can facilitate the student's ability to make choices (McInnis & Treffry, 1982).

Communication is the key to social interaction. Social spheres are, in part, determined by the number and quality of communication partnerships, thus communication is considered the primary concern of persons who are deaf-blind at all stages of life (Maxon, Tedder, Lamb, Geisen, & Marmion, 1989). The importance of communicative relationships is highlighted by comments made by Robert Smithdas (1976), an adult who is deaf-blind, who lost his vision and hearing at age five:

> Deaf-blindness creates serious problems of communication which are extremely isolating and cause an acute sense of loneliness and frustration. Communication is their [deaf-blind persons'] link with the environment and relationships which can provide the assurance they need that they are accepted by society. (p. 36)

Learners who are deaf-blind need, and are entitled to, meaningful relationships with friends in inclusive settings. A central focus upon communication and strategies to facilitate relationships must be the cornerstone in teacher education in deaf-blindness.

Developer of Communication Systems The teacher is a developer and implementor of a variety of communication systems used effectively by the learner who is deaf-blind. Most individuals who are deaf-blind are unable to use speech as a primary mode of communication. The challenges created by the heterogeneity of the population who are deaf-blind requires the teacher to have a flexible approach and a broad-based knowledge of augmentative communication, ranging from the use of body movements, vocalizations, objects, pictures, gestures, signs, finger spelling, written words or braille, to computerized augmentative systems. The choice of the augmentative systems used by

the learner who is deaf-blind depends upon his or her communication abilities and needs and the demands of each communication environment. For example, a student may use signs with his or her teacher, but may use pictures to request choices of clothes in a store where people do not sign. Learners who are deaf-blind should be encouraged to use multimodes of communication (Musselwhite & St. Louis, 1988). It is the teacher's role to develop systems and then to motivate and teach the learner to use the system. This involves teaching others how to use the system as well. Communication systems are important tools that allows persons who are deaf-blind to interact effectively with other people. The effective use of augmentative systems is crucial because the major, and most typical, tools of interaction in typical classrooms are speaking and listening.

Advocate and Resource for Families The teacher is an advocate and resource to learners who are deaf-blind and their families in obtaining and maintaining quality educational and community services. The Individuals with Disabilities Education Act (IDEA) (1990) mandates that parents are full and equal partners in the educational process. However, the intention of the law is not always put into effective practice. Teachers must be knowledgeable of state and federal laws and be able to interpret them, as they may be required to explain these laws to parents. Despite the national movement to educate students with disabilities in typical schools, some school systems still question the educability of children with severe disabilities.

The need for advocacy and knowledge of the law is illustrated by the following case. In 1980, the School District of Rochester, New Hampshire, began repeated attempts to deny education to Timothy W., a boy who was blind and had questionable hearing loss and severe multiple disabilities. The position of the school system was that Timothy W. could not benefit from education because his disabilities were so severe. This case was finally decided in 1989 in the United States Court of Appeals for the First Circuit in favor of Timothy W. (*Timothy W. v. Rochester, New Hampshire, School District*, 1989). The legal process took nine years. Timothy W.'s mother and his teachers were among his strongest advocates in this process.

Teachers must also be trained as advocates for systems change and reform in order to make the goal of inclusion a reality. A study by Izen and Brown (1991) of 148 teachers of students with profound or multiple disabilities and/or special medical needs showed that in more than 20% of the respondents' classes, integration strategies were not implemented. Respondents indicated that they did not attempt community and school integration either because they felt their students could not benefit or because the educators had inadequate resources or insufficient administrative support for such endeavors. The first reason, students being deemed unable to benefit from integration, calls for teacher educators to assure that the basic concept that all students with disabilities benefit from school and community integration is incorporated into teacher education. The other two reasons, inadequate resources and no administrative support, demand that teachers learn creative ways to influence the administrative systems to gain support for school and community integration (Izen & Brown, 1991).

Teachers must be prepared to be resources to families. Quality of life indicators considered important by parents of children who are deaf-blind (Giangreco, Cloninger, Mueller, Yuan, & Ashworth, 1991), the concept of Personal Futures Planning (Mount, 1992), and the McGill Action Planning System (MAPS) (Vandercook, York, & Forest, 1989) are helpful in setting a direction for

teachers' involvement with families. Teachers need skills to help them understand what families consider to be important to life and how to link quality of life indicators to the educational process. Most families and professionals would agree that strong determinants of one's quality of life include having a safe home; accessing a variety of places; engaging in positive activities; having meaningful relationships; having choice, control, and independence that match one's age; and being safe and healthy (Giangreco et al., 1991).

Another challenge facing teachers is to be flexible, sensitive, and responsive to families of diverse backgrounds who may have different perspectives and values. These skills are most challenging to incorporate into teacher training because they are difficult to teach from a textbook or lecture. The United States is changing from a country that took pride in being a melting pot to a country that celebrates its differences (Schlesinger, 1992). How teacher educators incorporate this philosophical shift into the educational system is pivotal to including all families in the education of their children.

Because more children who are deaf-blind are living and attending school in their home communities, teachers must work with families in partnerships to include the child who is deaf-blind in both family and community settings. Involving siblings so that normal interactions are facilitated is also important. The concept of inclusion is holistic and therefore encompasses the home and community environments. Helping families to obtain in-home support and respite services is an example of the kind of support that is likely to increase. Home support may be a particularly critical issue for families whose children are transitioned from residential schools and for those families whose children have complex medical needs.

Team Member   The teacher is an educator of other team members in the complex challenges imposed by combined vision and hearing impairments and an effective facilitator and collaborator in the team process. The learner who is deaf-blind faces complex challenges in all aspects of human development. Hearing and vision are the channels that give people most of their information about the world. Combined vision and hearing impairment deprives the individual of incidental learning opportunities and creates complex communication difficulties. The effects are not additive, they are synergistic, and therefore a teacher prepared in hearing impairments, and a teacher prepared in blindness may not adequately meet the needs of the learner who is deaf-blind. It is crucial that a teacher trained in deaf-blindness educate the other team members so they understand the impact of dual sensory impairments.

Teaming, collaboration, transdisciplinary team, and *team approach* are words that convey a positive connotation and are used with a high degree of frequency in both general and special education. Teacher educators must adequately prepare teachers with the necessary interpersonal skills to be effective participants. The present and future demand thorough research on what variables make a successful team member. In teacher preparation, other disciplines must be utilized, such as counseling psychology and social work, to help teachers evaluate and improve their interpersonal skills and ability to understand group dynamics. Teacher educators must model teaming in university-based coursework, which will require abandoning the lecture format and involving students in working in teams in classes at the university and in field experiences. This concept has a pragmatic appeal, but is most difficult when there is pressure at many institutions of higher learning to have high enrollment.

Coach The teacher is an effective coach of paraprofessionals and other professionals who facilitate the active participation of the student who is deaf-blind in school and social settings. Teacher shortages are likely to persist. Therefore, a major responsibility of the teacher is and will be to act as a coach to other professionals and paraprofessionals who will have the tremendous task of integrating and including children and young adults who are deaf-blind in school and community activities. Without question, learners who are deaf-blind can attend typical schools and make friends with peers without disabilities. They can fully participate in community activities. However, they need individualized support. Although this support person might be called by different names such as *intervenor, integration facilitator, interpreter-tutor,* or *teacher*, the fact is that this support person is crucial. A person who is deaf-blind requires someone to act as an interpreter of life's events. Anyone who has had the opportunity to know adults who are deaf or deaf-blind recognizes how very vital adequate and ongoing assistance is in achieving competence.

In addition to communication, paraprofessionals and general education teachers may need coaching in adapting the environment and in responding appropriately to the behaviors of learners who are deaf-blind. Adapting the physical and social environments can provide maximum opportunities for learners who are deaf-blind to interact with materials and their peers. This includes strategies such as adapting the physical environment, using cooperative learning, pairing or grouping students, and involving peers in the team process. Critical adaptations may allow for communication turn-taking and building relationships (O'Brien, Forest, Snow, & Hasbury, 1989). Service providers may also need coaching to prevent potential behavior problems, to recognize the communicative intent underlying some behaviors (Donnellan, Mirenda, Mesaros, & Fassbender, 1984), and to seek the consultation of a psychologist when necessary.

This role of the teacher as educator of professionals and paraprofessionals demands ongoing and effective coaching that incorpo-rates and then goes beyond traditional con-sulting. This role includes inservicing and also requires the specialist in deaf-blindness to create flexible partnerships with general education and support personnel. Personnel preparation programs need to be redesigned to determine the qualities that enable a teacher to be a competent instructor of other professionals and paraprofessionals. It is conceivable that a teacher might be an excel-lent instructor of children, but not a compe-tent teacher of adults. Therefore, teacher preparation must consider performance cri-teria that include working with a range of service providers.

Future Planner The teacher is an ongoing learner and future planner who integrates knowledge from the fields of general educa-tion, visual impairments, hearing impair-ments, severe disabilities, and deaf-blindness and adapts that knowledge to meet the needs of each individual learner who is deaf-blind. The stages of reflective learning that have been used in general teacher education have implications for teachers preparing in deaf-blindness. Preservice teachers progress through four stages:

1. Technical competence in teaching and management
2. Ability to analyze teaching
3. Understanding of the ethical and moral consequences of teaching
4. Sensitivity to the needs of learners with diverse characteristics (Freiberg & Wax-man, 1990)

Teachers must continue to revisit these stages on an ongoing basis. When teachers graduate from teacher preparation programs and assume roles, all of which are directed to improving the quality of life for students who are deaf-blind and their families, they are beginning a process of lifelong learning in teaching. The roles of teachers evolve and are driven by the actual needs of learners who are deaf-blind and their families. These needs should be the driving force of teacher education reform and set the directions of the future, which are addressed in the fol-lowing sections.

FUTURE DIRECTIONS IN TEACHER PREPARATION

A view of the future shows the need for at least 10 teacher preparation programs in deaf-blindness strategically placed through-out the country graduating a total of 80–100 graduates per year. Federal involvement is and has been a powerful and positive change agent in institutions of higher learning in teacher education in deaf-blindness (see chap. 2, this volume) and in severe disabili-ties (Reith, 1990). However, the future must be more than just a recreation of the past; and reform is necessary. The number of grad-uate teacher programs must be increased. They should collaborate with each other, es-tablish partnerships with schools, and share in research. Graduates must be placed where they are the most needed and teachers should be effectively supported following graduation. Determining where to place graduates of teacher preparation programs requires team collaboration that includes state coordinators of deaf-blind services, TRACES (Teaching Research Assistance to Children and Youth Experiencing Sensory Impairments) support, school personnel, and those involved in teacher preparation in deaf-blindness. Teacher education must also link with adult services and provide innova-tive leadership in training other personnel who provide services to infants, children, and youth who are deaf-blind and their fam-ilies (McLetchie, 1993).

Graduate Level Preparation and Collaboration

Teachers of the future will need to be better educated than ever before, especially if they are to be effective in training other personnel. Teacher education programs should be taught at the graduate level (Holmes Group, 1986). Teachers of students who are deaf-blind must have field experience and preparation in general education. One area of general education that may be particularly crucial is curriculum, especially because inclusion demands adaptation of the curriculum being used in general education settings. Universities most appropriate for teacher education in deaf-blindness would be those that already have strong expertise in general education and have demonstrated experience in teacher preparation in visual impairments, severe disabilities, and/or hearing impairments. This recommendation has educational as well as practical validity. Teachers of students who are deaf-blind must integrate knowledge from general education and specialty areas and adapt that knowledge to each child's unique needs.

Directions for the future are tempered with reality. Over the past decade, many universities have suffered debilitating losses in numbers of special education faculty and a reduction of special education programs. New programs and options in special education, including the field of deaf-blindness, need to integrate with one another and include general education applications. If a single university cannot provide the necessary coursework by linking and overlapping with its own curricula, mechanisms for partnerships with other universities should be established that could include satellite broadcasts. With careful, long-range planning, personnel preparation programs in deaf-blindness may be able to avoid elimination because of their interconnectedness with general education and other focus areas of special education at single universities, or groups of universities that share resources.

The teacher preparation programs that train teachers of students with deaf-blindness must connect with each other nationally. This collaboration is critical in developing standards that continue to evolve to assure that students with deaf-blindness are well served, to establish first-class practica and internship sites, and to share in much needed research in teacher education and placement of graduates.

Quality Internship Experiences Institutions of higher learning that prepare teachers to work with students who are deaf-blind and their families are in need of internship sites in typical schools. These sites must involve two critical people: 1) a student who is deaf-blind and 2) a cooperating teacher who is trained and experienced in teaching students who are deaf-blind. Sites should be those that have well-functioning, collaborative teams. Although more of these students are living and being educated in their home communities than in the 1980s, the reality is that their teachers are generally not qualified in teaching deaf-blindness. Teacher preparation programs must work in symphony to identify and establish high level practica experiences in typical schools. This will require university personnel to spend more time in schools creating partnerships with administrators and practitioners. Targeted sites should provide excellent information for university and school personnel to evaluate as a team. Use of videotapes, broadcasts from sites to universities, on-site observations, and co-teaching by university faculty and practitioners may provide much needed and valuable data on strategies for including students with deaf-blindness in typical schools and community-based settings and for studying the effects of inclusion on the learner who is deaf-blind.

Placement of Graduates Establishing innovative internship sites should include placing graduates of teacher education programs where they are most needed. Requiring university personnel to continue supporting and mentoring graduates after degrees are conferred is crucial. Graduated teachers, or at least a stipulated percentage in each of the federally funded personnel prep-aration programs, should be required to take positions where the teacher shortages have the greatest negative impact upon children who are deaf-blind and their families. For example, graduated students who received federal support could be required to teach in specified settings for a certain amount of time. Service would include teaching in both rural and inner-city settings where students who are deaf-blind may be at risk for not being adequately served. This effort will de-mand connectedness of the teacher prepara-tion programs nationally, with input from state coordinators for deaf-blind services, TRACES, and state and local education authorities. The ultimate beneficiaries of teacher preparation programs are the stu-dents. Ongoing and on-site follow-up of graduates may help to assure that children who are deaf-blind receive quality services. The benefits of networking teacher training programs in deaf-blindness include the es-tablishment of cutting edge internship sites, providing expertise to local schools, engag-ing in needed research, and creating a job bank in the field of deaf-blind education that spans the country.

Links Between Teacher Education and Adult Services

The future demands strong links between personnel preparation and services for deaf-blind adults. Education is lifelong; therefore, teachers must stretch their vision beyond yearly individualized education programs and stop thinking of education as only span-ning the years of birth to 21 or 22. If educa-tion services are in their childhood, services for deaf-blind adults are in their infancy (McNulty, 1992). This is a cruel paradox.

Teachers of the future must have actual experience with adults as part of their prepa-ration. Deaf-blind adults should be valued instructors in teaching modules in univer-sity-based courses. Although the actual pres-ence of a deaf-blind instructor is preferable, satellite interactive broadcasts or videos could be utilized. Aspiring teachers should be required to spend part of their practicum requirements in adult services. Without the critical perspective of the lives of deaf-blind adults, it is difficult for teachers to anticipate and plan for the futures of the children they serve.

Despite years of effort spent teaching stu-dents how to communicate effectively and make choices, many students leave school and enter adult life where there is no choice and often only loneliness and boredom. The doors of neighborhood schools have opened. However, in the future we must work cre-atively to provide inclusive communities for deaf-blind adults. As a profession, educators in deaf-blindness have always recognized the importance of working with families. Comparable recognition must be given to working with deaf-blind adults. Teacher ed-ucation in the future must be innovative, cre-ative, and in symphony with adult services. As a beginning, by having students do prac-ticum hours in adult programs, university personnel can establish mutually beneficial relationships with adult services providers. Working cooperatively with adult services is vital to the future of teacher education in deaf-blindness.

REFERENCES

Baldwin, V. (1991). Understanding the deaf-blind population. *TRACES, 1*(2), 1–3.

Braddy, N. (1933). *Anne Sullivan Macy.* New York: Doubleday.

Brandt, R. (1991). On teacher education: A con-versation with John Goodlad. *Educational Lead-ership, 49*(3), 11–13.

Collins, M. (1992). Reflections and future directions. *Proceedings of the National Conference on Deaf-Blindness: Deaf-Blind Services in the 90's.* Reno, Nevada: Hilton/Perkins National Program, Conrad N. Hilton Foundation.

Conlon, S. (1991, November). The federal government's role in educating people with dual sensory impairments. *American Speech-Language-Hearing Association, 42*–45.

Dickens, C. (1868). *American Notes.* London: Chapman & Hall.

Donnellan, A.M., Mirenda, P.L., Mesaros, R.A., & Fassbender, L.L. (1984). Analyzing the communicative functions of aberrant behavior. *Journal of The Association for Persons with Severe Handicaps, 9,* 201–212.

Farrell, G. (1956). *The story of blindness.* Cambridge: Harvard University Press.

Ferguson, D., Meyer, G., Jeanchild, L., Juniper, L., & Zingo, J. (1992). Figuring out what to do with the grownups: How teachers make inclusion work for students with disabilities. *Journal of The Association for Persons with Severe Handicaps, 17,* 218–226.

Freiberg, H.J., & Waxman, H.C. (1990). Changing teacher education. In W.R. Houston (Ed.), *Handbook of research on teacher education* (pp. 617–635). New York: Macmillan.

Giangreco, M.F., Cloninger, C.J., Mueller, P., Yuan, & Ashworth, S. (1991). Perspectives of parents whose children have dual sensory impairments. *Journal of The Association for Persons with Severe Handicaps, 16,* 14–24.

Goodlad, J.I., & Keating, P. (1990). *Access to knowledge: An agenda for our nation's schools.* New York: College Entrance Examination Board.

Hill, E., & Ponder, P. (1976). *Orientation and mobility techniques.* New York: American Foundation for the Blind.

Holmes Group. (1986). *Tomorrow's teachers.* East Lansing, MI: Author.

Individuals with Disabilities Education Act of 1990, (IDEA) PL 101-476, (October 30, 1990). Title 20 U.S.C. 1401 et seq: *U.S. Statutes at Large, 92,* 1103–1151.

Izen, C.L., & Brown, F. (1991). Education and treatment needs of students with profound multiply handicapping and medically fragile conditions: A survey of teachers' perceptions. *Journal of The Association for Persons with Severe Handicaps, 16,* 94–103.

Kauffman, J.M. (1989). The regular education initiative as Reagan-Bush education policy: A trickle down theory of education of the hard to teach. *The Journal of Special Education, 23*(3), 256–278.

Lane, H. (1984). *When the mind hears.* New York: Random House.

Lash, J.P. (1980). *Helen and teacher: The story of Helen Keller and Anne Sullivan Macy.* Delacorte Press.

Lilly, M.S. (1988). The regular education initiative: A force for change in general and special education. *Education and Training in Mental Retardation, 23,* 253–260.

Maxon, B., Tedder, N., Lamb, A., Geisen, J., & Marmion, S. (1989). The education of deaf-blind youth: Teacher characteristics and program issues. *RE: view, 21, 1.*

McInnis, J.M., & Treffry, J.A. (1982). *Deaf-blind infants and children: A developmental guide.* New York: University of Toronto Press.

McLetchie, B. (1993). Personnel preparation in deaf-blindness. In J.W. Reiman and P.A. Johnson (Eds.), *Proceedings of the national symposium on children and youth who are deaf-blind* (pp. 145–158). Monmouth, OR: Teaching Research Publications.

McNulty, J. (1992). Reflections and Future Directions. Reaction paper. In *Proceedings of the National Conference on Deaf-Blindness: Deaf-Blind Services in the 90's.* Reno, NV: Hilton/Perkins National Program, Conrad N. Hilton Foundation.

Mount, B. (1992). *Person-centered planning. Finding directions for change using personal futures planning.* New York: Graphic Futures.

Musselwhite, C.R., & St. Louis, K.W. (1988). *Communication programming for persons with severe handicaps.* Austin, TX: PRO-ED.

O'Brien, J., Forest, M., Snow, J., & Hasbury, D. (1989). *Action for inclusion: How to improve schools by welcoming children with special needs into the regular classroom.* Toronto, Ontario, Canada: Inclusion Press.

Pugach, M. (1987). The national education reports and special education: Implications for teacher preparation. *Exceptional Children, 53,* 308–314.

Reith, H. (1990). The politics of higher education and personnel preparation. In A.P. Kaiser & C.M. McWhorter (Eds.), *Preparing personnel to work with persons with severe disabilities.* Baltimore: Paul H. Brookes Publishing Co.

Schlesinger, A.M., Jr. (1992). *The disuniting of America: Reflections on a multicultural society.* New York: W.W. Norton.

Siegel-Causey, E. (1989). Research on the communication development of young children. In M. Bullis (Ed.), *Research on the communication development of young children with deaf blindness* (pp. 59–86). Monmouth, OR: Communication Skills Center for Young Children with Deaf-Blindness, Teaching Research.

Siegel-Causey, E., & Downing, L. (1987). Nonsymbolic communication development: Theoretical concepts and educational strategies. In L. Goetz, D. Guess, K. Stremel-Campbell (Eds.), *Innovative program design for individuals with dual sensory impairments* (pp. 15–48). Baltimore: Paul H. Brookes Publishing Co.

Smithdas, R.J. (1976). Implications of deaf-blindness. *Papers from the workshop on Usher's Syndrome.* Sands Point, NY: Helen Keller National Center for Deaf-Blind Youth and Adults.

Stainback, S., & Stainback, W. (1989). No more teachers of students with severe handicaps. *TASH Newsletter, 15*(2), 9.

Timothy W. v. Rochester, New Hampshire, School District, 875 F. 2d 954 (1st Cir. 1989).

Vandercook, T., York, J., & Forest, M. (1989). The McGill action planning system (MAPS): A strategy for building the vision. *Journal of The Association for Persons with Severe Handicaps, 14*(3), 205–215.

Van Dijk, J. (1967). The non-verbal deaf-blind child and his world. His outgrowth toward the world of symbols. In *Verzamelde Studies: I* (pp. 73–110). St. Michelsgestel: Instituut voor Doven.

Wade, W. (1904). *The blind-deaf.* (Monograph for private circulation). Indianapolis: Hecker Bros.

Waterhouse, E.J. (1975). *Education of the deaf-blind in the United States 1837–1967.* Unpublished manuscript, Perkins School for the Blind.

Writer, J. (1987). A movement-based approach to the education of students who are sensory impaired/multihandicapped. In L. Goetz, D. Guess, & K. Stremel-Campbell (Eds.), *Innovative program design for individuals with dual sensory impairments* (pp. 191–223). Baltimore: Paul H. Brookes Publishing Co.

Chapter 6

Developing Educational Plans to Support Valued Lifestyles

Lyle T. Romer
and Mary A. Romer

The content of education programs for students with deaf-blindness is influenced by numerous factors, including the advocacy efforts of family members; the training background of professional staff; leadership at the building and district level; and the availability of resources, both materials and educational specialists, to name just a few. However, the factor most influential in determining the content of education programs for students with deaf-blindness is societal values regarding education. These values influence program structure and curriculum as well as determine who participates in decision making and planning. The values held by the student, the student's family members and teachers, and by the culture in general, all play an important role in determining the content and accomplishments of education programs.

What is valued about a particular aspect of the student's culture is referred to as the *dominant paradigm*. In special education, a paradigm provides a model to follow in offering services and supports to students with disabilities. It also reflects how the culture thinks about people with disabilities. Brad-

ley and Knoll (1990) describe three paradigms that guided the efforts of professionals in the field of special education: 1) the medical model, 2) the developmental model, and 3) the community inclusion movement. In the medical model, people with disabilities are viewed as having conditions that render them ill, the result of which is an inability to function as a healthy person in society. In this model, the "treatment" for disabilities is separation from the healthy members of society in order to deliver services. There is little concern for habitation or teaching due to the opinion that such efforts would be unsuccessful.

Owing to a number of circumstances, chief among which were litigation efforts, the medical model was gradually replaced by the developmental model. In the developmental model, new hope was offered to people with disabilities and their families—a belief that everyone, regardless of the severity of disability, could learn. Unfortunately, this model tended to view people as being somehow "flawed" or "broken," and thus the best course of action was to "fix" people by teaching them to acquire new skills, new skills

To my sister Sally, I am deeply and lovingly grateful (M.A.R.). We both thank Justin Rohmer, Tom Witte, and Betty Hastings for the Personal Futures Planning graphics, and we thank Tommy and Sheila for sharing their invitation to discuss Tommy's future.

would make them more like "whole" people. These new skills would be best acquired in very specialized settings, designed for the purpose of affecting the necessary "repairs." Specialized services for people with disabilities were developed, in both the schools and communities. An entire continuum of services was constructed to fix people according to how broken they were, and, as people were repaired to a certain degree, they were moved on in the continuum for repairs at a more specialized level (Taylor, 1988).

As is usually the case in shifting paradigms, the medical and developmental models have coexisted for approximately the past 25 years. Although the medical model is waning, its influence can still be observed in many of the practices employed with people with disabilities, particularly in programs funded under Title XIX of the Social Security Act. Weick (1983) described a characteristic of the medical model that requires people to go through a process she referred to as "giving over." This principle, which can also be applied to the developmental model, is based upon a belief that the best way to help people is for them to seek professional or expert assistance; "giving over" can thus be defined as "a willingness to give someone else power to define one's personal reality" (Weick, 1983, p. 468). Evidence of this dynamic can be found in the belief that professional assistance is the best way to solve social problems.

Before readers leap to the conclusion that we are arguing for the abolition of professional expertise and knowledge, let us hasten to say this is not the case. However, the danger we do wish to point out is that an overreliance on the expertise of professionals leads people away from the knowledge that they inherently have about themselves and the knowledge and history that family members, friends, and other members of the school or community have about an individ-

ual. The role of expert knowledge is a crucial one, but it should be applied in support of decisions people make based on their knowledge of their own situation, and not as the prime determinant of what services should be offered (Cousins, 1976). Rappaport (1981) warned that relying too extensively on professionals and their expertise can result in a dependence on *convergent thinking*, in which there is one knowable and best answer to all problems. This may be true in engineering, but it is not the case in social issues. Rather, *divergent thinking* is likely to be the most productive manner of addressing social problems, wherein it is recognized that there can be many, even seemingly contradictory, answers to problems that are dependent, in large measure, upon the unique circumstances of the people facing them (Singer & Irvin, 1989). Starhawk (1988) alludes to how impoverished a perspective one has when one rejects the visions created by people who see from a different vantage point.

THE EMERGENCE OF COMMUNITY INCLUSION

A growing discontent with the results of the medical and developmental models has led to a reexamination of society's relationship with people with disabilities. The result is a concern about the way people with disabilities and their families are treated. Although individuals have moved away from large institutions (Lakin & Bruininks, 1985), they have moved into communities surrounded by specialized services. In essence, people with disabilities live in a world dominated by services, as opposed to social networks of friends and other community members. This form of "service" was once described as the "white corpuscle model" because, although people were in their communities, they were constantly surrounded by a white corpuscle of human services workers who acted as a filter for all the experiences of community, resulting in people who are in their community, without being a part of their community.

The tragic results of the giving over process are seen in the overreliance of people with disabilities and their families on professional assistance and services. Professionals are still presumed to know what is best for people, while the values held by students with deaf-blindness and their family members are largely ignored in determining the content of education programs. Schwartz (1992) points out how "professionalism, despite its benefits, displaces ordinary community processes . . . substituting an environment of service which can institutionalize people, even in their own homes" (p. 83). One need only look to the evidence that suggests that people with disabilities have an inordinately high number of people paid to provide them services, with a notable lack of friends and acquaintances to witness the result of the giving over process (Forest, 1989; Horner, Aaron, Ritchie, Stoner, & Twain, 1986). Ways of supporting people with disabilities that recognize the value of forming partnerships among those receiving services, their families, their friends, and other members of their communities are needed, with those partnerships based on an equality that no longer requires people to give over their own dreams and visions in exchange for professional expertise.

Identifying What Enhances Quality of Life

Over the past decade, increasing interest has been focused on planning services and supports with the intention of enhancing the quality of life enjoyed by people with developmental disabilities (Bellamy, Newton, LeBaron, & Horner, 1990; Emerson, 1985; Giangreco, Cloninger, & Iverson, 1993; Horner, 1991; O'Brien, 1987). The work of defining quality of life dimensions has centered on identifying the most important indicators, or accomplishments, associated with quality in lifestyle. Focusing on accomplishments, as opposed to behaviors or skills, allows one to determine if the ultimate valued outcomes are being attained (Gilbert, 1978). One can engage in a very elaborate set of behaviors that are, unfortunately, inefficient and ineffective with respect to achieving any worthy outcome. Although some behaviors may be associated with higher probabilities of achieving certain outcomes, it is still wise to separate the evaluation of outcomes from the behaviors used to achieve them.

The authors believe that educators should be concerned with supporting the development of behaviors in students with deaf-blindness that allow them to achieve valued consequences. Behaviors are not taught for their own sake, but rather to achieve a valued outcome. Unfortunately, sometimes the focus is on behaviors, or the settings in which behaviors occur, to a point where the intended outcomes or accomplishments are obscured. Focusing on inclusion as a goal, in and of itself, is a bit like confusing behaviors and accomplishments.

Inclusive education happens in a place where certain behaviors are more likely to help students achieve valued accomplishments. For example, if the valued accomplishment is developing a network of social support, attaining that goal will be enhanced if the student with deaf-blindness is supported to spend time with other students (Romer, Haring, Graham, Mace, & Rado, 1993). The accomplishment is not merely spending time with other students, but rather developing lasting, stable relationships with them. For students with deaf-blindness, skills such as braille reading and writing, orientation and mobility, and sign language (along with other alternative communication systems) are all important for achieving valued lifestyle accomplishments.

These skills should be taught in contexts that support students to achieve school presence, participation with peers, self-determination in lifestyle choices, greater competence, and the respect of others by offering contributions to one's friends and community. Focusing on valued lifestyle outcomes enables educators to prepare individualized education programs (IEPs) that are more likely to positively enhance students' quality of life by preparing them for full participation as members of their local communities.

A different way of looking at the lives of people with developmental disabilities would focus on providing services and supports that enhance the person's lifestyle, rather than merely teaching him or her new skills. But how is lifestyle defined? While there are certainly many varied aspects to each person's lifestyle, it may be possible to identify particular aspects, or indices, that all could agree are important to lifestyle quality. O'Brien (1987) articulated a set of five basic accomplishments that constitute a measure of lifestyle quality. Since the work of O'Brien, who recognizes the influence of Wolfensberger and Glenn (1975) and Wolfensberger and Thomas (1983) through their work in operationalizing the principles of *normalization*, several other researchers have put forth their own set of valued accomplishments that define quality in lifestyles. (Normalization is a principle by which the same patterns of daily life engaged in by people without disabilities are made available to people with disabilities.) Table 1 summarizes valued lifestyle accomplishments as defined by several researchers.

The five most common valued lifestyle accomplishments defined by researchers are:

1. Community presence or physical integration with others
2. Self-determination or the ability to make choices in one's life
3. Competence in obtaining those things that are important to maintaining one's lifestyle
4. Gaining the respect of other members of one's community by offering and making contributions
5. Developing a set of social relationships with other members of the community

These five lifestyle accomplishments should serve as the desired outcomes of educational services for students with deaf-blindness, with these accomplishments being most effectively and efficiently achieved in inclusive settings. Each of these valued lifestyle accomplishments are defined in greater detail in the following sections as they would apply to students with deaf-blindness in an inclusive school setting.

School Presence This accomplishment provides a sense of place. Belonging to places at school, such as where students learn (the classrooms), perform sports (the gym), join in club activities (classrooms), and eat lunch (the cafeteria) supports a sense of being a part of the school community through membership in varied aspects of that community. A sense of place also means obtaining one's needed goods and services from local vendors and one's educational services from the same schools that one's neighbors attend. Segregated or separate facilities and activities for people with disabilities often break the ties to a sense of place by concentrating all of the services that most people find in their school or community into the disability service system or special education.

Another problem often associated with community or school presence in specialized programs is that people enrolled in these programs often participate in the community in groups. This group factor inhibits the ability of people without disabilities to form relationships with specialized program participants because these individuals are seen as being with "their own kind." School pres-

Table 1. Valued accomplishments in lifestyle quality as defined by these researchers

O'Brien (1987)	Giangreco, Cloninger, and Iverson (1993)	Connecticut Department of Mental Retardation (1986)	Washington State Division of Developmental Disabilities (1988)	People First of Washington (1985)
Community presence	Access to a variety of places	Presence and participation in Connecticut town life	Integration in local communities	Being in the community
Choice	Personal choice and control that matches one's age	Opportunities to make choices	Power and choice	Making choices
Competence		Opportunities to develop competence	Competence	Being independent
Respect			Status	Getting respect and dignity
Community participation	Social network of meaningful relationships	Good relationships with family members and friends	Relationships	Meeting other citizens
	Being healthy and safe Having a safe, stable home		Health and safety	

109

ence is also crucial to achieving other valued lifestyle accomplishments, such as participating with other students without disabilities; experiencing and choosing valued lifestyle activities; becoming more competent in a range of valued lifestyle activities; and engaging in activities that offer opportunities for students with deaf-blindness to make contributions to others and, thus, earn respect from school and community members.

Self-Determination Self-determination is actually a more inclusive valued accomplishment than choice alone; it equates to an absence of tyranny in one's life, where one is subject to the control of others to an unneeded and unacceptable degree. Self-determination means making choices; it also means standing up for those choices in ways that others sometimes describe as noncompliant, stubborn, uncooperative, and so on. It is a crucial accomplishment in all matters of quality in lifestyle. Without some degree of self-determination, all other aspects of one's lifestyle diminish in value. Self-determination is, of course, a very complex issue for all of us, and especially so for people who have limited means of making themselves understood by others and for people who have had limited opportunities to participate in the diverse range of activities and events available to other students and community members. People with more significant disabilities, including deaf-blindness, can benefit from the support and understanding of others to make their choices more meaningful.

Support starts with the realization that self-determination in everyday matters (what to wear, what to eat, and so on) as well as life-defining ones (with whom to live, where to work) can be achieved if people are given supported experiences in making choices and evaluating thier consequences. Making choices is a significant way of defining one's own individuality. When others make choices

for us, we are seen as less capable and, therefore, less of a person in our own right.

One way of being supportive is by being sensitive to what people are communicating when they do so with nonsymbolic forms of communication (see chap. 10, this volume). People's behavior speaks very eloquently, not only of what their choices are, but also of how strongly they are committed to those choices (Carr & Durand, 1985). Watching behavior to understand a person's choices is a major factor in helping individuals achieve self-determination in their lifestyles. Communication instruction for students with deaf-blindness should help with the valued lifestyle accomplishment of self-determination.

Finally, it is sometimes necessary to support individuals to have the opportunity to develop long-standing, stable relationships with nonservice providers (friends, classmates, neighbors, and so on) in order to help interpret the individual's behaviors and communication in the area of self-determination. Selecting people other than service providers as friends and advisers mitigates the influence over choices that are more convenient for programs, school staff, or social service agencies, as opposed to those that are valuable for the students themselves.

Competence It should be noted immediately that there is a difference between *competence* and *independence*. Independence requires that a person meet his or her needs without any involvement or assistance from others, while competence implies that there are many different and varied ways to achieve one's objectives. People with severe disabilities are often isolated from other people in their lives, and adhering only to the attainment of independence often exacerbates this situation. More importantly, upon examination it appears that very few lives are lived independently, but are more likely to be lived *interdependently*, that is, in cooperation with one's friends and family. As long as lifestyle objectives are competently achieved, one's control is retained as part of an interconnected set of relationships. Students can be competent at achieving lifestyle accomplishments by receiving some support from friends, neighbors, and others; using adaptive equipment; or even purchasing certain services (laundry, housekeeping, and so forth). This view of competence has important implications in the area of personal assistance issues, where some people with severe disabilities could employ others to provide physical assistance for specific activities (Lyle-O'Brien, 1992).

Making Contributions   Respect is afforded to people on the basis of their contributions to others. People who are seen as occupying valued roles in the community are given respect by other community members. People with severe disabilities are often seen as being consumers, or takers, of goods and services, as opposed to contributors to their communities. Providing opportunities for students with deaf-blindness to be perceived as competent occupiers of valued social roles is an important part of enhancing quality in lifestyles. Occupying roles such as staff in the student store, rally squad members, student council representatives, and members of service societies provides opportunities for students with deaf-blindness to be seen as contributing positively to school life, thus earning the respect of their peers.

School Participation   Participating in school means developing a network of social relationships with a variety of peers. Often people with deaf-blindness are restricted in their social relationships to people who are paid to provide services (teachers, educational assistants, therapists, and so forth) and immediate family members. Relying on paid service providers for one's social support is risky because of the instability of relationships with

paid staff. Staff come and go at what is sometimes an alarming rate. Expecting social support from people who are likely soon to be gone means that the bonds that contribute to developing long-term, stable social relationships are frequently broken. On the other hand, relying solely on family for one's social support unfairly overtaxes those relationships. Certain needs, for example companionship, are best met by friends. Having a larger circle of social support also offers one opportunities to engage in activities when teachers and family are not available.

Planning for ways to enhance the lifestyle quality of a student with deaf-blindness means examining these five valued accomplishments. None of these five accomplishments exists in a vacuum. They all influence one another and certain choices in one, of necessity, limit choices in others. The degree to which people wish to be competent by being independent can have an effect on their social relationships. For example, choices about where to live and work, and with whom, affect community presence and respect. The authors believe that the education, and consequently the lifestyles, of students with deaf-blindness can be enhanced by supporting families and educators to focus their attention on these five lifestyle accomplishments.

Planning for Lifestyle Quality

Planning for lifestyle quality begins with the individual and those closest to him or her. It takes time to understand that person's current lifestyle and the visions that the person and his or her support network have for the future. This vision of the future is an extremely important element in all of our lives. Consuelo 'Connie' Martinez (1988) of Capitol People First (an organization of self-advocates) eloquently describes this need for vision in everyone's life:

My parents always had a dream for my brothers and sister for when they grew up, but nobody ever had a dream for me, so I never had a dream for myself. You can never have a good life if nobody has a dream for you, unless you learn to have a dream for yourself. That's what I had to do, and now I have a dream for myself—a little casa, a garden with flowers and peppers and tomatoes, and a loved one to share my life with—and more. Even if I don't get all those things, I know I'm alive now.

Discovering the resources needed to bring the vision closer to reality is the next step in planning for quality in lifestyles. The informal resources of the community (family, friends, co-workers, associations, and so forth) are seen as at least as important as the formal resources traditionally recognized as part of the developmental disability "system." The strategy for using resources is to create opportunities for community connections that will promote the student's desirable future. Sometimes the strategies mean teaching and sometimes they mean finding the right kind of support to achieve one or more of the valued lifestyle accomplishments.

Lifestyle planning (O'Brien, 1987) is known under at least two other labels: 1) *personal futures planning* (Mount, 1992; Mount & Zwernik, 1988) and 2) *MAPS* (the McGill Action Planning System) (Vandercook, York, & Forest, 1989). All three approaches to lifestyle planning have common assumptions as follows:

1. *Focus on individual's strengths:* Lifestyle planning is a positive, enhancing process, as opposed to being deficit seeking. The focus is on what makes people unique members of their communities and what they have to offer the community in the way of strengths and valued contributions. Continually focusing on a person's deficits causes the community to see the individual only in those negative terms. Imagine how frustrated you would be if you went to college and were informed that because your lowest entrance scores were in math you would be required to be a math major for the next 4 years in order to remedy this deficit? How long might it be before you developed "inappropriate" behaviors in an attempt to convey your frustration? Recognizing the contributions a person has to offer focuses the planners on empowering the individual to seek ways to make those contributions a part of his or her life (O'Brien & Mount, 1991).

2. *Individual ownership:* The lifestyle plan is owned by the individual, and not by any element of the service delivery system. Careful steps are taken to ensure this ownership. Lifestyle planning meetings are held in a place that is seen as belonging to the individual, for example his or her home, or at least a neutral meeting place in the community. Meetings should never be held at school, at the disability center, or any other institutional location. The person and his or her closest advocates invite other people who will attend the meeting. Invitations come from the focal person, not from an agency. Most importantly, the meetings are facilitated by someone who has no direct involvement in delivering services or supports to the focal person. The facilitator should take the time necessary to know the focal person's visions and dreams and be able to focus the meetings to arrive at a set of strategies that favor no one service element at the expense of these dreams and visions. When in doubt, the facilitator gives preferences to the visions of the focal person and his or her advocates.

3. *Formal and informal supports:* The lifestyle plan builds a set of formal and informal supports to achieve the person's desirable future. The detrimental effect of relying too heavily on human services to meet all of the needs of individuals with disabilities has already been mentioned in this chapter. Smull and Bellamy (1991) describe the use of informal support networks made up of family, friends, co-workers, and classmates to increase community connections for people with disabilities. They favor informal sup-

ports due to their flexibility and lower levels of intrusion in people's lives. Instances where co-workers assume more responsibility for on-the-job support, as opposed to job coaches, and where service providers go directly to the community for the purpose of building bridges and alliances with neighborhood associations, hold great promise for providing more effective ways to help people become connected to networks providing social support.

4. *A large and diverse social network:* No one person, or set of people, can meet all of the lifestyle needs of another person. Having only one or two people or agencies to go to for support results in dangerous levels of dependence on those people or agencies. The more connected people are to a social network, the less likely they are to lose a significant part of their social support if one individual is no longer involved with the person for whatever reason. People with disabilities are vulnerable to losing major sources of social support if they are dependent on staff and those staff change jobs, or the person is assigned to some other service. Given the diverse interests of most people, having a sufficient number of people with whom to engage in activities also increases the probability of satisfying a wider range of interests. Another advantage to having people who are not paid staff in a student's social network is the degree of safeguards they can provide through interest in the services and supports provided to a student by schools and social service agencies. Many times, having a balance of opinion about what may be important to a student and how to go about attaining goals results in a more representative plan than is possible when only one group of people are involved.

DEVELOPING LIFESTYLE PLANS

Planning to support a student's achievement of valued lifestyle accomplishments entails a series of initial meetings, plus an ongoing commitment to reconvening the planning group as often as necessary. Constructing a lifestyle plan may be thought of as involving four phases: 1) initial considerations, 2) developing a personal profile of the student, 3) creating a desirable vision of the student's future, and 4) formulating strategies to enhance the student's lifestyle accomplishments. The following sections explain how a lifestyle plan should be developed. Figures illustrating the case examples of "Maggie," a 10-year-old girl with deaf-blindness and developmental disabilities, and "Jamie," a 5-year-old girl with deaf-blindness and diplegic cerebral palsy, further explain lifestyle planning.

Initial Considerations

A lifestyle plan should be carefully considered prior to making plans for one. The commitment required to carry out a lifestyle plan is significant and should not be entered into lightly. While the process can be very satisfying and empowering, it can also be very disappointing to a student and his or her family if there is no follow-through.

When a Lifestyle Plan Should Be Made Not every one needs, or wants, a lifestyle plan. For many students, the questions addressed in a lifestyle plan are already being asked by the people committed to them. The lifestyle plan should not be thought of as a substitute for the individualized education program (IEP). Although the lifestyle plan can enhance and make the IEP more socially and educationally valid, the lifestyle plan does not replace the IEP. Lifestyle plans are usually thought of as being most helpful to students who are facing transitions in their lives (leaving school, moving to a new home, and so forth), are in a crisis of some nature (behavioral issues, dissatisfied with a job, major issues of medical or physical support, and so forth), or have suffered a loss in their life (losing a friend or loved one to death or moving out of town).

Who Should Attend the Lifestyle Planning Meeting Choosing people to attend the meeting should be done in consultation with the student and his or her family members. Ideally, participants will all have made a commitment to the focal student with deaf-blindness to make whatever changes they can to improve his or her educational services and quality of life. Professionals and lay people would make a good balance on a planning team. While the involvement and commitment of professionals is important, it is usually the family and other interested people who provide the stability that is crucial for the group's continuity over time. Although groups of varying sizes have been effective, groups of five to seven core members generally seem to function best. This number seems to facilitate the group process, as indicated by the work of Bales and Borgatta (1955). The group can easily expand its membership when the input, advice, or assistance of another person is needed. The people who attend the meetings have one thing in common, an interest in and commitment to the student. A partial list of the many people who might attend lifestyle planning meetings include:

- The focal student
- Family members
- Friends from school and the community
- Teachers
- Administrators and related services staff
- Family friends, neighbors, and pastors
- Bus drivers
- Job coaches, employers, and co-workers
- Residential support staff

When and Where the Meeting Should Occur The lifestyle plan can be used to provide IEP and ITP (individualized transition plan) documents with increased social and educational validity (Schwartz & Baer, 1991; Voeltz & Evans, 1983). As such, it is appropriate to schedule the lifestyle planning meeting prior to the IEP/ITP meeting in order for the content of the IEP/ITP to benefit from information in the lifestyle plan. Where the meeting is held is determined, in large part, by what is convenient to the participants. It is worthwhile to show deference to the family in trying to accommodate their schedule in where the meeting is held, as well as the time of day for the meeting. It is best to hold the meeting in a comfortable environment that is not associated with service agencies (school, residential support agency, and so forth). The family home, community churches, or libraries are often used for lifestyle planning meetings.

Invitations to the Meeting As the meeting is about and for the focal student, and it is that person's plan, it is appropriate that the student or his or her family invite people to attend. People to be invited often have connections to other important people, so it is worthwhile to consider how having some people present will influence the attendance of others; getting the people you want sometimes means making sure another person is invited. Figure 1 is an example of an invitation used by a mother and her son to invite people to attend the son's personal futures planning meeting.

Who Will Fill Certain Roles Conducting the planning meeting, and keeping the group together over time, requires that certain roles be occupied. One of the most important roles is that of the group facilitator. This is usually, but not always, a person paid by a social services agency to provide this sort of help to a group. It should be someone familiar with the process of lifestyle planning, who has very good skills related to bringing people together as a team. Mount, Beeman and Ducharme (1988) list several specific roles filled by the facilitator:

LYLE-YOU ARE INVITED TO:

TOMMY'S FUTURE

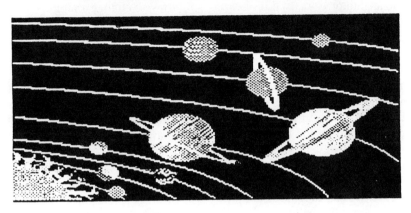

Saturday, April 24th, from 1:00–3:00 pm is a very special time, and you have been chosen to have the opportunity to participate in a very special process called "FUTURES PLANNING." Because you are so special in Tommy's life, we need your special insights so we can begin to build a picture of Tommy's future, and make plans, so we can facilitate him in achieving his highest potential.

There will be several different meetings that will be stretched out over time. The first meeting will be approximately two hours long. At this meeting, we will be sharing Tommy's history, likes and dislikes and many other things: from your own unique perspective. Because our group is small and we want as much input as possible, we hope that you will join us in unlocking doors into Tommy's exciting future.

If you have any questions call us at 111-1111. Thank you and we look forward to seeing you there.

With love and prayers.

Figure 1.   A sample invitation used by a mother and her son to invite important people to the son's personal futures planning meeting.

- Catalyst
- Enabler
- Broker
- Bridge-builder
- Advocate
- Chairperson
- Leadership developer
- Organizer
- Troubleshooter

The authors have found it best if the facilitator is not connected to an agency directly involved in providing services or supports to the focal student. This reduces the chance the facilitator, however unintentionally, will influence decisions made by the group. Because the facilitator is often paid by an agency not serving the student, it may be necessary for this person to move on eventually to assist other groups. Therefore, the facilitator might want to focus some of his or her efforts toward preparing someone from within the group to take over as facilitator. Given that the facilitator is focused on helping the group during the meeting so that they are free to participate fully, it is a good idea to rotate the role of notetaker among the other members of the group. Rotating this role means no one person has to be occupied with this duty all of the time.

Certain behaviors from group members enable the development of the lifestyle plan to proceed more effectively. It is a very good idea to have the group discuss and agree upon the norms of group behavior early in the process of lifestyle planning, for example:

1. Agree that meetings will start and end on time. Usually 2 hours is about the most people can manage when asked to engage in sustained, focused efforts at creative problem solving. Those arriving late should make up for what they miss after the meeting. Valuable meeting time will not be devoted to catching up latecomers.

2. Everyone has the responsibility to listen and participate actively in the discussions. All members agree to act as equals in the meeting; no one is allowed to dismiss the ideas of others. Members of the team agree to let go of their formal roles (deaf/blind specialist, school principal, job coach, and so forth) and remain focused on finding creative ways to further the student and his or her family's vision of a desirable future.

3. Everyone agrees to open themselves up to the process of new perspectives and changing the way services and supports are provided to the student. Group members agree to be on guard for phrases such as, "We've tried that before," "I agree with your philosophy, but

. . . ," "I am not in a position to make a decision," "Your idea may have worked there, but it won't work here." These kinds of remarks are recognized as resistance to change and noted as such when they are heard. Participants agree that all assumptions should be stated explicitly and are open to challenge at all times. If assumptions cannot be explained rationally and logically, they should be discarded. Group members do well in remembering the words of George Bernard Shaw: "You see things; and you say 'Why?' But I dream things that never were; and I say 'Why not?'" (Shaw, p. 7).

4. Group members agree that their focus is on the person, not on their professional "turf." They are in attendance due to their knowledge of, involvement with, and interest in the focal student, not strictly as the student's teacher, speech specialist, or school administrator.

5. Every member of the group agrees that they are there to make a personal commitment to the focal student and his or her desirable lifestyle.

Meeting Accommodations Involving the student, and possibly other group members, may entail the need to make certain accommodations. The planning should consider the need for interpreters for the student with deaf-blindness, as well as any other group members with hearing and/or vision impairments. Remember, it often takes time to locate and schedule interpreters, so allow enough time to do so. Also, check with any people needing interpreters about their preferences for certain interpreters or language requirements (e.g., Signed English, American Sign Language [ASL]). Any other necessary accommodations should be planned for at this time, such as wheelchair accessibility and so forth.

How Focal Student and Family Will Be Involved   The facilitator should meet with the family prior to the planning meeting to become familiar with the student and issues about which his or her family is concerned. The facilitator should be aware of any topics that the family may wish to avoid at the meeting. The role of the student and family at the meeting should also be discussed. Would they like to introduce other members of the planning group? Would they like to make any opening comments, thank people for attending, etc.?

Building a Personal Profile of the Student

The facilitator should begin the meeting by allowing the student and/or his or her family to make any desired opening comments. For the first meeting, it is helpful for the facilitator to give an overview of lifestyle planning and explain the process to be used. After making sure that everyone is comfortable with the process and understands what is to occur, the facilitator can begin to ask a series of questions to develop what is referred to as a personal profile of the student. The facilitator, or a recorder, writes down group responses on large pieces of poster paper hung on the walls. The posters not only help in recording information and agreements, their display helps to keep people focused and clear on what is said during the meeting. The recorder might use graphics to illustrate what is happening in the student's life. Drawing pictures often helps people to visualize patterns and relationships that may elude them in words. Sometimes people use certain conventions in recording information, for example, basic information is in blue; positive occurrences or talents, etc., are recorded in green; and negative occurrences or issues are recorded in red. This allows people to focus quickly on the positives to be enhanced as well as finding strategies to overcome or cir-

cumvent the negatives. In developing a personal profile, group members should consider the following questions.

What Are the Highlights of the Student's Life?   Figure 2 illustrates a sample timeline showing some highlights of "Maggie's" life. Group participants should consider the following when recalling the major events that have happened in the student's life:

1. When and where was the student was born?
2. Were there any unusual circumstances surrounding his or her birth?
3. Where did the family live throughout the student's life?
4. What schools did the student attend?
5. When did people important to the student first meet him or her?
6. Did any important people leave?
7. What milestones did the student reach (talking, walking, gaining employment)?
8. Were there any memorable trips or vacations?

Who Is Important to the Student?   This question helps ascertain who makes up the student's support network and how often these individuals spend time with the student. People involved in the student's life are then put into one of four groups: 1) family, 2) friends, 3) paid staff, and 4) community people (people the student is acquainted with, but who are not his or her friends). This question also attempts to identify the student's strongest allies or advocates. Who knows the student best? Are there any important people with whom the student has lost contact? Maggie's *relationship map*, also called *a circle of friends*, is represented in Figure 3.

Where Does the Student Spend His or Her Time?   This question seeks to know and understand the student's presence in the community. Are there places the student goes,

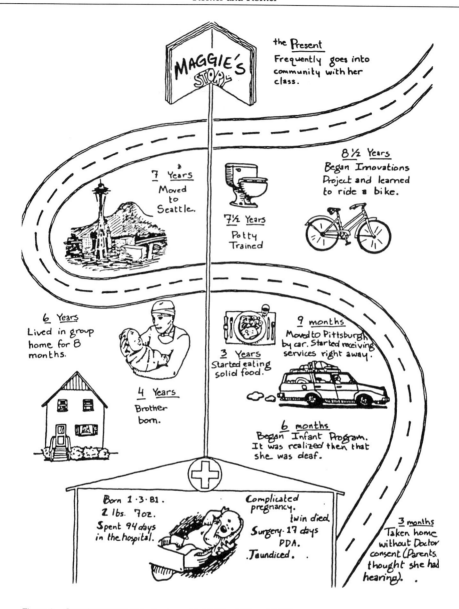

the **Present**
Frequently goes into community with her class.

8½ **Years**
Began Innovations Project and learned to ride a bike.

7 Years
Moved to Seattle.

7½ Years
Potty Trained

6 Years
Lived in group home for 8 months.

4 Years
Brother born.

3 Years
Started eating solid food.

9 months
Moved to Pittsburgh by car. Started receiving services right away.

6 months
Began Infant Program. It was realized then that she was deaf.

Born 1·3·81.
2 lbs. 7oz.
Spent 94 days in the hospital.

Complicated pregnancy.
twin died.
Surgery. 17 days
PDA.
Jaundiced.

3 months
Taken home without Doctor consent (Parents thought she had hearing).

Figure 2.   Sample timeline showing some highlights of "Maggie's" life.

groups that the student belongs to or spends time with on a regular basis? How often does the student go to those places? Are they open to everyone in the community or school or just to other people with disabilities? Does the person go to those places alone? With a group? Figure 4 shows the places Maggie spends time in her community. They are divided into places that are in her immediate neighborhood, a short drive away, and, outside the last circle, a distant commute. Figure 5 shows the places where she spends time at

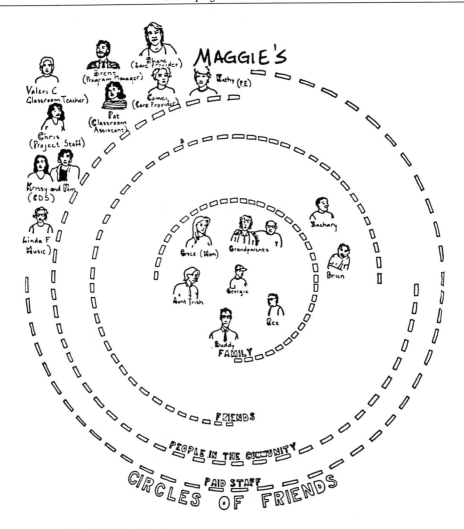

Figure 3.   Maggie's circles of friends.

school. The illustration is divided into special education activities and those that occur in the general education areas of the school.

What Choices Are Made By the Student? This area of developing a student profile entails asking another question as well, "What are the student's preferences?" Choices should be listed as those made by the student, those made by the student's family, and those made by other people. Remember that choices are very different for individuals as they grow in age and experience. The choices made by 5-year-olds are usually very different from those made by 18-year-olds. The choices Maggie makes, those made by her family, and those made by others are depicted in Figure 6. Maggie's preferences are shown in Figure 7.

What Are the Student's Gifts, Strengths, and Capacities? What do we know works and doesn't work for this student? What is this student very good at? What are his or her

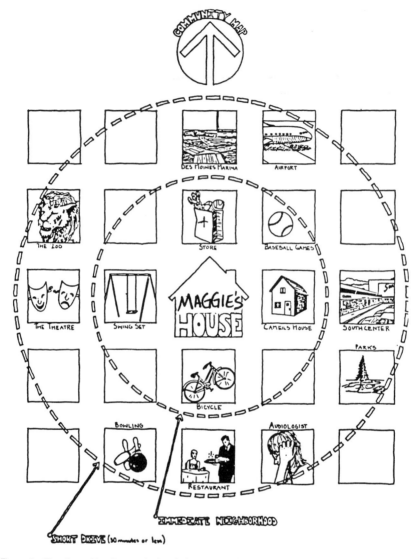

Figure 4. The places Maggie spends time in her community, divided into places that are in her immediate neighborhood, a short drive away, and a distant commute.

special talents? What do we know about working with this student that generates interest, enthusiasm, and excitement? Are there certain instructional strategies that work very well with this student? Are there other, noninstructional strategies that might also work well, such as environmental mod-ification or personal assistance from peers? What methods are known not to work, or to cause anger, frustration, or confusion? How can we stop using those? Table 2 shows the gifts, strengths, and abilities of a 5-year-old girl named Jamie. Figure 8 shows what works and doesn't work for Jamie.

Figure 5. The places Maggie spends time at school, divided into special education activities and those that occur in the general education areas of the school.

What Are the Student's Contributions? This question relates to the respect afforded the student by classmates, peers, teachers, and other members of the school and community. Valued social roles for the student might include: cheer leader, sports team manager, best friend, confidant, community activist, band member, and so forth. The student might contribute to the school and community by providing humor, helping others, encouraging others, volunteering for community activities, doing a good job at work,

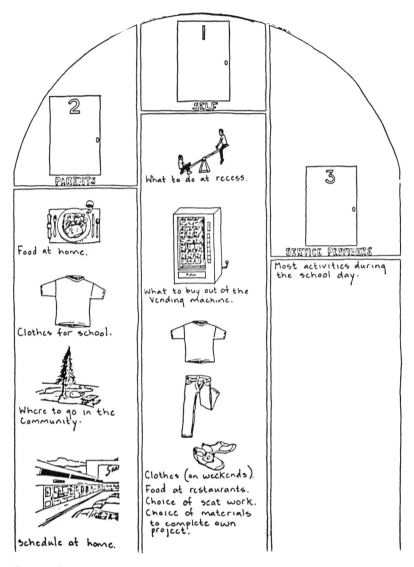

Figure 6.   Choices Maggie makes, those made by her family, and those made by others.

having a valued job (assembling medical equipment, assistant teacher in an early childhood program). Are there valued community roles that offer the student a chance to capitalize on his or her gifts, strengths, and abilities?

How Does the Person Communicate with Others?   This question was recently added to the lifestyle planning process by people at the University of Kentucky, with some help from the staff of the Helen Keller National Center and Dr. Beth Mount. They felt it was

Figure 7.   Maggie's preferences.

important to address this question in lifestyle plans for students with deaf-blindness because it is a very critical area in their lives. Questions about how a person currently communicates, in what modes, and with whom are important to thinking about how to achieve some of the five valued lifestyle accomplishments mentioned previously. How effective are the current communication modes? Are they used with a variety of people? In a variety of settings and activities? Creating a poster to help answer these ques-

Table 2.   Jamie's gifts, strengths, and abilities

I love books and can turn the pages.
I have a great smile.
I am curious, and I love music.
I can pull my socks off.
I can use the toilet.
I love to ride fast.
I can shake my head yes or no.
I can walk with my walker with stand-by assistance.
I can propel my wheelchair.
I can wash my hands.
I can tear off the towel myself.
I can reach for people I want.
I can grab, aim, and release.
I can scoot; I love to dance.
I can climb into a box.
I love to count.
I have a long attention span.
I can mark on paper.

tions entails first listing communication strategies that work well and those that do not work well. A sample of a communication poster is displayed in Figure 9.

Completing the communication poster discussed above ends the portion of the lifestyle plan called the personal profile. It is usually a good idea to stop at this point and allow people a week or two to reflect upon their experiences with the group before going on to the next phase—describing a desirable future and identifying strategies to enhance the student's lifestyle. Team members should try to identify themes they saw emerging in group discussions. Are there certain lifestyle accomplishments that are particularly lacking? Do people see any ways that they may be able to connect a high or low level of any of the lifestyle accomplishments to the presence or absence of others? What seem to be the student's most immediate needs?

Creating a Vision of the Student's Future

The next planning meeting starts with group members sharing what they thought and

learned about the student while completing the personal profile. Once again the facilitator asks the group members a series of questions that elicit their thoughts and feelings about the student's lifestyle. How would the group members describe the student's current quality of life? Are there current or upcoming opportunities or events that the group may wish to take advantage of in enhancing the student's lifestyle? Thinking about things that will happen to the student in the near future might identify upcoming events such as moving to a new school, graduating from high school, or a friend or sibling enrolling in the same school. Opportunities or events related to services might include support for new summer employment, an increase in funding available for transition, the availability of personal assistance support, or a new case manager. Finally, are there any new events or opportunities to take advantage of in the student's school or community (a new employer moving into town, a summer drama program starting at the town center)?

Conversely, the group should also think about the major obstacles or events that might affect the student's quality of life. The impending loss of a close family member or friend, limitations on classes to be offered next term, or changes in funding patterns for employment and residential support are all examples of events that could adversely affect the student's quality of life now or in the near future.

Next the group should reflect on what they see as a desirable future for the student. What visions would come to mind if nothing changed for this student? What would those visions look life if the group takes advantage of potential opportunities and develops strategies to overcome any obstacles? What are the most important things to happen for the student *right now*? Figure 10 displays short- and long-term visions of the future

WHAT WORKS

Giving me personal space

Giving me more than 1 choice to respond to

I need to know what activity is happening next and what you expect me
   to do (e.g., don't jerk a book out of my hand or walk me to the
   bathroom without telling me what is happening).

When speaking to me, use voice and sign.

Please do not talk "baby talk" to me.

Please watch my facial expressions and/or signs for things I want
   to tell you.

I have a definite "yes" and "no" response, I encourage you to use "yes
   & no" questions with me and wait for my answer.

Spending time with me & getting to know me.

WHAT DOESN'T WORK

Going too fast with questions of choices

Not waiting for me to complete my answer

Overstimulation (e.g., lots of movement around me with
   unexpected noise)

Being tired

Figure 8.   What works and doesn't work for Jamie

created by Jamie and the members of her planning group who met with Jamie to help her look at her future.

Identifying Strategies

Determining the strategies that will have the highest probability of improving the current and future quality of life for the focal student is best facilitated by reviewing the five valued lifestyle accomplishments previously discussed with an eye toward how they can be enhanced. Are there any activities, events, or elements that are part of the student's life that detract from achieving higher levels of

Communication by student				
Who interacts with the student and activity involved	**Methods**	**What for?**	**Examples of vocabulary**	**Responses from others**
Matty and day staff	*Gesture	Change shirt	Pulls at buttons	Provide different shirt & assist in changing it
Day and night staff	*Self injurious and other behaviors	Avoid task	Hits self	Provide choice to do different task
Matty and day staff	Object symbol	Bathroom	Wall tile	Assist in travel to bathroom
Matty and day staff	Actual objects	Choose breakfast food	Picks from 2 food items, e.g., cereal, waffle	Help him prepare the food he has chosen
Susan and night staff	*Manipulates others	Food or drink	Pulls staff to kitchen	Provide choices

Communication by others				
Who interacts with the student and activity involved	**Methods**	**What for?**	**Examples of vocabulary**	**Response from student**
Matty and day staff	Object	Indicate time to shower	Shampoo bottle	Walk toward bathroom
Day and night staff	*Object	Do next part of grooming task	Toothbrush, hairbrush, etc.	Begin task
Matty and day staff	Object symbol, sequence box	Anticipate what will immediately happen next (schedule)	Work card, scissors, lunch box	Holds object, waits for assistance
Susan and night staff	Pointing	Show where bathroom is	Pointing	Walks to bathroom on his own
Day and night staff	Individual sign language signs	Anticipate what will happen next	*"drink"; *"finish"; "toilet"	Do task

*= skilled/uses often

Figure 9.   Sample communication poster.

THE VISION

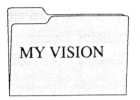 SHOULD NOT BE ⊘  IN A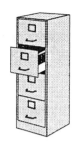

IT SHOULD BE REVIEWED BY EVERYONE  AGAIN & AGAIN & AGAIN

A YEAR FROM NOW

 I WANT MORE FRIENDS AND I WANT FRIENDS TO COME TO MY HOUSE. I ALSO WANT FRIENDS WHO ARE FLUENT IN ASL.

I WANT STUDENTS OR FRIENDS TO RESPOND TO MY ATTEMPTS AT COMMUNICATION. I WANT OTHER STUDENTS OR FRIENDS TO SIGN TO ME.

 I WANT STUDENTS TO ACCEPT AND APPRECIATE MY DIFFERENT MODES OF COMMUNICATION (E.G., SIGNING, BOARD, COMPUTER)

I WANT TO BE ABLE TO EXPRESS MY FEELINGS AND DESIRES & PEOPLE WILL RESPOND SUPPORTIVELY (E.G.,GOING TO THE RESTROOM).

Figure 10.   The short- and long-term visions for Jamie's future as created by Jamie and her planning team.

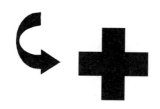

I WANT TO ONE DAY HAVE MY
LINDEMON PROCEDURE REVERSED
SO I CAN USE MY VOICE AGAIN.
I WANT TO MAINTAIN MY GOOD
HEALTH SO I NEED TO BE IN A
SAFE ENVIRONMENT. I WANT TO
KEEP LONG-TERM CONSISTENT
NURSES.

I WANT TO BE ABLE TO WRITE FRIENDS
ESPECIALLY MY NAME.

I WANT TEACHERS IN THE
FUTURE TO HAVE A POSITIVE
CHALLENGING VISION FOR ME.

5 YEARS FROM NOW

I WANT TO BE ABLE TO WRITE
LETTERS TO FRIENDS, READ
BOOKS, AND DRAW.

I WANT TO STAY CONNECTED TO
FAMILY RELATIVES & A GROUP
OF FRIENDS.

Figure 10. *continued*

I WANT TO EAT INDEPENDENTLY AT HOME & IN RESTAURANTS. I WANT TO MANAGE MY OWN PERSONAL NEEDS (E.G., DRESS-ING, PERSONAL HYGIENE, ETC.).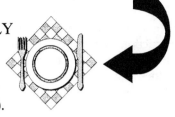

 I WANT TO BE ABLE TO COM-MUNICATE BY PHONE TO A FRIEND. I WANT TO BE ABLE TO TALK OR SIGN FLUENTLY.

I WANT TO WALK WITHOUT MY WHEEL-CHAIR OR WALKER. I WANT TO TAKE TAP OR CREATIVE MOVEMENT CLASSES. I WANT TO HAVE MORE LIFE EXPERIENCES (E.G.,CAMPING, FAST RIDES, GO TO PLAYS, SAILING, HORSE & TRAIN RIDE.

Figure 10. *continued*

the five valued lifestyle accomplishments? What can be done to eliminate or lessen their impact?

Community Presence Are there places suggested by the personal profile that the person is having trouble using? Are there ways that the person could become more competent at using those places, given instruction or support? Are there places that would be of benefit to the student to use in the community or at school? Pay attention to the student's preferences and gifts, strengths and abilities, to see if there may be community places that are congruent. Finally, ask what it would take to increase the frequency and variety of his or her school and community presence.

Self-Determination What decisions currently being made by others could be offered to the student with instruction and support?

What could be done to increase the choices made by the student in pursuing preferred activities? Are there particular communication strategies to be employed that could enhance the student's ability to indicate choices to others? When one person finds out about a new preference on the part of the student, how can that information be shared with others? What experiences can be provided to the student now that will help him or her exercise self-determination in the future (e.g., places to live and work)?

Competence What activities does the student want to learn that would positively affect choice, respect, community presence, and community participation? For example, communication skills could certainly enhance the student's ability to interact socially with peers. Learning to ride a bus could increase the number and variety of places a student can go in the community. What do we know about the most effective ways to provide instruction and support to the student? Reviewing the information on what works and doesn't work can help.

Making Contributions Are there specific community and school roles that relate to the student's preferences, gifts, strengths, and capacities that would allow the student to offer contributions to others that would enhance the student's status and respect? What would it take to support the student to spend more time in those roles? How does the student make contributions to his or her school or community? At what jobs does the student work? Does the student provide volunteer help at school or in the community? Are there any environmental characteristics that contribute negatively to the student's perceived contributions to the community and school? The team members should consider: 1) different schedules to which the student adheres; 2) how people talk about the student; 3) the activities the student engages in that no other, or only other, students with disabilities engage in; and 4) whether people express lowered expectations for the student's achievement of any of the five lifestyle accomplishments.

Community Participation How many people make up the student's social network? Are there any groups (family, friends) where few people are listed? What would it take to increase the number of friends in the student's network? Does the student have friends at school that he or she could also spend time with away from school? What support would be required for this to happen? Who are the student's strongest allies, advocates, friends? Are there people who were once important to the person with whom he or she has lost contact? What would it take to reestablish contact? Where do people with interests similar to the student's spend time at school? In the commu-

nity? What would it take for the student to spend time in those places? Is there any one in the planning group who could introduce the student to any of those people or places, or does anyone in the planning group know someone who could introduce the student to people with similar interests?

After reviewing what it would take to increase the levels of the five lifestyle accomplishments, the group can focus on what is most important to have happen right now for the student. Are there particular aspects of the student's lifestyle that need to be changed right now? In Maggie's lifestyle plan it became very apparent that she wanted to make more friends, and to do this, she needed to be able to communicate with them, and they with her. Her longer-range vision also included social relationships and communicating as well as mobility in the community and greater control over her life experiences. People in the planning group all agreed that they would work toward helping Maggie develop her communication skills and meet new people her own age.

For other individuals, it may be most important to find a good job or find an activity in which they may contribute to their community. Sometimes it becomes apparent in the planning meeting that what is most important for a person is to make new connections with people who could become part of his or her social network. When the only people attending a lifestyle planning meeting are service providers, and there is no one who really knows the person and speaks strongly for his or her interests, it is imperative that the focus become one of supporting the person to develop relationships with new people who will become involved and committed. Conducting a lifestyle planning meeting when no one present is an ally or advocate for the individual will not yield the results necessary to change his or her life for the better.

While the group should focus on the areas

of lifestyle most important to address right away, they should not be afraid to start small. For example, a young man with deaf-blindness, Julian, had very limited contacts with other students in his school, where he attended a self-contained classroom. People in the planning group decided it was important for him to meet other students and to be seen as making a contribution to the school community. After some thought, the group came up with the idea for Julian to work at the popcorn stand in the school. As students often came by to get popcorn between classes and during breaks they figured it was a good way for Julian to meet people. Julian had very limited formal language skills and was somewhat hesitant to touch or be touched by strangers. At first he was only handing the popcorn bags to customers. After he became more comfortable, he started taking their money and handing over the change. Some students became interested in knowing how to greet Julian, which led to them being able to use some signs to say hello. While Julian kept working at the popcorn stand, the planning group worked on getting him enrolled in his home school. When they finally succeeded, Julian's last day at his old school was one of bittersweet endings and beginnings. He was now leaving behind a number of students he had come to know through his work at the stand, but he was also moving on to meet new friends at the school in his neighborhood.

FOLLOW-UP MEETINGS

Once the planning group gets started they usually come back together every 6 weeks or so to review progress. They talk about what they tried since the last meeting and whether it worked or if a new strategy is needed. They spend time celebrating their small successes as well as their big ones. They continue to talk about the student's future vision and how it changes over time. They remember these words:

> Vision can be chosen, but it cannot be coerced. People don't finish with a vision; rather, as they work toward it, their appreciation of its meaning deepens and the words and symbols that communicate it grow richer and clearer. (O'Brien, 1990, p. 5)

REFERENCES

Bales, R.F., & Borgatta, E.F. (1955). Size of group as a factor in the interaction profile. In A.P. Hare, E.F. Borgatta, & R.F. Bales (Eds.), *Small groups: Studies in social interaction* (pp. 396–413). New York: Knopf.

Bellamy, G.T., Newton, J.S., LeBaron, N., & Horner, R.H. (1990). Quality of life and lifestyle outcomes: A challenge for residential services. In R.L. Schlock (Ed.), *Quality of life: Perspectives and issues* (pp. 127–137). Washington, DC: American Association on Mental Retardation.

Bradley, V.J., & Knoll, J. (1990). *Shifting paradigms in services to people with developmental disabilities.* Cambridge, MA: Human Services Research Institute.

Carr, E.G., & Durand, M.V. (1985). The social-communicative basis of severe behavior problems in children. In S. Reiss & R. Bootzin (Eds.), *Theoretical issues in behavior therapy* (pp. 219–254). New York: Academic Press.

Connecticut Department of Mental Retardation. (1986, February). *Mission statement.* Hartford, CT: Author.

Cousins, N. (1976, December). Anatomy of an illness (as perceived by the patient). *The New England Journal of Medicine,* 1458–1463.

Emerson, E.B. (1985). Evaluating the impact of deinstitutionalization on the lives of mentally retarded people. *American Journal of Mental Deficiency, 90,* 277–288.

Forest, M. (1989). *It's about relationships.* Toronto, Ontario, Canada: Frontier College Press.

Giangreco, M.F., Cloninger, C.J., & Iverson, V.S. (1993). *Choosing options and accommodations for children (COACH): A guide to planning inclusive education.* Baltimore: Paul H. Brookes Publishing Co.

Gilbert, T.F. (1978). *Human competence: Engineer-*

ing worthy performance. New York: McGraw-Hill.

Horner, R.H. (1991). The future of applied behavior analysis for people with severe disabilities: Commentary II. In L.H. Meyer, C.A. Peck, & L. Brown (Eds.), *Critical issues in the lives of people with severe disabilities* (pp. 607–612). Baltimore: Paul H. Brookes Publishing Co.

Horner, R.H., Aaron, G.L., Ritchie, K.K., Stoner, S.K., & Twain, K.R. (1986). *Comparison of the social networks of adults with and without developmental disabilities.* Unpublished manuscript, University of Oregon, Specialized Training Program, Eugene.

Lakin, K.C., & Bruininks, R.H. (1985). Contemporary services for handicapped children and youth. In R.H. Bruininks & K.C. Lakin (Eds.), *Living and learning in the least restrictive environment* (pp. 3–22). Baltimore: Paul H. Brookes Publishing Co.

Lyle-O'Brien, C. (1992). *To boldly go.* Georgia Governors Council on Developmental Disabilities.

Martinez, C. (1988, April). Untitled paper presented at the Quality of Life Conference, Washington, DC.

Mount, B. (1992). *Person-centered planning.* New York: Graphic Futures.

Mount, B., Beeman, P., & Ducharme, G. (1988). *What are we learning about circles of support?* Manchester, CT: Communitas.

Mount, B., & Zwernik, K. (1988). *It's never too early: It's never too late.* St. Paul, MN: Metropolitan Council.

O'Brien, J. (1987). A guide to lifestyle planning: Using *The Activities Catalog* to integrate services and natural supports. In B. Wilcox & G.T. Bellamy, *A comprehensive guide to The Activities Catalog: An alternative curriculum for youth and adults with severe disabilities* (pp. 175–189). Baltimore: Paul H. Brookes Publishing Co.

O'Brien, J. (1990). *What's worth working for: Leadership strategies to improve the quality of services for people with severe disabilities.* Lithonia, GA: Responsive Systems Associates.

O'Brien, J., & Mount, B. (1991). Telling new stories: The search for capacity among people with severe handicaps. In L.H. Meyer, C.A. Peck, & L. Brown (Eds.), *Critical issues in the lives of people with severe disabilities* (pp. 89–92). Baltimore: Paul H. Brookes Publishing Co.

People First of Washington, King County People First. (1985). *What we want from residential programs.* Unpublished manuscript.

Rappaport, J. (1981). In praise of paradox: A social policy of empowerment over prevention. *American Journal of Community Psychology, 9,* 1–25.

Romer, L.T., Haring, N.G., Graham, S.L., Mace, C., & Rado, E. (1993). *Innovations project final report* (Grant No. H086F90003). Washington, DC: U.S. Department of Education.

Schwartz, D.B. (1992). *Crossing the river.* Boston: Brookline Books.

Schwartz, I.S., & Baer, D.M. (1991). Social validity assessments: Is current practice state of the art? *Journal of Applied Behavior Analysis, 24,* 189–204.

Shaw, G.B. (1930). Back to Methuselah. *Bernard Shaw plays (vol. 16).* New York: William H. Wise.

Singer, G.H.S., & Irvin, L.K. (Eds.). (1989). *Support for caregiving families: Enabling positive adaptation to disability.* Baltimore: Paul H. Brookes Publishing Co.

Smull, M.W., & Bellamy, G.T. (1991). Community services for adults with disabilities. In L.H. Meyer, C.A. Peck, & L. Brown (Eds.), *Critical issues in the lives of people with severe disabilities* (pp. 527–536). Baltimore: Paul H. Brookes Publishing Co.

Starhawk. (1988). *Dreaming the dark.* Boston: Beacon Press.

Taylor, S.J. (1988). Caught in the continuum: A critical analysis of the principle of the least restrictive environment. *Journal of The Association for Persons with Severe Handicaps, 13,* 28–40.

Vandercook, T., York, J., & Forest, M. (1989). The McGill action planning system (MAPS): A strategy for building the vision. *Journal of The Association for Persons with Severe Handicaps, 14,* 205–215.

Voeltz, L.M., & Evans, I.M. (1983). Educational validity: Procedures to evaluate outcomes in programs for severely handicapped learners. *Journal of The Association for Persons with Severe Handicaps, 8,* 3–15.

Washington State Division of Developmental Disabilities. (1988). *Residential services guidelines.* Olympia, WA: Author.

Weick, A. (1983). Issues in overturning a medical model of social work practice. *Social Work,* 467–471.

Wolfensberger, W., & Glenn, L. (1975). *PASS 3.* Toronto, Ontario, Canada: National Institute on Mental Retardation.

Wolfensberger, W., & Thomas, S. (1983). *PASSING: Program analysis of service systems implementing normalization goals.* Toronto, Ontario, Canada: National Institute on Mental Retardation.

Using Social-Validity Assessments to Identify Meaningful Outcomes for Students with Deaf-Blindness

Ilene S. Schwartz _____

"Validity refers to the extent to which a test measures what its authors or users claim it measures. Specifically, test validity concerns the appropriateness of the inferences that can be made on the basis of test results" (Salvia & Ysseldyke, 1991, p. 145). Although the notion of validity (i.e., are we measuring what we say we are measuring, and are we measuring it well?) is important in any educational setting, the traditional methods of conceptualizing, evaluating, and interpreting evidence of validity are not appropriate when applied to students with deaf-blindness or other severe disabilities. The traditional methods of test validation are designed to be used on populations that are assumed to be homogeneous. These methods depend on a representative sample of persons on which to establish validity.

Although educators in deaf-blind education are also interested in issues of validity, traditional validation techniques are not useful in their research or practice. A defining characteristic of special education is celebrating the uniqueness of the students and their families. Relying on validation techniques that eschew the heterogeneity of students in special education is both inappropriate and nonfunctional. Thus, when working with students with deaf-blindness and their families, educators are faced with a dual challenge: 1) identifying what skills, outcomes, and behaviors should be measured, and 2) developing measurement systems that will provide reliable, meaningful, and valid information.

The concept of social validity is very useful to researchers, practitioners, and consumers in meeting this challenge. The purpose of social-validity assessment is to involve the consumers in evaluation of the program, particularly those consumers who are most directly affected. The "program" in this sense includes selecting goals, instructional

The author would like to thank Mary Martin, Susan Janko, and Stacey Glantz for their input on an earlier version of this chapter. Preparation of this chapter was supported in part by U.S. Department of Education Grant No. H023C20212 and Cooperative Agreement No. H086A20003. The content and opinions expressed herein do not necessarily reflect the position or policy of the U.S. Department of Education, and no official endorsement should be inferred.

strategies, location of the instruction, and desired outcomes. (Kazdin, 1977; Schwartz & Baer, 1991; Wolf, 1978). Similar to traditional methods of validation, social-validity assessments do not measure effectiveness. Instead, social-validity assessments measure how the program and its outcomes are *perceived* by people other than the program planners. In a dramatic departure from traditional concepts of validity, measures of social validity assess consumer satisfaction at the level of the individual program participant. Social-validity assessments are not designed to evaluate the acceptability of programming for a representative sample of students, rather they are intended to elicit feedback on a specific intervention for a particular individual in a prescribed context.

Social-validity assessments further differ from the traditional view of validation in that they offer an interactive method of program evaluation. Social-validity assessments consist of at least two essential parts: 1) canvasing consumers and 2) responding to consumer feedback by either maintaining satisfactory elements of the program or changing those elements that are unsatisfactory (Schwartz & Baer, 1991). Failure to implement either part of this process invalidates the procedures and changes the role of consumer from partner to disempowered informant. The purpose of this chapter is to define the concepts of meaningful outcomes and social validity, describe how social-validity assessments can be used to identify and achieve meaningful outcomes and goals, and to outline the methodology currently available to researchers and practitioners working toward improving outcomes for students with deaf-blindness and other significant disabilities.

DEFINING MEANINGFUL OUTCOMES

In the two decades since the passage of Public Law 94-142 (Education for all Handi-

capped Children Act of 1975) and the implementation of public education for all students with disabilities, the field of special education has demonstrated that people with severe disabilities can benefit greatly from these services; in fact, many of these students have exceeded all expectations. Our success in some arenas has been mitigated by our failure to create educational interventions that have a meaningful impact on the lifestyles of people with severe disabilities (Horner, Dunlap, & Koegel, 1988). This realization—that the technical effectiveness of an instructional strategy to teach a specific skill in a specific context was not sufficient to have a significant impact on the lives of the students and families involved—forced many researchers and practitioners to reframe the questions guiding their work. The question has shifted from asking whether a student with deaf-blindness can learn within the context of a public school, to asking what are the outcomes that a student with deaf-blindness must achieve within the context of a public school to affect his or her life in a meaningful way. The emphasis has shifted from a focus on specific skills and isolated instructional practices to a focus on meaningful outcomes. This shift in educational priorities has a tremendous impact on the selection of placement, activities, and appropriate instructional strategies for these students.

An essential component of developing an educational program for any student, using meaningful outcomes as a guideline, is the definition and identification of these outcomes. Identification of meaningful outcomes is, and must remain, a highly individualized activity. Meaningful outcomes are those classes of skills and behaviors that have a general effect on the quality of a person's life (Brown & Snell, 1993). It is impossible and presumptuous to assume that anyone but the student and his or her family can identify such outcomes. A shift toward programming focused on meaningful outcomes forces programming to become more family-centered, and therefore more socially valid, and requires professionals to work collaboratively with students and their families.

It is impossible to develop a generic curriculum or checklist of meaningful outcomes that is appropriate for all students with deaf-blindness. These goals must be developed with the student's and family's preferences, dreams, and priorities as the most important guideline. It is important in this activity, as in all family-centered services, to follow the family's lead and to provide as much support as deemed necessary by the family (see chaps. 3 and 17 for discussions of family-centered services). Professionals must respect the family's uniqueness, that is, the important cultural, linguistic, and educational factors, as well as the ability of the student to be an active participant in this process, and how these factors affect the challenging task of identifying meaningful goals and outcomes for a student with deaf-blindness.

This emphasis on a family-centered approach to identifying meaningful outcomes is reflected in the movement towards lifestyle planning for students with deaf-blindness (see chap. 6, this volume, for a review of lifestyle planning). Although students, families, and other connected individuals must identify meaningful outcomes for individual students, some general guidelines may be useful. The following sections identify some common elements of meaningful outcomes.

Accomplishment

Accomplishment, according to *The American Heritage Dictionary* (1985), is "something completed successfully; achievement" (p. 72). Using the idea of accomplishment, rather than isolated skills or behaviors, when determining meaningful outcomes will enable students and families to examine the impact of that outcome on the student's lifestyle (Gilbert, 1978). For example, learning to buy a drink from a vending machine or convenience store is a skill, but demonstrating the ability to *initiate* a trip to the convenience store with the appropriate amount of money to buy a drink when you are thirsty is an accomplishment.

Discussing accomplishments rather than skills encourages people to look at the way those accomplishments are integrated into a student's life and the role they play in his or her life. Viewing outcomes in this manner requires an examination of the opportunities in which the student has to exercise this achievement. In this way, meaningful outcomes selected by the student and family provide feedback regarding elements of a student's environment that must be in place. For example, if a student with deaf-blindness has demonstrated the ability to communicate choices during mealtime as part of a classroom exercise (Gothelf, Crimmins, Mercer, & Finocchiarto, 1993), but is never provided the opportunity to make choices during meals at home, this skill may not be functional or meaningful for the student. If family members are not willing to allow choices during meals, then teaching choice making at mealtimes is a meaningless exercise. Team members (i.e., school personnel and family members) must realistically examine the opportunities that exist or can be created in a student's environment before selecting target goals.

Social Importance

Meaningful outcomes must be of social importance to the student and his or her family; these skills must have an influence on the student's quality of life. Social importance needs to be judged by the student's family and immediate community, and membership in the community must be determined by the student and his or her family. For an outcome to be socially important, the student must have access and opportunity to practice and demonstrate the desired outcomes in contexts that are meaningful to the student, family, and immediate community. Baer, Wolf, and Risley (1987) illustrate the importance of this concept and the essential role of the social validation process in determining meaningful outcomes:

> We may have taught many social skills without examining whether they actually furthered the subject's social life; many courtesy skills without examining whether anyone actually noticed or cared; many safety skills without examining whether the subject was actually safer thereafter; many language skills without measuring whether the subject actually used them to interact differently than before; many on-task skills without measuring the actual value of those tasks; and in general, many survival skills without examining the subject's actual subsequent survival. (p. 322)

Functionality

Meaningful outcomes are functional for students. Opportunities to use functional skills occur regularly in the student's daily routine; occur naturally in school, home, and community settings; and help students gain access to a wider range of environments (Brown et al., 1979; Haring, 1988). Functional outcomes enable students to be more independent in inclusive environments. Although it is relatively common to identify self-care skills as functional skills, it is also important to consider functional skills in other domains including recreational (e.g., independent leisure skills), social-communicative (e.g., choice-making, expressing wants and needs), and community skills (e.g., independent movement between and within settings).

Chronological Age Appropriateness

When identifying meaningful outcomes for students with deaf-blindness, the issues of chronological age and individual appropriateness must be considered (Bredekamp, 1987;

Brown et al., 1979; Wehman & Schleien, 1980). With what types of activities are the student's typically developing peers involved? Where do they go after school? These are the activities and settings that should be considered when determining programs for students with disabilities. It is also important to consider the student's preferences when identifying age-appropriate activities. It is obvious that not all 16-year-olds like the same music, read the same books, or cheer for the same sport teams. Therefore, it is inappropriate to assume that a 16-year-old with deaf-blindness would not have his or her own individual preferences.

Family Uniqueness

In determining meaningful goals and outcomes, family uniqueness plays an essential role. Each family represents a unique blend of culture and tradition. These characteristics influence priorities and preferences, so it is important that students and families identify their own community. It is the norms and customs of this particular community that must be considered when identifying target goals, and it is the standards of this community that must be respected in developing students' educational plans. For example, some families place a great emphasis on independence, while others may not think that it is appropriate to encourage children to be too independent. The value that the individual family places on independence for all their children must be considered when identifying target goals and defining meaningful outcomes. Despite the growing respect for diversity in society at large and in education, the issue of respecting the family uniqueness of students with deaf-blindness and other severe disabilities has been largely ignored by special educators (Harry et al., in press).

All five of the elements of meaningful outcomes—accomplishment, social importance, functionality, chronological age appropriateness, and interest and importance to the student and his or her family—emphasize the importance of individuality and goodness of fit between the student and the outcome. It is impossible to identify meaningful goals and outcomes with the information that is usually generated through a traditional assessment and individualized education program (IEP) process. In addition to some of the more traditional domain-specific information, information about the student's lifestyle, wishes, dreams, and aspirations needs to be gathered. As students and families are the best source of this information, a new challenge to professionals is to support the active and meaningful involvement of families in identification and application of this information to identify meaningful outcomes for each individual student.

IDENTIFYING MEANINGFUL OUTCOMES

What to ask, whom to ask, and how to ask the questions necessary for obtaining the most reliable and useful information about a particular student are key concerns in identifying meaningful outcomes and planning corresponding education programs for students with deaf-blindness. Methodology from social-validity assessments can be of great assistance in addressing the first two issues. Generally, questions are asked regarding the importance and relevance of the goals; the acceptability of the procedures; and the satisfaction with the outcomes, including those outcomes that are short-term and long-term, intended and unintended (Wolf, 1978). By initiating the dialogue between the family and professionals, questions concerning current goals, procedures, and outcomes can serve as a solid basis for beginning to identify more meaningful outcomes and corresponding goals.

The issue of when these questions should be asked must also be addressed. The questions proposed by Wolf (1978) ask consumers about the goals of a program. In order for that information to impact the program of a specific student, information must be gathered before, during, and after program implementation. Input from students and families must be gathered prior to the identification of goals, and this information must influence the goal selection process. This dynamic use of social-validity assessments is a departure from their traditional use (Schwartz & Baer, 1991), but is an appropriate technique to meet the challenge of identifying meaningful goals and outcomes.

Who Should Participate in the Process?

The social-validity assessment methodology can also provide suggestions regarding whom to include in identifying and prioritizing goals and objectives for students with deaf-blindness. There is general consensus that the members of the student's family and community should be included in the goals identification process, but the more difficult questions are how to identify these people in a broadly inclusive manner, and how to identify and include those people who control the viability (i.e., the social validity) of the program. The important goal when identifying people to participate in the social-validity process is to include people who are interested and/or who can affect the viability or survival of a program. Therefore when talking about an inclusive school program, it is essential to include school administration representatives because whether or not they are interested in a particular student with deaf-blindness, their actions may directly affect his or her school program. Schwartz and Baer (1991) recommend that consumers from the following four groups be represented in any social-validity assessment.

Direct Consumers   Direct consumers of an intervention are the people who are the target of that intervention. In this case, the student with deaf-blindness is the direct consumer of services. Therefore, the student should be involved with discussions about goals and outcomes as much as he or she is able.

Indirect Consumers   Indirect consumers are those people who choose a program for someone else (e.g., parents are indirect consumers of their child's school program) and/or are strongly affected by the outcome of the program. This category usually includes family members and friends. It is extremely important that the student and family identify the people in this category. Although professionals can provide suggestions and feedback, and may even be members of this category if identified as such by the family, it is ultimately the family who defines the membership of this category.

Members of the Immediate Community
These individuals are people who interact with the direct and indirect consumers on a regular basis, but the effect of the program on their lives is diffuse. Members of this group might include typically developing students who attend the same school as the child with deaf-blindness, but are not really connected to the student; the parents of these typically developing students; other teachers in the school; patrons at the YMCA where the student with deaf-blindness swims; and the bus driver on the public bus route used by the student with deaf-blindness to travel in the community.

Members of the Extended Community   The extended community includes people who probably do not know or interact with the student with deaf-blindness, but who live in the same community. These people may influence the viability of programs by writing letters to the newspaper, school officials, or legislators. For example, when Al Shanker,

President of the American Federation of Teachers, takes out a paid advertisement in *The New York Times* to discuss the evils of inclusive education, he is affecting, whether directly or indirectly, the viability and survival of many inclusive education programs around the country. Although this group of consumers is the most difficult to identify and is almost always excluded from the process, they may be able to provide some of the most valuable information regarding program components that facilitate or impede program viability and survival.

Clearly, it is difficult, if not impossible, to include members from all of these categories when identifying meaningful outcomes or evaluating the social validity of education programs for students with deaf-blindness. The point of introducing these broad categories is to reinforce the idea that all students are educated within a social context, and many social aspects are often overlooked that can affect the implementation of the education program within its social context. The range of consumers also raises the issue of differential roles for participants. For example, the student, family members, and close friends may be actively involved in all parts of the process of identifying priorities and objectives, but other participants (e.g., agency representatives) may have a more limited role, such as brainstorming about the availability of different resources. The object is to include many people in the process and to respect the input of all participants. Although not all participants may agree, the multiple perspectives gathered may provide invaluable insight for developing programs that are viable and sustainable.

Professionals play an important role in collecting this information. Although it is essential that the student and family identify community members, it is incumbent upon the professional to support families in this process. The goal of this collaboration between the family and the professional should be to collect the type of information that will enable them to develop the best program possible for the student with deaf-blindness. As in all relationships, the exact role of the participants must be negotiated on an individual basis.

How Should the Information Be Collected?

After making decisions about what to ask and whom to ask, the really difficult issue of how to gather information in a credible, friendly, and efficient manner must be resolved. There is no one ideal technique for collecting these types of data. The selection of data collection/information gathering techniques must be based on a match among the people gathering the data, the purpose for which the data will be used, and the people providing the information. Most important, the information must be collected in a way that allows team members to use the data effectively. The team member collecting the information should have clear questions at the beginning of the social-validity assessment, and data should be collected, either qualitative, quantitative, or both, that allows those questions to be answered. The following sections provide some examples of information resources and data collection techniques.

Research Literature   One place to begin to look for the types of outcomes that may be considered meaningful for students with deaf-blindness and other severe disabilities in inclusive settings is in the research literature. For example, based on the results of ethnographic classroom observation over the course of 1 year for 20 students with severe disabilities in inclusive classrooms, Peck, Gallucci, Schwartz, and Staub (1993) identified three major categories of outcomes for these students: 1) development, 2) relationships, and 3) membership. Outcomes in

the area of development included academics, social-communication skills, and learning to participate in a group activity. Outcomes in the area of relationships included being a helper; receiving help; and experiencing friendship, play/companionship, nurturance, conflict, and protection. Outcomes in the area of membership included having a role in small groups (both social and academic), having a role in the classroom, and having a role in extracurricular activities. Students and families might want to examine the categories identified by Peck et al. when attempting to identify their own program goals.

Appropriate Comparison Groups   The strategy of observing what other children do who are the same age as the target student is also very informative. This is especially useful if it is difficult for families to imagine the types of activities that children the same age as their child engage in after school, or the kinds of jobs held by adults with deaf-blindness. The essential component of using this strategy is to find appropriate comparison groups. More than one comparison group may be observed in different contexts. For example, for more short-term planning it may be very important to identify what typically developing peers are doing after school and on weekends; however, for long-term planning, living options and job opportunities for adults with deaf-blindness should also be explored. The purpose of using comparison groups is not to "match to sample," but rather to expand the universe of possibilities and opportunities for the student throughout his or her lifetime.

Formal Assessment Tools   As providing inclusive educational services for students with deaf-blindness and other severe disabilities becomes more commonplace, this shift in philosophy and practice will be supported by more appropriate assessment and curricular materials. (See Brown & Snell, 1993, for a description of appropriate assessment tools.) One commercially available assessment instrument designed for planning programs in inclusive settings is *Choosing Options and Accommodations for Children (COACH): A Guide to Planning Inclusive Education* (Giangreco, Cloninger, & Iverson, 1992). A strong point of the COACH assessment is that it requires the family to first identify broad, meaningful goals and outcomes for their child; the rest of the assessment and program planning activities are then based on the priorities the family has identified. This assessment suggests broad goals and outcomes and then asks the family to prioritize these areas. A drawback to this type of approach is that some families may find the predetermined goals constraining. Many other families, however, may find the support of the predetermined categories very helpful.

Lifestyle Planning Activities   Another method used to involve the student, family, and members of the community in identifying meaningful goals and outcomes is lifestyle planning (e.g., O'Brien, 1987; Vandercook, York, & Forest, 1989; see also chap. 6, this volume). Lifestyle planning is more comprehensive than identifying meaningful goals and outcomes, but the identification and prioritization of these goals build the foundation of all future planning.

In summary, these four options for gathering information involve students, family members, and other interested parties at different levels. These options can be used together, or in conjunction with other techniques. When determining which of these strategies to use, it is important to look for the goodness of fit among the technique, the person collecting the information, and the people providing the information. There is no right way to proceed; it is a matter of finding a way that is acceptable (i.e., socially valid) to all the members of the team.

FUTURE DIRECTIONS

Throughout this chapter, the terms *meaningful outcomes* and *social-validity assessments* have been used almost interchangeably. Meaningful outcomes, by definition, must be agreed upon using some form of a social-validity assessment process. The purpose of social-validity assessments is to evaluate the acceptability and meaningfulness of an intervention to the people that it most directly affects. Clearly it is only these people (i.e., students, families, and other closely connected persons) who are in the position to identify a meaningful outcome. Researchers and practitioners must work with individuals with deaf-blindness to provide support when necessary, feedback when asked, and most important, to provide the expertise to translate these meaningful outcomes into relevant goals and effective education programs.

The social-validity literature from applied behavior analysis (e.g., Baer, 1986, 1987, 1988; Fawcett, 1991; Fuqua & Schwade, 1986; Hawkins, 1991; Kazdin, 1977; Schwartz & Baer, 1991; Winett, Moore, & Anderson, 1991; Wolf, 1978) provides some assistance in developing methods to identify and validate meaningful outcomes for students with deaf-blindness. Identifying and agreeing upon meaningful goals and outcomes, however, does not mean that an education program is effective. Like social-validity assessments, development of meaningful outcomes looks at how education programs make sense to consumers in the social realm, they *do not* assess (nor are they meant to assess) the effectiveness of any specific intervention or general program. This is an important distinction, for just as applied behavior analysts have had to learn how to integrate the results of social-validity assessments with the results of primary dependent variables that assess the effectiveness of an intervention, practitioners, researchers, and consumers of educational services for students with deaf-blindness must always consider the effectiveness of instructional programs in their search for meaning. Clearly the two are not mutually exclusive, but neither does meaningfulness necessarily guarantee effectiveness. The goal must be to create education programs that provide effective instruction in normalized settings that lead to optimal, meaningful outcomes for *all* students.

The movement toward using meaningful outcomes to guide the development of education programs for students with deaf-blindness and other severe disabilities (e.g.,

Brown & Snell, 1993; Giangreco et al., 1993; Horner et al., 1988; Meyer, 1991; O'Brien, 1987; Vandercook et al., 1989) can provide behavior analysts with an excellent applied example of social-validity assessments at work. This movement provides an outstanding lesson in how meaningful outcomes/ social validity must be assessed prescriptively and must be planned for from the outset of any educational plan. Identification of meaningful outcomes must begin early, and this process must be continued regularly if it is to have a proactive, rather than a reactive, effect on a student's program. The "train and hope" (cf., Stokes & Baer, 1977) method of achieving meaningful outcomes must no longer be used.

REFERENCES

The American Heritage Dictionary (2nd College Ed.). (1985). Boston: Houghton Mifflin.

Baer, D.M. (1986). In application, frequency is not the only estimate of the probability of behavioral units. In T. Thompson & M.D. Zeiler (Eds.), *Analysis and integration of behavioral units* (pp. 117–136). Hillsdale, NJ: Erlbaum.

Baer, D.M. (1987, March). *A behavioral-analytic query into early intervention.* Paper presented at the Banff International Conference on Behavioral Science, Banff, Canada.

Baer, D.M. (1988). If you know why you're changing a behavior, you'll know when you've changed it enough. *Behavioral Assessment, 10,* 219–223.

Baer, D.M., Wolf, M.M., & Risley, T.R. (1987). Some still-current dimensions of applied behavior analysis. *Journal of Applied Behavior Analysis, 20,* 313–327.

Bredekamp, S. (Ed.). (1987). *Developmentally appropriate practice in early childhood practice in early childhood programs serving children from birth through age 8.* Washington, DC: National Association for the Education of Young Children.

Brown, F., & Snell, M.E. (1993). Meaningful assessment. In M.E. Snell (Ed.), *Instruction of students with severe disabilities* (4th ed.) (pp. 61–98).

New York: Merrill.

Brown, L., Branston, M., Hamre-Nietupski, S., Pumpiam, I., Certo, N., & Gruenewald, L. (1979). A strategy for developing chronological age appropriate and functional curricular content for severely handicapped adolescents and young adults. *Journal of Special Education, 13*(1), 81–90.

Brown, L., Branston, M., Hamre-Nietupski, S., Pumpiam, I., Certo, N., & Gruenewald, L. (1979). A strategy for developing chronological age appropriate and functional curricular content for severely handicapped adolescents and young adults. *Journal of Special Education, 13*(1), 81–90.

Education for All Handicapped Children Act of 1975, PL 94-142. (August 23, 1977). Title 20, U.S.C. §1401 et seq: *U.S. Statutes at Large, 89,* 773–796.

Fawcett, S. (1991). Social validity: A note of methodology. *Journal of Applied Behavior Analysis, 24,* 235–240.

Fuqua, R.W., & Schwade, J. (1986). Social validation of applied behavioral research: A selective review and critique. In A. Poling & R.W. Fuqua (Eds.), *Research methods in applied behavior analysis: Issues and advances* (pp. 265–292). New York: Plenum.

Giangreco, M.F., Cloninger, C.J., & Iverson, V.S. (1993). *Choosing options and accommodations for children (COACH): A guide to planning inclusive education.* Baltimore: Paul H. Brookes Publishing Co.

Gothelf, C.R., Crimmins, D.B., Mercer, C.A., & Finocchiarto, P.A. (1993). Teaching students who are deaf-blind and cognitively disabled to effectively communicate choices during mealtime. *Deaf-Blind Perspectives, 1*(1), 6–8.

Haring, N.G. (Ed.). (1988). *Generalization for students with severe handicaps: Strategies and solutions.* Seattle: University of Washington Press.

Harry, B., Grenot-Scheyer, M., Smith-Lewis, M., Park, H., Xin, F., & Schwartz, I.S. (in press). Developing culturally inclusive services for individuals with severe disabilities. *Journal of The Association for Persons with Severe Handicaps.*

Hawkins, R. (1991). Is social validity what we are interested in? Argument for a functional approach. *Journal of Applied Behavior Analysis, 24,* 205–214.

Horner, R., Dunlap, G., & Koegel, R.L. (Eds.). (1988). *Generalization and maintenance: Life-style changes in applied settings.* Baltimore: Paul H. Brookes Publishing Co.

Kazdin, A.E. (1977). Assessing the clinical or applied importance of behavior change through social validation. *Behavior Modification, 1,* 427–452.

Meyer, L.H. (1991). Why meaningful outcomes? *Journal of Special Education, 25,* 287–290.

O'Brien, J. (1987). A guide to life-style planning: Using *The Activities Catalog* to integrate services and natural supports. In B. Wilcox & G.T. Bellamy (Eds.), *A comprehensive guide to The Activities Catalog: An alternative curriculum for youth and adults with severe disabilities* (pp. 175–189). Baltimore: Paul H. Brookes Publishing Co.

Peck, C.A., Gallucci, C., Schwartz, I.S., & Staub, D. (1993, November). *The inclusive education research project: A qualitative study of classroom practices affecting outcomes for children.* Paper presented at meeting of The Association for Persons with Severe Handicaps, Chicago.

Salvia, J., & Ysseldyke, J.E. (1991). *Assessment.* Boston: Houghton Mifflin.

Schwartz, I.S., & Baer, D.M. (1991). Social validity assessments: Is current practice state of the art? *Journal of Applied Behavior Analysis, 24,* 189–204.

Stokes, T.F., & Baer, D.M. (1977). An implicit technology of generalization. *Journal of Applied Behavior Analysis, 10,* 349–367.

Vandercook, T., York, J., & Forest, M. (1989). The McGill Action Planning System (MAPS): A strategy for building the vision. *Journal of The Association for Persons with Severe Handicaps, 14,* 205–215.

Wehman, P., & Schleien, S. (1980). Assessment and selection of leisure skills for severely handicapped individuals. *Education and Training of the Mentally Retarded, 15*(1), 50–57.

Winett, R.A., Moore, J.F., & Anderson, E.S. (1991). Extending the concept of social validity: Behavior analysis for disease prevention and health promotion. *Journal of Applied Behavior Analysis, 24,* 215–230.

Wolf, M.M. (1978). Social validity: The case for subjective measurement, or how behavior analysis is finding its heart. *Journal of Applied Behavior Analysis, 11,* 203–214.

Chapter 8

Collaborative Teaming to Support Participation in Inclusive Education Settings

Lyle T. Romer
and Andrew R. Byrne

Professionals from virtually every discipline have recognized for years the advantages of working together in groups. Educators have been apprised of the value of groups in schools for decades (Newman, 1974). In special education, the multidisciplinary team has been a legally required component since the passage of the Education for All Handicapped Children Act of 1975 (PL 94-142), known as the Individuals with Disabilities Education Act (IDEA) since its reauthorization in 1990. Within the past decade, the school restructuring movement has generated considerable support for the team structure as a mechanism for improving educational decision making (Abelson & Woodman, 1983; Friend & Cook, 1992), teacher empowerment (West, 1990), and inclusive practices (Stainback & Stainback, 1990).

The term *collaborative teaming* has been used by educators to refer to the group decision-making process used by teams (John-son & Johnson, 1987; Thousand & Villa, 1992). This chapter is about collaborative teaming and is divided into three sections. The first section contains the authors' synthesized definition of a collaborative team and examines the factors that have both promoted the emergence of collaboration, as well as interfered with its fruition, in North American education over the past 2 decades. The second section is devoted to a presentation of the authors' findings from an innovative project that used collaborative teams to increase the inclusion of students with deaf-blindness in typical education settings. All of the students in this project experienced some degree of developmental disability in addition to their visual and auditory impairments. Findings from this project are discussed as they relate to the knowledge base on collaborative teaming. Throughout this section, the experiences of one team that supported Julian, a student with deaf-blindness and developmental disabilities, are described in

The activity that is the subject of this report was supported in whole or in part by the U.S. Department of Education (Award Nos. H086F90003 and H025F10007). However, the opinions expressed herein do not necessarily reflect the position or policy of the U.S. Department of Education, and no official endorsement by the Department should be inferred.

depth. The third section presents recommendations for the continued use of collaborative teams to support the inclusion of students with deaf-blindness and developmental disabilities.

COLLABORATIVE TEAMING DEFINED

Present-day educators have used the terms *collaboration* and *teams* so widely that the words seem to have attained "buzzword" status. The two words, in fact, may be partly redundant because "teams may be described simply as collaborative work groups" (Friend & Cook, 1992, p. 32). The authors' definition underlies comments throughout this chapter and is based on the collaboration and group decision-making literature (Gray, 1989; Johnson & Johnson, 1987; Wood, Phillips, & Pederson, 1986), as well as the authors' own experiences conducting collaborative work groups. A *collaborative team* is a voluntary group of equal members who:

1. Represent all stakeholders (individuals, groups, or organizations who have an interest or "stake" in the particular issue or set of issues to be addressed)
2. Consider varying aspects of the issues to be addressed by bringing a variety of perspectives to the table
3. Engage in a series of systematic, face-to-face group discussions
4. Use their differences to create more comprehensive appreciation of the issues than any one of them could construct alone
5. Generate jointly agreed-upon strategies that exceed their own limited visions of the possibilities
6. Assume collective ownership of decisions and plans for implementing their strategies

Central to the success of collaborative teams is the concept of *interdependence* and the need to manage effective group discus-

sion. Johnson & Johnson (1987) describe interdependence as "the perception that one is linked with others in a way so that one cannot succeed unless they do" (p. 399). Thousand & Villa refer to it as "a mutual 'we are all in this together' feeling" (1992, p. 76). Gray (1989) urges us to consider the elephant parable to illuminate the importance of interdependence in collaborative teaming. As five people who are blind walk in the forest, they come upon an elephant. The first person touches the animal's tail and proclaims, "Ah, an elephant is like a rope." The next man feels the elephant's leg and exclaims, "No, it is a pillar." The third person rubs the animal's sides and argues, "You are both wrong, this animal is a wide and tall wall." The fourth man, upon feeling the animal's ear, exclaims with irritation, "Come on, everyone, any fool can tell that an elephant is shaped like a large leaf." Imagine the confusion and disbelief of the fifth individual who, after examining the trunk, shakes his head in disgust and says, "Haven't any of you people ever felt a snake before?"

Each individual's point of view in the parable is correct. Yet not until all five viewpoints have been heard is there hope for a common definition of an elephant's appearance. The five individuals are dependent on one another's perceptions of the elephant if they hope to create a common understanding of "elephantness" that goes beyond what their individual perspectives could produce. They have an opportunity to create a more complete understanding, but they need to communicate their unique perceptions without arguing about whose perception is correct and without developing resentments and power battles during the discussion.

EMERGENCE OF COLLABORATION IN NORTH AMERICAN EDUCATION

The call for collaboration has been loud and clear in education during the past 2 decades.

Multidisciplinary teams, child-study teams, cooperative learning, team teaching, parent–professional partnerships, school improvement teams, grade–level teams, and interagency partnerships are all examples of collaborative teams. What accounts for this proliferation of interest in collaborative teaming in education? Two factors seem especially relevant to this question: 1) changing social trends and 2) changing trends in schools toward including diverse groups in decision making.

Changing Trends in Society-at-Large

Futurists such as Alvin Toffler (1970, 1980) have argued that the information explosion of the late 20th century has made it virtually impossible for any one individual to access sufficient information to address the myriad new problems confronting people every day. Such rapid change creates uncertainty, combined with a need for more information from broader viewpoints, both to comprehend the issues and to generate potential solutions. This gives rise to the need for groups of people from various information bases to discuss issues and generate strategies—an ideal opportunity for collaboration.

Gray (1989) suggests that the trend toward rapid societal change produces several incentives to collaborate, including shrinking federal funding for social programs; a growing dissatisfaction with the judicial system for resolving problems; and a blurring of boundaries between business, labor, and government. Accordingly, individuals and organizations are turning to collaborative ventures as a way to address current issues, by means of such methods as employee participation in corporate decision making and quality circles.

Friend and Cook (1992) remind us that when America was founded, "rugged individualism" was important as pioneers moved into uncharted territory to face unknown dangers. However, the original notion of rugged individualism included a reliance on others to help accomplish the necessary tasks for settlement, such as barn raising and field clearing (Bellah, Madsen, Sullivan, Swidler, & Tipton, 1985). As technology developed, American settlers needed to rely upon others less for survival, which ultimately promoted the "lonesome cowboy" myth that seems to underlie much of the Western world's individualism. As the complexity of society increases, the notion of reliance on others is reemerging as individuals are less able to obtain the required information to make decisions or implement tasks. Thus society is being encouraged to "co-labor" once again.

Changing Trends in Educational Decision Making

Two decades ago, PL 94-142 mandated that school professionals use the team structure to assess and plan for the education programs of students with special needs. This legal mandate provided a strong impetus for educators to seek information and opinions from a diverse group of individuals who hold a stake in the educational planning for any given child, beginning with the child's family and many times including the child as well. The school reform movement has provided numerous examples of collaboration in schools. In this movement, "collaborative teams and teaming processes have come to be viewed as vehicles for inventing the solutions that traditional bureaucratic school structures have failed to conceptualize" (Thousand & Villa, 1992, p. 75). Reform efforts have included teacher empowerment through participation in educational decision making and site-based decision making to involve teachers in administrative as well as educational planning (Friend & Cook, 1992; Goodlad, 1984).

The emerging interests in diversity and inclusion offer educators two additional opportunities for collaboration. The need to construct curricula that are sensitive to the changing cultural face of America presents a set of demands that are ideally suited to collaborative teaming. Likewise, the drive toward inclusion of all children in general education presents another opportunity for general and special educators to collaborate with families (Halvorsen, Doering, Farron-Davis, Usilton, & Sailor, 1989). In both cases, people holding diverse viewpoints about educating our children are working together to create solutions that will be very different from those that any one person could discover alone.

OBSTACLES TO COLLABORATION IN THE SCHOOLS

With so many factors working to promote collaboration, why has it not become the norm among school personnel (Thousand & Villa, 1992; Timar, 1989)? There appear to be several obstacles preventing schools from fully embracing collaborative teaming. These obstacles are rooted in three major categories: 1) limited resources available to educators, 2) teachers' professonal socialization toward autonomy, and 3) the natural group phenomenon.

Resource Limitations in Schools

Realistically, teachers are one of the busier professional groups in existence. Finding time to meet beyond allotted instructional time is typically very difficult. The logistical steps involved in collaborative teaming may also be a discouraging factor. Identifying stakeholders, contacting them, encouraging them to participate, identifying meeting times, and securing space—these are only a sampling of steps involved in arranging a meeting. Busy teachers may have so much difficulty in simply arranging the first meeting that they become discouraged about continuing efforts toward initiating collaborative teaming.

Professional Socialization Toward Autonomy

Like many professionals, teachers are trained to become autonomous, expert problem solvers. University-based personnel preparation programs have placed emphasis on teachers becoming the sole authorities in managing their classrooms and directing their students' learning activities. As teachers demonstrate more competence, they are granted increased freedom from close supervision (in many cases, immediately after graduation and certification).

According to Friend and Cook (1992), all educational professionals are trained in the same basic steps of clinical problem solving: 1) assess the situation, 2) construct action plans to address the problem, 3) implement the action plan, 4) evaluate the plan, and 5) alter the plan as needed. These steps are carried out repeatedly and independently, and many teachers tend to ask for consultation only after determining that the problem is beyond their domain and within a consultant's purview. These traditional clinical problem-solving steps become disrupted by the extensive discussion and decision-making process required by collaborative teaming. Teachers considering teaming may feel that they can make decisions alone more effectively, more quickly, and with less aggravation. In this sense, it may appear that many teachers are professionally prepared and encouraged to find collaboration to be an interruption of their responsibilities, as opposed to a valued problem-solving tool.

The Group Phenomenon

As collaborative opportunities present themselves, it may be wise to remember the definition of a camel: "a horse designed by a committee." Groups hold the potential to generate creative solutions, but without concerted focus they have a tendency to produce less effective outcomes than individuals acting alone. Kieffer (1988) labels this tendency "collective incompetence" (p. 53) and argues that all group meetings should be approached with caution.

> Meetings are inherently risky enterprises, mobs in waiting, more susceptible to passions, pieties, persuasion, and manipulation of all kinds and degrees than are the individuals who participate in them. Taken another way, a meeting begins with the same risk of injury as a motor vehicle containing a steering mechanism at each passenger seat. (p. 55)

When a group of people meet, much more occurs than the expression of various viewpoints. Participants bring their respective information and opinions to meetings, but their communications during the course of the meeting interact with others' communications to form a chain of interactions. This chain of interactions is different from the input of any one participant, and it is shared in the memory of all in the form of collective understandings about group goals, decision-making history, and valued and devalued patterns of interaction.

Collective memory influences all future interactions of the group, and some of the tendencies of collective memory influence the future effectiveness of the team. If the team is unsuccessful in addressing these tendencies, then collective memory tends to create collective incompetence or *group think* (Janis, 1972). These tendencies are described by Kieffer (1988) as: 1) cognitive dissonance that occurs when new information contradicts the group's collective memory; 2) dissociation from task (or "spacing out") is found when one or more members of the group think that the rest of the team knows more about the topic under discussion, and therefore they drop out of the discussion even if they feel the specific proposal contains unacceptable elements of risk; 3) lowest common denominator has the tendency to be the result of group compromises simply to avoid conflict; and 4) the "risky shift effect," which describes the group tendency to

make far riskier decisions than they would if they were acting independently.

COMPONENTS OF EFFECTIVE COLLABORATION

Despite the overwhelming tendencies of groups toward collective incompetence, strong potential remains to harness these forces into collective genius. This section focuses on the question: What are the differences between collaborative teams that successfully forge collective genius and those that do not? Many have written about effective teaming, collaboration, and group decision making (Delbecq, Van de Ven, & Gustafson, 1975; Fox, 1987; Gray, 1989; Horowitz, 1970; Johnson & Johnson, 1987; Kraus, 1980; Thousand & Villa, 1992; Wood et al., 1986; Zander, 1982). A common theme runs through these writings—successful teams merge multiple perspectives into one common vision and create solutions with technical correctness and wide acceptability. Team effectiveness varies by how closely the members merge their respective viewpoints into a common vision.

Attaining common vision in and of itself, of course, is neither good nor bad. Yet the force to do so wields enormous influence on a team's collective self-image and future performance. Without careful monitoring by the participants, team discussions might produce an excess of unanimity due to groups' natural movement away from divisiveness and toward closure. This phenomenon has been labeled *group think* by Janis (1972), and it may be seen as an occupational hazard within the collaborative teaming process. Effective decisions cannot occur without common understandings, yet that commonality may be due to the pressures to conform and an unintentional suppression of conflict. Teams that succumb to group think value agreement above all else; many times such teams appear as a "tight ship on the wrong canal." Effective collaborative teams actively counteract group think by encouraging full disclosure and discussion of information that challenges emerging consensus.

Team decision-making procedures are useful gauges of the team's success at promoting full disclosure and discussion. Reilly and Jones (1974) describe six decision-making procedures that vary according to the proportion of team members who voice agreement with the actual decision. Teams can partially prevent group think by monitoring their use of the following decision making procedures: 1) lack of group response, 2) authority rule, 3) minority rule, 4) majority rule, 5) unanimous consent, and 6) consensus. These decision-making procedures are described in Table 1.

USING COLLABORATIVE TEAMS TO SUPPORT STUDENTS WITH DEAF-BLINDNESS

This section examines the findings from the *Innovations Project*[1], a federally funded demonstration project coordinated by the first author of this chapter. Discussed are the experiences of 12 teams, each of which supported efforts to include one student with deaf-blindness in education settings with peers without disabilities. First-person is sometimes used in this section to describe the first author's findings.

From September 1989 through August 1992, the 12 teams received support from two staff for the project who each had over 14 years experience working with students with deaf-blindness. Their support focused on: 1) creating a vision of inclusion for each student; 2) providing on-site technical assistance in goal setting, instructional planning, curricular adaptations, and team building among educational staff and family mem-

bers; 3) providing resource materials to teams; 4) arranging for workshop presentations on topics related to deaf-blindness and inclusion; and 5) arranging for on-site technical assistance from national experts in deaf-blindness. To accomplish these supports, project staff made weekly visits to school sites, attended monthly meetings of each team, and coordinated 2 team inservice days per year.

Demographic Information on Students and Other Team Members

The 12 students who received support from the teams attended seven school districts in the Seattle/Tacoma metropolitan area. Within those districts, they attended nine different schools. Three students attended the same class, and another two students were also classmates. In addition to deaf-blindness, all 12 students also had developmental disabilities to varying degrees. All assessments were carried out within a model that assumed the student had developmental disabilities. The reader should be aware that such an assessment approach with students with deaf-blindness can lead to errors of measurement due to the extreme difficulty in using traditional testing instruments. Table 2 summarizes the ages and characteristics of the students in the project.

Team membership was intended to represent all of the people affected by the inclusion of the student with deaf-blindness. Teams included:

- The student
- Family members
- Teachers (special and general education)
- Related services personnel (occupational, physical, and speech and language therapists; school psychologists; and school nurse)

[1]U.S. Department of Education Grant No. H086F90003.

Table 1. Group decision-making procedures

Lack of group response   This procedure involves the leader posing a decision and asking, "Any objections? No? Okay, done. Let's move on." While no objections might imply agreement by all, it is more likely to reflect suppression of conflict or lack of attention by members.

Authority rule   In effect, authority rule involves the leader saying, "We will do it my way." The acceptability of the decision to individual members is irrelevant during this decision-making process, although members are considerably less likely to provide support during the implementation of decisions made in this way.

Minority rule   In the authors' experience with work groups, minority rule is the procedure most often encountered. It is a dangerous decision-making procedure because it can create the illusion of consensus. A subgroup of participants actually carry the discussion with the remainder of the team being passively present. These discussions many times yield decisions that all *active* participants either support or can live with, leaving the impression of unanimity or consensus. However it is more likely to reflect incomplete disclosure and discussion by silent members.

Majority rule   A simple majority of 51% may be the decision rule, or teams may agree on higher percentages. The advantage of majority rule is its ease and clarity of implementation. Most everyone understands voting procedures. The disadvantage, of course, is that dissatisfied minority opinions often undermine the implementation of the decision or of future team decision-making success.

Unanimous consent   If literally every team member voices honest agreement, then unanimity has been achieved. Teams that require unanimous consent on decisions are more at risk for succumbing to groupthink, as the strong pressures to conform and to suppress conflicting opinions come into play. When everyone agrees, effective teams become suspicious and seek more disclosure of opinions by members, as a precautionary measure.

Consensus   Represents that status in the team decision-making discussion in which three elements are present:
1. Every member's input has been sought and received during the discussion
2. A high percentage of members voice agreement with the proposed decision
3. All dissenting participants are satisfied that they have had the opportunity to voice their perspectives, and that while they disagree with some parts of the proposed decision, they state their willingness to support the final decision

Adapted from Reilly and Jones (1974).

- School administrators (special education directors and building principals)
- Community service providers (residential and employment support agencies, developmental disability case workers)
- Deaf-blind specialists
- The student's peers

Not all teams were successful in recruiting members from each of these categories. Most notably missing from some teams were school administrators, peers, community service providers, and deaf-blind specialists. While not all the students were at an age where community service providers would be critical to planning for their future, certainly they all could have benefited from the input of deaf-blind specialists and student peers. We have encountered a great deal of fear and confusion (addressed in greater detail later in this chapter) when teachers who have no training in deaf-blindness have a child with these impairments assigned to their classroom. Although all of the teachers described in this chapter had experience working with students with developmental disabilities, none had ever had any training or direct experience with students with deaf-blindness. The fact that each team had a project staffperson assigned to it who was experienced in this area helped to overcome teachers' fears by making up for their lack of technical expertise in deaf-blindness. Without those project staff, it would have been absolutely critical to have another person with experience in the field of deaf-blindness to support the teams to function effectively.

Attendance at Team Meetings

Each team was scheduled to meet once per month during the school year. Meetings averaged approximately 1 hour in duration.

Table 2. Ages and characteristics of students in Innovations Project

Student	Age at 9/92 in years and months	Visual impairments	Hearing impairments	Intellectual assessment[a]	Other disabilities	School placement
JB	4-7	Legally blind	Moderate	Mild	Cerebral palsy; tracheotomy	Self-contained classroom
JV	8-5	Light perception only	Profound	Profound	Cerebral palsy	Self-contained classroom
NG	8-9	Myopia; legally blind	Moderate	Moderate	Down syndrome	Self-contained classroom
JL	9-10	Legally blind	Moderate	Moderate	CHARGE association syndrome	Self-contained classroom
FK	10-3	Light perception only	Moderate	Severe	None	Self-contained classroom
SR	10-7	Totally blind one eye; legally blind other	Moderate	Moderate	Cerebral palsy	Self-contained classroom
SU	11-0	Anopthalmic	Moderate	Severe	CHARGE association syndrome	Self-contained classroom
CP	11-8	Legally blind	Moderate	Moderate	None	Self-contained classroom
WC	12-5	Legally blind	Mild	Moderate	CHARGE association syndrome	Self-contained classroom
JM	16-0	Legally blind	Severe/profound	Severe	Cleft palate; trisomy 13	Self-contained classroom
JT	16-7	Light perception only	Moderate	Severe/profound	Cerebral palsy	Self-contained classroom
AR	17-4	Totally blind	Profound	Severe	Mild cerebral palsy	Neighborhood school, full inclusion

[a]These descriptions of intellectual assessment were taken directly from the school records of the students in the project.

During the meetings, goals and objectives set for the student by the team were reviewed, and modifications to those plans were discussed if deemed appropriate. (Teams used the procedures described in chap. 6 of this volume.) As the initial goals and objectives for the students were met, the team formulated new ones, along with action plans to support the student's achievement of the new goals. Minutes of the meetings were kept by members on a rotating basis; these minutes formed the basis of discussion at the next meeting. Team members also had frequent contact with one another between meetings and often had informal discussions during those times. Table 3 shows the makeup of each of the teams and the average percentage of total attendance at team meetings. Table 4 depicts the average attendance of team members by category of involvement with the student.

Table 3 reveals total average attendance at team meetings was 63%. Review of Table 4 indicates that parents and special education teachers showed the highest attendance at team meetings, followed closely by general educators. It is noteworthy that the teams with the best attendance were, for the most part, those with five to seven members, which are the optimal numbers cited for team membership by Bales and Borgatta (1955). Higher numbers of members often seemed to result in lower overall rates of attendance. Notable too is the fact that teams with the most related services personnel and peers had attendance in the 60%–67% range due, in part, to those two categories of team members showing lower rates of attendance as a group. Although it may be expected that meetings held in the special education classroom (where most meetings in this project did occur) would draw attendance from special education staff, it is very heartening to note that general educators were also able to attend at a 65% rate. Given

that general educators had many and varied responsibilities for other children, their dedication to attending meetings revealed a commitment to having children with deaf-blindness participate in their classes.

Members' Perspectives on the Team Process

The remainder of this section discusses the perspectives offered by team members on their experiences and their views on supporting students with deaf-blindness in typical education settings. Individual interviews were conducted with 43 team members between October 1991 and February 1992. Of the 43 team members interviewed, 9 were parents, 9 were related services staff, 13 were special education classroom staff, 5 were general educators, 1 was an administrator and 6 were peers. The total of 43 represents 52% of the team members listed in Table 2.

Interviews lasted approximately 30–45 minutes and were conducted, for the most part, at the student's school. The interviews were semi-structured and were guided by questions asked by a graduate student in special education who served as a project staff member. She engaged the interviewee in conversation based on questions related to how the team formed, how it conducted its work, its effectiveness, what worked well, what needed improvement, and how team decisions were made. She recorded all interviews on a portable tape recorder. Later, all interviews were transcribed verbatim for analysis.

A second major source of information regarding the teams comes from case histories kept by the two project staff who provided team support. In addition to the written case histories, the two staff were also interviewed for approximately 3 hours each to elaborate on their case history recordings. The information gathered from these staff members is best described as coming from participant observers, as these individuals served as

Table 3. Team membership and attendance

Student	Family	Special education staff	General education staff	Related services staff	Deaf-blind specialist	Community service provider	School administrator	Student peers	Total number of team members	Percentage of attendance
JB	1	1	2		1				5	75%
JV	2	2	2						7	71%
JL	1	4	1	1					7	72%
FK	1	1	1	2					8	60%
SR	1	1	2	5					6	62%
SU	2	2		6				2	10	66%
CP	1	2	1					4	8	61%
WC	1	1						1	3	98%
JM	2	2	1			1		1	8	67%
JT	1	3	1	2			1		7	81%
AR	1	3	3	3	1		2		13	60%
Total	14	22	14	19	2	1	3	8	83	63%

Table 4. Meeting attendance by category of involvement

Parents	75% (143/192)
Special education	81% (218/268)
General education	65% (77/118)
Related services	52% (116/223)
Deaf-blind specialist	35% (6/17)
Community service provider	70% (7/10)
Administrator	30% (11/36)
Peers	52% (28/54)

members of the teams for the length of the project. The use of participant observers is a widely recognized method for describing a range of human activities, most notably in the field of ethnography (cf. Edgerton, 1967).

Information provided from team member interviews, the team workshops, and participant observer interviews was analyzed in the same manner. The analysis was completed by the principal investigator and project coordinator of the project. Data were analyzed by the *constant comparative method* (Glaser & Strauss, 1967). In this method the first comment made by an interviewee is placed in a category by itself and labeled with a descriptive term, such as "lack of administrative support." Each subsequent comment is then compared to the first; if judged similar, it is placed into that category; if different, a new category is created. This process continued, with each comment compared to any existing categories, until all comments were assigned to a category. Once the initial categories were filled with all of the comments, any categories that were judged to be highly similar in their focus were combined and relabeled.

Review and subsequent analysis of the data resulted in the identification and elaboration of seven major themes. These themes included:

1. Overcoming fear and building trust
2. Commitment to the team's purpose
3. Positive interdependence among team members

4. Valuing each and every team member
5. Role release
6. Inclusion issues
7. Achieving positive results

The following sections discuss these themes as they relate to team efforts. The experiences of one team in supporting a student named Julian (also described in chap. 6, this volume) are highlighted to further illustrate the team process.

Overcoming Fear and Building Trust

Julian participates in weight training, wood shop, and homemaking classes as part of his high school curriculum. Although Julian has only been at his neighborhood high school a short time, this tall, muscular young man is already making new friends. Girls are particularly interested in talking with him outside class and getting to know him better. All these are normal high school activities for a 17-year-old boy. The major difference is that Julian is the only student without vision and hearing at his school. He communicates with tactile sign language, touch cues, and tactile cue cards, and until recently, attended an out-of-district self-contained classroom for students with severe disabilities. Julian's journey from that setting to his neighborhood high school is a story of fear and confusion, dreams and visions, and experiences that have all paved the way for Julian and left a pathway for other students with severe disabilities.

When Julian's family decided to bring him home from the state residential school to be educated closer to home, the local school district administrator was not sure where to enroll Julian. Until that time, the school district had never enrolled a student with deaf-blindness, and the administrator thought that a class for students with severe disabilities already in place in a neighboring school district seemed like the best option. Professionals at that school, however, were equally confused and reluctant. The communication development specialist stated, "When this lovely lady [Julian's mom] and her son came the very first day, we were fearful . . . we'd never [enrolled] a child like this." Julian's special education teacher told the district director that he wasn't "doing Julian or myself any good by putting us together because I have had no training with students with deaf-blindness." Despite their fears, however, the staff at the school quickly learned through in-service training provided by consultants from the local Educational Service District. These in-services focused on: 1) current "best practices" in inclusive education, 2) the values underlying inclusion and the value of diversity, 3) the increased benefits to students without disabilities, and 4) the increased relevance and functional outcomes of education when it occurs in inclusive settings.

Also at this time, Julian's family became members of a team supported by a grant through the University of Washington called *Innovations*, which focused on developing a plan to support Julian's increased inclusion in general education. The efforts of the team were instrumental in creating opportunities for Julian to be included with his peers in middle school. Julian's special education teacher remembers that "at first we were scared, then we were a team together, and we weren't afraid anymore."

One of the strongest messages we heard from the people we interviewed in the project was their fear when first presented with the prospect of trying to include a student with deaf-blindness in typical education settings. This should not be a surprising message, but it does seem to be one that is not often explicitly acknowledged. When we consider the fact that none of the participants, with the exception of project staff, had any direct training and background in the education of students with sensory impairments, it should come as no surprise that people were fearful of their own abilities to support such students in other settings. They were already feeling very uncomfortable with planning for the education of the student with deaf-blindness in the special education classroom; now, when presented with the prospect of designing an education plan that would, of necessity, be subject to more scrutiny by more people, it is no wonder that they were anxious about the plans for inclusion.

Fear of Fallibility The fear of fallibility (O'Brien, 1987) was a subtheme that arose from the interviews. Our society has created an aura of expertise and independence in educators (Friend & Cook, 1992) that makes them especially vulnerable to the fear of admitting that they really do not know everything about the education of all children. Although the special education teachers on the teams had a background in teaching students with developmental disabilities, they had no background in the education of students with deaf-blindness. They were expected to develop appropriate plans and supports for these students, yet they were placed in an extremely uncomfortable situation of either forging ahead with a job for which they knew they were not prepared, or admitting their inadequacy, something their professional training had not prepared them to do. One of our participant observers related that he saw fear in educators when they found themselves facing other professionals and parents in a meeting, as he put it, "the teaching profession, historically, has been, 'This is your room, go do your thing.' "

One of the participant observers related how a special education teacher felt upon first becoming involved with the project: "Gavin [special education teacher] asked Bill [project staff] to clarify his role during site visits and said that the visits make him nervous because of Bill's apparent skills and his [Gavin] being new and unprepared with the programs." This is a situation that requires special sensitivity. We may think, by offering an expert, that we are helping, but in reality, we are intimidating people who are afraid due to their perceived lack of skills. A special educator told us that sometimes her team was afraid to try something new, fearing that "if it fails, [others will] say, 'See, that didn't work.' " This level of professional expectation is, quite understandably, extremely difficult to deal with.

A related services staff member also told us about fear, saying, "I think [the team] really works because you get so many ideas, [but] sometimes I think we get stuck in our own philosophies and maybe are afraid to change them." General educators also expressed anxiety in their initial reactions to inclusion. One had this response about how she felt upon first being approached: "I was, of course, shocked at first. Deaf and blind in P.E. [physical education], now wait a minute, what are you expecting me to do?"

Fear of being fallible began to be overcome as evidenced by this remark from one of the participant observers:

> If they were team impaired, they would never ask for help. They would not know how to ask for what they needed. I started feeling really good about teachers when they knew what to ask for and knew what they didn't know.

From another participant observer we heard this same recognition of growth. "As people went along on the teams, [they began to realize] that they have permission not to know." Another way we saw fear of fallibility being faced was through team members recognizing the value of the "eye of the beginner," as in this comment from a special education aide: "Sometimes I'm right but don't always know what I'm talking about, but I'm valued as part of the team and they value my suggestions."

Knowing you will not be criticized for your ideas is an important part of defeating fear. This was also apparent in a comment from this related services staff person:

> I just sort of throw things out. We try them out and if they work, they work. If they don't, [we] table them and maybe bring them up another time. Pablo [the student] is the one who's showing us whether we're doing it right or not!

Being open to trying out ideas and basing your final judgments on how they affect the learner is another way of lessening the fear of how other people will judge a team member's ideas.

Another related services person told us that team members had to be comfortable with taking risks. "I was very comfortable saying I don't know how to sign, but I'm willing to learn." This comment came from a person on a team where many members were fluent signers and adept at alternative communication strategies. We knew they were on the way to accepting their fallibility when we heard comments like this: "You know it's really okay trying different things, we don't always know the answer first." If the educational profession could support the development of the "we don't know exactly how to do this, but let's figure it out together and see what we can learn" type of approach, educators would be moving ahead, instead of letting fear of fallibility paralyze their growth.

Fears Concerning Students without Disabilities Sometimes the fears we heard related to concerns for the children without disabilities. "Mekala [adaptive P.E. teacher] was concerned if Pablo might hold other students in the class back if he takes longer to learn an activity." The response to this fear came from another member of that team, the general education P.E. teacher, who said, "I'm not worried as long as the team develops strategies to teach Pablo the skills needed for specific activities." Another general education teacher related her experience when including a student with deaf-blindness in her classroom. "I'm afraid my initial reaction was selfish, thinking only of my own kids. The children were just wonderful. And they don't look upon her as a disabled child, they look upon her as just one more student in school." As is often the case, this fear was dealt with by exposure to real people and real situations, as opposed to abstract concepts of integration or inclusion.

Fear of Other Professionals' Reactions A closely related form of fear was how other professionals would react to the idea of inclusion. Often team members had to ask for the involvement of other teachers at school, especially those teachers who would be in charge when the student with deaf-blindness would be spending time with other students without disabilities. Sometimes the team members were afraid of asking for help because they feared the other teachers would reject their request to work with a student with deaf-blindness. However, they were frequently surprised by the responses of those other teachers, as in the following situation:

> For the first year we've been saying we (the team members) don't want him in Mr. Foster's class because he's the coach guy. But we ended up in his class. He came over one day and the regular education teacher, June, says we gotta get you a name sign . . . so Tony recognizes you. Well, he's got these massive arms and hands and so Mr. Foster says, "Well how about if I shake Tony's hand like this?" (grab his wrist, that's gotta be distinctive for Tony because Mr. Foster's hands are so big). I asked the special education teacher, Carl, if we could get Mr. Foster or somebody to have Tony dress down for P.E. in the locker room. Since I can't go in there, someone else has to do it. I said to Mr. Foster, "We need somebody that will dress Tony down in the locker room with the rest of the guys instead of me doing it up in the nurse's office." He said, "Yeah, we can do that." I said, "Do you want me to teach you how to do it, and you could start going down there [gym] and then gradually get one of the peers involved in doing it?" "Oh," he says, "Yeah." So I said, "In the next couple of days you can come up and I can teach you how to do it." He says, "Wait a minute, I'll see if Fred's in there to keep an eye on the boys and I'll come up now and you can show me how to do it."
>
> Sometimes it's us, like with Mr. Foster, we think it won't work, he's not a good match. Most of the time it's us. . . . Sometimes it only takes asking.

Trust, Mutual Responsibility, and Respect

What overcomes fear? We heard the answers to this question from the team members we interviewed: 1) building trust in the other members of your team, 2) developing a sense of mutual responsibility, and 3) recognizing the parity of all team members. People are willing to take more and bigger risks in a supportive environment. And how do you build this trust with people whom you don't

really know? Probably the most important element in building trust with other members of the team takes something that is often, unfortunately, in short supply for educators—time, time to get to know other people's values and beliefs, see how they take responsibility, find out if they are willing to do whatever it takes to reach a common goal. These are all crucial to building a basis for respect and, ultimately, for constructing the shared agenda and norms necessary for team success.

One parent told us that "regular contact is crucial to developing a trust among the team members and change in what is sometimes a 'them against us' feeling between parents and educators." An administrator echoed this thought. "It was more ongoing than an IEP team. The frequency is a big advantage in getting to know strengths and weaknesses." Also along those lines, another parent related, "I used to feel 'ganged up on' in the IEP meetings; now in the *Innovations* team meetings they view me as an expert. They ask for my input and respect what I know."

One of the participant observers saw that "an important part of having a group become a team was the commitment to the regular monthly meeting." Another comment on the importance of spending time together came from this parent who said:

> I think a 3-year time frame is important . . . because the first year you're just getting together what your goal is, and a lot of that time is just spent getting to know each other. So the next year you try it out. And the next year you change what didn't work last year and try to make it successful. Without some ongoing commitment to being together as a group, working on a shared commitment, a team simply cannot form. When the time is there, you get this. Time is what makes a difference, time is what will increase our effectiveness, more time to meet.

So, it seems unavoidable—if you want to have a team you must find the time to be together. Not surprisingly, we were told that the single biggest problem teams faced was finding time to meet. This issue is further addressed in the section on issues that teams faced in support of inclusion.

Commitment to Team Purpose

When Julian started middle school, the class was filled with junior and senior high school age students, but was actually located in an isolated wing of an elementary school adjacent to the middle school. Julian's special education teacher had a different vision though, one that included chances to be with other members of the student body. She noticed that in the adjoining middle school, there was a small room that was only occasionally used by staff. With this room, the teacher saw an opportunity for her students to have closer contact with their peers.

Moving from a spacious classroom set up for students with disabilities into a small room on the middle school campus was difficult, but as the teacher stated, "We gave up a lot to get something better." Previous attempts to move her classroom had been discouraged by the school administration, so when she saw the open classroom, she used a different strategy—she moved in! She told others, "We didn't ask permission because we'd been told, 'no, no, no,' so we asked for forgiveness *after* we moved in."

One of the first things a team had to do, after recruiting all its members, was to talk about what they would like to accomplish. As is usually the case, someone on the team had an idea on which to work. In Julian's case, it was one of the university-based project staff, but it could have been a building principal, a district administrator, a parent or other family member, or other students in the school. However, we learned that once a team conducts its first meeting, they need the space to define the team's purpose in their own way and on their own terms. We learned we could not, as project staff, come in and dictate a goal. It had to come from the team itself, whether or not we initially agreed with their goals. We also quickly learned that the team cannot be the reason for meeting. One of the participant observers put it this way:

"You have to have a mission. The goals get set because they all know what they're shooting for. But if it's just to hold the team together, people become suspicious." How many of us have had the experience of being on a committee or belonging to a group that doesn't seem to have any reason for existence outside of getting the same people in a room together?

We discussed people's intimidation when initially contacted to plan for the inclusion of a student with deaf-blindness. A participant observer noted that in order not to feel threatened, team members "want to negotiate that concept of integration, and they want to be able to manage it." Teams defined their own idea of inclusion by focusing on the particular student they were supporting. "The teams understand the goal by understanding the kid, and [they] understand the goal based in the realm of deaf-blindness." A parent elaborated on this idea of student-centered planning, saying:

You hear about projects like X that think all of education can be done in the regular education classroom. I don't know about that. I'll give you an example: Jorge going to an auditorium to hear a speaker or something like that. In my opinion, Jorge is not getting anything out of that. He can't hear the speaker, he can't see the speaker, he's in a seat and doesn't understand why, with nothing to do. I'm not for mainstreaming period, only when it enhances both sides.

Student-centered planning also supported teams in having a different view of the student. An administrator, summing up her feelings about the goal definition process, explained that the team could "accept the student's disability without that resulting in lower expectations." She continued, "the team allows one to focus on the things the kid can do" and promotes a "more complete view of [the student] as a person."

Once Julian and his classmates had more opportunities for meeting their peers, something had to happen to bring them closer together. Here the dream took on a new dimension. Julian's team looked into activities in which he could participate that would give him chances to interact with his peers. They came up with the idea of selling popcorn in the cafeteria during school hours as an objective. This meant a lot of work in developing communication systems for Julian and teaching the other students how to buy popcorn from him. Through this activity, Julian increased his communication skills, while meeting most of the other students at his school.

Once again, the dream expanded. The support team now approached a P.E. teacher and she began to include Julian in her classes with the general student body. She became enthusiastic about Julian's inclusion and tried to make socialization with the other students work for Julian. This teacher caught the sense of vision from the team, remembering how "the team was allowed to dream for Julian and see what happens." However, these dreams were backed up by hard work on the part of the team. They constantly sought out better ways for Julian to communicate with his peers and to adapt the curriculum so that he was learning as well as making new friends.

Julian's mom stated, "A parent has dreams and . . . shouldn't let those dreams die." Not only did the team not let them die, they had one more dream that seemed almost too incredible to believe could ever come true. Julian's mom had always wanted him to go to the same schools as his brothers. As Julian would soon need to transition into a high school, the team saw the opportunity to make this vision a reality. As the University of Washington consultant reasoned, "Wherever Julian would be transitioned, a program would have to be created, so why not use his home high school?" Julian's mother remained strong in her dream, but cautiously wanted to be sure it was best for Julian. "A lot of times you have the right to do something, but [sometimes] it's not the right thing to do for the child."

While members not only needed a chance to determine what their actual purpose as a team would be, they also needed a chance to enhance that purpose as they got further into developing supports. A participant observer saw it this way: "For a lot of them, the concept of integration was so new that they did tend to start small, but then when they were in there, they said, 'This isn't enough. We want more . . . How can we get more?'"

Of course, at this point, our initial faith in the team's ability to set its own agenda paid off. Momentum was now on the side of the team's commitment, we heard evidence of this momentum in the words of a general educator: "After you get results you stop looking at any kind of limitations for awhile. You know there's a way around every problem instead of [asking] 'Is it really going to work?'" Even new problems did not tend to stop a team once they got going: "We just kept going even when we took care of one barrier and another popped up, we just kept going." Lastly, we found out from an administrator that something special kept bringing people back to the meetings:

> Something about how the way the team operated, the way it was set up, the fact that it produced results got you hooked so you always wanted to come back for the next saga in the story of [the student].

Positive Interdependence of Team Members

Thousand and Villa (1992) define positive interdependence as a "mutual 'we are all in this together' feeling" (p. 76). A certain sign that trust building had succeeded was when team members recognized that no one member of the team could possess all the skills and strengths needed to bring the team's goals to fruition. Once the members saw that they were all interdependent, as opposed to independent, agents in supporting the education of the student, they truly began functioning as a team. However, most people will not willingly put themselves in a situation of being dependent upon others until they feel they can trust them. So, in this sense the chronology of becoming a team does seem to require trust as a prerequisite for working together interdependently.

One of the participant observers summed this up well:

> Everyone's issues or priorities are the whole team's priorities, instead of, "Oh, that's your

problem," or "That's your territory." They all problem solve together on issues that are important. What one person brings up, the whole team problem solves . . . together.

The idea of positive interdependence means building a sense of common responsibility and parity among team members and takes in the concept of give and take. No one can do it all, and we all have to give what we can, as well as take what we need. A general education teacher said, "I guess I think the team approach is good if they come in with ideas as well as expect me to have ideas." A related services staff remarked, "I consider myself an equal member, and not just in contributing, but in terms of receiving, it helps to know what other people's agendas are and what they're working on so there's consistency and opportunity." A counterproductive example of positive interdependence was found in this general educator's comment: "I wanted the team to be more directive rather than to ask what I thought." In other words, I can take from the team, but I have nothing to offer.

On a team where positive interdependence was achieved there also seemed to be a different kind of leadership that emerged. Thousand and Villa (1992) refer to this as *distributed leadership*, which was seen in the teams in the project. One team's leadership was described thus:

> We had 17 leaders. We had Carl, we had Miriam, and Kerry coming in once in awhile. We just had really outspoken people, Val. And then we had Justine, our regular educator, who . . . should be president. She has a dynamic opinion about everything.

People also felt comfortable with letting others lead at different times, depending on who had the most expertise about the issue at hand. "It's kind of like it expanded and contracted. But there was always a center."

Once team members recognized their shared interdependence, they were often able to avail themselves of support that might not have been there before the team formed. A special educator told us: "The team was the place I got support when I didn't get it from anywhere else in the school." Not everyone was afraid to be in a situation with people who might know more than they did, a new special education teacher pointed out that for her it was "neat, as a new teacher, having input from the team." Seeing the team as a place where they could get support made the goal of inclusion one that looked a lot more manageable than if they were on their own. As one special education teacher remarked, "It wasn't all put on me to do, which was nice. I had their support as well." Another general educator recognized that "without a team effort, it's going to be a lot harder," and a related services person told us about how working as a team was different from being on one's own with a student. "If you really blow it, you have someone to lean on."

Valuing different perspectives is a hallmark of positive interdependence. A related services person commented that when a new member joined the team, they "just accepted her and her ideas." A special educator on another team had this to say about a new team member: "We accepted her [childcare worker] right away. We were interested to hear [her thoughts] because she brought another whole setting to the situation." The idea of benefitting from different perspectives was also part of recognizing that there was always too much going on with a student for any one person to effectively handle. A related services person explained, "Things are too inter-related for just one person to make decisions. You can't make these decisions in isolation." Feeling like one is a part of something bigger is what comes from positive interdependence. As one special educator put it, "Instead of someone coming through here and saying, 'You should do A,

B, and C and those would be good for Jeff,' being part of the team made everybody feel like they had something to contribute, some ways to help Jeff."

A very poetic description of the idea of positive interdependence was offered by another special educator who said, "It's like a stone path where there are great gaps. I can see the stones, I know where the path will lead, but the quantum leaps between the stones aren't resolved." When people feel they are important and that they can rely on others for support, the "gaps between the stones" seem smaller.

Team Member Parity

In order to come together as a team, people needed to realize that each and every member of the group had a valuable perspective, set of skills, or other gift to offer the team. Although this may sound very similar to positive interdependence, it is slightly different. In positive interdependence, people come to realize that they could not be effective without all the other members of the team, that they complement each other. We heard people tell us that there were no team members whom they thought they could do without. In this way, teams acted like real communities; they included anyone who could help support the student with deaf-blindness. This valuing of the views and perspectives of each and every member was an empowering process for team members and is contained within the concept of team member parity.

Parents talked about how, often for the first time, they felt that their opinions and knowledge of their own child was considered important by professionals. One parent told us, "We are the experts, and now more people view us as such." Another parent felt valued because a team went out of its way to get parents' input, saying "Let me call Fraser or . . . Michelle and see what's good for them because it's their child we're talking

about." Along those lines we were told, again by parents, that team members "started to come to our house. They came in the evening after my wife got home from work, so [there] was a willingness."

A parent summed up the team experience this way when asked what was the most important thing the team accomplished: "Everyone respecting everyone else and communicating, supporting each other's importance." Respect for one another was also mentioned by administrators and related services people as an important part of being a team. A special education aide remarked, "I felt like I was welcome, like I was a part of it." A school nurse told one of the participant observers that she felt so welcomed by the team that she would be pleased to join them.

Role Release

How did people get from being independent agents, each with a unique and separate area of responsibility for a child, to becoming interdependent members of a group that made their collective views and strengths work to develop a better education for that child? How was parity among team members achieved? A large part of coming together as a team was contained in the concept of *role release,* whereby team members were able to let go of their professional role in favor of doing whatever it might take to improve the education of the student. All of the team members came together initially with very specific roles in relation to the student's welfare. There were special and general education teachers, occupational and physical therapists, communication development specialists, and so on. Along with those roles came an expectation that the person who occupied the role brought to the situation a specific area of expertise that was well defined, with certain boundaries. Communication specialists were not responsible for positioning; occupational therapists worked on fine motor issues (among others), not communication; and, of course, teachers did everything that the specialists did not claim as their professional "turf."

The concept of role release was best described in the words of the two participant observers. One had this comment: "As long as you're on somebody else's territory, if you don't know a way to communicate in a non-threatening manner or a way that the person can feel ownership, then teaming is never going to happen for that kid." If members held on to their individual turf, other people's input was devalued, and the whole development of a sense of positive interdependence was defeated. Once people could see that their expertise was still valued, then they could give up their preconceived, narrowly defined roles. Holding on to the specialist's role could result in a comment like this from a special education teacher:

> With our kids, we project turf issues onto other people, [saying] that they're not doing it my way and it's not right. If you're the teacher you're doing the only right thing in the building. Everyone else is on the other side, being criticized.

People began to give up their specialist roles when they were willing to take on any of the chores that might be important to creating an environment in which the student would learn:

> Bill and I both learned that . . . you get in there and do the toileting and the diaper changing, helping out at lunch time. Whatever needs to be done in order to say we're just one of the group here, we're one of the team, and we will do whatever we need to do, and oh, by the way, here's one way to teach language in this activity.

This idea of getting in and doing things beyond the specialist role really helped people feel like they were working together. A special education teacher remarked:

> I found out where I could help in the school. No one is going to help you out if you're not willing to help them out yourself. We got involved with the 100% club after I helped chaperone a skating party. Every spare moment I get I go up to the regular ed. teachers and spend time with them.

Rather than narrowly defined specialist roles, people began taking on more universal roles as they evolved as team members.

> People didn't hold on to their [professional] roles. For some reason the roles are less important . . . and they became [defined as] "I'm the person who clarifies things," or "I'm the person who keeps them on track." And that is a much healthier way of communicating, rather than to say this is my little part of the world.

Role release is well captured in this statement: "It isn't being the vice principal, it's being someone who wants to listen to that parent."

Inclusion Issues

If the process of developing a team were all that was needed, students with deaf-blindness would be a lot further down the road to inclusion. Once teams were formed, numerous problems had to be solved before their goals of inclusion could be realized. Teams faced negative attitudes of other people toward students with disabilities, logistical barriers related to space and large class enrollments, unnaturally large proportions of students with disabilities in segregated programs, and many other problems. The following sections focus on the two issues most frequently mentioned: 1) finding the time for team activities and 2) the impact of the students' disabilities on their inclusion.

Finding the Time The following quote is from a special education administrator and sums up all of the comments heard from other team members about not having enough time to be on teams for all the students who might benefit:

Teachers are really busy all of the time and that's a shame, because the whole concept of collegiality that is seen as such an important part of planning for kids just gets lost in the shuffle, you just don't have time to do it to any extent beyond the quick fix type of thing.

On one hand, team members said that supporting inclusion for students with deaf-blindness can best be accomplished through a team effort, while on the other hand they felt it was impossible to have that kind of time for each and every student. Rather than present all of the verbatim comments from team members on this issue, it was decided it might be better to recognize the seriousness of the problem and suggest some ways that might create more time for teams to do their work.

1. Let the team be the judge. The team will find a time for the meeting, even if it is at 7:00 A.M. for coffee or later in the day at the student's home.

2. Hold separate team meetings initially, and then combine them later. This may be an effective strategy for some team members who are on multiple teams supporting different children. Holding smaller team meetings separately at first allows the team to fully develop their vision of inclusion for each student. Once they begin working on strategies for inclusion, it may be possible to devote some portion of an agenda to discussing each child, thus avoiding the need to find the time to keep coming back for other meetings.

3. Run the meetings efficiently. If it is hard to find time to meet, it will be harder to find time to go to a meeting that is inefficient and/or ineffective. Nobody wants to waste valuable time at a meeting where nothing gets done. Have an agenda, with time allotments for each item, and stick to it. Agree that meetings start and end

on time and make sure this rule is followed. Make it known that people who are late will have to use their own time to catch up on what the team discussed before their arrival.

4. Hold meetings regularly. People can usually attend meetings more easily if they are at the same time and place on a regular basis. Agree to meet from 2:45 until 3:30, every third Monday, as opposed to negotiating a new meeting time each month. Have people agree that the meeting time is to be given highest priority over other committees, personal appointments, and so forth.

5. Involve administrators in the process of scheduling meetings early on to allow them to rearrange other school functions to meet the needs of team activities.

6. Release students 10–20 minutes early, once a month, so that teachers and other staff have time to meet.

7. Consider building into the school budget a permanent or semi-permanent substitute. The substitute could rotate throughout the day, allowing individual teachers time to meet with their teams.

8. Consider asking the school district to make child care available to parents at no cost so that they can attend meetings during school time. Some groups have worked out respite arrangements with state developmental disability agencies for the same purpose.

Impact of Disability on Student Participation

It was time to approach another local school administrator. With the support of Julian's team, his mom requested that Julian be allowed to attend his home high school where his brother was a senior. Because this high school did not have a special education class for students with severe disabilities, Julian would be enrolled in general education classes with his peers. To support his involvement in those classes, an educational assistant would accompany Julian as his interpreter. The team was given permission by the administrator to begin the transition planning process.

Several months were spent getting Julian used to changes in location, schedules, and activities. At the same time, through Julian's support team and "hands-on" experience, staff and students at the high school were learning more about people with deaf-blindness and particularly about Julian. His mother knew that the teachers were "scared at first that they might not be able to do the job," but this phase passed quickly as they came to know Julian as a real person, as opposed to some abstract idea of what a student with deaf-blindness might be like. Given the support of Julian's middle school team, most of the educational staff at the high school were supportive and willing to adapt their curricula into classes that were functional and meaningful for Julian. An important principle was stated by the consultant from the Educational Service District: "There are dignity issues involved with integrating Julian. It's nice to include him in a classroom, but I think it needs to have some meaning for him and it has to be an experience that the other kids can invest in."

The other major issue teams told us about, aside from finding time, related to the student's disabilities and the negative impact this had on participation in activities with typical students. Two strategies for dealing with this issue seemed to work for most teams. First, teams worked with general education teachers and typical students to discuss ways that they could partially involve the student with deaf-blindness in their activities (Baumgart et al., 1982). This often included getting the input of peers regarding activities that might be meaningful for the student with deaf-blindness. Partial participation also meant seeking alternative performance strategies for the student (White, 1980). Second, the teams saw the student's disabilities not as a barrier, but as an opportunity to increase the functionality of their teaching. This was seen in the case of a student with deaf-blindness who did not have a communication system to use with his peers. The opportunity to learn the use of communication systems with naive audiences is important for students with deaf-blindness

who spend time in their communities. The opportunity for typical students to learn how to communicate with their friends with deaf-blindness is also an important feature in addressing the issue of communication. It was frequently our experience that typical students who had an interest in the student with deaf-blindness were extremely motivated learners of American Sign Language.

Achieving Positive Results

In addition to the feelings of support created by a team, what also brought people to their positive attitudes concerning collaborative teaming were the outcomes they achieved together. Although the work was hard, the results were worth it. Team members told us about benefits to the professionals, students with deaf-blindness, school community, parents, and peers. A related services staff member told us that it is "a major step for a group of professionals to come together and have regular meetings and regular attendance for the sake of a child; I think it makes you feel good. I don't want to see it end."

Making popcorn at the middle school was one experience that gave Julian a chance to interact and develop friendships with other students. If anything, the opportunities at the high school were now even greater. An interaction Julian had with a new friend illustrates one of these opportunities. One day a student named Micki had lunch with Julian. As they walked to the cafeteria, she helped him find his way by showing him how, through his cane, he could feel the textures of the hallway, including the doormat. Julian, upon recognizing the mat, took two steps forward and knew right where to find the door handle. Julian sat next to Micki throughout lunch. By the smiles and teasing it seemed each thought the other was a real "kick." Micki would sometimes scratch Julian's back or give him a hug; he would smile and carefully try to steal her Coke can. Of course, Micki would see this attempt, wait until his hand found the can and then grab it and put it to her mouth. Julian's hand would stay on the can, and he would laugh as Micki drank. After this routine had occurred several times, Micki took the can and touched it to Julian's cheek, signing "cold" as Julian smiled. After eating, Micki signed "walk" into Julian's hands, and he stood up, took her elbow, and was guided by Micki to a group of her friends on the other side of the room. During the conversation, Micki showed two of her friends how to tactually sign "good" into Julian's hands. Julian appeared very casual as he "hung out" with the girls, while gently holding Micki's elbow. During this activity Micki and Julian acted as do so many friends in high school. They enjoyed each other's company, teased each other a little, communicated how they felt, and joined in with a larger group of their friends. Micki also taught a couple of her other friends how to begin to talk to Julian. This interaction, simply put, would never have happened in an isolated, self-contained education program for students with severe disabilities.

Benefits to the Student with Deaf-Blindness
People told us about a number of benefits they saw for the student with deaf-blindness as a result of greater inclusion at school. Some of the students were able to show a heightened awareness of their environments. One special education aide thought it was a benefit simply to have the other kids spend time with the student. Sometimes this increased awareness of environmental features is quite dramatic, as in this comment from a participant observer: "Suzanna has begun to open her eyes, literally, and attend to her environment."

By far the benefits to students with deaf-blindness most frequently mentioned related to social relationships. Having the opportunity to be with their peers afforded students the chance to get to know them better, to build trust, and to practice social skills in naturally occurring activities. A special education aide had this to say:

> He benefits because he has more contact with more people. He's learned things too. He's become a lot more comfortable taking a strange arm. He'll still hesitate, [thinking], "this person doesn't know what they're doing." Now he's a little more comfortable going off with another person. He doesn't get upset like he used to.

Learning to be comfortable with other people is a major benefit not usually enjoyed by students who are isolated from others. Learning how to act around other people is

important too, as in this comment from a parent: "What I really enjoy the most is seeing them teaching other kids how to communicate with Guy so that he will accept other people." The same parent spoke about how she used to think that her son did not like to be touched or want to make friends, but found that "it has really worked out well. I've been really pleased that he's made lots and lots of progress." Perhaps one of the most revealing quotes about the social benefits of inclusion comes from another parent who said that her son "needs little boys in his life to show him what being a little boy is all about." Finally, a special educator told us about changes in one of her students following inclusion:

> She's so much more social. The apathy that was there, whether from boredom or monotony of activities, has been replaced by somebody who I think is really excited about coming to school because good things are happening. She wants to be with other people now.

Another way of understanding how some people saw students with deaf-blindness benefiting from inclusion was to listen to what they thought things would be like if the team had not been around to help. A parent remarked, "If I were on my own, without the team, Emy would still be in her incline chair in her crib."

Finally, the change in the perceptions other people had of the students with deaf-blindness was another major benefit. It is so much easier to think a person is limited when they spend most of their time in an environment that does not really give them a chance to display their strengths. However, inclusive settings often supply the opportunity to show what one can do. As this special education teacher remarked, "We developed a new concept of Bonnie. In our minds, [we saw] her capabilities."

Benefits to Parents   The major benefits of teaming that parents reported were related to a sense of support from the team, the feeling of respect for the parents' knowledge about their child, and the opportunity to be involved in their child's education. One parent commented, "Together we've all shared information and solved a lot of problems. They've been great support to me, and I think the team itself . . . has been a valuable resource and advocate for me as a parent of a handicapped child." Team support for parents also came in the form of providing knowledge, as in this parent's statement: "The team helped prepare me mentally for what was going to happen next."

One parent spoke to us of how much she values and depends upon the team:

You have to have a team because people have a tendency to overlook a mother's wishes or knowledge because I'm not a professional. So the team is backing me up, especially this team. We've been close. We've been discussing everything, and without the team I don't think Tony would have been this far along.

Another parent explained:

Right now the team is my backup. I depend on them. And I don't want to lose that. Sometimes I say, "Oh my god, how am I going to cope with this?" The team just says, "Why don't you try this way? Or this way?" And it works. So everybody contributes to [my son's] needs, and to my needs.

Benefits to the School Community People also told us about the benefit to the school community as a whole. They saw the value in learning to appreciate each and every member of the school for their own personal contributions. The outcome of this acceptance of others and a recognition of their unique gifts was a reduction in negative attitudes toward students who were different. A general education teacher commented, "People who are exposed to people with disabilities will be less likely to be prejudiced, and therefore it would be a positive change for our society." The efforts of the teams and

the students with deaf-blindness were also seen as developing new pathways for other students with disabilities to be included in their school communities. One parent felt her son had helped create such pathways by "teaching the staff and students at this school that [he] and the other kids in the two classes here can be a part of this school." One of the participant observers noted that "the idea of integration started and there was no stopping it." An occupational therapist at a middle school said that her team "set the way for a lot of other kids." Finally, the successes of the teams brought about a renewed commitment to all the children in the school: "What we do for one, we try to do for all the kids we touch."

Benefits to Peers When we asked people about the benefits of the team process and what outcomes they saw as most significant, the most frequently mentioned area by far was the benefits to the typical peers of the students with deaf-blindness. We heard many stories about the typical kids growing in their ability to accept the diversity of people that make up, or perhaps we wish would make up, our communities. Typical students became less fearful of those who were different; they learned that they did not have to be afraid of people who may appear different once they recognized that everyone has common hopes and dreams and a need to be accepted by others. A general education teacher explained how she thought her students had learned a lot about accepting others:

It was interesting. Last spring two third-grade classes went to the aquarium, one from our school and one from another. That day another class of children with disabilities from a third school was also there. And our children responded to those kids because they were so familiar. They would wave and talk and then go on their way, whereas the other children from the other school who weren't around kids with disabilities were so distracted by the presence of children with disabilities that they couldn't even enjoy the aquarium. So I think that the children in our school, our student body, have gained so much in acceptance that [inclusion is] the best.

A similar view of the benefits of inclusion for peers was voiced by this special education teacher:

> When kids see other kids with a disability from afar they look real different. They make a lot of assumptions about what they're like and how they feel about it. When they get beyond those boundaries they realize this is another person who does have limitations, but it's not nearly as off-putting as it was at first. I think that is a big achievement for the first graders. Actually, this is a major achievement for anybody, to recognize the humanity of other people and to see their individual strengths and gifts.

We were frequently told about benefits that people saw for our communities in the future as a result of inclusion. A special education teacher put it this way:

> The community benefits because of what these [typical education] kids learn. These kids are the community as they grow up. They've learned that we're all more alike than different. And they have an understanding of their little world which gives them a better understanding of the rest of the world.

A similar view was expressed by this general education teacher who remarked:

> Some of these [typical education kids] are going to be doctors and nurses, and they are going to be dealing with these kinds of kids [students with disabilities]. It's just life and it's just there. I thought it was important for my whole class.

Our students are the future community. Are they learning to accept diversity, to value it, or are they learning that some people are to be isolated and kept apart from the places to which most people go? We need everyone in our communities if we are to regain that sense of community we seem to have misplaced (O'Connell, 1990). John Dewey had this advice over 80 years ago when he envisioned schools that would provide children with "an embryonic community life" that would, in turn, provide "the deepest and best guarantee of a larger society which is worthy, lovely, and harmonious" (Kidder, 1989, p. 299). The words of two peers involved in the project sum this idea up well:

> Well, I think [typical peers] should be able to communicate with other people of different kinds, and colors, and deafness, and blindness maybe . . . I think they should be able to communicate instead of having just one kind of school for those kind of people. Because they just know those kind of people. But if they're going to a school like this, then they could communicate with different people.

> I learned that I could accept any kind of people, including them. And how I couldn't really accept some people in my classes before third grade because I thought they were really different. But when I started working with [the students with disabilities], I thought well, if I can accept these people, then I can accept the [other] people in my class.

Peers learned two things that are important for the future of our communities through their relationships with their classmates with deaf-blindness: 1) the ability to see capacities and not just deficits in other people and 2) the gift of hospitality. We heard about learning to see capacities in this comment from a related services staff: "They are learning to see a special needs person survive in their environment . . . it can be done." A special education aide told us about seeing capacities in this comment:

> I was in class one day, they [typical education kids] had colored a picture of several butterflies. They laid one out next to [a girl with vision and hearing impairments], and she sat there and colored it identical. And they were just amazed. Cutting was another thing that they were amazed at because she could cut on the lines and glue them where they needed to go.

Once again, we find great wisdom in the words of one of the peers who said:

> Well, I learned . . . you can't take people by what they look like. You look at them and think, "oh." But, they're different I agree, but differences doesn't count because they really try. They taught me how to sign, how to have fun.

Hospitality came out in statements like this:

> Kids will come down and comb Jenny's hair and I . . . look at these kids and think that they would never want to do it, she's drooling, but it's no big thing now. And I've seen kids get Kleenex and wipe her mouth whereas 2 years ago they would have left.

A father of a preschooler with deaf-blindness was very pleased and touched by the hospitality he saw in his son's classmates:

> There's people at the school, little kids, every morning I take him to school, who say, "Hey, there's Jim's Daddy." I think they're kids not even in his class. I don't know where he met them. They're just walking around the school yard. "There's Jim." Five, six, seven years old. You have to give them credit.

This peer also told us about the hospitality of friendship:

> Well, I learned more sign language, that's for sure. And being around them I felt that I didn't have to act different. I could just be myself. I didn't have to give them very special treatment . . . I could just be like a friend.

RECOMMENDATIONS

When Julian's support team dreamed of and advocated and planned for more inclusion for Julian, opportunities opened up for other students as well. Julian's interpreter expressed that, initially, middle school teachers were not sure how students from the special education class would fit into general education. As time went on, the same teachers were disappointed if no students with disabilities were included in their classrooms. As the consultant for the Educational Service District stated, "The idea of integration started and there was no stopping it." The occupational therapist for the middle school said that Julian and the special education teacher have "set the way for a lot of other kids" and helped the school to know that they are all one community. Staff on the team used Julian's vision to affect the lives of other students. "What we try to do for one, we try to do for all the kids we touch." Julian's mother believes that her son is now opening the way for other students with severe disabilities to attend the local high school.

Collaborative teams are a powerful tool for supporting, developing, and implementing inclusive education plans for students with deaf-blindness. However, as noted in the opening sections of this chapter, there are numerous questions and reasons as to why collaborative teaming is not the norm in American education, special or general. With those reasons in mind, including a lack of resources, teacher training, and time for teaming, the authors forward these two recommendations. First, we believe it is imperative that preservice and in-service teacher training programs be redesigned. Preservice training should include class content devoted to collaboration and consultation with other professionals and family members, but even more importantly, should offer students opportunities to experience collaboration in actual team settings. Second, the authors add their recommendations to those of Stainback and Stainback (1992) and Villa and Thousand (1990) who encourage special educators to seek new ways of forming partnerships with their general education colleagues for the purpose of restructuring education to accommodate the input of a wider range of teachers, family members, and other stakeholders. This requires the commitment of educational administrators and policy makers to use collaborative teams to plan for the education of our children.

The authors believe that these two strategies, redesigning teacher preparation and restructuring educational planning, are both crucial and complimentary. Teachers trained in collaborative teaming, who experience its benefits and strengths, will be less likely to accept teaching in situations where opportunities for teaming are not present, thus placing additional pressure on administrators and school board members for change. The authors are convinced that once people experience the benefits of collaborative teaming they will exert the pressure required for further use of this resource. School districts will want to hire teachers who know how to operate in the team milieu, thus exerting pressure to change the structure of teacher training by hiring teachers from institutions where those skills are taught.

The authors truly believe this is the future of educational progress. Communities that are "worthy, lovely, and harmonious" begin with the models provided to our children while in school. Should the model continue to be an isolated, "one person can do it all" approach, or is society willing to work for harmonious communities by employing educational practices that model cooperation, mutual respect, and the power of "collective genius"?

_____

Through knowing Julian and the team of teachers, other professionals, family, and friends who supported his inclusion in high school, we have learned that dreams and visions should never be seen as finished or accomplished. Real dreams and visions only grow deeper and more meaningful as one begins to truly live them. We also found out that while dreaming is important, the hard work of developing new partnerships is equally important. Coming to understand that we all belong to each other in some way helps make the hard work worthwhile in the end.

_____

REFERENCES

Abelson, M.A., & Woodman, R.W. (1983). Review of research on team effectiveness: Implications for teams in schools. *School Psychology Review, 12,* 125–136.

Bales, R.F., & Borgatta, E.F. (1955). Size of a group as a factor in the interaction profile. In A.P. Hare, E.F. Borgatta, & R.F. Bales (Eds.), *Small groups: Studies in social interaction* (pp. 396–413). New York: Knopf.

Baumgart, D., Brown, L., Pumpian, I., Nisbet, J., Ford, A., Sweet, M., Messina, R., & Schroeder, J. (1982). Principle of partial participation and individualized adaptations in educational programs for severely handicapped students. *Journal of The Association for the Severely Handicapped, 7*(2), 17–27.

Bellah, R.N., Madsen, R., Sullivan, W.M., Swidler, A., & Tipton, S.M. (1985). *Habits of the heart: Individualism and commitment in American life.* Berkeley: University of California Press.

Delbecq, A.L., Van de Ven, A.H., & Gustafson, D.H. (1975). *Group techniques for program planning.* Glenview, IL: Scott, Foresman, & Co.

Edgerton, R.B. (1967). *The cloak of competence: Stigma in the lives of the mentally retarded.* Berkeley: University of California Press.

Education for All Handicapped Children Act of 1975, PL 94-142. (August 23, 1977). U.S.C. 1401 et seq: *U.S. Statutes at Large, 89,* 773–796.

Fox, W.M. (1987). *Effective group problem solving.* San Francisco: Jossey-Bass.

Friend, M., & Cook, L. (1992). *Interactions: Collaboration skills for school professionals.* White Plains, NY: Longman.

Glaser, B.G., & Strauss, A.L. (1967). *The discovery of grounded theory: Strategies for qualitative research.* Chicago: Aldine Press.

Goodlad, J. (1984). *A place called school.* New York: McGraw-Hill.

Gray, B. (1989). *Collaborating.* San Francisco: Jossey-Bass.

Halvorsen, A.T., Doering, K., Farron-Davis, F., Usilton, R., & Sailor, W. (1989). The role of parents and family members in planning severely disabled students' transitions from school. In G.H.S. Singer & L.K. Irvin (Eds.), *Support for caregiving families: Enabling positive adaptation to disability.* Baltimore: Paul H. Brookes Publishing Co.

Horowitz, J.J. (1970). *Team practice and the specialist: An introduction to interdisciplinary teamwork.* Springfield, IL: Charles C Thomas.

Janis, I.L. (1972). *Victims of group think.* Boston: Houghton-Mifflin.

Johnson, D.W., & Johnson, R.T. (1987). *Joining together: Group theory and skills* (2nd ed.). Englewood Cliffs, NJ: Prentice Hall.

Kidder, T. (1989). *Among schoolchildren*. New York: Avon Books.

Kieffer, G.D. (1988). *The strategy of meetings*. New York: Warner Books.

Kraus, W.A. (1980). *Collaboration in organizations*. New York: Human Sciences Press.

Newman, R.G. (1974). *Groups in schools*. New York: Simon & Schuster.

O'Brien, J. (1987). Embracing ignorance, error, and fallibility: Competencies for leadership of effective services. In S.J. Taylor, D. Biklen, & J. Knoll (Eds.), *Community integration for people with severe disabilities* (pp. 85–108). New York: Columbia Teachers College Press.

O'Connell, M. (1990). *Community building in Logan Square: How a community grew stronger with the contributions of people with disabilities*. Evanston, IL: Northwestern University, Center for Urban Affairs and Policy Research.

Reilly, A., & Jones, J. (1974). Team building. In J.W. Pfeiffer & J.E. Jones (Eds.), *The 1974 annual handbook for group facilitators* (pp. 227–237). La Jolla, CA: University Associates.

Stainback, W., & Stainback, S. (Eds.). (1990). *Support networks for inclusive schooling: Interdependent integrated education*. Baltimore: Paul H. Brookes Publishing Co.

Thousand, J.S., & Villa, R.A. (1992). Collaborative teams: A powerful tool in school restructuring. In R.A. Villa, J.S. Thousand, W. Stainback, & S. Stainback (Eds.), *Restructuring for caring & effective education: An administrative guide to creating heterogeneous schools* (pp. 73–108). Baltimore: Paul H. Brookes Publishing Co.

Timar, T. (1989). The politics of school restructuring. *Phi Delta Kappan, 71,* 265–275.

Toffler, A. (1970). *Future shock*. New York: Random House.

Toffler, A. (1980). *The third wave*. New York: Morrow.

Villa, R.A., & Thousand, J.S. (1990). Administrative supports to promote inclusive schooling. In W. Stainback & S. Stainback (Eds.), *Support networks for inclusive schooling: Interdependent integrated education* (pp. 201–218). Baltimore: Paul H. Brookes Publishing Co.

West, J.F. (1990). Educational collaboration in the restructuring of schools. *Journal of Educational and Psychological Consultation, 1*(1), 23–40.

White, O.R. (1980). Adaptive performance objectives: Form versus function. In W. Sailor, B. Wilcox, & L. Brown (Eds.), *Methods of instruction for severely handicapped students* (pp. 47–69). Baltimore: Paul H. Brookes Publishing Co.

Wood, J.T., Phillips, G.M., & Pederson, D.J. (1986). *Group discussion: A practical guide to participation and leadership* (2nd ed.). New York: Harper & Row.

Zander, A. (1982). *Making groups effective*. San Francisco: Jossey-Bass.

Chapter 9

Adapting Environments to Support the Inclusion of Students Who Are Deaf-Blind

Jeanne Glidden Prickett
and Therese Rafalowski Welch

Typical classroom settings and activities are characterized by information gathering and exchange. Students get information from teachers, each other, and a variety of media. Teachers receive information from students to track their learning and overall progress. The information exchanged in typical classroom settings is primarily visual and auditory. Therefore, each student's sensory functioning is a vital factor in how she or he gathers the information needed for learning. For students who have combined visual and auditory impairments, getting the information to be effective in all of the environments in which they participate can be extremely difficult, especially so in their typical learning environments. Still, adaptations and modifications can be made that support full participation of students who are deaf-blind in typical classroom settings and activities. This chapter outlines the rationale for making sensory adaptations and the ways in which adaptations can be made to meet the needs of a student who is deaf-blind.

SENSORY INFORMATION AND LEARNING

Five basic sensory systems are available for a typical individual to gain information about the world. Two of the systems, vision and hearing, are used primarily to gain information at a distance. These two "distance" senses allow an individual to gather information that is not immediately proximate in the individual's environment (Freeman, 1985; McInnes & Treffry, 1982; Welch & Huebner, in press). Distance information that is visual, for example, would allow an individual to check weather conditions without actually being outdoors or to identify a road sign half a mile away. Auditory information can be used, for example, to note a first-floor doorbell from a second-floor bedroom or an approaching ambulance that is still blocks away from the listener. Distance senses provide a learner with access to incidental information that is vital for concept building and learning, both in classrooms and other environments. When an individual experiences an impairment to either vision or hearing, access to this vital information is greatly compromised.

Sensory Input for Cognitive Development

Infants and toddlers interact with their environments, getting sensory inputs from all five sensory systems. From this repeated exposure, they learn to attach meaning to the sensory information they receive from objects, people, events, and other phenomena. Spoken language is used to mediate this sensory information. With the sensory input, families typically talk to children, for example, to draw their attention to visual and other sensory features of objects or to label them. Events and people are also described and named. Concepts are classified, for example, tables, chairs, and beds belong to the category of "furniture." Young children also establish conceptual subcategories based on sensory information and descriptive language. They typically describe, label, and categorize the concepts they have learned using spoken language. Eventually, children's language concepts are used for learning written language, which in turn allows for more abstract learning and development to occur. Written or spoken language is used daily in typical academic settings, as well as in adult situations and activities.

Different Sensory Functioning: Implications for Learning

The early experiences of infants and toddlers with distance sense losses are clearly affected by the reduced or distorted sensory information they receive when they interact with their environments. Children with vision losses are not as adversely affected in academic participation that depends on hearing and using language as may be children with hearing losses (Warren, 1984). For children with vision losses, experiences modified with

tactile input and explanation are usually satisfactory to support concept development.

Children receive linguistic input about their sensorimotor experiences from parents or other caregivers. This input supports cognitive development by providing labels and explanations about the world. However, children who have hearing losses may differ in cognitive development because they have not experienced the same linguistic input. Speechreading may be helpful, but even expert speechreaders can miss significant amounts of what is spoken to them. Consequently, children with hearing losses can experience significant delays in abstract concept development.

Still, children with hearing impairments whose families sign or make other adaptations and who communicate with them frequently can move beyond the sensorimotor stage because they have language to support their cognitive development. Children who are deaf may generally interact appropriately in their early environments, especially during preschool years, but may be at a disadvantage once they enter classroom environments, without appropriate adaptations, where the work is language based.

Deaf-Blindness and Learning

Children who are deaf-blind are at a greater disadvantage for gathering sensory information for learning than are their peers with single sense losses. With the combined distance sense losses, a child's sensorimotor input and experiences can be reduced (McInnes & Treffry, 1982), and overall development may be pervasively delayed. The combined losses are not considered "additive," that is, the child does not have a vision loss with deafness added or hearing loss with blindness added (McInnes & Treffry, 1982). Instead, the combination creates a very different disability because the alternate distance sense is not available to the child to allow for filling in of gaps in information. The pervasive developmental delays that may occur as a result of deaf-blindness can be ameliorated, with supplemental and supporting experiences and input that begin early in infancy. Most students who are identified as deaf-blind do have some residual vision and hearing that are useful for learning, and educators and families should capitalize on the remaining senses (Downing & Eichinger, 1990; Fredericks & Baldwin, 1987; Freeman, 1985; McInnes & Treffry, 1982). Adaptations and modifications to information-gathering strategies can be initiated early and continued into school-age years; additional adaptations and modifications that are specifically designed for school participation will also support learning in typical environments. Factors for making visual and auditory adaptations in school programs for students who are deaf-blind are described in the following sections.

REASONS FOR ADAPTING THE SCHOOL ENVIRONMENT

The most crucial reason for making adaptations to typical classroom settings for students who are deaf-blind is that without such adaptations, students seldom can participate effectively (Downing & Eichinger, 1990). As mentioned previously in this chapter, conventional instructional activities in typical classrooms rely on visual and auditory information sources (teachers, materials, media). Adaptations must be implemented to somehow provide the student who is deaf-blind with access to the visual and auditory information that facilitate learning.

Instructional settings are also important social environments because students participate and interact with peers as well as with educators. Students are socialized to the knowledge and customs of their own cultures in instructional settings much as they are at home with their families. Visual factors in social environments include the visual features of the people interacting within them, objects and materials used within the settings and activities, and pragmatic interaction factors such as making eye contact to indicate a desire to participate. Auditory features, such as tone of voice, give students clues about the social environment of an instructional setting, as do bells to indicate class change.

Interaction in social environments, especially instructional settings, is particularly complex for individuals who are deaf-blind. The process of interacting with another person requires several steps: 1) identifying that the individual is in proximity, 2) determining another way to come into contact with that individual (e.g., by telephone), 3) indicating intent to interact, and 4) proceeding to interact with a mutually understood mode (most often spoken or written language). Conventional ways of interacting require vision and hearing to identify an individual in the immediate environment and carry on the interaction. Because visual and auditory information are inaccessible, the student who is deaf-blind can have difficulty even knowing when others enter and leave the immediate environment and how to approach others for interaction. Thus, instructional environments drive the quality of participation for students who are deaf-blind, including those who also have additional disabilities. Adapting the features of instructional environments to facilitate effective participation is a necessary activity for education program planning and implementation.

A second compelling reason for making adaptations to a typical classroom setting so that a child who is deaf-blind can participate is that it is law. Sufficient legal support for making adaptations has been enacted for more than 20 years. Section 504 of the Rehabilitation Act of 1973 (PL 93-112) has afforded all students with disabilities the right to reasonable accommodations. Section 504 of this law covers elementary and secondary education specifically.

The new Americans with Disabilities Act of 1990 (ADA) (PL 101-336) is another major act that defines the rights of persons with disabilities and affords children who are deaf-blind the right to participate in general education with reasonable accommodations. The Individuals with Disabilities Education Act of 1990 (IDEA) (PL 101-476) and the regulations to implement it (34 C.F.R., Part 300) mandate that students be educated in the *least restrictive environment*, in which accommodations are made to facilitate participation.

Finally, some authorities view the Fourteenth Amendment of the Constitution itself as affording the most promising protection of an individual's right to accommodation in typical classrooms, including visual and auditory adaptations (Martin, 1993). The Fourteenth Amendment prevents the removal of an individual's life, liberty, or property without due process and equal protection under the law. This has been interpreted to mean that a child should only be removed from a typical classroom setting when there is strong evidence that accommodations made in the setting will not be sufficient to facilitate participation. Litigation and Office of Civil Rights rulings have supported the interpretations of these pieces of legislation to ensure that children who have disabilities, including those who are deaf-blind, can participate in typical classroom settings and activities with appropriate adaptations.

Who Adapts

Without a doubt, individuals who are deaf-blind themselves make many of the adaptations that allow them to participate in everyday life. Individuals who are deaf-blind find alternate ways of getting vital information

that will give them the details they need for decision making. This is true of individuals who are deaf-blind with advanced abilities, as well as those with cognitive disabilities. For example, a child who cannot see or hear and wants to know what is coming into her mouth may clamp her mouth shut as a spoon touches her lips, grab the caregiver's hand with the spoon in it, stop it, and smell the food before accepting or rejecting it. A typical child would likely look at the food first, and while he may or may not smell it first, he would have enough visual information based on previous experiences to accept or reject the food simply from visual scanning. Regardless of the ages or the abilities of individuals who are deaf-blind, compensatory strategies for information gathering tend to be developed individually over time.

Certainly, the individual who is deaf-blind will have communication partners who must make adaptations to everyday interactions as well. These partners include family members, peers, service providers, and people in the individual's wider community. In school settings, the most frequently encountered communication partners are peers, classroom teachers, teaching assistants, other school personnel, and related service providers. Communication partners learn very rapidly that interaction with an individual who has a combined distance sense loss needs modification for meaningful communication to occur (Prickett, in press-b).

Because neither visual nor auditory information is sufficiently accessible at a distance to most individuals who are deaf-blind, close proximity affords more satisfactory reciprocal information exchange and interaction. Optimal communication distance for an individual who is deaf-blind often means direct physical (tactile) contact, which makes one-to-one interaction imperative (Downing & Eichinger, 1990; Prickett, in press-a). For some individuals who have low vision or some useful hearing, optimal communication distance may be anywhere from inches away from the partner to just a few feet away. In both cases, the optimal proximity required to communicate effectively may be very unlike that used by typical people when they communicate (Prickett, in press-a). Touching another person as a systematic part of the communication process may be very new to some communication partners who are making such adaptations for the first time.

Other adaptations may be needed for individuals who are deaf-blind with peripheral visual field losses. Again, communication partners, as well as the individual who is deaf-blind, will need to make modifications in proximity. In these cases, instead of close contact the opposite is needed. Effective communication using a visual mode such as signing would require a moderate increase in distance of 5–15 feet between the individual who is deaf-blind and the partner. It may also be necessary to reduce the dimensions of the signing range to best accommodate the individual's visual field restrictions.

Peers and service providers are likely to need some training to interact effectively with students who are deaf-blind (Downing & Eichinger, 1990). Formal or informal training sessions will be helpful in giving potential communication partners the skills to communicate. In some cases, peers and service providers might take sign language instruction or train in the use of an augmentative communication system with the individual who is deaf-blind. Also, training for such activities as traveling together safely and efficiently through the school will enhance interaction between a student who is deaf-blind and others in the school setting (see chap. 11, this volume, for more information on social relationships with peers).

One-to-one interaction with tactile components or very close visual interaction are not standard behaviors for most people, yet these techniques ensure that the majority of individuals who are deaf-blind will get sufficient information to interact effectively with each communication partner. For example, a preschool student with low vision and a severe bilateral hearing loss may need to handle and look closely at instructional materials, receive visible sign language at a range of 1–3 feet, and may even need tactile sign language as she learns early language concepts, just to clarify fine details of sign language hand shapes and movement. A high school student may prefer tactile sign language, even though he has low vision, because of the eye fatigue brought on by watching all day through classroom lectures, discussion, and reading enlarged print. In both of these cases, one-to-one close interaction affords the student who is deaf-blind with necessary information and fine details of communication; this kind of contact is not a group activity. It is important to note, however, that one-to-one support may be needed for the student to participate *as* a group member, which is the case with the older student described above. For information gathering and communication, this highly individualized quality is the single most important adaptation that many individuals who are deaf-blind and their communication partners must address. One-to-one support is often cited as not being cost-effective, yet is often the only reliable way that students who are deaf-blind can fully participate and get information from instructional activities and social interactions with teachers and peers.

When and How Much to Adapt

According to Stratton (1990), "adapted materials are essential to enable some children to learn, but for many children, they should serve as a means to an end, not become the end itself" (p. 5). Teachers and families need to adapt in ways that focus on children's natural environments, including typical classrooms, so that activities are meaningful. Within those instructional environments, adaptations to items, materials, and procedures should be only the most necessary ones (Prickett & Prickett, 1991; Stratton, 1990).

Teachers have far more choices in availability of commercial materials for instruction than ever before in the history of education. Many typical instructional materials that are commercially available for typical students are also appropriate for students with disabilities, including those who are deaf-blind and/or those with multiple disabilities. Teachers can use such materials, adapting them if and as much as is necessary. For some kinds of contemporary instructional materials and techniques, no adaptations are actually needed, and therefore none should be made that could further set the student with a disability apart from his or her peers (Prickett & Prickett, 1991; Stratton, 1990). For example, metric system measuring rods are commercially available as mathematics teaching aids. These are divided into 1-centimeter lengths, 10-centimeter lengths, and similar metric measures. Children can handle the rods, moving them together or apart to add and subtract them, and talk about lengths using both visual and tactile terms ("Ten centimeters feels bigger than one centimeter. It is longer."). These rods do not need braille or large type adaptations, and they can be used as they are by both children who are sighted and those who have visual impairments. The rods are colored, but color is not a major variable in using the length factors; touch is adequate for the mathematical purposes.

Stratton (1990) describes a decision-making tool that teachers can use in determining how much adaptation might be appropriate for an instructional activity:

The principle of least restrictive materials is proposed as a guide to determining the extent to which adapted and specially designed materials are appropriate. . . . It is defined as the principle of utilizing materials in the child's natural environment to the fullest extent possible, adapting only when and to the extent necessary to ensure optimum learning. A hierarchy for using adapted materials may be constructed. . . . On Level 1, the child is able to learn from the natural environment with only the guidance usually given to any child. On Level 2, the child is able to learn from the natural environment, but needs mediation by another person to initiate and guide learning. Mediation is less intrusive than adapting the environment. For example, a blind child can learn to sort silverware, but initially may need verbal and manual guidance to distinguish size and shape. On Level 3, the child does not yet have the skills to learn directly from the environment and needs adapted materials to develop these skills. . . . On Level 4, the only way the child can gain access to the environment or to parts of it is by the use of adapted or specially designed materials, which represent a permanent need. For example, a child may need to use large print instead of regular print or use speech-adapted equipment to access a computer. (Stratton, 1990, p. 3, 5)

Adaptation of instruction and materials depends on many variables, all of which must be determined individually for each student's needs. The following should be considered:

- The amount of useful vision and hearing a student may have
- The student's age
- The student's physical and cognitive abilities
- The student's overall skills

As each variable is considered and the child's needs are defined, the adaptations that are selected must support the goals identified for the instructional program, the materials and activities to achieve the goals, and the demands of the learning environments. Adaptations should be made when they are necessary within the parameters of the overall program for a student who is deaf-blind, and only as much as is necessary to support the program. As a child grows and learns, adaptations used in previous work may be discontinued, and new kinds of adaptations implemented (more information on issues in decision making for adaptations is included later in this chapter). Such modifications are incorporated as an ongoing part of education program planning for each student who is deaf-blind. Each adaptation should support interaction and full participation comfortably and effectively for that student.

SPECIFIC ADAPTATIONS FOR STUDENTS WHO ARE DEAF-BLIND

Classrooms and other instructional situations present multiple environmental challenges for students who are deaf-blind, including those who have additional disabilities. Teachers who understand these environmental features and can identify them in specific settings can make decisions about adaptations to facilitate the full participation of their students who are deaf-blind. The features of typical instructional environments that most frequently require adaptations are described in this section.

Most teachers adapt daily without even realizing the extent and kinds of adaptations they have made. When a class has students of various reading levels, for example, a teacher will adapt by using a variety of materials and forming several reading groups to meet the needs of individual students. Individualized attention is facilitated by such management strategies. Students who are deaf-blind need somewhat more specialized adaptations; still, members of a student's educational team can make these adaptations by analyzing information about a student's

visual and auditory abilities and determining what modifications will be most effective. Both formal ophthalmological and audiological assessments and informal site-specific or task-specific assessments will yield vital information on which to base individual adaptations.

Readers should keep in mind that many children with losses of either vision or hearing also experience fluctuations in the functioning of the residual information received by the senses. Fluctuations may occur from such phenomena as ear infections that reduce motility of the eardrum, further reducing the amount of auditory information that is available to a child who has a partial, permanent hearing loss. Fluctuations may also occur as a result of the cause of the loss itself, for example, glaucoma. With congenital glaucoma, a child may experience even daily changes in ocular pressure that influence his or her ability to use the remaining vision functionally. All of these factors will affect a child's ability to gather information for learning in a typical classroom setting, and any combination of the adaptations described in this chapter may be used to support participation. Often, adaptations will be subject to ongoing modifications and redefinition because of such fluctuating losses. Several specific areas of adaptation that are commonly made for students based on auditory and visual needs are outlined in the following sections.

Visual Adaptations

Total blindness and total deafness are comparatively rare; in fact, most students who are "deaf-blind" have at least some useful vision, and instructional adaptations can capitalize on the remaining vision as a learning tool. A student who is able to use residual vision to participate in class activities should be encouraged and guided to do so. Visual adaptations do not always require the assistance of a teacher who specifically serves students with visual impairments, although technical assistance from local specialists in visual impairment can be helpful (Prickett & Prickett, 1991). Basic visual adaptations fall into several categories; each student's visual needs must be considered individually in terms of the most effective adaptations within these particular categories.

Lighting   Classroom lighting that is most cost-effective for schools usually combines natural lighting from windows with overhead fluorescent lighting (Carter, 1983). Most students with low vision require lighting to provide maximum contrast for the materials they read, while a few visual conditions are better suited to reduced levels of lighting (e.g., *albinism* [an absence of pigment in the eyes that can affect use of vision relative to lighting] and some other conditions with light sensitivity factors). Natural lighting, when it is available, is very effective for most students with low vision. Fluorescent lighting is the least effective for students with low vision, even though it is most prevalent in classroom settings (incandescent lighting is recommended second to natural lighting, but is rarely used in school environments) (Carter, 1983; Prickett & Prickett, 1991). Essential modifications can include:

- Monitoring lighting levels so optimal lighting is available for student needs (either reduced or maximum, depending on the visual impairment and functional use)
- Monitoring and minimizing glare from all sources of light, especially windows (window blinds and drapes can be used effectively for these adjustments)
- Providing a desk lamp for the student with low vision to give additional lighting for seated activities, especially those that require reading (Hicks & Hicks, 1983)
- Arranging student seating and teacher

position so that glare from windows does not affect visual use
- Monitoring rapid changes in lighting, for example, moving inside (darker) from outside (brighter) after recess, or into a dimly lit auditorium from a brighter hall (Carter, 1983; Prickett & Prickett, 1991)
- Monitoring other illumination factors, such as light absorption or reflection from wall surfaces, ceiling tiles, floors, and other items in rooms (Carter, 1983)

Positioning and Seating   The findings from a student's formal and informal visual assessments should provide information about the distance and position in space at which the student can best view objects or other people. To maximize use of visual information, instructors should ensure that materials or individuals requiring visual attention are positioned for the student's optimal viewing. The student should also be guided to position himself or herself in such a way that he or she can most comfortably and efficiently use residual vision.

In addition to seating arrangements that minimize glare from natural light sources (i.e., windows), other seating factors can affect visual use in a typical classroom setting. For students who have low vision, especially those with significant hearing losses, relative position in a class will be an important consideration (Prickett & Prickett, 1991). Students who have visual losses that reduce both central and distant vision, such as *optic atrophy* or high *myopia*, may need seating very close to the teacher. This way, visual clues from the center of class activities can be more accessible.

Conversely, a student who is deaf-blind due to *Usher syndrome* generally has good central vision, but lacks peripheral vision and has night blindness, which rarely affects daytime class participation. Optimal seating for this student is often toward the middle or back and center of the class. With such a position, the student with Usher syndrome will need to turn less to locate a peer who is speaking, and can still see the teacher clearly with distant central vision. If the student uses an interpreter, the interpreter must be seated so that the student with Usher's syndrome can: 1) receive all of the necessary class information from the interpreter, 2) see the teacher as much as possible, and 3) see peers to facilitate interaction when appropriate. If the student uses residual hearing with speechreading (lipreading) to communicate, finer visual use is required than with sign language or fingerspelling. This student may need to be seated within 10 feet of the primary source of activity, usually the teacher. Speechreading is possible, even with partial sight, at these distances (Elioseff & Robbins, 1983, Prickett & Prickett, 1989).

Classroom Setup and Instruction Teachers can make simple adaptations in how they manage and conduct instruction that will help students who are deaf-blind to participate more effectively. Some adaptations to physical features are suggested below, as well as modifications of instructional procedure.

Classroom Setup Teachers use specific features of classroom arrangements and displays in delivering instruction. Displays such as bulletin boards should have background colors that contrast sharply with the material on them, and neutral backgrounds are preferable (Hicks & Hicks, 1983; Prickett & Prickett, 1991). Colors and materials that reduce glare should be used, especially in instructional areas, so that a student with low vision can see the teacher and peers "clearly and comfortably" (Prickett & Prickett, 1989, p. 15). Visual clutter in instructional displays can also interfere with a student's use of residual vision for learning, and therefore should be monitored and decreased. Furniture in instructional areas should allow easy, safe, independent mobility for all students, includ-

ing students who are deaf-blind. Classroom furniture arrangements should provide "considerable freedom in open spaces . . . free from sharp edges" (Hicks & Hicks, 1983, p. 4-55). Teachers should also evaluate other potential hazards, especially steps or overhanging objects, such as open cabinet doors, that a student with low vision might not detect until he or she is too close to avoid them.

Chalkboard Use Most teachers use chalkboards or marker boards for instruction. Students with limited distance vision may not have clear access to what is written on such instructional aids. For a student with low vision who may have special seating arrangements and can see a chalkboard, written information should be "in upper and lower case (avoiding use of all capital letters), and 3–4 [inches] high for easy reading" (Hicks & Hicks, 1983, p. 4-55). Chalkboards should be kept clean to increase contrast, and black background with yellow chalk provides maximum contrast for most students with low vision (Prickett & Prickett, 1991). Green boards or white boards that require felt-tip marker do not provide as much contrast for students with low vision.

When information is written onto a chalkboard, it should also be read aloud for a student with a vision impairment and interpreted if needed or copied into a medium that the student can use, for example, braille. Other students in the class can benefit from this supplemental information as well. If assignments are posted on a chalkboard, they should be in the same place and format daily, and the student who is deaf-blind can walk to the board during specified times to copy the information or have it read and/or interpreted.

Instructional Management Teachers tend to move around their rooms as they teach. For a student who is deaf-blind, especially one with low vision, this can present a challenge for keeping up with an instructional activity.

During group instruction, especially for new information or discussion, a teacher should maintain a stationary position in the classroom. This allows the student who is deaf-blind with some useful vision (and hearing) to follow the teacher and the lesson and thus participate more easily. As noted earlier, it is vital that the teacher stay away from areas that will produce glare for the student, and thereby reduce useful visual information.

When a student who is deaf-blind participates in a group of any size, large or small, typical interaction patterns used by individuals who are sighted and hearing must be modified. First, the student who is deaf-blind must have access to the same information the others are receiving to be a full participant. An individual or several individuals (e.g., a teacher, teaching assistant, interpreter, peers, or volunteer) will need to have responsibility so the student who is deaf-blind receives the information in a one-to-one tactile or close vision format. Without such provisions, it is likely that the student who is deaf-blind can miss information that others receive, as no single facilitator will ultimately be responsible to assist the student with vital information gathering. It is incorrect to assume that the student who is deaf-blind, even with some useful residual vision or hearing, can get all the information without facilitation by others.

Several easy adaptations can be made for a student who is deaf-blind to participate in a group activity more effectively (Prickett, in press-b). These will establish the parameters of the interaction, give the student who is deaf-blind more information about who is speaking, allow more time to process information, and facilitate keeping up with the interchange.

1. Before discussion begins, each group participant should identify himself or herself, and the student who is deaf-blind should be given a sense of the general location of each member (if the discussion is occurring in a familiar class situation, the student will already have had this kind of orientation to the group, so it will not be necessary).

2. As discussion proceeds, the leader (teacher or peer) should recognize in turn each person who wishes to comment or ask a question. This allows the student who is deaf-blind and his or her interpreter/facilitator to be alerted to the next speaker and redirect their attention. A student with low vision and useful hearing may wish to look at each speaker, and this procedure allows time to locate a speaker visually and auditorily.

3. As a speaker begins to respond with a comment or question, he or she can self-identify again, for example, "This is Sara (or "This is Sara speaking"). I want to be on the planning committee for the school play, too." The repetition of the speaker's name allows the interpreter/facilitator to direct the attention of the student who is deaf-blind to the new speaker, and gives confirming information about the speaker. Because students who are deaf-blind can miss much incidental information in daily class activities, reinforcing peers' names (and name signs) gives information that will enhance peer communication at other times as well.

4. The leader should monitor if the interpreter/facilitator or the student who is deaf-blind seems to be keeping up with the interchange, especially if it is rapid. The leader can remind group members to slow down and be recognized before they speak in turn. This is a facilitating technique, not a disciplinary one. It is especially effective when one or more participants do not effectively follow a group discussion using the ordinary vi-

sual and auditory information that is exchanged.

Small and large group activities are some of the most vital in typical instructional settings. Usually, little instruction occurs entirely with individual student–teacher contact (see additional information on group participation with communication support in the following sections on auditory adaptations). Adaptations made for group activities define the degree to which a student who is deaf-blind can truly become a group participant as well as the quality of that participation.

Instructional Materials: Visual Features Instructional materials are generally visual, auditory, or a combination of both. Pictures, audio and videotaped materials, films and filmstrips, and written materials are most often used as teachers' instructional aids. Lowell and Quinsland (1973) surveyed students who were deaf with low vision and found that they had distinctly ranked preferences for formats of instructional materials:

1) Desk-top printed materials or information
2) Chalkboard information
3) Videotapes and colored slides
4) Overhead projections with colored acetate
5) Opaque projector (p. 741)

Materials that could be used by the student immediately and at close range were clearly preferred. Information or materials requiring use of distant vision were less preferred. Specific adaptations for visual features of such materials will be outlined in the following sections.

Picture-Based Materials Picture-based materials have several visual elements that can be monitored and adapted. Adaptations should be made that support satisfactory discrimination and understanding of the visual information, so that a student who is deaf-blind can use vision functionally for learning. The most important factors are the color, contrast, size, angle, or distance at which materials are viewed, and the complexity of the materials (Prickett, Rowland, & Schweigert, in press). These factors affect how a student processes visual information, which in turn can affect his or her class participation (Prickett, in press-a). Picture elements that should be monitored and can be adapted include:

- *Color:* Bright and primary colors are easiest to discriminate. Young children perceive red and orange first developmentally (Goetz & Gee, 1987). Color in pictures helps students with low vision discriminate details, especially if color is a factor in what is pictured, for example, an apple is red (the apple's distinctive shape also helps with discrimination).

- *Contrast:* Materials with distinctly contrasting colors are more easy to discriminate. Black or navy blue symbols/pictures against a white or ivory background provides optimum contrast for most students with low vision; yellow against white is an example of poorly contrasting materials. To sharpen contrast on dittos or weak photocopied materials, place yellow acetate over the material.

- *Size:* Pictures that are either very small or very large may be difficult for a student with low vision to discriminate. Pictures that are very small, however, may be brought closer to the eye. Those that are too large may be moved away, but may then be out of useful range before the student can take in all the details in one viewing, so large pictures should be avoided. The student's visual needs dictate what is considered "too large" or "too small."

- *Angle or distance:* Visual materials are more easily discriminated if they are near enough to the student with low vision or are at an angle that does not require the student to bend over to look at them. Fatigue can result from bending too much to use visual materials, so slanted desks or desk-easels can be used by the student to adjust the angle and distance of materials. As noted previously, the relative size of a picture or visual material can be modified by moving the materials closer to or father from the student. Some students have visual fields with "missing" areas, so they may view "eccentrically" (Watson & Berg, 1983, p. 335). For these students, visual displays or presentations may need to be at the side or away from midline, depending on the portion of the field that is most useful for viewing.

- *Complexity:* Pictures and other visual materials that are "cluttered" with visual details or have movement (e.g., computer images, videotaped materials) are more difficult for a student with low vision to discriminate. Simplify pictures by:
  - Cutting out background details and placing important parts of the picture onto a plain background
  - Using line drawings or schematic pictures for a student who seems to discriminate them more readily, adding color if appropriate
  - Controlling speed of slides or filmstrip frames, so the student with low vision has more time to absorb visual details (seating should also be close to the screen)
  - Controlling speed of computer image movement by modifying software, if possible, or using slower-moving programs with students who have low vision

For picture-based materials that cannot be controlled, for example, some videotaped materials or films, teachers and communication facilitators should attempt to provide as thorough a description of action and dialogue for the student as possible. If the material is important for specific learning objectives, it may be possible to obtain a transcript of the auditory information to read individually with the student and to replay the visual material with pauses for explanation.

When picture-based materials are used with students who are deaf-blind, regardless of vision levels, it is important that teachers monitor student comprehension. Students who have no useful vision will need to have the details of picture-based classroom materials explained to them if these concepts are vital to instructional objectives. Students with low vision may be asked to give feedback about the illustrated concepts so their teachers can check comprehension.

Written Materials Large print and braille are the most common adaptations made to written instructional materials. The same visual features that are important with picture-based materials must be monitored with printed materials (i.e., color, contrast, size, distance/angle, and complexity). For students with low vision who read in print, the primary factor is size. Most students with low vision can read print if it is larger than typical print. Print materials can be enlarged in several ways:

- Hand enlarged, usually with a felt-tip marker
- Computer enlarged, with scalable font or enlargement software
- Photocopy enlarged
- Offset in large type
- Electronically enlarged with a closed-circuit television (CCTV)
- Enlarged with a low-tech device, such as a hand-held magnifier, or with a low vision aid prescribed by a low vision specialist
- Moved closer to the reader with a modified desk or reading stand (not a true enlargment, but effective for some readers with low vision)

Printed materials may be sized appropriately but lack adequate contrast, for example, poor photocopies or faded dittos (Prickett & Prickett, 1991). Students with low vision can have difficulty working with these materials. Adapting these papers can be done by simply tracing over the information with a narrow black or blue felt-tip marker, so that the contrast increases between the paper background and the printed letters or illustrations in the foreground. If time for such an adaptation is unavailable, making a new photocopy from a master copy on a darker setting can also solve the contrast problem. As noted with picture-based materials, contrast can also be sharpened by placing yellow acetate over dittos or weak photocopied materials (Prickett & Prickett, 1991).

Some students who are deaf-blind will require braille materials to participate effectively in typical classrooms. Materials can be put into braille by:

- Computers using braille "monitors" or peripherals that have refreshable braille displays comparable to print monitors that can be used for everyday work, and can be attached to typical printers so that a student can print out homework that any teacher can read without needing to know how to read in braille
- Computers using braille translation programs (software) with embossing equipment (hardware) can be used for hard copy braille that the student can read
- Standard braille writing devices, for example, the *Perkins Brailler* or *Mountbatten* braille writing device
- Braille slate and stylus
- Braille label maker (specifically for plastic label tape)

With a computer braille translation program and an electronic embosser (the equivalent of a braille printer), transcription can be done by an individual who is not an expert in reading the braille codes. A transcriber can take materials on disk, for example, a test or work paper prepared in a common word processing program, add appropriate transcription symbols to the print materials according to directions in the transcription software, and prepare braille paper copy.

Overheads and similar projected materials are often used in typical instructional settings. For students who are deaf-blind with some useful vision, overheads can be copied onto plain paper and used individually. Also, a student with low vision can sit next to the overhead to read, although glare may be a problem. Like information on a chalkboard, information on overhead can also be read aloud and/or interpreted to reinforce student learning and give the student who is deaf-blind access.

Other Resources for Visual Adaptations
Some students who have useful residual vision can benefit by using low vision aids, which can assist students to see printed materials, chalkboards, signs and clocks, and other such objects. Students can be referred to service providers in low vision for assessment and recommendations or prescriptions for aids. Optical and nonoptical aids are available, some of which have been described in this chapter. Nonoptical aids are used essentially for improved illumination or contrast or to make the user more comfortable when performing visual tasks (Jose, 1983b), but they do not change actual refraction of visual information. For example, a slanted desk easel is a nonoptical aid because it does not use any sort of lens for magnification or other feature that would change light ray convergence mechanically. A student's need for a nonoptical aid may be assessed and recommended by a low vision specialist; some of these aids can be tried without specific recommendations.

Conversely, a hand-held 10X magnifying lens is optical (Jose, 1983b). It changes the way visual information, or light information, is refracted. This kind of aid is specifically recommended or prescribed and obtained following a low vision evaluation, and training can be arranged based on individual needs. Many local education agencies (LEAs) provide low vision services, either through the LEA itself or through a contractual agreement with another agency. In some cases, ophthalmologists or optometrists will evaluate and prescribe specific aids, particularly optical aids. Some orientation and mobility (O&M) specialists also perform low vision evaluations.

Orientation and mobility instructors can be valuable resource persons for teachers in general education settings who want to support safe movement and travel within the classroom and school building. Even for students who are deaf-blind and do not receive direct instruction in O&M, consultation with teachers can be helpful. An O&M instructor can assist with troubleshooting and arrangement of instructional areas, establishing safe and meaningful routes for students to travel, and training school personnel and peers in safe guiding techniques. Also, an O&M instructor can help identify sounds that will be important for a student who is deaf-blind in travel situations within the school and community. These sounds can be used for auditory training and to support safe, purposeful travel. (See chap. 14, this volume, for more on orientation and mobility instruction.)

Auditory Adaptations

Many students who are identified as deaf-blind have some useful hearing. They should be encouraged and guided to use that hearing for learning, especially because spoken language and its written derivative are the primary means by which information is exchanged in typical classrooms. Some of the most common adaptations for auditory information are included in the following sections.

Positioning and Seating   Students who are deaf-blind and have some useful hearing should be positioned so that the most significant sound sources are accessible. For example, if a student has one ear with good residual hearing and the other with very reduced reception, the "better" ear should be faced toward the instructor or other sound source. The findings from a student's formal and informal auditory assessments should provide very useful information for such decision making.

Interpreters, Intervenors, and Assistants   Few students who are deaf-blind receive all the necessary information, especially auditory, from typical classroom settings without some human assistance. Most need some form of communication support to participate effectively with complete information. Specially trained and certified interpreters can be used, although these individuals would be primarily trained and certified to interpret from spoken language into sign language for people who are deaf, rather than deaf-blind. Still, regular sign language interpreters can interpret for individuals who are deaf-blind. More often in elementary and secondary school settings, individuals who do not have full certification through the Registry of Interpreters for the Deaf, Inc. (RID) will interpret. These communication facilitators may or may not have extensive formal training, and they may or may not need it, based entirely on the student's individualized needs according to the requirements of the instructional setting. If a certified interpreter is used, that individual's role is defined by specific parameters of ethics and confidentiality that may alter the individual's level and degree of participation as an educational team member. Fees for such a person are sometimes calculated differently than are those of teaching assistants.

Some school systems, however, employ *interpreter/aides*, a category of communication facilitator that is unique to elementary and secondary school settings, and for which the job description includes supporting individualized instruction in addition to the interpreting of general class information. An individual who is employed as an interpreter/aide may assume some duties that are similar to those of other instructional assistants, with added responsibilities for interpreting. Individuals hired as interpreter/aides should be evaluated for their abilities to meet the needs of the child in the areas of instruction as well as interpreting.

When a student's needs for communication support are assessed, it is vital for the student's long-term achievement that the most competent individual for that child's needs be selected. An "interpreter" with only a beginning sign language course as background is unlikely to meet the highly technical needs of a student who is deaf-blind and attending a high school program full-time and competitively with peers without disabilities. Conversely, a student who is deaf-blind and does not use formal language may have more need for communication support from an individual with less training in sign language. If, however, the student who is deaf-blind shows potential to use sign language, all of the service providers around the student should be competent enough to give him or her a satisfactory language base. Communication partners, including interpreter/aides, will want to provide a student who is deaf-blind with a rich communication environment, and the most effective way to do that is to be highly competent themselves.

Intervenors are individuals who assist people who are deaf-blind to gather information for daily living. Intervenors are most widely used in Canada; the model is currently being investigated in the United States. The role of an intervenor may involve interpreting, and can include reading information, such as mail, or driving an individual who is deaf-blind to an appointment, to do business, or

to shop as well as interpreting during such activities.

For a student who is deaf-blind, a teaching assistant may support communication and materials adaptation. This service provider may have minimal sign language skills, but may have other skills, for example, braille production. The student who is deaf-blind and does not use sign language may need a teaching assistant rather than a trained interpreter. A student who is deaf-blind with additional or severe disabilities may be effectively served by teaching assistants. A teaching assistant is still responsible for ensuring that the student who is deaf-blind gets the information necessary from the environment for learning, especially facilitating instruction and interaction with peers, teachers, and other service providers.

Regardless of the type of communication facilitation that is provided in a typical setting for a student who is deaf-blind, this service provider's responsibilities go beyond conventional interpreting (Prickett, in press-c). Service provision can include guiding, reading materials from print when the student is unable to do so, assisting others to communicate with the student who is deaf-blind, and many other duties that are unique to deaf-blindness. This human services provision also supports full inclusion with access to information and effective participation for the student who is deaf-blind.

Assistive Technology Technological devices that can assist a student who is deaf-blind to use residual hearing for learning, or to get auditory information in another way, are called *assistive listening devices* (Bess & Humes, 1990). Some assistive listening devices are auditory and require assessment and prescription by audiologists. These range from personal hearing aids to individual frequency-modulated (FM) systems that amplify significant sounds, primarily a teacher's voice. Teachers may be responsible for monitoring such devices for younger children or to teach older ones to do so themselves, to ensure that they are working properly. Audiologists and resource specialists in hearing impairments can help teachers become familiar with such devices and their care.

Other assistive technology that provides more complete information for students who are deaf-blind can include flashing-light systems for waking up, fire alarms, doors, stove timers, and telephone rings. Some of these devices also have intense-volume sound signals to give more information for individuals with some hearing. While some of these technological items do not seem to have relevance for an instructional setting, learning to use them appropriately can be a part of an individualized education program. Even in a typical instructional setting, these items might be used to give the student who is deaf-blind more information for participation and new skills for adult life. For example, a flashing alert signal might be installed at the door to a classroom in which a student participates who is deaf and has low vision. When visitors come to the door, they can "ring" the alert signal, and all of the children in the class will be alerted that someone is at the door. This way, the student who is deaf and has low vision has access to the same information about a visitor at the door that peers are receiving. Other sound alert signaling devices might be used for the class-change bell sounds, again so that the student who is deaf and has low vision gets the same information and learns appropriate responses.

Assistive listening devices with tactual outputs are also available. Some audiologists have expertise in assessing and prescribing use of tactile devices. For students who are deaf-blind and have little or no useful hearing and vision, the vibrotactile information from these devices may be very helpful, both for specific environmental sounds and for

some speech sounds (Bess & Humes, 1990; Northern & Downs, 1991). For example, an individual who wears a tactile aid might have a microphone that picks up the sound of a doorbell or telephone, which is converted to vibrating signals and fed to an output component placed in a pocket or on the wrist. The individual will know that someone is ringing the bell and can respond to it appropriately. Vibrating alarm clocks are also available to help individuals who are deaf-blind awaken in the morning; these can be purchased without formal prescriptions or fittings.

A TTY/TDD (telephone-teletype/telecommunication device for the deaf) can be used with a regular telephone to facilitate telephone use. This technology can also be used in a classroom by typical peers or others who are unable to sign to communicate with an individual who is deaf-blind. Both communication partners can sit and take turns typing into the keyboard, which is similar to that of a standard typewriter. The TTY/TDD readout can be read by some individuals with low vision, and can be adapted with a peripheral that enlarges print. Also, the Telebraille from Telesensory, Inc., can be used for "face-to-face" communication. Both of these devices can be used for interpreting, and are especially useful for interpreters who type but do not sign or fingerspell well enough to convey information efficiently.

Classroom Setup and Instruction   Auditory adaptations to a classroom environment can be made similarly to visual adaptations. Monitoring and reducing "clutter," or background noise, is most important. Students who are deaf-blind and use residual hearing for learning depend on getting optimal auditory information from teachers and peers, without extraneous noises such as outside traffic, a boiler from the furnace room next door, or overhead airplanes. Any background noise from people or machines will mask the useful auditory information a student gets, even with optimal amplification.

Several kinds of classroom adaptations are appropriate. Classroom location must be determined even before students arrive for a new school year. If a student who is deaf-blind is assigned to a specific class, instructional planning team members and administrative personnel should check prospective classrooms to determine ambient noise levels. Noise levels will change once students are in the rooms. The quietest settings will generally be the best for a student with a hearing impairment. Rooms away from street and playground noise, cafeteria noise, stairs, furnaces, or other machinery are desirable.

Physical adaptations that are most often used include:

- Carpeting on part or all of the classroom floor
- Noise-reducing draperies
- Noise-reducing ceiling tiles or materials, cork room dividers, or wall panels

Some of these modifications can be viewed as costly, and cannot be readily moved from room to room with a student. While carpeting and noise-absorbing draperies provide the best noise reduction, often temporary and portable noise-reduction panels can be used instead to reduce costs to school programs and to "follow the student" through his or her school career. These items also do not require as much maintenance.

Instructional management techniques include the adaptations described earlier in this chapter for structuring group discussions that reduce noise levels. Also, maintaining a relatively quiet instructional atmosphere is beneficial for the student who is deaf-blind and uses residual hearing because it allows the student more access to clear auditory information in all classroom activities. While this may seem difficult in an active learning environment, other students will respect the need for it if it is explained carefully.

Tactile Adaptations

Many students who are deaf-blind, even those with residual hearing and vision, use tactile information as a primary learning tool or a supplemental tool. Tactile adaptations are essential to concept development for many students who are deaf-blind (Downing & Eichinger, 1990; Freeman, 1985; McInnes & Treffry, 1982). As with visual and auditory adaptations, tactile adaptations should be made when and if they are clearly necessary (Downing & Eichinger, 1990; Stratton, 1990). If adaptations can capitalize on the natural context, they can be more effective in supporting learning (Downing & Eichinger, 1990). For example, using fabric with a texture identical or very similar to that of a child's coat to communicate, "get your coat on," will support that child's understanding of the concept.

Tactile adaptations for academic materials (other than braille, which was described earlier) can usually be made with readily available materials and some creativity. Maps, graphics, and other visual materials used for learning can be adapted in two ways:

1. Application of tactile markers or materials (including braille, if there are printed words on the visual materials and the child reads) directly onto the visual materials
2. Development of a new aid that is entirely tactile, and which does not necessarily bear a strong resemblance to the visual materials it represents

Applying tactile features to an already existing visual material may take less time and

Table 1. Table in visual format

Genetics of Eye Color for Students in Biology I

	Student eye color		
Student sex	Blue	Brown	Total
Female	8	5	13
Male	10	7	17
Total	18	12	30

effort for the teacher or assistant and allows the child who is deaf-blind to use the same materials used by his or her peers. Sometimes, however, the visual features are so complex and so abstract for a child with limited vision that a specially developed tactile graphic or aid will be superior for the instructional purpose (Edman, 1992). Then, development of a tactile aid does not have to follow visual norms or rules, but can be schematic, incorporating only the most relevant details and excluding others. In fact, visual scanning of graphics and tactual scanning differ enough that some adapted visual displays will not make sense tactually.

For example, information that is given in table form visually, with rows and columns of information, is viewed according to its spatial arrangement. A braille reader would have some difficulty with this kind of information, if presented in braille, because braille is read in a strictly linear fashion. The fingertips are used to read in braille, and information that is not directly under the fingertips is inaccessible until the hands are moved. It could take considerable piecing together of the tactile information from the spatial table format, requiring more comprehension time. Instead, the braille version of the information might be more effectively used in a linear format.

Table 1 presents a table in visual format. Table 2 presents the same information in a tactile format. Even less complex spatial arrangements, like the primary mathematics worksheet in Figure 1, can be difficult to view and interpret tactually. An adaptation is shown in Figure 2 that would present the work paper in linear format for use by students who are deaf-blind.

For tactile information modified from visual displays that are spatially oriented, such as maps with spatial relationships defining where points of interest are located compared to one another, the spatial relationships must be faithfully adapted. These can often be done with textured materials, yarn, glue, and other items with tactile qualities.

Table 2. Table in tactile format

Genetics of Eye Color for Students in Biology I
There are three columns with the following information: Student eye color—blue/brown/total
There are three rows with the following information: Student sex—female/male/total
The cells have the following information:
Females: brown eyes—5, blue eyes—8; total females—13
Males: brown eyes—7, blue eyes—10; total males—17
Students with blue eyes (both sexes), total: 18
Students with brown eyes (both sexes), total: 12
Grand total of all students: 30

Note: This is one of several formatting possibilities. Certified transcribers follow very specific formats for tabular information. Note that print is presented here, although the table would actually be constructed in braille. This table is not intended to be visually attractive, rather, its purpose is to convey the information effectively in a tactile format.

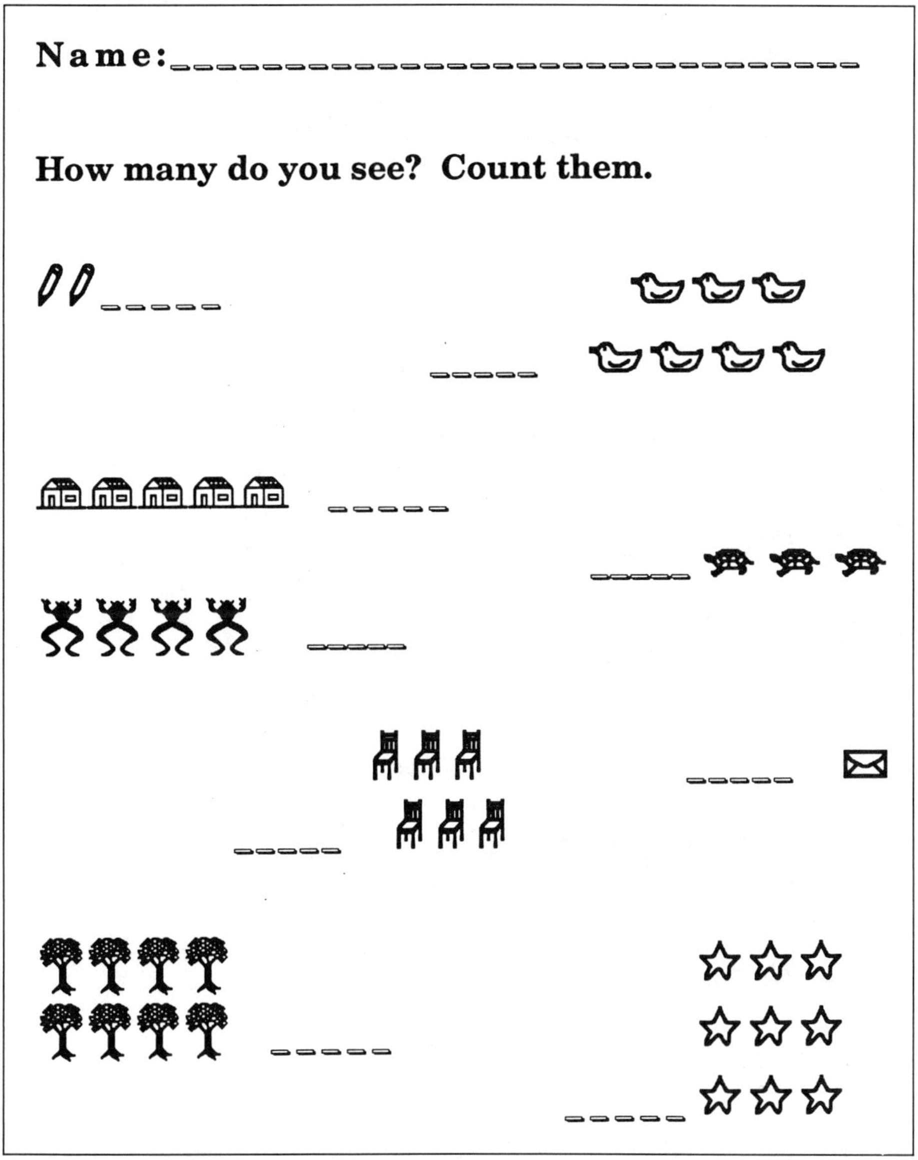

Name:_____

How many do you see? Count them.

0 0 _ _ _ _ _

_ _ _ _ _

_ _ _ _ _

_ _ _ _ _

_ _ _ _ _

_ _ _ _ _

_ _ _ _ _

_ _ _ _ _

_ _ _ _ _

_ _ _ _ _

Figure 1.   Primary mathematics worksheet: Standard form.

Edman (1992) noted that "one of the most difficult problems to solve is proportion" (p. 4). Often, a tactile graphic must be larger than its visual counterpart in order to have all elements spatially related for accuracy of both position and proportion. These tactual relationships may need explanation for a child who is deaf-blind (Edman, 1992); this can be combined with experience whenever possible to support concept development. For example, a schematic map of the school building can be traveled and described or

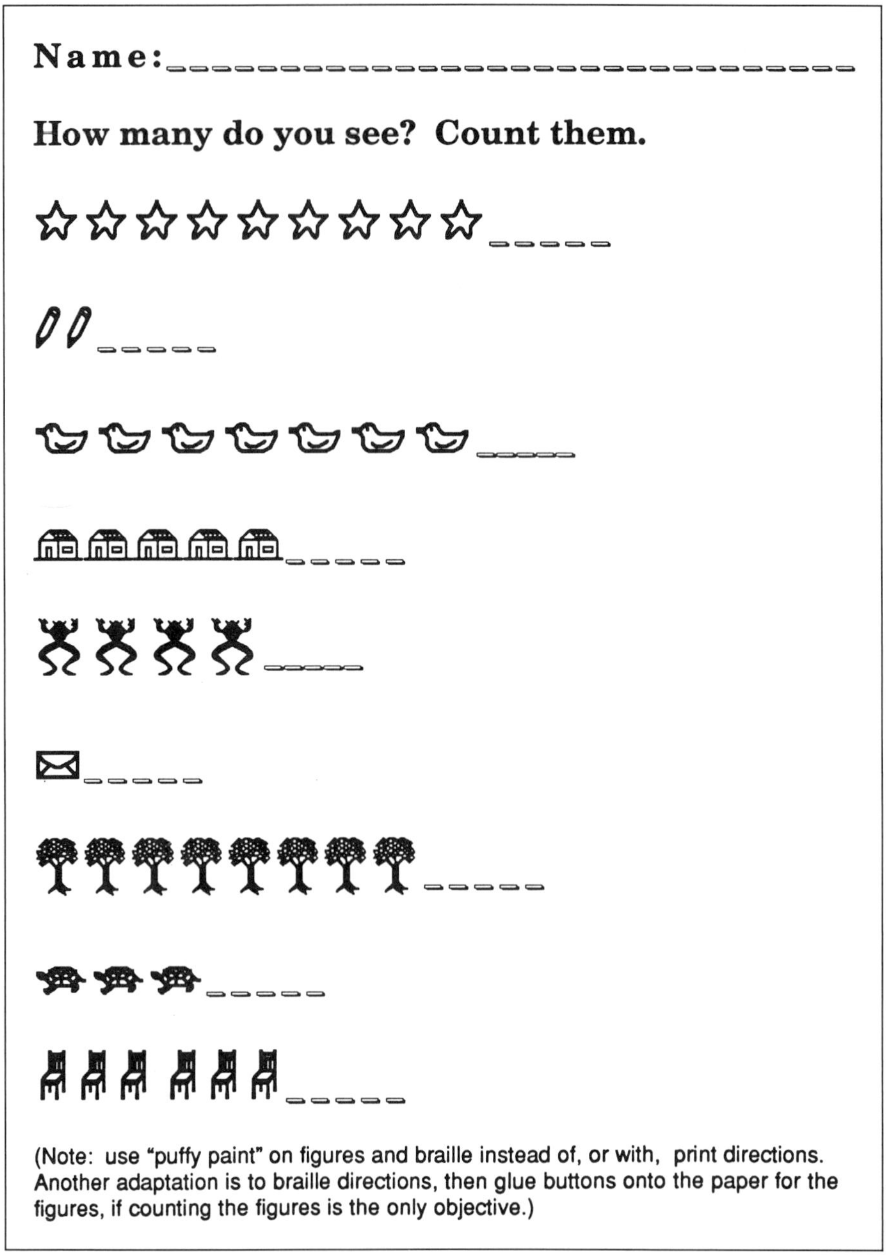

Name:_____

How many do you see? Count them.

☆ ☆ ☆ ☆ ☆ ☆ ☆ ☆ _____

𝟞 𝟞 _____

🐦 🐦 🐦 🐦 🐦 🐦 🐦 _____

🏠 🏠 🏠 🏠 🏠 _____

🐸 🐸 🐸 🐸 _____

✉ _____

🌳 🌳 🌳 🌳 🌳 🌳 🌳 🌳 _____

🐢 🐢 🐢 _____

🪑 🪑 🪑 🪑 🪑 🪑 _____

(Note: use "puffy paint" on figures and braille instead of, or with, print directions. Another adaptation is to braille directions, then glue buttons onto the paper for the figures, if counting the figures is the only objective.)

Figure 2.   Primary mathematics worksheet: Adapted form.

demonstrated using the tactile graphic map. An important consideration in making a tactile graphic is that touch must be combined with movement of the fingers across the item to be meaningful (Edman, 1992; Olson, 1981). Tactual perception does not require a single fixation on the display, as would visual perception, but a sweeping movement for tactual reception of the relevant features.

Linguistic information (e.g., words, symbols) from a visual display must also be clear and complete. Some visual displays, such as posters explaining school rules, may simply need to be put into braille on an individual paper for the use of a student who is deaf-blind.

Solutions for tactile adaptations can be easy or complex, based on the information the student needs to have. The significant consideration is that the information for the student is accessible and useful. Teachers in typical class settings can often make tactile adaptations themselves (Downing & Eichinger, 1990), or they may wish to consult vision specialists for assistance and ideas.

DECISION MAKING: HOW CHOICES ARE MADE FOR ADAPTATIONS

All school programs have limited resources. These parameters influence the kinds and amounts of adaptations that can be made for any student with a disability, especially for a student who is deaf-blind with intensive adaptation needs. As decisions are made concerning which adapatations are the most vital for full participation, many variables must be considered. The child's amount and quality of participation will be affected not only by his or her abilities and skills, but also by the appropriateness and thoroughness of the modifications that allow him or her to get optimal information from the visual and auditory features of the instructional environment. Educational planning team members must review all of these factors to recommend and pursue the most appropriate adaptations from all of those described in this chapter.

First, team members must remember the *principle of least-restrictive materials* (Stratton, 1990), which recommends making all the necessary adaptations, but no more than are necessary. Second, team members must deliberate and agree on whether resources of time, money, and personnel preclude some modifications and which of these must be accomplished to guarantee that a student who is deaf-blind has access to instructional information. For example, if carpet and drapes are not feasible because they are costly and difficult to maintain in a class of young students, noise-reducing portable dividers might eliminate enough noise to make the critical difference for a child who has a significant hearing loss.

Those team members who communicate best with the child who is deaf-blind have important roles in working in cooperation with other service providers. For example, if a child who is deaf-blind will be evaluated at a low vision clinic or by an ophthalmologist, team members who are most familiar and who communicate most effectively with the student can ensure that full information is gained during evaluation. This in turn provides the decision-making team members with guidance for understanding the child's needs and making adaptations appropriately.

The decision-making process may be lengthened because of the more complex approach required for gathering information about the student during assessment and the instructional modifications that are necessary. The student who is deaf-blind, especially one with additional disabilities, may receive and process information more slowly due to altered methods of information gathering. Additional time may be needed for decision making about which adaptations seem to be effective and which are not. Such adaptations as low vision aids or specific classroom management strategies may need trial periods to demonstrate their effectiveness. Decision making should accommodate the time needed by a student for these adaptations to be implemented and tested.

As they work together, teachers, family members, and other educational planning team members need to keep in mind that for every decision and adaptation made, the amount of information received by a student who is deaf-blind may be altered. Decision making controls the flow of information, whether the control that is imposed is inadvertent or deliberate. The student who is deaf-blind may have no other reliable way of receiving vital information for participation

except through the adaptations that have been determined by others on his or her behalf.

There can be a significant gap between minimal and optimal levels of adaptation. The concept of "adequate" also varies from student to student. Even for two students whose learning profiles seem almost identical, the ways in which visual and auditory information are used by each student will vary so that necessary adaptations will be different. The student may not be able to compensate for what is not supplied when a model of minimal adaptations is used. That student is at a disadvantage for effective participation. However, when decision making has been deliberate and systematic, adaptations can be made that support inclusion and full participation, in many cases, competitive participation, for the student who is deaf-blind with his or her peers in typical instructional settings.

REFERENCES

Americans with Disabilities Act of 1990 (ADA), PL 101-336. (July 26, 1990). Title 42, U.S.C. 12101 et seq: *U.S. Statutes at Large, 104,* 327–378.

Bess, F.H., & Humes, L.E. (1990). *Audiology: The fundamentals.* Baltimore: Williams & Wilkins.

Carter, K. (1983). Assessment of lighting. In R.T. Jose (Ed.), *Understanding low vision* (pp. 403–414). New York: American Foundation for the Blind.

Downing, J., & Eichinger, J. (1990). Instructional strategies for learners with dual sensory impairments in integrated settings. *Journal of The Association for Persons with Severe Handicaps, 15*(2), 98–105.

Edman, P.K. (1992). *Tactile graphics.* New York: American Foundation for the Blind.

Elioseff, J., & Robbins, N. (1983). Deafness and retinitis pigmentosa: On the education and management of deaf adolescents for whom blindness can be predicted. In N. Robbins (Ed.), *Deaf-blind education: Developing individually appropriate communication and language environments* (pp. 4-29–4-32). Watertown, MA: New

England Regional Center for Services to Deaf-Blind Children, Perkins School for the Blind.

Fredericks, H.D., & Baldwin, V. (1987). Individuals with sensory impairments: Who are they? How are they educated? In L. Goetz, D. Guess, & K. Stremel-Campbell (Eds.), *Innovative program design for individuals with dual sensory impairments* (pp. 3–12). Baltimore: Paul H. Brookes Publishing Co.

Freeman, P. (1985). *The deaf/blind baby: A programme of care.* London: William Heinemann Medical Books.

Goetz, L., & Gee, K. (1987). Functional vision programming: A model for teaching visual behaviors in natural contexts. In L. Goetz, D. Guess, & K. Stremel-Campbell (Eds.), *Innovative program design for individuals with dual sensory impairments* (pp. 77–97). Baltimore: Paul H. Brookes Publishing Co.

Hicks, W., & Hicks, D. (1983). The Usher's syndrome adolescent: Programming implications for school administrators, teachers and residential advisors. In N. Robbins (Ed.), *Deaf-blind education: Developing individually appropriate communication and language environments* (pp. 4-50—4-59). Watertown, MA: New England Regional Center for Services to Deaf-Blind Children, Perkins School for the Blind.

Individuals with Disabilities Education Act of 1990 (IDEA), PL 101-476. (October 30, 1990). Title 20, U.S.C. 1400 et seq: *U.S. Statutes at Large, 104,* 1103—1151.

Jose, R.T. (1983a). Optics. In R.T. Jose (Ed.), *Understanding low vision* (pp. 187—210). New York: American Foundation for the Blind.

Jose, R.T. (1983b). Treatment options. In R.T. Jose (Ed.), *Understanding low vision* (pp. 211—248). New York: American Foundation for the Blind.

Lowell, N., & Quinsland, L. (1973). Vision utilization training for deaf children. In *Proceedings of the Forty-Sixth Meeting of the Convention of American Instructors of the Deaf.* Washington, DC: U.S. Government Printing Office.

Martin, R. (1993, February). *Legislation and litigation.* Paper presented at the Third Annual United States Department of Education, Office of Special Education Programs Technical Assistance and Dissemination Conference, Arlington, VA.

McInnes, J.M., & Treffry, J.H. (1982). *Deaf-blind infants and children: A developmental guide.* Toronto, Ontario, Canada: University of Toronto Press.

Northern, J.L., & Downs, M.P. (1991). *Hearing in children* (4th ed.). Baltimore: Williams & Wilkins.

Olson, M.R. (1981). *Guidelines and games for teaching efficient braille reading.* New York: American Foundation for the Blind.

Prickett, H.T., & Prickett, J.G. (1991, June). Vision loss in deaf students: What educators need to know. In S. Powlowe-Aldersley, P. Schragle, V. Armour, & J. Powlowe (Eds.), *Proceedings of the Fifty-fifth Biennial Meeting of the Convention of American Instructors of the Deaf* (pp. 144—148). New Orleans, LA.

Prickett, J.G. (in press-a). Deaf-blindness and communication. In K.M. Huebner, J.G. Prickett, T.R. Welch, & E. Joffee (Eds.), *Hand in hand: Essentials of communication and orientation and mobility for your students who are deaf-blind.*

New York: The American Foundation for the Blind.

Prickett, J.G. (in press-b). Deaf-blindness: Implications for learning. In K.M. Huebner, J.G. Prickett, T.R. Welch, & E. Joffe (Eds.), *Hand in hand: Essentials of communication and orientation and mobility for your students who are deaf-blind.* New York: The American Foundation for the Blind.

Prickett, J.G. (in press-c). Manual and spoken communication. In K.M. Huebner, J.G. Prickett, T.R. Welch, & E. Joffee (Eds.), *Hand in hand: Essentials of communication and orientation and mobility for your students who are deaf-blind.* New York: The American Foundation for the Blind.

Prickett, J.G., & Prickett, H.T. (1989, June). *Usher's syndrome: Educational implications and visual adaptations.* Paper presented at the Fifty-Fourth Biennial Meeting of the Convention of American Instructors of the Deaf, San Diego, CA.

Prickett, J.G., Rowland, C., & Schweigert, P. (in press). Communication systems, devices and modes. In K.M. Huebner, J.G. Prickett, T.R. Welch, & E. Joffee (Eds.), *Hand in hand: Essentials of communication and orientation and mobility for your students who are deaf-blind.* New York: The American Foundation for the Blind.

Rehabilitation Act of 1973, PL 93-112. (September 26, 1973). Title 29, U.S.C. §701 et seq: *U.S. Statutes at Large, 100,* 1807—1846.

Stratton, J. (1990). The principle of least-restrictive materials. *Journal of Visual Impairment and Blindness, 84*(1), 3, 5.

Warren, D.H. (1984). *Blindness and early childhood development* (2nd ed.). New York: American Foundation for the Blind.

Watson, G., & Berg, R.V. (1983). Near training techniques. In R.T. Jose (Ed.), *Understanding low vision* (pp. 317—362). New York: American Foundation for the Blind.

Welch, T.R., & Huebner, K.M. (in press). The deaf-blind child and you. In K.M. Huebner, J.G. Prickett, T.R. Welch, & E. Joffee (Eds.), *Hand in hand: Essentials of communication and orientation and mobility for your students who are deaf-blind.* New York: The American Foundation for the Blind.

SECTION III

SCHOOL DYNAMICS

FACILITATING COMMUNICATION AND FRIENDSHIPS

Functional Communication in Inclusive Settings for Students Who Are Deaf-Blind

Kathleen Stremel
and Richard Schutz _____

Communication intervention for individuals who are deaf-blind must begin with a conceptual understanding of the individual's *ecosystem*, the system of mutual relations between organisms and their environment. Any environment in which an individual interacts is an ecosystem that is composed of physical (i.e., objects, locations, activities) and social (i.e., personal relationships) elements that are interconnected with elements of a larger social and cultural context that indirectly and directly influences communication interactions. This conceptual framework is increasingly important as more students who are deaf-blind are entering inclusive school, home, and community environments. For example, a change in one's physical environment, as in a student's inclusion in a typical classroom, may change the social relationships in which that person is involved. Additionally, the inclusion of the student in the typical classroom will also affect the attitudes and behaviors of others in the school.

In order to define *functional communication*, we must have a perspective of the individual and all aspects of his or her ecosystem. A number of aspects of functional communication include communication that:

- Is interactive
- Mediates subsequent events (Warren & Rogers-Warren, 1985)
- Can be used effectively in everyday settings with both adults, children, and peers
- Achieves material and social outcomes
- Progresses to higher levels of efficient and effective communication

When discussing functional communication, the *form, function,* and *content* of the communication must be considered. The forms of communication are the ways in which people can communicate. Communication forms may include body movement, touching, gestures, manual signs, and speech words. The functions of communication are the reasons for the communication, that is, how individuals use the communication to impact another person. Different functions include protesting, making choices, requesting continuation, offering, commenting, and so forth. Finally, the content of the communication refers to what one is communicating about. Content may include persons, objects, actions, events, and feelings.

Intervention efforts toward developing functional communication for any individual student who is deaf-blind must encourage effective communication exchanges between the student and all other interactors across many different environments. Functional communication for students who are deaf-blind must include the communication efforts of others communicating with the student as well as the student's own attempts at communication. Aspects other than form, function, and content need to be considered in the development of communication interventions for students who are deaf-blind. A means toward this end is the application of *contextualistic behavior analysis*, where a communication interaction is viewed within the larger sociocultural, environmental, and motivational context in which it occurs. Contextualistic analysis of behavior is similar to ecobehavioral analysis in that both approaches focus on the interrelationship between behavior and the environment and on functional control as a means of understanding variables that control behavior (Baer, Wolf, & Risley, 1987; Haring, 1992; O'Neill, Horner, Albin, Storey, & Sprague, 1990).

An important difference between contextualistic behavior analysis and ecobehavioral analysis is that the former also focuses on the purpose of behavior within and across settings, whereas ecobehavioral analysis does not focus on the purpose of the behavior (or motivation). Applying a motivational aspect, a skill has to be understood in relation to the goals that a student has for his or her communicative behavior, the quality of support

that the communicative behavior receives from others, and the power of the simple presence and responsiveness of others in the student's natural settings in order to increase occurrences of the behavior (Haring, 1992). In other words, a more contextualistic analysis considers the goals and functions of communicative behavior from the student's perspective as well as the responses that the student receives in interaction with others that reinforce the student's communicative behavior.

The intent of this chapter is to provide some perspectives on and strategies for considering factors of an individual's social and physical environments to achieve a shared communication system. This chapter also emphasizes a person-centered approach to the development and implementation of a functional communication system for students who are deaf-blind.

COMMUNICATION PRACTICES

Past Practices

Stillman (1992) emphasizes that *deaf-blindness* is a descriptive category, with individuals displaying differences in the degree of sensory impairment, age of onset, and the presence and extent of additional disabilities. Baldwin (1992) indicates that many students who are deaf-blind are identified as also having cognitive and/or other disabilities. Downing (1993) points out that the composition of the population that is deaf-blind is perhaps the greatest hindrance to the development of effective communication interventions. However, possibly a greater hindrance is the tendency of service providers not to consider the unique human characteristics of an individual or the accommodations that need to be determined when interacting with a student who is deaf-blind. Many of the past intervention practices summarized in the following list reflect the lack of individualization and inclusion of individuals who are deaf-blind:

1. Students who are deaf-blind and have severe disabilities were often ruled "ineligible" for speech and language services based on their level of cognitive functioning.
2. There was an emphasis placed on language and not on communication; therefore, early and nonsymbolic forms of communication were often not responded to or were ignored.
3. Students who did receive services were often "pulled-out" of their classroom for language and communication intervention.
4. Many of these students were being taught skills that were neither functional nor age-appropriate in settings that were segregated from their peers without disabilities. Many of these students were also separated from their families and their communities.
5. Many intervention efforts could be described as being stimulating rather than responsive, directive rather than interactional, and service provider driven rather than consumer driven.

Current Practices

Rowland and Stremel-Campbell (1987) have described communication as a shared process in which the form, perspective on a topic, intent, and social roles are understood and utilized by at least two communicative partners. Sharing in any one of these areas cannot be assumed, but must be achieved for effective communication to occur (Stillman, 1992). Currently, practices observed in many classrooms and schools do not fully reflect a shared process of communication. The following list of current practices is based on the first author's observations across over 50 classrooms in 32 different states.

1. Many students remain on manual signing programs in which they are physically assisted to make many signs without initially demonstrating *nonsymbolic communication* (the use of body movement, gestures, facial expressions, eye gaze, and/or vocalizations to communicate an intention to another person).
2. The same procedures of taking the student's hands and physically assisting the student are often used for both receptive input as well as expressive output.
3. The beginning, middle, and end of multiple routines and activities are not being fully utilized for more active participation or for communication interactions.
4. Even when more functional or inclusive peer activities are being targeted as outcomes, very few opportunities for communication are available. Teaching remains very unidirectional, with the primary exchange being directed by the service provider.
5. In the more progressive classrooms that are targeting nonsymbolic behaviors, such as body movement (student opening his mouth, turning his head, moving forward) or assisting the teacher, there are few attempts to "up-the-ante" or to teach the student a higher form or function of communication. In many cases, each student in the classroom is being taught identical forms, even though they may demonstrate differences in cognitive and social development.
6. In both segregated and inclusive classrooms, there are few demonstrations of actively teaching the student how to make choices and providing multiple opportunities for choices. If students are not given choices for the lesser decisions in life (i.e., what to eat, where to go, what to wear), they, in all probability, will not be prepared to make choices about the more important aspects of life

(i.e., where to work, where to live, whom they want as friends).

Current Perspectives and Best Practices

During the past 10 years, the majority of current perspectives on and best practices and approaches in communication intervention for infants, children, and youth have been the result of federally funded research and demonstration projects. One of the first of these projects was the Communication Skills Center for Young Children with Deaf-Blindness, which was funded from 1983 to 1988. This project consisted of a multisite, consortium model, which examined approaches of assessment and intervention for infants and young children across multiple settings (Bullis, 1987, 1989). During the same period of time, Stillman and Battle (1984) were conducting research and demonstration projects at the Callier Center for Communication Disorders, which concentrated on the development of communication interventions for school-age students who are deaf-blind. Many of the current perspectives and best practices specific to communication interventions for children and youth who are deaf-blind have resulted from these combined efforts (Bullis, 1987, 1989; Goetz, Guess, & Stremel-Campbell, 1987; Siegel-Causey & Guess, 1989). Recommendations from these and other studies include the following:

1. Multiple assessments conducted over time and across varying contexts are necessary to provide useful information for assisting a team to plan how to best integrate communication into routines, functional activities, and inclusive placements (Halle, 1993; Peck, 1989; Reichle & Yoder, 1979; Reichle, York, & Sigafoos, 1991; Rowland, 1987). Methods of assessment may include interview formats, direct observation, and systematic manipulations/ structured protocols (Halle, 1993).

2. Team planning formats, such as the *Personal Futures Planning* model (Mount & Zwernik, 1988; O'Brien, 1987), provide the family and important others the means to determine factors in the student's physical and social environments, current and future desired outcomes, the student's strengths and limitations, and service provision barriers.

3. A social interaction approach to training communication that includes different communication partners across varied environmental contexts is necessary for effective communication skills to be acquired, maintained, and generalized (Rowland & Stremel-Campbell, 1987).

4. Students who are deaf-blind need to be included in typical home, school, and community environments (Rainforth, York, Macdonald, & Dunn, 1992), with student outcomes being directed toward productive work, typical living options, and social interactions in the community.

5. Effective communication and other critical skills can best be accomplished through inclusive programming (Campbell, 1987, 1989; Dunn, 1991; Giangreco, 1990) and inclusive teams (see chap. 8, this volume).

6. Routines and functional activities provide the context from which interpersonal communication, sensory, and physical needs of the student can be addressed (Halle, 1988; Jackson, 1988; Stremel et al., 1990; chap. 13, this volume).

7. Receptive communication for students who are deaf-blind has, until recently, been an under-emphasized area of training (Rowland & Stremel-Campbell, 1987). Through the communication partner's use of different touch cues, object cues, gestures, pictures, and manual/tactile sign modalities, students who are deaf-blind will begin to

develop an understanding of their social and physical environments and learn daily life and vocational skills needed to function as members of society.

8. Nonsymbolic forms of communication must be considered if many students are to express different intents within the context of interpersonal interactions (Downing & Siegel-Causey, 1988; Rowland, Schweigert, & Stremel, 1992; Siegel-Causey & Downing, 1987; Siegel-Causey & Guess, 1989; Stillman & Battle, 1984; Stillman & Siegel-Causey, 1989).

9. Assessment of the potential communicative function of challenging behavior and the design of appropriate interventions has provided families and services providers new means for addressing challenging behaviors (Carr & Durand, 1985; Durand, 1993; Durand & Crimmins, 1988; Horner & Day, 1991).

10. Microswitch technology for early communication (Rowland & Schweigert, 1991; Schweigert, 1989) and more appropriate assessments and interventions for the use of augmentative and alternative communication have given service providers more options for addressing the students' needs.

Stillman (1992) points out that many approaches to teaching communication have been documented, with each approach working for some students who are deaf-blind and failing for others. He aptly points out that current practices might best be described as eclectic. Overall, service providers are recognizing that nonsymbolic behaviors can serve as communication. There has probably been a decrease in the emphasis of teaching "language" at the expense of communication. There is also a recognition that different forms of receptive communication

(or input to the student) need to be used for individual students, based on the severity of their vision, hearing, motor, and cognitive impairments, in order for them to understand the message of the communication partner.

Although these are positive developments in current practices, a number of additional practices must be emphasized. First, service providers should approach communication as a "process" rather than an "end product." There is a critical need in teacher training programs to teach collaborative teaming and decision making in a "process format." Stillman (1992) points out that service providers have often not received training to understand the progressive nature of communication acquisition. He states, "The result is that they spend considerable time nurturing affective displays that do not contribute substantively to the student's overall development of communication skills" (p. 132). Second, Certo and Kohl (1984) point out that for students with severe disabilities, the majority of their interactions fall into the "receive" category. Data collected by Houghton, Bronicki, and Guess (1987) strongly indicate that educational service providers: 1) infrequently respond to the communication attempts of students with severe, multiple disabilities and 2) provide infrequent opportunities for communication to occur. Third, there remains a lack of opportunities for choice making with students who are deaf-blind. Mirenda, Iacono, and Williams (1990) indicate that communication access and opportunities are perhaps the only prerequisites to communication. Fourth, perhaps the most important factors that need attention are the limited, so-called "interactions" and the types and quality of interactions for the student who is deaf-blind with important others in the home, school and community environments. Communication cannot be learned or taught if frequent and quality interactions do not occur (Stremel,

1994). Additionally, social bids and meaningful social relationships will be more feasible if a conventional communication system understood by other persons (i.e., gestures, pictures, words) is utilized by a student who is deaf-blind.

UTILIZING THE TEAM PROCESS OF PLANNING AND DECISION MAKING

Planning communication interventions for an individual student who is deaf-blind should not begin with the selection of a form (ways to communicate) or function (uses for communication) or the *referent* (object, action, person, event being referred to) to be expressed. Even though decisions concerning each of these critical features of communication will need to be addressed, forms and functions may be viewed as vehicles used between two or more persons in an interpersonal transaction. There must be a recognition that in order for functional communication to be developed, the vehicle will change along the way, and different vehicles may be necessary across different environments. Therefore, a communication "map" should be developed and modified for each individual student as an outgrowth of a life planning process conducted by a team. Four individuals are referred to in the following sections to provide a case example of the development of one student's education and communication program. These individuals include:

- Joshua Lyton, a 15-year-old young man who is profoundly deaf, with only light perception, and who is ambulatory
- Ms. Ann, Joshua's teacher
- Sam, Joshua's peer buddy
- Chris, who is doing his student-teaching practicum with Joshua
- Joshua's parents and siblings

The Lifestyle Planning Process

The growing number of demonstrations of inclusive community living and the increasing number of interpersonal relationships among people with disabilities and their peers without disabilities have led to several innovations in individualized education and human services planning strategies. First, individuals with disabilities, family members, friends, and community members are increasingly assuming key roles in the planning process (Forest & Lusthaus, 1987; Mount & Zwernik, 1988; O'Brien, 1987; Vandercook, York, & Forest, 1989). Consequently, planning is increasingly involving the persons who can provide both continuity and support to an individual throughout his or her lifetime. This development, in part, reflects an increasing focus on a socially inclusive lifestyle. Social inclusion addresses participation in social relationships across the entire range of human intimacy and support dimensions (i.e., from interacting with store clerks to the maintenance of long-term relationships), as opposed to physical or functional inclusion, which focuses on the placement of individuals with disabilities in nonsegregated school and community environments (Haring, 1991; Horner, Meyer, & Fredericks, 1986; Schutz, Williams, Iverson, & Duncan, 1984).

Second, planning strategies are evolving to focus on the desired future for an individual and to determine methods to realize these visions of an inclusive lifestyle (Forest & Lusthaus, 1987; Mount & Zwernik, 1988; O'Brien, Forest, Snow, & Hasbury, 1989). The *lifestyle planning* process developed by O'Brien and Lyle (O'Brien, 1987; O'Brien & Lyle, 1987) centers on basic questions associated with five outcomes, or accomplishments, identified as essential for achieving an acceptable quality of life:

- Community presence
- Choice
- Competence
- Respect
- Community participation (O'Brien, 1987; Mount & Zwernik, 1988; see also chap. 6, this volume).

The lifestyle planning process moves service providers, family members, and friends of the individual through three planning activities: 1) describing a desirable future for the individual, 2) delineating a schedule of activities and supports necessary to move toward that desired outcome, and 3) accepting responsibility for using available resources and dealing with the reality of those resources and supports that are not available.

The *Personal Futures Planning* model (Mount & Zwernik, 1988) is a second future-oriented planning process and is drawn directly from the lifestyle planning framework. Lifestyle planning and futures planning have been used most often for adults with disabilities and focus on their presence and participation in home, work, and general community environments. A third process, the *McGill Action Planning System* (MAPS), is a planning process that places primary emphasis on the inclusion, participation, and learning of students with disabilities in general education classes and other inclusive school settings (Forest & Lusthaus, 1987; Vandercook et al., 1989).

Joshua's team for assisting in envisioning his future includes his parents, siblings, friends, pastor, teacher, other related service personnel, and Chris (his student teacher). A facilitator who is skilled in drawing out the MAPS and leading the team through the life planning process has agreed to meet with the group throughout the year to plan and update the team's progress. A counselor for adults who are deaf-blind from the Voca-

tional Rehabilitation agency is also a major team member.

Envisioning Future Lifestyles

Common to the lifestyle planning strategies for Joshua is that a desirable future for him is one in which he is a participating member of a family and is included in community activities. In both the education and habilitation programs, his planning team's vision of where and with whom Joshua will go to school, live, work, spend leisure time, and use other community facilities establishes the focus for deciding what to teach him. Until this focus or vision is established, Joshua's planning team has no clear direction and cannot ensure the relevance of the curricular content.

In contrast to older planning models that were based on a deficit orientation (Hamill & Bartell, 1975; Salvia & Ysseldyke, 1985), envisioning a future lifestyle for Joshua requires team members to utilize a holistic approach to attain knowledge regarding his interests, assets, challenges, and needs. Planning team members can generate a vision of a desirable future for an individual by discussing such questions as:

1. Who is Joshua?
2. What is the desirable future for him?
3. What is the future to be avoided?
4. What are his interests and strengths?
5. What are Joshua's greatest challenges?
6. What are his greatest needs? (Forest & Lusthaus, 1987; Vandercook et al., 1989).

These questions may be posited for each of the four basic types of natural settings: 1) school, 2) home/neighborhood, 3) vocational, and 4) community. A vision of a desired future for Joshua can, and most probably will, change over time. Such changes would result from periodic updates of the lifestyle plan.

The shared vision for Joshua, developed through the lifestyle planning process, assists the team members to maintain a holistic view of him as a person rather than a collection of deficits. In addition, the shared vision of the future leads to a more unified view of the purpose and design of education or habilitation programs. For Joshua and all students who are deaf-blind, the development of a communication map within the lifestyle planning process is critical.

Considerations in Developing a Communication Map

Planning efforts for Joshua must address special considerations. First, due to the severity of Joshua's sensory losses, he may not have the advantage of communicating at a distance. Second, persons interacting with Joshua will also not have the advantage of being able to communicate at a distance. Therefore, a major *interferer* (person, object, or event that hampers or obstructs the actions of another person) in communicating will be distance. This may be an interference for several reasons including: 1) persons in our culture do not routinely use touch as a means of communicating unless they have a close relationship, and 2) it is more time-consuming to communicate at near distance than at a distance of more than 3 feet. Finally, in many cases, the potential interactors will have to learn a new skill (*touch cues, manual signs, tactile signs*) in order to communicate or other types of tangible systems (Rowland & Schweigert, 1989) will have to be developed and constructed.

Examples of touch cues include touching specific parts of the body to communicate (e.g., touching the arm to communicate "stand up," tapping fingers for "give me"). Manual signs include signs made by hand movements, configurations that can be seen visually and may mean, for example, "stop," "love," or "more." Tactile signs are signs made by hand movements, configurations that are made within and felt by a person's hand(s) if the person cannot see.

SELECTING AND ANALYZING PHYSICAL ENVIRONMENTS, ROUTINES, AND ACTIVITIES

In the past, Joshua's access to different environments was based, in part, on his social behaviors. Social behaviors, communication skills, and cognitive skills were often used as "prerequisites" to deny him access to different physical environments and the routines and activities that these environments afforded. The physical environments that Joshua has access to, or potential access to, define many of his social partners and social interactions. However, new social relationships can encourage Joshua and his family to select different physical environments in which he will work, play, worship, eat, and shop.

Range of Environments

Joshua's planning team decided that the major environments in Joshua's milieu will consist of home, school, work, and community. Subenvironments exist in each of these environments. The subenvironments in Joshua's community domain will include a laundromat, the grocery store, the bank, the gym, and fast food restaurants. The activities that Joshua will perform there, such as shopping in a convenience store, will determine the purpose of his communication and the vocabulary that is needed both for him and the persons interacting with him. Certo and Kohl (1984) stress that social interactions that occur must be linked to a functional purpose in home, school, and community contexts. This is especially true for the majority of social interactions between a student who is deaf-blind and his or her communication partner (see section, "Communication Partners," this chapter). Unless the student demonstrates high cognitive abilities or the onset of one of the sensory losses occurs later in life (as in Usher syndrome), the social interactions and communication content will be based on the activities in the present situation.

There are a number of features of the physical environments selected that will "set the occasion" for Joshua to increase his social interactions and communication exchanges. These include:

1. The presence of persons without disabilities who can be potential partners for communication
2. Functional and age-appropriate activities that provide a rich context in which Joshua has something to communicate about
3. Activities within these environments that should increase Joshua's dignity or at least not diminish it
4. Organized, predictable, and engaging situations (Stremel, 1994) that can facilitate the probability that communication will occur

Access to different physical environments will increase the availability of different communication partners and social interactions. However, access will not guarantee that communication will occur. *Communication intervention* (systematic instruction to change or increase the student's communication behavior) through social interactions must be an active process within each physical environment.

Context and Content of Environments

Activities carried out in a range of environments provide two critical variables that are necessary for communication to occur: context and content. The process for determining the specific context and content of an activity for Joshua will depend on: 1) his age,

2) the noncommunication-related outcomes desired, and 3) other communication partners who may be sharing an activity. The locations, objects, typical actions, and other persons involved in the activities can be used as the content or referents in any communication exchange. In many cases, the communication exchanges that are mandatory to carry out the activity may be minimal. Joint activities between Joshua and other persons provide more natural opportunities for communication to occur.

DEFINING SOCIAL INTERACTIONS AS A BASIS OF COMMUNICATION

It is critical that communication and language intervention for all individuals with disabilities begin with a conceptual framework regarding the meaning of social interaction. Schutz et al. (1984) point out that the difficulties in defining, teaching, and measuring skills associated with social interactions are due largely to the complexity of social activities. Schutz et al. indicate that interpersonal interaction assumes a sensory exchange (visual, auditory, or tactile) between two or more people. They further state that to measure the frequency and quality of an interaction, there must be a focus on the participants and the social context of an interaction.

Based on Joshua's Personal Futures Plan, Ms. Ann, Joshua's teacher, has outlined the current and future environments in which Joshua will be included. Analysis of these environments provides a basis for Joshua's team to determine: 1) the functions of the communication to be taught, 2) the content of both receptive and expressive communication, and 3) the training needs of other persons in these environments. The physical environments and activities for Joshua's education and vocation programs include:

- Shop, home economics, gym, and vocational education in typical classrooms
- Breakfast, dinner, and cleaning in the school cafeteria
- Walking to his locker and the bathrooms in the school hallways
- Shopping at the local mall
- Loading the soda machines in the teachers' lounge
- Gaining job experience cleaning at a local bank
- Shopping at the grocery store
- The school courtyard
- A local fast food restaurant
- The school library
- The school office

The Communication Act

Although different social interaction models have been described to discuss communication (Certo & Kohl, 1984), there seems to be a continuing trend to highlight the forms and functions of the communication system and then mention that these should be taught within a social interaction. The focus of communication intervention for Joshua will begin with a "theoretical framework that reduces all communicative behavior down to a small set of fundamental roles, then provides a basis for developing pragmatic categories that reflect the expression of these roles in everyday communication" (Jackson, 1988, p. 8). Jackson (1988) points out that the basic unit in a social communication exchange is the *communication act* (Searle, 1969). The communication act may be nonsymbolic, symbolic, or a combination within a specific social interaction. The communication act may serve one function or it may serve multiple functions. Jackson (1988) states, "Communication acts provide exchange participants access to social and material *outcomes*, and pragmatic functions are reflected in the efforts of communicating individuals to predict and control these out-

comes under continuously changing environmental, interpersonal, and intrapersonal conditions" (p. 9).

Within this perspective, communication acts are used so that individuals both realize their own needs and accommodate themselves to the needs of others. Figure 1 demonstrates a model of communication competence (Jackson, 1988). The basic components include a potential provider and a potential recipient, with both communication partners exchanging these roles (see "Role Exchange," this chapter). Each communication partner may initiate, maintain, or terminate an interaction. The basic model proposed by Jackson (1988) includes both the potential provider providing/offering or withholding/withdrawing and the potential recipient requesting/receiving or preventing/rejecting. The proposed model may be extended to four additional categories including:

1. Control of attention within a social interaction
2. Control of material and informational resources within a social interaction
3. Control of relationships within a social interaction
4. Representation of knowledge

For a communication act to be successful, there is an *expressive–receptive* demand placed on both partners. For example, any potential provider needs to express his or her message to Joshua in a way in which he, as receiver, will understand the message. Traditionally, communication and language programs have approached expressive and receptive skills as two relatively separate areas. It is imperative that the nature of expressive and receptive communication behaviors for students who are deaf-blind be viewed within the context of any social exchange (Rowland & Stremel-Campbell, 1987).

Communication Partners   The major persons to communicate with Joshua initially

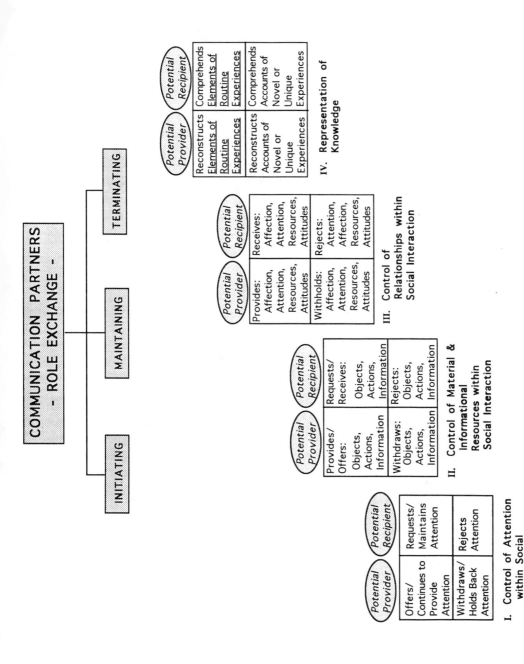

Figure 1. A model of communication competence using the communication act theory where communication partners initiate, maintain, and terminate an interaction. (From Jackson, L.B. [1988, October]. *Assessing the communication competence of persons with multiple impairments*. Paper presented at the 1988 Biennial Conference of the International Society for Augmentative and Alternative Communication, Anaheim, CA; reprinted by permission.)

will include Ms. Ann, Chris, Sam, and his family. The speech-language pathologist (SLP) will be instrumental in assisting the teaching staff and Joshua's family to determine the current and future forms and functions of Joshua's communication. However, it will be the major interactors who will *adapt, accommodate, and augment* Joshua's communication within a social exchange. van Dijk (1986) indicates that the relationship between the student who is deaf-blind and his or her teacher is critical. Also, the student needs to be able to control or influence his or her environment. The service provider must become skilled at participating in and observing the student's milieu (Murray-Seegert, 1989).

Role Exchange

Role exchange refers to two persons who are communicating with one another by taking on or exchanging the roles of speaker and listener. Any attempt at a social interaction may consist of only an *initiation*, in which a communication partner is not available to respond or exchange roles. Often, students with vision and hearing impairments, and possible motor disabilities, may not have the means to access a partner unless accommodations are made to the environment (such as having a calling device, peers who understand the communication forms). A study by Houghton et al. (1987) demonstrated that classroom staff responded at very low rates to student-initiated expressions. An initiation by a student may be *terminated* by the potential recipient's rejection of the social interaction.

For example, initially Sam did not respond to Joshua's body movement signal of leaning back to indicate he was finished eating because it is not a shared system of communication. This may be the lack of sensitivity discussed by Siegel-Causey and Guess (1989), or in Sam's case, no one had taught him the

meaning of Joshua's body movement signals. As Ms. Ann taught Chris how to observe and acknowledge Joshua's signals, Chris then became responsible for teaching Sam. Sam became more observant and noticed that Joshua reached out to touch him when he wanted a drink of water. Sam was then taught to help Joshua get a cup to represent his request for drink. In this way, other peers could more easily understand Joshua's request. Interactions may consist of an initiation and a termination in which the service provider offers material resources and the student receives or requests by making a communicative response. Finally, an interaction may be initiated, maintained, and terminated by either partner.

Future Desired Outcomes of Joshua's Current Communication Acts

Table 1 displays examples of current communication acts for Joshua and acts that may be included as future desired outcomes. This model puts part of the ownership of intervention on the communication partner. That is, a student cannot receive a request or an offer unless one is made by the potential provider. The nonsymbolic and symbolic forms that are used as the "vehicle" to accomplish the communication act within any interaction need to be examined for both communication partners.

Table 1. Developing new outcomes from Joshua's current communication acts

Current communication acts	Desired outcomes
Receives attention by hitting self	Requests attention by pressing a buzzer device
Receives objects, actions	Requests objects and actions from service providers and peers
Rejects attention and offers	Receives requests and offers

For example, typical peers sometimes tried to talked to Joshua (before he was fitted for hearing aids), and then would attempt to assist him. Joshua would often scream at them or jerk away. Thus, he was rejecting the social interaction. One strategy to change Joshua's behavior was to determine if hearing aids would improve his performance. However, another strategy would be to teach the peers to use object cues (e.g., handing Joshua a meal ticket to cue lunchtime or a screwdriver to cue shop class) and touch cues (e.g., tapping Joshua's arm to communicate "come with me").

DETERMINING NONSYMBOLIC AND SYMBOLIC FORMS FOR COMMUNICATION PARTNERS

Service providers need to have an awareness that there are many different signals that they can use to communicate with a student, and many signals that may be available for use by the student. The severity of the visual, auditory, cognitive, and motor disabilities and the onset of the loss of the senses are factors to consider in designing a communication map. For example, the SLP responsible for Joshua's communication intervention will provide in-service training to Ms. Ann, Chris, Sam, and Joshua's parents specific to the communication process. The in-service may include an introduction to the following ideas:

1. There is a process of communication acquisition that should be part of the knowledge base for decision making (Stillman, 1992).
2. There are numerous forms of communication that can be used by either Joshua or his partner.
3. Nonsymbolic forms for both Joshua and his partners must be considered, with

the knowledge base that using a person or a symbol as a vehicle to drive the communication act represent two very separate classes of behavior (Reichle, 1991).

4. The better maintained and generalized a response, the more difficult it will be to replace it with a more effective or readable response (Reichle, Feeley, & Johnston, 1993; Stillman, 1992). Therefore, the longer Joshua is able to communicate only by moving his body or touching a person, the more difficult it will be to teach him other, more conventional forms of communication, such as a headshake to mean "no."

Communication Process

Stillman (1992) points out that purposefulness or intentionality is a key issue in the communication process. Any behavior can serve as an index. However, often these behaviors are affected by *distancing features* and may not be used to intentionally affect others and achieve desired outcomes.

Distancing Features

Werner and Kaplan (1963) discuss the progressive distancing between the speaker and the listener, the referent and the communication form as an individual learns to represent actions and ideas with words. A number of researchers developing communication interventions for students who are deaf-blind have used these distancing features within the communication acquisition process (Downing & Siegel-Causey, 1988; Rowland, 1990; Rowland & Schweigert, 1989; Siegel-Causey & Downing, 1987; Stillman & Battle, 1984). Distancing features may include spatial, temporal, and similarity features.

For example, a young child may take her mother's hand to get the mother to continue feeding her. Later, the child may extend her cup to her mother to get more to drink. As the child develops, she will point to the cup or food or say the name of the object ("drink") when she sees it. Still later the child may say the word "dog" to indicate that she saw the dog yesterday. Therefore, there is a distancing between: 1) the way in which the child or student communicates, 2) the person who is being communicated to, and 3) that which is being communicated.

Distancing Between the Form and the Referent   There exists a continuum in which there is a process of differentiation or "distancing," in *representation*. For example, there is a gradual distancing of the behavior used to communicate and the referent. Werner and Kaplan (1963) discuss that an infant does not represent events, but initially simply responds to them by changes in movement. These early movement patterns may be reactive or co-active. Initially, the communication partner moves with the student in that the communication act and the action are the same event. The concept of movement in shaping communication has been discussed by van Dijk (1967) and Stillman and Battle (1984). There is a possibility that if this movement pattern is maintained and generalized for too long, the distancing process will be more difficult to achieve.

Students must also have a knowledge of objects (e.g., the smell or feel of a desired food), so that objects can be used as ways to communicate. Gradually, the student may use the communication partner's hand as a way to communicate; later, the object or an *object representation* (something that "stands for" the actual object or location) (Rowland & Schweigert, 1989) may be used as the way to communicate. If students have enough vision, a pointing response or gestures may be used as a way to refer to the object or action when the person is at a distance. Speech words or signs, which are used in a 1:1 relationship where the form represents a specific

referent, are the beginning of true symbolic behavior. Up until this point, the nonsymbolic forms are used to indicate more generalized meanings.

Distancing Time   The concept of distancing is also expressed in terms of time. For example, a student may be physically assisted to gesture his or her desire to eat. The student may initially continue the gesture or imitate the gesture. Gradually, he or she may make the gesture (*delayed imitation*) during the meal even though it was not immediately preceded by a model or direct assistance. Gradually, the student may be able to use a gesture or an object representation during the context of the activity without the object being presented to him or her.

Distancing Context   The concept of distancing in terms of location or context is important to the communication process. A student may communicate through some form that he wants to go to the convenience store, or that he wants to eat, even though he is not actually in the physical location where shopping or eating usually takes place.

Distancing Communication Partners   Initially, communication exchanges may occur primarily between one important partner and the individual who is deaf-blind. For a young child, this partner will be his or her primary caretaker. Gradually, the student who is deaf-blind will use a previously learned response to communicate with a peer who shares his or her system of communication. Therefore, concepts such as maintenance and generalization of the system of communication become important.

Using Multiple Forms Across Multiple Contexts   The use of multiple forms becomes an important consideration, especially as the student becomes older and has access to more communication partners and more social environments. For example, an older student may use signs at school and home, and a communication board in the workplace.

Nonsymbolic and Symbolic Forms Used By the Communication Partner

Symbols serve the function of representing meanings. The establishment of a symbolic form in the communication process is truly complex. Yet, as the need for symbolic forms becomes greater, service providers often attempt to begin to develop a communication program with a student who is deaf-blind. Unfortunately, there is no "cookbook" approach to this gradual process of differentiation across the communication process for any one student. The only approach is one of continual team decision making.

As Joshua is included in a greater number of social environments, it will be necessary for other persons to communicate with Joshua at a close distance. It is important that this communication act be accomplished with as little intrusion as possible. For example, if Sam grabs Joshua's hands to sign "cafeteria" as a directive for "Let's go to the cafeteria," his act may be described as intrusion without meaning. If Joshua does not indicate that he is ready to receive a message, and the form being used by Sam has no meaning, there may be a tendency for Joshua to reject the attempt at social interaction. Initially, nonsymbolic forms, such as touch and object cues, may need to be used by everyone who interacts with Joshua in order for their messages to be meaningful. There are many different types of receptive, or input, forms that may be effective with different students at different stages of the communication process.

Natural Contextual Cues Natural contextual cues may be movement-based cues (e.g., the service provider feeding the student or moving the spoon with the student) or cues that are routinely part of an activity, such as the smell or taste of a food, or the removal of the wheelchair strap when in transition. The more a student is involved in routine activities, the more these types of cues will be associated with the activity. At first, a student may lack an awareness of another person even being involved in the routine or activity. As there is more of an awareness of a social partner, there is a need to expand the communication partner's system of communication input forms. What is critical at this point in the process is that a student begins to anticipate the next step in the interaction. For example, when Joshua was younger, his mom reported that he would simply "receive" as she offered him another bite of food. As Joshua became older, she waited before continuing an activity and/or offered an object/activity before proceeding, so that Joshua made some movement as a signal to maintain the interaction/activity.

Tactile/Touch Cues Initially, a few touch cues may be used to "request attention" (e.g., using Joshua's name cue or a signal to gain his attention). This indicates to Joshua that someone is available to interact. Additional tactile or touch cues simply provide information to him (e.g., "I'm going to move your chair.") or issue a directive (e.g., "Get your coat."). At first, only a few cues will be used in routines or activities that occur the most frequently (e.g., "up," "go").

As Joshua indicated that he could learn the meaning of new touch cues in a short period and/or generalize these cues, cues were added that were more difficult (e.g., "give me," "get it," "search for it"). Transition routines and daily life activities, such as eating, were then analyzed to determine which cues would provide the most critical information to Joshua. As Joshua increases in his understanding of different forms, touch cues may be used for different communication acts, for example, requesting a motor response by tapping him twice on his shoulder, or providing him feedback as in "good job." At an even higher level of difficulty, cues such as asking, "Which or what do you want?" by holding two objects out and then moving them up and down, may serve as communication acts that request information from Joshua and encourage him to make choices. These communication acts then involve more than just a receiving function on the part of the student. Gradually, the student may provide information, objects, or actions in response to the communication partner's initiation.

Object Cues Rowland and Schweigert (1989) and Rowland and Stremel-Campbell (1987) provide examples of different object cues that may be associated with activities and routines. Initially, the actual object should be used to develop a knowledge of objects. Because Joshua has no vision, this may not be a simple process for him. Joshua does not have limited grasping responses, but for students who do, the desired outcomes may be multiple. That is, a student may be more motivated to retain a grasp on an object that has meaning, such as a spoon, than on an object that is not directly used in the context of an activity.

Rowland and Stremel-Campbell (1987) describe the gradual relationship between objects at a concrete level and objects at a more abstract level. Concrete objects, such as a spoon, will be added to Joshua's receptive communication this year and will later include:

1. *Miniature objects* (e.g., a small book that stands for library)
2. *Partial objects* (e.g., the pull-tab off the top of a soda can that stands for soda or for going to the soda machine)
3. *Associated objects* (e.g., the computer disk stands for the computer or working at the computer)
4. Those objects having only one shared feature with the actual object (e.g., a piece of tin to represent Joshua's locker at the high school)

More abstract objects may be used for higher functioning students, such as a triangle to indicate that it is time to choose a leisure activity. It is important to note that there are distancing features that can be gradually incorporated into the receptive communication process.

Picture Cues For students with residual vision, line drawings or pictures may be used. Some students may be able to detect large line drawings more easily than photographs due to clarity in foreground and background. The use of line drawings may involve a high level of cognitive ability.

Gesture Cues Gesture cues are a conventional form of communication. Some gestures may be cross-cultural in that persons from different cultures understand the same meaning (e.g., pointing to an object). Other gestures may be culturally specific in that the meaning is primarily understood only by persons in that culture (e.g., Native American gestures used within their dance rituals). Gestures may also be very contextually based or more abstract, for example:

- A gesture that continues and terminates in touch, such as a gesture for "up" or holding out one's hand for "come to me"
- A gesture may be a motor-gesture that indicates the activity, as in "let's dance"
- A gesture may include the function of a specific object, as in drinking
- A gesture may indicate the shape of the object, as in holding out one's hand as if holding a soda can
- Gradually, gestures may be used that are proto-signs, as in "want, finished, and throw away"

If students have residual vision, gestures may become a viable vehicle in the communication act. Facial gestures may also provide the student with additional information. For example, a gesture for "no" paired with either a stern expression or a smiling expression can indicate two different messages.

Tactile Signing Research on the development of tactile signs is limited. It is the authors' opinion that if students are not reaching out to receive a message by means of object and touch cues, they are not apt to receive messages well when a partner intrusively grasps their hands. The process of changing from visual–manual signing to tactile signing for students with Usher syndrome (congenital nerve deafness and progressive loss of vision) must also be considered. For these students, the loss of vision will necessarily change the vehicle in which communication acts are carried out by both partners. An interpreter may need to be employed to translate the messages of various partners, rather than teaching each potential partner to become proficient at a complex language system that is delivered completely through tactual means.

Manual Signing An initial consideration in using manual signs as receptive/input communication will be the distancing factor. Does the student see the signs if they are presented more than 12 inches from his or her face? If a student is not responding to conventional gestures (such as gestures to express "no," "give," "put," "bye," "come here," "yes," "want," "finished"), manual signs may need to be initiated at a later point. The same distancing features for symbolic formation must be considered in manual/tactile signing and speech words. Signs may represent the function or the object, or may be highly abstract.

Speech Communication partners should always use speech in their interactions and use it expressively. Some students, hopefully, will be benefiting from hearing aids or auditory amplification and will learn that different intonation patterns and syllabic patterns have different meanings, especially as they

are used in conjunction with one or more of the previously discussed forms. The use of speech with a student who has no hearing, but has some vision, allows him or her to see the communication partners' expressions as they talk. Additionally, the use of speech adds dignity to the student as typical peers observe interactions between the service providers and the student.

Functions Expressed in the Communication Act

If we look at a rather typical communication act between Joshua and his teacher last year (via videotapes), we may describe it as the partner providing a *directive* for Joshua to receive and perform a motor act. Clearly, the outcome was controlled by the teacher. The functions or uses of a partner's communication become critical even prior to a routine or activity. The following process may be used as any person interacts with Joshua:

1. Approach Joshua and wait a short time to provide any olfactory cues that he may use to identify you.
2. Draw a "J" on his chest for his name sign to let him know that an interaction is to begin.
3. Use your *personal identification cue* (e.g., draw attention to your ring, watch, beard) to let Joshua know who is communicating with him.
4. Wait for Joshua to extend his hand or orient to you (this behavior will need to be taught).

It is critical for all potential communication partners to realize that Joshua may not know where he is being taken or what is about to happen because the typical visual and auditory cues may be absent for him. Therefore, communication partners should never act upon him without first letting him know what is about to happen and where he is going. Ms. Ann or Chris would provide in-service training for typical peers. This training should include: 1) letting peers select their own identification cue, 2) teaching them Joshua's name cue, and 3) teaching them to use the appropriate form (touch, object, gesture, tactile sign) to give Joshua information in the least intrusive manner.

The functions or uses of communication should extend beyond providing directives or commands to the student. The following list indicates Joshua's current functions(*) and the new functions of communication that will be added as Joshua learns more forms and generalizes old functions.

1. Attention*
2. Information*
3. Feedback*
4. Rejection/protest*
5. Social (greetings)*
6. Comments
7. Offer/transfer
8. Directives/commands*
9. Questions or requests for communication that provide choices for the student
10. Models for communication forms

Stremel (1991) discusses the need to use differentiated tactile cues in order for the student to understand the intent of the communication partner. For example, even students with 100–200 word vocabularies often imitate the last word that is signed to them. Without hearing intonation patterns, not clearly seeing the partner's face, and having a limited understanding of semantic and syntactic relations, these students often do not understand the intent of their partner. For example, is the partner requesting them to get to work, requesting information about work, or providing them feedback about their work? It may be important to include tactile cues to differentiate: 1) imitation, 2) requests for action, 3) requests for information, and 4) feedback. There are no standardized cues

used to share this information. However, Strong et al. (1993) have developed a videotape that demonstrates many functional tactile signs that can be used to teach students who are deaf-blind.

Nonsymbolic and Symbolic Forms of Expressive Communication Across Acquisition Stages

Many of the forms that are used to express a message and an intent to Joshua may, at a later point in time, become his form of communication. For example, Joshua currently uses objects, miniature objects, and associated objects as cues indicating where to go and what to do. As Joshua learns the meaning of these objects, he can use them to communicate to others. There are different models used to differentiate the levels or stages of communication and language development (McLean & Snyder-McLean, 1978; Rowland & Stremel-Campbell, 1987). Analyzing the many forms of communication within stages provides service providers and teams with the process of communication acquisition. The stages of communication and language development described by Dunst (1978) are used in this section to describe the process of nonsymbolic communication acquisition.

Figure 2 represents the possible forms of communication within the stages of communication acquisition and the notion that many of the forms may be used concurrently. The various forms are represented in a stair-step fashion to show that a student's communication acquisition should contain both horizontal and vertical movement. First, one form may be used across a number of communication partners to indicate a variety of meanings (e.g., more drink, more interaction). Second, one form (such as body movement) may be used to indicate both rejection and continuation. Third, a new form within the same stage may be used to indicate an old function or intent (e.g., pointing to an object

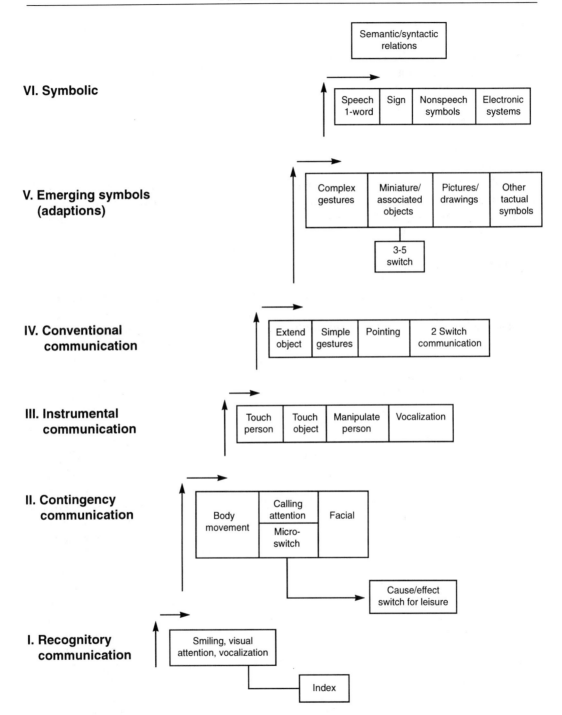

Figure 2.   Horizontal and vertical movement of expressive forms of communication across acquisition stages.

to receive it rather than actually touching it). Fourth, forms within higher stages of communication gradually replace the more primitive means of communication. The following paragraphs describe expressive forms of communication across acquisition stages.

Recognitory Communication During the first stage of communication acquisition, Joshua first realized the presence of a person outside of himself and indicated his notice. For students with some vision, these forms of notice or recognition may include visual regard, smiling, changing facial expressions, or maintaining their body in close proximity to another person. These behaviors are not intentional communication, but may indicate or serve an index of recognition or affect. Intervention procedures including the movement approach (Writer, 1987) or nurturance and sensitivity (Siegel-Causey & Guess, 1989) may be used to increase behaviors at this stage.

Contingency Communication At stage two, Joshua began to understand that if he behaved in some way something would happen. For some students, this may be a very gradual process that depends on a caregiver or communication partner beginning an activity, then stopping the activity. Initially, the student may simply continue the movement or use a behavior as an anticipatory response. Movement through this stage may depend on many repeated opportunities in which the student is given an opportunity to display intentional behavior. At this point the student may not realize that the outcome of his or her behavior is specifically controlled by another person.

During repetitive social interactions, the student must not only indicate a recognition of another person, but indicate rejection or request continuation of the action/activity. The student's early forms of behavior may be extremely subtle and require careful obser-

vation on the part of the communication partner. These forms of behavior may include:

1. Changes in posture or tone
2. Specific or general body movement
3. Facial changes
4. Eye movement
5. Vocalization
6. Smiling

Initially, these forms of behavior may not be used intentionally in that they are not directed to another person with a clear intent to impact the communication partner to respond. However, these early forms of behavior may become more intentional as different communication partners respond consistently to them.

A *microswitch*, a small device that is used to make, break, or change the connections in an electric or battery circuit (e.g., a plate switch that activates light or music by a touch), may be used by the student at this stage as a calling or attention-getting device. A looped tape-recorded message that says, "come here, please," may be made by using a person's voice of the same age and sex who is unknown to the student or child. The student then presses a switch to activate the recording. The switch may contain a vibration device to cue a student with a profound hearing loss. This allows a student with or without some hearing ability to initiate a communication act if he or she is unable to approach another person.

Instrumental Communication At this stage, a student is either acting on a person or acting on an object to communicate. For example, teaching Joshua to use touch (person or an object) as a form of communication, rather than using body movement, provided him with an increased orientation to his family, Ms. Ann, Chris, and Sam. Again, teaching Joshua to touch was accomplished in a nonintrusive manner. Initially, the communication partner moved her hand to touch Joshua's hand, rather than physically assisting him to touch her. Gradually, Ms. Ann moved her hand away so that he demonstrated an intentional touch. A receptive, or input, cue of "more" was used so that Joshua began to understand that continuation of an activity was available and that he should make a response. At this stage, some students may also use the partner as a "tool" in that they guide the partner's hand to the desired object or to repeat an action. Whereas touching and manipulating a partner are forms that do communicate, the communication map should include more conventional forms and strategies to expand the student's forms of communication to a higher level. During the instrumental stage of communication, Joshua will have forms with which to indicate: 1) attention, 2) protest/rejection, 3) continuation, and 4) choice between at least two objects or activities.

Conventional Communication The forms of communication at this stage include forms of communication that typical persons use each day of their lives. Teaching these forms (extending objects, pointing, and gesturing) will depend on an individual student's motor ability (or interferers) and vision. Microswitches and other devices may need to be considered for some students with physical disabilities. For students such as Joshua, who may have the potential to use manual signs, an extensive gestural vocabulary will be targeted. These gestures may include: come, bye, finished, want, more/again, give me, take, mine, drink, and eat. Joshua's routines and activities will guide the selection of gestures that are needed for him and his communication partner(s) to jointly carry out the activity.

Emerging Symbols At this stage, more complex gestures; miniature, partial, or associated objects; pictures/drawings; and other

tactual forms of communication become more abstract. Initially, these forms may be paired with the actual objects used in the previous conventional stage so that pairing and a gradual shift occur in expanding Joshua's system to a higher level. For students who do not have the motor ability to use signs or who have a limited range of motion, the communication map may indicate that the emerging symbols may be placed on a communication device, which may have a digitized voice output.

Symbolic Many students who are deafblind may indicate one or two "signs," such as "eat" or "more." These initial signs may actually function as generalized gestures that mean "I want." At this stage, it is critical to determine if the signs, words, or nonspeech symbols are being used to denote the specific referent for which they stand. For example, teaching would include letting Joshua select the item he indicated by a sign or a symbol to make sure that there is a 1:1 correspondence of the sign to the referent. Initially, he may indicate a want or need only if the activity (eating, swimming) has already begun. Teaching would include gradually distancing the activity and the location so that Joshua can make a choice even though it is not tactually present. Students who do not have cognitive disabilities may learn braille at this stage as their typical peers are learning to read. Braille and written words are also symbolic, as are signs, speech words, and phrases.

INTEGRATING COMMUNICATION ACTS INTO ROUTINES AND ACTIVITIES

The Personal Futures Planning process and IEP should drive the routines and activities that are critical for Joshua to achieve interdependence across work, daily living skills, play/recreation/leisure activities, and community access. In turn, the targeted routines and activities should drive the assessment, planning, implementation, and evaluation of the communication acts, forms, functions, and content for both present and future environments. Figure 3 shows a communication map for Joshua that could also be used as a basis for any student. Forms that Joshua is currently using are shaded dark. New forms to be targeted throughout the school year are shaded light. Forms that may be potentially targeted in the future are shown in the dotted areas. Forms and functions to be taught are based on the Personal Futures Planning summary on the right-hand side of the figure. Specific content (vocabulary) will be based on the persons, locations, and activities included in the summary. This "map" provides a student's family and all his or her service providers with a direction and indicates a progression in the communication acquisition process.

Analyzing Routines and Activities

There are a number of steps in analyzing a routine or activity. First, the beginning, middle, and end of a routine or activity must be included. Second, the student's level of partial participation to carry out the routine or activity must be considered. Third, the mandatory receptive or input forms to teach the steps in the activity must be determined. The desired outcomes for both the caregiver (parent) and the student, the integration of receptive cues, levels of partial participation, and the opportunities for expressive communication are indicated in the sample activity analysis for Joshua shown in Figure 4.

Changing the Routine or Activity

It is critical that the individual's routines and activities be dynamic, not static. Although desired outcomes for students will include participating in an activity with as much independence as possible, the activity should change once the student demonstrates the desired outcome. Table 2 shows that as routines and activities change from isolated tasks to cooperative tasks, the roles of the service provider, parent, and peers may change as well.

Role of Teacher Initially, in teaching Joshua any routine or activity, there will be frequent use of receptive cues as part of the teaching sequence. There may be a tendency for Ms. Ann or Chris to provide too much physical assistance and too few touch or object cues for Joshua in teaching the task. Unfortunately, many routines and activities can be carried out with little or no need for students to communicate. When Joshua is learning a new task, there will be a highly predictable sequence in which Ms. Ann controls the outcome.

Role of Partner In an isolated task, the student is ultimately responsible for completing the task (making sandwiches), although he or she may require some physical assistance. In a cooperative task, the task is completed by two to three persons who perform different skills in order to complete the task. For example, one person can make dinner and clean up (isolated task), or the entire family can participate (cooperative task).

As Ms. Ann changes the activity from an isolated task to a cooperative task, she becomes more involved, and the receptive forms and functions change as well. As Joshua learns the task, fewer directives will be needed, and Ms. Ann will be able to comment on Joshua's actions, indicating to him what she is going to do, commenting on her own actions, and requesting that he assist her in some way. These changes in the task and social roles set the occasion for Joshua to model, and at a later point, offer objects and comment as well, rather than just request. At this point, Ms. Ann and Chris should use time delay procedures and more indirect

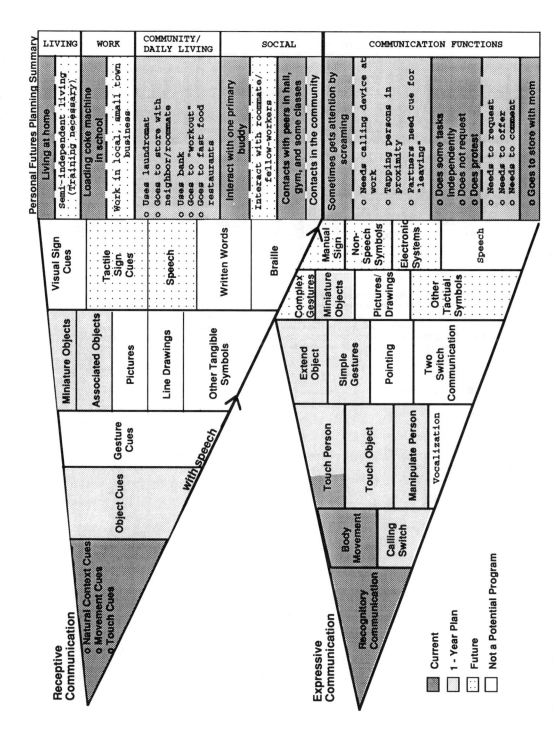

Figure 3. Communication map for Joshua.

219

LEARNER CHARACTERISTICS

AGE:	15 years
COMMUNICATION:	Level III & IV
MOTOR:	Ambulatory
VISION:	Blind
HEARING:	Profound

RECEPTIVE COMMUNICATION OBJECTIVES

EXPRESSIVE COMMUNICATION OBJECTIVES

o To respond to <u>touch cues</u>

o To respond to <u>object cues</u>

o To respond to a few <u>tactile gesture cues</u>

o To "touch people" to request

o To "touch objects" to request

o To "extend objects"

o To use "simple gestures"

DOMAIN: Community   **ACTIVITY:** Hair cut with brother

PREPARATION

o Mom provides an object cue for <u>hair cut</u>.

o Mom tactually gestures <u>money</u>.

o J extends his hand for "money."

o J puts money in his wallet.

o J gets keys and "extends" to brother.

o J and brother drive to mall.

o Brother used as sighted guide and cues for <u>step up</u> and <u>open door</u>.

o

o

PARTICIPATION

o Brother gives choice of who goes first.

o J gestures <u>me</u>.

o Barber lets J feel the cape.

o Barber lets J feel the water.

o J pushes his hand away for <u>no</u>.

o Barber gestures "finished."

o J assists taking the cape off.

o Brother uses touch cue for <u>my turn</u> and <u>sit down</u>.

o

o

o

TERMINATION

o Brother gestures "I finished."

o J "extends money."

o J "extends his hand" for the change.

o Brother gestures <u>go</u>.

o

o

o

o

Figure 4.   Sample activity analysis to determine receptive and expressive communication.

220

Table 2. Changes in social roles of communication partners as routines and activities change from isolated tasks to cooperative tasks

Role of teacher	Role of partner	Role of mediator	Role of observer
Teaching the task until student can carry out the task without prompts	Changing the task to a cooperative task	Introducing peer to 3-way communication exchange	Fading out of the exchange for a peer–student interaction
Student performs task in isolation	Teacher and student complete task together	Teacher, student, and peer perform task together	Student and peer perform task together
• High use of receptive communication	• Different use of receptive communication (teacher role)	• Model lighter forms/functions of receptive communication (teacher role)	• Provide nonintrusive feedback
• Minimal use of student's expressive system (few opportunities)	• Expansion of activity (teacher role)	• Differences in activity (student role)	• Provide redirection to direct student's communication to peer
• High predictability of sequence (teacher controlled)	• Functions change	• Functions change (student role)	• Little predictability of sequence (student and peer have control)
	• Maximal use of expressive communication (student role, more opportunities)	• Maximal use of expressive communication (student role)	
	• Lower predictability of sequence (student has more control)	• Lower predictability of sequence	

221

cues to maximize Joshua's differentiated use of communication. As the sequence of the routine or activity becomes less predictable, Joshua will have more control over the outcomes of the interaction.

Role of Mediator   Initially it may be advantageous to have only one peer buddy or friend or sibling included in the cooperative task. The activity will change to include a three-way communication exchange. Ms. Ann will initially verbalize: 1) the receptive cues (go, more, pay, finish) that she is using, 2) why she is using them (information, directive, comment), and 3) specifically how they are to be used (touch, object, gesture). Sam can then model these and ask questions. There will be increased opportunities to expand the content and forms (e.g., letting Joshua know that Sam is buying potato chips). As Sam and Joshua take more control of the outcome of the activity, Ms. Ann will fade out and there will be a very low predictability of the sequence. For example, Sam may go to the rest room in the convenience store and ask Joshua to buy him something. Joshua may request money if Sam did not offer it. Joshua must then get the item requested by Sam, as well as his own, and pay for both items. Joshua must then give the change back to Sam.

Role of Observer   It is important that Ms. Ann fades out of the exchange and only observes the continued interactions of Sam and Joshua. She may include Sam in a second activity with Joshua. Peers should not be placed in the role of buddy or friend without receiving in-service training, which would include individualized modeling and coaching techniques. It is the role of the service provider, teacher, or SLP to make sure that the student and peer have a shared system of communication. Teacher training should also include training peers specifically on communication exchanges.

MEASURING POSITIVE OUTCOMES

The goals of functional communication for an individual student can only be determined by a team. Decisions in this process include assessing the quality and frequency of the student's forms, functions, content, and interactors across different contexts or activities. Communication with peers with and without disabilities can also be assessed. A 10-minute receptive communication sample (see Figure 5) will be taken for Joshua by the SLP across different tasks. These samples may be taken across three to four activities each month. A check mark is made to indicate the type of form and function made by the person communicating to Joshua and Joshua's response. Therefore, the goals of communication should include goals for the interactors (communication partners) as well as for Joshua himself.

Expressive communication samples can also be taken (see Figure 6). For example, if Joshua is currently using approximately five communication behaviors to communicate in Levels II and III (touch person or objects), short-term goals may include increasing the frequency of opportunities for communication and expanding his forms to include extending objects and using gestures. Samples taken in the subsequent month will allow the team to determine if goals have been met and to determine new goals. New goals may include an increase in peer communication and an increase in initiations. Ms. Ann, Chris, and Sam will need to employ different techniques of teaching (time delay, pairing/shifting, etc.) (see Halle, 1988) for these goals to be accomplished. The data reflected in these samples are used to determine: 1) positive outcomes in communication exchanges across different partners and activities and 2) new outcomes once old outcomes have been met.

Receptive Communication Sample (10 Minute)—Videotaped

Name: Joshua
Observer: Kat
Ratio-Adults/Students: 1:2

1-11 Peer buddy not included
2-8 Peer buddy included

Date: 1-11-94—Isolated
2-8-94—Cooperative
Domain: Community
Setting and Activity: Going to convenience store after school
NOTES: Going to convenience store after school

Content	No Cue	Environmental	Touch	Object	Gesture	Picture	Miniature Object/Association	Visual sign	Tactile sign/gesture	Speech	Attention	Inhibit	Model	Command	Request for	Information	Comment	Social	No Response	Facial/Body	Act on Object	Direct Response	Teacher	Assistant	SLP	OT/PT	Peer with Disabilities	Typical Peer
Go store				✓												✓						✓	✓					
Get money									✓					✓							✓		✓					
Open door									✓					✓								✓	✓					
Get Coke			✓											✓							✓		✓					
Get chips			✓											✓							✓		✓					
Go register									✓					✓								✓	✓					
Pay money			✓											✓							✓		✓					
Get change			✓											✓								✓	✓					
Where go?									✓						✓							✓						✓
I go									✓							✓						✓						✓
What need?									✓						✓							✓						✓
Get me ___									✓					✓								✓						✓
Have money				✓												✓					✓							✓
Give it			✓												✓							✓						✓
Thanks J			✓															✓		✓ (smile)								✓
I'll get straws									✓							✓			✓									✓
Let's sit			✓												✓							✓						✓
Mine's cold too			✓													✓				✓								✓
Ready?			✓												✓							✓						✓

Rows "Go store" through "Get change" are bracketed as 1–11*
Rows "Where go?" through "Ready?" are bracketed as 2–8*

*Entire sequence is not provided

Figure 5. A 10-minute receptive communication sample for Joshua.

223

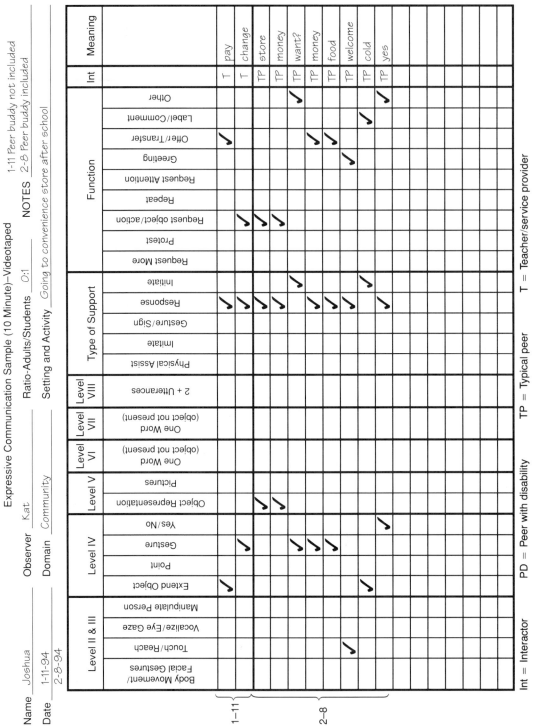

Figure 6. A 10-minute expressive communication sample for Joshua.

224

POSSIBLE CHALLENGES TO IMPLEMENTATION

In general, effective communication interventions should include the following:

1. A long-term planning process that includes both current and potential future milieus
2. Team planning, in which the individual and his or her family, peers, siblings, service providers, and persons from the community are included
3. Consideration of social context and social interactions (Seigel-Causey & Downing, 1987)
4. Analysis of different relevant physical environments (Stremel, 1994)
5. Consideration of important communication partners
6. Consideration of receptive communication in reciprocal communication exchanges
7. Active interactions with the student, rather than an isolated approach to teaching daily life skills outside of his or her natural social context
8. Analysis of nonsymbolic and symbolic communication forms for both the student and communication partner
9. Various communication uses
10. Content that is critical within any routine or activity

Inclusive environments provide only the potential for more frequent and more effective communication exchanges for students who are deaf-blind. Even inclusive environments do not provide a guarantee that communication will occur. Team planning and in-service training must be a continuous process to assure that the components listed above remain critical in the decision-making process.

Collaborative team planning is also necessary to identify potential barriers to implementation and to develop strategies to overcome these challenges. It is critical to evaluate student outcomes. Often, students who are deaf-blind display limited communication because the planned interventions were not fully implemented. For example, one might see that Joshua's Personal Futures Planning and communication map have been developed collaboratively by a team, with substantial family input. However, if one were to observe several times in the inclusive environment, few opportunities for Joshua to communicate might be seen. The observer might note that Joshua's calling device is on a shelf on the other side of the room. Sam may approach him and guide him to the cafeteria or his locker without using cues. So what are the problems with implementation? There are not always easy answers or simple solutions to this question.

Implementation takes discipline and work on everyone's part. Joshua will not, in all probability, began to communicate at a higher level without opportunities to communicate and without the use of active teaching procedures. The following are a number of problems that may have to be analyzed and solved by teams, the administration, and families if they are interfering with interventions being implemented:

1. Inadequate time for teams to plan and measure outcomes
2. Inadequate time and resources to purchase or construct necessary switches, devices, and systems
3. Inconsistent use of systems across school and home environments
4. Lack of strategies for problem solving
5. Inadequate training of peers and natural school supports
6. Need for total teacher/adult control of activities
7. Not taking the time to communicate at near-distance

8. Lack of teacher training opportunities for teaching observational skills
9. Lack of teacher training experiences to work directly with students who are deaf-blind and their families
10. Lack of knowledgeable instructors (at the preservice level) to develop communication systems for students who are deaf-blind

Perhaps the greatest hindrance to the acquisition of effective and efficient functional communication for students who are deaf-blind is people's reluctance to communicate *with* them as equal communication partners. We, as service providers, parents, siblings, and peers tend to tell them what to do and what not to do. Therefore, many students remain as recipients in too few communication acts. Our perspective has to change to reflect equal participation in at least some activities, thereby reflecting the same variation and level of predictability that would occur between any two people engaged in a com-

munication act. Two people in the same environment (e.g., grocery store, laundromat, church) rarely exhibit consistent, identical behaviors.

There are often different communication partners available to us and different topics of communication. There needs to be an expectation on our part that the student is a potential provider in a communication act. One message must be clear as we interact with students who are deaf-blind: "I enjoy interacting with you as a person, I know that you can communicate to me in some way and understand my communication; if you indicate to me that my form or function of communication is not understood, I will try another way." The more frequently we interact with a student who is deaf-blind, the more opportunities there will be for communication acts to occur between both parties. Increased opportunities for communication acts will provide a context in which the forms and functions used by both the student and the communication partner can be expanded.

REFERENCES

Baer, D.M., Wolf, M.M., & Risley, T.R. (1987). Some still-current dimensions of applied behavior analysis. *Journal of Applied Behavior Analysis, 20,* 313–328.

Baldwin, V. (1992). Population/demographics. In J.W. Reiman & P.A. Johnson (Eds.), *Proceedings of the National Symposium on Children and Youth Who Are Deaf-Blind.* Monmouth, OR: Teaching Research Publications.

Bullis, M. (1987). *Communication development in young children with deaf-blindness: Literature review III.* Monmouth: Teaching Research Division, Oregon State System of Higher Education.

Bullis, M. (1989). *Communication development in young children with deaf-blindness: Literature review IV.* Monmouth: Teaching Research Division, Oregon State System of Higher Education.

Campbell, P. (1987). The integrated programming team: An approach for coordinating professionals of various disciplines in programs for students with severe and multiple handicaps.

Journal of The Association for Persons with Severe Handicaps, 12(2), 107–116.

Campbell, P. (1989). Students with physical disabilities. In R. Gaylord-Ross (Ed.), *Integration strategies for students with handicaps* (pp. 53–76). Baltimore: Paul H. Brookes Publishing Co.

Carr, E.G., & Durand, V.M. (1985). Reducing behavior problems through functional communication training. *Journal of Applied Behavior Analysis, 18,* 111–126.

Certo, N., & Kohl, F.L. (1984). A strategy for developing interpersonal interaction instructional content for severely handicapped students. In N. Certo, N. Haring, & R. York (Eds.), *Public school integration of severely handicapped students* (pp. 221–241). Baltimore: Paul H. Brookes Publishing Co.

Downing, J. (1993). Communication intervention for individuals with dual sensory impairments. In L. Kupper (Ed.), *The second national symposium of effective communication for children and youth with severe disabilities: A vision for the future* (pp. 231–256). McLean, VA: Interstate Research Associates.

Downing, J., & Siegel-Causey, E. (1988). Enhancing the nonsymbolic communicative behavior of children with multiple impairments. *Language, Speech, and Hearing Services in Schools, 19,* 338–348.

Dunn, W. (1991). Integrated related services. In L.H. Meyer, C.A. Peck, & L. Brown (Eds.), *Critical issues in the lives of people with severe disabilities* (pp. 353–377). Baltimore: Paul H. Brookes Publishing Co.

Dunst, C. (1978). A cognitive social approach for assessment of early nonverbal communicative behavior. *Journal of Childhood Communication Disorders, 2*(2), 110–123.

Durand, V.M. (1993). Using functional communication training as an intervention for the challenging behavior of students with severe disabilities. In L. Kupper (Ed.), *The second national symposium on effective communication for children and youth with severe disabilities: A vision for the future* (pp. 89–108). McLean, VA: Interstate Research Associates.

Durand, V.M., & Crimmins, D.B. (1988). Identifying the variables maintaining self-injurious behavior. *Journal of Autism and Developmental Disorders, 17,* 99–117.

Forest, M., & Lusthaus, E. (1987). The kaleidoscope: Challenge to the cascade. In M. Forest (Ed.), *More education/integration* (pp. 1–16). Downsview, Ontario, Canada: G. Allen Roeher Institute.

Giangreco, M.F. (1990). Making related service decisions for students with severe disabilities: Roles, criteria, and authority. *Journal of The Association for Persons with Severe Handicaps, 15*(1), 22–31.

Goetz, L., Guess, D., & Stremel-Campbell, K. (Eds.). (1987). *Innovative program design for individuals with dual sensory impairments.* Baltimore: Paul H. Brookes Publishing Co.

Halle, J.W. (1988). Adapting the natural environment as the context of training. In S.N. Calculator & J.L. Bedrosian (Eds.), *Communication, assessment, and intervention for adults with mental retardation* (pp. 155–185). Boston: College Hill.

Halle, J.W. (1993). Innovative assessment measures and practices designed with the goal of achieving functional communication and integration. In L. Kupper (Ed.), *The second national symposium on effective communication for children*

and youth with severe disabilities (pp. 201–252). McLean, VA: Interstate Research Associates.

Hamill, D.D., & Bartell, N.R. (Eds.). (1975). *Teaching children with hearing and behavior problems.* Newton, MA: Allyn and Bacon.

Haring, T.G. (1991). Social relationships. In L. Meyer, C.A. Peck, & L. Brown (Eds.), *Critical issues in the lives of people with severe disabilities* (pp. 195–218). Baltimore: Paul H. Brookes Publishing Co.

Haring, T.G. (1992). The context of social competence: Relations, relationships, and generalization. In S.L. Odom, S.R. McConnell, & M.A. McEvoy (Eds.), *Social competence of young children with disabilities: Issues and strategies for intervention* (pp. 307–320). Baltimore: Paul H. Brookes Publishing Co.

Horner, R.H., & Day, H.M. (1991). The effects of response efficiency on functionally equivalent competing behaviors. *Journal of Applied Behavior Analysis, 24,* 719–732.

Horner, R.H., Meyer, L.H., & Fredericks, H.D. (Eds.). (1986). *Education of learners with severe handicaps: Exemplary service strategies.* Baltimore: Paul H. Brookes Publishing Co.

Houghton, J., Bronicki, G.J.B., & Guess, D. (1987). Opportunities to express preferences and make choices among students with severe disabilities in classroom settings. *Journal of The Association for Persons with Severe Handicaps, 12*(1), 18–27.

Jackson, L.B. (1988, October). *Assessing the communication competence of persons with multiple impairments.* Paper presented at the 1988 Biennial Conference of the International Society for Augmentative and Alternative Communication, Anaheim, CA.

McLean, J., & Snyder-McLean, L. (1978). *A transactional approach to early language training.* Columbus, OH: Merrill.

Mirenda, P., Iacono, T., & Williams, R. (1990). Communication options for persons with severe and profound disabilities: State of the art and future directions. *Journal of The Association for Persons with Severe Handicaps, 15,* 3–21.

Mount, B., & Zwernik, K. (1988). *It's never too early, it's never too late: A booklet about personal futures planning.* St. Paul, MN: Metropolitan Council.

Murray-Seegert, C. (1989). *Nasty girls, thugs, and humans like us: Social relations between severely disabled and nondisabled students in high school.* Baltimore: Paul H. Brookes Publishing Co.

O'Brien, J. (1987). A guide to life-style planning: Using The Activities Catalog to integrate services and natural support systems. In B. Wilcox & G.T. Bellamy, *A comprehensive guide to The Activities Catalog: An alternative curriculum for youth and adults with severe disabilities* (pp. 175–189). Baltimore: Paul H. Brookes Publishing Co.

O'Brien, J., Forest, M., Snow, J., & Hasbury, D. (1989). *Action for inclusion.* Toronto, Ontario, Canada: Frontier College Press.

O'Brien, J., & Lyle, C. (1987). *Framework for accomplishment.* Decatur, GA: Responsive Systems Associates.

O'Neill, R.E., Horner, R.H., Albin, R.W., Storey, K., & Sprague, J.R. (1990). *Functional analysis of problem behavior: A practical assessment guide.* Sycamore, IL: Sycamore Publishing.

Peck, C.A. (1989). Assessment of social/communicative competence: Evaluating effects of environments. *Seminars in Speech and Language, 10,* 1–15.

Rainforth, B., York, J., Macdonald, C., & Dunn, W. (1992). Collaborative assessment. In B. Rainforth, J. York, & C. Macdonald , *Collaborative teams for students with severe disabilities: Integrating therapy and educational services.* Baltimore: Paul H. Brookes Publishing Co.

Reichle, J. (1991). Describing initial communicative intents. In J. Reichle, J. York, & J. Sigafoos, *Implementing augmentative and alternative communication: Strategies for learners with severe disabilities* (pp. 71–88). Baltimore: Paul H. Brookes Publishing Co.

Reichle, J., Feeley, K., & Johnston, S. (1993). Communication intervention for persons with severe and profound disabilities: An overview. In L. Kupper (Ed.), *Second national symposium on effective communication for children and youth with severe disabilities: A vision to the future* (pp. 147–200). McLean, VA: Interstate Research Associates.

Reichle, J., & Yoder, D. (1979). Communication behavior for the severely and profoundly mentally retarded: Assessment and early stimulation strategies. In R. York & E. Edgar (Eds.), *Teaching the severely handicapped. Vol. 4* (pp. 180–218). Seattle: American Association for the Education of the Severely/Profoundly Handicapped.

Reichle, J., York, J., & Sigafoos, J. (1991). *Implementing augmentative and alternative communication: Strategies for learners with severe disabilities.* Baltimore: Paul H. Brookes Publishing Co.

Rowland, C. (1987). Perspectives on communication assessment. In M. Bullis (Ed.), *Communication development in young children with deaf-blindness: Literature review III* (pp. 1–22). Monmouth: Teaching Research Division, Oregon State System of Higher Education.

Rowland, C. (1990). Communication in the classroom for children with dual sensory impairments: Studies of teacher and child behavior. *Augmentative and Alternative Communication, 6,* 262–274.

Rowland, C., & Schweigert, P. (1989). Tangible symbols: Symbolic communication for individuals with multisensory impairments. *Augmentative and Alternative Communication, 5,* 226–234.

Rowland, C., & Schweigert, P. (1991). *Analyzing the communication environment.* Tucson, AZ: Communication Skill Builders.

Rowland, C., Schweigert, P., & Stremel, K. (1992). *Observing and enhancing communication skills: For individuals with multisensory impairments.* Tucson, AZ: Communication Skill Builders.

Rowland, C., & Stremel-Campbell, K. (1987). Share and share alike: Conventional gestures through emergent language. In L. Goetz, D. Guess, & K. Stremel-Campbell (Eds.), *Innovative program design for individuals with dual sensory impairments* (pp. 49–75). Baltimore: Paul H. Brookes Publishing Co.

Salvia, J., & Ysseldyke, J.E. (1985). *Assessment in special and remedial education.* Boston: Houghton Mifflin.

Schutz, R.P., Williams, W., Iverson, G.S., & Duncan, D. (1984). Social integration of severely handicapped students. In N. Certo, N. Haring, & R. York (Eds.), *Public school integration of severely handicapped students* (pp. 15–42). Baltimore: Paul H. Brookes Publishing Co.

Schweigert, P. (1989). Use of microswitch technology to facilitate social contingency awareness as a basis for early communication skills: A case study. *Augmentative and Alternative Communication, 5*(3), 192–198.

Searle, J. (1969). *Speech acts.* Cambridge, England: Cambridge University Press.

Siegel-Causey, E., & Downing, J. (1987). Nonsymbolic communication development: Theoretical concepts and educational strategies. In L. Goetz, D. Guess, & K. Stremel-Campbell (Eds.), *Innovative program design for individuals with dual sensory impairments* (pp. 15–48). Baltimore: Paul H. Brookes Publishing Co.

Siegel-Causey, E., & Guess, D. (1989). *Enhancing nonsymbolic communication interactions among learners with severe disabilities*. Baltimore: Paul H. Brookes Publishing Co.

Stillman, R. (1992). Communication. In J.W. Reiman & P.A. Johnson (Eds.), *Proceedings of the National Symposium on Children and Youth who are Deaf-Blind* (pp. 129–140). Monmouth, OR: Teaching Research Publications.

Stillman, R., & Battle, C.W. (1984). Developing prelanguage communication in the severely handicapped. *Seminars in Speech and Language, 5*, 159–170.

Stillman, R., & Siegel-Causey, E. (1989). Introduction to nonsymbolic communication. In E. Siegel-Causey & D. Guess, *Enhancing nonsymbolic communication interactions among learners with severe disabilities* (pp. 1–13). Baltimore: Paul H. Brookes Publishing Co.

Stremel, K. (1991, November). Communicating with people who have multiple sensory impairments. *American Speech-Language-Hearing Association, 30*–31.

Stremel, K. (1994). Instructional strategies. In P. Cipkowski (Ed.), *Teacher self-study curriculum: AFB deaf-blind project*. New York: American Foundation for the Blind.

Stremel, K., Molden, V., Leister, C., Matthews, J., Wilson, R., Goodall, D., & Holston, J. (1990). *Communication systems and routines: A decision making process*. Hattiesburg: University of Southern Mississippi, Department of Special Education.

Strong, C., Clark, T., Barringer, D., Watkins, S., Walden, B., & Williams, S. (1993). *Using tactile signals and cues with children who are deaf-blind*. Logan, UT: HOPE.

Vandercook, T., York, J., & Forest, M. (1989). The McGill action planning system (MAPS): A strategy for building a vision. *Journal of The Association for Persons with Severe Handicaps, 14*(3), 205–215.

van Dijk, J. (1967). The non-verbal deaf-blind child and his world: His outgrowth toward the world of symbols. *Proceedings of the Jaarverslag Institiuut voor Doven* (pp. 73–110). Sint Michielsgestel, Holland.

van Dijk, J. (1986). An educational curriculum for deaf-blind multi-handicapped persons. In D. Ellis (Ed.), *Sensory impairments in mentally handicapped people* (pp. 375–382). London: Croom-Helm.

Warren, S.F., & Rogers-Warren, A.K. (1985). *Teaching functional language*. Baltimore: University Park Press.

Werner, H., & Kaplan, B. (1963). *Symbol formation*. New York: John Wiley & Sons.

Writer, J. (1987). A movement-based approach to the education of students who are sensory impaired/multihandicapped. In L. Goetz, D. Guess, & K. Stremel-Campbell (Eds.), *Innovative program design for individuals with dual sensory impairments* (pp. 191–223). Baltimore: Paul H. Brookes Publishing Co.

Chapter 11

Social Relationships Among Students with Deaf-Blindness and Their Peers in Inclusive Settings

Thomas Haring,
Norris G. Haring,
Catherine Breen,
Lyle T. Romer,
and Jennifer White

Due to the inclusion of persons with deaf-blindness in typical school and community settings, there has been a greater interest in investigating how research and intervention can facilitate further social integration of such students. The development of social relationships among students with deaf-blindness and their peers is not just a matter of possessing the required social skills. Although some of these skills are indeed important, such as sharing a common communication system, they are insufficient, in and of themselves, to guarantee the development of long-term, stable social relationships. Rather, to build more inclusive educational settings for students with deaf-blindness and other severe disabilities, much broader issues must be considered. Special educators would be remiss if they only designed interventions that taught students specific social skills, without also considering the activities in which the students normally engage with their peers, the interests and preferences of the students with and without disabilities, prevailing attitudes and practices with respect to students with disabilities in a given school, and the frequency with which students have opportunities to interact with one another.

One of the primary goals of inclusion is participation of students with deaf-blindness in social relationships across the entire range of human intimacy, from casual relationships (e.g., socially greeting retail service personnel) to long-term relationships and friendships. Until very recently, difficulties with the development of friendships and other social relationships among students with deaf-blindness and their peers have been viewed as: 1) an inherent characteristic of the social isolation created by having deaf-blindness, 2) a skill-deficit problem that could be remedied through targeting and training appropriate interaction skills, or 3) a communication problem that could be alleviated through proper language training using highly specialized methods developed specifically for students with deaf-blindness. From a traditional educational perspective, viewing the isolation of students with deaf-blindness as a primary result of social and communication skill deficits makes a great deal of sense. Those deficits (were they to be the actual fundamental causes of isolation) are correctable through changes in instructional objectives and practices that clearly relate to the way many teachers select and prioritize targets for instruction. That is, attributing the source of the problem to an inherent developmental problem such as social or language skill deficits ties well into the view that students' problems are primarily a result of a lack of skills across traditional domains, not as a lack of opportunities to interact and develop social relationships.

Although there is a great appeal and traditional support for viewing the problems of students as primarily related to basic skill deficits (see, e.g., Peck, 1991), increasingly educators are becoming aware that providing instruction in skills, be they independent living, social interaction, or language skills, may not be the most effective approach to achieve the facilitation of social relationships in inclusive settings. The best way for a student to learn new skills is to receive instruction in those skills, but the most effective route to achieving full inclusion is to provide students with access to routine, ongoing, intensive contact with one another. The result of such ongoing contacts should be the development of long-term, stable relationships among some subset of students. This change

in perspective from a focus on skill deficits to viewing social integration as a primary purpose of schooling can affect all aspects of teaching, including the priorities that teachers value in selecting curricula, the settings for instruction, and the instructional procedures selected to achieve educational goals.

SOCIAL RELATIONSHIPS ARE CENTRAL TO INCLUSION

Although instruction aimed at fixing skill deficits clearly plays an important role in preparing students to participate in more inclusive schools, there has been a shift in focus in special education from a primary concern with teaching basic skills to a focus on creating situations and positive attitudes that facilitate the social support of students with deaf-blindness in typical education settings. The following paragraphs address some of the reasons why social relationships should be viewed as a key indicator and defining characteristic of inclusive services.

Quality of Life

Social relationships contribute substantially to quality of life. Few people without disabilities would choose to live a life with little social support, yet many people with developmental disabilities living in community settings report feelings of loneliness and isolation. This problem was illustrated in a study by Bercovici (1981). She found that in 6 out of the 10 group homes that were studied, staff members tended to discourage or prohibit residents from maintaining contacts or friendships with others outside of the program. More recently, Falvey (1986) found that social relationships were important factors in improved performance in school and in successful transitions to less restrictive settings. Other researchers have documented similar findings on the value of social relationships in the lives of students with severe disabilities (Sailor, 1986; Voeltz, 1980). It is clear that feelings of self-fulfillment and satisfaction with one's life are highly associated with the attainment of a stable social network (e.g., McKinney, Fitzgerald, & Strommen, 1982). The development of emotional intimacy is an important experience for all adolescents and adults regardless of ability (cf. Erikson, 1959).

Functional Participation in Community Activities

Social interaction skills are necessary for functional participation in many community activities. An analysis of social interactions reveals that the overall pattern of behavior is remarkably consistent across a wide variety of community events. For example, it is frequently necessary to ask for help when making purchases. It is necessary to interact socially with cashiers to attend movies and other life-enhancing recreational events. Indeed, the nonverbal exchange behaviors that are characteristic of completing a purchase are identical in pattern to the exchange behaviors of playing a game or holding a conversation and are equally social in that they involve a reciprocal exchange of responses between two people.

Social Reinforcers

Many critical skills are maintained by complex schedules of remote and more immediate reinforcers that are frequently social in nature. For example, while some high school students respond to the infrequent reinforcer of attendance provided by grades, others are more responsive to the daily reinforcers of being with their friends. It is actually more likely that typical high school students are reinforced for their attendance at school by some combination of these consequences.

Similarly, in many vocational settings, the key daily reinforcers are social contacts available at the job site, combined with monetary rewards on some less frequent schedule. Certainly, the longer-term complex contingencies of school and work are powerful determinants of behavior (see Michael, 1986, for a theoretical analysis), but in the absence of daily social contingencies, these are often insufficient to maintain behavior. Thus, contacts with members of valued social networks are mitigating circumstances that provide some immediate reinforcement for engaging in work-related activities that may be, in and of themselves, considered somewhat aversive by the participants.

Reduction in Challenging Behaviors

There is a relationship between the development of social skills and the reduced need for programming based on behavioral control. For example, Carr and Durand (1985) demonstrated a functional relationship between socially acceptable communicative behaviors and a reduction in the occurrence of problem behaviors, such as self-injury and physical aggression. Their research has had a powerful impact on viewing the instruction of social communicative skills as a primary intervention for seriously disruptive and potentially life-threatening behaviors. From this perspective, all behaviors, including those that are challenging, are viewed as potentially communicative attempts to control the behavior of others (e.g., to escape unwanted tasks). Because of the inherent communication challenges for people with deaf-blindness, socially undesirable behaviors, such as aggression and self-injury, have often been the only effective avenue of expression. Thus, the building of social competence reduces challenging behaviors that stigmatize some people with deaf-blindness. Additionally, the reduction in challenging behaviors also removes what is sometimes used as a rationale for the further isolation of students with deaf-blindness in programs specifically designed to deal with these types of behaviors.

Removal of Social Barriers

There is an increasing awareness that disability is more an attitude held by professionals and people without disabilities than it is a property or defining characteristic of the person with disabilities (Gartner & Lipsky, 1987; Lane, 1988). The greatest obstacles to inclusion are social barriers erected by people without disabilities, who have little, if any, personal contact with people with disabilities. Sociological analyses have indicated that such social barriers may reflect an underlying ideology that people with disabilities do not possess the full range of characteristics that make people "human" (Goffman, 1963; Wolfensberger, 1972). We should recognize that communities of deaf-blind adults exist across the United States and that those communities, as well as sighted-hearing peers, represent important sources of social support for students with deaf-blindness. When people with deaf-blindness are viewed as fully accredited members of communities the ultimate goal of inclusion will be realized.

Thus, there are many reasons to view the development of social relationships as central to inclusion. At the level of the individual, social relationships are an important source of happiness and self-perceptions of quality of life. At the pragmatic level, social interaction within the context of a stable social network is an important means of support for engaging in functional life activities, maintaining complex skill repertoires in the absence of direct tangible reinforcement, and reducing aberrant responding. At the broadest societal level, social inclusion is an important indicator that people with deaf-blindness are accepted as valued members of a common, pluralistic culture.

PEER SOCIAL SUPPORT NETWORKS TO FACILITATE INCLUSION

A variety of support networks provide essential resources for responding to the needs of students with deaf-blindness to function effectively at home, in school, and in the community. These networks may be considered broadly in two major categories: 1) formal and 2) informal. While experiences may certainly be shared among these two categories of support, the first category is typically seen as being highly organized and specialized, and primarily made up of paid professionals (e.g., interdisciplinary services, special education, family counseling, medical clinics). The second category is less formal and is voluntary (e.g., family friends, neighbors, social organizations). Students with deaf-blindness find a lack of balance in the resources they gain from these two network sources; given the natural distribution, their support comes mainly from the formal network. Generally the support acquired from the informal networks, that is, friends and family, is far too sparse to provide any measure of quality in their life. Romer (1991) has outlined a framework of four necessary points to assist people in building satisfactory social networks.

1. People's abilities are more important than disabilities. Trying to help people shouldn't always be an exercise in finding out what's wrong with them. Successful integration is built upon people recognizing in each other common interests, mutual commitments to beliefs and values, and the mutual satisfaction of spending time together.
2. People need more in their lives than services. The benefits of friendships cannot be purchased as we purchase services for people, but they are just as important, if not more so. It is often more important to have a circle of friends when you are looking for a ride to work (transportation), a new apartment (residential program), a job closer to home (vocational placement), or a new activity to learn (educational ser-

vices) than it is to have a "service system."

3. What happens on a day-to-day basis in people's lives is what is truly important. Focusing on building skills is not the only method needed to help people become members of friendship networks. Rather, one should be looking for those patterns of activities that define the person as a unique individual and what [this person] wants to have happen in [his or her] life.

4. No one person should try to be everything for another person. Having only one or two people or agencies one goes to for support results in dangerous levels of dependence upon those people or agencies. The more people you are interdependent with, the less likely you are to lose an important source of support from your network if someone leaves. People are very vulnerable to losing parts of their networks when they are overly dependent upon professional staff to make up their social networks and those staff change jobs or a person goes to a different service or classroom. Furthermore, depending upon only a small number of people for friendship and support almost always means a person will be restricted in his/her activities. Given the diverse interests of most people [most individuals need] to know a variety of people who share some common activity interests. (Romer, pp. 9–10)

Building and Maintaining Peer Support Networks

Social support networks grow out of a need to build a social structure that can provide continuing social relationships—relationships or networks that can provide students with deaf-blindness a social network of friends with and without disabilities with whom they can share the many contributions of friendships. Clearly, social support networks do not form readily. We have seen from our research and have confirmed from others, that students with deaf-blindness have practically no informal friendship networks. A few students have only one friend, usually another child with disabilities, to respond to the many needs that arise from having sen-

sory and mobility impairments (Horner, Reed, Ritchie, Stoner, & Twain, 1986).

The purpose, then, for employing strategies for building social support networks is to develop a more permanent structure for students with deaf-blindness to enjoy satisfying and supportive interpersonal relationships. First, building and maintaining peer support networks assumes that students with deaf-blindness are included in typical classrooms and that they have natural daily opportunities to interact with peers without disabilities. Second, although natural opportunities for social interaction with peers without disabilities are provided daily, that does not assure that interaction will occur. In fact, the actual interactions tend to be low in frequency, of poor quality, and not often repeated with the same peer (Romer & Haring, 1993). In other words, providing an inclusive context for social relationships is not sufficient intervention for formulating lasting friendship structures.

Peer Support Research Project

To test our ideas about a social network intervention, we set up a small study with three students with severe to moderate disabilities (Breen, Kennedy, & Haring, 1991). In addition to these 3 students, 21 peers without disabilities participated in our initial investigation of the use of peers to support students with disabilities in contexts (specifically, breaks between classes, recess, and lunch) in which teachers had found it difficult to program social skills intervention, contexts whose structure was constantly changing, contexts in which any teacher intrusion would prove to be more stigmatizing than facilitative. The three students we worked with were males ages 12, 13, and 14 years old who were attending typical junior high and elementary schools. The classroom programs in which the students were enrolled were highly committed to integration, normalization, and social development, and each had made extensive efforts to increase the amount of contact and improve the quality of relationships among peer groups of students with and without disabilities. As part of this effort, each of the three students was mainstreamed into at least one typical education class.

Regardless of these efforts, however, prior to beginning the network intervention, the students had few opportunities for interaction with peers, interacted appropriately with peers at very low rates, and overall had no friendships or relationships with their peers without disabilities at school. Many of our previous efforts and the efforts of the classroom teachers had been toward facilitating specific interactions between one of the three students and one peer without disabilities. While we could increase the interactions between members of the dyad within those contexts in which we systematically programmed, we found that the interactions did not generalize very well to nontrained contexts and really did not maintain over time.

Moreover, when looking at the quality of the interactions and the quality of the relationship between the two people, we had a hard time calling it a friendship. We decided that there were a few flaws in our logic. First, what we as adults think would be "cool" to talk about or to do together may not be what children or adolescents actually talk about or do together. We needed to change our focus from adult-centered decision making to child-centered decision making. Second, interactions and friendships among youth generally do not occur at the dyadic level, but within groups or cliques. Typically, adolescents will be friends with someone else as long as their other friends are supportive of that friendship. We needed to move from trying to structure dyadic interactions to structuring interactions and relationships within groups of peers who are already part of existing cliques. Third, interactions need to be flexible. Teaching students specific scripts may be useful in terms of increasing a specific interaction within a specific context, but this approach does not serve to increase the participation of students across multiple contexts. We needed to find a way to teach the three students more generic and more natural strategies for being with their peers without disabilities throughout the school day.

We looked at the contexts in which each of the students had the most opportunities for interaction with familiar peers; generally, this was within the mainstreamed class. We found one or two peers in this context who shared an interest with the focal student (for example, for one student, this interest was playing the trumpet; for another student it was playing soccer), and we asked these peers if they would be interested in "hanging" with and including the student with disabilities in their normal activities during these difficult-to-program contexts (i.e., breaks during the school day) and if they had any friends who also might like to participate. The peers were all accepting of the idea, although initially hesitant about their individual involvement. Once the group of friends was put together and had all participated in the introductory meeting of the focal student and his peers and the first few team meetings were held, their level of enthusiasm increased tremendously. The peers were asked to hang out with the student at least one time per day in a place and time convenient to both the peer and the student. They were asked to participate as a group in deciding how best to facilitate the inclusion of the student into their clique and into school activities in general. Finally, they were asked to support each other as well as the student with disabilities in making the program work.

As a result, all of the peers involved in each of the three support networks not only interacted with and supported the participation of the student with disabilities in ongoing school activities, but also developed a real friendship with the student as well. The friends of the peers involved in the support networks also became more accepting of the student and began to look past the disability at the person. Parents of both the students with disabilities and the peers participating in the program were highly supportive, as were the school administrators, with all adults emphasizing how positive the effects had been on the self-esteem, attitude, and school affiliation of all of the children involved.

To conclude, then, the effects of this program were lasting, and even affected peers who were not directly involved. The effects spilled into contexts that never were targeted (e.g., after school and weekend activities, phone calls, transitioning into new schools). We have been in the business of improving the social interaction skills and integration of students with disabilities for 10 years. Never before have we seen such a powerful force for change as networks of peers.

Selecting and Recruiting Peers without Disabilities for Inclusion in a Social Support Network

We have found that the following practices and approaches for teachers serving as facilitators for building social networks in school increase the likelihood of friendships forming among students with deaf-blindness and their peers:

1. *Be accessible:* Special education teachers should make themselves accessible to the general education faculty and student body. Be visible in the halls, at lunch, at school activities, in general education classes, and in faculty meetings. If teachers are going to sell the idea of inclusion of students with disabil-

ities into the general education system, they must be perceived as wanting to be a part of that system. Teachers should be seen by the student body as individuals who are accessible, friendly, caring, and enthusiastic. Teachers will be spending some time with the members of the support groups in order to recruit peers for participation; peers must see the teacher as someone with whom they might want to spend time.

2. *Develop a list of potential peers:* Develop a list of peers with whom the student comes into contact at least one time per day. Contacts may occur in mainstreamed classes, peer-tutoring sessions, sports activities, when passing from class to class, during breaks, or at lunch. This information can be gathered through: a) interviewing the student with deaf-blindness regarding those peers with whom he interacts, b) direct observation by the supervising staff member, or c) nominations of the general and special education teachers.

In this initial survey, teachers should get some general information regarding how often an interaction with a specific peer occurs, and most importantly, the quality of the interactions. Are the interactions respectful or at least *typical* of interactions that occur among peers without disabilities? From this information the teacher can develop a list of peers who already have some familiarity with the student and generally exhibit a positive *intent* when interacting with the student. At this point, peers may have positive intent when interacting with a student, but may attempt to interact in a manner that is somewhat age-inappropriate, stigmatizing, or incorrect with regard to deaf-blindness (e.g., talking to a student who is deaf, gesturing to a student who is blind). At this point, some of this type of interaction is okay, the intent is probably more critical. The manner in which students interact can and will be a focus of later peer-group meetings.

3. *Watch students interact:* Observe and/ or talk to each of the peers from the list of potential friends. Identify one or two peers with whom the student has shared interests. Students may be similarly attracted to music, art, sports, fashion, books, food, cars, computer or video games, and so on.

4. *Discuss peer networks:* Explain the program in general terms to each of the peers. Describe the overall goal as increasing the number of friends for student A and to make student A more a part of the school. Anecdotally assess each peer's attitude toward the student and toward participation in a social support netowrk.

5. *Choose an initial peer:* Select for inclusion in the program the peer who demonstrates the greatest interest or enthusiasm.

6. *Have initial peer choose some of his or her friends:* Request that the peer identify three to five friends who might know student A or be interested in participating in a social support network. The most critical element in identifying a social support group is to ensure that members selected are *already* friends.

7. *Send invitations for the first peer network meeting:* Invite the four to six peers to an introductory meeting to discuss the purposes and procedures of the social network and to enlist their participation. This meeting is usually held at lunch or over pizza after school.

8. *Hold the first meeting:* Conduct the introductory meeting following the outline provided in the next section, "Explaining the Network to Peers." Obtain a verbal commitment from all members who wish to participate. If the number of students willing to participate drops below four, recruit new members from the same social clique. *Note:* limit the number of participants to less than six; four or five peers without disabilities appears to be ideal.

Explaining the Network to Peers

When some interested students are identified, the teacher/facilitator should try to provide them with some basic information about disabilities and deaf-blindness, the specific student with deaf-blindness, and the idea of a peer social network. Inviting a presentation by a deaf-blind adult is often very effective. Table 1 presents basic questions and answers for introducing peers to the network concept.

Facilitating Interactions Among Social Support Network Members

When students begin spending time together, they need support from teachers (or more experienced peers) to facilitate interactions with their new friend with deaf-blindness. We have found the following procedures to be helpful:

1. *Obtain student schedules:* During the introductory meeting, obtain the daily schedules of each member, including the time, location, and activities in which the students engage.

2. *Review schedules:* Compare the schedule of the student with deaf-blindness with each peer schedule. Identify those times and places in which there is shared participation between the student and the peer. Identify the context in which the shared participation takes place as a natural time for an interaction between that member and the peer with deaf-blindness. Produce a schedule for interaction for the student with deaf-blindness that ensures an opportunity for interaction with at least one member of the group during all contexts in which you would like an interaction to occur. Produce copies of the schedule for each member, highlighting those times and places when they are scheduled to meet the student with deaf-blindness. *Note:*

Table 1. Introducing peers to the peer support network

What?	Have a group of students who are already friends include a new person into their social clique.
Why?	Lots of reasons:
	1. People need friends for an acceptable quality of life.
	2. People learn *how* to hang out with other people by being with friends who give them feedback and model appropriate behavior, skills, and appearance.
	3. This will help students with disabilities to become a greater part of the school.
	4. People without disabilities need to see people with disabilities as being a part of their school or community.
	5. This person offers something to the social clique that can be valued and enjoyed.
Why us?	Friendships develop from things that people have in common. You and (student) both like (music, sports, fashion, riddles, science, art). You and (student) have a class together; therefore, you have already established a reason for a friendship.
Who?	(Student) and five peers who would be willing to support him or her throughout the school day, and an adult group facilitator.
How?	As a group we will map out all of the things (student) does during his or her school day and map out all of the things that you do during the school day and find those times and places where you and (student) are in the same place at the same time. During those times, we are asking you to include (student) in whatever it is you are doing with your friends or alone. Together we will decide how you should include him or her and how we should teach him or her how to hang out with you. We will also teach you the skills you need to communicate with your new friend with deaf-blindness. You and (student) will have an opportunity to mark down the times that you interact and briefly evaluate the interaction on data sheets that I will provide.
When?	At least one time per day when we have identified you and (student) ate with each other, and whenever else you see (student) and feel like including him or her. One time per week we will meet as a group during lunch to talk about the interactions you have had with (student), and the procedures that we as a team want to try to increase the number and quality of your interactions. After the group is up and running and everyone feels comfortable with the process, we will decide if we need to continue to meet weekly. Whatever you want to do, we will do.
Commitment?	From students:
	1. See this as a good thing—it makes sense, it's right.
	2. See this as a good thing for you and for your social group. It has to be positive for you; if it is perceived as a burden before you start, then it is not for you.
	3. Include (student) as one of your friends whenever it matches with your schedule.
	4. Attend group meetings once a week until we decide to change the frequency. Be open and honest in your feedback during group meetings.
	5. As much as you want, take simple data on your interactions.
	6. Talk to the group facilitator and/or the classroom teacher immediately if you start to feel yourself "burning out" or if you are unhappy with anything that is going on; don't wait until the group meeting.
	From teachers/facilitators to students:
	1. We will not ask you to change your schedule to make this work; we do not want to make your life difficult.
	2. We will work out all schedules once you provide us with initial information as to where you are and when.
	3. We will provide you with all written information that you might need.
	4. We will be sensitive to your feelings.
	5. We will work hard to teach (student) ways to interact and hang out with you. We will also teach you the things you need to know about interacting with your friend with deaf-blindness, such as how to communicate, move around, and other social issues.
	6. We will use your suggestions and be responsive to your comments.

For friendships to develop, daily contacts appear to be necessary; therefore, schedule one interaction per member per day. However, avoid scheduling more than one interaction with the same member per day to avoid "burnout" of the peer. It is beneficial if more than one interaction spontaneously occurs between members, but a greater frequency of interaction should (and will) occur because it is desired, not because it is required.

3. *Negotiate interaction schedules:* During the second group meeting, provide each member (including the student with deaf-blindness) with a schedule. Go over the times and places when students should meet each other. The student with deaf-blindness may require a modified version of the interaction schedule (e.g., large print, tactile symbol, braille). Photographs of each group member in the targeted location organized according to time may facilitate the usefulness of the schedule for students with some residual vision. If the student is fully blind, a calendar box with tactile symbols should be considered. If a calendar box is used for the student with deaf-blindness, a schedule with photographs will still be needed for the peers (see p. 245, this chap., for information on self-monitoring strategies).

4. *Explore interaction activities:* Discuss strategies for socializing with the student with deaf-blindness. Encourage the peers *not* to change their natural routine in any way. That is, if they normally go to their locker and hang out with a group of friends between second and third period, then they should have the student with deaf-blindness join them in that activity. They should not remove themselves from their typical activities in order to have an isolated conversation with the student with deaf-blindness. The idea is to include peers with deaf-blindness in ongoing natural activities as much as possible.

Discuss communication strategies, such as touch or sign language, that peers will utilize with the student with deaf-blindness. Those strategies should be taught in reasonable increments, with reference to the activities in which the students are engaging. It will also be necessary to provide ongoing support and review of those strategies already taught as well as adding new strategies as needed.

5. *Talk about interaction strategies:* Discuss strategies for behavior management and prompting of specific social behavior. Role playing and ongoing reinforcement of peer interactions are useful tools in teaching instructional strategies to the members of the group. The most critical element in teaching interaction strategies is instructing peers to respond normally and to have age-appropriate expectations for the targeted student's behavior and skills. Members of the group must learn to respond to and include the student in the same way that they do their peers without disabilities.

6. *Invite a deaf-blind adult to a network meeting:* Discuss strategies for introducing deaf-blind adults to the focal student. These adults can serve as important role models for the student with deaf-blindness as well as members of his or her support network. Also, explore agencies that provide services to people with deaf-blindness. Students can learn to use those resources to expand their knowledge base regarding communication systems and deaf-blindness in general.

Conducting Network Meetings

Some of the most valuable information on what teachers and other interested adults may do to support the continued development of the friendship network comes from discussions during network meetings. The following meeting procedures are suggested:

1. *Determine a meeting schedule:* Initially meet with the group one time per week during lunch or after school for 40 minutes to 1 hour. Once the group is demonstrating independence in terms of ongoing interactions among members, reduce the frequency of group meetings to a schedule that is satisfactory to both the members and the group leader/facilitator. For example, in one of the groups that we facilitated, the members met weekly for the first 3 months of the group

until they felt comfortable handling all situations that came up, including inappropriate social behavior, noncompliance, other students teasing, and simply creating an easygoing social situation. After 3 months, the group met generally every 2 or 3 weeks, with an option to call a weekly meeting as needed to problem solve within the group context. In addition, we found that after a few months, members of the group began to trust the problem solving and decision making of their fellow members and would talk to each other outside of a group meeting context. Eventually there was less reliance on the adult facilitator for input.

2. *Discuss how to include the student with deaf-blindness:* Inclusion of the student with deaf-blindness in the weekly group meeting must be determined for each individual. Much of the group discussion focuses on the member with deaf-blindness. If this can be done with the student present, in a respectful way and with positive outcomes, then the student should be invited to attend the weekly meetings. Be sensitive to the responses and satisfaction of the student with deaf-blindness during and following all group meetings. Make sure all people present identify themselves at the start of the meeting, say (or sign) who they are when they speak, and notify the student with deaf-blindness when they leave the room. Be sensitive to the degree of participation in the group by each member. Some members may not feel comfortable talking about the student with him or her present. If the student with deaf-blindness has an interpreter at school, he or she should attend the meetings. If the student does not already have an interpreter the issue should be raised with school administrators.

3. *Review issues from previous meetings:* During each meeting, review the previous week's interactions among members of the group, looking at the following areas:

a. Assess whether the members were able to get together when scheduled. If not, what can be changed to better facilitate their interactions?

b. Assess the substance of the interactions. When they did get together, what did they usually do? Were they engaged in activities or routines that were typical, or did they do things that they wouldn't normally do? Problem solve about how to better normalize their activities.

c. Assess the quality of the interactions. Did the student respond appropriately, did the student stay with the peer, did the student participate in the interaction? Problem solve about how to increase new skills and reinforce existing ones.

d. Assess the reaction of people outside of the group. If negative, discuss how the members can respond and how the members feel about other's reactions. Encourage the group to support each other's participation.

4. *Identify skills for instruction:* Through peer input, identify those skills that are in greatest need of change and develop procedures for impacting these skills during subsequent meetings. The skills identified should be seen as critical by members of the group. That is, without the skill or without the reduction of a specific behavior, the members feel that a friendship between themselves and the student is unlikely. Specific skills and procedures targeted will differ across students. Overall, the emphasis should be placed on teaching normalized skills using natural, less intrusive instructional strategies. Natural peer feedback and peer modeling may be sufficient to teach new skills or strengthen existing ones. Prioritize the skills to be worked on by the group members. Work on one skill at a time. Encourage the group to be patient and to look for subtle changes in the student's interactions.

5. *Monitor progress:* Assess the progress of the goals set during the previous meeting. This can be done either through anecdotal discussions of how each member perceives the group's progress, or through charting of interaction data gathered by members of the group or by the group facilitator. With either format, focus on the times and contexts when the interactions were successful, and discuss why they were successful. Identify those things that the member(s) did that might have encouraged success. Problem solve as to how those things can be applied to less successful situations. Remind the members that the process is slow, but that what they have done has already made an impact on this student and on their relationship with the student. Charted data can be highly reinforcing to some students, especially when the actual behavior change is subtle. The biggest reason for peer burnout is the sense that the peer has failed. If the peers believe that they are making a difference in a student's life, there will be a greater likelihood for continued motivation to participate.

Facilitating Problem Solving

Perhaps the most effective way to get peers to interact with a student with deaf-blindness in the same way that they do with their friends without disabilities is for the group facilitator to model age-appropriate interactions with both the peers and the student with deaf-blindness. That is, teachers should attempt to take on the same style of verbal and nonverbal language and behavior that is typical of the age cohort. The peers will model the teacher's behavior. If the facilitator acts like a teacher—responding in a "teacher voice" with "teacher words" to teacher-determined situations and behaviors—the peers will come to act toward the student in the same way as the teacher. This is not a good foun-

dation for establishing a friendship. If the facilitator acts like a 13-year-old in a group of 13-year-olds—responding in a 13-year-old voice with 13-year-old words to situations and behaviors that are determined by 13-year-old minds—the peers will also act like 13-year-olds and interact with the student in a manner appropriate to 13-year-old interactions.

Peers will often ask, "What do we do when . . .?" In most cases, the teacher can respond to the peers with, "What would you do if your other friends did that?" (See chap. 10, this volume, for information on how to address issues of communication.) In this way, the teacher is stressing typical responding and typical patterns of interaction. While the emphasis should remain on typical responding, behavior management strategies that are specific to a particular behavior of a student may need to be taught to the group members. Management strategies must make sense to the group members; otherwise, they may feel uncomfortable and disinclined to use them. Therefore, discuss the rationale behind a behavior management strategy and how it works, and solicit feedback from the peers regarding its usefulness in natural settings. Make changes to your management plan as deemed necessary by the group discussions.

Peers will often hesitate before giving advice or negative feedback to the student because they are afraid of "hurting his feelings" or because they just don't think the student will understand. Again, emphasize that they should respond exactly the same way that they would with a friend without disabilities. Protecting him or her from the truth (just because of a disability) will not help the student. Feedback can be given in a constructive, nonconfrontational fashion. Assess what they would typically say to a friend who did something that they didn't like.

Translate the content of their message to fit the communication style or language system of the student with deaf-blindness, then role play giving that same kind of feedback to the student with disabilities.

At first the peers will want the facilitator to solve situations for them, because after all he or she is the teacher as well as the expert. We encourage teachers to ask peers (in a very supportive way) to deal directly with most day-to-day situations. Encourage them to: 1) respond immediately and naturally to situations that they don't like (e.g., if the student is kissing them, they should tell the student that they do not want to be kissed and that kids at school just say hi); 2) use the group as a time to problem solve among themselves with the group facilitator assisting in the discussion; 3) get advice from the facilitator and other group members whenever they are unsure about a situation; they should not wait until the group meeting; and 4) give feedback (positive and negative) directly to the student during group meetings. Crisis situations or situations that occur because of administrative management problems will of course need to be dealt with immediately by the adult facilitator or the classroom teacher. Sometimes it is important to help students define the difference between situations that require adult intervention and those that do not. Time in the group can be used to discuss when adults are needed. With younger students especially, issues of toileting and challenging behavior may arise where they will need adult guidance and support. Addressing these concerns can alleviate fears of being asked to act as a teacher. Otherwise, for most of the issues that arise, students generally have the capabilities and willingness to address those issues themselves. The danger with an adult stepping in to solve a situation is that the peers may come to depend on the adult to

intervene rather than attempt to use their own strategies for interaction. Friendships will not develop if the presence of an adult mediator is needed to sustain or to promote interactions.

The group should continuously develop inventories of what they feel are the greatest needs of the student or the peers in terms of achieving greater inclusion. Peers tend to have more realistic and more normalized suggestions for what needs to be taught than what adults might suggest is appropriate. Teachers should encourage peers to give them assignments for skills to target in the classroom, including teaching appropriate responses to often asked questions, teaching students to initiate interactions with their peers, teaching other peers that making close contact with a student with deaf-blindness is often needed to communicate with them, and teaching age-appropriate appearance skills. Although teachers may find that the majority of this type of instruction of the student occurs during natural interactions with their friends, there may be additional need for greater practice of skills through teacher intervention in the classroom.

The teacher should follow the interaction schedule. Make sure that the student with disabilities is in the right place at the right time. Once members of the group have gotten together, the teacher should remove herself from the interaction entirely. The presence of an adult is generally stigmatizing to the student, disruptive to the ongoing interaction, and can serve to encourage the members of the group to rely on the teacher rather than themselves to manage the interaction. However, in some instances the student will have an interpreter who will be present during interactions. Teachers should be prepared to provide information to peers on how to utilize an interpreter in such a way that it does not detract from their interactions.

Evaluating the
Effectiveness of Peer Support Groups

Once a peer support group is in place, it should be evaluated on a regular basis. The following procedures are recommended for evaluating group effectiveness:

1. *Assess network member interactions:* Anecdotal feedback gathered during weekly group meetings will provide general information regarding the frequency of interactions and the nature of interactions among members of the group.

2. *Determine network member satisfaction:* Anecdotal feedback gathered during weekly group meetings will provide general information regarding the satisfaction of the group members regarding participation in the network.

3. *Review actual data on interactions:* Systematic data gathered by the peers either continuously or intermittently will provide more specific information regarding the frequency of interaction and the nature of interactions among members of the group. Figure 1 provides an example of a data format that can be used by the peers to collect information regarding their ongoing interactions. Inclusion of peer data collection methods is beneficial in providing teachers with specific information regarding the acquisition and generalization of social responses. In addition, the data collection form allows peers to objectively record information that may be either too sensitive to discuss openly during group meetings or forgotten over the span of a few days.

Another example of peer data collection is having students keep journals. At the end of their time together, students with and without disabilities sit and write or draw about their experiences of the day. Photos can be added when available. The journal can double as a communication vehicle for some students, that is, when concepts of time are difficult to discuss, students can refer to pictures in the journal.

Note: The use of peer data collection procedures should depend on the needs and desires of the network members. Teachers may find that while some of the members like the opportunity to record their interactions, some members find data collection too intrusive or burdening, and some members adopt the procedures inconsistently. The best solution is to provide ongoing opportunities and support for data collection by the peers, without placing restrictions on how or when the data are collected.

Bill   Monday
Assigned time: after school   Assigned place: class to bus

Was there an interaction?	Yes		No
Who started the interaction?	Me		(Student)
Was the interaction 1 turn or longer?	1 turn		Longer
Did (student) respond appropriately?	Yes	Some	No
Did (student) hang out appropriately?	Yes	Some	No
Were there other people around?	Yes		No
Did other people react okay?	Yes	Some	No
Interaction was	Good	OK	Not good

Comments: _____

_____

_____

Figure 1.   Sample peer data collection form.

4. *Review actual data on member satisfaction:* Systematic evaluations of peer satisfaction conducted intermittently will provide more specific information regarding the satisfaction of the group members toward participation in the network.

5. *Use self-monitoring systems:* Self-monitoring systems can be used by the student with disabilities to monitor the frequency and nature of his or her interactions with peers. Student self-monitoring can provide the teacher with additional evaluative data regarding the effectiveness of the group intervention. Self-monitoring can reflect, generally, the occurrence of an interaction or, specifically, the presence of a target behavior within an interaction (e.g., initiations, responses, elaborations, turn-taking, conversational repair, maintaining appropriate social distance and attention). Many systems for self-monitoring of student behavior exist and can be modified to meet the specific needs of the individual, including the use of wrist counters to count the frequency of appropriate social responding within a social interaction, peer review cards on which the peer records a (+) or a (−) to reflect the overall appropriateness of a specific interaction, or tally sheets on which the student records the occurrence or nonoccurrence of an interaction with a specific group member.

Figure 2 presents a sample self-recording system that can be used by students with adequate residual vision to record interaction data. In this system, a notebook is placed by the classroom door that includes photographs of each peer group member arranged according to time and place of interaction, and a tally sheet directly below the appropriate picture. As the student exits the classroom, he identifies from the photograph the friend with whom he will spend time. In returning to class, the student records on the tally sheet in the corresponding box a (+) or a (−) to reflect the occurrence or nonoccurrence of an interaction. This system can be modified to provide for the tactile identification of peers or students with little or no residual vision. These data can then be used by the teacher to reinforce the participat-

	Photo of Tom	Photo of Ann	Photo of Max	Photo of Group	Photo of Mary	Photo of Bill
	1st-2nd Tom, Bill Max	2nd-3rd Ann, Mary	3rd-4th Max, Tom	Lunch Boys: T, Th Girls: W, F	5th-6th Mary	After School Bill, Ann
Monday						
Tuesday						
Wednesday						
Thursday						
Friday						

Figure 2. Sample form for student self-monitoring of interactions.

ing members of the group and to structure problem-solving discussions within the group meetings as to the reasons for members not interacting.

6. *Adult data sources:* Systematic data gathered by the teacher or adult network facilitator will provide specific supplemental data to that collected by the peers and the student with disabilities. Adult observation data collection systems can be used to gather baseline information regarding ongoing interactions between students with and without disabilities, normative information regarding typical patterns of interaction among students without disabilities, and postintervention information used to evaluate the effectiveness of specific group interventions. How the observation data will be used will help to determine how frequently data should be taken. For baseline data and normative data, it is suggested that those contexts that will be targeted for intervention be observed three to five times to obtain a pattern of interaction. Data gathered following the inception of intervention will vary according to the completeness of the data provided by the group members. As a guideline, however, an adult should attempt to observe targeted contexts an average of 1 day per week per context.

CONCLUSIONS

The use of peer social support networks has been shown to be a highly effective way to promote interactions and develop friendships among students with and without disabilities. Peers can be effective change agents if they are reinforced for their efforts by their peer with disabilities, by adult group facilitators, and most importantly by the other members of their social clique. Peer pressure is a tremendously powerful social element. By including multiple members of an intact social clique in a peer network, the strength of peer pressure can be used to an advantage. The authors have found that because individual members of the network support each other for their participation, few members leave the group or fail to follow through with commitments that they have made to the group. There is tremendous positive pressure to maintain and continue and little pressure from other members of the social clique to discontinue involvement.

The procedures presented for implementation and evaluation of peer support networks have been validated with students with moderate and severe disabilities, including students with challenging behaviors. The authors cannot advocate more for the use of this system in terms of its impact on students with and without disabilities. This system has produced tremendous satisfaction from the students, friends outside of the network, parents, teachers, and site administrators. The natural abilities and desire of peers to facilitate new friendships is a tremendous untapped resource to which all should direct a greater focus.

REFERENCES

Bercovici, S. (1981). Qualitative methods and cultural perspectives in the study of deinstitutionalization. In R.H. Bruininks, C.E. Meyer, B.B. Sigford, & K.C. Lakin (Eds.), *Deinstitutionalization and community adjustment of mentally retarded people* (pp. 133–144). Washington, DC: American Association on Mental Deficiency.

Breen, C., Kennedy, C., & Haring, T. (Eds.). (1991). *Social context research project: Methods for*

facilitating the inclusion of students with disabilities in integrated school and community contexts. Santa Barbara, CA: University of California.

Carr, E.G., & Durand, V.M. (1985). Reducing behavior problems through functional communication training. *Journal of Applied Behavior Analysis, 18,* 111–126.

Erikson, E.H. (1959). *Identity, youth, and crisis.* New York: Norton.

Falvey, M.A. (1986). *Community-based curriculum:*

Instructional strategies for students with severe handicaps. Baltimore: Paul H. Brookes Publishing Co.

Gartner, A., & Lipsky, D.K. (1987). Beyond special education: Toward a quality system for all students. *Harvard Education Review, 57,* 367–395.

Goffman, E. (1963). *Stigma: Notes on the management of spoiled identities.* Englewood Cliffs, NJ: Prentice Hall.

Horner, R.H., Reed, B., Ritchie, K.K., Stoner, S.K., & Twain, K.R. (1986). *A study of the structure and adequacy of social networks of adults with developmental disabilities.* Unpublished manuscript, University of Oregon, Center for Human Development, Eugene.

Kennedy, C., & Haring, T. (1992). *Establishing and extending choice-making during social interactions for students with profound multiple disabilities.* Unpublished manuscript, University of California, Santa Barbara.

Lane, H. (1988). Is there a psychology of the deaf? *Exceptional Children, 55,* 7–21.

McKinney, J.P., Fitzgerald, H.E., & Strommen, E.A. (1982). *Developmental psychology: The adolescent and young adult.* Homewood, IL: Dorsey Press.

Michael, J. (1986). Repertoire-altering effects of remote contingencies. *Analysis of Verbal Behavior, 4,* 10–18.

Peck, C.A. (1991). Linking values and science in social policy decisions affecting citizens with severe disabilities. In L.H. Meyer, C.A. Peck, & L. Brown (Eds.), *Critical issues in the lives of people with severe disabilities* (pp. 1–16). Baltimore: Paul H. Brookes Publishing Co.

Romer, L. (1991). *Friends for Life Technical Proposal.* Unpublished manuscript, University of Washington, Experimental Education Unit.

Romer, L., & Haring, N.G. (1993). *The social participation of students with deaf-blindness in educational settings.* Manuscript submitted for publication.

Sailor, W. (1986). *Community intensive instruction: Research and implementation strategies.* Paper presented at Marshall University Conference on Generalization and Maintenance, Huntington, WV.

Voeltz, L.M. (1980). Children's attitudes toward handicapped peers. *American Journal on Mental Deficiency, 84,* 455–464.

Wolfensberger, W. (1972). Social role valorization: A proposed new term for the principle of normalization. *Mental Retardation, 21,* 254–259.

SUPPORT STRATEGIES

Chapter 12

Behavioral Support in Inclusive School Settings

Felix F. Billingsley,
Robert Huven,
and Lyle T. Romer

Attempts to manage the challenging behaviors of people with deaf-blindness have not differed markedly from attempts to manage similar behaviors displayed by individuals with other forms of disability. Disruptive, disturbing, or stereotypic behaviors have been dealt with, for example, by response cost procedures (Luiselli & Lolli, 1987), aversive tastes (McDaniel, Kocim, & Barton, 1984), water mist (Reilich, Spooner, & Rose, 1984), differential reinforcement of other behaviors (DRO) (Barton, Meston, & Barton, 1984), and overcorrection (Barton & LaGrow, 1983).

Unfortunately, such behavior management procedures have often been selected without consideration of the variables that actually control target behaviors and have frequently included the application of aversive stimuli (e.g., water mist, monetary fines). As a result, they are likely to generate their own set of problems (see, e.g., Azrin & Holz, 1966; Carr, Robinson, & Palumbo, 1990; Donnellan, LaVigna, Negri-Shoultz, & Fassbender, 1988; Sidman, 1989). These problems may include at least the following: 1) dramatic in-

stances of countercontrol on the part of the learner; 2) the inadvertent reinforcement of unwanted behaviors; 3) reduced opportunities for learners to participate in instructional programs (e.g., various forms of time out); 4) negative reactions from community members and peers; and 5) the recovery of undesirable behaviors following the withdrawal of punishing consequences, unless those consequences are very intense. In addition, individuals may be denied the opportunity to communicate effectively, make choices, and engage in meaningful social interactions because although they have been taught what *not* to do, they have not been taught what *to* do to achieve desired outcomes in acceptable and efficient ways.

Considerable interest has emerged in recent years in shifting from traditional techniques that are designed primarily to suppress challenging behaviors (a *control* perspective) to an approach that promotes the development of functional, adaptive behaviors (an *educational* perspective). The latter approach, which is also characterized by the simultaneous application of multiple treatment strategies and an emphasis on preserving and supporting human dignity, has come to be known as *positive behavioral support* (cf. Horner, Dunlap, et al., 1990). A growing research base indicates the value of a positive behavioral support orientation to the management of a wide variety of challenging behaviors across individuals who experience diverse disabilities. Included in that research base are data to suggest the considerable potential of positive, functional techniques for application to individuals with deaf-blindness (Durand & Kishi, 1987). This chapter presents a number of procedures that might be used effectively within a program of positive behavioral support for persons with deaf-blindness and provides recommendations for intervention within inclusive public school settings.

THE PREVENT–TEACH–REACT MODEL

Janney, Black, and Ferlo (1989) have developed a model that groups intervention components into three categories representing those that: 1) *prevent* challenging behaviors, 2) *teach* the individual new behaviors to meet his or her needs, and 3) *react* in productive ways when the behavior does occur. Strategies to prevent challenging behaviors are designed to produce rapid reductions in the frequency and/or intensity of target behaviors and should therefore have a number of positive effects. First, they should act to reduce the number of opportunities the student has to "practice," and be reinforced for, performing challenging behaviors. Second, many stimuli (e.g., staff, surroundings) in the student's environment that previously set the occasion for undesirable behaviors should begin to set the occasion for desired behaviors. Third, conditions for teaching and learning in the classroom should improve as a result of the elimination of distractions that

often accompany challenging behaviors and associated teacher responses. Fourth, rapid reductions in target behaviors should reduce "wear and tear" (Janney et al., 1989, p. 24) on staff and students alike and should reduce the temptation to use nonfunctional, aversive strategies.

Teaching new behaviors that provide effective and efficient alternatives to challenging behaviors is a critical step in maintaining the success that has been achieved by prevention methods. All persons behave to achieve some outcome; in other words, behaviors have a function. Simply because challenging behaviors have been prevented or suppressed, it does not necessarily follow that the student will no longer attempt to achieve the outcome produced by that behavior. In fact, in the absence of an acceptable alternative to the challenging behavior, the individual may develop new, and equally unacceptable, ways to serve the same function. Thus, the teaching component of the model proposed by Janney et al. (1989) provides for a "win–win" solution to behavior problems; that is, educators, parents, peers, and others no longer have to deal with challenging behaviors and the student continues to achieve desired effects from his or her actions. Obviously, this outcome is satisfying both practically and ethically.

Because it is relatively unusual that any plan, regardless of how thoughtfully conceived and implemented, will result in the immediate and total elimination of target behaviors, it is necessary to identify ways to react when those behaviors do occur. Reactions should indicate to the student that target behaviors will no longer be successful, and they should prevent harm to the student or to others (Janney et al., 1989; Meyer & Evans, 1989). The necessity for such reactions, however, should rapidly decline if effective procedures have been selected for preventing and teaching.

The model proposed by Janney et al. (1989) not only shares elements recommended by others (e.g., Meyer & Evans, 1989; Pyles & Bailey, 1990), but also seems highly consistent with needs and conditions in educational settings. In the sections that follow, methods are described by which teachers of students with deaf-blindness can implement each of the intervention components of the prevent–teach–react model. In order to select the most appropriate methods, however, it is first necessary to develop a hypothesis or theory regarding the purpose or purposes target behaviors serve for the student. If, for example, Todd engages in stereotypic behavior, does it serve a self-regulatory function or has he learned to use the behavior to escape from task demands? Does Sheila scream because she is hungry, because she doesn't know where she is or who is around her, because she needs help with a task, because she wants company, or some combination of reasons? Certainly, interventions would differ depending on the function of the behaviors displayed by Todd and Sheila. A *functional assessment* provides the basis for formulating a theory regarding the purpose(s) of challenging behaviors and for developing program planning based on this theory.

Functional Assessments

It is beyond the scope of this chapter to address functional assessment procedures in detail, and the reader is referred to such sources as Iwata, Vollmer, and Zarcone (1990); Janney et al. (1989); O'Neill, Horner, Albin, Storey, and Sprague (1990); Pyles and Bailey (1990); Touchette, MacDonald, and Langer (1985); and Wacker et al. (1990) for thorough discussions. Briefly, however, functional assessments are designed to suggest a theory regarding the function of challenging behaviors and to contribute to program planning by identifying the conditions under

which challenging behaviors do *and* do not occur.

Identifying those conditions is usually a team process (see "Behavioral Support Teams," p. 269, this chap.) and requires that the team obtain answers to questions such as:

1. What are the characteristics of the undesired behaviors? This question calls for a precise statement regarding the specific, observable actions that are considered challenging and their topography (e.g., "bites hand and forearm") rather than general labels (e.g., "mean and aggressive") (Janney et al., 1989; O'Neill et al., 1990). As Janney et al. (1989) have indicated, general labels "tell us more about how we feel about the behavior than the behavior itself" (p. 12). In addition, data must be available regarding the frequency of target behaviors, their duration, and their magnitude or intensity.

2. What ecological or physiological events may affect the behaviors? Information related to this class of events would include, for example, the potential influence of medications and/or the medical condition of the individual (e.g., allergies), dietary concerns, and the general conditions that exist in the environment(s) in which target behaviors occur (e.g., lighting, temperature). The student's sleep cycle (disturbances are common among children with sensory impairments before consistent routines are established), the extent to which he or she is exposed to a variety of activities throughout the day, and the results of tasks and activities in which he or she is involved (i.e., boring to, or preferred by, the student) should also be considered. For students with deaf-blindness, it is particularly important to obtain information regarding the use of residual

vision and/or hearing (Fewell & Rich, 1987; Niswander, 1987; Prickett & Prickett, 1992). For example, a problem behavior may be triggered by an ill-fitted or inadequately adjusted hearing aid; the frequent flinging of glasses or hearing aids could indicate a need to retest hearing and vision.

3. What specific events occur before, during, and after the behavior? Specific events of particular concern might include *who* is present (or coming or going) when the behavior occurs, *what* is going on at the time (e.g., activities or nature of tasks in which the student is involved), and what happens following the behavior (e.g., teacher-provided consequences, reactions of classmates). Other critical information regarding specific events includes an indication of *when* target behaviors are performed (e.g., the time of day or particular days of the week) and *where* it is probable that behaviors will be observed; that is, is the student likely to perform the challenging behavior more often in the classroom or on the playground, at the grocery store and restaurant or in the home, and so forth. It should be noted that it is equally important for the educational team to determine and document those "who, what, when, and where" conditions under which challenging behaviors *seldom* or *never* occur.

A number of methods may be used to collect functional assessment data, including interviews and questionnaires (cf. Durand & Crimmins, 1988; Janney et al., 1989; Willis, LaVigna, & Donnellan, 1989), checklists (cf. Pyles & Bailey, 1990), direct naturalistic observation (cf. O'Neill et al., 1990; Touchette et al., 1985), direct controlled observation in analog situations (cf. Iwata et al., 1990; Wacker et al., 1990), or some combination of

those techniques. When the data are collected, the behavioral support team uses them to determine whether it is possible to predict circumstances under which challenging behaviors are probable and to develop a theory regarding the function of the student's behavior. A failure of team members to agree regarding the predictability and/or function of target behaviors is a good sign that more information should be obtained. When agreement is reached, however, team members must then apply their conclusions regarding behavioral predictability and function to the development of the prevent-teach-react plan.

Many of the sources cited above provide excellent discussions regarding the relationship between functional assessment and programming, and Janney et al. (1989) and Meyer and Evans (1989) outline important considerations in a team approach to the development and implementation of positive behavioral support programs. Team functions are addressed more fully in the section, "Behavioral Support in Inclusive Settings," p. 266. In the sections that follow, specific interventions that might be used within the prevent, teach, and react components of behavioral support programs for students with deaf-blindness are presented.

Preventing Challenging Behaviors

Some strategies applied to prevent challenging behaviors may be permanent if they are acceptable in typical community settings; for example, a student might be excused from participating in some nonpreferred recreational activity or his schedule of medication might be modified. Many preventive strategies, however, are considered to be temporary measures that will be systematically removed as the student becomes better able to achieve desired outcomes in acceptable ways, and as his or her environment becomes discriminative for appropriate behaviors. Often, the methods used for prevention are stimulus based (cf. Carr, Robinson, Taylor, & Carlson, 1990). These and other methods are described in the following sections and summarized in Table 1.

Introduce Stimuli that Control Low Rates of Problem Behavior Functional assessment results will usually reveal certain conditions under which target behaviors seldom or never occur. Increasing the extent to which those conditions are present in the student's environment could be one way to reduce the

Table 1. Some strategies and tactics for preventing challenging behaviors

Strategies	Tactics
Introduce low-rate stimuli	• Introduce specific stimuli • Increase predictability
Modify high-rate stimuli	• Modify environmental stimuli • Modify tasks • Modify response requirements
Embed stimuli	• Mix low-rate task demands among high-rate demands • Precede high-rate task demands with low-rate demands
Build stimulus control	• Confine behavior to specific circumstances in which it can be tolerated • Confine behavior to circumstances that can be faded
Modify curricula	• Distribute practice • Increase instructional pace • Increase probability of success and achievement of critical effect • Try total task instruction • Promote generalization • Move ahead to more difficult step or skill
Change condition of the individual	• Attend to medical and medication-related conditions • Provide adequate levels of exercise and rest • Implement dietary modifications
Implement differential reinforcement of other behavior (DRO)	• Use events that maintain challenging behaviors as reinforcers in DRO program

likelihood of such behaviors. Was it found, for instance, that Roger never scratched one particular instructional assistant or that Gina engaged in less hand flapping when she was actively participating in group activities? In these cases, perhaps Roger's schedule could be temporarily rearranged so that he spends most of his time with the "preferred" instructional assistant, and Gina's programs could be constructed in such a manner that most of her instruction occurs within a group context. Likewise, it might have been noted that Steve gouged his eyes when left alone without anything to do, but seldom eye-gouged in the presence of certain toys or other manipulable items. It would be a relatively simple matter, then, to provide him with engaging objects whenever he is not interacting with others (see, e.g., Cancio, Young, Macfarlane, West, & Blair, 1991).

An important consideration for many students with deaf-blindness relates to the extent to which their environments are predictable. Certainly, many of us feel uncomfortable and may even "act out" when our routines are unexpectedly disrupted or when we are unsure of what is going to happen next. For example, consider your feelings and, possibly, your behavior on the first day you were left alone at school by your parents. Prediction could be particularly difficult for students with deaf-blindness. Unless appropriate steps are taken by the teacher, leisure, transitions, and "down time" could all be perceived as periods of chaos.

It has been noted that increasing predictability by the use of picture schedules has resulted in decreases in aberrant behaviors by individuals with a variety of disabilities including autism (Schrader & Gaylord-Ross, 1990). Similar strategies could be appropriate for children with deaf-blindness where assessments have indicated that predictable situations were characterized by lower levels of challenging behaviors than at times of change and potential uncertainty. Tactile cues, or cues relying on other senses such as smell (e.g., a distinctive fragrance worn by the teacher), could be used to help the student recognize teachers or social partners, become familiar with the layout of the environment, identify destinations, provide representations of daily routines, and so forth (Murray-Branch, Udavari-Solner, & Bailey, 1991).

Actual objects could also be used to represent upcoming activities or events that would be provided when the student completed some task (Rowland & Schweigert, 1989). Tony, for example, was unable to anticipate any positive events in his day until he learned to recognize a piece of the laundry basket as the symbol of his favorite job (washing clothes). He found the vibrations of the washer and the warmth of the dryer pleasant. His mother was able to remind him of this approaching task as a way to interrupt his injurious behavior of falling on the floor and striking his face. The critical message here is that a situation that may be clear and enjoyable to many people may be one that is highly ambiguous and perhaps terrifying to the student.

Modify Stimuli that Control High Rates of Problem Behavior

Just as it is likely to be found that there are certain conditions under which challenging behaviors rarely occur, other conditions may be identified in which occurrences are particularly frequent, intense, or of extended duration. An appropriate initial step in programming, then, might be to modify or eliminate those conditions. For example, it was previously noted that Gina engaged in less stereotypic behavior when involved in group activities. It is possible that another student (Stephanie) would be found to engage in such behaviors at a very high rate when she had to be around large numbers of peers in confined and noisy areas. In Stephanie's case, it might be possible to change her placement to a classroom with lower enrollment and in which the teacher's style resulted in somewhat less movement and chatter by students. In other instances, environmental pollutants might be reduced (e.g., by avoiding temperature extremes or adjusting hearing aids for a noisy situation), certain types of demands could be minimized, the length of instructional sessions could be lessened, or task difficulty could be simplified.

Some ways to simplify task difficulty could include requiring only partial participation, giving single- rather than multiple-step directions, or providing highly salient stimulus prompts that would allow the student to use any functional vision more effectively. Teachers might also completely revise the nature of tasks so that they could be completed primarily through the use of movements already in the student's repertoire or employ assistive technology (such as tactile communication or a light box for picture board communication).

Keep in mind that everyone has certain activities that they can choose to avoid. A range of such choices should also be made available to students with deaf-blindness. If it is found that there are activities during which levels of challenging behavior increase, it may be because that activity is simply boring or unpleasant to the student. In such cases, it should be determined whether the activity is one in which the student should be able to choose *not* to participate, either temporarily or permanently.

Embed Stimuli

Embedding stimuli that control high rates of problem behaviors with those that control low rates is a strategy that is often used to improve student compliance to directions and may take a number of forms. In one variation, difficult task demands that have been associated with considerable problem behavior are mixed among requests for easy skills that the student has in his repertoire and almost always performs (e.g., Winterling, Dunlap, & O'Neill, 1987). In another form of this method, requests that are likely to result in compliance *precede* requests that are likely to be followed by noncompliance (see e.g., Mace et al., 1988; Singer, Singer, & Horner, 1987).

Singer et al. (1987) referred to the latter intervention as *pretask requesting*. In their investigation, which focused on students with moderate to severe mental retardation, three requests for which there was a high probability of compliance were presented in rapid succession prior to a request for which the probability of compliance was low. High-probability requests included such instructions as "give me five" or "shake hands," and low-probability requests involved transition from a preferred to a less preferred activity. It was found that the presentation of pretask requests substantially increased compliance with the low probability requests. In a later study, Horner, Day, Sprague, O'Brien, and Heathfield (1991) demonstrated that a similar procedure could also be used effectively to reduce levels of aggression and self-injury by a student with severe disabilities.

Following the logic of embedding procedures, if a student experiences difficulty in performing activities that require extensive use of residual vision and often emits challenging behaviors when requested to engage in such activities, the requests might be preceded by, or mixed with, those that involve behaviors more enjoyable to the student and that are not as vision dependent. Such strategies may obtain desired results because reinforced pretask requests "come from the same class of responses as the target response (i.e., compliance with requests)" (Singer et al., 1987, p. 289). Another possibility is that the increased reinforcement that follows

compliance with high probability requests establishes a *behavioral momentum* that carries through to requests that are of lower probability (Mace et al., 1988).

Build Stimulus Control   Sometimes, a target behavior is a "challenge" simply because it occurs in inappropriate situations. Other target behaviors may require elimination in all situations, but elimination can be promoted if, initially, the behavior is confined to certain teacher-selected conditions. In such cases, it may be of value to bring the target behavior under the control of some specific set of stimuli (Andrews & Billingsley, 1991; Donnellan et al., 1988; LaVigna & Donnellan, 1986). Intervention, therefore, consists of reinforcing challenging behaviors when those behaviors occur in the presence of particular conditions, but not in the presence of others.

One example of this stimulus control approach was provided by LaVigna and Donnellan (1986) who reported that the public masturbation of a 5-year-old girl was treated by providing reinforcers when masturbation was limited to the privacy of the bathroom. In another example, spitting on shiny objects was reduced by first reinforcing spitting on a mirror. When spitting occurred only in the presence of the mirror, the availability of the mirror was faded (LaVigna, Willis, & Donnellan, 1989). Specific guidelines for developing and applying stimulus control methods in response to challenging behaviors have been provided by Andrews and Billingsley (1991) and LaVigna and Donnellan (1986).

Modify Educational Curricula   Modifying educational curricula associated with problem behaviors includes those interventions that relate to the way tasks are presented for instruction and the nature of the skills being taught. Some ways to potentially reduce behavior problems by manipulating task presentation are to: 1) vary tasks in a distributed practice format rather than devoting an extended block of time to repetitive instruction of a single task (cf. Winterling et al., 1987) and 2) increase the pace of instruction (Dunlap, Dyer, & Koegel, 1983). Moving ahead quickly to more difficult tasks or steps in the curriculum rather than continuing instruction on a skill far beyond the point of skill acquisition can also be used to avoid or reduce challenging behaviors related to specific instructional programs (White, 1985).

In addition, it may be important to present tasks in such a way as to increase the probability that the learner will be successful and will be able to recognize how the task "makes sense." By way of illustration, it might be observed that Leslie screamed and banged her head when instructed to perform certain skills in a backward chaining format (teaching the last step of a task first). Perhaps those behaviors simply indicated that Leslie needed more antecedent teacher assistance, which would later be faded, to be able to work through the task successfully from start to finish (i.e., a total-task instructional format; cf. Neel & Billingsley, 1989). Such assistance would help Leslie to achieve consequences related to successful performance and would help her define the purpose of the entire task, in terms of its product, through movement.

Methods for task presentation (e.g., variations in settings, materials, and/or persons) that increase the probability that skills will be generalized are also important from a behavior management perspective. A failure to achieve acceptable generalization can result in instructed skills being performed in situations in which they should not occur (e.g., disrobing in public places) or in skills not being performed where they should occur. While either situation can be interpreted as a "behavior problem," the relationship of generalization failures to observed behaviors may be particularly hard to recognize when instructed skills do not occur in appropriate circumstances. Because the student cannot identify the skill that ought to be performed, or because he or she is frustrated or embarrassed due to an inability to select the appropriate behavior, undesirable responses (e.g., stereotypic behavior, aggression, running away) that are also performed in a variety of other contexts may be emitted.

Educators should consider generalization training to be a particularly high priority for students with deaf-blindness due to the difficulties those students may experience in identifying natural environmental cues for instructed behaviors. Complete discussions of methods to promote generalized responding may be found in such sources as Haring, (1988) and Horner, Dunlap, and Koegel (1988).

At a more basic level, challenging behaviors may occur because skills selected for instruction are simply meaningless or boring to the individual (i.e., they result in no *critical effect*) (Evans & Meyer, 1985; Green, Canipe, Way, & Reid, 1986; Meyer & Evans, 1989; Neel & Billingsley, 1989). As Meyer and Evans (1989) suggested, tantruming or engaging in self-injurious behaviors may be the student's way of bringing about a change in a routine or of introducing excitement into an otherwise boring situation. A reevaluation of the extent to which skills selected for instruction will actually contribute to fulfilling the learner's needs may be highly appropriate where excess behaviors appear closely related to specific tasks (cf. Meyer & Evans, 1989). If it is determined that their necessity to the learner is insubstantial, a reasonable approach would be to delete these skills from the student's curriculum and substitute more functional instructional targets.

Change the Condition of the Individual
The term *setting events* refers to a wide range of events that affect preexisting stimulus–

response relationships (Carr, Robinson, Taylor, et al., 1990). Many of the strategies described thus far involve a change in setting events. Such events, however, also include those that relate to the condition of the learner (Helmstetter & Durand, 1991). Illness, pain, discomfort, allergies, and medication side effects are but a few of the many possible learner conditions that could act as setting events to influence the appearance and maintenance of problem behaviors.

If, for example, a student is nauseous as a result of a particular medication used to control seizures, it would not be surprising if he refused food, did not want to play with other children, and appeared generally noncompliant (Pyles & Bailey, 1990). Perhaps a change in dosage or medication schedule (e.g., provide the medication just before bedtime rather than at breakfast) would resolve the problem. A child with deaf-blindness could become increasingly nonresponsive to verbal directions and requests as a result of an ongoing sinus problem or middle-ear infection (cf. Moss, 1992). Appropriate medical treatment to restore available conductive hearing might restore attentiveness and compliance. Interventions that result in a change in the student's condition therefore should not be neglected as a potentially effective class of behavior management tactics.

Illustrations of the effective application of methods designed to change the condition of the individual have been provided by such researchers as Bachman and Sluyter (1988); Lobato, Carlson, and Barrera (1986); and Pyles and Bailey (1990). Bachman and Sluyter observed reduced levels of stereotypic movements, off-task behaviors, and inappropriate vocalizations by two adults with severe disabilities following the participation of those individuals in daily aerobic dance exercise sessions. Lobato et al. used a satiation treatment involving the provision of unlimited quantities of low calorie foods to re-

duce the chronic rumination of two clients. Finally, Pyles and Bailey documented the case of a woman with disabilities who cried and sobbed the majority of the day. Their analysis indicated that "she was hungry, thirsty, wet, fatigued, and suffered from PMS" (p. 391). The crying and sobbing was eliminated when the woman's care routine was revised so that she was offered food and drink on a regular schedule, was provided with opportunities for morning and afternoon naps, and had her clothing checked frequently for urination.

It must be emphasized that there is an ethical need to attempt to provide the individual with deaf-blindness a form with which to express pain and well-being. Sensory losses should be accommodated by the use of symbols, signs, or gestures to promote communication with others. The role of communication instruction in behavioral support programs will be addressed more fully in the "Teaching Alternative Skills" section of this chapter.

Use Differential Reinforcement of Other Behavior (DRO) Procedures Differential reinforcement of other behavior procedures have been widely described in the behavior management literature (see, e.g., Deitz & Repp, 1983; LaVigna & Donnellan, 1986; Lennox, Miltenberger, Spengler, & Erfanian, 1988). As Vollmer and Iwata (1992) have noted, DRO "involves the delivery of reinforcement contingent on the nonoccurrence of the target response for a prespecified interval of time" (p. 395). Unfortunately, the reinforcers delivered have often been selected arbitrarily and, possibly as a result, the outcomes of the application of DRO have been mixed, particularly in the case of self-injurious behaviors.

It is likely that DRO outcomes could be improved substantially if the reinforcers were selected on the basis of a functional assessment (Vollmer & Iwata, 1992). In such a case, an effort would be made to identify the events that maintained the target behaviors and then to employ those events in the context of the DRO program. It might be found, for example, that face hitting functioned to obtain attention. The DRO procedure would then involve the provision of attention, rather than food items or toys, following established time intervals during which the individual did not hit his or her face. Concurrently, of course, more appropriate attention-getting behaviors could become the focus of instruction. For additional information regarding issues and procedures in DRO application, see sources such as LaVigna and Donnellan (1986) and Vollmer and Iwata (1992).

Teaching Alternative Skills

As previously noted, a major outcome of the functional assessment process is to develop a theory regarding the function the challenging behavior serves for the student, that is, to determine its purpose. Steps taken to prevent problem behaviors usually result in short-term solutions such as temporarily eliminating certain tasks that are critical to adaptation within natural community settings, and therefore must generally be reintroduced; teaching individuals to participate in a range of activities that extend beyond a small number that are highly preferred; and so forth. The teaching component of intervention plans, therefore, is intended to provide learners with acceptable alternative skills that will allow them to achieve the same outcomes that were achieved through the use of challenging behaviors (cf. Carr, Robinson, & Palumbo, 1990; Helmstetter & Durand, 1991; Meyer & Evans, 1989). Implicit in a focus on outcomes is that the emphasis in selecting new behaviors for instruction should be on the *functional incompatibility* of those behaviors with target behaviors rather than on *topographical incompatibility*, that is, incompatibility based on performing a target behavior (e.g., throwing

a truck) at the same time as a new behavior (e.g., rolling the truck).

Teaching alternative skills as a behavior management strategy is based on work that suggests that excess behaviors often represent an expression of skill deficits (Schrader & Gaylord-Ross, 1990). In order to promote the maintenance of low levels of challenging behaviors across multiple situations, then, it is critical to assure that the skill deficits that contributed to the appearance of those behaviors are remediated.

Teaching Specific Skills   Deficits displayed by students might be in the performance of specific skills or in the ability to receive and/or express communications effectively. Good examples of specific skill instruction have been provided by Donnellan et al. (1988) and Rincover, Cook, Peoples, and Packard (1979). Donnellan et al. (1988) related how Jennie, who worked in a restaurant, picked the skin on her face and arms when under stress, causing sores that endangered her continued employment in the restaurant setting. As an alternative replacement behavior, her vocational counselor taught her to carry a tube of skin moisturizer cream and to apply the cream when she felt stressed rather than picking. In the investigation conducted by Rincover et al. (1979), the stereotypic movements of four youngsters with autism (one of whom also had severe visual impairments) were successfully and dramatically reduced. The intervention consisted of training the children to play with toys that produced the same type of sensory input (proprioceptive, auditory, or visual) that the stereotypic behaviors were hypothesized to produce.

The work of Rincover and colleagues underscored the need to teach skills that are functionally incompatible with challenging behaviors. The learners were actually taught to play with two types of toys: one that produced the sensory input presumed to result from the student's stereotypic behavior and another that produced a different form of input. In all cases, the students played only with the toy that provided input consistent with their particular stereotypic behavior (i.e., served the same self-regulatory function). The investigation was also instructive in that it illustrated that it cannot be assumed that, given toys or other leisure options, individuals with disabilities will know how to use them or to participate without specific instruction. Rincover et al. observed that none of the learners played with the toys until they were provided training, even though the toys were available.

In that regard, it should be pointed out that learners with deaf-blindness may be unfamiliar with many items or activities that are quite familiar to their peers who do not have identified disabilities or even to individuals with other forms of disability. Therefore, although engagement in leisure pursuits could be an effective alternative to stereotypic or other challenging behaviors for students with severe visual and hearing impairments, the findings of Rincover et al. (1979) and others (Favell, McGimsey, & Schell, 1982) indicate that the simple provision of access and opportunity may not yield desired results. Where learners have not learned how to interact with materials or how to participate, specific training will be required. In addition, in order for training to be effective, adaptations to common materials and activities may be necessary to promote engagement by individuals with sensory losses.

Communication Training Although teaching alternative specific skills can play a useful role in behavior management, the provision of instruction designed to improve communicative competence has received particularly widespread visibility and support in recent years (e.g., Carr & Durand, 1985a, 1985b; Carr et al., 1994; Donnellan, Mirenda, Mesaros, & Fassbender, 1984; Neel & Billingsley, 1989). Neel and Billingsley (1989)

have indicated that students with disabilities use communication for at least the following purposes:

1. To make requests to satisfy needs and wants, seen and unseen
2. To request help
3. To protest
4. To respond to social initiatives
5. To initiate social interaction
6. To maintain social interaction
7. To ask for reward or affection
8. To seek comfort
9. To express an interest in the environment
10. To communicate experiences not shared by others
11. To play act or pretend (pp. 24–26)

Another function that might be served within several of the categories listed above is "making choices."

The variety and nature of communicative functions indicates the primacy of communication in the lives of most individuals. Further, for persons with deaf-blindness, those functions may often be specific to the special needs of coping with a sensory loss (e.g., requesting a sighted guide, protesting a scary prompt to touch an unknown object, agreeing to explore the environment with a friend's encouragement). It is, therefore, easy to understand why an individual who did not have the means to initiate or receive communications by using acceptable forms might engage in whatever unacceptable forms would result in reliable access to valued outcomes. If a pupil has not been taught to sign that he wants a change in activities, he might throw materials in order to obtain the change. If another student has not learned to use a textured communication system (cf. Murray-Branch et al., 1991) to indicate that she needs help finding her way, she might attempt to obtain assistance by striking her face with her hands. If the teacher uses modes of communication that a third student does not understand, that student might communicate his or her failure to understand by screaming.

Considerable success has been achieved in replacing challenging behaviors with alternative communication forms (see, e.g., Carr & Durand, 1985a; Horner & Budd, 1985; Horner, Sprague, O'Brien, & Heathfield, 1990; Hunt, Alwell, & Goetz, 1988). As an example of the general method, Bird, Dores, Moniz, and Robinson (1989) taught a young man (Greg) diagnosed with blindness, autism, and profound mental retardation to use a token exchange as a request for a 1-minute break from task demands. The token exchange communication form was employed as an alternative to the high-rate, intense self-injurious behaviors (SIB) Greg had previously used to escape demands.

Initially, token exchanges were prompted, and subsequent breaks from work were provided to Greg immediately following his compliance with a very simple request for performance. Following Greg's acquisition of the token exchange as a mode of communication, the level of demand difficulty was systematically increased in several steps. Access to the token that could be used to ask for a break was delayed until task-related responses were completed.

During the last 6 weeks of the investigation, it was found that Greg emitted no SIB responses following requests for performance of relatively complex task sequences. In addition, his involvement in functional communication training seemed to be associated with the appearance of spontaneous gestural requests to work. Similar results were documented for a second individual when manual signs were taught as functional alternatives to SIB and aggression.

Conditions for Successful Behavior Replacement Training   Although teaching alternative behaviors can play a major role in behavior management programs, they are unlikely to be maximally effective unless several conditions exist. These conditions include the following points: (cf. Billingsley & Neel, 1985; Carr, 1988; Horner, Sprague, et al., 1990; Schrader & Gaylord-Ross, 1990):

1. Target behaviors and alternative behaviors are members of the same response class; that is, both produce the same critical environmental effect. Once again, a thorough functional assessment is necessary to develop a hypothesis regarding the effect that the learner achieves by using the challenging behavior.
2. Alternative behaviors are more efficient than challenging behaviors in producing effects in the sense that the alternative behaviors: a) require less physical effort and/or b) achieve quicker results. If new signs or symbols are to be taught to a student, it is important to ensure that those signs or symbols will be easily and widely understood. When the appropriate communication form is not understood, the student may find that a quicker response can be achieved by using an inappropriate form (i.e., problem behavior).
3. Alternative behaviors are more reliable than challenging behaviors in producing effects. For example, use of a speech synthesis device (turned to an appropriate volume) might result in gaining teacher attention on every occasion, whereas biting one's own arm might achieve that result only sporadically. Synthesized speech, therefore, might serve as an effective replacement for arm biting.

Comprehensive Programs   It should be noted that more is likely to be required in the teaching component of behavior management programs than a "one-to-one replacement of negative behaviors with positive alternative substitutes" (Meyer & Evans, 1989,

p. 68). Meyer and Evans (1989) have noted that the most durable effects and quality-of-life improvements may require a more general approach that recognizes complex behavioral relationships. As they point out, if aggressive behavior in the workplace was triggered by co-worker criticism and teasing, a reasonable approach would be to teach the aggressive worker to use an assertive social skill. Such a skill might be to ask the co-workers not to make offensive comments. However, as Meyer and Evans also suggested, the aggression in such a case reveals more complex and fundamental socialization problems, one of which might be poor self-control across a variety of areas. In that case, a broad program of self-control training in different situations would also be indicated.

Reacting to Challenging Behaviors

A thoughtfully developed "prevent and teach" plan should have an immediate and substantial impact on the appearance of challenging behaviors. Target behaviors, however, may still occur during the initial stages of most interventions, albeit at a greatly reduced frequency. A behavioral support plan, therefore, should indicate how to respond to those behaviors.

The react portion of the plan again requires input from team members involved in the functional assessment of target behaviors as well as in the implementation of the prevent and teach strategies. The elimination of challenging behaviors depends on consistent responses in all environments. Involving family members; teaching staff; support persons such as occupational therapists, sensory impairment specialists (Downing & Eichinger, 1990), and psychologists; and other interested persons in the team effort toward consistency is critical (Janney et al., 1989; Varney, 1988).

For every team involved with a person with deaf-blindness, the plan for reacting to challenging behaviors will be unique. There are, however, documented strategies from which to choose (Janney et al., 1989; Meyer & Evans, 1989), keeping in mind that the presence of sensory impairments supports the rejection of some widely used interventions (Luiselli, 1984). For example, individuals who are deaf-blind and without well-planned supports tend to be withdrawn and often remain unaware of the potential for positive interactions with others (Downing & Eichinger, 1990). More than any other disability, a combined sensory loss demands close, consistent contact with another person for most learning opportunities and for participation within unfamiliar situations. Therefore, the common strategy of using "time-out" and isolation in response to challenging behavior is likely to pose problems.

Because decreasing stimulation in the hope of eliminating the target behavior may tend to promote the individual's withdrawal from the environment, positive behavioral support techniques that emphasize learning effective and acceptable ways to meet one's needs or to cope with difficult situations are considered preferable (Durand & Kishi, 1987; Sisson, 1992). The careful use of such techniques will contribute to the understanding of the individual with deaf-blindness that the target behaviors will no longer be useful and that interacting with others will promote more effective choices. Furthermore, individuals with deaf-blindness experience events and learn many skills through tactile input and through consistent series of movements (van Dijk, 1986). They must learn to trust that familiar movement routines will affect the environment in predictable ways. Therefore, strategies that confuse established routines (e.g., overcorrection) should be considered highly intrusive and possibly aversive.

As alternatives to more traditional modes of reacting to challenging behaviors, such techniques as *ignore–redirect–reward* proce-

dures and the use of natural and logical consequences are appropriate for inclusion in
behavioral support plans for individuals with
deaf-blindness. Crisis management procedures for behaviors that threaten the safety of
the individual or others around the person
may also need to be identified. These alternatives are addressed in the following
sections.

Ignore–Redirect–Reward   The close interactions and continued input of stimuli inherent in the ignore–redirect–reward strategy
allows for the positive supports required by
individuals with deaf-blindness. Unlike extinction or time-out techniques that involve
ignoring the individual until the behavior
stops, this approach requires that the target
behavior be ignored while the learner is redirected to the next step in the routine (Janney et al., 1989). For example, attention can
be shifted by changing the hand positions of
the instructor and learner. Successful use of
traditional training techniques that rely on
vision and hearing (e.g., modeling and verbal instructions) can be hindered by the
presence of sensory impairments (Durand &
Kishi, 1987). Therefore, a student might be
guided through a task sequence with the instructor grasping the student's hands and
manipulating them through the task. Should
the control inherent in this molding technique result in problem behaviors, the instructor could provide the student with the
next tactile prompt in the sequence by slip-
ping a hand under the student's hand and
guiding the student to voluntarily "look" at
what happens next. If the student was familiar with the task, she could be encouraged to
remove her hands from the instructor's in
order to complete the task independently.
This redirection strategy encourages learning from the behaviors of another individual
and allows the student to control the level of
stimuli because she can remove her hands
without struggling to gain their release.
Learning to use one's hands to actively "look

at," and gain information from, the actions
of another person is an important skill for a
student with little or no vision.

A variation of the above is for the instructor to continue modeling the remaining steps
in a task after a target behavior occurs, rather
than having the student complete the task.
The student is simply asked to remain attentive with her hands over the instructor's as
the task is shown to her. This strategy works
well for newly introduced tasks, or when a
familiar task is being generalized to a new
setting. By keeping her hands on the instructor's hands to watch the activity, the student
receives the expected reward when the task
is completed (e.g., praise, moving to another
anticipated activity, enjoying the sandwich
just made). The intent, then, is to provide
reinforcers for engaging in tactile observation. As students become more adept at observing others by using their hands, residual
visual or auditory sensations may also be
strengthened.

The best outcomes for individuals who respond most effectively and appropriately
within predictable routines are likely to occur where the natural flow of events can be
maintained in spite of the occurrence of a
challenging behavior. While grooming, for
example, Jolinda would often flap her hands
and attempt to hyperventilate. Her support
team developed the hypothesis that Jolinda
exhibited those target behaviors when she
was under- or over-stimulated and became
increasingly withdrawn as she self-regulated
visual and physical stimuli. The reaction plan,
therefore, required that the instructor prompt
her to put away the hair brush while emphasizing the remaining steps in the grooming
sequence. This emphasis might be added by
flicking the lights over the mirror off and
on and briefly squeezing the atomizer for
Jolinda's perfume.

Activating an object required for the completion of a task can be an excellent form of
brief response interruption designed to use a

powerful stimulus to draw attention towards completing a task, and away from a target behavior that, if continued, would isolate the student from environmental input. By having Jolinda put the brush away, the instructor informed her that they are moving on in the sequence of grooming activities. The light flashing might work to get her visual attention because Jolinda used her eyes and examined the environment only when extremely motivated. The smell of the perfume indicated an object in the environment that was needed for a following activity.

In another setting, Dale screamed and began to poke his eyes as a peer mistakenly guided him toward the hallway while the other students gathered coats and backpacks from the classroom closet. His teacher recognized his confusion and encouraged the peer to turn and guide Dale's free hand to touch the wall as a landmark. While Dale and his friend waited for the other students to move past, the teacher brought over Dale's pack, showed it to him, and guided him to the closet. Dale's companion signed for them both to don their coats and they proceeded out the door and onto the bus, ending the day like any other.

Another variation of the ignore–redirect–reward strategy specifically targets strengthening communication skills (Durand & Kishi, 1987; Sisson, 1992). As previously noted, a target behavior might indicate an attempt to communicate for at least 11 different purposes (Neel & Billingsley, 1989). The instructor, therefore, could acknowledge the intent of the communication by showing the student how to access tactile choices that are appropriate in the context of the current situation (Berg & Wacker, 1989). The student's hand might be guided to the next compartment of a divided sequence box that contains tactile descriptions of the landmark events of the day (Rowland & Schweigert, 1989; Stillman & Battle, 1984). In the box he would find three objects representing appropriate choices such as an alternate learning activity, the opportunity to take a break, or a trip to the drinking fountain.

Natural and Logical Consequences Natural and logical consequences are similar to the ignore–redirect–reward approach, but can be harder for the student with deaf-blindness to comprehend. A natural consequence for throwing ice cream is to be redirected to another activity and not receiving more ice cream. A logical consequence for wandering off the playground might be to return to the building early and practice the route to the classroom. The white cane used for mobility that was in the student's backpack while he was playing could be used as a tangible symbol to represent this change in schedule.

Such procedures are more complex than strategies that remain in the context of one activity. Learners successfully responding to these more sophisticated methods are likely to be those who tolerate changes in routine, make choices, and might return to finish a task at a more convenient time. Other individuals with deaf-blindness may require much more consistency in the entire daily schedule and will become confused by consequences that lead to unpredictable changes in activities.

Crisis Management Target behaviors do not always slip away as a student resumes familiar tasks. Especially in the beginning periods of a positive plan for supporting an individual's behaviors, problems might exacerbate to the point of being damaging or dangerous. In cases where an individual has caused physical damage or has seemed to pose a threat to someone else's or his own physical safety, a responsible team will anticipate and describe specific instances of crisis management. Such strategies will be considered temporary and not as a reason for continued restraint or as a substitute for any of the other positive methods explored above (Horner, Dunlap, et al., 1990; Sisson, 1992).

In addition, strategies for reacting to problem behaviors must be socially acceptable in inclusive settings. If an apparently extreme intervention is necessary for safety reasons, it should be introduced carefully in specifically chosen settings and faded as quickly as possible.

Families and staff must be able to choose from a variety of specific tactics for different situations in which a crisis might develop. For example, Trisha, a middle school student, might have to be quickly guided to the car from the grocery store to prevent head banging and eye gouging. Until Trisha learns to understand available choices represented on her communication board, the wisest tactic to cope with the possibility of injury would be to maintain a quick pace with a sighted guide to keep her attention on movement and away from other behaviors. If she was at risk of continuing self-injury while walking, store visits would require that two staff or family members be available, one to offer sighted guidance and the other to keep her hand away from her head. Once in the car, a tactile symbol for "calm down" (e.g., a large pillow at first and, eventually, a soft texture on her board) would be presented, and Trisha would be encouraged to sit in the middle seat. For crisis situations to be resolved safely, and to support learning of alternative communication methods, the support team must be well-prepared before risking new environments. Therefore, in this example, Trisha should experience using the calm down symbol in familiar settings and begin to make choices within routines before being asked to cope with new situations.

Teams planning crisis intervention strategies must be mindful of the unique nature of relationships for a person with deaf-blindness. van Dijk (1986) emphasized the interactive nature of physical contact and the building of trust through predictable relationships in consistent routines. Although physical intervention to prevent injury may sometimes be necessary, consideration must be given to how such interventions might cause the learner with deaf-blindness to tolerate less input from another person. Some things that may help an individual with sensory impairments perceive safety are pillows, a safe and consistent place to go, warm temperatures or a cooling fan, or a calming person with a favored cologne. Such items, persons, or conditions communicate that as soon as the danger has past the world will return to a predictable form.

BEHAVIORAL SUPPORT IN INCLUSIVE SETTINGS: PLANNING AND IMPLEMENTATION

Does behavioral support differ markedly when implemented in inclusive settings, as opposed to segregated or self-contained special education classrooms? On the one hand, the answer is no; the principles of behavioral support do not change from setting to setting. On the other hand, it is equally true that the environments encountered in typical segregated or self-contained classrooms differ substantially from those of inclusive settings. Inclusive settings are characterized by access to a different, and perhaps wider, range of stimulus and response characteristics. For example, a student with deaf-blindness in an inclusive setting will, presumably, associate with other students who display a wider range of behaviors than those students enrolled in self-contained classrooms. An inclusive situation also presents greater variety in materials, social interaction opportunities, environmental features (classroom equipment, decorations, etc.), and available activities.

This broad range of environmental responses and stimuli may cause concern on the part of some educators. Given the degree to which special education teachers can control the behavioral responses and the stimulus features of self-contained classrooms, it would not be surprising if some teachers assumed that a student's behavior in an inclusive setting would be problematic due to a loss of that control on the part of the educational staff. However, while self-contained classrooms offer a teacher more control over a student's behavior through manipulations of the environment, students may be exposed to a narrower and more contrived range of environmental features. Given the importance of naturally occurring reinforcers that maintain a desired behavior (Horner et al., 1988; Stokes & Baer, 1977) and natural cues and correction procedures (Falvey, Brown, Lyon, Baumgart, & Schroeder, 1980) to both generalization and maintenance, access to the wider range of stimuli

and events that may be available in inclusive settings should promote the development of adaptive behaviors by students with deaf-blindness.

The contrast in segregated and inclusive environments is illustrated in Figure 1. The shaded portion of the figure illustrates that segregated environments are typically characterized as being high in teacher control, with a contrasting lessening of natural maintaining contingencies. Conversely, inclusive environments have less teacher control, with a higher degree of natural contingencies that maintain behaviors.

Horner, Dunlap, et al. (1990), Meyer and Evans (1989), and O'Neill et al. (1990) indicated the need for behavioral support to include an analysis of a wide range of stimulus features in order to develop the most effec-

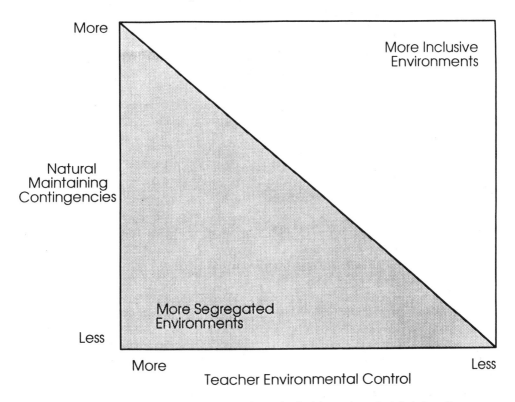

Figure 1.   Relationship of control in segregated settings and natural maintaining contingencies in inclusive settings.

tive plans. Whereas the analysis of behaviors once focused on a narrow band of antecedents and consequences, referred to as *ABC analysis* (Bijou, Peterson, & Ault, 1968), the focus has now broadened to include "lifestyle" measures (Meyer & Evans, 1989), setting events (Horner, Albin, & O'Neill, 1991), and contextual factors (Baer, Wolf, & Risley, 1987; Greenwood, Delquadri, Stanely, Terry, & Hall, 1985). The focus on larger patterns of behavior and the contingencies that shape them suggests the need to more comprehensively analyze the range of stimuli encountered in inclusive environments.

Taking full advantage of the naturally occurring contingencies in inclusive environments requires a thorough and careful analysis of the myriad factors that influence behaviors, both positively (appropriate role models, natural consequences) and negatively (increased frequency of stimuli that control problem behavior). Greenwood, Carta, and Atwater (1991) referred to this approach as *ecobehavioral analysis* and describe it as a combining of "the ecological psychologists' concern for the broader aspects of the environment or habitat with the applied behavior analysts' strategies of behavioral assessment and experimental design" (p. 60).

Functional Assessment in the Inclusive Setting

As previously noted, it is important to consider the difference in the complexity and the range of environmental variables associated with an inclusive setting as opposed to the more traditional self-contained special education classroom. Where the relatively less complex environment of the special education classroom could reasonably be analyzed by the teacher alone, the complexity of inclusive settings requires a corresponding increase in the breadth of the procedures required to complete a thorough assessment of any student's behavior patterns. How does

one accomplish this increased breadth of analysis? The answer is to work with the larger numbers of people who are in contact with the students and who potentially have valuable knowledge about those students and the features of the inclusive environments. This means working with a collaborative team of individuals whose task is to perform a functional assessment of the interaction of the student's behavior and the environment and to develop, implement, and evaluate a behavioral support plan for that student.

Although technical assistance to teachers and other school personnel in the area of behavioral management has been employed for a number of years (Durand & Kishi, 1987; Horner, Diemer, & Brazeau, 1992; Janney & Meyer, 1990; O'Neill, Williams, Sprague, Horner, & Albin, 1993) the model typically used has been one where an outside "expert" consults with a teacher and, after some period of time to study the situation, provides a behavior management plan for the teacher to follow. A number of problems may be associated with this approach. For example, individuals who are not part of the development process may have less ownership in the plan and, therefore, may not be prone to implement the plan with an acceptable degree of fidelity (Durand & Kishi, 1987). The more serious shortcoming of the expert consultant model of technical assistance, however, is revealed in the attempts of any single outsider, no matter how well versed in the principles of behavioral analysis, to assess the full range of variables that are potentially associated with a student's behavior in an inclusive educational setting.

Given these shortcomings, it seems far wiser for the outside expert (where "outside" means anyone not in daily contact with the focal student) to build a framework within which the people most familiar with the student and the environment actually identify the elements of the support plan themselves. This approach increases the probability that a plan will be implemented because of the investment in its development by those who will implement it. This process also facilitates the identification of potential problems that may be encountered in the implementation phase. An opportunity then exists to address those issues (e.g., the social acceptability of support plan components and the logistical demands of proposed plans) prior to program initiation.

Behavioral Support Teams

The benefits of collaborative teaming in educational settings are now widely recognized (Giangreco, Cloninger, & Iverson, 1993; Stainback & Stainback, 1990; Thousand & Villa, 1992). Collaborative teaming is a method for identifying critical issues and defining options for students that recognizes the complexity of a student's behavioral support needs in inclusive settings. (See chap. 8, this volume, for a fuller description of the elements of collaborative teams.)

Choosing Team Members Deciding who should participate on a behavioral support team and enlisting their assistance is the first step to be completed. Behavioral support teams should be representative of the individuals who have a stake in the focal student's behavior in the inclusive setting. It is perhaps best to view the membership on the behavioral support team as consisting of two groups: 1) a primary or "core" group and 2) a secondary group comprised of persons who attend meetings as the need arises for their input. The core group would consist of the focal student and his or her general education teachers, special education teachers or consultants, family members, a behavioral support specialist, and the student's peers without disabilities (the input of peers may be solicited from two or three classmates) (cf. Vandercook, York, & Forest, 1989). Other

individuals may be important, depending upon where the target behaviors occur, the elements of the support plan, and the need for modifications in school routines that may require administrative input. For students who are employed, job coaches, co-workers, and employers may be important members of the team; for those students who receive residential support, relevant staff may also need to be consulted.

Setting the Agenda The work of the behavioral support team should focus on the following agenda items: 1) identifying the target behavior(s), 2) defining those behaviors in objective and measurable terms, 3) identifying those conditions that predict the occurrence and nonoccurrence of the target behavior(s), 4) generating a hypothesis that defines the possible functions of the behavior(s) and the consequences that are maintaining them, 5) conducting observations that confirm or negate the hypothesis, 6) defining the elements of the behavioral support plan, and 7) monitoring the plan's implementation.

Determining Team Members' Roles A basic role for all team members is to provide the team with their individual input regarding the student's behavior and be prepared to listen to the input of all other team members. Teams function best when all of the members trust each other to offer nonjudgmental responses.

Behavioral Support Specialist The behavioral support specialist has an especially important role to play as the facilitator. This individual should be focused on ensuring that all team members are providing their input and that no one is being left out of the process. Mediating the opinions of team members when it comes time to decide on the elements of a support plan is also a crucial task for the behavioral support specialist. A valuable tool for gathering the information needed to complete the first four items on the team agenda as indicated above is the *Functional Analysis Interview Form* (O'Neill et al., 1990). This form can be used successfully in a group setting where the input of all members is recorded on the form. The facilitator engages the team in discussion and records information in response to all of the items on the form.

Family Members   The input of family members in the development of the behavioral support plan focuses on their intimate knowledge of the student. The student's past history, especially in the area of behavioral support plans, is critical. Questions about the student's general health; sleep patterns; use of medications; and preferences for people, activities, and items are best answered by members of the student's family who have known him far longer than school personnel. Any contrast in the occurrence or nonoccurrence of the target behaviors between the school and home can also be noted through the families' participation on the team.

General and Special Education Teachers   General and special education teachers are a source for information related to student behavior at school. In addition to the information sought on the *Functional Analysis Interview Form*, teachers can best determine what educational modifications are important and feasible to make. As noted previously, changes in curriculum, such as reducing task difficulty (Carr, Newsome, & Binkoff, 1980) and modifying instructional procedures (Gaylord-Ross, Weeks, & Lipner, 1980; Horner, Day, et al., 1991), have been used effectively to decrease problem behaviors. Hitzing (1992) suggested that teachers ask themselves several questions focused on student motivation for learning particular tasks at school. These questions are all directed toward determining what the student really wants to learn and how to make the tasks being taught relevant and functional. There are certainly times

when students may benefit from learning something that, at the time of initial instruction, seemed irrelevant (e.g., certain math skills). What is desirable in the curriculum is a balance of skills that have immediate, functional relevance for the student with a smaller proportion of skills that may have more relevance over time.

General education teachers' input about the type and extent of environmental modifications that can be made in their classrooms has a crucial impact on support plan development. Student seating arrangements, the assignment of students to instructional groups, classroom lighting, noise levels, and the placement of equipment can all affect student behavior. (See chap. 9 of this volume for a thorough discussion of classroom environmental adaptations for students with deaf-blindness.)

Related Services Staff   Occupational, physical, speech and communication therapists; school psychologists; and other related services staff are important team members when and if the expertise of their disciplines is related to the student's target behavior(s). For example, functional communication training is widely recognized to play a major role in the development of many behavioral support plans (Carr & Durand, 1985a; Durand, 1990). Improper student positioning can also be related to the occurrence of problem behaviors, while proper positioning can allow students to engage in more functional tasks that reduce the occurrence of stimuli for problem behaviors. Appropriate specialists would, therefore, be involved in behavioral support teams where plans would be likely to include communication or positioning components.

Peers   Finally, the peers of a student with deaf-blindness can be valuable sources of information in developing support plans as well as effective elements in the plan's implementation. Forest and Pearpoint (1990) suggest several steps in involving peers in behavioral support plans. Talking to peers about the student's behavior should be done frankly, while also informing the peers that their opinions and their advice are important. Peers should be respected as members of a group that includes the student with deaf-blindness and should have the right to be involved in determining what forms of behavior are valued by this group. Their assistance in shaping and responding to the student's behaviors is critical to long-term changes in those behaviors.

Building the support plan itself entails the selection of a variety of procedures that were described in this chapter. The selection of those procedures is directly related to the contingencies that maintain challenging behaviors. By using a collaborative team approach to building the behavioral support plan, the probability is increased that the plan will: 1) be based on accurate and thorough information about the target behavior(s) and the features of the environment, 2) be directly related to the function the behavior fulfills for the student, and 3) be implemented with a high degree of fidelity.

Effective behavioral support cannot be achieved by basing the selection of methods primarily on the nature of the problem behavior and the desire to achieve rapid results (Carr, Robinson, & Palumbo, 1990). Rather, the characteristics of the pupil and the context in which target behaviors occur must be carefully considered by those who know the pupil, and the context, the best. A team approach to plan development and implementation is not only desirable, but crucial.

REFERENCES

Andrews, P.E., & Billingsley, F.F. (1991). Stimulus control of personally intrusive behavior. *Precision Teaching, 8*(2), 13–24.

Azrin, N.H., & Holz, W.C. (1966). Punishment. In W.K. Honig (Ed.), *Operant behavior: Areas of research and application* (pp. 380–447). New York: Appleton-Century-Crofts.

Bachman, J.E., & Sluyter, D. (1988). Reducing inappropriate behaviors of developmentally disabled adults using antecedent aerobic dance exercises. *Research in Developmental Disabilities, 9*, 73–83.

Baer, D.M., Wolf, M.M., & Risley, T.R. (1987). Some still-current dimensions of applied behavior analysis. *Journal of Applied Behavior Analysis, 20*, 313–327.

Barton, L.E., & LaGrow, S.J. (1983). Reducing self-injurious and aggressive behavior in deaf-blind persons through overcorrection. *Journal of Visual Impairment and Blindness, 77*, 421–424.

Barton, L.E., Meston, L.A., & Barton, C.L. (1984). Reduction of stereotypic behavior in a deaf-blind student via response blocking and applied differential reinforcement procedures. *B.C. Journal of Special Education, 8*, 157–165.

Berg, W.K., & Wacker, D.P. (1989). Evaluation of tactile prompts with a student who is deaf, blind, and mentally retarded. *Journal of Applied Behavior Analysis, 22*, 93–99.

Beukelman, D.R., & Mirenda, P. (1992). *Augmentative and alternative communication: Management of severe communication disorders in children and adults.* Baltimore: Paul H. Brookes Publishing Co.

Bijou, S.W., Peterson, R.F., & Ault, M.H. (1968). A method of integrating descriptive and experimental field studies at the level of data and empirical concepts. *Journal of Applied Behavior Analysis, 1*, 175–191.

Billingsley, F.F., & Neel, R.S. (1985). Competing behaviors and their effects on skill generalization and maintenance. *Analysis and Intervention in Developmental Disabilities, 5*, 357–372.

Bird, F., Dores, P.A., Moniz, D., & Robinson, J. (1989). Reducing severe aggressive and self-injurious behaviors with functional communication training. *American Journal on Mental Retardation, 94*, 37–48.

Cancio, E.J., Young, K.R., Macfarlane, C., West, R., & Blair, M.E. (1991). Eliminating self-injurious behavior through the use of a functional analysis, antecedent interventions, reinforcement procedures, and data-based decision making. *Journal of Precision Teaching, 8*(2), 25–33.

Carr, E.G. (1988). Functional equivalence as a mechanism of response generalization. In R.H. Horner, G. Dunlap, & R.L. Koegel (Eds.), *Generalization and maintenance: Life-style changes in applied settings* (pp. 221–241). Baltimore: Paul H. Brookes Publishing Co.

Carr, E.G., & Durand, V.M. (1985a). Reducing behavior problems through functional communication training. *Journal of Applied Behavior Analysis, 18,* 111–126.

Carr, E.G., & Durand, V.M. (1985b). The social-communication basis of severe behavior problems in children. In S. Reiss & R.R. Bootzin (Eds.), *Theoretical issues in behavior therapy* (pp. 219–254). New York: Academic Press.

Carr, E.G., Levin, L., McConnachie, G., Carlson, J.I., Kemp, D.C., & Smith, C.E. (1994). *Communication-based intervention for problem behavior: A user's guide for producing positive change.* Baltimore: Paul H. Brookes Publishing Co.

Carr, E.G., Newsome, C.D., & Binkoff, J.A. (1980). Escape as a factor in the behavior of two retarded children. *Journal of Applied Behavior Analysis, 13,* 113–129.

Carr, E.G., Robinson, S., & Palumbo, L.W. (1990). The wrong issue: Aversive vs. nonaversive treatment; The right issue: Functional vs. nonfunctional treatment. In A.C. Repp & N.N. Singh (Eds.), *Perspectives on the use of nonaversive and aversive interventions for persons with developmental disabilities* (pp. 361–379). Sycamore, IL: Sycamore.

Carr, E.G., Robinson, S., Taylor, J., & Carlson, J.I. (1990). Positive approaches to the treatment of severe behavior problems in persons with developmental disabilities: A review and analysis of reinforcement and stimulus-based procedures. *Monograph of The Association for Persons with Severe Handicaps, 4.*

Deitz, D.E.D., & Repp, A.C. (1983). Reducing behavior through reinforcement. *Exceptional Education Quarterly, 3*(4), 34–46.

Donnellan, A.M., LaVigna, G.W., Negri-Shoultz, N., & Fassbender, L.L. (1988). *Progress without punishment: Effective approaches for learners with behavior problems.* New York: Teachers College Press.

Donnellan, A.M., Mirenda, P.L. Mesaros, R.A., & Fassbender, L.L. (1984). Analyzing the communicative functions of aberrant behavior. *Journal of The Association for Persons with Severe Handicaps, 9,* 201–202.

Downing, J., & Eichinger, J. (1990). Instructional strategies for learners with dual sensory impairments in integrated settings. *Journal for The Association for Persons with Severe Handicaps, 15,* 98–105.

Dunlap, G., Dyer, K., & Koegel, R.L. (1983). Autistic self-stimulation and intertrial interval duration. *American Journal of Mental Deficiency, 88,* 194–202.

Durand, V.M. (1990). *Severe behavior problems: A functional communication training approach.* New York: Guilford Press.

Durand, V.M., & Crimmins, D.B. (1988). *The motivation assessment scale: An administration manual.* Unpublished manuscript, State University of New York at Albany.

Durand, V.M., & Kishi, G. (1987). Reducing severe behavior problems among persons with dual sensory impairments: An evaluation of a technical assistance model. *Journal of The Association for Persons with Severe Handicaps, 12,* 2–10.

Evans, I.M., & Meyer, L.H. (1985). *An educative approach to behavior problems: A practical decision model for interventions with severely handicapped learners.* Baltimore: Paul H. Brookes Publishing Co.

Falvey, M., Brown, L., Lyon, S., Baumgart, D., & Schroeder, J. (1980). Strategies for using cues and correction procedures. In W. Sailor, B. Wilcox, & L. Brown (Eds.), *Methods of instruction for severely handicapped students* (pp. 109–133). Baltimore: Paul H. Brookes Publishing Co.

Favell, J.E., McGimsey, J.F., & Schell, R.M. (1982). Treatment of self-injury by providing alternate sensory activities. *Analysis and Intervention in Developmental Disabilities, 2,* 83–104.

Fewell, R.R., & Rich, J.S. (1987). Play assessment as a procedure for examining cognitive, communicative, and social skills in multihandicapped children. *Journal of Psychoeducational Assessment, 2,* 107–118.

Forest, M., & Pearpoint, J. (1990). Supports for addressing severe maladaptive behaviors. In W. Stainback & S. Stainback (Eds.), *Support networks for inclusive schooling: Interdependent integrated education* (pp. 187–197). Baltimore: Paul H. Brookes Publishing Co.

Gaylord-Ross, R.J., Weeks, M., & Lipner, C. (1980). Analysis of antecedent, response and consequence events in the treatment of self-injurious behavior. *Education and Training of the Mentally Retarded, 15,* 35–42.

Giangreco, M.F., Cloninger, C.J., & Iverson, V.S. (1993). *Choosing options and accommodations for children (COACH): A guide to planning inclusive education*. Baltimore: Paul H. Brookes Publishing Co.

Green, C.W., Canipe, V.S., Way, P.J., & Reid, D.H. (1986). Improving the functional utility and effectiveness of classroom services for students with profound multiple handicaps. *Journal of The Association for Persons with Severe Handicaps, 11*, 162–170.

Greenwood, C.R., Carta, J.J., & Atwater, J. (1991). Ecobehavioral analysis in the classroom: Review and implications. *Journal of Behavioral Education, 1*, 59–77.

Greenwood, C.R., Delquadri, J., Stanley, S.O., Terry, B., & Hall, R.V. (1985). Assessment and eco-behavioral interaction in school settings. *Behavioral Assessment, 7*, 331–347.

Haring, N.G. (Ed.). (1988). *Generalization for students with severe handicaps: Strategies and solutions*. Seattle: University of Washington Press.

Helmstetter, E., & Durand, V.M. (1991). Nonaversive interventions for severe behavior problems. In L.H. Meyer, C.A. Peck, & L. Brown (Eds.), *Critical issues in the lives of people with severe disabilities* (pp. 559–600). Baltimore: Paul H. Brookes Publishing Co.

Hitzing, W. (1992). Support and positive teaching strategies. In S. Stainback & W. Stainback (Eds.), *Curriculum considerations in inclusive classrooms: Facilitating learning for all students* (pp. 143–158). Baltimore: Paul H. Brookes Publishing Co.

Horner, R.H., Albin, R.W., & O'Neill, R.E. (1991). Supporting students with severe disabilities and challenging behaviors. In G. Stoner, M. Shinn, & H.M. Walker (Eds.), *Interventions for achievement and behavior problems* (pp. 269–287). Washington, DC: National Association of School Psychologists.

Horner, R.H., & Budd, C.M. (1985). Teaching manual sign language to a nonverbal student: Generalization of sign use and collateral reduction of maladaptive behavior. *Education and Training of the Mentally Retarded, 20*, 39–47.

Horner, R.H., Day, M., Sprague, J.R., O'Brien, M., & Heathfield, L.T. (1991). Interspersed requests: A nonaversive procedure for reducing aggression and self-injury during instruction. *Journal of Applied Behavior Analysis, 24*, 265–278.

Horner, R.H., Diemer, S.M., & Brazeau, K.C. (1992). Educational support for students with severe behavior problems in Oregon: A descriptive analysis from the 1987–1988 school year. *Journal of The Association for Persons with Severe Handicaps, 17*, 154–169.

Horner, R.H., Dunlap, G., & Koegel, R.L. (Eds.). (1988). *Generalization and maintenance: Life-style changes in applied settings*. Baltimore: Paul H. Brookes Publishing Co.

Horner, R.H., Dunlap, G., Koegel, R., Carr, E.G., Sailor, W., Anderson, J., Albin, R.W., & O'Neill, R.E. (1990). Toward a technology of "nonaversive" behavioral support. *Journal of The Association for Persons with Severe Handicaps, 15*, 125–132.

Horner, R.H., Sprague, J.R., O'Brien, M., & Heathfield, L.T. (1990). The role of response efficiency in the reduction of problem behaviors through functional equivalence training. A case study. *Journal of The Association for Persons with Severe Handicaps, 15*, 91–97.

Hunt, P., Alwell, M., & Goetz, L. (1988). Acquisitioning conversation skills and the reduction of inappropriate social behaviors. *Journal of The Association for Persons with Severe Handicaps, 13*, 20–27.

Iwata, B.A., Vollmer, T.R., & Zarcone, J.R. (1990). The experimental (functional) analysis of behavior disorders: Methodology, applications, and limitations. In A.C. Repp & N.N. Singh (Eds.), *Perspectives on the use of nonaversive and aversive interventions for persons with developmental disabilities* (pp. 301–330). Sycamore, IL: Sycamore.

Janney, R., Black, J., & Ferlo, M. (1989). *A problem-solving approach to challenging behaviors: Strategies for parents and educators of people with developmental disabilities & challenging behaviors*. Unpublished manuscript, Child-Centered Inservice Training and Technical Assistance Network, Syracuse University, Syracuse, NY.

Janney, R.E., & Meyer, L.H. (1990). A consultation model to support integrated educational services for students with severe disabilities and challenging behaviors. *Journal of The Association for Persons with Severe Handicaps, 15*, 186–199.

LaVigna, G.W., & Donnellan, A.M. (1986). *Alternatives to punishment: Solving behavior problems with non-aversive strategies*. New York: Irvington.

LaVigna, G.W., Willis, T.J., & Donnellan, A.M. (1989). The role of positive programming in behavioral treatment. In E. Cipani (Ed.), *The treatment of severe behavior disorders: Behavior analysis approaches* (pp. 59–83). Washington, DC: American Association on Mental Retardation.

Lennox, D.B., Miltenberger, R.G., Spengler, P., & Erfanian, N. (1988). Decelerative treatment practices with persons who have mental retardation. A review of five years of the literature.

American Journal on Mental Retardation, 92, 492–501.

Lobato, D., Carlson, E.I., & Barrera, R.B. (1986). Modified satiation: Reducing ruminative vomiting without excessive weight gain. *Applied Research in Mental Retardation, 7,* 337–347.

Luiselli, J. (1984). Treatment of an assaultive, sensory-impaired adolescent through a multicomponent behavioral program. *Journal of Behavior Therapy and Experimental Psychiatry, 15,* 71–78.

Luiselli, J.K., & Lolli, D.A. (1987). Contingency management of a blind child's disruptive behaviors during mobility instruction. *Education of the Visually Handicapped, 19*(2), 69–70.

Mace, F.C., Hock, M.L., Lalli, J.S., West, B.J., Belfiore, P., Pinter, E., & Brown, D.K. (1988). Behavioral momentum in the treatment of noncompliance. *Journal of Applied Behavior Analysis, 21,* 123–141.

McDaniel, G., Kocim, R., & Barton, L. (1984). Reducing self-stimulatory mouthing behavior in deaf-blind children. *Journal of Visual Impairment and Blindness, 78,* 23–26.

Meyer, L.H., & Evans, I.M. (1989). *Nonaversive intervention for behavior problems: A manual for home and community.* Baltimore: Paul H. Brookes Publishing Co.

Moss, K. (1992, Spring). Hearing loss and communication. *Traces,* pp. 3–4.

Murray-Branch, J., Udavari-Solner, A., & Bailey, B. (1991). Textured communication systems for individuals with severe intellectual and dual sensory impairments. *Language, Speech, and Hearing Services in Schools, 22,* 260–268.

Neel, R.S., & Billingsley, F.F. (1989). *IMPACT: A functional curriculum handbook for students with moderate to severe disabilities.* Baltimore: Paul H. Brookes Publishing Co.

Niswander, P.S. (1987). Audiometric assessment and management. In L. Goetz, D. Guess, & K. Stremel-Campbell (Eds.), *Innovative program design for individuals with dual sensory impairments* (pp. 99–126). Baltimore: Paul H. Brookes Publishing Co.

O'Neill, R.E., Horner, R.H., Albin, R.W., Storey, K., & Sprague, J.R. (1990). *Functional analysis of problem behavior: A practical assessment guide.* Sycamore, IL: Sycamore.

O'Neill, R., & Williams, R., Sprague, J., Horner, R.H., & Albin, R.W. (1993). Providing support for teachers working with students with severe behaviors: A model for providing consulting support within school districts. *Education and Treatment of Children, 16,* 66–89.

Prickett, H.H., & Prickett, J.G. (1992). Vision problems among students in schools and programs for deaf children. *American Annals of the Deaf, 137,* 56–60.

Pyles, D.A.M., & Bailey, J.S. (1990). Diagnosing severe behavior problems. In A.C. Repp & N.N. Singh (Eds.), *Perspectives on the use of nonaversive and aversive interventions for persons with developmental disabilities* (pp. 381–401). Sycamore, IL: Sycamore.

Reilich, L.L., Spooner, F., & Rose, T.L. (1984). The effects of contingent water mist on the stereotypic responding of a severely handicapped adolescent. *Journal of Behavior and Experimental Psychiatry, 15,* 165–170.

Rincover, A., Cook, R., Peoples, A., & Packard, D. (1979). Sensory extinction and sensory reinforcement principles for programming multiple adaptive behavior change. *Journal of Applied Behavior Analysis, 12,* 221–233.

Rowland, C., & Schweigert, P. (1989). Tangible symbols: Symbolic communication for individuals with multisensory impairment. *Augmentative and Alternative Communication, 5,* 226–234.

Schrader, C., & Gaylord-Ross, R. (1990). The eclipse of aversive technology: A triadic approach to assessment and treatment. In A.C. Repp & N.N. Singh (Eds.), *Perspectives on the use of nonaversive and aversive interventions for persons with developmental disabilities* (pp. 403–417). Sycamore, IL: Sycamore.

Sidman, M. (1989). *Coercion and its fallout.* Boston: Authors Cooperative.

Singer, G.H.S., Singer, J., & Horner, R.H. (1987). Using pretask requests to increase the probability of compliance for students with severe disabilities. *Journal of The Association for Persons with Severe Handicaps, 12,* 287–291.

Sisson, L.A. (1992). Positive behavioral support: New foci in the management of challenging behaviors. *Journal of Visual Impairment and Blindness, 86,* 364–369.

Stainback, W., & Stainback, S. (Eds.). (1990). *Support networks for inclusive schooling: Interdependent integrated education.* Baltimore: Paul H. Brookes Publishing Co.

Stillman, R.D., & Battle, C.W. (1984). Developing prelanguage communication in the severely handicapped. An interpretation of the van Dijk method. *Seminars in Speech and Language, 4*(3), 159–170.

Stokes, T.F., & Baer, D.M. (1977). An implicit technology of generalization. *Journal of Applied Behavior Analysis, 10,* 349–367.

Thousand, J.S., & Villa, R.A. (1992). Collaborative teams: A powerful tool in school restructuring. In R.A. Villa, J.S. Thousand, W. Stainback, & S. Stainback (Eds.), *Restructuring for caring and effective education: An administrative guide to creating heterogeneous schools* (pp. 73–108). Baltimore: Paul H. Brookes Publishing Co.

Touchette, P.E., MacDonald, R.F., & Langer, S.N. (1985). A scatterplot for identifying stimulus control of problem behavior. *Journal of Applied Behavior Analysis, 18,* 341–343.

Vandercook, T., York, J., & Forest, M. (1989). The McGill action planning system (MAPS): A strategy for building the vision. *Journal of The Association for Persons with Severe Handicaps, 14,* 205–215.

van Dijk, J. (1986). An educational curriculum for deaf-blind multi-handicapped persons. In D. Ellis (Eds.), *Sensory impairments in mentally handicapped people* (pp. 374–382). San Diego: College-Hill Press.

Varney, G. (1988). *Building productive teams: An action guide and resource book.* San Francisco: Jossey-Bass.

Vollmer, T.R., & Iwata, B.A. (1992). Differential reinforcement as treatment for behavior disorders: Procedural and functional variations. *Research in Developmental Disabilities, 13,* 393–417.

Wacker, D., Steege, M., Northup, J., Reimers, T., Berg, W., & Sasso, G. (1990). Use of functional analysis and acceptability measures to assess and treat severe behavior problems: An outpatient clinic model. In A.C. Repp & N.N. Singh (Eds.), *Perspectives on the use of nonaversive and aversive interventions for persons with developmental disabilities* (pp. 349–359). Sycamore, IL: Sycamore.

White, O.R. (1985). Decisions, decisions. . . . *B.C. Journal of Special Education, 9,* 305–320.

Willis, T.J., LaVigna, G.W., & Donnellan, A.M. (1989). *Behavior assessment guide.* Los Angeles: Institute for Applied Behavior Analysis.

Winterling, V., Dunlap, G., & O'Neill, R.E. (1987). The influence of task variation on the aberrant behaviors of autistic students. *Education and Treatment of Children, 10,* 105–119.

Chapter 13

Supporting the Medical and Physical Needs of Students in Inclusive Settings

Philippa H. Campbell

Students with deaf-blindness may also have additional medical problems as well as impaired movement abilities. Although students whose primary disorders involve vision and hearing may have minor difficulties with moving around their environments or special health problems such as asthma or allergies, this chapter focuses on those students with deaf-blindness and substantial posture and movement disabilities and/or health problems. Students such as these may be counted by states under the categories of *deaf-blind, orthopedically handicapped, other health impaired,* or *multiply handicapped* (Bullis & Otos, 1988). The classification label applied to a particular student may not differentiate among the actual needs of the student as much as it may reflect the practices of a particular state education agency and its policies (Fredericks & Baldwin, 1987).

All students, even those with the most complicated and multiple disabilities, can be educated in their neighborhood (home) schools when sufficient resources and services are provided. Services are designed to support students in these normal and least restrictive environments (LREs) rather than to remediate or *fix* a student's disabilities. Services that support student participation in the activities and routines of typical educational, community, and home environments assist students to develop as much independence as possible through skill improvement (learning) and use of compensatory strategies, devices, and aids. The natural home, school, and community environments that characterize the life of a particular student and his or her family and friends can be described in terms of the activities and routines that are carried out within those environments. These activities and routines provide a base from which the special sensory, physical, and health needs of students may be addressed (Campbell & Forsyth, 1993).

Students with disabilities may be physically or socially included in typical environments; however, achieving instructional inclusion may be difficult when students have multiple disabilities. *Physical inclusion* occurs when students are physically a part of school and community environments. This means, for example, that students with physical disabilities have correctly fitting equipment that not only positions them properly but does so in ways that do not isolate students from their peers (Campbell, 1993). Without correctly fitted and working hearing aids, students with hearing impairments are not physically included in school or community environments. *Social inclusion* occurs when students with disabilities interact socially and develop friendships with their peers. *Instructional inclusion* means that needed special services and supports for students with disabilities are provided within typical educational environments and classrooms.

Many students, especially those with multiple disabilities, are unable to perform skills independently that seem to be needed for full inclusion into typical educational and community settings. When students are unable to speak, move independently around an environment, or take care of their own needs, concerns may be expressed about both the ability of the student to benefit from general education programs and the capacity of the setting to address the needs of the student. Integrated programming enhances the use of activities and routines as a basis for providing services and support to students with even the most severe disabilities in typical environments (Campbell, 1987a, 1989). This type of programming has been described as a variation of a transdisciplinary team model where specialists, general education personnel, family members, the student's friends and advocates, and the student (where chronologically age appropriate) work together collaboratively to:

1. Define desired outcomes
2. Determine the best ways for services and supports to be provided
3. Plan and implement the most efficient ways for routines to be delivered
4. Identify ways in which a student can participate in typical activities

5. Determine specific strategies that will be used to infuse inclusive strategies within routines and activities
6. Monitor the effectiveness of the team's decisions as well as the impact of those decisions on student participation and performance

These collaborative efforts lead to full inclusion of students in typical home, school, and community environments (Rainforth, York, & Macdonald, 1992; see also chap. 8, this volume, for a full discussion of collaborative teaming).

PHYSICAL AND HEALTH FACTORS THAT INFLUENCE INDEPENDENCE

Students with deaf-blindness are likely to have delayed acquisition of movement skills when they are infants and toddlers due to the difficulties imposed by sensory impairments (Michael & Paul, 1991; Stremel et al., 1990). These infants and toddlers learn movement skills at a later age, with or without special services such as physical or occupational therapy. Other infants may have brain dysfunction that results in motor disorders, such as cerebral palsy, that accompany vision and hearing disorders. The posture and movement abilities of these infants are likely not only to be absent or delayed, but also to be characterized by atypical ways of achieving these skills. These students may not acquire motor abilities without use of special strategies associated with disciplines such as physical and occupational therapy.

Some children may have special health care needs in addition to sensory impairments, particularly if vision and hearing impairments are associated with prematurity (e.g., de Vries, Dubowitz, Dubowitz, & Pennock, 1990; Fitzhardinge & Pape, 1982). These health care needs may include special methods for feeding and nutrition; management of respiration through oxygen therapy, ventilation, mechanical suctioning, or chest physical therapy (CPT); infection control; management of bowel and bladder functions; medications; or other related procedures (Campbell & Bailey, 1991; Graff, Ault, Guess, Taylor, & Thompson, 1990; Kohrman, 1991). The need for special health management procedures may decrease with age. Infants, especially those who have been recently discharged from an NICU (neonatal intensive care unit), may require the use of procedures until they are sufficiently stable to have acquired more independent ways of achieving nutrition, respiration, or other functions (Jaudes, 1991). For example, some infants may continue to require oxygen therapy following hospital discharge during high periods of energy use or stress. Babies such as these may receive oxygen only during feedings, with therapy discontinued when the infant is able to eat with efficient use of the oral musculature.

Some children may continue to have special health care needs throughout their lifetimes, and some of these needs may increase with age. For example, children with prolonged and chronic lung disease may require more complex procedures in order to continue to manage the lung disease as they get older (Caldwell & Kirkhart, 1991). Students who were once able to achieve sufficient nutritional status through oral feeding alone may require supplemental or total feedings through external means such as gastrointestinal tubes (G-tubes). These students are likely to have special health care needs in combination with other disabilities such as cerebral palsy and sensory impairments (Holvoet & Helmstetter, 1989).

Understanding the Physical Disabilities of Students

Students with severe physical disabilities require management of caregiving needs as well as opportunities to improve their skill performance. Factors associated with their physical disability may interfere negatively with independent performance of care routines such as dressing or eating, full participation in typical activities, and acquisition of functional skills such as mobility or communication. Other factors such as motivation, cognition, and vision and hearing may further complicate the possibility of full independence.

Disorders of Posture and Movement Physical disabilities may result from many situations including damage to the brain and central nervous system, neuromuscular disorders, or maternal infection (see Batshaw & Perret, 1992, for a full description of the various physical disabilities). The physical disabilities most often associated with other impairments, such as in the visual or auditory systems, derive from central nervous system dysfunction and include diagnoses such as cerebral palsy or brain damage. The principle manifestation of these types of diagnoses in relation to motor abilities are:

- Differences in muscle tone
- Absense of or atypically achieved posture against gravity
- Absence of or atypically coordinated movement patterns
- Tendency to acquire secondary physical disabilities such as diminished muscle strength, limitations in joint range of motion, reduced endurance, or orthopedic disorders (see, e.g., Campbell, 1991a)

Genetic syndromes involving chromosomal alterations may also result in similarly manifested disorders of muscle tone, difficulties with posture and movement skills, and secondary physical changes. Many of these syndromes may include visual and auditory disorders in addition to motor disabilities.

Many students with motor disorders are considered to have multiple disabilities due to the disorders in the visual and auditory systems or in overall health that, in combination with motor disorders, affect the strategies that will be needed to maximize student learning. When students have combined vision and hearing impairments, the primary disability may not always be the motor disability; however, when students have significantly reduced motor abilities, the motor disorder must be considered even when visual and/or auditory impairments or deafblindness accompanies limited performance of motor skills. A mild or moderate problem with posture and movement is often more obvious when students with deaf-blindness are infants, toddlers, or preschoolers and are learning how to control and move their bodies. As these students get older and acquire motor abilities, their sensory disabilities may become more prominent.

Some individuals with physical disabilities have too little muscle tone (i.e., *hypotonia*), whereas others have too much muscle tone (i.e., *hypertonia*). Muscle tone may change in all individuals by becoming increased at some times and decreased at other times. The degree of tension (or tone) present in muscles throughout the body allows for: 1) posture against the influences of gravity and 2) initiation and performance of coordinated patterns of movement of the head, the extremities (i.e., arms and legs), and the whole body. Body postures vary in terms of the extent to which these positions require antigravity control. Lying on one's back or stomach, for example, does not require antigravity control because these postures position the body neutrally in relation to gravity. Sitting on the floor or on a chair requires antigravity control of the head, trunk, and arms, and standing requires the entire body to be upright against the influences of gravity. The body musculature must have sufficient tone to withstand these gravitational influences. Muscles must be able to shorten

and lengthen in order to initiate and perform coordinated movement, and they must work together in groups to produce movement at body joints. When one muscle group is shortening, the opposite muscle groups must become longer. These reciprocal relationships among muscle groups allow the head to change position, the arms and legs to move, and the whole body to change position in space.

When muscle tone is either decreased (i.e., hypotonic) or increased (i.e., hypertonic), coordinated initiations and performance of movement patterns of the head, extremities, and total body are likely to be affected. In extreme variations of tone, movements may be impossible to initiate; with less extreme variations, movements may be produced but are likely to be poorly coordinated or performed with compensations. Furthermore, changes in the muscles, joints, or soft tissues in muscles or around joints may occur secondary to muscle tone deviations and atypically coordinated movement patterns. These changes include shortening or overlengthening of muscles, tightening of joint structures, diminished muscle strength, or orthopedic changes (e.g., dislocated hips, spinal scoliosis or lordosis, malalignment of the spine and rib cage). Those individuals with extremely decreased muscle tone are at greatest risk for acquiring secondary disabilities. Those students with significant spasticity (i.e., increased tone) are equally at risk for acquiring secondary disabilities that are linked directly to the distribution of spasticity throughout the body.

Muscle tone provides a basis for antigravity posture and movement, and differences in muscle tone may negatively influence an individual's ability to perform functional activities. Many of the activities or skills that are important for an individual to perform require movements such as reaching or grasping objects, using body movement to express oneself, or moving around the environment. These activities and skills may be influenced by atypical muscle tone. Students who have difficulty seeing and who also have, for example, low muscle tone may have difficulty locating objects visually and may also be limited in the ability to locate objects by using their hands to scan due to difficulties initiating reaching or moving the arms. Individuals with poor head control due to low muscle tone in the neck and trunk muscles may maintain a posture where the head is held down. This posture makes it difficult for an individual to use any residual sight that may be available and may also make the person look disinterested or unavailable for social interaction. Many of the strategies that are used by individuals with visual impairments involve the use of movement as a compensation for poor sight. When individuals have difficulty with posture and movement, these compensations may not be as readily available as when muscle tone is within normal range and posture and movement abilities are performed easily.

Key Physical Factors   The primary factors involving posture, patterns of movement, and secondary physical disabilities are outlined and defined in Table 1. These factors are those that typically interfere with student independence and are organized within the following categories: 1) posture and alignment against gravity, 2) movement of body parts (e.g., arms, legs, mouth), 3) movement

Table 1.   Performance factors associated with physical disabilities

Performance area	Performance factor	Definition
Posture and alignment against gravity	Anterior/posterior weight shift	Shifting of body weight in front of or behind the line of gravity within the anterior/posterior plane of space
	Body adjustment	Changes in postural alignment within the same position; adjusting body alignment in sitting, standing, and other positions
	Position	Restriction of performance to only one position (e.g., student is mobile only on hands and knees, but not in walking)
	Trunk posture against gravity	Maintenance of the trunk in an anti-gravity position such as sitting or standing
	Trunk stability/tone	Extent to which sufficient tone is present to support the trunk against gravity
Movement patterns of body parts	Eye/facial movement	Movement of the eyes or facial musculature
	Foot position in weight bearing	Position of the foot (or feet) when weight bearing is required such as in standing or walking
	Lower extremity movement patterns	Movement of the hips, legs, and feet
	Manipulation/hand use	Use of small muscle groups for controlled movements, particularly in relation to objects or for activities such as signing for communication

(continued)

Table 1. *(continued)*

Performance area	Performance factor	Definition
	Upper extremity movement patterns	Movement of the arms and shoulders
	Oral motor movements	Coordination of the oral-pharyngeal musculature for controlled movements
Movement of whole body in space	Movement between positions within the same activity	Ability to move from one posture to another within an activity (e.g., moving from standing to sitting to use the toilet)
	Movement during transition	Ability to move from one posture/activity to another posture/activity (e.g., moving from the reading to the math area of the classroom or moving between classrooms)
Secondary physical disabilities	Endurance	Sustaining of cardiac, pulmonary, and musculoskeletal exertion over time
	Joint stability	Co-contraction of muscles around a joint to hold the joint in place to allow movement at other joints or to hold the body against gravity
	Muscle length/range of motion	Capacity of the muscles to lengthen or shorten from resting length; limitations may restrict muscle length to a shortened length due to tightness or to an overlengthened (overstretched) length due to insufficient activation or position
	Orthopedic deformities	Specific conditions that involve the bones, joints, or muscles of the body, including deformities such as scoliosis (spine) or hip/shoulder dislocations

of the whole body in space, and 4) secondary disabilities. An understanding of these factors is important for two reasons as follows.

First, each of these factors may become an interferer in terms of a student achieving independence in routines, activities, or functional skill improvement. Identifying these factors and the extent to which each interferes with or facilitates independence forms the basis for *integrated programming* or *integrated therapy*. These terms are used to describe programming that integrates strategies drawn from a variety of different disciplines (Campbell, 1991a; Campbell & Forsyth, 1993). A student may receive services from a vision specialist, hearing specialist, teacher, physical therapist, occupational therapist, and speech and language pathologist. These services may be coordinated through a variety of team structures (e.g., multidisciplinary, interdisciplinary, transdisciplinary). When particular strategies from one or more disciplines are linked together for the purposes of helping a student achieve a particular outcome or goal, integrated programming results. The second reason these factors are critical is that the integrated programming plan is directed toward improving or compensating for each of these factors through routines, activity participation, and infusion of strategies. Each student's unique pattern of physical needs can be addressed by the programming team when all members understand the impact of specific factors.

Posture and Alignment Factors associated with posture and alignment against gravity may prevent a student from being able to assume or maintain body position and posture against gravity or may influence the ways in which the position is maintained. When a student is unable to assume or maintain a body position independently or when severe malalignment in that position occurs, adaptive equipment may be necessary to promote independence and to maintain postural alignment. Holding the body in reasonable alignment is important in order to: 1) provide supports that will allow movement of the head, arms, or legs; 2) prevent secondary physical disabilities that are acquired due to malalignment of the body (e.g., spinal deformities such as scoliosis); and 3) support the student's body in a comfortable position. Some students with less severe physical disabilities may learn to assume and maintain one or more body positions against gravity independently. Other students with severe physical disabilities may never learn to assume or maintain these positions independently. Supporting these students' bodies enables them to learn to use their arms for a variety of tasks within routines and activities. For example, these students may be able to put their arms through sleeves and use their arms to help pull themselves into a standing position for transfer to the toilet or to activate a joystick switch on a motorized chair or communication device.

Movement Patterns of Body Parts Movement of the head and extremities is a critical skill for students with the most severe physical disabilities. Arm movement is a key compensation when muscle tone in the trunk is reduced. The arms, for example, can support the trunk in sitting on the floor, hold onto a walker for independent (but assisted) mobility, and assist in moving the body from one position to another (e.g., can push the body upright from floor lying to floor sitting.) The arms locate objects and can be used to express communication through gestures. Arm movement is a critical skill for promoting partial participation and/or full independence within most caregiving routines and within many activities. Hand movement is also important. Whereas arm movement brings the hand to a particular location, hand movement is used to feel, manipulate, or express oneself through manual communication. Functional skills such as mobility, communication, recreation/leisure, and learning can be achieved through movement of the arms alone, or in combination with hand manipulation and/or eye and facial or oral–motor movement.

These extremity skills are the most crucial skills to establish and maintain when students have physical disabilities or when students have significant visual impairment or deaf-blindness, alone or in combination with physical disabilities. As mentioned earlier, movement is a primary compensation for visual impairment. Reach and manipulation provide a means to use the hands to locate and feel objects, such as food and utensil placement, or communication symbols, such as object cues or even braille. Students who have difficulty with movements in the hands may not be able to easily learn to express themselves through manual signing and may have greater communication success with object cues or, if hearing is sufficient, with auditory scanning communication devices. When a student with deaf-blindness is unable physically to use arm and hand movements, intensive interactions with adults and peers may be necessary to expose the individual to the many objects and people in his or her environment. A primary method for establishing these basic movement skills is to require their use within as many routines and activities as possible.

Movement of Whole Body in Space The ability to move the whole body in space allows students to be independently mobile through crawling or walking (as well as through other forms such as scooting in a sitting position) and to change their bodies from one position to another. Movement of the body results when an individual is able to shift body weight in various planes of space. To stand up from a chair, for example, an individual must shift the weight of the body forward onto the feet, thus moving body weight from the hips onto the feet. To walk, an individual must shift weight from side to side to alternately unweight one leg and foot. Shifting body weight can be very difficult for students with either decreased or increased muscle tone. When muscle tone is decreased, the body may sink into gravity or the base of support may be so wide (to maintain position against gravity) that weight shift may be impossible. Assistance in learning necessary weight shifts is important for students with physical disabilities. Strategies to facilitate weight shifts can be incorporated into routines and activities. For example, the weight shift required to move from sitting to standing can be incorporated into caregiving routines (e.g., moving from a wheelchair to the toilet; standing up when dressing in order to pull up slacks or underpants).

Secondary Physical Disabilities Secondary physical disabilities are not present when children with physical disabilities are infants or toddlers. These disabilities are acquired as children are moved and as they learn to move themselves. When present, these secondary physical disabilities function to influence postural alignment and to restrict possible movement patterns. Secondary physical disabilities are also related to postural and movement compensations. A student with one dislocated hip may sit with body weight over the nondislocated hip, thereby causing the spine to curve in a "C" position. The maintenance of the spine in this "C" curve may result in imbalance of the spinal muscles or in the development of a permanent scoliosis. A student who cannot fully extend the arm in reaching may compensate and learn to reach objects by rounding the upper back or contracting the muscles in the upper trunk, thereby overlengthening the spinal muscles and creating permanent tightness in those muscles that attach the arms to the trunk. The resultant outcome is further limitation in upper extremity movement.

Secondary physical disabilities may be preventable by incorporating strategies within activities and routines that maintain full range of motion and prevent compensatory postural malalignment or movement patterns. Once acquired, however, these disabilities require specific procedures, typically administered by physical or occupational therapists or by orthopedic surgeons. These procedures are ones that are provided through direct hands-on therapy or through surgery and are not likely to be easily incorporated into activities and routines.

Understanding Student Health Needs

Students may have a variety of health care needs including:

- Nutrition/feeding
- Management of respiration through a variety of procedures or devices
- Bowel and bladder management
- Infection control
- Seizures
- Medications

Students with complicated health problems require supports in order to fully participate in activities and routines across school and community environments. Health issues frequently accompany conditions that result in multiple disabilities and may be more dramatic during infancy and the early child-hood years than with older students. Not all students with deaf-blindness will have sig-nificant health care needs. However, when the visual and auditory impairments are re-lated to central nervous system damage (as may be the case with children who are very prematurely born), medical issues may also be present. Medical equipment as well as in-dividuals who are knowledgeable in provid-ing health routines are the two primary sup-ports needed (e.g., Holvoet & Helmstetter, 1989). Some of these health care procedures can be implemented within other activities and routines, while others may require re-moval of a student from an activity in order to administer the procedure.

Educational administrators and direct ser-vice personnel may be fearful of the health needs of students as well as reluctant to ad-minister health care procedures within school environments. Some students with severe health needs may come to school with a nurse or health aide who is available to ad-minister needed procedures. This support is most often provided when the family's health insurance will finance a nurse or with students who are participants in Medicaid-financed health waiver programs. When a nurse accompanies a student to school and is present throughout the day, the role of this individual within the classroom and school needs to be defined by the team of individ-uals working with the student (Caldwell & Kirkhart, 1991). A student attends school to enjoy the benefits of opportunities for physi-cal, social, and instructional inclusion. An extra adult within a classroom may inadver-tently function in ways that restrict the social and instructional inclusion of the student unless this individual's role is well-defined.

Health Factors Students may require con-sideration of their health needs, if not direct provision of one or more health routines, when planning activity participation and

functional skill improvement. Typical health care needs are listed and defined in Table 2 as factors that may influence or impact upon student participation. These factors are ad-dressed through integrated programming in the unique design of instructional methods and through compensatory strategies.

ACTIVITIES AND ROUTINES

Activities are defined as those events that oc-cur in natural home, school, or community environments. Gym, swimming, art, or an after-school club are examples of activities that occur in typical school settings. Com-munity activities include going shopping or to the dry cleaners, attending the movies or a church Sunday school class, eating in a res-taurant, or playing in a park with other chil-dren. Eating meals, watching television, or doing chores are examples of activities that occur in homes. The particular activities as-sociated with environments may vary de-pendent upon factors such as the student's age; choices made by individuals or their families; the culture, values, and lifestyles of families that define the unique importance of activities; as well as opportunities available within, and the practices adopted by, partic-ular communities.

Routines occur repeatedly within and across environments. Routines include those actions necessary to move (or transition) a student from one position or place to an-other; provide care by feeding, dressing, toi-leting, or bathing; or implement medical/health routines by suctioning, ventilating, or managing seizures or respiratory crises. En-vironmental routines, such as standing in lines, occur across school and community. These routines may be necessary to purchase groceries or a movie ticket or to select food from the school cafeteria. Table 3 lists exam-ples of various types of transitional move-

Table 2.   Performance factors associated with special health care needs

Performance area	Performance factor	Definition
Nutrition/feeding	Frequency of eating	Number of times per day that the student must be fed
	Special devices	Need for devices such as tubes or syringes
	Special equipment	Need for equipment such as pumps or special formulas used in parenteral nutrition
Respiration	Frequency of management	Number of times per day that the student may require procedures such as chest physical therapy (CPT) and oral or tracheostomy suctioning
	Special equipment	Need for equipment such as suctioning machines, ventilators, or monitors
	Cardiopulmonary endurance	Sustaining of cardiopulmonary exertion over time
	Ease of management	Prevalence of crises that require use of emergency procedures such as CPR
Bowel and bladder management	Frequency of needed elimination	Number of times per day that bladder and bowel functions must be managed
	Special devices or procedures	Need for use of devices such as catheters or procedures such as scheduling
Infection control	Susceptibility	Extent to which student easily gets infections
Seizures	Occurrence and type	Extent to which seizures are controlled through medication, diet, or other procedures
	Ease of management	Ease by which seizures are managed when they occur and impact on student following a seizure
Medications	Frequency of administration	Frequency that medications need to be administered
	Method of administration and length of time required	Method used to administer medication (e.g., orally, by tube, by infusion) and length of time required to administer

ment, caregiving, health, and environmental routines.

Both activities and routines provide a context in which student participation can be promoted. Some students will never be fully independent in particular activities or routines, but all students, even those with the most multiple disabilities, can participate in at least one or more aspects of an activity or routine. Participation requires a student to use a skill or behavior already existing in his or her repertoire. For example, a student who can vocalize to signal "more" can be required to participate more fully in an eating routine by using vocalization to signal "more food/another bite." A student who is able to reach both arms forward can be required to do so before being lifted from the floor.

In addition to participating by using existing abilities, students can also learn new skills within the context of activities and routines. Instruction, therapy, nursing, and other specialized services may be provided for students by infusing individualized strategies into activities and routines (Campbell, Cooper, & McInerney, 1984; Dunn, 1991). Skill infusion differs from participation in that a student is learning a new skill(s) rather than using an existing skill(s) and is being taught this new skill within the context of one or more activities and routines. Instructional strategies necessary to teach a student to learn a new skill are designed by the team working with the student and are likely to integrate information from a variety of perspectives (Campbell, 1987b). A student who

Table 3.   Examples of different types of routines

Transitional movement	Physical care	Health care	Environmental
Lifting and carrying a student from one location to another	Feeding a student orally	Feeding a student using medical equipment (e.g., nasogastrostomy tube, gastrointestinal tube, pump)	Entering school and going to the correct classroom or location
Repositioning from one piece of equipment or one position to another	Dressing and undressing	Suctioning a student through the mouth, nose, or a tracheostomy	Going to the cafeteria, playground, or other school locations
Holding a young infant or child	Changing diapers or assisting with toileting	Providing oral or tubed medications	Changing classes
Assisting a student to move from one location to another	Washing/bathing or assisting with bathing	Performing respiratory procedures such as chest physical therapy (postural drainage) techniques	Getting out of bed in the morning or going to bed at night
	Performing or assisting with oral hygiene (tooth brushing, flossing)	Performing CPR (cardiopulmonary resuscitation)	Standing in lines (to purchase tickets, wait to go to the bathroom, etc.)

is learning to use arm movement might be required to reach toward objects or people within the context of activities, such as art class, or caregiving routines, such as eating. The particular strategies used to facilitate reaching reflect the unique characteristics of the student's abilities and reflect the input, for example, of vision and hearing specialists and therapists for a student with deafblindness and physical disabilities.

ASSESSMENT AND PLANNING STRATEGIES THAT PROMOTE FULL INCLUSION

Activities and routines are characterized by both the skills required from the participating students and the environmental characteristics associated with the activity or routine (Rainforth, York, & Macdonald, 1992). An environmental routine such as walking down the hall of a school requires mobility on the part of the student. The environmental characteristics of this activity, however, are different when a student is walking to

the office when other students are in classes or to the cafeteria when all students are going to lunch. In the first instance, the student may be the only person in the hall, whereas in the second instance, the student may have to cope with many people who are also walking in the same direction. Thus, differences in environmental characteristics can change the level of difficulty involved in various activities and routines.

A student's functional abilities influence success in performing activities and routines with full independence. Limitations in vision or hearing, posture and movement, or overall health influence the ways in which students participate in activities and routines. As previously mentioned, all students can participate to some extent in all activities and routines. The principle of partial participation promotes student participation in one or more aspects of an activity or routine through use of strategies that modify all or part of the activity or routine or provide compensations that promote student participation (Baumgart et al., 1982; Ferguson &

Baumgart, 1991). An understanding of the functional abilities of students in relation to the requirements of particular activities and routines helps determine the specific strategies to promote maximal student participation (Rainforth, York, Macdonald, & Dunn, 1992). In addition to promoting participation in an activity or routine, specific functional abilities may be taught across one or more identified activities or routines. Abilities required within a routine or activity and that may not be learned (or easily learned) by a student can be compensated for through strategies and equipment or devices. In these ways, students with even the most multiple disabilities can be participants in the activities and routines of general education (and other typical community or home environments), receive needed specialized services, and learn skills and abilities that are unique to their individual needs.

Beginning with Outcomes: A Top–Down Assessment

A top–down assessment model is more likely to lead to meaningful inclusion than are traditional evaluation models that identify strengths and weaknesses of student performance exclusive of the environments in which skills may be needed (e.g., Campbell, 1991b; Campbell & Forsyth, 1993). The top–down assessment is used to determine the ways in which a student will be able to achieve desired outcomes (or goals) within a particular environment. The process for conducting a top–down assessment is diagrammed in Figure 1.

Desired outcomes "drive" the assessment process in contrast to more traditional approaches where evaluation and assessment determine the selection of outcomes or goals. The desired outcomes may be identified by the student and his or her family or by a team of individuals that includes professionals, family and friends, and the student. Outcomes are expressed globally in terms such as: "I would like John to walk," "I would like Janey to have friends in our neighborhood with whom she can play after school," or "Susan needs to have a job after she finishes school." Outcomes are an expression of a situation that one or more people involved with a particular student, or the student, would like to have happen in the future. Most outcome statements can be classified as: 1) performance of or inclusion in a particular activity (e.g., "I would like Jared to have art with other second graders in his school."), 2) improvement of a routine (e.g., "Suctioning needs to be implemented with Harrison throughout the day."), or 3) improvement in performing a particular functional skill (e.g., Sarah needs to learn to be independent in getting around the house and yard"). Outcomes are not judged as realistic (or unrealistic) or written in measurable or behavioral terms, nor is a student viewed as having (or not having) the potential to attain the outcome (Campbell, Strickland, & LaForme, 1992).

Once the desired outcomes are determined, the assessment process draws upon a number of different assessment strategies to: 1) identify student performance interferers and facilitators that influence achievement of a particular outcome, 2) identify environmental interferers and supports, and 3) establish the strategies that will be used to bypass student performance and environmental interferers or improve student performance. The outcome of the assessment process is a written intervention plan that outlines specific objectives, the methods that will be used to achieve those objectives, and the ways in which achievement will be evaluated. Ongoing assessment allows team members to determine the extent to which the intervention plan is working and to make decisions concerning any needed programming changes.

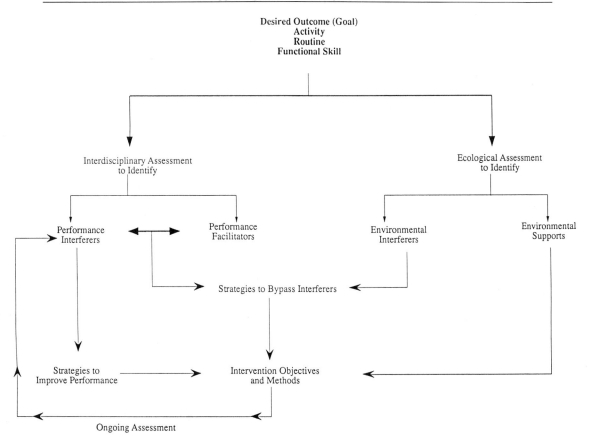

Figure 1.   The top–down assessment model includes interdisciplinary assessment and ecological assessment procedures that are used to identify performance interferers and facilitators and environmental interferers and supports.

Impairments in vision, hearing, physical abilities, or health status are likely to interfere with attainment of a desired outcome. Student performance interferers, however, may not be the only factors that interfere with or influence success. Environmental factors such as the number of students in a particular class (or classroom), the location of the class within a school building, or the availability of adaptive equipment and devices or needed services or supports may interfere to a greater degree with the attainment of an outcome than may the performance interferers associated with the student. Likewise, factors associated with a particular environment may support student success despite the student's disability. The focus of the assessment process is to identify the interferers and supports associated both with student abilities and with the environment. Strategies that bypass or reduce the influence of interferers, as well as those designed to improve the environment and improve student performance, can be designed on the basis of assessment information.

Identifying Student Performance Interferers and Strengths   Several assessment strategies are used to determine the abilities of a particular student in reference to attainment of a specific outcome. A team of individuals, including those professionals with expertise related to a student's disabilities, the student, family and friends, as well as other individuals, may be needed to obtain all the necessary information. Each discipline uses clinical or systematic observation strategies as well as other assessment measures to determine the impact of student performance factors on the desired outcome. The impact of performance factors on the desired outcome are rated in terms of degree using the following categories:

NA No problems are identified through assessment.

0   A problem is suspected, but is not currently influencing performance; follow-up may be required.

1   A problem is present and influences performance, but is not likely to impact in major ways; simple interventions such as environmental modifications may be sufficient to address needs.

2   A problem is present and interferes with performance significantly; interventions directed to the problem may be necessary.

3   A problem is present and prevents acquisition or use of the functional skill; jointly designed interventions that integrate input from all team members are necessary.

Typical performance factors associated with particular categories of activities and routines have been developed into assessment grids that result in a synthesized profile of student performance (see Campbell, 1991a, or Campbell & Forsyth, 1993, for a detailed explanation of the use of these grids with students with multiple disabilities). An example of one such assessment grid is presented in Figure 2, which shows assessment information from team members working with a 10-year-old student, "Rachael," who was classified as deaf-blind with physical disabilities and health care needs. The desired activity outcome in this assessment was participation in recess. Rachael was placed in a regular fifth grade classroom in her neighborhood (home) elementary school where she and her classroom teacher received support services from physical and occupational therapists, a vision specialist, a speech language pathologist, and a health aide.

As can be seen from reviewing the grid, programming designed to ensure Rachael's success in participating in recess needed to account for the following interferers:

1. Position
2. Anterior/posterior weight shift
3. Movement between postures within the same activity
4. Upper extremity movement patterns
5. Manipulation/hand use
6. Physical access to environments
7. Vision
8. Hearing
9. Health issues

Motivation and cognition were strengths as were Rachael's abilities to use adaptive equipment and assistive devices.

Identifying Environmental Interferers and Supports Ecological assessment procedures offer a strategy for observing the requirements of a particular environment during a specific activity and for determining the strategies that might best address a student's individual pattern of performance (Baumgart et al., 1982; Campbell, 1989, 1992; Linehan, Brady, & Hwang, 1991; Rainforth, York, & Macdonald, 1992). An outcome of observing environments is the identification of environmental interferers and supports. Full inclusion of students into activities and routines associated with a particular environment can be accomplished with no change in

Infants and Young Children
Functional Outcomes Assessment Grid

Functional Outcome: Play/Leisure

Activities or Routines: Recess
Student: Rachael

Performance Areas	Performance Components	NA	0	1	2	3	Comments
Posture & alignment against gravity	Anterior/posterior weight shift		X				
	Asymmetry/symmetry patterns	X					
	Position				X		
Movement patterns of body parts	Lower extremity movement patterns		X				
	Manipulation/hand use					X	
	Upper extremity movement patterns				X		
Movement of the body in space	Movement between postures within same activity					X	
Secondary physical disabilities	Joint stability	X					
	Orthopedic factors			X			
Use of behavior	Choice-making				X		
	Initiation					X	
	Response			X			
Sensory systems	Vision				X		
Integration	Motivation/cognition	X					
Health issues			X				
Assistive equipment or devices	Expression aids	X					
	Performance aids	X					
	Postural equipment	X					
Other							

Figure 2.   Sample functional outcomes assessment grid for "Rachael." (NA—No problems are identified through assessment. 0—A problem is *suspected* but currently is not influencing functional development. 1—A problem is present and *influences* functional performance but is not likely to be a primary interferer. 2—A problem is present and *influences* functional performance significantly [i.e., is a principle interferer]. 3—A problem is present and *prevents* acquisition or use of the functional skill.)

student performance, but with changes in environmental factors. For example, maintaining the physical continuity of a preschool classroom environment over time may be an important factor in ensuring that a student with visual impairments can safely and successfully participate in the activities and routines of a preschool classroom. Reducing the amount of classroom furniture may allow a student in a wheelchair to be independently mobile within that classroom. Adding electrical outlets to a classroom or locating the classroom near the nurse's office can enable a student with health problems to be accommodated within the school environment.

The ecological inventory of recess in the elementary school attended by Rachael is illustrated in Table 4. By using the assessment information summarized on Rachael's performance profile (see Figure 2) and obtained from the ecological inventory, the team working with Rachael was able to design programs and supports to facilitate her participation and inclusion in school recess. Participation in recess was increased by using object cues for communication and choice making and by having a friend assist Rachael during recess activities. Observation indicated that Rachael preferred activities such as sliding down the sliding board and being pushed by another child in "running the bases" in baseball or during a relay race; therefore, these activities were made available for choice making. Two children from Rachael's "circle of friends" were selected each day by the teacher to assist Rachael with choice making, communication, and participation. These students also helped to infuse skills of reaching and vocalization within all activities. The students learned how to facilitate reaching in activities such as reaching toward her locker and throughout the playground activities. They also encouraged Rachael to vocalize to signal "more," for example, to express her desire to continue an activity.

Table 4. Ecological inventory: Participation in recess

Inventory of typical participation	Inventory of Rachael	Suggested integrated stategies and adaptations
Goes to locker	Needs to be pushed in chair to get to locker	Object cueing will be used: a piece of material will be placed in Rachael's hand to let her know she is going to get her clothing. A friend can push Rachael to her locker, placing her sideways next to the door.
Gets outside clothing from locker	Cannot open locker or reach in to get clothing	Rachael can locate the handle on which a large loop of material will be hooked to the handle; she can reach forward and, with assistance from her friend, place her arm through the loop and move her arm to open the locker. Her friend will get her clothing out.
Puts on outside clothing	Cannot select or put on clothing without assistance	Her friend will help Rachael put on her sweater or coat; Rachael will straighten her arm to put it through both sleeves.

(continued)

Table 4.   (continued)

Inventory of typical participation	Inventory of Rachael	Suggested integrated stategies and adaptations
Stands in line	Stays in line in her wheelchair if placed there	Object cues of a toy plastic sliding board will be placed in Rachael's hand when communicating to her that she is going outside to play. Her friend will wheel her into line to go outside.
Goes out to playground	Needs to be pushed in chair to get to the playground	Her friend will push her outside to the playground.
Decides activity in which to participate	Can decide activity with assistance	Activities in which Rachael can participate will be available. Object cues will be determined for each activity. These cues will be placed in front of Rachael, and she will be assisted to manipulate (feel) each one and to select one by pointing or by vocalizing.
Plays an organized game (e.g., hide and seek; jump rope)	Can participate in some games with assistance	Rachael will participate in the selected activity with the assistance of one or more friends.
Plays an organized sport (e.g., baseball)	Cannot play an organized sport without assistance and modification	Rachael will participate in the selected activity with the assistance of one or more friends.
Plays on playground equipment (e.g., slide, swings, merry-go-round)	Can go down slide, if placed at top; cannot sit on swing without assistance; cannot operate merry-go-round	Rachael will participate in the selected activity with the assistance of one or more friends.
Interacts with other children; follows game or participation rules; asks for assistance, when needed	Vocalizes as part of activities she enjoys; initiates some contact with other students; vocalizes for assistance	Friends will stop activity periodically and ask if Rachael wants to continue to participate using the object cue; vocalization will be an indication of interest in continuing.
Responds to signal for going inside by stopping activity	Stops activity with assistance	Friends will tell Rachael when activity is ending.
Lines up to go inside	Stays in line in her wheelchair if placed there	Friend will move her into the line using an object cue of the material (for clothing) to indicate she is going to her locker.
Removes outside clothing and puts in locker	Cannot remove clothing or place in locker without assistance	Friend will help Rachael take off her outside clothing and will hang clothes in her locker.
Goes inside classroom	Can go inside classroom when pushed in her chair	Object cue of a plastic desk will be used to indicate the classroom and will be placed in Rachael's hand before her friend pushes her into the classroom.
Sits at desk (or in location specified by teacher) to begin next activity	Can sit at desk in her wheelchair or another location when placed there	Friend will push Rachael to her desk (or whatever location selected by her teacher).

SUPPORTS AND PROGRAMMING TO ATTAIN FULL INCLUSION

Physical, social, and instructional inclusion of students with multiple needs are a challenge to the team of professionals, family members, and friends associated with a student. Meeting this challenge requires collaboration among agencies, sharing of financial resources and expertise, and agreements among team members to focus upon and support all aspects of inclusion. Safe and efficient routines support physical inclusion. Social inclusion results when neither the routines needed by a student nor support personnel function to isolate the student from other individuals within school or community environments. Instructional inclusion occurs when students participate in all activities associated with school or community environments and when opportunities are provided for skill improvement through infusing integrated strategies within activities and routines.

Supporting Physical Inclusion Through Routines

Students with deaf-blindness who have physical or health care needs may require significant amounts of assistance with moving around the environment and with basic care activities and health maintenance. These routines are likely to be carried out many times during the day. The caregivers (e.g., family members and professionals) who provide these routines on a daily basis develop their own routine ways for addressing student needs. The routines used by an adult become highly practiced, especially with students where a particular routine is administered frequently throughout the day. Family members, for example, may become so adept at suctioning through a student's tracheostomy that they can hear a child's breathing and know that suctioning is re-

quired, turn on the machine, and suction while carrying on a conversation with another adult. Routines may become *done to* rather than *with* students, and opportunities where a student might participate in the routine are missed.

All transitional movement, caregiving, and health routines should be carried out as safely and efficiently as possible. Carrying out these routines with students should be as easy as possible and should not require a great deal of time. Students should be active participators in one or more aspects of the routine, even when students are not expected to become fully independent in the routine. Most routines are carried out frequently with students and therefore provide an ideal opportunity for infusing skill improvement objectives into the routine. Skills may be infused into routines when adding this additional component to the routine does not require significantly increased time to accomplish the routine.

Transitional Movement Routines Students with deaf-blindness with physical disabilities may require assistance to move from one location to another or one position to another. Changing the position of a student with physical disabilities may require use of adaptive equipment including adaptive seating; standing equipment, such as supine standers; or other types of equipment (e.g., sidelyers). Equipment is designed to maintain a student in a position that the student is unable to assume or maintain independently. Transitional routines provide an opportunity to teach students independence in changing locations or positions, but for those students whose physical disabilities are severe, transitional routines may provide opportunities for partial participation or skill improvement. Professionals with expertise in teaching students with deaf-blindness are the most logical personnel to develop strategies for teaching independence and for training all individuals associated with a student in the proper use of those strategies. When students have additional physical disabilities, physical or occupational therapists, in collaboration with vision and hearing professionals, determine both the extent to which a student's physical disabilities preclude full independence and the strategies for promoting participation in one or more aspects of the transitional routine.

An ambulatory student with deaf-blindness may be able to initiate hand placement or movement along the wall to be guided by an adult when learning to move around a room or from room to room. A student with multiple disabilities may be able to reach forward with the arms to assist in being lifted or hold onto the adult when being carried. Transitional movement routines provide many opportunities for infusing skill improvement strategies. The specific aspects of transitional movement routines that are selected to provide opportunities for skill improvement, as well as the skills that will be improved, are determined by team members and implemented by everyone who assists a student with transitional movement.

Transitional movement routines need to be accomplished quickly and efficiently in most environments. When a great deal of time is required to move a student from one location or position to another, the routine may serve to isolate the student from participating in the activity for which the location and position are being changed. Only the degree of student participation possible that does not significantly lengthen the time required to carry out the routine is advised. As student participation increases or skill improvement is noted, additional requirements for participation and skill independence can be added.

Physical Care Routines Students with deaf-blindness who also have severe physical disabilities may need to be fed, toileted, dressed, or bathed. Whereas bathing is most likely to take place in the home, other caregiving routines will be implemented in home, school, and community environments. Those students with severe physical disabilities may never be able to care for themselves independently, without assistance or supervision, due to limitations of movement. Toileting, dressing, and bathing require substantial abilities to move the body in space and to use the arms and hands independently. Although most students with even the most severe movement disabilities can learn to eat independently (or with supervision and occasional assistance from another person), many will not be able to dress and undress, bathe, or toilet themselves without help from another person.

When students have visual or auditory impairments, as well as severe physical disabilities, strategies for compensating for the visual impairment may also be difficult to perform. For example, a student with deaf-blindness and difficulty moving may learn to move a spoon or cup to the mouth, but may be unable to use hand movements to determine the depth of liquid in a cup or the location of food on the plate. When the motor disabilities are mild, students with deaf-blindness may learn to perform more components of a caregiving routine. For example, a student may be able to put a shirt on independently when sitting on the floor, but may lack the fine motor/manipulation abilities necessary to determine the position of the shirt in relation to the body (e.g., front/back) or to use cues to select matching clothing. While physical assistance may not be necessary to put on the shirt, supervision and assistance may be required to put the shirt on correctly or to identify an appropriate shirt to wear with another piece of clothing (e.g., pants or a skirt).

Who Can Assist in Physical Care As with transitional movement routines, caregiving routines need to be provided for students in safe and efficient ways in classroom and community environments by everyone who is associated with a student. Other students in a classroom may be able to assist with routines such as feeding, toileting, or putting on clothing. Having another student(s) provide or assist in caregiving routines promotes social inclusion though interactions with other students. Decisions about who can assist in these caregiving routines include consideration of the following factors:

1. How difficult is the routine?
2. Are there students available who are interested in learning how to help the student with disabilities?
3. Can the students be taught to perform the routines safely?
4. Can the needed routine be carried out sufficiently quickly so that time for education is not lost for either the student or the peer helper?

Physical and occupational therapists, another professional, or family members may train other persons to carry out the routines and should then monitor implementation periodically. This training is especially important when students have multiple disabilities or when very specialized procedures may be necessary to provide safe caregiving.

Some routines with some students may be very difficult or may require a great deal of time to implement. A teacher, for example, may have a great deal of difficulty getting the stiff arm of a student with spasticity (i.e., increased tone) through coat sleeves. A classroom assistant may struggle through trying to feed a student in a reasonable amount of time. A family member may find bathing difficult with a child who is not able to sit independently and who is fearful of water. Consultation from physical or occupational therapists or other specialists may be helpful in identifying easier ways to carry out the routine. For students with physical disabilities, use of adaptive equipment such as a bathing chair or changes in the ways in

which a student is positioned may make the routine easier. When caregiving routines are difficult or time-consuming, the purpose of consultation is to improve the ease and decrease the length of time by which the routine is provided.

Partial Participation Caregiving routines offer many opportunities for participation and for infusion of functional skill improvement. Specific instructional strategies may be used during dressing to teach an arm extension movement by using therapeutic facilitation procedures to put the arm through the sleeve of a shirt or coat. Partial participation in a feeding routine can be required by placing the spoon in the student's hand and guiding the spoon to the mouth or by requiring a student to use an existing "yes/no" communication during eating. A risk in using caregiving routines as a context for instruction is that the routine may be made more difficult or time-consuming. For example, a second grader who requires over an hour to eat may miss recess or some other activity in which peers, who are likely to take 30 minutes to eat, are participating. Two primary considerations in deciding whether to provide instruction within the context of routines are: 1) the impact that instruction will have on the length of time required to implement the routine and 2) the importance of the instruction in relation to missed activities.

Health Care Routines   Most students with special health needs can attend school without a full-time nurse if school personnel have been well-trained and are monitored in the implementation of needed health routines. Decisions concerning a student's participation in school and community activities are best made by the team of individuals involved with the student, including the student's family and medical personnel. The services that a student needs, who will be responsible for providing the needed routines, and any plans for teaching a student to be independent in self-administration should be included on the student's individualized education program (IEP) (Council for Exceptional Children, 1988).

Procedures to reduce the risk of liability in schools or other environments should be in place before a student is included in those environments. Such procedures include:

1. Obtaining prescriptions and specific directions for performing any needed procedures
2. Training all individuals who are involved with the student, including personnel such as specialty subject teachers and bus drivers; making sure that both primary personnel (e.g., classroom teacher) and back-up personnel (i.e., individuals who will provide procedures when the primary personnel are absent) are trained in both health routines and emergency procedures
3. Providing information about the student to the companies that service the school (e.g., electric company) as well as to the local emergency medicine personnel

These activities require agreement among parents, physicians, and school and community personnel and documentation on a student's IEP (or other plan) or in some other written form. All parties sign the written form as an indication of both agreement with and knowledge of the occurrence of the activities (Caldwell, Todaro, & Gates, 1989).

Much of the medical equipment that may be needed by students with the most severe health care needs requires electricity to operate, although battery-operated versions of some equipment are available. Classrooms must be equipped with back-up generators when students are dependent on equipment for life-sustaining functions. Procedures that control infection are of great importance. Such procedures include good handwashing technique, washing of toys and materials, and limiting or preventing of contact with other students who may have an infection. Training personnel in both needed health routines and emergency procedures is essential when including students in school and community environments. Parents, nurses providing home care for students, or nurses associated with a particular school or community program may serve as trainers of all the individuals who will be involved with a student. Table 5 outlines recommendations for training personnel and emphasizes the need for all personnel to be competent in im-

Table 5. Recommendations for training personnel to administer health routines and emergency procedures

1. Secure individualized prescriptions and protocols including warning signs and symptoms; develop protocols in collaboration with parents and health care providers.
2. Begin training prior to a student's inclusion in educational or community environments and programs.
3. Train a primary provider (e.g., teacher) and at least one backup provider (e.g., classroom aide, school principal) to administer health routines.
4. Train all personnel who are involved with a student, including the school secretary or principal, to administer emergency procedures.
5. For a designated period, an expert (e.g., trained parent, nurse, other health care provider) should be present for continued training and on-site back-up; length of back-up is determined by the school or community personnel's competency and comfort. At least five administrations of each required health routine with 100% accuracy should be documented before school or community personnel work independently.
6. Document training using an individualized checklist that follows each health routine protocol.
7. Regular rechecks of provision of both health routines and emergency procedures by school and community personnel must be provided by the expert.

plementing ongoing health routines as well as emergency procedures.

Health routines are not as ideal for participation and infusion as are other routines because addressing student health needs is of primary importance. Some students may ultimately achieve independence in health routines, such as administration of medications or simple procedures. Those with severe health needs may be dependent upon other individuals to manage equipment, provide procedures, or deal appropriately with emergencies. For these reasons, health routines should be administered compassionately and as quickly as possible. Prolonging the routine through requirements for participation or new learning may also serve to prolong any unpleasantness associated with the routine.

Many health routines are unpleasant, and students often have no choice about whether the routines are administered. Other choices may be possible within the context of some routines. Some medications, for example, are administered as needed; students may be able to participate in decisions about taking these types of medications. They may also be able to share in decisions about who can administer a particular procedure or when and where the procedure will be provided. When students, even those with multiple disabilities, require a great deal of management of health procedures, only limited control over their own lives may be possible. However, providing opportunities to participate in the routine itself or in decisions concerning the routine allows students opportunities to achieve some measure of independence from caregivers.

Environmental Routines There are many routines that are associated with one or more environments that either have to be provided by another person or performed independently by a student. Standing in lines, getting up in the morning or going to bed at night,

answering the phone, and moving out of a building when the fire alarm has sounded are all examples of these types of routines. These routines are used across environments and by individuals of all ages. In contrast with other types of routines, students need to participate as fully as possible in these routines and, ideally, learn to perform them without assistance from another person. Strategies that compensate for vision, hearing, movement, health, or other disabilities can be used to enable student independence. A student with physical disabilities may be taught to "stand in line" using a wheelchair, or a student with hearing impairments may learn to watch for a blinking light (instead of listening for the fire alarm) or to read the cues of other people in the environment to learn to exit a building.

Environmental routines may be learned initially as part of participation in one or more activities. For example, a student may first learn to stand in line to check out books from the school library and later may transfer this ability to purchasing tickets for a movie, buying groceries, or using an automated bank teller machine. Having learned a routine in one environment helps some students to transfer performance of the routine to another environment or situation. Other students will need assistance in using the routine each time the environmental characteristics or requirements change. For example, a student who has learned to leave the elementary school building during a fire drill may not automatically transfer this skill to the high school and may need to be taught how to exit the high school building. Similarly, a student who has learned how to check a book out of the school library may need assistance to perform this same routine independently in the community library. School programming should be directed toward ensuring student competence in a variety of community environments, and family

members and friends should be knowledgeable about the best ways of teaching a student so that additional learning opportunities are provided.

Promoting Social Inclusion

A main purpose of fully including students
with disabilities in typical home, school, and
community environments is to provide opportunities for students with and without
disabilities to interact socially and to develop
friendships (Brown, Long, Udvari-Solner,
Davis, et al., 1989; Brown et al., 1991).
Adults in any environment model interactions with students with disabilities for the
other students in that environment. When
adults are unsure about interacting with a
student with disabilities, their behavior may
be learned by other individuals in that environment. Similarly, when adults are confident about ways of interacting with students with disabilities, other individuals are
more likely to model accepting interactions.

Special services (e.g., therapies, tutoring,
resource room) needed by some students
with disabilities, as well as caregiving and
health routines, may interfere with social interactions in several ways: 1) the student
with disabilities may be removed from the
environment or activity for administration of
the service or routine, 2) the activity from
which the student is removed may vary in
terms of opportunities for social interactions,
and 3) the need to be removed may "isolate"
the student with disabilities or make him or
her appear significantly different from the
other students in the classroom. For example, when a student is taken to the health
room during lunchtime to be fed by the school
nurse through use of the gastrostomy tube,
the student has been removed from an activity that is highly conducive to social interactions and is made to look significantly different from other students who are eating
lunch in the school cafeteria. Social interac-

tions are more likely to be promoted when a
student who needs to be fed using a tube receives food during lunchtime and in the cafeteria with the other students.

A first step in promoting social inclusion of
students with disabilities is to ensure that
special services and administration of routines do not reduce the number of opportunities for social inclusion. Both the number of times and the length of time a student
is removed from typical environments or
activities should be held to a minimum. Furthermore, the activities from which a student is removed should be those during
which social interactions do not typically occur (e.g., seatwork in an elementary grade,
study hall in a high school).

Social interactions and friendships will
not necessarily develop spontaneously just
because students with disabilities are physically present in the same environments and
activities as their typical-age peers. Social
inclusion can be promoted by use of special
approaches and methods that support social
inclusion (Giangreco & Putnam, 1991; Haring, 1991; Vandercook, York, & Forest, 1989;
see also chap. 11, this volume). In general,
various methods for promoting interactions
and friendships among students with and
without disabilities have included: 1) programs of special friends where students
without disabilities provide access to social
activities that may not be easily accessible by
students with disabilities, 2) models where
students without disabilities function as
helpers or "peer tutors" for those with disabilities, and 3) approaches that attempt to
promote friendships among students with
and without disabilities such as the *Circle
of Friends* model (Vandercook, York, & Forest, 1989). All of these approaches help students with deaf-blindness and those with
physical or health needs participate more
fully in the social life of their schools and
communities.

Ensuring Instructional Inclusion

Responsibility for providing appropriate specialized services is the work of the team of professionals, family members, and friends who are associated with each student. A number of professionals are typically included as members of teams of students with deaf-blindness, including nurses and other medical personnel, physical and occupational therapists, and speech language pathologists, psychologists, job coaches, or transition specialists in addition to general and special educators, vision and hearing specialists, and mobility specialists (Brown, Long, Udvari-Solner, Davis, et al., 1989; Campbell, 1987a; Downing & Eichinger, 1990; Giangreco, 1990). These team members are collectively responsible for supporting the instructional inclusion of students within typical educational and community environments. This responsibility includes ensuring that each student receives maximal opportunities for learning and skill improvement.

Support Teams Supporting instructional inclusion requires professional team members to function in somewhat different ways than have been required in traditional interdisciplinary or transdisciplinary team models. Key differences between traditional team models and support teams are shown in Table 6. A critical difference between the two types of teams is the underlying purpose for each team. Traditional teams have as their purpose the improvement of student performance as well as the remediation of student performance deficits. The purpose of support teams is to enable students with disabilities to be successful within typical environments by promoting participation in activities through supportive assistance and improvement of student performance.

Participation in Activities General education programs can be categorized by their activities and routines. The specific activities that characterize a school differ depending on the age of the students as well as on the teaching practices and philosophy of the

Table 6. Differences between traditional special education teams and school support teams

Function	Traditional teams	Support teams
Evaluation	Deficit-based; result is to identify and focus upon skills that students are unable to perform	Determine eligibility for services (and types of services for which student is eligible)
Assessment	Professionally generated	Generated collaboratively by family members and professionals
Goal setting	Professionals set goals based on evaluation results, either individually by each team member's discipline or collectively by all members	Families establish desired outcomes; may be supplemented by additional outcomes identified by other team members
Type of goals	Developmental or functional skills that a student needs to learn; typically deficit-based; written in measurable or behavioral terms	Activity participation, improvements in routines, or functional skill improvement expressed generically as outcomes, rather than as measurable objectives
Measurement of progress	Continuous or probed measurements of skill performance; professional judgment of degrees of goal attainment	Validation by families or team members of change in outcome status; continuous or probed measurements of skill performance
Services	Determined by professionals; provision model relies on direct service, but may include monitored services or consultation	Determined by families or collectively by team members; provision model combines collaborative consultation, monitored, and direct services

school. A primary goal of educational support teams is to involve all students in school and classroom activities. The expertise of disciplines that are not traditionally part of general education is likely to be required to achieve participation of students with disabilities. Support teams work collaboratively to devise unique means for participation through use of the strategies described in the following paragraphs and illustrated in a case example.

1.   *Modify the materials used:* Many students are able to perform the same activity as their peers by using different instructional materials or supports. A student with both visual impairments and physical disabilities may be able to perform seatwork or written assignments by using a computer equipped with a special keyboard and voice output. A student who is deaf-blind, but without significant physical disabilities, may be able to perform the same tasks using large-print (or large-sized picture) materials. Students who are able to perform the same or similar activity content as their peers are supported in doing so through the use of materials that compensate for their disabilities.

2.   *Modify the requirements of the activity:* A student who is unable to work as fast as other students can be required to do fewer math problems or read fewer pages than other students in the class. A student with disabilities in a general preschool program can be required to participate in two learning stations when other children are expected to work at three or four stations. Life jackets and other swimming equipment can be used to teach a student to move in the water while other students may be learning to swim. The support team identifies ways in which students with disabilities can learn in relation to their individual needs while still participating with peers who may be learning different skills within the same content area.

3.   *Substitute skills:* Substitute skills that a student can do independently for those that

a student is unable to perform. Magnetic letters that can be manipulated by a student with deaf-blindness may be used in learning to "write" letters when other students are learning to write stories. A student with visual impairments can learn to find his or her locker by recognizing a particular tactile stimulus taped to the outside, rather than by reading his or her name.

4.   *Use peers to provide assistance:* Peers can be taught to provide assistance for students with disabilities. For example, another student can help a student with disabilities complete an art project, manage containers during mealtime, or select a book or videotape from the library. When other students assist their peers with disabilities, social interactions can occur that are not possible when all assistance is provided by adults.

5.   *Substitute another activity:* When students with disabilities are deficient in many skills, ensuring participation in particular activities may be difficult without total assistance by an adult. It makes little sense to provide one-on-one assistance from an adult in an activity that requires skills a student may never learn to carry out independently. For a student who is deaf-blind and is not yet able to add and subtract, it is more appropriate to provide tutoring in braille or to teach mobility during an eighth-grade algebra class than to have an adult help the student do math in the back of the class. Teaching a student to perform a job within school or at a community site may be more appropriate for a student with severe disabilities than attending a ninth-grade history class. Decisions concerning activity substitution are made by support team members by weighing the relative merits of removing a student to provide participation in another activity.

The strategies described here were used by the support team for an 8-year-old student with deaf-blindness and physical disabilities named Michael, who was enrolled in his neighborhood school in a typical second-grade classroom. Michael's first full inclusion in a general education classroom began in this second-grade class. Michael had received specialized services for children with deaf-blindness since infancy, but he had been partly included in kindergarten and first grade in this same neighborhood school. Because Michael had benefited considerably from interactions with the other children, a decision was made to fully include him in the second grade.

The second grade included both academic activities (e.g., reading groups, arithmetic, language arts, science) and nonacademic activities (e.g., field-trips, art, music, physical education, lunch, recess). In addition, the school sponsored a number of after-school activities including sports, special interest clubs, and groups such as Boy Scouts. The general education teacher and the support team members worked together closely to problem solve and implement strategies that would ensure Michael's maximum participation in all school activities. An essential feature of this cooperative relationship was planning. The general education teacher completed her lesson plans 1–2 weeks in advance and shared her plans with the specialists working with Michael. Knowing what information the teacher was planning to teach (e.g., content) and how she planned to teach the information (e.g., strategies, teaching methods) provided the support team with data that would help them work out ways for Michael to participate as fully as possible.

Michael was not yet able to read and was unable to recognize letters visually, even when they were presented in large print and with different visual contrasts. Michael's hand manipulation skills were limited due to spasticity in his hands, which were held closed (or in a fisted position) most of the time. Michael's hearing was his strong sensory area and appeared better when aided by an auditory trainer. The support team determined that Michael could best participate in reading in two ways. First, several students in the classroom who were learning to read out loud were placed in a reading group with Michael. These students took turns and used a phonic system to provide amplification for Michael when they were reading out loud. The teacher also used the amplification system when asking comprehension questions and leading a discussion about the content of what the students were reading. The students answered these questions verbally. Michael was also asked questions, although he was unable to respond verbally by talking. The teacher frequently simplified the language of the questions addressed to Michael and initially phrased questions so that Michael was able to respond with "yes," "no," or "I don't know." These three responses were available to him through a switch-operated device that connected each of three switches to three tape recorders with fixed loop (i.e., answering machine) tapes. The switches used were large so that Michael was able to activate the correct switch by banging it with his closed fist.

During this discussion activity, Michael was encouraged to respond verbally and to open his hand so that the switch was activated with an open hand. The teacher achieved this by allowing Michael to respond in any way possible and then encouraging him or having another student assist him to activate the switch with an open hand. Michael learned not only to listen to the story and its contents, but to comprehend and correctly answer simple questions about the story. In addition, over time the other children and the environmental demands in general functioned to "teach" Michael to activate the switches consistently and independently with an open hand. This movement was important for Michael because eventually he would need to learn to isolate a finger for use at a voice-output computer that allowed him to express himself more fully.

In the second grade, the teacher and the support team members accomplished several things. First, they planned ahead so that sufficient time was available to make any necessary modifications. Second, they assisted Michael so that he not only participated, but he also was able to learn a new skill (hitting the switch with an open hand and vocalizing) that would provide a basis for future learning. Finally, they recognized that the activity provided Michael with an opportunity to learn essential skills such as touching an object with an open hand and vocalizing in response to a question. The team used strategies of modifying the requirements of the reading activity, substituting skills that a student can do independently for those that a student is unable to perform, and using peers to provide assistance in order to ensure Michael's full participation in second grade reading instruction.

Infusing Instructional Strategies for Skill Improvement Students with severe or multiple disabilities may never learn to participate in activities independent from supports or may need to learn skills that are more basic than those required in an activity. Teaching individually needed skills within the context of one or more activities provides a means for addressing student instructional needs while achieving physical and social inclusion. Many activities provide a context within which other skills can be taught. Motor skills such as reaching, pointing, holding, or object manipulation are ideally infused within many typical activities (Campbell, 1987b). Communication skills are also easily infused. A student may be taught within the context of activities to signal using vocalization, a communication device, or words or signs (see chap. 10, this volume).

Specific strategies that will be used to teach a student a desired behavior (or skill) are infused within the particular activity and held constant across other activities. These strategies reflect and combine the expertise of support team members in order to design strategies that are unique to student needs. Strategies for teaching a student with deaf-blindness and physical disabilities to communicate using object cues would reflect sensory needs as well as the physical abilities of the student to grasp objects (Rowland & Stremel-Campbell, 1987). Designing unique instructional strategies that integrate the input from several disciplines has been described as a critical feature of integrated programming teams (e.g., Campbell, 1987a; Dunn, 1991). These integrated strategies increase the likelihood that students with multiple disabilities will acquire the desired skills because they provide increased opportunities for students to practice a desired behavior.

REFERENCES

Batshaw, M.L., & Perret, Y.M. (1992). *Children with disabilities: A medical primer* (3rd ed.). Baltimore: Paul H. Brookes Publishing Co.

Baumgart, D., Brown, L., Pumpian, I., Nisbet, J., Ford, A., Sweet, M., Messina, R., & Schroeder, J. (1982). Principle of partial participation and individualized adaption in education programs for severely handicapped students. *Journal of The Association for Persons with Severe Handicaps, 7*(2), 17–27.

Brown, L., Long, E., Udvari-Solner, A., Davis, L., VanDeventer, P., Ahlgren, C., Johnson, F., Gruenewald, L., & Jorgensen, J. (1989). The home school: Why students with severe intellectual disabilities must attend the schools of their brothers, sisters, friends, and neighbors. *Journal of The Association for Persons with Severe Handicaps, 14*(1), 1–7.

Brown, L., Long, E., Udvari-Solner, A., Schwarz, P., VanDeventer, P., Ahlgren, C., Johnson, F., Gruenewald, L., & Jorgensen, J. (1989). Should students with severe intellectual disabilities be based in regular or in special education classrooms in home schools? *Journal of The Association for Persons with Severe Handicaps, 14*(1), 8–12.

Brown, L., Schwarz, P., Udvari-Solner, A., Kampschroer, E.F., Johnson, J., & Gruenewald, L. (1991). How much time should students with severe intellectual disabilities spend in regular education classrooms and elsewhere? *Journal of The Association for Persons with Severe Handicaps, 16*(1), 39–47.

Bullis, M., & Otos, M. (1988). Characteristics of programs for children with deaf-blindness: Results of a national survey. *Journal of The Association for Persons with Severe Handicaps, 13*(2), 110–115.

Caldwell, T.H., & Kirkhart, K. (1991). Accessing the education system for students who require health technology and treatment. In N.J. Hochstadt & D.M. Yost (Eds.), *The medically complex child* (pp. 122–135). United Kingdom: Harwood Academic.

Caldwell, T.H., Todaro, A., & Gates, A.J. (1989). *Community provider's guide: An information outline for working with children with special needs in the community.* New Orleans, LA: Children's Hospital.

Campbell, P.H. (1987a). The integrated programming team: An approach for coordinating professionals of various disciplines in programs for students with severe and multiple handicaps. *Journal of The Association for Persons with Severe Handicaps, 12*(2), 107–116.

Campbell, P.H. (1987b). Integrated programming for students with multiple handicaps. In L. Goetz, D. Guess, & K. Stremel-Campbell (Eds.), *Innovative program design for individuals with dual sensory impairments* (pp. 159–188). Baltimore: Paul H. Brookes Publishing Co.

Campbell, P.H. (1989). Students with physical disabilities. In R. Gaylord-Ross (Ed.), *Integration strategies for students with handicaps* (pp. 53–76). Baltimore: Paul H. Brookes Publishing Co.

Campbell, P.H. (1991a). *Assessment strategies for determining intervention approaches, models, and methods for infants and toddlers.* Akron, OH: Children's Hospital Medical Center of Akron.

Campbell, P.H. (1991b). Evaluation and assessment in early intervention for infants and toddlers. *Journal of Early Intervention, 15*(1), 36–45.

Campbell, P.H. (Ed.). (1992). *The preschool integration network training manual.* Akron, OH: Children's Hospital Medical Center of Akron.

Campbell, P.H. (1993). Physical management and handling procedures. In M. Snell (Ed.), *Instruction of students with severe disabilities* (pp. 248–263). Columbus, OH: Macmillan/Merrill.

Campbell, P.H., & Bailey, K. (1991). Issues in health care in the education of students with the most severe disabilities. In M.C. Wang, M. Reynolds, & H. Walberg (Eds.), *Handbook of special education. Vol. IV* (pp. 143–160). Oxford: Pergamon Press.

Campbell, P.H., Cooper, M.A., & McInerney, W.F. (1984). Therapeutic programming for students with severe handicaps. *American Journal of Occupational Therapy, 38*(9), 594–602.

Campbell, P.H., & Forsyth, S. (1993). Integrated programming and movement disabilities. In M. Snell (Ed.), *Instruction of students with severe disabilities (4th ed.)* (pp. 264–289). Columbus, OH: Macmillan/Merrill.

Campbell, P.H., Strickland, B., & LaForme, C. (1992). Enhancing parent participation in individual family services plan. *Topics in Early Childhood Special Education, 11*(4), 112–124.

Council for Exceptional Children's Ad Hoc Committee on Medically Fragile Students. (1988). *Report of the council for exceptional children's ad hoc committee on medically fragile students.* Reston, VA: Council for Exceptional Children.

de Vries, L.S., Dubowitz, L.M.S., Dubowitz, V., & Pennock, J.M. (1990). *Color atlas of brain disorders in the newborn.* Chicago: Year Book Medical Publishers.

Downing, J., & Eichinger, J. (1990). Instructional strategies for learners with dual sensory impairments in integrated settings. *Journal of The Association for Persons with Severe Handicaps, 15*(2), 98–105.

Dunn, W. (1991). Integrated related services. In L.H. Meyer, C.A. Peck, & L. Brown (Eds.), *Critical issues in the lives of people with severe disabilities* (pp. 353–377). Baltimore: Paul H. Brookes Publishing Co.

Ferguson, D.L., & Baumgart, D. (1991). Partial participation revisited. *Journal of The Association for Persons with Severe Handicaps, 16*(4), 218–227.

Fitzhardinge, P.M., & Pape, K.E. (1982). Follow-up studies in the high-risk newborn. In G.B. Avery (Ed.), *Neonatology* (2nd ed.). Philadelphia: J.B. Lippincott.

Fredericks, H.D.B., & Baldwin, V.L. (1987). Individuals with sensory impairments: Who are they? How are they educated? In L. Goetz,

D. Guess, & K. Stremel-Campbell (Eds.), *Innovative program design for individuals with dual sensory impairments* (pp. 3–12). Baltimore: Paul H. Brookes Publishing Co.

Giangreco, M.F. (1990). Making related service decisions for students with severe disabilities: Roles, criteria, and authority. *Journal of The Association for Persons with Severe Handicaps, 15*(1), 22–31.

Giangreco, M.F., & Putnam, J.W. (1991). Supporting the education of students with severe disabilities in regular education environments. In L.H. Meyer, C.A. Peck, & L. Brown (Eds.), *Critical issues in the lives of people with severe disabilities* (pp. 245–270). Baltimore: Paul H. Brookes Publishing Co.

Giangreco, M.F., York, J., & Rainforth, B. (1989). Providing related services to learners with severe handicaps in educational settings: Pursuing the least restrictive option. *Pediatric Physical Therapy, 1*(2), 55–63.

Graff, J.C., Ault, M.M., Guess, D., Taylor, M., & Thompson, B. (1990). *Health care for students with disabilities: An illustrated medical guide for the classroom.* Baltimore: Paul H. Brookes Publishing Co.

Haring, T.G. (1991). Social relationships. In L.H. Meyer, C.A. Peck, & L. Brown (Eds.), *Critical issues in the lives of people with severe disabilities* (pp. 195–217). Baltimore: Paul H. Brookes Publishing Co.

Holvoet, J.F., & Helmstetter, E. (1989). *Medical problems of students with special needs: A guide for educators.* Boston: College Hill Press.

Jaudes, P.K. (1991). The medical care of children with complex home health care needs: An overview for caretakers. In N.J. Hochstadt & D.M. Yost (Eds.), *The medically complex child* (pp. 29–60). United Kingdom: Harwood Academic.

Kohrman, A.F. (1991). Medical technology: Implications for health care and social service providers. In N.J. Hochstadt & D.M. Yost (Eds.), *The medically complex child* (pp. 3–13). United Kingdom: Harwood Academic.

Linehan, S.A., Brady, M.P., & Hwang, C. (1991). Ecological versus developmental assessment: Influences on instructional exceptions. *Journal of The Association for Persons with Severe Handicaps, 16*(3), 146–153.

Michael, M., & Paul, P. (1991). Early intervention for infants with deaf-blindness. *Exceptional Children, 57*(3), 200–210.

Rainforth, B., York, J., & Macdonald, C. (1992).

Collaborative teams for students with severe disabilities: Integrating therapy and educational services. Baltimore: Paul H. Brookes Publishing Co.

Rainforth, B., York, J., Macdonald, C., & Dunn, W. (1992). Collaborative assessment. In B. Rainforth, J. York, & C. Macdonald, *Collaborative teams for students with severe disabilities: Integrating therapy and educational services.* Baltimore: Paul H. Brookes Publishing Co.

Rowland, C., & Stremel-Campbell, K. (1987). Share and share alike: Conventional gestures to emergent language for learners with sensory impairments. In L. Goetz, D. Guess, & K. Stremel-Campbell (Eds.), *Innovative program design for individuals with dual sensory impairments* (pp. 49–75). Baltimore: Paul H. Brookes Publishing Co.

Stremel, K., Molden, V., Leister, C., Matthews, J., Wilson, R., Goodall, D., & Holston, J. (1990). *Communication systems and routines: A decision making process.* Hattiesburg: University of Southern Mississippi, Department of Special Education.

Vandercook, T., York, F., & Forest, M. (1989). The McGill action planning system (MAPS): A strategy for building the vision. *Journal of The Association for Persons with Severe Handicaps, 14*(3), 205–215.

Chapter 14

Orientation and Mobility

Access, Information, and Travel

Kathleen Gee,
Joan Houghton,
Rona L. Pogrund,
and Richard Rosenberg

Rich McGann, an individual with deaf-blindness as a result of Usher syndrome, reveals what it was like growing up with a profound, bilateral hearing loss and, at least initially, a substantial amount of useful vision:

> I was a good speech reader and I had a neighbor who knew sign language, but going to the deaf club, I would depend on an area where there was a lot of light so I could catch signing and speech reading at the same time. When it got dark, I was at a loss. I guess I was hiding my vision impairment to my friends because I was afraid that I wouldn't be accepted [because of] the fact I was going blind. (Virginia Commonwealth University & Helen Keller National Center, 1993)

Mr. McGann relates how reduced vision, caused by retinitis pigmentosa (RP), affected his ability to travel:

> Sometimes when I'd go into restaurants, walking from a lighted area into a dark area, I would kick the tables in the restaurant or bump into them. I would be asked to leave, or was thrown out of restaurants, because people were under the impression that I did not have all my faculties about me. . . .

> Before I met my future wife I did not use the cane, but when I met her I shared my experiences with her. She said that I had to accept it and start using a cane. I said no, no I thought it was negative—it was a negative reflection of myself. She said, no cane, no marriage. I thought about that and decided I would use the cane. So, one morning I went to work on the bus. As I got off the bus, I knew that this intersection was extremely busy, and traffic was going back and forth. I took out my folding cane and started across the street for the first time. I could see some of the traffic coming because I still had a little vision. I noticed cars actually stopped for me as I crossed the street. When I reached work I called my wife and said how amazing it was that the traffic stopped for me because they were able to identify that I had a visual impairment. Since then, I have used a cane everyday. (Virginia Commonwealth University & Helen Keller National Center, 1993)

Mirika, a seven-year-old student with CHARGE Association, has a fluctuating, mixed loss in one ear and a profound sensorineural loss in the other ear. She has reduced visual functioning in one eye; the other eye has been removed. Mirika also has heart disease and motor disabilities in her lower extremities, and she is fed by a gastrostomy tube. When one of the authors, an orientation and mobility (O&M) consultant, asked Mirika's mother where she would like Mirika to travel and what Mirika's travel needs were, her mother responded:

> I want her to be safe. My biggest fear is she will leave the house and crawl out in the country somewhere and we would not know it. We would never be able to find her . . . or she could be bitten by a rattler out in the field. Also, I would like for her to be able to tell somebody if she got lost or was in danger, but that is a little too much to expect. I would like to work on something where she could go to the back door or her bathroom to play in the tub if she wanted to. Right now, she will scream if she wants to go there and I end up carrying her. It is getting hard on my back—me lifting her and all.

The above testimonies describe a small piece of the impact that vision and hearing losses have on an individual's ability to travel, communicate, work, adjust, and live. Parents of infants and toddlers with deaf-blindness have consistently reported the need for early intervention that includes orientation and mobility, as well as communication skills training, to compensate for their child's reduced ability to receive and give information through the primary learning senses (Alsop, 1993; Cornelius, 1994; Morgan, 1992; O'Donnell & Livingston, 1991). The nature of deaf-blindness requires individuals to construct concepts and knowledge from depleted sources of information. This has a significant impact on the individual's mobility and the ways in which she or he accesses people and things in the environment. In turn, this affects cognitive and social growth as well as

the development of self-esteem and social relationships (Downing & Eichinger, 1990; Gee, 1993).

With the development of inclusive school practices and the passage of the Americans with Disabilities Act of 1990 (PL 101-336), the issues in service delivery for individuals with deaf-blindness of all ages are receiving increased attention. National and local surveys; national symposiums; and interviews with consumers, technical assistance providers, and syndrome-specific groups have attempted to delineate the priority needs of individuals with deaf-blindness (Chen, 1992; Collins, 1992; Davenport, 1992; "Deaf-blindness," 1990; Enos, 1993; Kennedy, 1990; Seiler, Everson, & Carr, 1992; Watson, 1992; "Which problems," 1980). Results from the majority of surveys revealed work, communication, travel, and community living as the priority needs reported by consumers and their families ("Deaf-blindness," 1990; Watson, 1992; "Which problems," 1980). In addition, the surveys have reported the need for technical assistance to the agencies who provide services to individuals with deaf-blindness (Seiler et al., 1992). These findings are consistent across both educational and adult services (Collins, 1992; Davenport, 1992; Kennedy, 1990; Watson, 1992). Chen (1992) has also identified the need for family services and supports, and program models for early intervention programs.

Speculation as to why these identified priorities exist includes such possible explanations as: 1) limited availability of services, living arrangements, and employment opportunities; 2) the specific and varied receptive and expressive communication modes needed across many environments; and 3) the varied orientation and mobility skills needed across environments (Seiler et al., 1992). Inclusive schooling and the changing standards of positive outcomes from school to work and community living make safe, efficient mobility an important goal for all students with deaf-blindness. Indeed, quality of life for individuals with deaf-blindness often includes a discussion of mobility in addition to communication and social relationships.

Despite the instructional technology now available, there is a relatively small data base of validated strategies to teach orientation and mobility to individuals with deaf-blindness, including infants and young children and those individuals with cognitive and/or physical disabilities in addition to deaf-blindness (cf. Bailey & Head, 1993; Bryant & Jansen, 1980; Chen, 1992; Cioffi, 1994; Davies, 1990; Everson, 1994; Gamble, 1980; Gee, Harrell, & Rosenberg, 1987; Houghton, 1993, in press; Lubecki, 1994; Michaud, 1990; Sauerburger, 1994). Early orientation and mobility techniques, as well as an understanding of some of the underlying processes of independent travel (Eisenberg, 1979; Hill & Ponder, 1976; Welsh & Blasch, 1980), were developed primarily by professionals focusing on persons whose only disability was a visual impairment or blindness. However, since the 1940s the field of orientation and mobility has expanded rapidly. After World War II, the long cane and the touch technique method of travel were developed. It was not until 1953, at the first conference on mobility, that an expansion of orientation and mobility services provided to blind war veterans was considered for children and civilian adults (Welsh & Blasch, 1980).

Professional licensing for O&M instructors began in 1959, and the 1960s brought the introduction of specific training strategies and sequences. Services were still primarily limited to persons whose only disability was blindness. For these individuals, orientation and mobility instruction has been community-based and functional in nature. Instruction of travel skills is provided in the person's home, school, community, or work environment. This instruction includes conceptual and discrimination skills and other aspects of orientation considered necessary for successful, independent travel. Instruction is, however, based on a strictly ordered curriculum sequence.

Since the 1960s there has been an expanding application of orientation and mobility sequences and techniques with a wider, more varied population, including individuals with low vision; elderly persons with acquired visual impairments; and infants, preschoolers, and individuals with multiple disabilities. Traditional applications of orientation and mobility assessments and curricula to persons with deaf-blindness and/or other severe disabilities, however, have been known to exclude these individuals from the opportunity to increase their mobility. Instruction typically stresses the acquisition of certain presumed, prerequisite abilities—conceptual, psychomotor, and affective—on a step-by-step basis prior to the introduction of travel skills. Many persons with severe, multiple disabilities may never acquire the "prerequisites" to begin instruction in travel skills. The heavy reliance on the use of verbal instruction and verbal feedback (Lolli, 1980) that is also typical of traditional orientation and mobility instruction may exclude young children, persons with deaf-blindness, and persons with cognitive disabilities.

Although it is recognized that the level of one's conceptual, motor, communicative, and social abilities will directly influence the speed and degree of acquisition of orientation and mobility skills, some professionals in the field of O&M have also recognized the importance of *semi-independent travel*, and the positive effects of successful *independent and semi-independent movement* for individuals with severe, multiple disabilities (Bailey & Head, 1993; Bryant & Jansen, 1980; Gamble, 1980). Others have begun to recognize that alternative instructional strategies and curricular decisions are necessary for teaching O&M skills successfully to individuals with deaf-blindness (Chen, 1992; Cioffi, 1994; Collins, 1992; Davies, 1990; Everson, 1994; Gee et al., 1987; Houghton, in press; 1993; Lubecki, 1994; Michaud, 1990; Sauerburger, 1994).

The purpose of this chapter is to provide a framework for the development of instructional programs designed to teach orientation and mobility skills to individuals with deaf-blindness, including individuals with additional cognitive, physical, or behavioral disabilities. It is an attempt to utilize the techniques of safe, efficient travel developed by the field of orientation and mobility in conjunction with current effective, best instructional practices within inclusive schools and communities. The model is based on the premise that the contexts for instruction of orientation and mobility skills, from the most basic to the most advanced, should be motivating, natural situations (participation in the contexts of general class and school activities, the community, and work environments) that require movement or travel.

RATIONALE AND THEORETICAL PERSPECTIVE

Traditionally, literature from the field of O&M has focused on assessment and intervention programs that stress the development of prerequisite sensory, motor, and conceptual skills (Harley, Wood, & Merbler, 1975, 1980). A precise teaching approach to O&M skills using a developmental/sequential approach was developed by Harley, Wood, et al. in 1975 and later adapted by the same authors (1980). The resulting assessment and programmed instruction, known as the *Peabody Mobility Scale*, was successful in teaching basic O&M skills to students with moderate, multiple disabilities. In another report, Merbler and Wood (1984) concluded that there

was a moderate to high correlation between students' performance scores on the sensory, concept, and motor subscales and their performance on the mobility skills scale. Additional authors have outlined many developmental concepts believed to relate to O&M skills (Foulke, 1971; Hapeman, 1967; Kay, 1974; Welsh & Blasch, 1980). This body of literature is often used as the basis to support the use of certain sensory, motor, and conceptual skills as prerequisites for instruction in independent travel and cane use and, in many instances, for the receipt of O&M services.

Despite the increasing use of various O&M assessment tools and instructional techniques, authors have noted as problems the wide variability among learners and the lack of knowledge of the interactions among the processes of perception, spatial learning, and actual mobility (Bailey & Head, 1993; Heydt, 1992; Schingledecker & Foulke, 1978; Welsh & Blasch, 1980). Conflicting reports regarding the processes involved in mobility and the complexity of travel within natural environments cast doubt on the ability to determine the specific cognitive, sensory, and motor skills necessary for successful mobility within various environments (Houghton, in press; Miller, 1982; Reiser, Gruth, & Hill, 1982; Strelow, 1985). Miller (1982) concluded that there was little relationship between the level of mobility and the development of positional concepts and that, in fact, they are two separate entities. Singer (1966) demonstrated high task specificity among individual motor abilities, supporting Miller's conclusion that the development of conceptual skills and levels of mobility are highly specific, yet equally important, skills.

In a comprehensive discussion of cognitive and perceptual processes related to mobility, Strelow (1985) describes the ability to travel as involving no single principle; rather, any or all perceptual and conceptual strategies could be involved in any particular instance of travel. He discusses certain mobility tasks as being purely perceptual as well as other situations where concepts and memory play a more important role. Strelow states that the person's ability to take in information useful for travel and the ability to use this information based on previous experience will determine successful mobility. He further proposes that the difference in travel without sight is found in the informational bases available to the traveler. Determining information sources and the actual information most useful to a student on each part of any particular route is a difficult task, made even more complex by the everchanging stimulus field created as the student moves.

Although relatively little is understood about the relationship between mobility and discrete travel skills, many mobility programs still require successful performance on certain sensory discrimination tasks, as well as demonstrated understanding of certain spatial and positional concepts prior to instruction in movement and travel or more advanced skills in these areas. Recommended instruction for students with multiple, severe disabilities has tended to follow the same basic sequences, but at a slower pace (Bryant & Jansen, 1980; Hill & Ponder, 1976; Heydt, 1992; Jacobson, 1993). Some programs suggest adaptations and modifications within skill sequences and environments to enhance the acquisition of travel skills for students with additional disabilities including deaf-blindness. Other programs emphasize receptive and expressive communication skills needed during travel for community members who are not familiar with sign language or tactile communication modes. These skills are used when an individual needs to request information, ask for assistance, and seek emergency aid (Pogrund, Healy, et al., 1993; Sauerburger, 1993). Many programs discuss the importance of student participation in activities that include O&M skills training within functional environments.

During the last decade, orientation and mobility training for infants and preschoolers has received increased attention as a content area of priority in early intervention programs for children with visual impairments (American Foundation for the Blind, 1983; Hill, Rosen, Correa, & Langley, 1984; Joffee, 1988; Warren, 1978). There has been a growing recognition of the importance of providing young children with opportunities to explore and gain purposeful movement with or without the use of mobility aids (Blind Children's Center, 1993; O'Donnell & Livingston, 1991). Areas typically emphasized in early instructional materials for the development of orientation and mobility skills are:

- Sensory skills
- Concept development
- Motor development
- Environmental awareness
- Community awareness
- Formal orientation and mobility techniques (Dodson-Burk & Hill, 1989b; Hill et al., 1984; Joffee, 1988)

Adaptations to Standard Practice

Rather than continue with a readiness model, some authors have suggested that adaptations to the standard practice be made (Hill & Ponder, 1976) and that *splinter skills* or *route travel* be taught to individuals with deaf-blindness in order to increase independence and participation in daily activities (Gamble, 1980). Drawing a distinction between route travel and independent travel skills, Gamble suggests that students can be taught specific routes to home, work, and recreational areas even if they are unable to learn skills that will make them successful independent travelers in unfamiliar environments. She also suggests that splinter skills—

skills specific for a particular response, but often not transferable to another situation—be taught to assist the student to function in present and future environments. Careful evaluation of the student and his or her skills is recommended to ensure that the right decision is made when teaching splinter skills versus generalizable mobility skills.

Teaching O&M Skills Within Naturally Occurring Routines

Despite the fact that instructional activities that are functional, meaningful, preferential, and socially integrated have been proven to be effective for students with deaf-blindness and multiple disabilities to acquire and maintain skills (Downing & Eichinger, 1990; Gee, 1993; Gee, Alwell, Graham, & Goetz, 1994; Gee, Graham, & Goetz, 1994; Goetz, Guess, & Stremel-Campbell, 1987; Utley & Nelson, 1991), few programs address the need for O&M instruction to occur in a distributed fashion, within naturally occurring routines that are student-centered, age-appropriate, and useful (Bailey & Head, 1993; Gee et al., 1987; Goetz & Gee, 1987a, 1987b; Houghton, in press). In one study, Gee and Goetz (1985) taught four students with severe disabilities, including blindness, four specific O&M skills (i.e., a modified trailing technique, maneuvering around obstacles, trailing around corners, and crossing short open spaces with no trailing surface) within the context of several functional travel routes. Despite their failure to pass the conceptual and sensory skills on the *Peabody Mobility Scale*, these students were able to learn the O&M skills successfully. These same students were also able to generalize the use of these O&M skills to new and unfamiliar routes and environments. In addition, they demonstrated evidence of incidental learning of the landmarks, clues, and memory tasks specific to the training routes. The students acquired semi-independent travel

—travel with supervision and occasional assistance—to specific destinations and activities within designated environments. They also gained valuable O&M skills that are basic to travel in almost any environment or route.

Pogrund, Healy, et al. (1993) included a separate section in their curriculum for working with students who have multiple disabilities. They stated:

> It is the responsibility of the orientation and mobility instructor to pick and choose skills to be taught. The decision can be made by skipping around, starting lower on the hierarchy, or applying the skill to specific settings or activities. (p. 22)

Instructional strategies in Pogrund, Healy, et al.'s curriculum specific to students with multiple disabilities include: 1) using a team approach, 2) teaching within daily routines and activities that are meaningful and reinforcing to the student, 3) building a good relationship with the student, 4) using different types of prompts, 5) reducing the level of prompts once proficiency is demonstrated, 6) using different prompts during different parts of the lesson, 7) using repetition and consistency to achieve progress, 8) knowing which students would not benefit from teaching skills in a hierarchy, 9) using community-based instruction, 10) being familiar with the student's communication, 11) incorporating flexibility, and 12) having high expectations.

Early O&M Intervention

An abundance of curricular guides, screening instruments, skills checklists, and activities of orientation and mobility for infants and preschoolers with visual impairments have recently become available to practitioners and parents (Blind Childrens Center, 1993; Bolton, 1989; Chen, Friedman, & Calvello, 1990; Dodson-Burk & Hill, 1989a, 1989b; Morgan, 1992). The majority of scales and curricular guides are designed for children with visual impairments without accompanying disabilities and are developmental in nature; however, there are a few resources available that include strategies for infants and toddlers with deaf-blindness, with or without additional disabilities (Alsop, 1993; Blind Childrens Center, 1993; Chen et al., 1990; Pogrund, Healy, et al., 1993). Skill development within these particular curricular guides includes enriched sensory environments, concept development, establishing routines and instructional sequences, possible environmental adaptations, gross motor development, positioning, orientation, purposeful movement with or without a mobility device, and protective techniques. Although most of these guides emphasize the importance of prerequisite skill development, several include suggestions for partial participation, functional and embedded skills, environmental modifications and adaptations, and meaningful activities regardless of whether the child has met prerequisite skills (Pogrund, Healy, et al., 1993).

Another recent development in orientation and mobility for toddlers and children is the use and instruction of adaptive mobility devices (Clarke, 1988; Foy, Kirchner, & Waple, 1991; Foy, Von Scheden, & Waiculonis, 1992; Kronick, 1987; Morse, 1980; Pogrund, Fazzi, & Lampert, 1992). Two of the first published uses of adaptive mobility devices were modifications made on long canes, one for a student with deaf-blindness (Morse, 1980) and one for a student with visual impairments and multiple disabilities (Kronick, 1987). These devices were designed for students who did not have the skills necessary to manipulate a traditional long cane for efficient travel within their environments. Researchers believed that adapted canes provided these students with: 1) protection from drop-offs and barriers and 2) environmental

information to make decisions for maneuvering around barriers and obstacles within their paths of travel.

Alsop (1993) and Clarke (1988) described the use of push toys as appropriate mobility devices for young toddlers who are beginning to demonstrate self-initiated movement and exploration outside of their immediate environments. Alsop (1993) noted factors that restrict movement in a child with deaf-blindness. She stressed the importance of providing children with tools that will allow access to their environments and the necessity to build self-confidence in travel. Clarke (1988) emphasized the importance of determining whether the mobility toy or device serves an an enabler, allowing the child opportunities to interact with the environment or barrier, or limits interactions with objects and people. Some of the push toys included large wooden trucks and weighted kiddie grocery carts.

Foy et al. (1991) developed a mobility device specifically for the use of preschoolers called the Connecticut Precane, which took the place of the previously used hulahoop. The advantages of the Precane included: 1) protection, 2) ease of use, 3) minimal training, 4) inexpensive cost, and 5) detection of barriers and drop-offs. Pogrund, Fazzi, and Schreier (1993) reported the use of "kiddy canes" (a child-size long cane) for preschoolers. Kiddy cane advantages they identified were: 1) a child-size grip that promoted proper finger position, 2) lightness in weight for easier handling, and 3) provisional feedback to keep the tip pointing downward. Skellenger and Hill (1991) reported that the primary reason O&M specialists used the long cane for preschoolers was to increase their confidence in movement. The most common factor that influenced O&M specialists to begin long cane instruction for preschoolers was the opportunity for self-initiated movement.

Discrepancies exist in the literature as to whether to begin instruction with the pre-cane and then move to a kiddy cane or to start instruction with a kiddy cane imme-diately (Clarke, Sainato, & Ward, 1994; Po-grund et al., 1992; Pogrund & Rosen, 1989). Foy et al. (1991) and Foy et al. (1992) in-tended the precane to be used by preschool-ers who did not have their motor skills suffi-ciently developed to manipulate a long cane, but still needed a device that would provide them with safety and protection during move-ment. After preschoolers acquired the skills of hand position and arc swing and were able to detect obstacles consistently with the pre-cane, they were moved on to a kiddy cane. Pogrund, Fazzi, et al. (1993) noted factors to consider when deciding to use a precane or a kiddy cane: 1) the child's motivation, 2) other disabilities that would interfere with the child's ability to be protected by a kiddy cane, and 3) whether the device is socially and age appropriate. Clarke et al. (1994) conducted a study to determine the effec-tiveness of long cane and precane devices of four preschoolers with visual impairments. The results revealed that: 1) the precane pro-vided more protection for the participants than did the long cane, 2) all of the children used the precane device more effectively than the long cane (they received training on both devices), 3) the children maintained skills when using precane devices, and 4) the majority of parents felt the precane had more positive effects on their childrens' travel skills.

Person-Centered Instruction

LaShawn, a 20-year-old with deaf-blindness as a result of rubella, has a moderate, bilateral, sen-sorineural hearing loss and a bilateral visual condi-tion as a result of secondary glaucoma. LaShawn wears bilateral hearing aids and tinted prescriptive lenses. He has an acuity loss and a 30-degree visual field in both eyes. LaShawn was sent to a private re-habilitation center for training in adult life skills.

When interviewed about the types of environments that he travels at home, he signed, "a quiet rural set-ting." The downtown area of his home town consists of two blocks and does not have any traffic controls; there are no sidewalks. LaShawn wanted to learn how to cross the street safely in a downtown area with no traffic controls and how to travel from a rural neighborhood to town. After an assessment of mo-bility in both indoor and outdoor environments, it was determined that LaShawn did not remain "in-step" on the sidewalks, could not detect driveways, and did not demonstrate appropriate rhythm when walking in a residential neighborhood. Before in-struction could be conducted in a small business area, LaShawn had to "graduate" from the residen-tial travel unit. After two sessions walking up and down the same sidewalk in a small residential com-munity, LaShawn signed in frustration:

> Why do I need to learn this? I don't want to learn this. I don't even have sidewalks in my neighbor-hood at home. This is very different. We don't have cars or driveways. I am not going to remem-ber this stuff when I go home. And, I'm not going to use my cane when I go home.

Orientation and mobility instruction for all persons with visual disabilities, regardless of cognitive, physical, or auditory ability, must be based on a person-centered plan (Forest & Lusthaus, 1989; Mount & Zwernick, 1988; Turnbull & Morningstar, 1993) that reflects ecologically sound decisions (Goetz et al., 1987), the right to make choices, and the need for access to information and relation-ships that are meaningful to the student. Based on the most recent research and dem-onstrations (Alsop, 1993; Bailey & Head, 1993; Bolton, 1989; Chen, 1992; Davies, 1990; Goetz & Gee, 1987a, 1987b; Lubecki, 1994; Michaud, 1990; Pogrund, Healy, et al., 1993; Sauerburger, 1994), the remainder of this chapter proposes a model that facilitates the learning of O&M skills for students with deaf-blindness and/or severe and multiple disabilities. It is an expansion of a student-centered model developed in the 1980s (Gee & Goetz, 1985; Gee et al., 1987), and it is de-signed to teach the interrelationships of the skills necessary for movement and mobility through the direct application of systematic instruction within the actual contexts in which the student is expected, and motivated, to move or be mobile.

O&M SKILLS DEFINITIONS

The skills needed for individuals with visual impairments or deaf-blindness to travel independently, safely, and effectively have traditionally been defined using two terms: *orientation* and *mobility* (Cioffi, 1994; Welsh & Blasch, 1980). Orientation skills are described as knowing: 1) where the body is in space and the destination of travel (Sauerburger, 1994), 2) where the body is in relationship to other objects within environments (Gothelf, Rikhye, & Silberman, 1988; Hill & Ponder, 1976; Houghton, in press), and 3) how to construct a mental map of environments (Chapman & Stone, 1988). Mobility skills are described as: 1) facilitation of independent or assisted movement (Gothelf et al., 1988; Jacobson, 1993), 2) movement from place to place (Alsop, 1993; Dodson-Burk & Hill, 1989b), and 3) purposeful movement to a desired location (Cioffi, 1994). Hill and Ponder (1976) stated that "the ultimate goal of orientation and mobility is to enable the student to enter any environment, familiar or unfamiliar, and to function safely, efficiently, gracefully, and independently by utilizing a combination of these two skills" (p. 1).

A variety of assessment instruments and curriculum guides have been developed for evaluating the current O&M levels of infants, children, youth, and adults with visual impairments or deaf-blindness (see Table 1). Most of these assessment tools and curriculum guides (with the exception of one or two) are in the form of developmental sequences or checklists of skills and are often conducted in isolated settings that have little meaning to the student. There appears to be a trend within more recent assessments and curriculum guides for recommending that evaluations and instruction be conducted within functional and meaningful environments (Pogrund, Healy, et al., 1993; Utley & Nelson, 1991). Bailey and Head (1993) state that, although O&M curricular strategies are typically conducted in functional environments, many of the activities used for instruction or assessment have little contextual meaning.

Table 1 includes checklists for basic O&M skills, concept development, functional vision, and motor development. Many informal checklists have also been developed by various school districts, private agencies, and O&M specialists. While these assessment tools and curriculum guides can be useful in identifying potential curricular content areas for instruction, they should be used with careful scrutiny for students with deaf-blindness, with or without concomitant cognitive, physical, or behavioral disabilities (Gee et al., 1987). As discussed earlier, there is little empirical evidence that training of certain concept skills, such as body image, prior to the instruction of travel skills will indeed improve the student's performance on these travel skills (Bailey & Head, 1993; Gee et al., 1987; Joffee & Rikhye, 1991; Strelow, 1985).

Educators who work with an O&M specialist may gain a greater understanding of the potential services this specialist can provide to students with deaf-blindness if they are aware of the traditional scope and sequence of successful O&M training for students whose only disability is a serious visual impairment or blindness. A basic outline of the O&M sequence is shown in Table 2 (Eisenberg, 1979). It is utilized by students in, and graduates of, mobility training programs as a reference guide for sequencing skill instruction. It is developmental in nature, going from "simple skills related to basic mobility needs to advanced techniques

Table 1.   O&M assessment scales and curriculum guides

Assessing Infants Who are Visually Impaired or Deaf-Blind for Functional Vision and Orientation and Mobility—Assesses the developmental acquisition of skills and behaviors that are important for future O&M development of infants who have or are suspected of having visual impairments (Davies, 1990)

First Steps: A Handbook for Teaching Young Children Who Are Visually Impaired—Designed as a developmental curriculum and activity guide, including content areas, such as behavior management, speech and language development, sensorimotor integration, and O&M for parents and practitioners of infants and toddlers who have visual impairments (Blind Children's Center, 1993)

Functional Vision Inventory—Assessment of vision in children who have low vision and mental retardation (Langley, 1980)

Hill Perfomance Test of Selected Positional Concepts—Developed to assess spatial concepts needed in O&M by children from ages 6 to 10 who have visual impairments (Hill, 1981)

INSITE Resources for Family Centered Intervention for Infants, Toddlers, and Preschoolers Who Are Visually Impaired—Designed as a developmental assessment and curriculum guide, including content areas, such as vision, clues and landmarks, tactile skills, and braille for toddlers and young children to age 5 (Morgan, 1992)

Learning Together: A Parent Guide to Socially Based Routines for Visually Impaired Infants—Designed as a developmental activity guide, including teaching techniques, such as establishing routines, and implementation strategies and content areas, such as communication, cognition, and motor development for parents of infants with visual impairments (Chen, Friedman, & Calvello, 1989)

A Model for Assessment and Intervention on Visual and Visual-Motor Skills of Persons with Multiple Disabilities—Assesses a person's localization acuity using a variety of size categories within three distances in natural contexts for students who have limited vision and accompanying disabilities (Utley & Nelson, 1991)

Move with Me: A Parent's Guide to Movement Development for Visually Impaired Babies—Designed as a developmental activity guide, including teaching techniques, such as the importance of positioning during play and movement in space for parents of premature infants and infants with visual impairments (Hug, Chernus-Mansfield, & Hayashi, 1993)

One Step at a Time: A Manual for Families of Children with Hearing and Vision Impairments—Designed as a developmental guide, including content areas such as communication, eating, play, and motor development for parents of young children with visual impairments (Bolton, 1989)

An Orientation and Mobility Primer for Families and Young Children—Designed as a developmental guide to early O&M skills; provides answers of commonly asked questions regarding O&M development and services for parents of young children with visual impairments (Dodson-Burk & Hill, 1989a)

Peabody Developmental Motor Scales and Activity Cards—Assesses sensory and motor functions (Folio & Fewell, 1983)

The Peabody Mobility Kit—Assesses sensory and motor function of children with mental disabilities, visual impairments, and low vision (Harley, Henderson, & Wood, 1975)

Peabody Mobility Scale—Designed for measuring O&M skills of children with visual impairments and multiple disabilities (Harley, Wood, & Merbler, 1980)

Preschool Orientation and Mobility Screening—Assesses programming needs in orientation and mobility, identifies current levels of functioning, and identifies the need for O&M services of infants and toddlers (birth to 5 years) with visual impairments and accompanying physical, cognitive, or behavioral disabilities (Dodson-Burk & Hill, 1989b)

Reaching, Crawling, Walking . . . Let's Get Moving: Orientation and Mobility for Preschool Children—Designed as a developmental curriculum and activity guide specifically for beginning orientation skills and mobility skills of infants and toddlers with visual impairments (Simmons & Maida, 1993)

A Resource Manual for Understanding and Interacting with Infants, Toddlers, and Pre-School Age Children with Deaf-Blindness—Designed as an assessment and curriculum guide including content areas, such as O&M, communication, cognition, motor development, vision, and hearing for toddlers and young children to age 5 (Alsop, 1993)

Teaching Age-Appropriate Purposeful Skills (TAPS): An Orientation and Mobility Curriculum for Students with Visual Impairments—Designed as a comprehensive orientation and mobility assessment and curriculum guide (primarily for students ages 3–21), which provides a tool for systematic evaluation of student progress over time (Pogrund, Healy, Jones, Levack, Martin-Curry, Martinez, Marz, Roberson-Smith, & Vrba, 1993)

(continued)

Table 1.   *(continued)*

For more specific information, contact a local O&M instructor or write to:

The American Foundation for the Blind
Orientation and Mobility Consultant
15 West 16th Street
New York, NY 10011

Helen Keller National Center
111 Middle Neck Road
Sands Point, NY 11050-1299

The National Office of the Association for Education
and Rehabilitation of the Blind
and Visually Impaired (AER)
206 North Washington Street, Suite 320
Alexandria, VA 22314-2528

for complex independent travel in the extended geographical outdoor world" (p. iv). When instructed, each skill area is expanded into many more steps. This sequence assumes that the individual moves from the concrete to the abstract and that the goal is independent travel in any environment, whether familiar or unfamiliar. The skills of orienting oneself within an environment, that is, knowing where one is in space, where the destination is in space, and a way of ordering what must be done to arrive at that destination (Hill & Ponder, 1976), are taught in conjunction with movement skills.

A brief description of orientation and mobility skills follows. It is not intended to be a comprehensive discussion of all techniques available, but rather a summary useful for parents and educators with primary responsibility for an individual who is deaf-blind and/or who has other multiple disabilities. The reader is referred to the texts by Hill and Ponder (1976), Welsh and Blasch (1980), and the sequence by Eisenberg (1979) for more detailed descriptions of O&M techniques.

Concept Skills

Generally, when O&M specialists refer to concept skills they are indicating three basic areas: 1) body, 2) spatial, and 3) environmental. Body concepts refer to the student's body image and body schema (Welsh &

Blasch, 1980). The sequence of instruction includes body parts, functions, surfaces, and relationships. Spatial concepts include positional and relational concepts of the body and the environment (such as beside, under, lateral, internal, external, etc.), concepts of measurement, and action concepts such as the terms for various movements (i.e., turn at 45 degrees, 90 degrees, right-angle turn; move; scoot; creep; crawl; roll; walk; run).

Table 2.   Traditional scope and sequence of O&M

Concept development
Basic techniques
  Sighted guide
  Protective and information gathering
  Forearm technique
  Trailing
  Lower body protective technique
  Independent room orientation
Introduction to cane techniques
  Touch technique
  Training with the touch technique
  Diagonal cane technique
  Touch and slide technique
  Stair travel
  Congested area cane technique
  Entering and exiting doorways, cars, and so on
  Touch and drag technique
  Three-point touch technique
Residential travel
Light business travel
Major metropolitan travel
Rural travel
Snow travel and other adverse conditions

Adapted from Eisenberg, 1979.

The environmental concepts emphasized by Welsh and Blasch (1980) are those related to travel. Their list is a series of terms such as *traffic light, city, business district, road, crosswalk*, and so on. In addition, they include topography concepts, such as *side, border, flat*, and *straight*, and concepts of texture, such as *pavement, stone, slick*, and *gravel*. Their list also includes temperature concepts important to the traveler, such as *hot, cold, muggy*, and *chilly*.

Orientation Skills

Hill and Ponder (1976) refer to six components of orientation: 1) landmarks, 2) clues, 3) indoor and outdoor numbering systems, 4) measurement, 5) compass directions, and 6) self-familiarization. Landmarks include "any familiar object, sound, odor, temperature, or tactile clue that is easily recognized, is constant, and that has a known permanent location in the environment" (p. 4). Landmarks are used to establish and maintain direction, to locate specific destinations, to use for perpendicular or parallel alignment for straight-line travel, or to obtain information about an area such as a floor. Examples of landmarks are the drinking fountain next to the gymnasium entrance or the bump in the hallway floor right before the turn to the locker room.

Clues are not necessarily permanent. They refer to tactile, auditory, visual, and olfactory stimuli that give the student information about his or her direction, position, and orientation relative to specific landmarks or locations. For example, the student may smell the food in the cafeteria and use it as the clue that he or she must turn left and head toward the door.

Indoor and outdoor numbering systems refer to the arrangement of numbers of rooms in a building and the addresses on streets within a town or city. Compass directions are transferable from one environment

to another and, once understood, are a valuable aid to the person with a visual impairment. Self-familiarization is the ability to tie together all the orientation concepts as one becomes familiar with a strange environment. Hill and Ponder (1976) have outlined a specific process for self-familiarization in which the student enters a room or building and systematically explores and notes all the necessary landmarks and positions of objects in relation to one another.

Basic Mobility and Cane Techniques

A list of mobility skills and techniques, both basic and advanced, are shown in Table 3. The reader can see that these skills follow a sequence from what has been considered "easier" skills to more advanced skills. Working with a sighted guide, the student is expected to learn many travel concepts that can be used later while using a cane. Similarly, the student is taken through a series of skill-building procedures while using a sighted guide prior to learning the use of the cane.

Since the mid-1980s, many O&M specialists and teachers have begun to use the cane with preschool students, toddlers, and students with multiple disabilities, even though these students have not mastered many of the skills that precede the cane techniques on the list (Bailey & Head, 1993; Gee & Goetz, 1985; Gee et al., 1987; Houghton, 1993, in press; Pogrund, Healy, et al., 1993). For example, an 18-year-old student with deaf-blindness and cognitive disabilities, who had never been independently mobile before, learned to trail, cross open doorways, and follow a straight line of travel, while also learning to use the cane in the diagonal position. A 6-year-old student with severe cognitive disabilities and deaf-blindness learned to move independently, trail, maneuver around obstacles, and turn corners, while learning to hold the cane in a diagonal position (Gee & Goetz, 1985).

Table 3.   Mobility skills and purposes

Skill	Purpose
Sighted guide Basic Adapted Transferring Narrow passages Reversing Accepting and refusing aid Stairways Doorways Seating	To travel safely and efficiently with a sighted person within different environments and under varying conditions.
Self-protection Upper hand and forearm Lower hand and forearm Alternate hand and lower forearm Modified forearm Trailing Traversing open doorways Direction taking Search patterns Dropped objects Squaring off Aligning	To travel efficiently, safely, and independently, primarily within familiar indoor and outdoor environments affording the maximum protection, with or without the use of a mobility aid.
Basic cane skills Walking with a guide Transferring sides with a guide Doorways with a guide Accepting and refusing aid Placement of the cane Cane maintenance	To travel safely, efficiently, and independently within familiar and unfamiliar indoor and outdoor environments.
Diagonal cane technique Changing hands Contacting objects and obstacles Traversing doorways Trailing Stairways Cane manipulation Adapted	To travel independently, primarily within a familiar indoor environment, with some degree of protection.
Two-point touch technique Basic Adapted Trailing Changing from diagonal to two-point touch technique Examining objects Constant contact technique	To detect drop-offs and objects, and maintain a line of direction in the vertical plane within familiar and unfamiliar indoor and outdoor environments. To detect drop-offs and objects, and maintain a line of direction in the vertical plane by always keeping the cane tip on the ground within familiar and unfamiliar indoor and outdoor environments.
Adapted mobility devices Basic Trailing Examining objects Changing from an adapted mobility device to the long cane Negotiating doorways Negotiating stairs Push toys	To detect drop-offs and obstacles, maintain a line of direction, and process sensory feedback in the vertical plane by always keeping the device on the ground within familiar and unfamiliar indoor and outdoor environments. To detect obstacles and maintain a line of direction in the vertical plane by always keeping the toy on the ground within familiar indoor environments.

(continued)

Table 3.   (*continued*)

Skill	Purpose
Outdoors: residential	
Car familiarization	To enter and exit cars safely and independently.
Shorelining	To establish and maintain a desired line of travel and to locate specific objects perpendicular to the line of travel.
Sidewalk recovery Touch and slide technique	To detect textual changes, such as subtle drop-offs or wheelchair ramps, primarily within familiar and unfamiliar outdoor environments.
Touch and drag technique	To detect curbs, expansion joints, elevated walkways and platforms, and maintain a line of direction by using the shoreline in a vertical plane, primarily within familiar and unfamiliar outdoor environments.
Three-point touch technique Adapted	To detect objects off to the side and above the vertical plane of travel (e.g., sidewalk to one-step entrances) and maintain the line of travel, primarily used within familiar and unfamiliar outdoor environments.
Street crossings Communication: expressive and receptive	
Outdoors: commercial Street crossing with traffic controls Street crossing with no traffic controls Pedestrian traffic control Soliciting aid Communication: Expressive and receptive Public transportation (e.g., buses, taxis, subways, trains, airplanes) Primary commercial facilities Escalators and elevators Revolving doors Parking lots Mall travel	
Special considerations Inclement weather Night travel Rural travel Dog guides Electronic travel devices (ETDs) Emergencies	

Adapted from Alsop, 1993; Hill and Ponder, 1976; Jacobson, 1993; Pogrund, Healy, Jones, Levack, Martin-Curry, Martinez, Marz, Roberson-Smith, and Urba, 1993; Sauerburger, 1993; Stroud and Higgins, date unknown.

When the student's combination of disabilities, such as deaf-blindness, suggests that the typical assessment instruments and instructional sequences may be inappropriate, it is recommended that alternative assessment and instructional methods such as the ones defined in this chapter be utilized. Regardless of additional multiple disabilities, it is also suggested that all students with vision impairments needing O&M instruction will benefit from some aspects of the person-centered approach described.

ORIENTATION AND MOBILITY PROGRAM DEVELOPMENT

There are four basic premises to the program development model that follows. First, instruction of orientation and mobility skills, from the most basic to the most complex, takes place within and across the activities and environments that naturally require performance of the skills selected based on consumer needs and preferences. The contexts for assessment and instruction are selected as part of a person-centered, inclusive, and community-based model (see chap. 16, this volume). The priority classes, school activities, work settings, and leisure and community activities designed by the family-centered team are thus the contexts in which the consumer's teacher(s) determine the most effective means of increasing successful orientation and mobility skills (see the following case study). Numerous consumers such as LaShawn (see previously, this chapter), families, and professionals have expressed the superiority of a consumer-driven planning process that ensures that instruction will generate meaningful skills useful to the consumer in the places in which the individual and his or her family choose to go to school, live, work, and play (Gee, Alwell, et al., 1994; Mount & Zwernick, 1988; Rainforth, York, & Macdonald, 1992; Stainback & Stainback, 1992; Turnbull & Morningstar, 1993).

Jordan is an active 10-year-old with diplegic cerebral palsy and cognitive disabilities who is also deaf-blind. Jordan's team looked at the fifth grade schedule of classroom and nonclassroom activities, as well as his after-school activities, to determine the most motivating settings in which to teach him new O&M skills. The teachers also used context analyses of each setting to determine the way in which Jordan needed to move and to gain access to information.

Jordan's new mobility system involved the use of a walker, which required adapted forms of the typical sequence leading to the use of a cane. His team set movement with the walker as an educational priority, as well as searching for materials, orienting equipment and materials to himself, standing still with the walker, using his hand to intermittently scan and/or trail surfaces, and so on. The instruction was carried out during most opportunities to move from place to place within the classroom and school. Jordan used a wheelchair in the community and worked on his orientation objectives as well as other communication and sensory discrimination objectives during community activities.

The second premise to O&M program development is an integrated service delivery system. Central to providing successful services to individuals with deaf-blindness is the concept of the integrated team, transdisciplinary team, or integrated therapy model (Campbell, 1993; Dunn, 1991; Gee, Graham, et al., 1994; Goetz et al., 1987; Lyon & Lyon, 1980; Rainforth et al., 1992). When teams use an integrated service delivery approach, specialists on the team share expertise and provide training to others on the team to implement specific programs and teaching strategies throughout the day (Rainforth et al., 1992). This avoids isolated instruction and instruction done out of context and increases opportunities for instruction. There is a fairly large data base supporting the instruction of motor and mobility skills (and other basic skills) within and across natural, motivating activities referenced to same-age peers (Gee, Graham, Sailor, & Goetz, in press; Sailor, Gee, & Karasoff, 1993; Sailor, Goetz, Anderson, Hunt, & Gee, 1987; Sailor et al., 1986; Snell, 1993).

Shortages in professionally trained O&M instructors make the integrated team concept a necessity for effective implementation of programs. Currently, many individuals are still not provided with O&M instruction because of this shortage. In turn, many students who have multiple disabilities are put at the bottom of the list. An integrated service delivery approach allows persons with the extra training and expertise in O&M to provide not only assessment and program development, but also consistent instruction to the other support personnel (i.e., teachers, therapists, paraprofessionals, and parents or family members) who work with an individual on a daily basis so that O&M instruction can continue in the absence of the O&M professional.

The third premise is the use of *contextual* and *constructivist* teaching approaches (Gee, Graham, et al., 1994; Grennon-Brooks & Brooks, 1993; Sailor et al., 1986). Constructivist teaching stresses the larger context, cognitive strategies, self-regulated learning, distributed or embedded instruction, and responsive instruction. Students with multiple disabilities are more successful in the acquisition of new skills when those skills are embedded within understandable, meaningful, and motivating routines or contexts (cf. Sailor et al., 1987; Snell, 1993). Contextual instruction has been shown to be an effective tool for teaching individuals with deaf-blindness and/or severe and multiple disabilities (Gee, 1993; Gee et al., 1987; Gee, Graham, et al., 1994). Similarly, the use of ongoing routines enhanced by contextual input has been shown to be a useful strategy (Siegel-Causey & Guess, 1989; van Dijk, 1986, 1989) for creating critical instructional moments (Gee, Graham, Sailor, & Goetz, in press).

The fourth premise is the use of systematic, embedded instruction. Variations will exist as to specific teaching strategies; however, it is recommended to use antecedent fading or systematic use of most-to-least assistance prompting procedures when students are receiving context instruction and/or during the initial acquisition phases. Time delay procedures are suggested for students in the "fluency" stage of instruction. The student learning basic O&M skills may not be initially required to perform all the skills necessary to get from one place to another in

a given route or activity. Rather, he or she may be taught two or three skills that are required within a route of travel. These skills are required at various points along the route and thus are instructed when their performance is necessary (embedded). The instructor assists the student on all other parts of the route or activity, stopping and giving planned instruction when the skills designated are required (Gee et al., 1987). As the student passes the initial objectives, more of each route or new activity skills can be added. Consistent, planned methods of instruction with useful measures of progress are necessary.

When developing orientation and mobility programs, the authors suggest the following process:

1. Utilize a person-centered/family-centered approach to program development to determine priority activities, environments for instruction, and goals.
2. Assess students within and across these meaningful settings using an ecological approach to curriculum.
3. Conduct context analyses to determine when and where to teach priority objectives as well as the natural cues and motivation for particular skills.
4. Utilize contextual instruction strategies.
5. Embed systematic instruction.
6. Evaluate and reevaluate progress using an integrated team.

Assessment of the Individual's Current O&M Skills

As stated earlier, the individual's priorities within the realm of orientation and mobility must be set by a consumer-driven team. A person-centered planning meeting (see chaps. 6 & 8, this volume) including the parents and the consumer will provide key information as to the types of classes, activities, and community settings in which the individual has been or will be spending his or her time. Priority objectives are also discussed with the whole team in terms of functional outcomes (i.e., What does this individual need to learn in order to have increased access to his or her environment, mobility, and information?). The outcomes of this planning meeting provide the key teachers with the contexts in which to conduct assessment and instruction as well as a tentative list of priority goals.

Prior to the direct assessment, the team reviews information from several sources. Among individuals with deaf-blindness there is great variation in visual ability, which occurs in conjunction with a wide range of auditory abilities and varying levels of cognitive and physical ability. Each individual's combination of disabilities will influence his or her ability to orient and be mobile. Understanding an individual's vision problem thoroughly will assist in developing appropriate O&M goals and objectives. If a field loss exists in the lower quadrants, for example, the use of a cane or special scanning procedure may be necessary, even though the student has a great deal of functional vision. Based on the recommendation and/or prescription made by a qualified eye care specialist, low vision devices, contact lenses, sunglasses, and so forth may also be appropriate for students to maximize their remaining vision. Objectives should reflect strategies to teach the use of any functional vision within mobility routes. The team will also need accurate information regarding the individual's hearing loss in order to plan assessment and instructional strategies. The special education teacher, speech and language specialist, audiologist, and/or teacher of the deaf and hearing impaired should be able to provide the team with relevant information for programming.

An individual's needs change over a lifetime as a result of increased or decreased vi-

sion and hearing skills, improved technology, improved assessment procedures, and general life demands (Cioffi, 1994; Everson, 1994; Houghton, in press; Kennedy, 1990). As previously described by consumers, vision and hearing losses impact an individual's ability to travel independently within home and community environments. Orientation and mobility skills are also influenced by the age of onset of the dual disabilities. Cioffi (1994), Lessard and Lolli (1973), and Lolli (1980) identified four categories for onset of occurrences that directly impact an individual's ability to travel. These categories are: 1) congenitally deaf-adventitiously blind, 2) adventitiously deaf-congenitally blind, 3) adventitiously deaf-blind, and 4) congenitally deaf-blind. Rich McGann explains:

There are differences because those who are deaf first and then lose their vision, know what colors are like, what shapes look like, what the world around [them] looks like, they know sign language and facial expressions. They keep these visions in their memories so they continue with those when they go blind.

But, if they are blind first then lose their hearing—they don't know the importance of facial expressions, sign language, or what colors look like. They tend to use fingerspelling for their mode of communication. This is true for individuals who are deaf-blind or are going to be deaf-blind in the future. (Virginia Commonwealth University & Helen Keller National Center, 1993)

Other considerations regarding an individual's vision and hearing loss include whether:

1. The losses are partial or total.
2. The losses are stable or progressive.
3. The vision loss is central or peripheral.
4. The hearing loss is sensorineural, conductive, or mixed.
5. The hearing loss is bilateral or unilateral.
6. The losses fluctuate due to the nature of the syndrome, disease, medication, or medical intervention (Cioffi, 1994; Houghton, 1993).

Information from physical and occupational therapists regarding such concerns as the student's balance, reflexes, trunk control, and wheelchair guidelines is also necessary in the development of an O&M program. The student's physical abilities will affect his or her ability to learn to travel. The primary support teacher and/or speech-language therapist will also have valuable information for the team to consider regarding the student's primary mode of communication and best learning styles.

Planned Observations Across Settings and Activities   The initial step in conducting a functional assessment of O&M skills is to structure planned observations of the performance of specific skills identified from previous experience with the student, parent and family input, and team input. The teacher observes the student using each specific skill at a time when there are natural cues for its performance. In order to use this strategy adequately, the teacher and O&M specialist must review the skills they wish to assess, determine functional age-appropriate contexts in which the skills are necessary, and arrange for the opportunity to observe or gather baseline data on the student in those contexts. Examples of some O&M skills and contexts in which they might be assessed are shown in Table 4.

Through general structured observations within the activities and contexts identified as priorities through the person-centered plan, an ecological assessment (Brown et al., 1979; Falvey, 1992; Harrell & Rosenberg, 1986; Houghton, 1993) can be conducted. In this process, the instructor takes a more holistic view of the student as she or he functions within an activity or environment. The O&M instructor or teacher first outlines the route or activity components, then through direct observation and assistance, notes areas of need and identifies new target skills that require instruction. Figures 1, 2, & 3 de-pict ecological inventories for three different individuals. Figure 1 depicts a young child during the activities preceding her bathtime. Figure 2 depicts a student traveling from his classroom to the school cafeteria, and Figure 3 depicts an inventory for an individual at work. Each of these inventories includes observational notes taken by the O&M instructor or support teacher regarding current abilities and suggestions for adaptations and instructional targets.

Determining Contexts for Instruction   While completing planned observations across priority contexts in order to become familiar with the student's performance levels, instructional staff can begin to select contexts for systematic instruction. It is recommended that instruction be given in as many contexts as possible. Four main factors should be considered in route/context selection. First, routes of travel or activities should be chosen that will be used on a regular and continuing basis. For example, a kindergarten student may travel regularly from his or her classroom to the playground, the cafeteria, the library, and the gym. A 15-year-old student may travel between the school locker room, cafeteria, and science lab, in addition to transitions between each class period, travel from the school to the bus stop, or travel to a work placement in the community.

Second, it is preferable to choose activities or contexts in which the student can be most practically instructed, given teacher–student ratios and availability of trained peers. In addition to the instructional time provided by the O&M specialist, in an integrated service delivery model the student's teacher and other staff carry out the mutually agreed upon O&M programs across the day (following training from the O&M specialist). There may be certain times during the day when there are more staff available, allowing the kind of close one-on-one assistance that is often necessary for mobility instruction.

Table 4. Contexts in which O&M skills are essential

Category	Skill	Function	Age-appropriate contexts in which the student can demonstrate skill performance	
			3–7 years	13–18 years
Underlying basic skill	Tactile discrimination	To determine differences among tactile stimuli	Stop or sit down on the rug with the group after noticing the difference in surface (in the school gym)	Stop or slow down and cautiously approach the swimming pool when students' bare feet touch the tile surrounding the edge of the pool
Underlying basic skill	Sound localization	To recognize the direction from which a sound came	Turn toward the sounds from other children on the playground	Turn toward the sounds coming from the bus arriving at the corner
Orientation skill	Utilize clues	To change movement or direction based on an environmental clue	Move or attempt to leave when the bell rings for recess	Stop and turn left down a hallway when the flow of air hits face
Orientation skill	Utilize landmarks	To change movement behavior or direction based on recognition of a landmark	Slow for the stairway when the railing is felt with the hand	After passing the drinking fountain, enter the next doorway
Mobility skill	Trailing	To move continuously using a guiding surface	Follow the hallway at home to the bathroom	Follow the classroom wall to the coat rack
Mobility skill	Crossing a defined open space 14'–30'	To move continuously across a defined space in a purposeful and relatively straight path	Cross the hallway leading to the school cafeteria	Bring dishes to the sink from the table in the kitchen

Environment: Home
Subenvironments: Hallway, bathroom
Activity: Water play before bathtime

Steps of Skill Sequence	+/−	Adaptations/Target Skills	Route Description
Travel from play area to bathroom door.	−	Give child wash cloth with soap scent to cue. Walk with one hand assist to wall. Pause. With one hand on wall, trail; continue using one hand assist. Have bathroom light on and door open.	Square off at couch. Travel straight line to wall, turn left. Trail to door with light on in bathroom (clue). Have same soap scent on washcloth in bathroom (clue).
Get pail and toys out of cabinet.	+/−	Got lost and resisted in bathroom. Orient child to everything in bathroom initially in systematic fashion. Use door guard on cabinet doors except one. Have toys in that cabinet. Child able to locate toys and pulled out of cabinet.	Turn right in door way. Explore which door will open. Sit and pull out toys.
Drop toys in tub to play.	+/−	Picked up toys but would not drop. Did not appear to know water was in tub. Have water running in tub and same scented soap (bubble bath) (clues).	Crawl in straight line from cabinet to tub with water running and same scented soap as on washcloth (clues).
Undress and enter tub.	+/−	Pulled arm out of sleeves and pant legs. Lifted into tub. Used wash cloth to scrub. Let child touch wash cloth then begin scrubbing with child's assistance.	

Figure 1.   Ecological inventory for toddler during bathtime. (+ indicates independent performance, − indicates no independent performance, and +/− indicates partially independent performance.)

The third factor is motivation. If the routes lead to some desirable activity that occurs regularly on arrival, the student's motivation for movement may increase. Thus, the teacher may choose to train O&M skills on the way to the swimming pool if the student enjoys swimming, to a worksite where the student interacts with friends, or simply within the classroom where the student enjoys being mobile with peers.

Lastly, consideration should be given to variations in the skills required in the routes/activities. The team may decide, for example, that certain routines require too many advanced skills or that some routes are too short to allow enough practice. It is preferable to train across routes that allow several opportunities for practice on each skill. The information gathered from the route/activity analysis described in the next section will assist in this decision.

Baseline Route/Activity Analysis After a route or activity has been chosen for more direct instruction, the team analyzes the activity or travel route to determine two things: 1) the most efficient path for the student to travel using the most efficient movement and 2) the O&M skills required for traveling or moving through the route or activity. Routes of travel are analyzed by the O&M

Environment: School
Subenvironments: Classroom, hallway, and cafeteria
Activity: Lunch

Steps of Skill Sequence	+/−	Adaptations/Target Skills	Route Description
Stands up and pushes chair under desk.	+/−	Classmate taps arm and tactually signs lunch. Locates cane by self. Can stand up and push in chair using velcro tabs.	Velcro tabs used for orientation.
Stands in line in back of room.	+/−	Squares off from back of chair. Uses constant contact to travel to back wall. Greets classmate in line using tactual sign.	Squares off from back of desk using tactual markers to align body. Walks in straight line to back wall of classroom that contains coat rack (landmark).
Walks to cafeteria.	−	Uses constant contact for travel and is cued to use overhead lights to maintain line of direction. Needs to have classmate assist in counting two doorways using tactual signs. Travels from side to side of hall—veers left.	Turns body right and approaches classroom door. Turns right and counts two doorways (clues) before reaching cafeteria door. Also uses overhead lights in the hallway to determine line of travel.
Locates cafeteria door.	+		Locates cafeteria by smells (clue). Turns right to enter cafeteria door.
Gets tray and silverware.	+/−	Locates and gets tray independently. Classmate cues to brailled labels under individual silverware containers. Keeps cane hook in pocket.	Proceeds down the cafeteria line trailing the tray shelf.
Gets food and drink.	+/−		Touch cues by cafeteria worker to locate plate and put plate on tray. Classmate cues to brailled labels listed under choices of drink.
Goes to table and sits down.	−	Need to teach use of plastic mat and cane skills to locate chair at first table. Can find chair at table once arrives.	At end of the line, turns left following plastic mat (clue) on the floor to chair at the end of the first table.

Figure 2. Ecological inventory for student going to the cafeteria. (+ indicates independent performance, − indicates no independent performance, and +/− indicates partially independent performance.) (From Houghton, J. [1993, July/August]. Incorporating functional orientation and mobility skills in the ecological process. *Indiana Deaf-Blind Services Project Information Update, 12*; reprinted by permission.)

specialist and/or teacher to write down each component and organize the route for safety, efficiency, and appearance (see section, Setting Performance Criteria, this chapter). Every change in direction, change of hand or foot, turn, shift of cane, landmarks, and so on is considered to be a separate component of the route. The O&M specialist advises the teacher of the path of travel or series of movements that would be recommended for a per-

Environment: Vocational
Subenvironments: Work area
Activity: Sealing machine operation

Steps of Skill Sequence	+/-	Adaptations/Target Skills	Route Description
Exits bus and walks to front door of shop.	+/-	Needs card to communicate to bus driver this is stop. Assistance when exiting bus stairs. Walked to front door using touch and drag. Telephone pole was cue to turn to door.	Exited bus. Crossed sidewalk. Turns right when encounters pole (clue). Walks straight to front door.
Enters shop and goes to locker room.	+	Squares off to side of door and uses constant contact to counter. Greets receptionist by waving hi. Travels to locker room.	Squares off to side of door and travels in straight line to counter. Turns left at counter and trails to locker room door.
Locates locker and puts lunch and equipment away.	+/-	Needs to clear area after opening door. Has trouble locating locker. Checks everyone until finds one that is open. Maybe need to attach braille label with name.	Opens door, trails straight line of lockers.
Leaves locker room to work area.	-	Waits for peer to provide sighted guide. Peer talks rapidly to student behind student's back. Student does not respond. Peer drags student to work area. Needs sighted guide techniques to peer and instruction on talking to student. Teach student route for open space maybe through map. Sets vibrowatch to signal break.	Turns so left shoulder is touching locker. Trails to door. Turns left. Pop machine is home base (landmark). Trails to equipment shelves (landmark). Turns left, squares off, and walks in straight line to work area.
Places pre-cut plastic bag on edge of machine and presses lever.	+/-	Could locate pre-cut bag on edge of machine and press lever. Needs to wear heat-resistant safety gloves, ear protection, and goggles.	
Releases lever to empty bag into box. Checks periodically to see if box is full. Full box is loaded onto cart.	+		
Cart is full—takes to equipment shelf and unloads.	+		Turns left. Feels end of table on left side. Puts hands in middle of cart and pushes until comes in contact with equipment shelves (landmark).

(continued)

Figure 3.   Ecological inventory for student at work. (+ indicates independent performance, − indicates no independent performance, and +/− indicates partially independent performance.) (From Houghton, J. [in press]. *Orientation and mobility for youth with deaf-blindness*. Sands Point, NY: Helen Keller National Center.)

Steps of Skill Sequence	+ / −	Adaptations/Target Skills	Route Description
Takes cart back to work area and repeats sequence.	+		Uses wall by equipment shelf to square off with left shoulder touching equipment shelf. Pushes cart in straight line to work area.

Figure 3. (*continued*)

son with only a visual impairment, and together they determine any adaptations that might be necessary for a student with deaf-blindness. For example, on a route from the classroom to the front entrance of the school building, there may be a section where the independent blind traveler would cross a crowded, open area with no surface to trail continuously, in order to reach a series of steps. The teacher and O&M specialist may decide to have the student with deaf-blindness and/or severe disabilities take a different path at that point in the route, allowing the student to follow a wall that eventually leads to the steps. While less efficient, it may allow the student more independence.

Table 5 depicts two routes that have been analyzed for two students with deaf-blindness (see the following case studies). The first is the route from the classroom to the corner bus stop (down the block from the school) for Tim, a 17-year-old high school student who is learning cane travel for parts of his routes. The second route is for Rebecca, a 5-year-old elementary school student who uses a walker to travel from another kindergarten classroom back to her own classroom daily.

Tim is fully included in an urban high school. He spends 4 periods of his day included in general classes, uses the cafeteria for lunch 3 days a week, eats off campus twice a week, and spends 3 periods a day at a job in the xerox and mail room of a large insurance company. Tim is deaf and blind. He has no residual vision or hearing to use for informational purposes. Tim is 17 years old but has only recently received the services of an O&M instructor. Prior to

this point he was denied O&M services because of his cognitive disabilities. Without O&M instruction, Tim developed some patterns of movement and prompt dependency that now need to be remediated in order for him to become more independent.

Rebecca's schedule is the same as her kindergarten peers. In addition to their own classroom, they spend some time during the week in the gymnasium, the art room, and another kindergarten room down the hall. They use the cafeteria and the playground daily. Rebecca has severe glaucoma and cataracts. She can recognize people she knows at about a 3-foot distance. Rebecca also has a severe sensorineural hearing loss. She wears hearing aids that assist her to hear environmental sounds and to let her know when someone is speaking. She is not able to discriminate speech, however. Rebecca has begun to use a tactile symbol system in conjunction with co-active gestures for communication. Rebecca has cerebral palsy and uses a walker to be mobile.

Determine Instructional Components Unlike some activities in which one instructional procedure can be used across several steps, each mobility route requires the use of many different skills. Each skill may require a different instructional approach. Instructional procedures are written for each of the varied skills required within and across the routes.

Like many activities, however, the instructional components can be divided into two categories: 1) skills that can be used across many travel routes or activities and 2) skills that are specific to a particular route or activity. The first category, skills that are *noncontext bound*, includes basic movement skills, sighted guide techniques, cane techniques, and basic orienting skills. These skills can be practiced across many contexts and can be generalized to new and unfamiliar contexts (Gee & Goetz,

Table 5. Task-analyzed routes for Tim and Rebecca

Tim's route from classroom to corner bus stop	Rebecca's route from other classrooms to her own kindergarten room
1. Open door of classroom	1. Exit classroom
2. Trail around right corner	2. Follow short wall on left
3. Cane in left hand	3. Cross hallway
4. Trail the wall	4. At wall, turn right
5. Three obstacles: garbage can, chair, chair	5. Follow wall
6. Trail around right corner	6. At end of wall, go around corner
7. Down first set of stairs	7. When walker hits stairs, move walker to right
8. Trail wall	8. Grasp railing—both hands
9. Down second set of stairs	9. Go upstairs (5 steps)
10. At bottom of stairs, turn left	10. At top of stairs, grasp walker
11. Follow bottom step with cane	11. Follow wall
12. At end of stair, walk straight	12. Cross open doorway
13. Cross open space	13. Follow wall
14. When cane hits short stairs, turn left	14. When reach children singing, stop and turn right
15. Find wall	15. Cross hallway
16. Down 3 steps	16. Find doorknob
17. Turn left	17. Open door of classroom
18. Cross open space	18. Enter kindergarten class
19. When cane hits stairs, find railing	
20. Down 3 steps	
21. Find doors	
22. Push open doors/exit	
23. Cross open space to outside steps	
24. Down four steps without railing	
25. At bottom, turn left, wait for guide	
26. Walk one block on sidewalk with sighted guide	
27. At curb, stop and wait for bus	

1985). Performance of these skills will be the same on any route. The technique to travel up and down stairs with a railing, for example, will be the same across most routes. Similarly, trailing a wall, making turns, crossing doorways, and other movement skills can be used in many environments.

The second category, skills that are *context bound*, includes the steps that are only necessary to the particular route being analyzed. Landmarks and clues are usually included in this category. While the ability to use landmarks and clues may be general for the more advanced student, each clue or landmark must be remembered and used in its specific location on the route. The student may need to remember, for example, that the large pole in the front hallway of the high school is the landmark to begin using the cane to search for the steps. That clue or landmark is specific to exiting the high school building.

A format for doing a contextual analysis of routes and activities and collecting baseline data was developed by Gee & Goetz (1985). Figure 4 depicts a partial baseline route analysis for Tim's route from the classroom to the bus stop. At the top of the form the instructor notes any adaptations that have previously been made (see Adaptations and Technology section, this chapter), and the current status

Baseline Route Analysis

School site or other community site: _____

Student: Tim — 17 _____

Route: Classroom to front entrance and bus stop on corner _____

Communication System: A few tactile signs and gestures _____

Vision Status: No vision   Hearing Status: Profound Loss

* = Indicates that data from this step is to be combined with data on the same objective from other routes.

*Stairs without railing	*Open classroom door	Route memory	Open large front doors	*Turn, square off	*Sighted guide	*Shift cane	*Correct position on stairs — down	*Trail with cane only	*Cross defined open spaces	*Maneuver obstacles	*Continue to hand trail while turning corner	*Maintain trailing — diagonal and hand	Route description by objective — Cane with marshmallow tip in use	6/7/84	6/8/84	6/20/84
	x												Open door of classroom	-	-	■
	x											x	Trail around right corner	-	-	-
	x					x							Cane in left hand	-	-	■
												x 23	Trail the wall (23 trials)	+1	+6	+7
										3 x			3 obstacles: garbage can, chair, chair	- - -	- - -	- - -
	x											x	Trail around right corner	-	-	+
							x						Down 1st set of stairs	-	+	■
												x 2	Trail wall	- / -	+ / +	+ / -
													Down 2nd set of stairs	-	-	■

. . . etc.

Goal: 4 routes within school building

Date: 6/21/86, steps chosen for instruction: trailing with hand cane at diagonal; trail around corners; maneuver around obstacles in trailing path; cross defined open spaces using diagonal techniques.

Figure 4. Baseline route analysis: Tim. (From Gee, K., Harrell, R., & Rosenberg, R. [1987]. Teaching orientation and mobility skills within and across natural opportunities for travel: A model designed for learners with multiple severe disabilities. In L. Goetz, D. Guess, & K. Stremel-Campbell [Eds.], *Innovative program design for individuals with dual sensory impairments* [p. 144]. Baltimore: Paul H. Brookes Publishing Co.; reprinted by permission.)

of the student's vision, hearing, and communication mode. In the vertical column on the right side of the form the steps of the route are listed in order. Several columns for data are available. The instructor uses the columns to the left of the route to indicate the O&M skills for each corresponding step. The specific skills are written in at the top of the columns and the boxes that are parallel to the step are checked. Skills that are non-context bound (i.e., trailing, maneuvering obstacles) receive their own column. Skills that are context bound (i.e., remembering landmarks, clues, etc., specific to the route from the classroom to the front door of the building and then to the bus stop) are included under *route memory* for Tim. By organizing the baseline in this fashion, the teacher(s) can begin to see the many points within an activity at which particular skills are necessary.

The columns on the right side of the form are used to collect baseline data, probe data, post-test data, and so on before or after instruction. On 6/7 and 6/8, Tim's teacher collected pretest data by going through the route with him and providing opportunities to perform each of the skills listed. Based on his performance, four skills were chosen for instruction: 1) trailing walls with his cane in the diagonal position, 2) trailing corners, 3) maneuvering around obstacles, and 4) crossing open spaces (e.g., hallways). Baseline data on these four skills were then taken on 6/20, after criteria had been set and context instruction had occurred (see section on context instruction).

Pretest Data   The purpose of the first baseline or pretest is to determine the present level of the student's performance, possible instructional techniques, and where instruction is necessary. The instructor uses a format of least-to-most assistance with a constant time delay throughout the route, allowing the student to demonstrate any current ability to perform the step required. Changes in performance criteria or the route itself may be indicated. It may be discovered, for example, that rather than trailing with the cane, the student can benefit from learning the more advanced touch technique, or rather than the diagonal technique, an adaptation should be made. Following baseline it was determined that Tim's method of travel in buildings would be trailing with the cane held in the diagonal position, rather than using open space travel techniques. His team members felt that Tim should focus on independent movement versus the most advanced means of travel.

The route anlysis will be different for each route, and each student will have an individualized set of movement skills depending on his or her abilities. Rebecca, for example, must travel without a cane because she needs both hands on her walker to ambulate. The skills represented by steps that indicate traveling down hallways, across rooms, and along sidewalks will be different than the skills used by the student with a cane. A route analysis for Rebecca traveling from the upstairs kindergarten classroom back to her own kindergarten classroom is shown in Figure 5. To get up and down the stairs Rebecca holds the railing with both hands, supporting her weight and moving at the same time. Tim uses a different method because he is able to walk independently and is learning to use a cane.

Setting Performance Criteria

Before setting the performance criteria on long- and short-term objectives, it is useful to consider the criteria that the O&M specialist would set for a person whose only disability is blindness. Based on the data from the pretest/baseline observations, the criteria can be adapted temporarily or permanently to suit the student with multiple disabilities. *Safety, efficiency*, and *appearance* are the three levels of competency that are considered within the traditional orientation and mobility paradigm. The same levels should be considered when defining goals and objectives for the student with deaf-blindness or who has other additional disabilities. Adaptations to the program and materials can be made accordingly.

The first priority in O&M instruction is the safety of the student. Ensuring that the student has the necessary skills to move about safely in familiar and unfamiliar environments is essential before independent travel is considered. Protective techniques for confronting low and overhanging obstacles are essential if the student with visual impair-

Baseline Route Analysis

School site or other community site: _____

Student: Rebecca — 4

Route: Other K-classroom to own kindergarten classroom.

Communication Status: Uses 3–5 tactile signs receptively

Vision Status: Residual peripheral vision and spots on right side.

Hearing Status: Severe loss in both ears.

* = Indicates that data from this step is to be combined with data on the same objective from other routes.

*Turn, square off	*Localize to sound	*Use one arm to balance	*Walk upstairs—no walker	*Move walker aside	*Corners	*Cross open space	Route memory	*Follow walls in walker	Route Description by Step — Four legged rollator walker in use. Instructor carries walker upstairs and places in position	Date of baseline/posttest (open squares indicate the objectives to be tested).		
							x		Exit classroom.			
								x1	Follow short wall on left.			
						x			Cross hallway.			
							x		At wall, turn right.			
								x4	Follow wall (4 trials).			
					x				At end of wall, go around corner 24			
				x			x		When walker hits stairs, move walker to right.			
							x		Grasp railing—both hands.			
			x						Upstairs — 5.			

(continued)

Figure 5. Baseline route analysis: Rebecca. (From Gee, K., Harrell, R., & Rosenberg, R. [1987]. Teaching orientation and mobility skills within and across natural opportunities for travel: A model designed for learners with multiple severe disabilities. In L. Goetz, D. Guess, & K. Stremel-Campbell [Eds.], *Innovative program design for individuals with dual sensory impairments* [pp. 146–147]. Baltimore: Paul H. Brookes Publishing Co.; reprinted by permission.)

ments is to move freely in various environments. It is often a disservice to the student to unnaturally modify his or her environment to make it safe. It is preferable to teach the student how to recognize hazards and how to safely maneuver around them.

The second area of emphasis in O&M instruction is efficiency. A variety of skills, strategies, and "tricks of the trade" make traveling easier for individuals with visual impairments. Locating a door knob, for example, by rotating one's wrist and holding one's cane vertically an inch off the ground while moving it across the door is a much faster way to find the door knob than groping aimlessly all over the door with one's free hand.

The third area of emphasis in O&M instruction is appearance. Teaching appropriate posture, gait, and coordinated move-

Figure 5.   (continued)

•Turn, square off	•Localize to sound	•Use one arm to balance	•Walk upstairs—no walker	•Move walker aside	•Corners	•Cross open space	Route memory	•Follow walls in walker	Route Description by Step Four-legged rollator walker in use. Instructor carries walker upstairs and places in position.	Date of baseline/ Posttest (open squares indicate the objectives to be tested.)		
	x							x	At top of stairs, grasp walker.			
								x2	Follow wall (2 trials).			
						x			Cross open doorway.			
								x2	Follow wall (2 trials).			
x	x								When reach children singing, stop and turn right.			
						x			Cross hallway.			
									Find doorknob.			
	x							x	Open door of classroom.			
								x	Enter kindergarten.			
	1	2			1			9	= Trials Score =			

Goal: Four routes within building with minimal assistance.

Date: 1/86, steps chosen for instruction:
      1) localize to sound;
      2) use one arm to balance;
      3) follow walls;
      4) go around corners and continue to follow wall.

ments will assist the individual to appear capable and efficient. A comfortable and relaxed appearance also provides image enhancement and self-esteem in inclusive settings.

The need for instruction in each of these three areas of competency must be decided individually in relation to each student. Safety should always be given first consideration; however, efficiency and appearance should also be considered. For example, the O&M specialist may choose to forgo efficiency and appearance for a particular student who is able to travel safely to his or her after-school job, even though he or she is not always efficient and might appear awkward. Performance criteria must ultimately be based on the student's abilities.

Another aspect of setting the performance criteria is determining how to *systematically measure* the student's use of particular techniques. As shown in the baseline analyses, some routes have multiple opportunities to practice particular skills and few opportunities for others. In addition, a student may be expected to trail using the diagonal cane technique down a very long hallway at one point, and for a very short distance at another point. Taking quantitative data on the student's performance requires some equal measure across data points; thus, the instructor(s) must determine points at which data will be taken and what the criteria will be. For example, during the first phase of Tim's instruction, his team determined that for trailing with the cane, they would define an instructional trial as approximately every 7 feet. Tim might travel down a long hallway getting 6 trials of trailing technique, or he might travel a short span and practice 2 trials (approximately 14 feet). In this manner, the team had some equal measures of his ability to master the technique across routes. Many skills, such as maneuvering around obstacles, will not be subject to distance measures and can easily count as one opportunity.

The other aspect to determining the performance criteria is *quality*. How much of the skill will be expected during the first instructional objective? Based on the initial assessment, past experience and instruction, and baseline data, the team determines how much more the student will learn in the next instructional period and defines the criteria clearly. For some students the initial criteria for using a sighted guide may simply be keeping their hand on the elbow of the guide. A student using a wheelchair may have the criteria of holding her hand on the moving milk cart, as someone pushes her to her school job.

Context Instruction and Second Baseline

Based on a series of research studies, an instructional practice known as *context instruction* has been shown to be effective with students with deaf-blindness and other multiple disabilities (Gee, 1993; Gee & Goetz, 1985; Gee et al., in press; Gee, Graham, et al., 1994; Gee, Graham, Oshima, Yoshioka, & Goetz, 1991). Context instruction is designed to establish the context and the motivation for travel or movement. It is used to "bring the environment to the student" in order to compensate for the student's lack of distance senses and experience with the information sources sighted and hearing persons have readily available.

Before receiving O&M instruction, many individuals with deaf-blindness and/or other severe and multiple disabilities either use a sighted guide or, unfortunately, are pushed or pulled through most environments. As a result, they have not experienced the landmarks and clues, the surfaces, or any of the other steps in the routes they travel in any systematic or useful fashion. It cannot be assumed that the individual understands the natural cues for travel along a particular route, nor the presumed motivation of the activity at the end of a movement or route of travel, just because they have been involved in it in the past.

During context instruction the student is assisted to travel through each route in the manner in which she or he will eventually be expected to travel independently. This phase is an adaptation of the initial training used to develop independent travel in a frequently used indoor environment for a person who is blind. The instructor calls attention to tactile, auditory, and other situational cues and manipulates the student's body through moving, turning, holding the cane, and any other components necessary to reach the destination. The one demand placed on the student is cooperation in participation. No data are collected during this phase. Rather, the purpose is to: 1) establish a level of expectation in the student of events that take place within and at the end of the route and 2) provide opportunities to learn the natural cues available for the route memory.

Depending on the student's typical learning rate, the instructor implements context instruction for a period of time that will vary (5 days, 10 days, etc.) and then takes a second baseline measure.

Data from the second baseline reflect the student's ability to perform the skills after a set of expectations and anticipated clues have been established through context instruction. These sessions are run identically to the first baseline/pretest. Baseline data on particular basic movement skills (e.g., taking steps independently, trailing, moving up and down stairs) following context instruction have been shown to demonstrate a higher level of performance than the data on the initial baseline (Gee & Goetz, 1985). Presumably, the students may learn some of the skills by simply being put through the movements during the context instruction phase. The data may also reflect the student's knowledge or anticipation of events within and at the end of the route. With these expectations available, the student has a script of the activity in mind and may be more likely to continue to move along the route and at least attempt to continue travel.

Instruction and Evaluation

Instructional objectives for students with deaf-blindness may range from very basic movement skills to more advanced cane skills. A few general guidelines for setting objectives follow. First, based on the data from Gee and Goetz (1985) indicating that many route memory steps (landmarks, clues, and so forth specific to each activity) can be learned incidentally, it may be preferable to begin instruction on the basic motor movement skills (e.g., holding the sighted guide, maintaining context with a moving object while being pushed in wheelchair, turning corners, trailing) and cane techniques that will get a student from place to place—the heart of the ability to be mobile. As the stu-

dent meets the criteria on the initial movement objectives, more steps within the route can be added to the student's repertoire. Second, the number of opportunities for practice on the skill is another variable to consider. If the necessity to use a particular skill only arises once out of several trailing routes, it may not be a priority. Third, age will also influence the objectives. The older student will travel to more environments in the community, requiring skills that are not restricted to a particular building. It may also be more advantageous to make adaptations for older students who have only a short amount of time left in school to receive instruction.

Table 6 depicts a long-term goal and two short-term mobility objectives for Tim. Also included are definitions of the targeted skills for purposes of instruction and measurement. These objectives were taught in the context of four natural travel routes, including travel between the bus stop, school entrance, and classroom; the classroom and restroom; and from the classroom to a store in the community.

A wide variety of instructional strategies are available to the teacher and O&M specialist (cf. Rainforth et al., 1992; Snell, 1993; Wolery, Ault, & Doyle, 1992). Shaping and gradual fading of physical assistance and reinforcement are commonly used in the initial phase of instruction. Physically assisting the students through the correct motions may be an effective means to let them know exactly how the correct movements feel. Students can easily become prompt-dependent, however, from too much physical attention and verbal prompting, learning that if they stop moving someone will make contact with them or talk to them to initiate movement. Careful use of tactile and verbal feedback can help avoid the problem. Another effective means to avoid prompt dependence is the use of time delay (Snell, 1993; Touchette,

Table 6.   Objectives and definitions for Tim

Goal: Tim will be able to travel at least four routes independently under supervision within the school building.

Objective #1: While traveling within the school building to specific destinations, Tim will be able to trail the walls using correct position for his hand and the diagonal cane position, continuously moving until encountering an obstacle or a route marker, with at least 90% accuracy maintained for 2 weeks.

Objective #2: While traveling within the school building to specific destinations, Tim will be able to maintain the diagonal trailing position with hand and cane while going around corners, with 100% accuracy, maintained for at least 2 weeks.

Objective	Instructional trial definitions
1. Trailing by hand with the cane	Approximately every 7 feet, using natural markers in the fence, wall, and so on, or masking tape to mark each trail
2. Corners	Each time the student has to turn a corner while trailing, and continue trailing

1971) in conjunction with gradual fading of physical assistance (Gee et al., 1991; Gee & Goetz, 1985). Time delay is an instructional technique that gradually increases the amount of time between the natural cue to use an O&M skill and the prompt that will initiate it (Snell, 1993).

An important component of the instructional program is placement of the instructional trials within route travel or within the activity. This means that parts of the route (the components being systematically instructed) must be performed to the criteria designated in the program, but the teacher assists the student to perform the remaining components of the route. Using this method, the teacher can begin with instruction on one, two, or three objectives and continue to gradually add more components to the route as objectives are mastered.

Periodically, it is advisable to run a probe session. During a probe session, the teacher requires performance on all steps of the route, thus providing a baseline for all the nontraining steps in the route. The data will point out any steps that have been incidentally learned or partially trained.

Implementation and Data Monitoring

Instruction should be data-based, that is, regularly evaluated using both quantitative and qualitative measures. Data may be collected daily or on a varied schedule basis

(e.g., every third day). For practical purposes, the instructor may choose only to collect data on one objective at a time and periodically probe all objectives (components) across the route. The data from the skills used across more than one training route can be compiled into graphs that show overall performance on each skill. The teacher gathers the scores from all the routes for each skill and plots the student's performance. The number of trials per skill will depend on the performance criteria and the number of opportunities for practice across all the training routes.

Figure 6 shows a partial data sheet for teaching trailing on Tim's route from the classroom to the bus stop. Data from trailing trials (route steps 4 and 8) are combined with trailing data from other routes. On 7/5, the next objective, trailing around corners, was probed. On 7/11, the entire route was probed. The data suggest that trailing around corners is being learned incidentally as part of the contextual training package.

In addition, the teacher can plot the student's performance on each individual route. This can be done simply by adding the number of components in the route that the student can perform correctly and plotting the data on a graph. As previously mentioned, periodic probes should be conducted to determine performance on steps not yet being instructed. The data sheets and graph also

Instruction on objective #1 only: Trailing
Student: Tim
Route: Classroom to bus stop

Route steps	Trials ↓ Date →	Probe trailing corners					Probe entire route		
		7/1	7/2	7/3	7/5	7/8	7/9	7/10	7/11
1. Open door of classroom									−
2. *Trail around right corner					+				+
3. Cane in left hand									−
4. *Trail the wall	23	+7	+11	+10	+15	+17	+19	+21	+20
5. *Obstacles	3								+ + −
6. *Trail corner to the right					+				+
7. Down first set of stairs									+
8. *Trail wall	2	+ −	+ +	+ +	+ +	+ −	+ +	+ +	+ +
9. Down second set of stairs									+
10. At bottom of stairs, turn left									−
11. Square off									−
12. Follow bottom steps with cane									−
13. At end of stair, walk straight									+
14. Cross open space	2								+ −
15. When cane hits stairs, turn left									−

. . . etc. for remainder of route

Figure 6.　Sample data sheet: Tim. (From Gee, K., Harrell, R., & Rosenberg, R. [1987]. Teaching orientation and mobility skills within and across natural opportunities for travel: A model designed for learners with multiple severe disabilities. In L. Goetz, D. Guess, & K. Stremel-Campbell [Eds.], *Innovative program design for individuals with dual sensory impairments* [p. 151]. Baltimore: Paul H. Brookes Publishing Co.; reprinted by permission.)

provide a means for the O&M specialist and the teacher to communicate about the student's progress in order to make decisions about the program based on objective criteria.

Adaptations and Technology

The intent of all mobility techniques is to provide protection and information for individuals with visual impairments to allow them to move within and between various environments successfully and safely. Basic instructional formats and procedures may need to be adapted to accommodate the unique needs of each student. Many adaptations are programmatic in nature and require no special materials; however, modifications from traditional techniques or criteria are often needed. If it is determined by the O&M specialist that the use of a long cane is necessary, for example, modifications from the traditional touch technique may be necessary. The cane serves as a bumper and probe. It protects the traveler from contacting low obstacles, and it provides tactile and auditory feedback. The long cane is traditionally thought of as an extension of the index finger as it explores the path in front of the person who is blind. The touch technique involves keeping the hand and arm centered as the cane is extended out from the midline of the body. As the cane tip moves slightly off the ground in an arc to the right, the left foot steps forward, alternating foot and cane as one walks. All cane movements are to emanate from the wrist, and a rhythmic movement is necessary to remain in step and keep a safe arc size. Significant coordination and integration of body movements are needed when utilizing the traditional touch technique.

Problems of balance, cognitive disabilities, and/or limited range of motion may interfere with the acquisition of advanced cane skills. The diagonal technique is sometimes more beneficial for the student with coordination problems. This technique provides a degree of protection and serves as a bumper. The cane is held diagonally across the body in a stationary position. This technique does not provide optimum protection; however, it is better than no technique and is often easier to learn.

When students have difficulty with coordination and with learning to rhythmically tap the cane, or have trouble interpreting tactile feedback, the use of the constant contact technique may be helpful. The cane stays in continuous contact with the ground while moving back and forth in an arc movement. This technique allows for more tactile information about varying surfaces, contours, and obstacles. A disadvantage of the constant contact technique is that the cane often gets stuck in cracks, holes, and so forth.

Modifying the cane itself is beneficial for many students. One modification is the "marshmallow tip," a 1¼-inch diameter white nylon tip developed by Wurzburger (1980) that provides the student with as much tactile input as possible. Its weight encourages the student to keep the cane on the ground, and the tip slides across the surface more easily than the traditional tip. Another cane adaptation was developed by Morse (1980) for use by students with deaf-blindness. A diagonal cane extension was attached to the long cane at a point less than halfway from the ground, so that the secondary tip touched the opposite side from where the primary cane tip arc touched, thus providing body-width coverage without having to move the cane. This modification proved to be useful for students who had trouble coordinating the back and forth movements of the touch technique. Another modification for a student with a physical disability might be to paint a support crutch or three-pronged cane white with a red tip to signal the presence of a visual impairment. When properly used, the crutch will also identify obstacles.

For the student who has visual impairments and uses a wheelchair, the teacher may attach curb detectors to the wheelchair, to inform the student of obstacles and/or allow the student to trail a wall, curb, or building. Curb detectors are also useful in identifying intersecting corridors or doorways.

Adaptations to assist in route retention or in asking for help from the public are also important. The student who is nonverbal may use a route card with printed questions or a voice-output communication device that ask for assistance at particular crossings, for example, "Please help me cross Main Street," or, "I need to take the 104 uptown and get off at Main Street." The cards have a tactile cue so the student knows which card to use. The cards should be as subtle as possible. For the student with low vision, using a thick black marker on a white card has been successful. Picture cards have also been utilized with the student who has low vision and is also a nonreader.

For the student with a hearing loss in one ear, adaptations can be made, such as having the student walk on the side of the street with his or her hearing ear to the traffic. Wearing thin-soled shoes assists in obtaining more tactile input while traveling. It is also important to understand how the use of a hearing aid can seriously distort sound localization in loud traffic and inclement weather.

Electronic travel aids (ETAs) or devices (ETDs) (Pogrund, Healy, et al. 1993; Warren, Horn, & Hill, 1987) can provide supplemental information about the environment to an individual with visual impairments by enhancing sensory awareness beyond the distance provided by a cane or dog guide. ETDs are operated by emitting signals (through ultrasounds or laser beams) that reflect off objects or surfaces within the path of travel. These signals return to the device and are then translated into auditory or tactile sensations that need to be interpreted by the indi-

vidual. These devices may either be worn on an individual's head, hung on the chest, or carried in the hand (Jacobson, 1993; Sauerburger, 1994). ETDs are typically divided into three categories: 1) "go–no-go" devices, 2) primary travel devices, and 3) secondary travel devices (Pogrund, Healy, et al., 1993).

Even though some researchers have indicated that individuals with visual impairments have benefitted from using these devices (Warren et al., 1987), other researchers have reported that individuals with visual impairments have had little interest in using them for a variety of reasons including cost and limited availability (Jacobson, 1993). Michaud (1990) and Sauerburger (1994) reported individuals with deaf-blindness whom they instructed or interviewed did not feel that ETDs were particularly useful during travel for other reasons, including maintenance of the devices, familiarity with travel routes (e.g., used landmarks and clues for orientation), constant vibrations in crowded areas, and additional equipment they had to carry (e.g., canes, communication cards, writing devices).

Jacobson (1993) and Pogrund, Healy, et al. (1993) reported that more commonly accepted ETDs used by individuals with visual impairments are the Mowat Sensor, Pathsounder, Laser Cane, and the Sonicguide. Sauerburger (1994) indicated ETDs with tactile feedback were more appropriate for individuals with deaf-blindness. These ETDs included the above mentioned devices as well as the Wheelchair Pathfinder. A vibrotactile device that may be useful in detecting sounds, but not moving traffic, from a busy street is a TACTAID II +.

Gee et al. (1987) discussed the potential use of ETDs for students with multiple disabilities. The Pathsounder, developed by Lindsay Russell, is a small battery-operated sonar device that is mounted on the chest. It warns the user of objects within the path of travel by emitting ultrasounds (Jacobson, 1993). The feedback is both auditory and tactile through vibrations in a neck strap. The Pathsounder has been used with students with deaf-blindness and students who use wheelchairs; however, it is less popular because it is handmade, bulky, and unattractive. It is a member of the "go–no-go" category for ETDs (Pogrund, Healy, et al., 1993).

Nurion Industries developed two ETDs: the Polaron and the Laser Cane. The Polaron is a compact hand-held or chest-mounted aid for persons with visual impairments or deaf-blindness. It detects objects at 4, 12, or 6 feet (Sauerburger, 1993) and emits a sound or vibration. The chest mount or a headband sensor mount make it useful for persons using walkers, crutches, or wheelchairs. It is also considered a member of the "go–no-go" category for ETDs (Pogrund, Healy, et al., 1993).

The Laser Cane uses three lasers to detect objects in different directions from the body; one laser detects objects that are ahead in the path of travel, the other laser detects objects that are above the cane (in front of the individual's face) (Sauerburger, 1993), and the third laser detects objects below the cane (Pogrund, Healy, et al., 1993). These lasers are translated into auditory and tactile signals that determine the location of the obstacle. It can not detect glass, and the cane may give false signals if directed toward shiny surfaces. These canes are members of the category for primary travel devices (Pogrund, Healy, et al., 1993).

The Mowat Sensor is another ETD that is hand-held and has a vibrating output. This often is used with a long cane or dog guide (Jacobson, 1993) to locate doorways, obstacles, other landmarks, and pedestrians by emitting ultrasounds and signals. It can detect objects at a distance of 4–12 feet. This device does not detect drop-offs (e.g., curbs or stairs). It is a member of the category for secondary travel devices (Pogrund, Healy, et al., 1993). TACTAID II + is a device that is commonly worn on the wrist. It can detect sound frequencies between 200–7000 Hz. This device can be used to detect busy intersections or crowded pedestrian areas (Sauerburger, 1993).

Both programmatic and material adaptations should be specified and included in the instructional program. Generating functional adaptations and modifications of O&M teaching strategies and techniques for the student who is deaf-blind and students with other multiple disabilities has only recently begun. With the increase in technology, future optimism for increased independence is justified. Continued research and program development in this field will advance our ability to assist individuals with deaf-blindness to be as independently mobile as possible. Further efforts directed at integrated, transdisciplinary service delivery and innovative methods of expanding services to all individuals, regardless of ability level, will, no doubt, produce new and promising educational techniques and service delivery models in the field of orientation and mobility.

REFERENCES

Alsop, L. (Ed.). (1993). *A resource manual for understanding and interacting with infants, toddlers, and pre-school age children with deaf-blindness.* Logan: Utah State University, SKI*HI Institute.

American Foundation for the Blind. (1983). *Minutes of the National Task Force on Early Childhood Development.* New York: Author.

Americans with Disabilities Act of 1990 (ADA), PL 101-336. (July 26, 1990). Title 42, U.S.C. 12101 et seq. *U.S. Statutes at Large, 104,* 327–378.

Bailey, B.R., & Head, D.N. (1993). Orientation and mobility services to children and youth with multiple disabilities. *RE:view, 25*(2), 57–66.

Blind Children's Center. (1993). *First steps: A handbook for teaching young children who are visually impaired.* Los Angeles: Author.

Bolton, S. (1989). *One step at a time: A manual for families of children with hearing and vision impairments.* Monmouth, OR: Teaching Research Publications.

Brown, F., & Snell, M. (1993). Meaningful assessment. In M. Snell (Ed.), *Instruction of students with severe disabilities* (4th ed.). New York: Merrill/Macmillan.

Brown, L., Branston, M.B., Hamre-Nietupski, S., Pumpian, I., Certo, N., & Gruenewald, L. (1979). A strategy for developing chronological age appropriate and functional curricular content for severely handicapped adolescents and young adults. *Journal of Special Education, 13*(1), 81–90.

Bryant, N.W., & Jansen, W. (1980). Topic: The mentally retarded visually impaired person. In R. Welsh & B. Blasch (Eds.), *Foundations of orientation and mobility* (pp. 452–459). New York: American Foundation for the Blind.

Campbell, P. (1993). Integrated programming and movement disabilities. In M. Snell (Ed.), *Instruction of students with severe disabilities.* New York: Macmillan.

Chapman, E.K., & Stone, J.M. (1988). *The visually handicapped child in your classroom.* London: British Library Cataloging in Publication Data.

Chen, D. (1992). Early intervention: Presentation. In J.W. Reiman & P.A. Johnson (Eds.), *Proceedings from the National Symposium on Children and Youth Who Are Deaf-Blind* (pp. 37–51). Monmouth, OR: Teaching Research Publications.

Chen, D., Friedman, C.T., & Calvello, G. (1990). *Learning together: A parent guide to socially based routines for visually impaired infants.* Louisville, KY: American Printing House for the Blind.

Cioffi, J. (1994). Orientation and mobility issues and support strategies. In J. Everson (Ed.), *Supporting young adults with deaf-blindness in their communities: A guide for service providers, family members, and friends.* Baltimore: Paul H. Brookes Publishing Co.

Clarke, K.L. (1988). Barriers or enablers: Mobility devices for visually impaired and multihandicapped infants and preschoolers. *Education of the Visually Handicapped, 20*(3), 115–132.

Clarke, K.L., Sainato, D.M., & Ward, M.E. (1994). Travel performance of preschoolers: The effects of mobility training with a long cane versus a precane. *Journal of Visual Impairment & Blindness, 88,* 19–30.

Collins, M.T. (1992). Educational services: Presentation. In J.W. Reiman & P.A. Johnson (Eds.), *Proceedings from the National Symposium on Children and Youth Who Are Deaf-Blind* (pp. 165–178). Monmouth, OR: Teaching Research Publications.

Cornelius, N. (1994, April). Orientation and mobility . . . for infants? *California Deaf-Blind Services reSources,* 1–2.

Davenport, S. (1992). *Usher syndrome needs document.* Bloomington, MN: Vision Screening Project.

Davies, J. (1990). *Assessing infants who are visually impaired or deaf-blind for functional vision and orientation and mobility.* San Diego: San Diego City Schools.

Deaf-blindness. (1990). *Rehab Brief,* 1–4.

Dodson-Burk, B., & Hill, E.W. (1989a). *An orientation and mobility primer for families and young children.* New York: American Foundation for the Blind.

Dodson-Burk, B., & Hill, E.W. (1989b). *Preschool orientation and mobility screening.* Alexandria, VA: Division IX of the Association for Education and Rehabilitation of the Blind and Visually Impaired.

Downing, J., & Eichinger, J. (1990). Instructional strategies for learners with dual sensory impairments in integrated settings. *Journal of The Association for Persons with Severe Handicaps, 15,* 98–105.

Dunn, W. (1991). The sensorimotor systems: A framework for assessment and intervention. In F. Orelove & D. Sobsey, *Educating children with multiple disabilities: A transdisciplinary approach* (2nd ed.) (pp. 33–78). Baltimore: Paul H. Brookes Publishing Co.

Eisenberg, R.A. (1979). *Orientation and mobility.* Unpublished manual, California State University, Los Angeles.

Enos, J. (Ed.). (1993). *Usher syndrome and transitions for the future.* Sands Point, NY: Helen Keller National Center.

Everson, J.M. (Ed.). (1994). *Supporting young adults with deaf-blindness in their communities: A guide for service providers, family members, and friends.* Baltimore: Paul H. Brookes Publishing Co.

Falvey, M.A. (1992). *Community-based curriculum: Instructional strategies for students with severe handicaps* (2nd ed.). Baltimore: Paul H. Brookes Publishing Co.

Folio, M.R., & Fewell, R.R. (1983). *Peabody developmental motor scales and activity cards.* Allen, TX: DLM Teaching Resources.

Forest, M., & Lusthaus, E. (1989). Promoting educational equality for all students: Circles and maps. In S. Stainback, W. Stainback, & M. Forest (Eds.), *Educating all students in the mainstream of regular education*. Baltimore: Paul H. Brookes Publishing Co.

Foulke, E. (1971). The perceptual basis for mobility. *Research Bulletin of the American Foundation for the Blind, 23*, 1–8.

Foy, C.J., Kirchner, D., & Waple, L. (1991). The Connecticut precane. *Journal of Visual Impairment & Blindness, 85*(2), 85–86.

Foy, C.J., Von Scheden, M., & Waiculonis, J. (1992). The Connecticut precane: Case study and curriculum. *Journal of Visual Impairment & Blindness, 86*, 178–181.

Gamble, S.M. (1980). Topic: The visually handicapped person with cerebral palsy. In R. Welsh & B. Blasch (Eds.), *Foundations of orientation and mobility* (pp. 445–452). New York: American Foundation for the Blind.

Gee, K. (1993). *An experimental and qualitative investigation into the motivation and competence of peer interactions involving students with severe, multiple disabilities in middle school classrooms*. Unpublished doctoral dissertation, University of California, Berkeley.

Gee, K. (1994). The learner with deaf-blindness: Constructing context from depleted sources. In K. Gee, M. Alwell, N. Graham, & L. Goetz (Eds.), *Inclusive instructional design: Facilitating informed and active learning for individuals with deaf-blindness*. San Francisco, CA: San Francisco State University, California Research Institute.

Gee, K., Alwell, M., Graham, N., & Goetz, L. (1994). *Inclusive instructional design: Facilitating informed and active learning for individuals with deaf-blindness*. (Manual produced on the Active Interactions Project, OSERS Validated Practices: Children and Youth with Deaf-Blindness, Grant No. HO 86G00003). San Francisco: Department of Special Education, San Francisco State University, California Research Institute.

Gee, K., & Goetz, L. (1985). Outcomes of instructing orientation and mobility across purposeful travel routes in natural environments. Unpublished manuscript, San Francisco State University, Department of Special Education.

Gee, K., Graham, N., & Goetz, L. (1994). *Context instruction: Effects of a method for increasing initiation and participation for students with multiple physical and sensory disabilities*. Manuscript submitted for publication, San Francisco State University.

Gee, K., Graham, N., Oshima, G., Yoshioka, K., & Goetz, L. (1991). Teaching students to request the continuation of routine activities by using time delay and decreasing physical assistance in the context of chain interruption. *Journal of The Association for Persons with Severe Handicaps, 16*, 154–167.

Gee, K., Graham, N., Sailor, W., & Goetz, L. (in press). Use of integrated, general education and community settings as primary contexts for skill instruction of students with severe, multiple disabilities. *Behavior Modification, 1*.

Gee, K., Harrell, R., & Rosenberg, R. (1987). Teaching orientation and mobility skills within and across natural opportunities for travel: A model designed for learners with multiple severe disabilities. In L. Goetz, D. Guess, & K. Stremel-Campbell (Eds.), *Innovative program design for individuals with dual sensory impairments* (pp. 127–157). Baltimore: Paul H. Brookes Publishing Co.

Goetz, L., & Gee, K. (1987a). Teaching visual attention in functional contexts: Acquisition and generalization of complex visual motor skills. *Journal of Visual Impairment & Blindness, 81*, 115–118.

Goetz, L., & Gee, K. (1987b). Functional vision programming: A model for teaching visual behaviors in natural contexts. In Goetz, L., Guess, D., & Stremel-Campbell, C. (Eds.), *Innovative program design for individuals with dual sensory impairments*. Baltimore: Paul H. Brookes Publishing Co.

Goetz, L., Guess, D., & Stremel-Campbell, K. (Eds.). (1987). *Innovative program design for students with dual sensory impairments*. Baltimore: Paul H. Brookes Publishing Co.

Gothelf, C.R., Rikhye, C.H., & Silberman, R.K. (1988). *Working with students who have dual sensory impairments and cognitive disabilities: A handbook for special education teachers and related services personnel*. Albany: New York State Education Department.

Grennon-Brooks, J., & Brooks, M.G. (1993). *The case for constructivist classrooms*. Alexandria, VA: Association for Supervision and Curriculum Development.

Hapeman, L. (1967). Developmental concepts of blind children between the ages of three and six as they relate to orientation and mobility. *International Journal for the Education of the Blind, 17*, 41–48.

Harley, R.K., Henderson, F.M., & Wood, T.A. (1975). The development of a scale in orientation and mobility for multiply impaired blind children. *Education of the Visually Handicapped,* 7, 1–5.

Harley, R.K., Wood, T.A., & Merbler, J. (1975). Programmed instruction in orientation and mobility for multiply impaired blind children. *The New Outlook for the Blind,* 69, 419–422.

Harley, R.K., Wood, T.A., & Merbler, J. (1980). An orientation and mobility program for multiply impaired blind children. *Exceptional Children,* 46, 326–331.

Harrell, R., & Rosenberg, R. (1986). *Best practices in orientation and mobility for individuals who are multihandicapped vision impaired.* Unpublished manuscript, California State University, Los Angeles, and Whittier Union High School District.

Heydt, K. (1992). Orientation and mobility. In C. Cushman, K. Heydt, S. Edwards, M. Clark, & M. Allon (Eds.), *Perkins activity and resource guide: A handbook for teachers and parents of students with visual and multiple disabilities.* Watertown, MA: Perkins School for the Blind.

Hill, E.W. (1981). *The Hill performance test of selected positional concepts.* Chicago: Stoelting.

Hill, E.W., & Ponder, P. (1976). *Orientation and mobility techniques: A guide for the practitioner.* New York: American Foundation for the Blind.

Hill, E.W., Rosen, S., Correa, V.I., & Langley, M.B. (1984). Preschool orientation and mobility: An expanded definition. *Education of the Visually Handicapped,* 16(2), 58–72.

Houghton, J. (1993, July/August). Incorporating functional orientation and mobility skills in the ecological process. *Indiana Deaf-Blind Services Project Information Update,* 1–2.

Houghton, J. (in press). *Orientation and mobility for youth with deaf-blindness.* Sands Point, NY: Helen Keller National Center.

Hug, D., Chernus-Mansfield, N., & Hayashi, D. (1993). *Move with me: A parents' guide to movement development for visually impaired babies.* Los Angeles: Blind Childrens Center.

Jacobson, W.H. (1993). *The art and science of teaching orientation and mobility to persons with visual impairments.* New York: American Foundation for the Blind.

Joffee, E.(1988). A home-based orientation and mobility program for infants and toddlers. *Journal of Visual Impairment Blindness,* 82, 282–285.

Joffee, E., & Rikhye, C.H. (1991). Orientation and mobility for students with severe visual and multiple impairments: A new perspective. *Journal of Visual Impairment & Blindness,* 85, 211–216.

Kay, L. (1974). A sonar aid to enhance spatial per-ception of the blind. *The Radio and Electronic Engineer,* 44, 605–627.

Kennedy, C.R. (1990). Interview with Rich McGann, Resource & Media Director for Western Pennsylvania School for Blind Children. *TASH Newsletter,* 5.

Kronick, M.K. (1987). Children and canes: An adaptive approach. *Journal of Visual Impairment & Blindness,* 81, 61–62.

Langley, M.B. (1980). *Functional vision inventory.* Chicago: Stoelting.

Lessard, K.J., & Lolli, D. (1973). *Some thoughts on mobility for deaf-blind.* Watertown, MA: Perkins School for the Blind.

Lolli, D. (1980). Topic: Deaf-blind persons. In R. Welsh & B. Blasch (Eds.), *Foundations of orientation and mobility.* New York: American Foundation for the Blind.

Lubecki, C. (1994). O&M techniques for special populations. *RE:view,* 25(1), 25–27.

Lyon, S., & Lyon, G. (1980). Team functioning and staff development: A role release approach to providing integrated educational services for severely handicapped students. *Journal of The Association for Persons with Severe Handicaps,* 5, 250–263.

Merbler, J., & Wood, T.A. (1984). Predicting orientation and mobility proficiency in mentally retarded visually impaired children. *Education and Training of the Mentally Retarded,* 19, 228–230.

Michaud, M. (1990). Making the difference for deaf-blind travelers in mass transit. In M. Uslan, A. Peck, W. Wiener, & A. Stern (Eds.), *Access to mass transit for blind and visually impaired travelers.* New York: American Foundation for the Blind.

Miller, H. (1982). Relationship between mobility level and development of positional concepts in visually impaired children. *Journal of Visual Impairment & Blindness,* 78, 149–152.

Morgan, E.C. (Ed.). (1992). *INSITE resources for family centered intervention for infants, toddlers, and preschoolers who are visually impaired.* Logan: Utah State University, SKI*HI Institute.

Morse, K.A. (1980). Modifications of the long cane for use by a multiply impaired child. *Journal of Visual Impairment & Blindness,* 76, 15–18.

Mount, B., & Zwernick, K. (1988). *It's never too early, it's never too late: A booklet about personal futures planning.* St. Paul: Minnesota Governor's Planning Council on Developmental Disabilities.

O'Donnell, L.M., & Livingston, R.L. (1991). Active exploration of the environment by young children with low vision: A review of the literature. *Journal of Visual Impairment & Blindness, 85,* 287–289.

Pogrund, R.L., Fazzi, D.L., & Lampert, J.S. (1992). *Early Focus: Working with young blind and visually impaired children and their families.* New York: American Foundation for the Blind.

Pogrund, R., Fazzi, D.L., & Schreier, E.M. (1993). Development of a preschool kiddy cane. *Journal of Visual Impairment & Blindness, 87,* 52–54.

Pogrund, R., Healy, G., Jones, K., Levack, N., Martin-Curry, S., Martinez, C., Marz, J., Roberson-Smith, B., & Vrba, A. (1993). *Teaching age-appropriate purposeful skills (TAPS): An orientation and mobility curriculum for students with visual impairments.* Austin: Texas School for the Blind and Visually Impaired.

Pogrund, R.L., & Rosen, S.J. (1989). The preschool blind child *can* be a cane user. *Journal of Visual Impairment & Blindness, 83*(9), 431–439.

Rainforth, B., York, J., & Macdonald, C. (1992). *Collaborative teams for students with severe disabilities: Integrating therapy and educational services.* Baltimore: Paul H. Brookes Publishing Co.

Reiser, A., Gruth, T.S., & Hill, B.W. (1982). Mental processes mediating independent travel: Implications for orientation and mobility. *Journal of Visual Impairment & Blindness, 76,* 212–218.

Roseborough, D. (1994). Orientation and mobility. From a parent's perspective. *California Deaf Blind Services reSources,* p. 3.

Sailor, W., Gee, K., & Karasoff, P. (1993). School restructuring and full inclusion. In M. Snell (Ed.), *Systematic instruction of persons with severe handicaps* (4th ed.). Columbus: OH: Charles E. Merrill.

Sailor, W., Goetz, L., Anderson, J., Hunt, P., & Gee, K. (1987). Research on community intensive instruction as a model for building functional generalized skills. In R. Horner, G. Dunlap, & R. Koegel (Eds.), *Generalization and maintenance in applied settings* (pp. 67–98). Baltimore: Paul H. Brookes Publishing Co.

Sailor, W., Halvorsen, A., Anderson, J., Goetz, L., Gee, K., Doering, K., & Hunt, P. (1986). Community intensive instruction. In R.H. Horner, L.H. Meyer, & D.B. Fredericks (Eds.), *Education of learners with severe handicaps: Exemplary service strategies* (pp. 251–288). Baltimore: Paul H. Brookes Publishing Co.

Sauerburger, D. (1993). *Independence without sight or sound: Suggestions for practitioners working with deaf-blind adults.* New York: American Foundation for the Blind.

Sauerburger, D. (1994, April). Why orientation and mobility? *California Deaf-Blind Services reSources, 1,* 7.

Schingledecker, C.A., & Foulke, E. (1978). A human factors approach to the assessment of the mobility of blind pedestrians. *Human Factors, 20,* 273–286.

Seiler, L.H., Everson, J.M., & Carr, T.S. (1992). *A needs-assessment of agencies serving individuals with deaf-blindness: A national profile of transitional services.* Sands Point, NY: Helen Keller National Center.

Siegel-Causey, E., & Guess, D. (1989). *Enhancing nonsymbolic communication interactions among learners with severe disabilities.* Baltimore: Paul H. Brookes Publishing Co.

Simmons, S.S., & Maida, S. (1993). *Reaching, crawling, walking . . . let's get moving: Orientation and mobility for preschool children.* Los Angeles: Blind Children's Center.

Singer, R. (1966). Interlimb skill ability in motor skill performance. *Research Quarterly, 37,* 406–410.

Skellenger, A.C., & Hill, E.W. (1991). Current practices and considerations regarding long cane instruction with preschool children. *Journal of Visual Impairment & Blindness, 85,* 101–104.

Snell, M.E. (1993). *Instruction of students with severe disabilities.* (4th ed.). New York: Macmillan.

Snell, M., & Browder, D. (1986). Community referenced instruction. Research and issues. *Journal of The Association for Persons with Severe Handicaps, 11,* 1–11.

Stainback, S., & Stainback, W. (1992). *Curriculum considerations in inclusive classrooms: Facilitating learning for all students.* Baltimore: Paul H. Brookes Publishing Co.

Strelow, E.R. (1985). What is needed for a theory of mobility: Direct perception and cognitive maps—lessons from the blind. *Psychological Review, 92,* 226–248.

Stroud, M., & Higgins, N. (unknown). *Orientation and mobility tips.* Sands Point, NY: Helen Keller National Center.

Touchette, P. (1971). Transfer of stimulus control: Measuring the moment of transfer. *Journal of the Experimental Analysis of Behavior, 15,* 347–354.

Turnbull, A., & Morningstar, M. (1993). Family and professional interaction. In M. Snell (Ed.), *Instruction of students with severe disabilities.* New York: Merrill/MacMillan.

Utley, B.L., & Nelson, G.L. (1991). *A model for assessment and intervention on visual and visual-*

motor skills of persons with multiple disabilities. Unpublished manuscript, University of Pittsburgh.

van Dijk, J. (1986). An educational curriculum for deaf-blind multihandicapped persons. In D. Ellis (Ed.), *Sensory impairments in mentally handicapped people* (pp. 375–382). London: Cross-Helm.

van Dijk, J. (1989, July). *Techniques for working with children who are deaf-blind.* Paper presented at symposium on deaf-blindness, University of Washington, Seattle.

Virginia Commonwealth University & Helen Keller National Center. (Producers). (1993). *Sensory disabilities and supported employment* [Videotape]. Richmond: Virginia Commonwealth University.

Warren, D.H. (1978). Childhood visual impairment: Services and uses of knowledge. *Journal of Visual Impairment & Blindness, 72,* 404–411.

Warren, S.F., Horn, E.H., & Hill, E.W. (1987).

Some innovative educational applications of advanced technologies. In L. Goetz, D. Guess, & K. Stremel-Campbell (Eds.), *Innovative program design for individuals with dual sensory impairments.* Baltimore: Paul H. Brookes Publishing Co.

Watson, D. (1992). Adult services: Presentation. In J.W. Reiman & P.A. Johnson (Eds.), *Proceedings from the National Symposium on Children and Youth Who Are Deaf-Blind* (pp. 201–212). Monmouth, OR: Teaching Research Publications.

Welsh, R.D., & Blasch, B. (Eds.). (1980). *Foundations of orientation and mobility.* New York: American Foundation for the Blind.

Which problems are most severe? (1980). *Rehab Brief,* p. 3.

Wolery, M., Ault, M.J., & Doyle, P. (1992). *Teaching students with moderate to severe disabilities.* New York: Longman.

Wurzburger, P. (1980). Wurzburger Mobility Aids. Concord, CA: Author.

Chapter 15

Instructional Strategies in Early Intervention Programs for Children with Deaf-Blindness

*Ilene S. Schwartz
and Bonnie McBride*

The field of early childhood special education (ECSE) has changed dramatically in the last 20 years. Currently, special education services for preschool children ages 3–5 are mandated in all 50 states, and with the passage of PL 99-457 (Education of the Handicapped Act Amendments of 1986), early interventionists, family members, and policy makers are hard at work across the nation to extend this mandate to birth. Not only are early intervention services much more available as of this writing than they were 20 years ago, but the form of these services has changed significantly. Early childhood special education services are becoming increasingly family focused and community based. Similarly, the goal of early intervention has changed. Early intervention services, ranging from Head Start to programs for children with severe disabilities, are not viewed as an inoculation to "fix" children who are at risk or who have identified disabilities, but rather as the beginning of a lifelong partnership to enhance the competence and confidence of the children and families being served.

Current recommended practices in early childhood special education also reflect this shift in philosophy. These recommended practices include: 1) individualized programming in inclusive, community-based settings; 2) multidomain assessments; 3) use of normalized instructional strategies; 4) planning for transitions; 5) family-focused intervention; and 6) outcome-based programming (Bailey & Wolery, 1992; Carta, Schwartz, Atwater, & McConnell, 1991; Division of Early Childhood, 1993; McDonnell & Hardman, 1988). Young children with deaf-blindness present some of the greatest programming challenges facing early childhood special education personnel. It is indeed a complex task to incorporate the changing role of early interventionists and current recommended practices without compromising the spe-

Preparation of this chapter was supported in part by U.S. Department of Education Grant H023C0212 and Cooperative Agreement H086A20003. The contents and opinions expressed herein do not reflect the position or policy of the U.S. Department of Education, and no official endorsement should be inferred.

cialized needs of young children with deaf-blindness and multiple disabilities.

The purpose of this chapter is to outline nine recommended practices for early intervention programs, and to discuss how these practices can be implemented in inclusive settings serving young children with deaf-blindness and multiple disabilities. The nine program characteristics that are discussed in this chapter are displayed in Table 1. These nine program characteristics are not intended to be an exhaustive description of ECSE. Clearly it is beyond the scope of this chapter to discuss in adequate detail all the necessary components of an effective early intervention program for children with deaf-blindness. Rather, it is the authors' intent to highlight important issues and provide a propaedeutic outline that can be used by practitioners in program development and by families in evaluating prospective programs. Readers who would like more information on early intervention programs in general should refer to some of the textbooks in this area (see, e.g., Allen, 1992; Bailey & Wolery, 1992; Bricker, 1989; Meisels & Shonkoff, 1990; Odom & Karnes, 1988; Peterson, 1987; Raver, 1991).

RECOMMENDED CHARACTERISTICS AND PRACTICES OF INCLUSIVE EARLY CHILDHOOD PROGRAMS

Inclusive and Community Based

Across the United States, more and more children with disabilities are being served in inclusive classrooms in their neighborhood schools and other community-based programs (e.g., community centers, recreational programs, childcare centers). The social, moral, and legislative imperatives driving this movement are firmly embedded, and the integration of children with diverse abilities is well-established as a goal for schools of the

Table 1.   Recommended program characteristics and practices of early childhood special education

- Inclusive and community based
- Comprehensive and adaptable
- Multidomain assessments
- Individualized programming
- Normalized instructional methodologies
- High levels of active engagement
- Transition planning for future placements
- Family-focused intervention
- Outcome-based programming

future (e.g., Brown et al., 1989; Peck, Odom, & Bricker, 1993; Salisbury, 1991; Salisbury & Vincent, 1990; Taylor, 1988; Vincent, Brown, & Getz-Sheftel, 1981). Throughout the country, evidence demonstrates that inclusion is no longer viewed as "an experiment to be tested, but [is now viewed as] a value to be followed" (Ferguson & Asch, 1989, p. 137). The challenge facing researchers, practitioners, and parents at this point is not to demonstrate that inclusive education programs are effective for children with multiple disabilities, but to identify instructional strategies that can be used within inclusive settings to support the unique needs of children with deaf-blindness. The issue of *support* for children means that our goal must be to enable *all* children to fully participate in and benefit from inclusive programming. Support may include specialized instructional strategies, ongoing staff training, and technical assistance. The key to providing high-quality inclusive programs is that the support is provided within the context of a high-quality, early childhood education program.

Providing inclusive school programs for preschool children, however, introduces a new variable into the equation. The majority of children under the age of five are not served by the public schools; yet public schools are mandated to serve preschool children with disabilities. The question becomes, what is the most natural setting and least restrictive environment (LRE) for young children with deaf-blindness? What practices must be in place to make the setting effective? How can a public school system provide an inclusive classroom for a four-year-old with multiple disabilities when the district does not provide any services for typically developing four-year-olds? Is an elementary school the most appropriate setting for an early intervention program for young children with disabilities?

This is where the issue of community-based services becomes essential in providing high-quality and inclusive services to preschool children with disabilities. Although the majority of children under the age of five are not being served by the public school system, they are participating in some out-of-home educational or childcare arrangements. These types of programs include private preschools, Head Start, center-based childcare, and family childcare. Outside of the home, these types of community-based programs may be the most natural environment for young children, and must be considered viable placement options for young children with deaf-blindness (Hanline & Hanson, 1989; Hanson & Widerstrom, 1993). Researchers, practitioners, and families must expand their view of possible placement and service delivery options and work with the staff of community-based programs to develop appropriate guidelines for inclusion. Inclusive programs for children with deaf-blindness must meet the following dual quality standards: 1) standards developed to assess the quality of early childhood programs and 2) additional standards used to evaluate early childhood special education programs. One of the challenges in implementing inclusive early intervention programs is to maintain the programmatic features of a high-quality early childhood program (e.g., providing a variety of high-interest, meaningful activities that encourage children's

participation), while providing adequate support for children with deaf-blindness to participate and learn in the setting.

Comprehensive and Adaptable

The needs of young children with disabilities, especially children with deaf-blindness, are varied and complex. Early childhood special education programs must be prepared to address these needs by providing a wide range of services and supports to young children and their families. Programs for young children with special needs should offer a range of services that vary in intensity based on the needs and preferences of the children and families they serve. The range of services required will vary across families and children, and it is quite likely that no child in a school district will receive the same package of services and supports as another. Services included in an early intervention program for children with deaf-blindness may include:

- Orientation and mobility training
- Vision and hearing services
- Communication intervention
- Occupational therapy
- Physical therapy
- Medical services
- Social services
- Recreational services
- Family support services

The trend in early childhood special education is toward providing services for all children through a *transdisciplinary approach* (e.g., Bricker, 1989; Klein & Campbell, 1990; Peterson, 1987; Raver, 1991). In a transdisciplinary approach, professionals from various disciplines, along with family members, work together in planning, implementing, and evaluating services. This differs from an *interdisciplinary approach* where professionals from different disciplines may work together in a more parallel manner. An essential element in the transdisciplinary approach is that professionals share a common philosophy and goals and educate each other about their discipline-specific practices so that all professionals can implement the different components of a child's program.

There is no set prescription outlining the members of a transdisciplinary team, although all of the disciplines working with the child and his or her family should be represented. Most transdisciplinary teams have at least a family member, teacher, communication specialist, social worker, occupational and/or physical therapist (if there are motor concerns), and nurse (if there are health or nutrition concerns). Transdisciplinary teams serving children with deaf-blindness should also have as active members a vision specialist, an audiologist, and a specialist in deaf-blindness who can address the child's unique needs (Michael & Paul, 1991). The needs associated with sensory impairments will most likely be the primary focus of the transdisciplinary team; therefore, it may be appropriate for a specialist in the area of deaf-blindness to be the service coordinator and/or team leader. It will be the responsibility of this specialist to educate the other members of the team on the unique needs of a child with deaf-blindness. In districts where specialized personnel are not available (see chap. 5, this volume, for a discussion of personnel needs), members of the transdisciplinary team should seek the participation of appropriate consultants or additional training for one or more team members.

A transdisciplinary approach to early intervention allows children and their families to receive services that are based on a holistic view of the child within the context of the family, rather than on a segregated view of development that addresses one domain of a child's behavior at a time. For example, the physical therapist cannot limit her input to gross motor issues, and the special education teacher cannot restrict his view to academic concerns. "Interaction across discipline lines permits professionals to get a more balanced picture of the whole child" (Raver, 1991, p. 31). When working with a young child with multiple disabilities, the need for transdisciplinary assessment, planning, intervention, and evaluation are accentuated. The needs demonstrated by these children and their families cut across traditional developmental domains and professional boundaries. To provide comprehensive and effective services that meet the needs of children with deaf-blindness, professionals must work as members of cohesive and interactive transdisciplinary teams. Transdisciplinary teaming requires practitioners to abandon preconceived notions of professional responsibilities. This type of collaboration enables team members to develop programs that are more reflective of the needs of individual children and their families than more traditional special education programs.

Early intervention programs must also provide flexibility in the location, format, and duration of services provided. At various points in the child's life, the child and family may require differing amounts and types of services. These service delivery options include home-based intervention (e.g., a therapist and/or teacher works with the child and the family in their home), center-based intervention (e.g., the child attends a school program), and community-based intervention (e.g., a therapist and/or teacher works with the child at a childcare setting, or a teacher works with the child and the family in a specific community activity such as attending church or eating in a restaurant). Most children and families will require a combination of all three of these service delivery options.

In addition to considering where the intervention services will be provided, transdisciplinary intervention teams must also decide when and by whom the services will be provided. Any home-based services should be provided when the primary caretakers are available. If both parents are involved in the child's care, visits should be scheduled to include both parents and/or other important caretakers (e.g., primary babysitter, grandmother, siblings). This type of flexibility may not be supported institutionally, but teachers, therapists, and families should attempt to work with the school and their employers to arrange a workable schedule.

Services should be scheduled to support the child's greatest needs. For example, if feeding is a primary concern for the family, some visits should be scheduled around mealtimes to address this issue in "real time." Likewise, if supporting the child in a childcare setting is a primary concern for the family, the teacher and/or therapist should work with the family and the childcare provider to address the child's needs in that setting.

Providing services that are comprehensive and adaptable is essential in meeting the needs of young children with deaf-blindness and their families. There may not be a typical program for children with deaf-blindness in the district; rather, an individual program is developed for every child depending on his or her unique strengths and needs. This type of service delivery model is fraught with administrative difficulties; however, given the diverse and complex needs of young children with deaf-blindness, flexibility is essential. A challenge facing professionals on transdisciplinary teams is to overcome these barriers and develop services for individual children based on specific needs rather than static program descriptions.

Multidomain Assessments

The purpose of assessment in early childhood special education is to provide comprehensive information regarding the strengths and needs of a young child and his or her family, which can then be used to develop an intervention program. For young children with deaf-blindness, a major purpose of the assessment process will be to identify strengths and preferred learning modalities (e.g., residual vision and hearing); determine the appropriate mode of communication; determine appropriate and functional goals; assess preferred activities, objects, and other forms of reinforcers and motivation; and assess family priorities and concerns. There is growing consensus among professionals in early childhood special education that the use of standardized measures to assess developmental levels is both inadequate and inappropriate (Neisworth & Bagnato, 1992). This is good news for early interventionists working with children with deaf-blindness and their families. Families and professionals have long recognized the low instructional utility of standardized assessments for these children and have advocated for a more prescriptive approach to assessment.

The implementation of PL 99-457 has sparked interest in developing assessment instruments that are more appropriate and functional for young children. The new public law requires assessments of young children to be interdisciplinary and multidimensional; practitioners and families call for the assessments to be ecologically valid and have a high degree of instructional utility. This means that assessments must cross multiple domains, use multiple measures, include multiple informants and sources of information gathering in the process, observe children in natural environments, and assess functional skills. Assessments should also be ongoing to monitor progress and changing needs.

Assessment of Child Behavior The use of multidimensional assessment is crucial for a child with deaf-blindness. In addition to the more traditional developmental domains (e.g., cognitive, motor, communication, self-care, social, play), assessments of young children with deaf-blindness must include thorough and functional assessments in vision, hearing, and orientation and mobility. Functional vision and hearing assessments may be the most important components of an assessment battery for these children. The purpose of these assessments is not only to determine the extent of the hearing and vision loss, but more importantly, to determine any residual use of these senses and make recommendations for intervention strategies to accomodate and enhance them. This information is essential for planning an effective intervention program. (For more information regarding vision and hearing assessment, see Goetz & Gee, 1987; Lundervold, Lewin, & Irwin, 1987; Niswander, 1987.)

A functional orientation and mobility assessment must also be included in an assessment battery for young children with deaf-blindness. Orientation and mobility skills are keystone skills (Wolery, 1991) to facilitate children's success in inclusive programs. A child's ability to move independently within his or her environment will increase opportunities for participation, active engagement, child initiations, and peer interactions. Although orientation and mobility training has traditionally been conducted with older students exclusively, the work of Clarke and colleagues (Clarke, Sainato, & Ward, 1993) demonstrates the effectiveness and positive side effects of this training with preschool children. (See chap. 14, this volume, for more information on orientation and mobility issues.)

Assessment of Classroom Ecology Assessment of the classroom ecology is an important component of a comprehensive educational assessment for young children with deaf-blindness. Components of the classroom ecology can have a facilitative or deleterious effect on children's behavior (Bailey & Wolery, 1992; Carta, Sainato, & Green-

wood, 1988; Sainato & Carta, 1992). A thorough assessment of classroom ecology can identify elements that can be modified to optimize a child's success in an early intervention setting and therefore play an important role in planning for intervention.

The classroom ecology consists of static and dynamic elements (Carta et al., 1988). The static elements of a classroom environment include activities, materials, location of activities (e.g., at tables or on the floor), size of group, student–teacher ratio, and group composition (e.g., the number of children with disabilities and the number of typically developing children). Dynamic elements of the classroom environment include teacher behavior and child behavior. An assessment of classroom ecology should describe how a child spends his or her day (e.g., what activities, alone or with peers, independent or with assistance), the frequency and quality of adult–child interaction, and the opportunities that exist for the child in the classroom. The latter component of the assessment may be most important for a child with severe disabilities and may have the greatest impact on practice. This portion of the assessment should address the following questions:

- Are materials functionally accessible (e.g, can the children access the materials independently)?
- Do materials have appropriate adaptations (e.g., switches)?
- Is the classroom free of barriers inhibiting mobility?
- Are there activities in the classroom in which the child can participate independently?
- Are there activities and materials available in the classroom that are of high interest to the child?
- Do teachers and typically developing peers know how to communicate with the child with deaf-blindness (e.g., teach-

ing peers greeting and name signs using manual sign and/or tactile communication systems)?

- Are there typically developing peers proximal and available for interaction?

Answering these questions will provide necessary information for developing a classroom environment that facilitates interaction and supports children with severe disabilities.

Another component of the classroom ecology that should be assessed is the amount and types of environmental prompts and supports that are available in the classroom. These prompts may include routines, use of multisensory cues (e.g., calendar boxes), and use of peer buddies. The use of routines can be extremely beneficial for young children with severe disabilities. A child's ability to learn a routine and modifications to the routine should be assessed and considered an adaptive skill that can be used to teach new behaviors, activities, and facilitate independence in new settings.

Using Assessments in Planning and Evaluation For teachers and other professionals working with children with deaf-blindness on a daily basis, the planning and evaluation aspects of assessment will be the most important. To facilitate functional and appropriate program planning and ongoing evaluation, early childhood special educators should use a linked system of assessment and intervention (Bricker, 1989; Bricker & Littman, 1982). The key characteristics of a linked system are to use the information gathered during assessment to develop the individualized family service plan (IFSP) or the individualized education program (IEP), base the selection of instructional strategies on the individual learning objectives, center the ongoing evaluation activities on the IFSP or IEP goals, and use the evaluation information to guide future intervention goals. This type of system increases the likelihood that

priorities identified during assessment will be addressed in intervention and that these priorities will serve as the baseline for further assessments. Using a linked system of assessment and intervention helps to increase the efficiency and accountability of early intervention services.

Individualized Programming

Special education is built upon the concept of individualization. The philosophy of inclusion reinforces the importance of individualization and extends this concept to all children. An ongoing challenge in early childhood special education programs is to conduct a careful analysis of the strengths and needs of the children in the program, and develop goals and objectives that support and challenge the child.

Building an individualized program for young children with significant developmental delays requires professionals and family members to assess the "goodness of fit" (Thomas & Chess, 1977) between the child and the program. The fit or the match with the program depends on goals, objectives, activities, and instructional strategies being individually appropriate, developmentally appropriate, and chronologically age-appropriate. Goals and objectives must also be functional and help to increase the independence and competence of the child.

Developing individualized programs for children with deaf-blindness also involves decisions about the language strategies (e.g., American Sign Language [ASL] or signed English) that will be used. Parents and professionals must work together to share information and preferences honestly, and to use this information to make this difficult and important choice. Professionals must individualize programs to support the different needs, priorities, and choices of individual families.

It is extremely important for children with deaf-blindness in inclusive settings to have an individualized program. Many early childhood settings base their programs on the *Developmentally Appropriate Practice* guidelines (Bredekamp, 1987) developed by the National Association for the Education of Young Children (NAEYC). Although these guidelines are based upon the concepts of age appropriateness and individual appropriateness, they do not account for the specialized intervention needs of young children with disabilities. These guidelines alone are not sufficient as a basis for an early intervention program for children with special needs (Carta et al., 1991; Carta, Atwater, Schwartz, & McConnell, 1993; Wolery, Strain, & Bailey, 1992). A challenge for early interventionists working in inclusive early childhood programs is to integrate the *Developmentally Appropriate Practice* guidelines and explicit and systematic instructional strategies into a comprehensive and individualized program for a child with deaf-blindness.

An important first step in developing a truly individualized program is to select appropriate goals. Goals must be functional and must address the child's needs in school and nonschool settings, incorporate the child's strengths and preferences as well as needs, teach the child skills that enable him or her to impact the environment, and include the family in the goal selection process. For children with deaf-blindness, programs must also individualize the mode of communication used, the type of orientation and mobility training conducted, the kinds of cues given to indicate routines and activities, the type of adaptations to materials and the classroom environment necessary to facilitate independent engagement, and the kinds of reinforcers that will be used to strengthen behavior.

Normalized Instructional Methodologies

Wolfensberger (1972) defined normalization as the "utilization of means which are as culturally normative as possible, in order to establish and/or maintain personal behaviors and characteristics which are as culturally normative as possible" (p. 28). Normalized instructional strategies are contextually based, are the least intrusive possible, and capitalize upon natural patterns of interaction. Researchers and practitioners working in both the fields of early intervention and in the education of children with deaf-blindness have a history of recognizing the importance of normalized instructional strategies. The efficacy of teaching in the natural environment, teaching across the child's day, and taking advantage of naturally occurring "teachable moments" are well established in these professions (e.g., Bricker & Cripe, 1992; Hart & Risley, 1975, 1980; Noonan & McCormick, 1993; Stillman & Battle, 1984; van Dijk, 1966; Warren & Kaiser, 1988). These professionals have moved best practices toward instructional strategies that work to "develop functional skills that capitalize on the daily interactions of children with their social and physical environment" (Bricker & Cripe, 1992, p. 2).

Intervention programs that rely on normalized instructional strategies are not haphazard or accidental. Rather, they require careful planning, environmental arrangement, and staff training. A variety of activities must be planned that catch and maintain the interest of children with diverse abilities, the classroom environment must facilitate and support their participation, and classroom personnel must be able to identify and take advantage of these teachable moments by matching the most appropriate strategy to the appropriate goal while maintaining the ecological validity and contextual integrity of the interaction. In addition to meeting the criterion of normalization, instructional strategies for young children with deaf-blindness must also be effective, efficient, and functional (Bailey & McWilliam, 1990).

That is, instructional strategies must result in skill acquisition, make good use of instructional time, and lead to behavior changes that are generalizable and meaningful.

Clearly, there is not one strategy that will be effective for all children at all times. The effectiveness of an instructional strategy depends upon the match with the target goal, the current context, and the child's motivation. Teachers must be able to implement a range of instructional strategies (McWilliam & Bailey, 1992; Noonan & McCormick, 1993). In general, normalized instructional strategies occur within the natural stream of interaction in the classroom; take advantage of multiple, brief, and distributed trials; are focused on an activity or object of interest to the child; and use natural consequences (Warren & Kaiser, 1988).

Normalized instructional strategies should provide students with adequate support to participate successfully in a wide variety of classroom activities. Children with more severe disabilities may require additional support to benefit from the rich environments offered in inclusive early childhood settings. It is important to use instructional strategies that allow teachers to find the appropriate balance of directive and explorative/discovery learning for individual children.

A child's need for direction or support may vary across activities and times of the day. Children should have opportunities within their programming day to make choices, initiate activities, and demonstrate independence. There will also be times within the day when children need to participate in teacher-directed activities. Children with deaf-blindness may require systematic and explicit instruction in both child-initiated and teacher-initiated activities. They may also require direct instruction to explore materials and environments and to respond to peer and adult initiations. That is, children may need systematic instruction to learn to take advantage of a well-planned and interesting environment.

The effectiveness of an instructional strategy must be determined for individual children in specific situations. Rather than deeming instructional strategies uniformly effective or ineffective, professionals must assess when different strategies are most appropriate in every child's school career. For young children with deaf-blindness, the consistent use of normalized, efficient, effective, and functional instructional strategies is an essential component in facilitating their success in inclusive early childhood programs.

High Levels of Active Engagement

Recently, researchers and practitioners in early childhood special education have focused more attention on the relationship between a young child's level of active engagement and the acquisition and maintenance of new skills (Carta, Greenwood, & Robinson, 1987). Because young children learn primarily through play, exploration, and participation in naturally occurring events in the environment, it is important that the child be actively involved in his or her environment in order to ensure optimal learning (McWilliam & Bailey, 1992). Children with disabilities, particularly children with multiple disabilities, typically show low levels of engagement (Krakow & Kopp, 1983; McWilliam & Bailey, 1992). As engagement is linked to a child's ability to attend to stimuli in the environment, increasing engagement is an important component to learning (Hays, Ewy, & Watson, 1982). For children with deaf-blindness, learning to become actively engaged in the environment can improve mobility, communication, social interaction, and independence (Liberty, Haring, & Moran, 1990). Active engagement in early childhood environments provides children with multiple "opportunities to respond" (Hall, Delquadri, Greenwood, & Thurston, 1982), and these opportunities facilitate the acquisition and maintenance of a variety of functional skills (Carta et al., 1987). Regardless of the instructional methods employed for skill acquisition, a child's level of engagement should be an important consideration across activities and settings.

Engagement has been defined as the total amount of time a child spends actively involved in activities that are behaviorally and contextually appropriate (McWilliam, 1991). Therefore, a child who is engaged interacts with and is involved in the environment for sustained periods of time. Engagement is defined individually for children based on developmental level and experience in the environment. For example, with most activities the type of material exploration expected of a child with deaf-blindness is different from what would be expected of a typically developing child or a child with mild language delays. Although one might be pleased to see a child with deaf-blindness engaged in repetitive object manipulation (e.g., repeatedly dumping toys out of a bin and putting them back in the bin), this same behavior would not be considered developmentally appropriate engagement for a child with more advanced play skills.

There are many advantages to programming for high levels of engagement. Risley (1986) identified three rationales that support the importance of focusing on engagement as a viable outcome for programs serving young children with deaf-blindness. First, high levels of engagement result in higher levels of learning because when a child is engaged in an activity, opportunities to teach skills appropriate to that activity are increased. Second, if a child is actively engaged, behavior problems are less likely to occur; this increases the likelihood that more normalized contingencies for controlling difficult behavior can be established. Third, by promoting high levels of engagement, professionals are focusing on the importance of interesting

and more normalized environments for children with deaf-blindness.

Evaluating Current Goals and Objectives
One of the first steps professionals working with young children with deaf-blindness can implement to promote engagement in inclusive programs is to evaluate children's current goals and objectives. Educational goals should be functional and relevant to the child. One way to assess whether a goal is functional and relevant is to determine if the child would have the opportunity to use the skill in at least two different contexts and to ensure that the skill is taught in the contexts in which the child would naturally use that skill. Functional behaviors also enable a child to gain access to a wider range of activities and environments, increase a student's reinforcing value, reduce the child's need for custodial care taking (e.g., by promoting self-care skills) and support, and provide the child with recreational and leisure skills (Haring, 1988). Functional skills are most often thought of as self-care and adaptive skills. For young children with multiple disabilities, however, teaching play skills may be the most important skill to promote engagement and independence in inclusive settings (Finn, Fewell, & Vadasy, 1988).

Appropriateness of the Classroom Environment In addition to the appropriateness of program goals, the physical and social environments are important factors in increasing engagement (Bailey & Wolery, 1992). The physical arrangement of the classroom can be a particularly important issue for children with deaf-blindness. It is important to provide a physical space that is safe and easy to access. The physical space should be a modified open room arrangement (Sturmey & Crisp, 1986), with smaller spaces within the room that are separated by low barriers (Dunst, McWilliam, & Holbert, 1986). This allows the teacher to supervise the different activity areas and still increase the likelihood that the child will be engaged with the materials, because smaller spaces have been shown to promote higher levels of involvement and social interaction (Sainato & Carta, 1992). Other considerations when arranging an early childhood environment to meet the needs of children with deaf-blindness include: 1) defining consistent landmarks to facilitate orientation and mobility, 2) lighting that is neither too bright nor too dim, and 3) materials that are stored in consistent locations (see chap. 9, this volume, for a thorough discussion of environmental adaptations).

The materials available within the classroom should represent a wide range of interests and developmental levels. Every classroom should include a range of toys so that there are at least some toys that are interesting and challenging to children representing the full range of abilities. The toys should be accessible to the children, and they should be rotated; this ensures that they remain interesting and novel (Bricker & Cripe, 1992; Ostrosky & Kaiser, 1991). There should be a variety in the types of toys and activities available. Toys and activities should promote social, constructive, manipulative, and motor play. They should have multiple uses and promote creativity. For children with deaf-blindness, it is also important to include activities that have a sensory component (e.g., sand or water table, musical instruments, Lite Brite, vibrating tables, small trampoline).

Classroom Schedule and Routines   The classroom schedule can also influence levels of engagement. Assigning staff members to activity areas instead of to individual children is a more efficient way to manage classroom resources (LeLaurin & Risley, 1972). This type of scheduling ensures that staff are available to facilitate and support the children's engagement. This staffing pattern also allows children to be more independent and decreases the amount of time spent in teacher-directed transitions.

The structure of classroom routines is another important component to promote en-

gagement. A classroom schedule should be developed and followed in a consistent manner; this is particularly important to children with deaf-blindness. The use of a calendar box to teach the schedule can help these children become more responsive and independent in the classroom. Children will benefit from a predictable environment in which to practice new skills. Consistent use of routines promotes increased levels of engagement and independence in the classroom.

Teacher Behavior   Teacher behavior is another important component of the classroom ecology that can be used to promote engagement. Teachers need to support children's exploration in the classroom. For children with deaf-blindness, this support is essential for them to begin to construct meaning from the activities and routines in the classroom. This support or scaffolding must be dynamic, that is, it must be responsive to the child's changing needs and abilities. Teachers should provide adequate support to facilitate engagement, while encouraging opportunities for independence and growth.

Transition Planning for Future Environments

Preparing for transitions to different education programs is an important part of all comprehensive early intervention programs. For children with deaf-blindness who may have limited communication skills and may need extensive support to function safely and independently in community-based settings, transition planning becomes essential to the success of the program. Young children experience many transitions before they reach school age: the transition from home to infant-toddler programs, to preschool programs, and to kindergarten. Children in childcare situations may experience additional transitions. Every transition is filled with new challenges and opportunities for children, families, and service providers (Atwater, Orth-Lopes, Elliott, Carta, & Schwartz, 1994; Fowler, Hains, & Rosenkoetter, 1990;

Fowler, Schwartz, & Atwater, 1991; Hanline, 1993; Johnson, Chandler, Kerns, & Fowler, 1986; Noonan & Kilgo, 1987). New programs require children to learn new routines, make new friends, learn new skills, and develop bonds with new teachers. New programs require families to modify schedules; develop relationships with new staff; adjust to different levels of communication and family involvement; and adjust to seeing their child in a new setting, with new peers. Transitions require service providers to say good-bye to children and families with whom they have developed relationships, to welcome new children into the program, and to work collaboratively with professionals from other programs to facilitate a smooth transition with minimal disruptions in service provision for all participants. Successful transitions can be facilitated by cooperation and careful planning.

Preparing the Child for Transition   Preparing the child for a transition to a new educational setting is an important part of the transition planning process, and usually involves teaching skills that are valued in the future setting. These skills can be identified by conducting an environmental inventory of the future environment (Allen, 1992; Anderson & Schwartz, 1986; Carta, Atwater, Schwartz, & Miller, 1990; Fowler, 1982; Rule, Fiechtl, & Innocenti, 1990; Vincent et al., 1980). The purpose of these future environment surveys is to identify differences in the behavioral and social expectations between the current placement and the new placement.

The expected and valued skills that are different in the two environments have been called *keystone* or *survival* skills (Vincent et al., 1980; Wolery, 1991). These are the skills that will facilitate a child's success and independence in the new setting. For example, in a preschool classroom, children may be required to take their cup and placemat to the sink after a snack. This is not required in the toddler program the child currently attends. A simple way to help prepare the child for transition is to begin to teach the child to clear his or her place approximately a month before the transition. Being familiar with this simple routine can help the child through the bewildering days in a new program. When using a skills approach to preparing children for a transition, it is essential to remember that the ability to demonstrate these keystone skills is optimal, but not required. Making a transition into an inclusive program or into a program with chronological age-appropriate peers is not based on a "readiness" model or on meeting a set of behavioral prerequisites (Salisbury & Vincent, 1990).

Preparing the Child's Family   Transitions are often critical events for families (Bailey & Simeonsson, 1988). The stress associated with transitions can be assuaged through information and support. Transition planning with families should begin 6–12 months before the estimated date of transition. Families should receive adequate information explaining the transition process and the rights, responsibilities, players, options, and opportunities associated with the process. Information should be provided in a medium that is understandable to and is available for the family to refer back to throughout the process. A family interview can help to determine family concerns and priorities.

Preparing Professionals   Teachers and other direct services staff are the professionals most often involved in the transition process. Although administrative support plays a key role in successful transition planning, the direct services staff will conduct the majority of the transition activities. Professionals from both the sending program and the receiving program need to be active members of the transition team and should exchange information about their respective programs. Information can be exchanged through classroom visits or via videotapes. Professionals should work together to determine keystone skills that the sending teacher and/or family can address before the transition and to identify key supports that the receiving teacher can implement to facilitate the child's successful entry into the new program (e.g., Gallaher, Maddox, & Edgar, 1984; Rosenkoetter, Hains, & Fowler, 1993).

Professionals from other programs who serve the child but are not directly involved in the transition (e.g., childcare providers) can also supply important information and support for transition planning. During a transition in school programs, the childcare program may remain constant. These professionals should also be involved as members of the transition team, as they may be integrally involved in preparing the child for and supporting the family during the transition.

Children and families will experience a number of transitions in their lifetimes. The success of transitions during early childhood can help set the tone for future transitions. If the early childhood transitions are smooth and well-planned and facilitate involvement from all members of the transition team (i.e., family members, professionals from the sending program, professionals from the receiving program), they can help relieve some of the stress often associated with transition and help families to become active participants in future transition planning.

Family-Focused Intervention

In recent years the field of early childhood special education has adopted a new focus on working with families of children with disabilities (Dunst, 1985; Turnbull & Turnbull, 1990; Turnbull et al., 1993). This new focus stresses the importance of viewing the child with disabilities in the context of his or her family and community. Professionals who work with young children ages birth through five are in the unique position of being part of the first experiences that families have with the educational system. This is an important role because these early experiences can set the stage for children and their families. That is why it is critical that early childhood professionals help families build a support network in their communities and that parents become full partners in all decision making concerning their child's education.

Historically, parent involvement has been seen as attendance at meetings, participation in planning meetings for their child's IEP, and direct instruction of their child in the home or at school. While there are data to support the value of parental participation in the acquisition, maintenance, and generalization of new skills, some parents do not choose or have the desire to take on the role of "special educator" in the home (Turnbull & Turnbull, 1990; Turnbull et al., 1993). The view of parents as "educators" by professionals has been seen by many parents as a burden placed on them by the educational community and has resulted in the needs of the whole family being overlooked.

Traditional parent training programs where the parent is trained as "teacher" may not be the panacea once envisioned. Baker, Heifetz, and Murphy (1980) conducted a follow-up study comparing the traditional parent training approach with teaching parents to use more naturalistic teaching techniques for specific skills (e.g., identifying natural contexts for instruction, such as teaching body parts during bathing). They found that a significant number of the parents were still using the naturalistic teaching techniques months after the training program, whereas only a small percentage were using a more traditional teaching approach. Perhaps these naturalistic techniques built upon the already established parent–child interactions and emphasized the importance of that relationship. Naturalistic teaching techniques also lend themselves more readily to use in home and community settings (e.g., restaurants, parks) and may be more appropriate for addressing specific skills that parents want to address at home (e.g., play, social behaviors).

The need to involve family members in early intervention in a more meaningful way has sparked a revolutionary change in the role of families. This new approach is a hallmark of ECSE and is called family-focused intervention. This approach recognizes the child as a part of a dynamic family system and acknowledges that changes (e.g., intervention) to any part of the system influence all parts of the system (Barber, Turnbull, Behr, & Kerns, 1988; Bronfenbrenner, 1979).

Components of Family-Focused Intervention For young children with multiple disabilities, a change in the focus and context for intervention has taken place. Now, the family and the community are seen as the center of the service delivery system instead of educational agencies or institutions because natural contexts for infants, toddlers, and preschoolers are the home and the community (Winton, 1993). There are several components to a family-centered approach that are particularly relevant to families of children with deaf-blindness. The following list is by no means exhaustive, but represents an overview of a philosophical shift in the way families are viewed in early intervention programs.

1. *Professionals should recognize and respect each family's strengths and differences.* Families are diverse, complex, and ever-changing systems. Because of this, it is vital that professionals have the knowledge and skills to provide services that are sensitive to cultural differences, flexible, and supportive (Lynch & Hanson, 1992; Shelton, Jeppson, & Johnson, 1987). Regardless of the make-up of the family, it is essential for professionals to re-

spect that system and take it into consideration when designing an intervention program. As with other disabilities, children with deaf-blindness are not born into families of only certain segments of our society; all types of families, regardless of socioeconomic status, education, or ethnic background could have a family member with this disability. This is why it is critical that a nonjudgmental, supportive system be established that will support the family and help promote the integration of the child into his or her family and community. This may be especially important in helping families to learn to interact in an optimal manner with their infants with deaf-blindness, as these interactions may be affected by the child's sensory deficits. While teaching parents facilitative interaction skills, it is essential to recognize and respect the cultural norms of social relationships that are important to the family.

2. *The design of educational systems should be such that they are accessible and responsive to the needs and priorities of the family.* In the past, families with children with disabilities, particularly those with children with multiple disabilities, were viewed from a deficit or dysfunctional model that assumes that all families with children with disabilities have problems. Family-focused philosophy and intervention practices have helped to change this antiquated view (Barber et al., 1988; Dunst, 1985; Turnbull & Turnbull, 1986; Turnbull et al., 1993). It is becoming more commonplace to focus on the strengths and existing resources of the family, and the possibility that a child with disabilities could exert a positive effect on his or her family members. It is important that ongoing family assessments identify the existing resources and strengths of the family as well as their priorities and needs in order to build on existing resources and support existing

strengths (Bailey, 1987; Turnbull & Turnbull, 1993).

3. *Parent and professional collaboration should be facilitated on all levels of program planning.* Decision making about program components concerning children with deaf-blindness should be controlled by *families* rather than by educators or interventionists. Professionals should empower families with knowledge and skills that will increase their competence and confidence in their ability to act as advocates and experts concerning the needs and educational priorities of their child (Bailey, 1987). In the past, parental participation in the educational planning process consisted of attendance at the IEP meeting. Clearly, attendance does not ensure active participation in the decision-making process (Harry, 1992). Many of the decisions made by professionals concerning programming priorities for a child with multiple disabilities are value laden. The skills that will enable a child to participate more fully in his or her community and family life are best determined by the parents, with assistance from teachers, support staff, and other professionals.

4. *There should be ongoing communication among families and service providers.* The role of the family in the intervention process should be as individualized as each child's educational goals. Not all families will choose to play the same role in the educational process. The needs and priorities of families continually change. Early interventionists need to maintain systematic communication with families in order to ensure that mutually valued goals are continually addressed (McDonnell & Hardman, 1988).

5. *Skill development should be planned within the context of naturally occurring family routines.* The use of more naturalistic teaching techniques has gained widespread support in the field of early childhood special ed-

ucation. For families, teaching children skills during already existing family routines such as bath time, diaper changing, play, and so on creates a more normalized environment for the child with multiple disabilities as well as for other family members. In addition, there is reduced need for programming for generalization of skills because the child is learning, practicing, and using the skill in the appropriate context. Teaching parents to use more naturalistic teaching methods can also alleviate stress placed on them to set aside special time each day to work on skills in the home (Hanson & Lynch, 1989).

6. *Programs should include activities for all family members.* Programs serving young children with deaf-blindness should include support for all members of the family. Typically, mothers have been identified as the main caregivers for children with disabilities, and much of the focus of family intervention has been centered on them. However, in many cases, fathers, siblings, and grandparents also play an important role in the caregiving needs of a child with multiple disabilities (Meyer & Vadasy, 1987; Meyer, Vadasy, & Fewell, 1987). Thus, it is important to address the need for support for and information to and from all family members.

Outcome-Based Programming and Ongoing Evaluation

Accountability is the bedrock of early childhood special education. As services for young children with severe disabilities are increasingly being provided in inclusive and community-based settings, the challenges to maintain standards of accountability are increased. Inclusion does not mean that educational services will be less intense, effective, or accountable (Taylor, 1988). Early interventionists are mandated to provide intervention services that are educationally beneficial (*Board of Education of Hendrick Hudson School v. Rowley*, 1982). This means the effectiveness of the educational services provided to young children with deaf-blindness must be assessed regardless of the setting in which the services are provided.

Inclusion alone is not an outcome. Inclusion is a descriptor of the *context* in which services are provided. It does not describe the quality of the services or the goodness of fit between the child and the services. It does not describe the amount of time a child is engaged in meaningful activities or is interacting with typically developing peers. It is incumbent upon early interventionists to determine the effectiveness of the services provided to every child and family involved in their program by defining and measuring important outcomes.

Outcome-based programs depend on objective and ongoing program evaluation (Carta et al., 1991). These evaluation activities should be linked to other assessment activities (Bricker, 1989; Bricker & Littman, 1982). Program evaluation must also be multifaceted. Evaluation questions should address individual child progress, appropriateness of objectives and instructional strategies, quality of implementation of programmatic components, and the satisfaction of program consumers.

Evaluation of Child Progress Child progress is the level of program evaluation most frequently conducted. In program evaluation, the form of these assessments may not be different; however, the function of the assessment information is different. In prescriptive child assessments, interventionists are interested in information that will lead to functional and appropriate objectives; in program evaluation, they are interested in determining the amount of progress the child has made. The information is then used to help determine the efficacy of the intervention program. This type of outcome-based

approach assumes that all children can and will learn and that student failure should be viewed as instructional failure. Rather than attributing the child's disability as the cause for a lack of progress, professionals must view the amount of progress as a barometer of the effectiveness of the intervention itself and the lack of progress must be seen as an opportunity and a challenge to improve instructional practices and the system of classroom supports.

Evaluation of Selected Goals and Instructional Strategies Outcome-based programs must also evaluate the appropriateness of selected goals and instructional strategies. Goals must be functional, individually appropriate, and chronologically age appropriate. Goals should address family priorities, build on child strengths and preferences, and enable the child to increase his or her independence in the setting. The primary criterion for instructional strategies is effectiveness. If instructional strategies are not effective, they should not be used. If instructional strategies are effective, they must meet the additional criteria of sustainability, ecological validity, and social validity. Ongoing evaluation of the instructional strategies used in the program is an important component of outcome-based services. To warrant continuation, however, instructional strategies must pass tests for both effectiveness *and* acceptability.

A third type of program evaluation that must be conducted in early intervention programs is procedural reliability or treatment fidelity (Billingsley, White, & Munson, 1980; Peterson & McConnell, 1993). The effectiveness of an intervention cannot be evaluated unless the intervention is implemented consistently and correctly. Factors including training, support, and the acceptability of the intervention may all influence treatment fidelity; however, there is a strong relationship between how well an intervention is implemented and the effectiveness of the intervention (Atwater et al., 1994; Peterson & McConnell, 1993).

Finally, an outcome-based early intervention program must be judged to be socially valid (i.e., acceptable and effective) by its consumers. Social validity is the degree to which a program meets the expectations and respects the community standards of a set of consumers (Fuqua & Schwade, 1986; Schwartz & Baer, 1991; Wolf, 1978). The effectiveness of an intervention and the acceptability of the program are separate issues, and therefore should be evaluated differently. Acceptability without effectiveness is insufficient for an early intervention program, and effectiveness without acceptability violates the tenets of family-focused programming. Information provided through social validity assessments can help early interventionists determine priorities and develop instructional strategies that are effective in community-based programs. Involving consumers (e.g., parents, teachers) in a meaningful way in program evaluation will provide important information about the acceptability of program goals, methods, and outcomes. This information is essential to improving the quality of early childhood special education for young children with deaf-blindness.

FUTURE DIRECTIONS FOR RESEARCH AND PROGRAM DEVELOPMENT

The field of early childhood special education has matured a great deal in the past 25 years. Educators in this field are developing a unique professional identity and are leading the way in meaningful transdisciplinary collaboration. Researchers and practitioners in ECSE have developed an assortment of effective practices. Our current challenge is to incorporate these components into a unified and meaningful strategy for meeting the needs of young children with severe disabilities in inclusive, community-based settings.

Inclusion is an accepted value and goal in ECSE. It is no longer appropriate to ask the research question, "Does inclusion work?" It is more appropriate to ask the question, "How can we facilitate the meaningful inclusion of young children with disabilities into community-based programs?" Researchers and practitioners desperately need to ask this question in regard to children with deaf-blindness and other severe disabilities. These children are often the last children to be included, and they offer some of the greatest challenges to service providers.

A related issue is the challenge to make ECSE programming meaningful and responsive to children and their families. ECSE is becoming increasingly family-centered; however, there is still much work to be done in determining how to address the diverse and complex needs of different families. The notion of "family" must also be expanded to include parents, siblings, grandparents, and other people who play a significant role in the child's life.

Finally, the ultimate goal of ECSE is to support young children with disabilities in their community. Therefore, interventions need to be developed, evaluated, and disseminated that are ecologically and socially valid and sustainable in community-based settings. Early interventionists must build upon the unique strengths of different community-based programs, while responding to the needs and concerns of the consumers of special education, namely children, families, and service providers. It is only through being responsive to these consumers that educators will be able to improve the quality of early intervention services so that these services can have a meaningful impact on the lives of young children and their families.

REFERENCES

Allen, K.E. (1992). *The exceptional child: Mainstreaming in early childhood education* (2nd ed.). Albany, NY: Delmar.

Anderson, S.R., & Schwartz, I.S. (1986). Transitional programming. In F.J. Fuoco & W.P. Christian (Eds.), *Behavior analysis and therapy in residential programs* (pp. 76–100). New York: Van Nostrand Reinhold.

Atwater, J.B., Orth-Lopes, L., Elliott, M., Carta, J.J., & Schwartz, I.S. (1994). Completing the circle: Planning and implementing transitions to other programs. In M. Wolery & J. Wilbers (Eds.), *Including children with special needs in preschool programs* (pp. 167–188). Washington, DC: National Association for the Education of Young Children.

Bailey, D.B. (1987). Collaborative goal-setting with families: Resolving differences in values and priorities for services. *Topics in Early Childhood Special Education, 7*(2), 59–71.

Bailey, D.B., & McWilliam, R.A. (1990). Normalizing early intervention. *Topics in Early Childhood Special Education, 10*(2), 33–47.

Bailey, D.B., & Simeonsson, R.J. (1988). *Family assessment in early intervention.* Columbus, OH: Merrill.

Bailey, D.B., & Wolery, M. (1992). *Teaching infants and preschoolers with disabilities* (2nd ed.). New York: Macmillan.

Baker, B.L., Heifetz, L.J., & Murphy, D. (1980). Behavioral training for parents of mentally retarded children: One-year follow-up. *American Journal of Mental Deficiency, 85,* 31–38.

Barber, P.A., Turnbull, A.P., Behr, S.K., & Kerns, G.M. (1988). A family systems perspective on early childhood special education. In S.L. Odom & M.B. Karnes (Eds.), *Early intervention for infants and children with handicaps: An empirical base* (pp. 179–198). Baltimore: Paul H. Brookes Publishing Co.

Billingsley, F., White, O.R., & Munson, R. (1980). Procedural reliability: A rationale and an example. *Behavioral Assessment, 2,* 229–241.

Board of Education of Hendrick Hudson School v. Rowley, 458 U.S. 176 (1982).

Bredekamp, S. (Ed.). (1987). *Developmentally appropriate practice in early childhood programs serving children from birth through age 8.* Washington, DC: National Association for the Education of Young Children.

Bricker, D. (1989). *Early intervention for at-risk and handicapped infants, toddlers, and preschool children.* Palo Alto, CA: VORT.

Bricker, D., & Cripe, J. (1992). *An activity-based approach to early intervention.* Baltimore: Paul H. Brookes Publishing Co.

Bricker, D., & Littman, D. (1982). Intervention and evaluation: The inseparable mix. *Topics in Early Childhood Special Education, 1*(4), 23–33.

Brofenbrenner, U. (1979). *The ecology of human development.* Cambridge, MA: Harvard University Press.

Brown, L., Long, E., Udvari-Solner, A., Davis, L., VanDeventer, P., Ahlgren, C., Johnson, F., Grenewald, L., & Jorgenson, J. (1989). The home school. *Journal of The Association for Persons with Severe Handicaps, 14,* 1–7.

Carta, J.J., Atwater, J.B., Schwartz, I.S., & McConnell, S.R. (1993). Developmentally appropriate practices and early childhood special education: A reaction to Johnson & McChesney-Johnson. *Topics in Early Childhood Special Education, 13.*

Carta, J.J., Atwater, J.B., Schwartz, I.S., & Miller, P.A. (1990). Applications of ecobehavioral analysis to the study of transitions across early education settings. *Education and Treatment of Children, 13,* 298–315.

Carta, J.J., Greenwood, C.R., & Robinson, S.L. (1987). Application of an ecobehavioral approach to the evaluation of early intervention programs. In R. Prinz (Ed.), *Advances in the behavioral assessment of children and families* (Vol. 3) (pp. 123–156). Greenwich, CT: JAI.

Carta, J.J., Sainato, D.M., & Greenwood, C.R. (1988). Advances in the ecological assessment of classroom instruction for young children with handicaps. In S.L. Odom & M.B. Karnes (Eds.), *Early intervention for infants and children with handicaps: An empirical base* (pp. 217–239). Baltimore: Paul H. Brookes Publishing Co.

Carta, J.J., Schwartz, I.S., Atwater, J.B., & McConnell, S.R. (1991). Developmentally appropriate practice: Appraising its usefulness for young children with disabilities. *Topics in Early Childhood Special Education, 11*(1), 1–20.

Clarke, K.L., Sainato, D.M., & Ward, M. (1994). A comparison of the effects of mobility training with a long cane and a precane device on the travel performance of preschool children. *Journal of Visual Impairments, 88,* 19–30.

Division of Early Childhood. (1993). *DEC recommended practices: Indicators of quality in programs for infants and young children with special needs and their families.* Pittsburgh: Author.

Dunst, C.J. (1985). Rethinking early intervention.

Analysis and Intervention in Developmental Disabilities, 5, 165–201.

Dunst, C.J., McWilliam, R.A., & Holbert, K. (1986). Assessment of preschool classroom environments. *Diagnostique, 11,* 212–232.

Education of the Handicapped Amendments of 1986, PL 99-457. Title 20, U.S.C. 101 et seq: *U.S. Statutes at Large, 100,* 1145–1177.

Ferguson, P., & Asch, A. (1989). Lessons from life: Personal and parental perspectives on school, childhood, and disability. In D. Biklen, A. Ford, & D. Ferguson (Eds.), *Disability and society* (pp. 108–140). Chicago: National Society for the Study of Education.

Finn, D.M., Fewell, R.R., & Vadasy, P.S. (1988). The play of young children who have dual sensory impairments. In M. Bullis & G. Fielding (Eds.), *Communication development in young children with deaf-blindness: Literature review* (pp. 149–163). Monmouth: Oregon State System of Higher Education.

Fowler, S.A. (1982). Transition from preschool to kindergarten for children with special needs. In K.E. Allen & E.M. Goetz (Eds.), *Early childhood education: Special problems, special solutions* (pp. 309–335). Rockville, MD: Aspen.

Fowler, S.A., Hains, A.H., & Rosenkoetter, S. (1990). The transition between early intervention services and preschool services: Administration and policy issues. *Topics in Early Childhood Special Education, 9*(4), 55–65.

Fowler, S.A., Schwartz, I.S., & Atwater, J.B. (1991). Perspectives on the transition from preschool to kindergarten for children with disabilities and their families. *Exceptional Children, 58,* 136–145.

Fuqua, R.W., & Schwade, J. (1986). Social validation of applied behavioral research: A selective review and critique. In A. Poling & R.W. Fuqua (Eds.), *Research methods in applied behavior analysis* (pp. 265–292). New York: Plenum.

Gallaher, J., Maddox, M., & Edgar, E. (1984). *Early childhood interagency transition model.* Bellevue, WA: Edmark.

Goetz, L., & Gee, K. (1987). Functional vision programming: A model for teaching visual behaviors in natural contexts. In L. Goetz, D. Guess, & K. Stremel-Campbell (Eds.), *Innovative program design for individuals with dual-sensory impairments* (pp. 77–98). Baltimore: Paul H. Brookes Publishing Co.

Hall, R.V., Delquadri, J., Greenwood, C.R., & Thurston, L. (1982). The importance of opportunity to respond to children's academic success. In E. Edgar, N. Haring, J. Jenkins, & C.

Pious (Eds.), *Serving young handicapped children: Issues and research* (pp. 107–140). Baltimore: University Park Press.

Hanline, M.F. (1993). Facilitating integrated preschool service delivery transitions for children, families, and professionals. In C.A. Peck, S.L. Odom, & D.D. Bricker (Eds.), *Integrating young children with disabilities into community programs: Ecological perspectives on research and implementation* (pp. 133–146). Baltimore: Paul H. Brookes Publishing Co.

Hanline, M.F., & Hanson, M.J. (1989). Integration considerations for infants and toddlers with multiple disabilities. *Journal of The Association for Persons with Severe Handicaps, 14,* 178–183.

Hanson, M.J., & Lynch, E.W. (1989). *Early intervention: Implementing child and family services for infants and toddlers who are at-risk or disabled.* Austin, TX: PRO-ED.

Hanson, M.J., & Widerstrom, A.H. (1993). Consultation and collaboration: Essentials of integration efforts for young children. In C.A. Peck, S.L. Odom, & D.D. Bricker (Eds.), *Integrating young children with disabilities into community programs: Ecological perspectives on research and implementation* (pp. 149–168). Baltimore: Paul H. Brookes Publishing Co.

Haring, N.G. (Ed.). (1988). *Generalization for students with severe handicaps: Strategies and solutions.* Seattle: University of Washington.

Harry, B. (1992). *Cultural diversity, families, and the special education system: Communication and empowerment.* New York: Teachers College Press.

Hart, B.M., & Risley, T.R. (1975). Incidental teaching of language in the preschool. *Journal of Applied Behavior Analysis, 8,* 411–420.

Hart, B.M., & Risley, T.R. (1980). In vivo language training. Unanticipated and general effects. *Journal of Applied Behavior Analysis, 12,* 407–432.

Hays, L.A., Ewy, R.D., & Watson, J.S. (1982). Attention as a predictor of learning in infants. *Journal of Experimental Child Psychology, 34,* 38–45.

Johnson, T.S., Chandler, L.K., Kerns, G.M., & Fowler, S.A. (1986). What are parents saying about family involvement in school transitions? A retrospective transition interview. *Journal of the Division of Early Childhood, 11,* 10–17.

Klein, N.K., & Campbell, P. (1990). Preparing personnel to serve at-risk and disabled infants, toddlers, and preschoolers. In S.J. Meisels & J.P. Shonkoff (Eds.), *Handbook of early childhood intervention* (pp. 679–699). Cambridge: Cambridge University Press.

Krakow, J.B., & Kopp, C.B. (1983). The effects of

developmental delay on sustained attention in young children. *Child Development, 54,* 1143–1155.

LeLaurin, K., & Risley, T.R. (1972). The organization of day-care environments: "Zone" versus "man-to-man" staff assignments. *Journal of Applied Behavior Analysis, 5,* 225–232.

Liberty, K.A., Haring, N.G., & Moran, D.C. (1990). *Differences in engaged time and communication when students with dual sensory impairments and profound disabilities enter less restrictive educational situations.* Unpublished manuscript, University of Washington, Seattle.

Lynch, E., & Hanson, M. (Eds.). (1982). *Developing cross cultural competence: A guide for working with young children and their families.* Baltimore: Paul H. Brookes Publishing Co.

Lundervold, D., Lewin, L., & Irwin, L. (1987). Rehabilitation of visual impairments: A critical review. *Clinical Psychology Review, 7,* 169–185.

McDonnell, A., & Hardman, M. (1988). A synthesis of "best practice" guidelines for early childhood services. *Journal of the Division of Early Childhood, 12,* 328–341.

McWilliam, R.A. (1991). Targeting teaching at children's use of time: Perspectives on preschoolers engagement. *Teaching Exceptional Children, 23,* 42–43.

McWilliam, R.A., & Bailey, D.B. (1992). Promoting engagement and mastery. In D.B. Bailey & M. Wolery (Eds.), *Teaching infants and preschoolers with disabilities* (2nd ed.), (pp. 229–253). New York: Macmillan.

Meisels, S.J., & Shonkoff, J.P. (Eds.). (1990). *Handbook of early childhood intervention.* Cambridge: Cambridge University Press.

Meyer, D.J., & Vadasy, P.S. (1987). *Grandparent workshops.* Seattle: University of Washington Press.

Meyer, D.J., Vadasy, P.S., & Fewell, R.R. (1987). *Living with a brother or a sister with special needs: A book for siblings.* Seattle: University of Washington Press.

Michael, M.G., & Paul, P.V. (1991). Early intervention for infants with deaf-blindness. *Exceptional Children, 57,* 200–210.

Neisworth, J.T., & Bagnato, S.J. (1992). The case against intelligence testing in early intervention. *Topics in Early Childhood Special Education, 12*(1), 1–20.

Niswander, P. (1987). Audiometric assessment and management. In L. Goetz, D. Guess, & K. Stremel-Campbell (Eds.), *Innovative program design for individuals with dual sensory impairments* (pp. 99–127). Baltimore: Paul H. Brookes Publishing Co.

Noonan, M.J., & Kilgo, J.L. (1987). Transition services for early age individuals with severe retardation. In R.N. Ianacone & R.A. Stodden (Eds.), *Transition issues and directions* (pp. 25–37). Reston, VA: Council for Exceptional Children.

Noonan, M.J., & McCormick, L. (1993). *Early intervention in natural environments: Methods and procedures.* Pacific Grove, CA: Brooks/Cole.

Odom, S.L., & Karnes, M.B. (Eds.). (1988). *Early intervention for infants and children with handicaps: An empirical base.* Baltimore: Paul H. Brookes Publishing Co.

Ostrosky, M.M., & Kaiser, A.P. (1991). Preschool classroom environments that promote communication. *Teaching Exceptional Children, 23,* 6–10.

Peck, C.A., Odom, S.L., & Bricker, D.D. (Eds.). (1993). *Integrating young children with disabilities into community programs: Ecological perspectives on research and implementation.* Baltimore: Paul H. Brookes Publishing Co.

Peterson, C.A., & McConnell, S.R. (1993). Factors affecting the impact of social interaction skills interventions in early childhood special education. *Topics in Early Childhood Special Education, 13*(1), 38–56.

Peterson, N. (1987). *Early intervention for handicapped and at-risk children.* Denver: Love.

Raver, S.A. (1991). *Strategies for teaching at-risk and handicapped infants and toddlers: A transdisciplinary approach.* New York: Merrill.

Risley, T.R. (1986, May). *Behavioral engagement as a fundamental variable in treatment quality.* Paper presented at the Association for Behavior Analysis 12th Annual Convention, Milwaukee, WI.

Rosenkoetter, S.E., Hains, A.H., & Fowler, S.A. (1993). *Bridging early services for children with special needs and their families: A practical guide for transition planning.* Baltimore: Paul H. Brookes Publishing Co.

Rule, S., Fiechtl, B.J., & Innocenti, M.S. (1990). Preparation for transition to mainstreamed post-preschool environments: Development of a survival skills curriculum. *Topics in Early Childhood Special Education, 9*(4), 78–90.

Sainato, D.M., & Carta, J.J. (1992). Classroom influences on the development of social competence in young children with disabilities. In S.L. Odom, S.R. McConnell, & M.A. McEvoy (Eds.), *Social competence of young children with* disabilities: Issues and strategies for intervention (pp. 93–109). Baltimore: Paul H. Brookes Publishing Co.

Salisbury, C.L. (1991). Mainstreaming during the early childhood years. *Exceptional Children, 58,* 146–155.

Salisbury, C., & Vincent, L. (1990). Criterion of the next environment and best practices: Mainstreaming and integration ten years later. *Topics in Early Childhood Special Education, 10*(2), 78–89.

Schwartz, I.S., & Baer, D.M. (1991). Social validity assessments: Is current practice state of the art? *Journal of Applied Behavior Analysis, 24,* 189–204.

Shelton, T.L., Jeppson, E.S., & Johnson, B.H. (1987). *Family-centered care for children with special health care needs.* Washington, DC: Association for the Care of Children's Health.

Stillman, R.D., & Battle, C.W. (1984). Developing prelanguage communication in the severely handicapped: An interpretation of the van Dijk method. *Seminars in Speech and Hearing, 4*(3), 159–170.

Sturmey, P., & Crisp, T. (1986). Classroom management. In J. Coupe & J. Porter (Eds.), *The education of children with severe learning difficulties: Bridging the gap between theory and practice.* London: Croom Helm.

Taylor, S.J. (1988). Caught in the continuum: A critical analysis of the principle of the least restrictive environment. *Journal of The Association for Persons with Severe Handicaps, 13,* 25–36.

Thomas, A., & Chess, S. (1977). *Temperament and development.* New York: Bruner/Mazel.

Turnbull, A.P., Patterson, J.M., Behr, S.K., Murphy, D.L., Marquis, J.G., & Blue-Banning, M.J. (1993). *Cognitive coping, families, and disability.* Baltimore: Paul H. Brookes Publishing Co.

Turnbull, A.P., & Turnbull, H.R. (1986). Stepping back from early intervention: An ethical perspective. *Journal of the Division of Early Childhood, 10,* 106–117.

Turnbull, A.P., & Turnbull, H.R. (1990). *Families, professionals, and exceptionality: A special partnership* (2nd ed.). New York: Merrill.

Turnbull, A.P., & Turnbull, H.R. (1993). Participatory research on cognitive coping: From concepts to research planning. In A.P. Turnbull, J.M. Patterson, S.K. Behr, D.L. Murphy, J.G. Marquis, & M.J. Blue-Banning (Eds.), *Cognitive*

coping, families, and disability (pp. 1–14). Baltimore: Paul H. Brookes Publishing Co.

van Dijk, J. (1966). The first steps of the deaf-blind child towards language. *The International Journal for the Education of the Blind, 15*(4), 112–114.

Vincent, L.J., Brown, L., & Getz-Sheftel, M. (1981). Integrating handicapped and typical children during the preschool years: The definition of best educational practices. *Topics in Early Childhood Special Education, 1*(1), 17–24.

Vincent, L.J., Salisbury, C., Walter, G., Brown, P., Gruenewald, L.J., & Powers, M. (1980). Program evaluation and curriculum development in early childhood special education. Criteria of the next environment. In W. Sailor, B. Wilcox, & L. Brown (Eds.), *Methods of instruction for severely handicapped students* (pp. 303–328). Baltimore: Paul H. Brookes Publishing Co.

Warren, S.F., & Kaiser, A.P. (1988). Research in early language intervention. In S.L. Odom & M.B. Karnes (Eds.), *Early intervention for infants and children with handicaps: An empirical base* (pp. 89–108). Baltimore: Paul H. Brookes Publishing Co.

Winton, P.J. (1993). Providing family support in integrated settings: Research and recommendations. In C.A. Peck, S.L. Odom, & D.D. Bricker (Eds.), *Integrating young children with disabilities into community programs: Ecological perspectives on research and implementation* (pp. 65–80). Baltimore: Paul H. Brookes Publishing Co.

Wolery, M. (1991). Instruction in early childhood special education: "Seeing through a glass darkly . . . knowing in part." *Exceptional Children, 58,* 127–135.

Wolery, M., Strain, P.S., & Bailey, D.B. (1992). Reaching potentials of children with special needs. In S. Bredekamp & T. Rosegrant (Eds.), *Reaching potentials: Appropriate curriculum and assessment for young children* (pp. 99–111). Washington, DC: National Association for the Education of Young Children.

Wolf, M.M. (1978). Social validity: The case for subjective measurement or how applied behavior analysis is finding its heart. *Journal of Applied Behavior Analysis, 11,* 203–214.

Wolfensberger, W. (1972). *The principle of normalization in human services.* Toronto, Ontario, Canada: National Institute on Mental Retardation.

Chapter 16

Facilitating Active and Informed Participation and Learning in Inclusive Settings

Kathleen Gee

There has been growing recognition in the field that inclusion of students with multiple disabilities in general education classrooms and school life, when implemented well, represents the maximal opportunity for social and instructional integration with their peers without disabilities (Halvorsen & Sailor, 1990; Rainforth, York, & Macdonald, 1992; Raynes, Snell, & Sailor, 1991; Sailor et al., 1989; Stainback & Stainback, 1992; Stainback, Stainback, & Forest, 1989; Villa, Thousand, Stainback, & Stainback, 1992). To educators collaborating to provide quality services to individuals with disabilities in inclusive schools, however, full inclusion signifies much more than the "mainstreaming" of persons with disabilities into general education classrooms. The full inclusion movement represents school improvement and school change on many levels for all students.

When full inclusion is implemented using best practices, students with disabilities lose neither services nor support, but gain the opportunity to grow in functional and meaningful ways in the social and learning contexts of their peers without disabilities (Ferguson, Meyer, Jeanchild, Juniper, & Zingo, 1992; Sailor, Gee, & Karasoff, 1993). Inclusion brings students together; however, whether their learning and social interactions will be successful (that is, lead to positive curricular, functional, and cognitive growth; self-esteem; the motivation for competence; social relationships; and friendships) is not determined simply by placement and opportunity. Across the country, educators and parents are seeking to provide the support, instruction, and facilitation that will enhance the quality of life of and provide a meaningful education for students with deaf-blindness and other disabilities in the school community.

There is a relatively small, but growing, knowledge base from which to recommend strategies to teachers attempting to fully include students with deaf-blindness (Downing & Eichinger, 1990; Ferguson, Ferguson,

Portions of the material presented in this chapter were developed as part of a research project conducted at San Francisco State University and federally funded by the Office of Special Education and Rehabilitative Services (Grant No. HO 86G00003).

& Taylor, 1992; Gee, 1993; Gee, Alwell, Graham, & Goetz, 1994; Hunt, Staub, Alwell, & Goetz, 1994; Rainforth et al., 1992; Sapon-Shevin, 1992; Snell, 1993; Stainback & Stainback, 1992; Thousand, Villa, & Nevin, 1994; Vandercook & York, 1989). Rainforth et al. (1992) have provided useful examples of the integrated teaming process, and Gee, Alwell, et al. (1994) have completed a manual that reviews teaming, curriculum, instructional strategies, and creating school community for use with students with deaf-blindness in inclusive classrooms.

Innovative general education models such as activity-based instruction, integrated curriculum, whole language, and literacy-based programs offer opportunities for meaningful instruction of students, with learning goals covering the entire range of intellectual ability (Englert, Tarrant, & Mariage, 1992). Cooperative learning has provided educators with a successful strategy for designing collaborative lesson plans for heterogeneous groups that allow for individual as well as group accountability (Putnam, 1994; Putnam, Rynders, Johnson, & Johnson, 1989; Thousand et al., 1994). Instructional paradigms such as invitational education (Purkey & Novak, 1984), "thoughtful" education (Hanson, Silver, & Strong, 1990), social constructivism (Grennon-Brooks & Brooks, 1993), and cognitive strategies (Brown & Campione, 1990; Herman, Aschbacher, & Winters, 1992) offer unique opportunities for general and special educators to focus on learning and motivation with particular attention to learning styles (see Englert et al., 1992; Ford, Davern, & Schnorr, 1992; and Villa & Thousand, 1992, for review). Authentic assessment (Herman et al., 1992; Marzano, Pickering, & McTighe, 1993) in general education provides another link to the individualized instruction that benefits all students.

Creative curricular adaptations and instructional organization strategies (Gee, Alwell, et al., 1994; Giangreco, Cloninger, & Iverson, 1994; Neary, Halvorsen, Alwell, & Kronberg, 1993; Rainforth et al., 1992; Udvari-Solner, 1992, 1994) that promote competent participation and growth within general school and classroom activities have been successful in allowing students with multiple disabilities (including students with deaf-blindness) to acquire meaningful curricular outcomes as well as functional skills while within general education instructional activities (Ford & Davern, 1990; Ford et al., 1992; Rainforth et al., 1992; Stainback & Stainback, 1992; Villa & Thousand, 1992; York & Vandercook, 1989). Time series research on the acquisition of specific cognitive, motor, sensory, social, and communication skills with students with deaf-blindness and additional cognitive skills within and across integrated, community-based settings has identified additional teaching practices specific to individuals with deaf-blindness (Gee, 1993; Gee, Graham, & Goetz, 1994; Gee, Graham, Oshima, Yoshioka, & Goetz, 1991; Gee, Graham, Sailor, & Goetz, in press; Goetz & Gee, 1987a, 1987b; Hunt, Staub, et al., 1994; Sailor, Goetz, Anderson, Hunt, & Gee, 1987). Qualitative research on the interactions of middle school students with deaf-blindness and their peers without disabilities in inclusive classrooms (Gee, 1993) has provided a closer look at issues related to social relationships (see chap. 11, this volume, for more information on social relationships).

This chapter is focused on methods for ensuring that students with deaf-blindness are active and informed members of the learning and social community in heterogeneous, inclusive schools and classrooms. It should be additionally emphasized, however, that the success of the individual with unique learning characteristics is linked directly to the use of effective teaching practices in the general education classrooms of which she or he is a member. The instructional strategies described are, therefore, linked to general education strategies for heterogeneous groups. It is through teaming and collaboration to provide excellence in education programs for all children that the educational staff supporting students with deaf-blindness will be able to provide the instruction for their students' additional needs.

DEVELOPING THE INDIVIDUALIZED PROGRAM

Persons with deaf-blindness are a highly diverse group of individuals with unique learning characteristics and a wide range of capabilities. This diversity parallels the diversity in the general student population that teachers in integrated and inclusive schools and classrooms are now serving. Persons with deaf-blindness have a variety of interests, strengths, and talents. Each has a different family, different background, and different personality. When teaching, working, or playing with an individual with deaf-blindness, the same bottom-line principles that are adhered to with other students, co-workers, and friends should also be followed, namely: 1) respect for the individual (and his or her choices and learning styles), 2) flexibility, and 3) cooperation.

In an inclusive educational model, the individual's needs and desired educational outcomes shape the goals and objectives selected for instruction without limiting or precluding the students' participation in the general education program. Similarly, the general education and community settings chosen as the learning contexts for the student shape the way in which the goals and objectives are instructed. The contexts for instruction are referenced to the student's same-age peers and are selected for their motivational, curricular, and socially integrative value.

Central to the provision of services to children and adults with deaf-blindness in full inclusion programs are the concepts of integrated service delivery and collaboration (Downing & Eichinger, 1990; Dunn, 1991; Rainforth et al., 1992). Several authors have recently described individual service delivery planning processes that have been successful in fully inclusive systems (see Giangreco et al., 1994; Neary et al., 1993; Stainback & Stainback, 1992; Rainforth et al., 1992; Thousand et al., 1994; York & Vandercook, 1989). Figure 1 depicts a curriculum planning process that has been successfully validated for students with deaf-blindness and students with severe, multiple disabilities in inclusive settings (Farron-Davis, Gee, & Goetz, 1994; Gee & Goetz, 1990; Gee and Goetz, 1994). A detailed description of the process and several case examples of students with deaf-blindness are provided in this chapter.

The quality of instruction and the achievement of IEP goals need not be abandoned for placement in a general education classroom/program when full inclusion is implemented carefully and collaboratively. Individuals with deaf-blindness are a unique group of individuals with a wide range of educational needs and interests. Because of their disabilities in information gathering, communication, and mobility, individuals with deaf-blindness, whether intellectually gifted or faced with additional cognitive disabilities, need a significant amount of support from a variety of sources. This requires careful teaming and collaboration among professionals, parents, staff, and peers. Inclusion also requires that roles and responsibilities be clearly defined. In many of the inclusive schools across the country, teaching teams

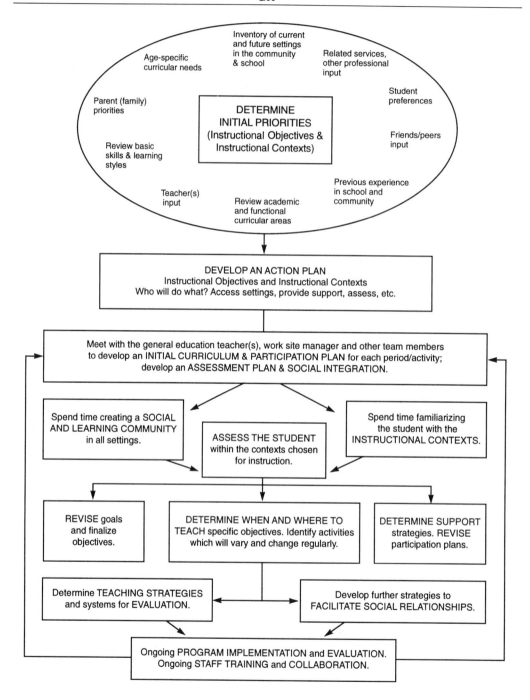

Figure 1. Flowchart of an individualized curriculum planning process.

have redefined their roles and responsibilities to ensure quality instruction (see Karasoff, Alwell, & Halvorsen, 1993, for review).

In the model presented here, there is always a special education teacher who functions as the student's *primary support teacher*. It is this teacher's responsibility to do the following:

1. Work directly and closely with the student's parents, general education teacher(s), and other support staff
2. Modify and adapt curriculum
3. Design instructional programs and strategies to meet the student's educational goals and objectives in a wide variety of settings
4. Train support staff (e.g., paraprofessionals, interpreters, other professionals) directly on effective teaching methods that are attentive to the student's sensory impairments
5. Facilitate social interactions and the development of social relationships and networks for the student
6. Train peers to collaborate in instruction and communication with the student

It is also this person's responsibility to ensure that specialized curricula specific to the student's sensory disabilities (such as braille, compensatory literacy techniques, orientation and mobility, instruction in sign or other augmentative communication systems, and so on) are integrated into the daily curriculum and that input from specialists is utilized for accessing educational technology and modifying and adapting curriculum.

The support teacher functions as a direct service teacher, co-teacher, team leader, and synthesizer. This teacher has the same student load as she or he would if teaching in a special education classroom or resource room. The students have at least the same amount of paraprofessional and/or interpre-

ter support as they would have in a special classroom. Paraprofessional assistance is provided as a support to the entire class.

The primary support teacher, the interpreter and/or facilitator, and the general education teacher share the responsibility for determining how the instruction will be implemented (i.e., the groupings, arrangements, activities, formats, teacher–student ratios, and so on) and for creating classroom community and student collaboration. As in all transdisciplinary teaming, the success of this model will depend on the team members' ability to collaborate and share information (see chap. 8, this volume, for further information on transdisciplinary and collaborative teaming in inclusive schools).

It is not uncommon to hear debate about the role of the interpreter for individuals with deaf-blindness. It is also common to hear debate about whether a person with deaf-blindness needs one-to-one adult facilitation. It is this author's position that if the individual with deaf-blindness is using sign language (or tactile sign language) as her or his primary receptive and/or expressive communication system, she or he needs a qualified interpreter who also functions as a facilitator of instructional and social relationships, similar to the other support staff who assist individuals not using sign language. This will require additional training from the primary support teacher and perhaps a revised job description.

As the goal of inclusion is to connect the student with his or her natural educational and social communities, the role of the facilitator, or any adult providing support to the individual, is extremely important. The facilitator is the student's link to the community of individuals available for joint learning and possible friendships and social networks. How much time the facilitator/interpreter spends one-on-one or in small groups with the student with deaf-blindness will be determined on an individual basis. However, we cannot ignore that individuals with deaf-blindness have a constant need for receptive and expressive communicative input in order to benefit from the educational and social activities of their peers.

It is important to note that the steps for developing an individualized program described in this chapter are not necessarily to be followed in a concrete order, as each individual student and school situation is different. Depending on the time of year, the newness of inclusion at the school, and many other factors, the primary support teacher using this model will facilitate the determination of an appropriate team timeline and action plan. Ongoing collaboration, program implementation and evaluation, and staff training are the keys to continuing a quality education program for each student.

Setting Goals

Prior to a group discussion and synthesis of goals, the primary support teacher meets with the student and his or her family members to review the student's strengths and needs as well as the student's current participation in activities at home and in the community. A family interview (Neary et al., 1993) or discussion concerning goals assists the individual and her or his family to solidify their priorities and needs. The support teacher discusses the use of a "person-centered" planning process at a pre-IEP (individualized education program) meeting for the significant team members, and together they determine a strategy for working collaboratively.

Various methods of team participation in the formulation of goals and objectives exist (see, e.g., Neary et al., 1993; Salisbury, 1992; Strully & Strully, 1989; Turnbull & Morningstar, 1993; Vandercook, York, & Forest,

1989). Chapter 8 of this text provides a detailed description of collaborative teaming. A primary rule in any team process is that the focus individual and his or her parent, guardian, family, and friends are given first consideration in stating the student's strengths, needs, and educational priorities. With student participation in the team process and the participation of the student's friends, co-workers, and advocates, the dynamic of the traditional IEP is changed. When a group of people come together to create and enhance the vision for a particular individual using person-centered planning strategies, everyone is placed on "equal ground" and the way in which the person with disabilities is viewed is changed. By continuing to meet on a regular basis, this group of people can positively influence the implementation of actions that will have a direct impact on the individual's future (Browder, 1991; Malette et al., 1992; Neary et al., 1993). The outcomes of a planning meeting used to *begin* the curriculum development process should at least include: 1) a list of agreed upon educational priorities or goals, 2) a schedule of classes and activities in which to accomplish these goals, and 3) an action plan for the implementation of the goals and schedule.

Determining Educational Priorities Educational priorities are chosen based on the input from all team members. If the student has not yet had the opportunity to be included in a general classroom, or if this is the first time he or she will be receiving instruction in a real work setting, the outcomes identified will be different from those of a student who has had numerous work opportunities or previous full general class placement. These objectives may change, be deleted, or be added to after the teacher and other team members have assessed the student within the contexts identified.

Identifying Appropriate Contexts and Activities The contexts and activities selected for the student consist of the general education teacher's class schedule of daily activities and other school and community contexts that are expected to be frequented by the students regularly (such as the cafeteria, the locker rooms, the gym, the yard, a local shopping center, worksites, etc.). This is essentially a tentative schedule of contexts and curricular periods throughout which instruction may take place. In order to prepare for this planning, it is helpful if the support teacher has done an inventory (Falvey, 1989) of all the possible classes, community sites, school environments, transportation, methods, and so forth that are available to the student. For elementary school students, the general class teacher's entire schedule is usually initially included in the context schedule, and alternatives are designed based on integrated assessment decisions. Depending on the teaching strategies utilized in the general education classroom and the needs of the individual student, some alternative activities and strategies within the classroom, the school, and the community may need to be developed.

For secondary students there may be a general class homeroom placement and, depending on decisions of the student's team, a general class schedule resembling that of the student's peers without disabilities. This schedule may also include instruction in other school contexts, school jobs, job rotation sampling in integrated real work placements in the community, and community instruction. The move to full inclusion from integrated special classroom models sometimes makes the balance between time spent at school and time spent in the community confusing for professionals. Numerous positions exist as to the amount of time that should be spent in the community versus the classroom and school environments for students with disabilities in various age groups (Brown et al., 1991; Sailor et al., 1989).

Teachers of secondary-age students particularly struggle with this issue as they seek to help the student form and maintain social relationships, increase social interaction skills, and prepare for real jobs and supported living in the community. Unfortunately, many programs give up a substantial amount of integration as they add community environments to their curriculum, and it is not uncommon to find students with disabilities in middle and high school programs spending large amounts of time in school and community settings in which peers or co-workers without disabilities may be present, but are not regularly available for interaction and social relationship development.

The PEERS Project (Neary, Halvorsen, & Smithy, 1991) has suggested a decision model for balancing classroom, school, and community time for secondary-age students. This decision model asks the team to look at several factors to individually determine community instruction time versus school instruction time, including:

- The student's age
- Student and parent/sibling preferences
- Effect on personal relationships
- Student ability to generalize
- Functional skill needs
- Prior history
- Availability of relevant school/community environments and use of community facilities
- General class and similar school experience compared to siblings and peers without disabilities
- Friendships
- Personal hygiene needs
- Home, recreation, vocation, and mobility skills
- Safety and health concerns

Preparation for the world of work and adult supported living takes a balance between time with peers acquiring important social skills and friendships, time spent learning specific curricular objectives and personal management skills, and time in various work situations identifying jobs that are most preferred and best performed by the student. As students who have been integrated and included in the general education program since preschool reach secondary programs, it is predictable that they (and their parents) will not wish to sacrifice the close friendships, peer support networks, and motivation generated by inclusion in the general education program. The contextual and cooperative instructional methods (Gee, Alwell, et al., 1994; Putnam, 1994; Thousand et al., 1994) and the co-worker support strategies (Nisbet & Hagner, 1988) that are increasingly present in general education classrooms and integrated work settings will become essential to these families and their educators. Individualized programs allow for variation in the amount of time spent in general classrooms, other school activities, and the community. Quality inclusive schools promote fluid instructional options for *all* students. A variety of groupings, formats, and strategies are used, depending on the situation, as well as a wide range of instructional settings.

Designing the Action Plan   The action plan includes a fairly detailed schedule of activities that are required to accomplish the desired goals, identify who is responsible for each activity, and suggest a timeline for the completion of the activities. The action plan should include activities to address both social and curricular priorities as well as transitional activities. Sometimes one action plan is designed by the support team; other times small groups meet to handle specific areas of the overall profile.

The team also negotiates the supports that will be necessary from other professionals and instructional staff in order for the student to benefit from his or her educational plan. A related service delivery plan is designed, and at this time team members coordinate participation in integrated assessments to be completed in the identified contexts. The team begins to coordinate the implementation of a service delivery plan (i.e., who will be responsible for the delivery of instruction and program monitoring in various contexts and objectives). If a specialized health care service delivery plan is needed, the team designates a timeline for its full operation. After baseline is complete, these plans can be revised and modified.

Another key part of the first action plan should include strategies to facilitate the student's social integration in the general classroom and any other school and community instructional contexts. The team determines the supports that will be facilitative of social interaction and peer support networks and lists the strategies that will be used to facilitate inclusion in various contexts. The team implements the action plan at the beginning of the school year and sets a timeline for the program development process to be completed and a date for the second primary team meeting. The team process of listing priorities, selecting appropriate contexts, and designing an action plan to achieve desired goals are illustrated in the following case example.

Ranelle is a second-grade student in Ms. Hughes class. She loves the "Lambchop" show, adores riding in the car, has fun on the Merry-go-round with friends, and enjoys exploring the piano. She has low vision with cataracts and glaucoma as well as a moderate/severe sensorineural hearing loss. She wears both corrective lenses and hearing aids. Ranelle also has spastic cerebral palsy with involvement on her right side.

Ranelle was in a special education class with some integration (two class periods) during her first grade year. Her school system has since moved to full inclusion, and she is now enrolled in the second grade as her full-time class placement with primary support from her special education teacher and additional support from the occupational therapist, speech therapist, and paraprofessional staff. Because of her physical and cognitive disabilities, signing was not possible as an effective communication system. Her support team switched to pictures paired with gestures for input and output, but she always uses verbal input as well. The team plans to move to a verbal output system that would be accessed through the same pictures.

———

Ranelle's support team listed numerous priorities (see Figure 2) and had to carefully examine her needs to come up with an operable list. Ms. Hughes ran a very creative class schedule that allowed for fluid options and alternative activities. For example, during the class "workshop" time, Ranelle was able to receive some instruction in the community with peers who were working on their own contextual objectives (e.g., a math problem). It was determined that Ranelle needed extra time for certain self-help tasks and eating, so she would need to come late or leave early for certain periods. The team tried to figure out which periods were most flexible. Figure 3 presents the action plan designed by Ranelle's team.

Name: *Ranelle*

Grade: *2nd, Ms. Hughes*

Dates information was gathered: *August 27*

INITIAL SUMMARY OF PRIORITIES

PARENTS/FAMILY
- Friends, kids to play with
- Self-care activities: get more independent/less assistance
- Communication system: output system, input
- Happy, have fun, not bother other kids
- Learn to recognize name
- The computer—as a tool for communication and other things in school
- Eating out, eating/mealtime manners, make snacks

FRIENDS
- Play more games
- "Say" what she needs to say
- Communicate
- Stop pulling on us or pulling our hair
- Write her name
- Have a class job
- Take turns
- Walk more easily

STUDENT
- Move around a lot
- Be with other kids
- Active & loud situations
- Snacks
- Visual assists, adaptations
- General classes vs. special ed. class
- Roy, Mary, Tia, Tamara, Elise, and Mr. Torey
- Routines
- Farm and Garden period w/2nd grade
- Music

TEACHERS/OTHER STAFF
- Utilize communication system: initially a book for WANT, then identify items/labels/activities for content
- Initiate
- Acknowledge interactions
- Match objects to adapted pictures
- Eating/drinking
- Adaptations for leisure time, recess
- Use right hand to help with self-care activities, eating, etc., by balancing or holding
- Learn to use white cane with 3 prongs on tip → (step up from walker)
- Negotiate obstacles
- Follow classroom routines and rules
- Utilize name stamp
- Community: mobility and accessing restaurants, stores
- Follow picture/gesture directions

Figure 2.   Ranelle: Initial summary of priorities.

Name:	_Ranelle_	**Date:**	_August 29_

Grade: _2nd - Mrs. Hughes_

Persons present: _Family, Mrs. Hughes, support teacher; Ray, Elise, Mary, Mr. Torey (principal)_

ACTION PLAN

LIST PRIORITY CURRICULAR CONTENT AND BASIC SKILLS. _Indicate any special assessment needs_	Team Members Responsible	Timelines	Date Complete
Communication system: start with picture/gesture combined with verbal; move to computer system with verbal output	Support teacher with speech/language person and O.T.	by 9/25	
Games and **turn-taking** with peers	Same as above	by 9/25	
General **class schedule with options for extending** lunch-time, extending time in bathroom for self-care instruction, and community instruction during "workshop" with other students _Interaction skills_	General ed. teacher and all above	by 9/30	
Computer access - microswitch use for beginning matching programs and discrimination; plus games with peers	Support teacher	by 9/25	
Walking with 3-prong cane	Support teacher, OT, & OM	by 9/30	
Basic O & M	Support teacher, OT, & OM	by 9/30	
LIST CONTEXTS, PERIODS, AND ACTIVITIES TARGETED FOR INSTRUCTION			
2nd grade routines and activities (class expectations) Circle/attendance/messages, etc. 　9:00–10:15 - blocked cores 　　　always Math 　　Mon.　-Journals, story 　　Tues.　-Science, story 　　Weds.　-Spelling, journals 　　Thurs.　-Handwriting, spelling, journals 　　Fri.　-Spelling, journals 　10:15–10:30 - Recess 　10:40–11:40 - Class Workshop: Individual & small groups; class job; community options with peers 　12:30–12:50 - Silent reading 　12:50–1:40 - M, W: Science; Tu - Farm; Th - Music; F - Library 　1:40–2:40 - M, W, F - P.E.; Tu-Th - Art	Support teacher and general ed. teacher, paraprofessional	by 9/25	
SPECIFY ANY SPECIALIZED HEALTH CARE NEEDS (attach reports, etc.). **SPECIFY ANY TECHNOLOGY OR EQUIPMENT NEEDS**			
3-prong white cane/walker	O&M consult	w/in 1 mo.	
Computer access switch	Support teacher	by 9/25	
Later in the year: voice output communication system	Support teacher & speech/language	Review in Nov.	

Figure 3.　Ranelle: Action plan.

As stated earlier, any number of styles for action planning could be used. Because students with deaf-blindness often have a variety of professionals collaborating to meet their needs, it is important to have a clear vehicle for coordinating efforts, improving communication, and reducing frustration.

Team Planning and Curriculum Organization

The primary task of the individual's core team is the development of assessment plans, participation plans, support plans, and instructional plans for each curricular period and nonclassroom activity. Whether this is done prior to entry in the class or shortly after entry, this process can have a significant influence on the success of the student in the general classroom(s). A collaborative planning effort brings the general class teacher(s), the support teacher, and any other support personnel who are involved on a regular basis within each class/context together to discuss "nitty-gritty" information regarding curriculum, strategies, and cognitive growth. These discussions and strategy meetings are ongoing based on changes in curricular units and changes needed in teaching formats, strategies, and supports.

In order to assist general and special educators to plan together around curriculum, Gee (1991) developed a worksheet that highlights key aspects of the decisions that need to be made. It is not the actual *participation plan* (see later in this chapter), but rather a planning guide, and it is especially useful as teachers first begin the process of determining meaningful outcomes and integrating curriculum (Farron-Davis et al., 1994; Gee & Goetz, 1994). This process consists of the following seven steps.

Step 1: Collaborating on the General Curriculum and Instructional Strategies As the general and special educators begin to collaborate regarding the instructional design of the class, a first step is to ask the general educa-

tion teacher to talk about her or his program and teaching strategies. From an ecological perspective (Rainforth et al., 1992), this is similar to a general class inventory. The author expands that notion here to include the teaching styles and general milieu created by the teacher and the students. It is most helpful if the support teacher has had an opportunity to observe in the classroom prior to the meeting; however, this may not always be possible. Step 1 offers the teacher a chance to share the types of learning activities she or he uses; her or his preferences and typical routines; and the teaching formats, groupings, and assessment strategies.

If the school is already operating with grade level, multigrade level, or departmental teams, the process of including a student with disabilities is much easier. Teachers in these schools are familiar with working cooperatively to plan curriculum, and special educators may already be assigned to various teams. The reader is referred to several sources for cooperative, collaborative teaching relationships (Putnam, 1994; Rainforth et al., 1992; Thousand et al., 1994).

At the beginning of the team relationship, Step 1 may be approached as a "getting to know you" process, and more general teaching issues may be discussed. It is also used as an opportunity to provide the general education teacher with positive feedback and to offer any assistance the support teacher(s) can provide. Most importantly, the focus at this point is on the general class curriculum. This gives all the participants at the meeting a chance to connect with each other on a professional level regarding curriculum, instructional design, students, and general issues in teaching. If this is a first meeting, the discussion may revolve around curricular organization and strategies of instruction in general versus focusing on a particular unit. The upcoming target units (e.g., a unit on medieval literature, fractions, the ecology of the Bay, and so forth) are then discussed in more detail at the same meeting or at a second meeting.

At a planning meeting for Ranelle, the young girl discussed in the previous case example, Ranelle's second grade teacher, Ms. Hughes, discussed her upcoming unit on water pollution with the other team members. Ms. Hughes let the group know that her primary objectives during science always include: cooperative working relationships, how to interpret information, strategies for seeking information, conflict resolution, and task completion. During this particular unit she is also working toward an understanding of the main impact of water pollutants in the Bay, how to conduct an experiment, how to interpret results, how to write clear sentences to describe sequence of steps, and how to generate creative solutions to problems.

Step 2: General Student Objectives and Expectations In the second step of the planning process, the general educator reviews his or her expectations for the general education students. This includes social and behavioral expectations, such as class rules, homework, group collaboration, and so forth, in addition to curricular objectives and expected instructional outcomes. Support teachers are often surprised at the variety of goals within each activity and that the expected outcomes for students in the general class cover such a wide range. As team members get to know one another, supportive relationships evolve and ideas are shared between professionals. A sense of mutual responsibility begins to develop, and the development of units is done with more joint collaboration (Rainforth et al., 1992). This process takes time and, as our schools are currently structured, requires teachers to break away from the typical individualistic style of organization (Johnson & Johnson, 1989; Skrtic, 1991). If the school is using teaching teams and teachers are planning units together regularly, some of this process may not be necessary. Students with deaf-blindness (and other significant disabilities),

however, will still need classroom expectations and instruction planned to suit their unique learning styles within the lessons designed.

Step 3: Student Profile/IEP Summary and Review After a discussion of the curriculum and units, the primary support teacher takes the opportunity to review the target student's learning objectives and the priorities that were set by the larger team (including the parent(s), peers, siblings, other staff, and so forth). A positive profile of the student is developed as the student's learning styles, communication techniques, and adaptations are reviewed. This affords the general educator the opportunity to ask questions and to learn more about the student, especially if he or she was not included in the initial planning meeting. It puts the persons present at the meeting on more equal ground in terms of their ability to contribute to the activity in the next step.

At this point in the process, some teams may elect to spend a couple of weeks with the student in the class(es) in order to gain some practical ideas for instructional inclusion. If the teachers have not worked together before, and/or this student is new to the support teacher, it may be difficult to predict how the student will be included (as is suggested in step 4). Allowing some time—informed time—for the support teacher to interact with the student within the classroom setting can be very helpful at this stage.

Step 4: Expectations and Outcomes for the Target Student The next step is to engage the group in brainstorming and problem-solving activities to determine the initial curricular and social expectations that will be set for the target student in the class. Each type of learning activity that the teacher uses (e.g., cooperative groups, individual work, small group, lecture) is discussed as well as the typical classroom routines. If the focus of the meeting is on a particular unit (as in the example of the science class in which Ranelle was included), the strategies will be more specifically outlined. If this is the first meeting the information will be more general.

The group generates ideas for embedding skill instruction within the content of the activities, adaptations, and ideas for participation. Curricular adaptations and the notion of embedding skills within natural activities are not new concepts (cf. Sailor et al., 1987; 1989; Snell, 1993, for review). The successful instruction of a wide range of objectives that vary from the "typical" student's objectives in the general class has also been documented in much of the recent literature (Englert et al., 1992; Rainforth et al., 1992; Stainback et al., 1989; Villa & Thousand, 1992; York & Vandercook, 1989).

Several authors have outlined various levels of curriculum adaptations (Ford et al., 1992; Giangreco et al., 1994). Udvari-Solner (1992, 1994) suggests that teachers consider changes in 1) instructional groupings; 2) teaching formats; 3) the environment, materials, or types of support; and 4) levels of support. It is also suggested that teachers think of outcomes and curricular goals in the following terms:

- *Multi-level curriculum:* Students are working in the same subject area, but are working at different levels of the curriculum.
- *Curriculum overlapping:* Students are involved in the same activity with other students, but may have goals from a different curriculum area.
- *Substitute curriculum/alternative activities:* Students with disabilities are working on alternative activities in the classroom or in other school or community environments; activities are preferably socially integrated.

Neary et al. (1993) suggest five categories for examining curriculum adaptation: 1) leave as is, providing physical assistance; 2) adapt materials; 3) multi-level curriculum; 4) curriculum overlapping; and 5) substitute curriculum. The teaching team is clearly influenced by the introduction of a learner with multiple disabilities. Teaching formats that are more conducive to heterogeneous groups and facilitative of the development of collaboration and cooperation in the classroom (e.g., cooperative learning, thoughtful education, learning styles) provide the anchor for successful development of meaningful instruction.

From experience and research, some additional guidelines for setting expectations and outcomes for students with deaf-blindness are highlighted in the following paragraphs.

Align Outcomes with Those of the Whole Class Consider a common set of outcomes with a wide range of ability within each. Many times the adaptations made from purely a "participation" viewpoint limit the student's true integration into the curriculum. By carefully considering the actual outcomes expected of the students without disabilities, a teacher can align outcomes more successfully for the student with disabilities.

One student observed during journal writing time was being asked to hold the crayon and draw on the paper. While the fine motor component of the activity may have been aligned with the other students, the central meaning of the activity (expressing oneself on paper, formulating information) was lost. After some thought, the teacher chose to have the student work on putting together picture sequences to express himself in symbolic form.

In another situation, a student with deaf-blindness was included in a language arts class. When the general education students discussed the literature piece they were reading, this student was brought to a table on the side of the room to listen to tapes through headphones. After some additional consideration, the support teacher decided that a reduced version of the book chapter could be read (through signing) to the student in a "Cliff Notes" fashion during the independent reading time. When the discussion occurred, the general education teacher could be coached on questions to ask the student, which she would then have the opportunity to answer.

Avoid Continual "Random" Participation   Students' instructional objectives should receive the same planned and systematic efforts that would occur in a smaller group or special class session. The primary support teacher, therefore, needs to organize and plan how instruction will be conducted within the general education class formats. If instruction on skills is totally random and participation is "on the spot," more often than not it will be difficult to ensure the consistent instruction necessary to move the student from acquisition to mastery and generalized usage of new skills.

Revise Initial Planning As Needed   After further assessment within each class/period/activity, curriculum planning to include students with disabilities will often need to be changed or improved. It is important to consider the first participation plans as initial, and stay open to revision. Often after spending time in the class or activity, the team's ideas change. In addition, the student's team needs to evaluate progress on a regular basis through ongoing, authentic assessment.

Create Integrated Alternative Activities   When alternative activities or instructional arrangements need to be created because of particular needs the student has or because the class period or activity is not one in which the student can benefit, the support teacher can often create alternatives that are still integrated with the rest of the class. Students from the class can accompany peers with disabilities in small groups doing alternate activities, or they can accompany students into the community or other parts of the school for enrichment activities that benefit all the students. Some examples follow:

One second grade teacher conducted her math instruction primarily through the use of worksheets and paper-and-pencil tasks. It was highly individualized. Because Roy (a student with deaf-blindness) was not working on any math objectives, his support teacher offered to conduct a "math workshop" during math time. About five students would go to the workshop area with Roy each day. The workshop activities supported the concepts being learned on paper in the current unit. The support teacher was able to provide some manipulatives instruction in an applied math format for the students without disabilities while gaining a small group activity in which to include Roy. Roy focused on some beginning communication symbols to request turns at the games and to seek assistance to participate.

A social studies teacher who had a student with deaf-blindness (Sara) in her class required a community experience project of all her students. During one particular unit, however, the work in class was primarily focused on reading and answering questions from the text. The support teacher assisted Sara to set up her community experience as a dog-walker for some senior citizens who were unable to give their dogs enough exercise. During this particular unit, the social studies teacher allowed two different students to accompany Sara each day as she walked the dog of one of the seniors who lived nearby.

One middle school support teacher who had two students needing extensive orientation and mobility experience in the community, advertised himself as the "contextual education" teacher. He connected with faculty who needed extra support for community-related projects and arranged periods during the day in which his students could join in on community projects and get extra time in the community for their O&M instruction.

Figures 4–8 provide some additional examples of thoughtful instruction within general education activities. In Figure 4, the decisions made by Ranelle's team regarding the unit on water pollution are depicted. As the reader can see, the team determined that during cooperative group time Ranelle could work on turn-taking, social interactions, and following a picture sequence versus the written step-by-step instructions given to the other students. Initiating interactions with peers using her communication system would also be a priority during group work. Her walking and mobility goals could be worked on during the field trip, and, by utilizing the computer, she could be responsible for participation in data entry.

Figures 5 and 6 depict an action plan and a planning and organization sample from the

Student: *Ranelle*   **Date:** *September 2*

Class Period(s)/Grade Level/Setting/Activities: **Team Members Involved:** *Ms. Hughes,*
2nd grade, Science, Monday/Wednesday   *Ms. Graham (support teacher), Robin (O.T.)*

TEAM PLANNING AND CURRICULUM ORGANIZATION

TYPICAL CLASS ACTIVITIES & ROUTINES	TYPICAL TEACHING STRATEGIES (if nonclass activity, describe context & routing)	EXPECTATIONS FOR GENERAL ED. STUDENTS	EXPECTATIONS FOR TARGET STUDENT (T-S-C)	How will Ranelle RECEIVE INFORMATION	How will Ranelle PROVIDE INFORMATION	FURTHER INTEGRATION AND SUPPORT IDEAS (Teacher & Paraprofessional)
12:50 - 1:40	• Listen to directions from teacher • Break into cooperative groups (heterogeneous) • Conduct experiment of activity Week 1: Water pollution experiment Week 2: Take bus to Bay and collect samples, analyze Week 3: Speakers from Lawrence Hall of Science Week 4: Groups generate solutions to problems and design poster campaign • Fill out group worksheet • Share with large group	• Work cooperatively (they have specific strategies they are working on) • Conflict resolution • Complete assignments in group This unit: • Understand impact of main pollutants on water in Bay system • Conduct an experiment and analyze results • Write clear sentences to describe • Create new solutions	• Turn-taking • Follow routines • Select partner & job using comm. book • Follow picture sequence • Social interactions • Finish job w/peer support • Mobility & walking goals • Matching pictures of water system used in labs • Use computer to assist peers for reporting • Collect samples, etc. • Assist to make poster	• Input for class directions & routines through picture cues combined with gestures - always use speech also • Periodically touch R. as you give group directions • Peer points to speaker • Peer partner provides cues which are precedent.	• Point to pictures for choices after getting attention of peer or adult through acceptable means • Computer selections • Stickers to put on page after peer puts key word answers on them • Matching	• Select a group with one or two of R.'s friends in it • Take 5 mins. at beginning of group to assist in determining R.'s job and partner, etc. • Students can rotate being partners • Allow group to choose participation, but spend time assisting them to know what R. <u>can</u> do and what she <u>needs</u>

Figure 4.   Ranelle: Team planning sheet for science class.

first meeting with Jacob's teacher (see the following case study). Figure 5 portrays a list of the objectives and contexts chosen as priorities for Jacob.

Jacob is a seventh grader in Ms. Garcia's literature/language arts class. Jacob enjoys rock concerts, MTV, listening to music, and lots of activity. As the result of a near-drowning incident when Jacob was only 14 months old, he has lost the use of his voluntary movement except for his breathing, some eye movements, and a slight head movement. He has no blink reflex, breathes through a tracheotomy tube, and requires numerous specialized health care procedures in order to maintain his life while at school. Jacob's vision is limited to the area directly in front of his face within about 12 inches, only at midline. The best test of his hearing suggested a mild to moderate loss. Because he had only recently gained access to an integrated school, Jacob's team designed numerous goals around friendships, social interactions, gaining control over voluntary behaviors, controlling the environment, understanding routines, nonsymbolic communication, and so forth. They determined that the best schedule for Jacob would be to include him with peers without disabilities in as many classes as possible that were active and exploratory in nature.

In Figure 6, the reader can see that this planning session was done at the beginning of the year. Ms. Garcia discussed her teaching strategies in general, and the group planned for overall methods of participation during the various types of learning activities. During reading aloud, for example, a peer would be asked to prerecord passages from the literature piece of focus so that Ms. Garcia could call on Jacob to read aloud during class. Jacob's objective would be to respond to the verbal instruction, paired with a tactile cue from a peer. Gradual fading of assistance would be used to teach Jacob to activate a microswitch attached to the tape recorder. During group debate, his goal would be to shift his gaze or change affect (i.e., blush, widen his eyes). His peers would read intent into his change and take it as a cue to move him to the other side of the debate (literally) in the class. Because Ms. Garcia used numerous interactive activities there would

be many opportunities for social interaction instruction. Jacob's computer objectives could be worked on with partners during independent study times.

Figure 7 depicts a planning sheet from Tiu's (see the following case study) 10th grade American History class.

The class is working on a unit regarding the period from 1900–1930. Tiu has been included in the general education program since entering high school in the 9th grade. Previously she attended a junior high where she was taught in a special education classroom for students who were deaf, with some integration into general education classes. Prior to junior high she attended a segregated elementary school for students with multiple disabilities. Because she has only recently been given the opportunity for full inclusion, she is behind on many concepts related to the curriculum content of the courses. While she learns very quickly and is extremely motivated, her communication system has only recently been developed. She is able to use speech as an output system, but cannot hear speech any more due to a deteriorating hearing loss. Her vision is very limited, but she is able to read large print with a magnifier and use of the V-tech (a device that enlarges printed materials). These adaptations are very slow, however, because she sees only a few letters at a time. Tiu is learning braille quickly, but because it was not offered to her before (teachers said she was a "behavior problem"), her braille ability is at a primary level.

Many of Tiu's goals are the same as her peers, but with slight modifications. Concepts and vocabulary need to be explained through extra time with her interpreter and support teacher during a study hall period. Two peers usually accompany her to assist in vocabulary definition and conceptual understanding. When Tiu is assisted to understand the vocabulary and is provided with background information, she is able to connect to the information with the same degree of intellectual understanding as her peers. She is provided with some "reduced length" readings and sometimes the teacher's lecture notes and syntheses so that she can read this material instead of the entire chapter/book. Some additional adaptations are made for

Name:	Jacob	Date:	September 2

Grade: 7th

Persons present: *Mrs. Garcia (Gen. Ed.), Nancy (R.N.), Ms. Tang (Support tchr.) Family, two General Ed. students*

ACTION PLAN

LIST PRIORITY CURRICULAR CONTENT AND BASIC SKILLS. *Indicate any special assessment needs*	Team Members Responsible	Timelines	Date Complete
Control over breathing to move head 1/4-in. to access switch for loop tape system	Support teacher and paraprofessional in conjunction with family		
Eye gaze control for communication	"		
Tactile symbol system for "anticipation" board; indicate to access activity continuation	"		
Respond to interactions --> affect, eye gaze	""		
Use switch to access computer --> beginning	"		
Continuing awareness	"		
Use switch to operate "conversation" book	"		
After school activities	"		
Friendships	"		
Regular classes/community access and awareness	"		

LIST CONTEXTS, PERIODS, AND ACTIVITIES TARGETED FOR INSTRUCTION			
Arrives at end of 1st period Period 2: Computer Class	Support teacher and Mr. Harris		
Period 3: Literature	Ms. Garcia		
Period 4: First half: Cafeteria with friends Period 5: Second half of 4th and all of 5th: Catheterization; other vital SHCN; reclined tube feeding (with peers)	Circle of Friends Paraprofessional		
Period 6: Social Studies Period 7: Language Arts core	Ms. Suchman		
Period 8: Electives: Band, Choir, Home Ec., Shop	Mr. Hubert		

SPECIFY ANY SPECIALIZED HEALTH CARE NEEDS. (attach reports, etc.) SPECIFY ANY TECHNOLOGY OR EQUIPMENT NEEDS			
See attached report on time schedule and supervision, etc. --> needs suctioning regularly (every 15-30 mins.); catheter; respiratory therapy; tube feeding; vital signs; meds; and other	Support teacher Supervising R.N. and paraprofessional		
Microswitches; tape recorder - loop tape; env. switches			
MAC LC with KNEX will arrive from other school - this should accompany him at all times			

Figure 5. Jacob: Action plan.

Class Period/Activity: *3rd Period Language Arts/Literature*

Team Planning & Curriculum Organization

TYPICAL CLASS ACTIVITIES & ROUTINES	TYPICAL TEACHING STRATEGIES	EXPECTATIONS FOR GENERAL ED. STUDENTS	EXPECTATIONS FOR TARGET STUDENT (T-S-C)	HOW WILL JACOB RECEIVE INFO.	HOW WILL JACOB PROVIDE INFO.	FURTHER INTEGRATION & SUPPORT IDEAS
Arrival Find seat Listen to directions The following happen *nearly every day:* 1. Group discussion 2. Journal question 3. Reading of focus piece for literature Other: 4. Small group or individual projects related to literature —writing —prose, poetry —analyze literature piece & present through variety of media	"Thoughtful Education Model" Large group discussions & debates Individual and group projects Values of diversity Independent Reading aloud, taking turns, teacher also reads, discussion Group work during class & at noon, after school Students work individually in class	Get to seat on time Observe class rules (see packet designed by students) Social interactions Listen to directions & participate actively in each part of the period Pick partners or groups if needed & work cooperatively Get work in on time *Writing:* grammar, spelling, style, critical thinking, semantics *Reading:* aloud, interpretive, grade level, understanding *Projects:* work independently or in groups, complete work on time, creativity, work skills *Literature:* critical thinking, variation, ??	Learn tactile & visual symbols for class period and routines Acknowledge interactions Initiate interactions Class job? Group discussion —remain w/group —debate, peers use J.'s nonsymbolic messages and assign intent —alternative: work on computer or utilize head phones and tapes Reading aloud Activate tape recorder with pre-determined passages read by peer or adult Journal writing —alternate: *computer* —contingency awareness programs & partner groups *Projects*—peer partners	Object calendar/ symbols with touch cues and verbal input Assign protocol—Important to use touch, object, visual, & verbal Peers give class directions Staff provide training input at designated times Peers determine participation Peers give verbal & symbolic input	Eye gaze shift & focus Acknowledge Activate loop tape in addition to eye gaze Initiate Loop tape and breathing loudly Info. related to topics on J.'s computer Conversation book with social info. Activate tape recorder with readings Computer Eye gaze Hand switch operation Head switch operation	Peers supply symbols and info. for J. as to what's happening next during the period Peers learn to watch for J.'s eye movement and breathing; head turn to activate loop tape Peers determine how J. will participate in group & partner projects Peer support group Peer partners for interaction games on computer

Figure 6.　Jacob: Team planning sheet for literature class.

| | Student: | Tiu | | Date: | September 10 |
| | | | | | Team Members Involved: |

Class Period(s)/Grade Level/Setting/Activities:

10th grade; History – American

TYPICAL CLASS ACTIVITIES & ROUTINES	TYPICAL TEACHING STRATEGIES (if nonclass activity, describe context & routing)	EXPECTATIONS FOR GENERAL ED. STUDENTS	EXPECTATIONS FOR TARGET STUDENT (T-S-C)	How will Tiu RECEIVE INFORMATION	How will Tiu PROVIDE INFORMATION	FURTHER INTEGRATION AND SUPPORT IDEAS (Teacher & Para-professional)
Monday/Wednesday • Class begins with independent newspaper reading or news magazines; students select article to share w/others in group --> select most noteworthy to share in class **Tu-Thurs-Friday** • Share news from eve. before • Students listen to plan for the day and activities, etc.; ask questions • Current unit: 1900-1930 **Methods:** • Reading from actual period text and newspapers • 2 paperbacks reflecting analysis of the period • Group project --> choose from project board in back of room • Discussion & debate format • Synthesis tests using various learning formats • Films • "Concept" discussions with group presentations to class	• Read & interpret current news; begin to form habits of paying attention to the news & critical reading • Speaking to the class • Follow directions & actively participate • Critical reading ⎫ • Gathering info ⎬ • Note-taking ⎭ • Interpret. reading ⎫ • Analyze & prepare one topic in depth; present in creative format • Articulate in writing synthesis of period • Engage in debate & discussion over topics	• Same; also, braille and note-taking skills • Same but through interpreter (tactile sign) • Same • Vocabulary • Same goals but braille reading at own level; large print reading is grade level but slow • Vocabulary and concept work • May require modified amount since vocabulary is behind • Questions need modification • Through interpreter	• Get readings to interpreter in advance • Tiu should read news article ahead of time & review notes during class • braille is preferred but a new skill, so large print & v-tech will be used also • Large print reading is at grade level – but slow; vocabulary needs to be addressed • Modify texts and use different notes where possible	• Tiu speaks but her speech is dwindling; encourage her to speak <u>and</u> sign • Remember, she doesn't hear you in return • Utilize interpreter in all group and whole class discussions • Encourage Tiu to ask questions	• Groups need some input on how to work with interpreter • Advise Tiu on modifications she can do for herself • Partner to practice class speaking delivery with Tiu • Vocabulary & concepts are difficult: use study period to review

Figure 7.   Tiu: Team planning sheet for U.S. history class.

the current events readings. Her team constantly battles time to give her the missing background information so that she can participate in the lessons of her peers, which she can master to the same degree. Her information input systems (braille, tactile sign language, and other adaptations) will require extra instruction in the summers in order to match her communication skills to the same level as her conceptual understanding. Tiu often asks why she wasn't previously allowed to learn braille and why she didn't learn about people and things such as the Native Americans and the constitution before. Table 1 provides additional examples of ways in which various students with deaf-blindness and other disabilities can learn and

participate in core curriculum activities, with outcomes that are aligned with their peers without disabilities.

Step 5: How Will the Student Receive Information? After the initial instructional targets have been outlined, the group generates ideas on how the student will *receive* information (both task-related and social information) most effectively within classroom routines and activities. Some of the planning in this area is specific to communication systems, such as establishing an object symbol for various activities or determining which information will be provided in braille as opposed to tactile sign language. Other planning involves determining whether peers, the general education teacher, or support

Table 1.   Examples of aligning learning outcomes for students with and without deaf-blindness

Expectations for students without deaf-blindness	Expectations for the student with deaf-blindness
5th grade: Writing the script, designing the puppets, and organizing the show for a puppet show related to ecology topics for kindergarten through 2nd grade students.	Adam: Using the computer to assist in designing the posters and the programs; facilitating one of the hand puppets in the show whose part requires little movement, with cues and support from a peer; selecting the fabric and trim for the costumes for the puppets. Sara: Assisting the group, with help from her interpreter, in designing the plot and the characters; providing a review of the story to the other deaf students in the school and a braille transcription of the program for another blind student.
9th grade English class: Write a research paper on a topic of interest. Learn outlining, note-taking, references, and so on. Share progress with cohort group regularly.	Suni: Work in partnership with two other students from the class writing separate papers. Suni's responsibilities include participation in public library searches, accessing community resources, and connecting with people resources related to the topic. Expectations include utilization of a communication device at a basic level, utilization of adaptations, community travel goals, and social interaction skills.
Kindergarten: Understand basic calendar, dates, year, days of the week, and so on.	Troy: Learn tactile symbols for daily schedule. Set up schedule inside portable notebook. Taylor: Learn braille calendar.
7th grade literature/social studies core: Group writes a skit about the death of Robin Hood and acts it out to the class.	Jacob: Plays the part of Little John who has been injured in a battle. Activates a tape recorder through a microswitch to "say" lines when cued by peer. During group planning time and practices, tape records discussion and plays it back for group confirmation.

staff (support teacher, interpreter, or paraprofessional/facilitator) will provide certain types of information.

Students with no physical or sensory disabilities have a number of pieces of information available to them to begin learning to interact with the materials and people integral to a new activity or learning context. They have a constant source of sensory information (cues) with which to learn to anticipate events and behaviors and the ability to access more information using their fine and gross motor capabilities. While they vary with respect to their intellectual mastery of these capabilities, they can interact with the environment by moving and acting on stimuli and can anticipate events and behaviors based on sensory information. The contextual referents or "script" of a social learning context are readily available through their primary distance senses (vision and hearing) and their ability to move to gain contact with the environment (Gee, 1993).

Sensory disabilities impact how a learner receives and takes in information. If we think of deaf-blindness as an information-gathering disability, it helps us to remember that adaptations must be made and instructional techniques must be used to ensure that the student with deaf-blindness receives the same amount of information about the activity, lesson, or topic as students who are taking in the information with intact vision and hearing. Our distance senses are continuously utilized to anticipate, recognize, and discriminate people, things, and events. When both the primary distance senses (hearing and seeing) are not intact, learners have much more difficulty discriminating, recognizing, or interpreting what is going on until they actually make physical contact with the people or things that are necessary to the activity. It is the reduction of distance sense capability that has such a profound impact on the learning and concept develop-

ment of individuals with deaf-blindness (van Dijk, 1989). Consider a shopping activity in a local grocery store where the student with deaf-blindness in the situation described below has: 1) received fewer pieces of information and 2) had less time to process it.

Students with their senses intact see the store, people entering, people getting carts, the cars in the parking lot, and so forth prior to entering the store. Some time passes between the visual and auditory cues before actually entering the store, allowing for some anticipation and processing of cues. Students who are deaf-blind have fewer natural cues that let them know they are approaching the store. There may be a pattern, however, that develops over time as to the number of curbs crossed, the traffic lights and the particular route, and so forth, but not on the first visit. The first cues the student will have are on impact when the store doorway is crossed, air rushes onto his or her face, and railing guides are felt on the way to get a cart. Smell is a distance sense, which at this point will provide information related to the store environment. If the student also has physical disabilities and is riding in a wheelchair, there may be fewer touch and kinesthetic cues available without assistance. Suddenly the student is in the store with a cart in hand, with few distance cues to indicate what the store is like and what people might be doing there.

The rich social and physical contexts for learning that are so readily available in inclusive school and community settings can thus be elusive to these students if the adults and peers providing support fail to consider two key factors: 1) how the student will become an *informed participant* and 2) how the student will become an *active participant* (Gee, 1993). An informed learner has had information delivered in a manner that is accessible, given his or her communication skills and sensory capabilities. Time has been allowed for the student to perceive the information, and concepts have been explained through the use of alternatives to observation and discussion. He or she has not only received, but has been given the opportunity to comprehend, clear cues for the sequences of behavior in an activity, a lesson, a job, or a class period. An active learner is a learner who has been given various means of control within the activity, meaningful ways to demonstrate knowledge, and the motivation to know what he or she needs to know (Gee, 1993).

A key responsibility of teacher planning for instruction of a student with deaf-blindness, therefore, is to determine what distance and impact cues will be available to the student naturally and what additional sources of information could be enhanced or added to ensure that the student understands and interprets the events, people, and things going on around her. The order of information delivery should respect the natural sequence in terms of distance to impact senses, and enough time must be allowed for processing of the information. The teaching team will also need to design a way of measuring whether the student in fact gains the information and can anticipate and interpret the situation adequately. More teacher preparation *prior* to activities may be needed to organize tactile and exploratory opportunities for the student and to design descriptive information. More individual interpreting of the events occurring in classrooms, the learning activities, and the environment at large will be necessary. Use of models and real settings and objects is required as well as a reduction of assumptions when explaining new concepts.

For example, Ranelle (see Figure 4) used a picture/gesture receptive input system. Peers and her teacher Ms. Hughes were encouraged to use the system throughout the day. Ms. Hughes was asked to seat Ranelle close to the center of the class where she could easily get to her. This allowed Ms. Hughes to walk near to Ranelle and to touch her and use her system while in the middle of giving directions.

Jacob (see Figure 6) utilized a tangible object system. He was just beginning to learn the objects, however, and staff, peers, and Ms. Garcia were taught to use the object visually and tactilely along with speech and touch to indicate the start of new activities or changes in a current activity. Touch cues to indicate continuation, affect, and the general social context were utilized continuously.

Tiu (see Figure 7) required advance brailled information as well as large-print versions of materials. She also utilized the V-tech for on-the-spot enlargement. She was in the process of learning tactile sign language as her receptive language system, although she could understand the speech of a few individuals if it was loud, close, and clear.

Step 6: Providing Information The next step in the process is to determine ways for the target student to *provide* information related to his or her goals, class activities, and other social situations. During this time, the group has a chance to talk specifically about how the student communicates and to generate adaptations that can be used in the class/activity. Most often students with disabilities are put in the role of *receiving* information or support. However, research conducted on a project serving students with deaf-blindness in inclusive settings (Gee, 1993) demonstrated that it is just as important for teachers to design systems for the student to provide others with information, both socially and throughout the curriculum, even if their communication ability is not yet sophisticated enough to interpret that type of information. By designing strategies to place students with deaf-blindness in the role of providing information about themselves (e.g., their family, what they did over the weekend), supplying information relevant or necessary to the curriculum unit, and offering feedback and demonstrating preferences, there was a distinct change in the social roles and relationships among middle students with and without disabilities participating in the study. Students without disabilities began to include the students with deaf-blindness in qualitatively different types of conversations. In addition, the students without disabilities directed their social attention to the target students in new ways. In general, by increasing their demonstrations of knowledge provision and choice, others in turn requested more interactions with them and chose to engage them in different types of conversations.

In one example, Jacob (see Figure 6) was provided with a "talking book" version of a conversation book (Beukelman & Mirenda, 1992; Hunt, Alwell, & Goetz, 1988). He activated taped messages corresponding to pictures of what was happening in his personal life to share with his friends. Jacob was also an integral part of the curriculum. Numerous ways for Jacob to connect with his classmates regarding content were designed. For example, in class, his teacher, Ms. Garcia, alerted the students one week by saying, "Sometime during the week you need to get back to Jacob and get the information on the Globe Theatre. He's got it in the computer for you." During another unit Jacob had the vocabulary words and definitions in his computer. Students interacted with him through a taped series of directions in order to learn to use the computer.

In her social studies class, Tiu was encouraged to share information with the class about the newspaper articles she read using her own speech, with assistance from her interpreter. Her brailled notes were transcribed for some of her peers to use as study notes/guides.

Step 7: Supports The final step is to determine other inclusive activities and peer supports that will be used in classroom activities, how peer support networks will be recruited and maintained, and ways in which the support teacher and general education teacher will communicate. This planning

will not only be specific to the particular class period being discussed in the meeting, but will also be connected to the overall social inclusion action plan that the team has designed. It is important to recognize, for example, that if peers will be providing some support through information provision, they will need some advising and instruction. This can be done easily through a group meeting or at the beginning of activities. If groups or partners will rotate, a system needs to be in place. As discussed in Chapter 11, peers need assistance and facilitation to provide meaningful supports.

At this point the support teacher, related service personnel, and the paraprofessional or interpreting staff also plan how to use their time with the students in the class with the general educator. The team needs to determine:

1. During which periods the student with deaf-blindness requires an interpreter or other adult to provide direct instruction or support within the small and large group or individual activities
2. During which periods the student can be supported by peers
3. How the adults will work together for the benefit of *all* the students in the class

INITIAL ASSESSMENT OF INCLUSION PLANNING

Team problem-solving approaches have been highly developed by Johnson and Johnson (1989) under the rubric of cooperative goal structures. Other sources have developed these strategies under the themes of integrated therapy (Campbell, 1993; Dunn, 1991; Rainforth et al., 1992), transdisciplinary teaming (Vandercook & York, 1989), and team collaboration (Giangreco et al., 1994; Thousand et al., 1994). Researchers and interventionists have found that teachers collaborating in this manner to serve students with disabilities will begin to review the instructional groupings, formats, delivery, and effective practices for all the students in the class. The introduction of a learner who requires careful planning for concept development and problem-solving skills and who exemplifies the need for learning communities can stimulate educators to rethink what they are defining as their typical practices (Ford et al., 1992; Gee, 1993).

Using a Matrix to
Review Instructional Priorities

At the end of the planning meeting(s), the team fills in a matrix, like the one drawn up by Ranelle's team (see Figure 8), to get an overall picture of the student's schedule of learning activities. On the left side of Figure 8, Ranelle's schedule is filled in; the top row depicts Ranelle's goals. The letter "D" represents those activities where the skill will be directly instructed, and the letter "I" indicates incidental instruction.

Matrices to depict the distribution of instruction over numerous contexts have been widely used in special education to demonstrate the efficacy of instruction on specific skills within and across numerous motivating and community-referenced settings. A review of the matrix helps the team determine if the instructional objectives are embedded successfully. This may be difficult to determine until further authentic assessments have been completed. It is important to recognize that *the matrix itself is not an assessment or participation plan*, but rather a means to summarize the current organization of when and where planned instruction will occur.

Ongoing Collaboration

The information generated from the planning meetings forms the basis for a more thorough context analysis and assessment, in which specific strategies for providing and receiving information, instructing the student, and "connecting" him or her with peers are identified. This initial plan also allows the team to get started establishing a learning and social community. Assessment and ongoing problem solving brings the team back together repeatedly to evaluate whether the target objectives are being met, whether the student is truly integrated into the curriculum and the social community, and whether changes in the instruction need to be made.

CREATING A SOCIAL
AND LEARNING COMMUNITY

It is extremely important to familiarize the student with the instructional contexts and learning situations of each classroom. It is equally important to establish communication strategies within the classroom and to develop a rapport among the direct instructional staff, student peers, and the student with deaf-blindness. Many general education teachers spend time creating community with the entire class at the beginning of the year and as an ongoing strategy through various community building techniques (see Grennon-Brooks & Brooks, 1993; Sapon-Shevin, 1992; Villa & Thousand, 1992, for review). The special needs of the individual with deaf-blindness can be integrated into these strategies. The reader is referred to Chapter 11 for further information on the social inclusion of the student with deaf-blindness.

As stated earlier, a large amount of social information is often missing for the individual with deaf-blindness. How loud people are talking in a particular setting and whether he or she is alone, with one person, or with several people will make a difference in expectations of behavior. Individuals with deaf-blindness have a right to privacy as well

Name: _Ranelle_

Date: _____

INSTRUCTIONAL SCHEDULE MATRIX
Student's Schedule of Activities, Contexts

[D = Direct; I = Incidental]

G o a l s

Schedule	Communication - Social Interaction	Games Turn-taking Skills	Computer Access	Mealtime Skills	Object/Picture Match, Dis-crimination	Self-Care Activities	O&M Walking with new cane	Community: Travel, Stores, & Restaurants	Classroom Routines & Rules
8:45–9:00 _Circle_	D	I				Arrival D	All Transitions		D
9:00–10:15 (Core) •_Math_ (M-F)	D	I			D				D
Journals (M,W,Th,F)	D	D	D		D		I		D
Story (M-F)	D	I	I		D				D
Spelling (W,Th,F)	I	D							D
Handwriting (Th)	I	I	D		D				D
10:15–10:30 _Recess_	D	D		I		D	D		D
10:40–11:40 _Workshop_	D	D	D				Direct	D	D
11:40–12:20 _Lunch/Recess_	D	D		D		D	D/I	D (periodic)	D
12:30–12:50 _Silent Rdg_	I	D	D				D		D
1:50–1:40 _Science_ (M,W)	D	D	D		D				D
Farm (Tu) _Music_ (Th) _Library_ (F)	I	I			I	I			D
1:40–2:50 _P.E._ (M,W,F)	D	I					D		D
Art (Tu,Th)	D	I				D			D

Figure 8. Ranelle: Instructional schedule matrix and student goals.

as a right to know who is around them. They should be informed of who is present and whether they are with one individual, a small group, or a large group. They should also be informed when people leave or return. These are pieces of information we often take for granted, but when they are not communicated adequately to an individual who is deaf and blind, they may be a source of irritation, confusion, or withdrawal. Deaf-blind "etiquette" tells us that we need to think about our approach to a person, identify a name sign for ourselves and others, and develop a set of consistent signals for common occurrences and social situations. Letting a person know when we leave the room, when we join a group, who is talking, and some information about the social context are all strategies that can become second nature to staff, peers, family, and friends after some practice, role playing, and feedback.

Participation in new social, instructional, and work settings will require a period of "context instruction" or establishment of familiar routines and cues (Gee, 1993; Gee, Graham, & Goetz, 1994). Often students who are labeled deaf-blind, in addition to having severe cognitive disabilities, may have serious reactions to placement in a new classroom or job or participation in a new social setting unless context instruction and social support is provided (see case studies below).

Holly, age 7, cried for the first few days of her new milk delivery job. She had no vision and hearing, a cognitive disability, and very limited movement ability. After her teacher organized a consistent plan for providing her with information all the way through the activity and the peers without disabilities involved in her program learned to provide consistent cues and feedback, her crying stopped and she soon enjoyed her new job.

Harry, age 15, banged his head on his wheelchair, or attempted to do so, with a much higher frequency than usual during his first week at his job training site at the V.A. hospital. He had a profound hearing loss,

limited light perception, a cognitive disability, and very limited movement. His paper shredding job was ideal because it could be done with minimal support and several adaptations, and it provided him with great tactile feedback (the machine vibrated heavily). His support staff and co-workers learned to provide him with a series of cues and tactile input to indicate the steps in his work routine from the moment he entered the hospital until he left. His head banging stopped as he became informed and gained a routine he could expect and anticipate.

Sally, age 12, entered the 7th grade in September along wither her same-age peers. She had a cognitive disability in addition to a moderate hearing loss and a severe vision loss. Her support teacher planned ahead with the general education teacher to have several peers participate in a support circle for Sally. These students sat near her; provided her with planned feedback and information regarding activities, discussions, movements, and so forth; and learned positive interaction methods to communicate with Sally in a respectful way. Orientation and mobility instruction provided assistance with orienting Sally to the room, the school, and the school grounds, as well as assisting the support teacher with ways to organize Sally's school materials, and so on. With this planning, Sally's outbursts were reduced to a minimum during the first weeks of school.

When communicating with or teaching communication to an individual with deaf-blindness, an integral responsibility is providing more than the semantic message. Supporting information to help clarify the message may need to be given. Emotional information such as squeezing a hand, giving a hug, or a planned set of cues for general social feedback may be necessary. Maintaining physical contact by holding a hand in between specific communications or having the person touch you in a particular place on your arm are other methods of communicating security, consistency, and dependability. As the support teacher enters into team relationships with families, general educators, and related service professionals, one important role she or he can provide is active modeling of communication and deaf-blind "etiquette" as well as sharing information about learning styles and communication techniques.

Ongoing Assessment and Instruction

The team may need to conduct more detailed activity-based assessments to determine specifically when and where the instruction of each skill will occur. Within scheduled activities that are easily task analyzed, a component analysis can be done to break down the parts of the activity and to determine the skills that need to be targeted for instruction (Brown & Snell, 1993). The curricular activities of general education classrooms, however, and the research indicating the effectiveness of constructivist and cognitive teaching strategies (Englert et al., 1992; Grennon-Brooks & Brooks, 1993) may not lend themselves to this model.

Often special educators who are trained in a task-analytic approach tend to think sequentially about their curriculum, using a more reductionist method, although many of the effective general education practices are more holistic or constructivist in their approach (Englert et al. 1992). If we take a closer look at the curriculum unit for an academic class, we find that there are several types of activities planned to teach particular concepts, basic skills, and higher order thinking skills and several means to demonstrate that knowledge or skill. By working closely with the general educator to understand the plan and the purposes of the learning activities, we can identify how the student with special needs will work on his or her objectives within the activities.

The team may also need to conduct functional assessments targeted at particular skill areas. For example, the team conducted a thorough assessment of Ranelle's communication skills shortly after her entry into the second grade as stipulated on the action plan. Recommendations were then made for program options (see Figure 3, Ranelle's action plans). Ongoing, authentic assessment strategies must also be established for use throughout the year.

After more thorough assessments are completed, the team can:

1. Revise the objectives
2. Determine the instructional strategies for each objective
3. Design a means for evaluation
4. Finalize supports for each activity/class period
5. Set up participation plans that organize instructional and facilitative supports

Organizing Instruction: Participation Plans and Student Notebooks

Whether the student is receiving instruction in the community, in general education classes, or other areas of the school (e.g., library, cafeteria, locker room), designing a *participation plan* for each typical educational activity of the day is one of the most important things the primary support teacher can do to facilitate the implementation of the student's program. The participation plan is like a management plan for each period of the day and includes the following:

- A general description of the class period/ or other school or community activity
- The objectives targeted for the period
- A description of the typical activities and routines that occur within the class period or other context
- How the student can participate during each activity/routine
- Expectations of the student with disabilities
- Strategies for providing information to the student
- How the student will communicate to others
- When and where direct or indirect instruction of each objective should occur
- What types of support will be provided
- How to facilitate peer interactions and student collaboration
- Evaluation procedures or note taking required

- Any other helpful hints and directions for staff

Some teachers may also include more specific instructional programs on the same sheet of paper; others may simply make reference to places where there is a systematic instructional plan that should be followed. The systematic instructional plans/strategies for particular objectives are not replaced by the participation plan. This tool is simply a means of organizing instruction. Figure 9 provides an example of a participation plan for Jacob in his 7th grade literature class; Figure 10 presents an example of a participation plan for Tiu in her 10th grade American History class.

The primary support teacher may wish to put together a student notebook to organize all the necessary information to facilitate smooth delivery of services and support. Depending on the student's abilities, the notebook may be one that the student assists to develop and uses on a daily basis, or, a notebook that the student's team members use in conjunction with the student and her or his peers. The notebook should contain an IEP summary, the student's schedule, the student's support staff schedules, a matrix of instructional delivery, participation plans, instructional programs, and any necessary information for communication, technology, specialized health care, and so forth. Depending on each team's preferences, the notebook may go with the student or be left in the classroom.

General Instructional Implications

Although the length of this chapter precludes a discussion of the research and application of effective instruction, some general guidelines for instruction follow.

Constructing Context from Depleted Sources
The learner with deaf-blindness is often missing the *context* for learning and interact-

ing. Aside from the specific cues for a requested skill or the specific communication from a peer or even an interpreter, this learner is often not given the additional information that most people use to make judgments about what they are going to say or do. In other words, the broader context of routines and events often shape our motivation and assist us in making discriminations. The peers or staff supporting a learner with deaf-blindness learn quickly that being a facilitator, an intervener, or an interpreter means more than just translating what is said or teaching others to use a student's communication system.

An interpreter for a person who is deaf, but has good use of vision, will not only interpret the conversation directed specifically to that person; the interpreter will also interpret conversations going on around the person who is deaf. In this way, the social context around the individual is captured. However, in this case, the individual can also see who is interacting, how he or she is behaving, and his or her facial expressions. An interpreter for a person with deaf-blindness using sign/tactile sign language has a bigger job (Smith, 1992). This interpreter will often describe the visual context around the learner in addition to interpreting the conversations, lecture, or discussion. He or she might tell the student about the person seated next to him who has a comic book inside his history book, or describe the facial expressions of the teacher as some students present a funny skit. The interpreter tries, to the best of his or her ability, to give the learner with deaf-blindness a visual picture of the social scene.

Obviously some compromises have to be made. The interpreter cannot provide all verbal and visual information that is going on at once in a highly exciting classroom or social event through the tactile sign mode. The job of the interpreter, therefore, also involves

Student: _Jacob_ **Subject/Class Period:** _3rd period_ **Room No.** _____

Literature (7th grade)

Primary Objectives for This Period: _Receptive tactile and object symbols, communication - using call device, using computer, using eye gaze for choice, using microswitch for computer and type to read aloud_

Informational Support Ideas	Typical Routine & Activities	Ways Student Can Participate & Things Student Should Work On (*systematic plan is below or attached)	Other Support Ideas
Use object & tactile symbol (book)	Enter & find seat Listen to directions	*Eye gaze *Respond to greetings *Initiate greetings	Remind kids to use symbols, etc. Peer support
Hand on his hand, still	Group discussion	If it's a debate or if he can go with his friends	Peers keep in contact, if long and not interesting for J., go back to computer
Rub his hands & cheek ahead of time	Read literature piece aloud	*Activate literature reading when asked by general ed. teacher	Peers can cue and assist
Symbol for computer, select friend	Journal question	Use computer during this time *Eye gaze	Ask for partners
Use symbol & sign (eye gaze)	Small group work	*Eye gaze Go with friends to a group Hold materials Record meeting on tape recorder	Peers support this
		Play back stuff, use computer	Gen. ed. teacher contact
	Large Group		Keep hand in contact
Communication symbols	Organize "stuff"	*Object/tactile calendar, *Respond to greetings	
"			Peers support this
	Dismissed	" " "	

Procedures: _Remind peers to provide info_

* See programs for details on responses required

_During journal or independent writing time, go to the computer and work with one or two partners if Ms. _____ says it's OK._

Figure 9. Jacob: Participation plan for literature.

Student: *Tiu*   **Subject:** *Social Studies*   **Room:** *109*

Activities:

1. *Independent news reading, share with class; discuss*
2. *Group projects*
3. *Large group debate*
4. *Synthesis of information - written*

Student Considerations:

Tiu enjoys the newspaper and the "news" in general. Encourage her to discuss what she thinks with a peer prior to whole class (rehearsal). Allow her to choose topics and group projects. Vocabulary and concepts need to be addressed during study period. Cliff notes for small books. V-tech for chapters. Braille for short items.

Goals/Objectives:

- *Read news and interpret events; ask questions (at fluid reading level)*
- *Identify words and concepts not understood; write them down - vocabulary*
- *Knowledge of American History unit --> modified concept knowledge*
- *Braille, V-Tech*   • *Asking peers for information*
- *Work in group*   • *Provide peers with information*
- *Express opinion, discuss, and debate*

	SUPPORT NEEDED:	
	Stay within activity	*Alternate activity*
Large Group	• Interpreter for input & output • Write down key words during lecture, especially those not understood; review with peer later • Discuss and debate (interpreter use)	• If particularly new topic, interpreter can use copy of teacher's notes and review the main concepts with Tiu during large lecture
Small Group	• Join group in which she knows some of the students • Determine pieces of work Tiu can accomplish, work with partner and interpreter	
Independent	• Utilize interpreter, but access V-tech and braille • Utilize note-taking skills vs. constant adult presence for questions	

Figure 10.   Tiu: Participation plan for U.S. history class.

some decision making and problem solving. Smith (1992) has outlined some suggestions for interpreters working with individuals with deaf-blindness. These suggestions provide an excellent glimpse into the world of an individual with deaf-blindness and are useful for *anyone* sharing a teaching or social relationship with these persons.

Because the majority of students with deaf-blindness have additional disabilities or have not received adequate services that have kept them at an appropriate grade level, there are a number of other decisions to be made. First, the peers and support staff facilitating for the student may not be doing so with sign language as the primary mode (Rowland & Stremel-Campbell, 1987; Siegel-Causey & Guess, 1989). Second, depending on the student's cognitive and communicative abilities and the student's previous concept development, additional problem solving will be needed to determine which information to interpret (or provide), how much can be given and understood at once, and how to do this effectively. The facilitator's role is, in part, to function as an "interpreter," even if the student is not using sign language as her or his communication system. Whatever the communication system chosen, whether it is nonsymbolic or symbolic, it must be used by the facilitator and peers to provide information as to the broader context of social and learning events taking place in addition to the specific learning and social interactions.

Allowing Extra Time for Processing Information Time is perhaps one of the most crucial yet overlooked variables when interacting with or instructing individuals with deaf-blindness. Just as there are conventions about "personal space," people tend to have typical expectations as to how quickly a person should respond to interactions or perceive information. The individual with deaf-blindness often needs extra time to process the information he receives because he is constructing concepts from adapted information. If using an augmentative system for communication, the individual may also need time to organize his or her response. Allowing time for processing of information of all kinds, not just direct communications, will ease the tension and avoid frustration for the learner.

When entering a new environment, for example, allow time for the learner to figure out where she is and to utilize the cues and adaptations described in previous sections. If the learner has multiple disabilities, allow even more time.

When Harry and his friends go out to recess, his friends give him the cues for recess and then pause and wait for him to smile or become quiet. They assist Harry in getting his things and then push his wheelchair outside. They put his hand on the brass handle to push the big school door open and then pause a minute when they get outside. This pause gives Harry some time to catch up and also gives him an opportunity to indicate where he would like to go, up toward the basketball courts or down toward the playground equipment, before his friends choose for him. When Harry goes to the library with his class, his friends put a book in his hand along with the stamp he uses for his name. When they enter the library, they pause inside the door for a few moments to allow Harry to sense the quieter atmosphere and smell the familiar smell of books and carpet in the library.

Tanya's teacher observed that during class discussion, Tanya would typically not respond to questions or provide input, even when she was sure that Tanya had answers or information to provide. She found that if she gave Tanya's facilitator some questions to discuss ahead of time that were typical of the discussion that was going to occur, Tanya was more likely to try to contribute. She also found, however, that if she gave Tanya a question, allowed some time, then went on to some other students, and came back to Tanya later, Tanya would very often have a carefully considered response.

Communication Choices and control for the student over any system of communication and within any learning situation will stimulate motivation and ownership of that system. If a student has technology such as a brailler, a V-tech, and print-to-braille computer software, for example, he or she needs to be given the choice as to which system is most useful in which class or situation. Likewise, a student who wishes to use his or her voice, even if an adaptation is needed for clarity, should not be asked to refrain from speaking. Other students may indicate their choices with nonsymbolic means or with a combination of nonsymbolic and symbolic means. For additional resources and references regarding communication assessment, instructional strategies for communication skills, and augmentative systems, see Chapter 10.

One way of establishing communication communities is to utilize peer support groups (Breen, 1991; Forest & Lusthaus, 1989; Gee, 1993) in which the support teacher can take extra time to model, role play, and discuss effective communication strategies. Whether the individual is using tactile symbols, gestures, signs, pictures, or nonsymbolic means to communicate, peers and teachers will require assistance and facilitation to be successful. A key role of the individual facilitating the student's participation in activities will be to connect him or her to the social context. If the student is using a large number of signs or is fluent in sign language, the interpreter and support teacher can start a signing club or signing class at the school. Many general education students are interested in sign language. While there may not be other individuals with deaf-blindness who use sign language fluently in that particular school district, there may be a cluster of students who are deaf at one particular school. Some families elect to place their child with

deaf-blindness at that particular general education school in order to have a community of fluent signers (if their child is learning sign language) available to join their child's social networks. It is still important, however, to assist the students who are deaf to understand how to interact with the individual with deaf-blindness because communication strategies may be very different depending on the degree of the student's vision loss.

DIRECTIONS FOR FUTURE RESEARCH

Many issues require further study. For example, increased technology is needed to support communication in, as well as access to, academic, social, and work settings for individuals with deaf-blindness. Literacy and communication research relevant to individuals with deaf-blindness and further study on linguistic and cultural communities that support and connect individuals with deaf-blindness, despite their low incidence, are also of high priority. Finally, additional work on both friendships and instructional techniques will provide the field with meaningful strategies to apply within classrooms.

Further research and demonstration efforts can develop valuable new ideas for creative educational innovations, but these efforts should spring from a base of what is already known to be best practice with regard to program development, service delivery, collaboration, and a person-centered approach to planning. Further outreach efforts are additionally necessary to make these practices typical of services for individuals with deaf-blindness rather than unusual.

REFERENCES

Beukelman, D., & Mirenda, P. (1992). *Augmentative and alternative communication: Management of severe communication disorders in children and*

adolescents. Baltimore: Paul H. Brookes Publishing Co.

Breen, C.G. (1991). Setting up and managing peer

support networks. In C. Breen & N. Haring (Eds.), *Social context research project: Methods for facilitating the inclusion of students with disabilities in integrated school and community contexts.* Santa Barbara: University of California.

Browder, D. (1991). *Assessment of individuals with severe disabilities: An applied behavior approach to life skills assessment* (2nd ed.). Baltimore: Paul H. Brookes Publishing Co.

Brown, A., & Campione, J. (1990). Communities of learning and thinking or a context by any other name. *Developmental Perspectives on Teaching and Learning Thinking Skills, 21,* 108–126.

Brown, F., & Snell, M. (1993). Measurement, analysis, and evaluation. In M. Snell (Ed.), *Instruction of students with severe disabilities* (4th ed.). New York: MacMillan.

Brown, L., Schwartz, P., Udvari-Solner, A., Kampschroer, E., Johnson, F., Jorgenson, J., & Gruenwald, L. (1991). How much time should students with severe intellectual disabilities spend in regular education classrooms and elsewhere? *Journal of The Association for Persons with Severe Handicaps, 16,* 39–47.

Campbell, P., & Forsythe, S. (1993). Integrated programming and movement disabilities. In M. Snell (Ed.), *Instruction of students with severe disabilities* (4th ed.) (pp. 264–289). New York: MacMillan.

Downing, J., & Eichinger, J. (1990). Instructional strategies for learners with dual sensory impairments in integrated settings. *Journal of The Association for Persons with Severe Handicaps, 15*(2), 98–105.

Dunn, W. (1991). The sensorimotor systems: A framework for assessment and intervention. In F. Orelove & D. Sobsey, *Educating children with multiple disabilities: A transdisciplinary approach* (2nd ed.) (pp. 33–78). Baltimore: Paul H. Brookes Publishing Co.

Englert, C., Tarrant, K.L., & Mariage, T.V. (1992). Defining and redefining instructional practice in special education: Perspectives on good teaching. *Teacher Education and Special Education, 15*(2), 62–86.

Falvey, M.A. (1989). *Community-based curriculum: Instructional strategies for students with severe handicaps* (2nd ed.). Baltimore: Paul H. Brookes Publishing Co.

Farron-Davis, F., Gee, K., & Goetz, L. (1994). Extended validation effort of the active interactions project. In *Final Report: Active Interactions Project.* (OSERS Validated Practices: Children and youth with deaf-blindness. Grant #HO 86G00003). San Francisco: San Francisco State University.

Ferguson, D., Meyer, G., Jeanchild, L., Juniper, L., & Zingo, J. (1992). Figuring out what to do with the grownups: How teachers make inclusion "work" for students with disabilities. *Journal of The Association for Persons with Severe Handicaps, 17*(4), 218–226.

Ferguson, P., Ferguson, D., & Taylor, S. (1992). *Interpreting disability: A qualitative reader.* New York: Teachers College Press.

Ford, A., & Davern, L. (1990). Moving forward with school integration: Strategies for involving students with severe handicaps in the life of the school. In R. Gaylord-Ross (Ed.), *Integration strategies for students with severe handicaps* (pp. 11–31). Baltimore: Paul H. Brookes Publishing Co.

Ford, A., Davern, L., & Schnorr, R. (1992). Inclusive education: "Making sense" of the curriculum. In S. Stainback & W. Stainback (Eds.), *Curriculum considerations in inclusive classrooms: Facilitating learning for all students.* Baltimore: Paul H. Brookes Publishing Co.

Forest, M., & Lusthaus, E. (1989). Promoting educational equality for all students: Circles and maps. In S. Stainback, W. Stainback, & M. Forest (Eds.), *Educating all students in the mainstream of regular education.* Baltimore: Paul H. Brookes Publishing Co.

Gee, K. (1991). *Team planning and curriculum organization format.* (Active Interactions Project). San Francisco: San Francisco State University.

Gee, K. (1993). *An experimental and qualitative investigation into the motivation and competence of peer interactions involving students with severe, multiple disabilities in middle school classrooms.* Unpublished doctoral dissertation, University of California, Berkeley.

Gee, K., Alwell, M., Graham, N., & Goetz, L. (1994). *Inclusive instructional design: Facilitating informed and active learning for individuals with deaf-blindness.* (Manual produced on the Active Interactions Project, OSERS Validated Practices: Children and Youth with Deaf-Blindness, Grant No. HO 86G00003). San Francisco: San Francisco State University, Department of Special Education.

Gee, K., & Goetz, L. (1990). *Final report: Integrated educational services: Options for all students.* (OSERS Demonstration and Research Project). San Francisco: San Francisco State University.

Gee, K., & Goetz, L. (1994). *Final report: Active interactions project.* (OSERS Validated Practices: Children and Youth with Deaf-blindness Grant # HO 86G00003). San Francisco: San Francisco State University.

Gee, K., Graham, N., & Goetz, L. (1994). *Context instruction: Enhancing initiation and cognitive engagement.* Manuscript submitted for publication, San Francisco State University.

Gee, K., Graham, N., Oshima, G., Yoshioka, K., & Goetz, L. (1991). Teaching students to request the continuation of routine activities by using time delay and decreasing physical assistance in the context of chain interruption. *Journal of The Association for Persons with Severe Handicaps, 16,* 154–167.

Gee, K., Graham, N., Sailor, W., & Goetz, L. (in press). Use of integrated, general education and community settings as primary contexts for skill instruction of students with severe, multiple disabilities. *Behavior Modification.*

Gee, K., Harrell, R., & Rosenberg, R. (1987). Teaching orientation and mobility skills within and across natural opportunities for travel: A model designed for learners with multiple severe disabilities. In L. Goetz, D. Guess, & K. Stremel-Campbell (Eds.), *Innovative program design for individuals with dual sensory impairments* (pp. 127–157). Baltimore: Paul H. Brookes Publishing Co.

Giangreco, M., Cloninger, C., & Iverson, V. (1994). *Choosing options and accommodations for children (COACH): A guide to planning inclusive education.* Baltimore: Paul H. Brookes Publishing Co.

Goetz, L., & Gee, K. (1987a). Teaching visual attention in functional contexts: Acquisition and generalization of complex visual motor skills. *Journal of Vision Impairment & Blindness, 81,* 115–118.

Goetz, L., & Gee, K. (1987b). Functional vision programming. A model for teaching visual behaviors in natural contexts. In L. Goetz, D. Guess, & K. Stremel-Campbell (Eds.), *Innovative program design for individuals with dual sensory impairments.* Baltimore: Paul H. Brookes Publishing Co.

Grennon-Brooks, J., & Brooks, M.G. (1993). *The case for constructivist classrooms.* Alexandria, VA: Association for Supervision and Curriculum Development.

Halvorsen, A., & Sailor, W. (1990). Integration of students with severe and profound disabilities. In R. Gaylord-Ross (Ed.), *Issues and research in special education* (Vol. 1). New York: Teachers College Press.

Hanson, J.R., Silver, H.S., & Strong, R.W. (1990). Thoughtful education: Staff development for the 1990's. *Educational Leadership, 48*(5), 25–29.

Helmstetter, E., & Guess, D. (1987). Application of the individualized curriculum sequencing model to learners with severe sensory impairments. *Innovative program design for individuals with dual sensory impairments.* Baltimore: Paul H. Brookes Publishing Co.

Herman, J., Aschbacher, P., & Winters, L. (1992). *A practical guide to alternative assessment.* Alexandria, VA: Association for Supervision and Curriculum Development.

Hunt, P., Alwell, M., & Goetz, L. (1988). Acquisition of conversation skills and the reduction of inappropriate social interaction behaviors. *Journal of The Association for Persons with Severe Handicaps, 13,* 20–27.

Hunt, P., Staub, D., Alwell, M., & Goetz, L. (1994). *The effects of heterogeneous cooperative math group instruction on the acquisition of targeted skills for students with severe, multiple disabilities and their nondisabled peers.* Unpublished manuscript, California Research Institute, San Francisco State University.

Johnson, D.W., & Johnson, R. (1989). *Cooperation and competition: Theory and research.* Edina, MN: Interaction Book.

Karasoff, P., Alwell, M., & Halvorsen, A. (1993). *Systems change: A review of effective practices.* San Francisco: California Research Institute, San Francisco State University and California PEERS Project.

Malette, P., Mirenda, P., Kandborg, T., Jones, P., Bunz, T., & Rogow, S. (1992). Application of a lifestyle development process for persons with severe intellectual disabilities: A case study report. *Journal of The Association for Persons with Severe Handicaps, 17*(3), 179–191.

Marzano, R.J., Pickering, D., & McTighe, J. (1993). *Assessing student outcomes: Performance assessment using the dimensions of a learning model.* Alexandria, VA: Association for Supervision and Curriculum Development.

Mount, B., & Zwernick, K. (1988). *It's never too early, it's never too late: A booklet about personal futures planning.* St. Paul, MN: Minnesota Governor's Planning Council on Developmental Disabilities.

Neary, T., Halvorsen, A., Alwell, M., & Kronberg, R. (1993). *Curriculum adaptations for inclusive classrooms.* San Francisco: California Research Institute, San Francisco State University and California PEERS Project.

Neary, T., Halvorsen, A., & Smithy, L. (1991). *Definition of inclusive education.* Sacramento, CA: PEERS Project.

Nisbet, J., & Hagner, D. (1988). Natural supports in the workplace: A re-examination of supported employment. *Journal of The Association for Persons with Severe Handicaps, 13,* 260–267.

Purkey, W., & Novak, J. (1984). *Inviting school success: A self-concept approach to teaching and learning.* Belmont, CA: Wadsworth.

Putnam, J. (1994). *Cooperative learning and strategies for inclusion: Celebrating diversity in the classroom.* Baltimore: Paul H. Brookes Publishing Co.

Putnam, J., Rynders, D., Johnson, R., & Johnson, D. (1989). Collaborative skill instruction for promoting positive interactions between mentally handicapped and nonhandicapped children. *Exceptional Children, 55*(6), 550–557.

Rainforth, B., York, J., & MacDonald, C. (1992). *Collaborative teams for students with severe disabilities: Integrating therapy and educational services.* Baltimore: Paul H. Brookes Publishing Co.

Raynes, M., Snell, M., & Sailor, W. (1991). A fresh look at categorical programs for children with special needs. *Phi Delta Kappan, 73*(4), 326–331.

Rowland, C., & Stremel-Campbell, K. (1987). Share and share alike: Conventional gestures to emergent language. In L. Goetz, D. Guess, & K. Stremel-Campbell (Eds.), *Innovative program design for learners with dual-sensory impairments* (pp. 49–75). Baltimore: Paul H. Brookes Publishing Co.

Sailor, W., Anderson, J., Halvorsen, A., Doering, K., Filler, J., & Goetz, L. (1989). *The comprehensive local school: Regular education for all students with disabilities.* Baltimore: Paul H. Brookes Publishing Co.

Sailor, W., Gee, K., & Karasoff, P. (1993). School restructuring and full inclusion. In M. Snell (Ed.), *Systematic instruction of persons with severe handicaps* (4th ed.) (pp. 1–30). Columbus, OH: Charles Merrill.

Sailor, W., Goetz, L., Anderson, J., Hunt, P., & Gee, K. (1987). Research on community intensive instruction as a model for building functional generalized skills. In R. Horner, G. Dunlap, & R. Koegel (Eds.), *Generalization and maintenance in applied settings* (pp. 67–98). Baltimore: Paul H. Brookes Publishing Co.

Salisbury, C. (1992). Parents as team members: Inclusive teams, collaborative outcomes. In B. Rainforth, J. York, & C. MacDonald (Eds.), *Collaborative teams for students with severe disabilities: Integrating therapy and educational services* (pp. 43–66). Baltimore: Paul H. Brookes Publishing Co.

Sapon-Shevin, M. (1992). Celebrating diversity.

In S. Stainback & W. Stainback (Eds.), *Curriculum considerations in inclusive classrooms: Facilitating learning for all students* (pp. 19–36). Baltimore: Paul H. Brookes Publishing Co.

Siegel-Causey, E., & Guess, D. (1989). *Enhancing nonsymbolic communication interactions among learners with severe disabilities.* Baltimore: Paul H. Brookes Publishing Co.

Skrtic, T. (1991). *Behind special education: A critical analysis of professional culture and school organization.* Denver: Love Publishing.

Smith, T. (1992). Presentation at the American River College Interpreter Training Program, Sacramento, CA.

Snell, M.E. (1993). *Instruction of students with severe disabilities* (4th ed.). New York: MacMillan.

Stainback, S., & Stainback, W. (Eds.). (1992). *Curriculum considerations in inclusive classrooms: Facilitating learning for all students.* Baltimore: Paul H. Brookes Publishing Co.

Stainback, S., Stainback, W., & Forest, M. (1989). *Educating all students in the mainstream of regular education.* Baltimore: Paul H. Brookes Publishing Co.

Strully, J., & Strully, C. (1989). Friendships as an educational goal. In S. Stainback, W. Stainback, & M. Forest (Eds.), *Educating all students in the mainstream of regular education* (pp. 59–68). Baltimore: Paul H. Brookes Publishing Co.

Thousand, J., Villa, R., & Nevin, A. (1994). *Creativity and collaborative learning: A practical guide to empowering students and teachers.* Baltimore: Paul H. Brookes Publishing Co.

Turnbull, A., & Morningstar, M. (1993). Family and professional interaction. In M. Snell (Ed.), *Instruction of students with severe disabilities* (4th ed.) (pp. 31–60). New York: MacMillan.

Udvari-Solner, A. (1992). *Curricular adaptations: Accommodating the instructional needs of diverse learners in the context of general education.* Topeka: Kansas State Board of Education.

Udvari-Solner, A. (1994). A decision-making model for curricular adaptations in cooperative groups. In J. Thousand, R. Villa, & A. Nevin (Eds.), *Creativity and collaborative learning: A practical guide to empowering students and teachers* (pp. 59–77). Baltimore: Paul H. Brookes Publishing Co.

Vandercook, T., & York, J. (1989). A team approach to program development and support. In J. York, C. Macdonald, & S. Wolff (Eds.), *Strategies for full inclusion* (pp. 21–44). Minneapolis: Institute on Community Integration, University of Minnesota.

Vandercook, T., York, J., & Forest, M. (1989). The McGill action planning system (MAPS): A strategy for building the vision. *Journal of The Association for Persons with Severe Handicaps, 14,* 205–215.

van Dijk, J. (1989, July). *Techniques for working with children who are deaf-blind.* Paper presented at Symposium on Deaf-Blindness, University of Washington, Seattle.

Villa, R., & Thousand, J. (1992). Student collaboration: An essential for curriculum delivery in the 21st century. In S. Stainback & W. Stainback (Eds.), *Curriculum considerations in inclusive sive classrooms: Facilitating learning for all students* (pp. 117–142). Baltimore: Paul H. Brookes Publishing Co.

Villa, R., Thousand, J., Stainback, W., & Stainback, S. (1992). *Restructuring for caring and effective education: An administrative guide to creating heterogeneous schools.* Baltimore: Paul H. Brookes Publishing Co.

York, J., & Vandercook, T. (1989). *Designing an integrated education for learners with severe disabilities through the IEP process.* Minneapolis: University of Minnesota, Institute on Community Integration.

Chapter 17

Joining the Community

Planning for Adult Life

Bob Huven
and Shepherd Siegel

Like anyone else, people who are deaf-blind dream dreams, set goals, and aspire to successful careers. The challenge to those in their families, or working in their schools and communities, is to give children who are deaf-blind a chance to dream. Professionals in schools and community services must facilitate a goal-setting process for deaf-blind youths and their families. Such an approach must include careful collaboration and planning among educators, families, the student, and community and adult service workers. Dreaming high will also mean setting realistic goals.

Furthering the dream challenges people working with adolescents who are deaf-blind to offer every possible experience that clearly supports their future goals. This chapter deals primarily with the transition planning that shapes an adult future in concert with the deaf-blind person's needs and abilities. Included are principles of normalization (Wolfensberger, 1972), person-centered futures planning (Mount & Zwernik, 1988; O'Brien, 1987), and school-to-work and adult life transition planning (Sowers &

Powers, 1991; Wehman, 1992; Wehman, Moon, Everson, Wood, & Barcus, 1988). These concepts are used to illustrate how plans may be developed to systematically provide deaf-blind individuals the access to success that our society is expected to offer all its citizens.

Persons who are deaf-blind range in cognitive abilities from profoundly challenged to extremely bright. But for anyone who is deaf-blind, limitations of both the primary senses of hearing and sight affect the person's relationship to the environment more profoundly than almost any other single disability. Thus, regardless of intellectual ability, there are always many difficulties to overcome when addressing the issues of deaf-blind individuals.

Despite the heterogeneity of people with disabilities, and in acknowledgment of the possible mistake made in putting such a diverse group into a single category, credible federal education policies require serving the transition needs of all students in special education. The most recent form, the IDEA legislation (Individuals with Disabilities Education Act of 1990), mandates the development of a formal transition plan by the time of a student's 16th birthday—14th if there is a significant need. The valid principle behind this policy is that students will ultimately benefit most from having individualized transition plans developed early and implemented in a systematic, ongoing manner (Wehman, 1992; Wehman et al., 1988).

Such plans are best conceived when they result from the efforts of an entire team of individuals who have come together to coordinate their services with the needs of the student. The literature provides many examples of how to form these teams for specific outcomes related to the transition of individual students (see, e.g., Barrett, 1992; Everson & Burwell, 1991; Everson, Rachal, & Michael, 1992; Gaylord-Ross et al., 1991; Hardman & McDonnell, 1987; Thorin & Irvin, 1992; Wehman, 1992; Wehman et al., 1988). Who should become members of such a team is discussed in the following section.

There is a parallel concept of a *systems change* team whose mission is more indirect: improving services to students who are deaf-blind by reshaping bureaucracies whose modes of operation most affect the transition process (Everson et al., 1992; Wehman et al., 1988). Specific to the needs of young people who are deaf-blind is the model developed by the Helen Keller National Technical Assistance Center, which supports team efforts for both individual case study/futures planning and for statewide systems change (Everson et al., 1992). This chapter describes optimum conditions, contingencies, possible scenarios, and the idiosyncrasies of the futures planning team for individual young people who are deaf-blind.

DEVELOPING A
TRANSITION PLANNING TEAM

Who is appropriate as a member of such a team? Team membership will be as individu-

alized as the goals and objectives of one particular student's plans for the future. A team for a young person with sensory impairments must include people who know and interact often with the individual. Their exacting job will be to provide opportunities for meaningful experiences in an organized fashion (Downing & Eichinger, 1990). Parents, teachers, friends, and someone who is skilled at making accommodations for deaf-blindness are all good candidates for transition team members. Their challenge will be to do more than maintain a single environment, but to engineer the almost always difficult transition from school to adult life, "the transition from less participation in mainstream society to more" (Siegel et al., 1993). Also, when geographically possible, teams benefit from the input of an adult member of the deaf-blind community.

The focal student's interaction with the team process can be shaped to meet his or her individual needs. All students who are deaf-blind can make choices and have a say in their lives. Some individuals who are deaf-blind will participate successfully in team meetings. Other individuals with more challenging communication needs may find the meetings confusing or aversive. Team members must create ways for young people who are deaf-blind to have input in the team planning process.

The following case study presents one family's efforts during the early steps in the transition to adulthood for a son who is deaf-blind.

Tony was born 15 years ago with no vision and a profound hearing loss. Some people thought he responded to music, but Maria, Tony's mother, was not too sure. His teachers sometimes remarked that Tony exhibited problem behaviors. He responded to some directions in sign language and made only several distinct signs to express a few choices.

Maria took the initial, critical steps in a transition plan informally and alone. She knew of no "professional" approach, but trusted her instincts, knowing her son's future should be headed toward life in their home community. She began making decisions. Maria wanted Tony returned to living at home instead of at the state residential facility.

Maria wanted Tony to learn how to interact with more people and to get along in the community where his family lived. The residential facility staff expressed their concerns and told Maria she was in for trouble and could not handle Tony's difficult behavior. She persisted and contacted her home school district. There, administrators told her they contracted with a larger district nearby for students like her son. Tony would be on the bus for 40 or so minutes each way to attend middle school. Maria met with the classroom teacher and talked with the principal. She decided that Tony would do okay at this school, even with it being so far from home, *if* he had a one-on-one aide able to sign with him and guide him through his daily routine. With his new teacher, Virginia's, support, the home district funded this aide position.

Virginia arranged meetings with the staff from Tony's first school and, with their help, began setting up a daily routine for him. The new aide, Keara, was quickly frustrated. Tony did not seem to understand or respond to any of her signs and he did not act like the deaf children she had worked with before. The tactile signing he needed was new to Keara, and anyway, she told Virginia, she was probably doing it all wrong. Tony would grab her hands and yank her toward the door, seeming to prefer spending his entire day walking outside. When confounded, he lay on the floor making distressing noises and banging a fist into his face. Keara and Virginia were both feeling overwhelmed.

The district had an itinerant teacher for students with vision impairments who knew about setting up routines and developing learning objectives for students with deaf-blindness. Together, she and Virginia set up a calendar box system with objects Tony easily recognized as being a part of the major events of his day. For example, a piece of running shoe tread meant "go for a walk," a sweat band was the symbol for "gym," and a lunch sack glued to a card meant "time for lunch." Using this structure made it easier for the aide to make transitions between activities clearer to Tony. Virginia, Keara, and others at school began to see the happy, active teenage boy that Maria described.

Around this time, Virginia agreed to participate in an inclusion project with specialists in deaf-blindness from a nearby university. Maria was willing to join in regular meetings (but told a project staff person she was shy about talking in front of the group). A mix of teachers and support staff began to meet with her and people from the university project. A team formed around the shared idea that Tony needed to enjoy more activities with his peers in a variety of environments. Maria suggested trying something like weight-lifting or track because Tony was happiest when moving. Team members invited the P.E. teacher to join, and together they planned activities

and made more textured symbols to use with Tony to describe this new set of activities.

This transition went smoothly from the start. Inspired, team members began talking about planning activities throughout the day, and they sought more ways to include Tony in the school community. Step by step, he learned to eat with other students, exercise with them, make popcorn and sell it, and soon his day was filled with activities that made sense, and which taught him important life skills through social interaction. Maria said she was pleased.

Later that year, Virginia and Maria began to wonder how Tony would do in high school. This district had a large, segregated special education program and Maria did not want him separated again and made to do vocational type tasks that she described as "busy work." She began talking with the inclusion team about making a plan to move to the high school near his home. The team met with the home district, and talk also started to focus on transition to life after school.

Maria did not have the steps of a formal, district-approved ITP (individual transition plan) brought to her by an established team of transition experts. She had a feeling about what might be a better life for her son and was brave enough to assert her opinion with skeptical professionals. Maria had realized her son was growing up away from home and instead wanted him learning to be a part of his family and community. Maria knew that her family would always be there for Tony. She nourished and treasured close relationships among her grown children and refused to have Tony separated from them.

Later, with the support of professionals and a written transition plan guiding a team effort, Maria led many more successful transition activities for her son. Building upon his growing understanding and toleration of daily events, Tony went to high school with neighbors, made friends, took P.E., art, agriculture, and studied his community by participating in it every day. Tony relies on the guidance of others for every activity. He responds to textured symbols for daily activities and uses them to make some clear choices. He has favorite friends and charms them with a handsome smile when they identify themselves to him.

A team effort to plan a school to adult life transition suggests a participant observer approach (Edgerton, 1967, 1984). That is, at least one service provider gains the trust of the individual who is deaf-blind and her or his ecosystem, which usually includes the family as well as other critical players. The participant observer can be seen as a knowledgeable guide, a mentor, and a monitor, someone interested in building trust and knowledge within the team and comparing their progress to team goals and current practices in the field of deaf-blindness. The participant observer does not have to be the team leader. In fact, encouraging members to share such leadership duties as setting agendas and chairing meetings is often more effective. The concept of participant observer is most powerful when the emphasis is placed equally on both words of the term it-self, that is, a person who acts as an active *participant* and also diligently *observes* the team process. The involvement required in such an approach allows for a heightened re-sponsiveness on the part of some partici-pants. Although attitudes of "professional distance" may remain among team mem-bers, they are gradually refined to build trust and interactive relationships instead of rein-forcing aloof professional behavior.

The above case study suggests a twist on a team strategy: reality proves that the com-plexities of human experience will impact any life planning process. Maria sought for, and encouraged, interactions with profes-sionals. From the start, she herself was the participant observer who was able to clearly state conditions as she experienced them. Many of her strategies relate to six important steps gleaned from the literature related to transition planning (see Table 1) and dis-cussed in the following sections.

STEPS TO TRANSITION PLANNING

The transition planning steps described here serve to sustain the team's focus and mo-mentum necessary for the successful transi-tion of a young deaf-blind person into adult community life. The steps are presented in order of how they typically occur; however, every situation is unique. There is an implied chronology, and some of the later steps rest upon the footings built earlier. Yet the steps often become interconnected as futures plan-

Table 1. Transitions: steps toward building satisfying futures for persons who are deaf-blind

Step 1: Organize an individualized transition planning team when the student reaches the age of 14.
- Inform student and family members of the process and enlist their participation.
- Identify school personnel with needed expertise.
- Identify resource people from adult services.

Step 2: Hold the initial transition meeting, as part of an annual IEP meeting, and raise the idea of meeting more frequently.
- Do some "futuring" by expressing dreams and fears, mapping progress and choices, and so forth.
- Gather, generate, and maintain assessment infor-mation, including ecological inventories of learning settings and functional vocational assessments. En-list input from specialists in sensory impairments.
- Develop an individualized transition plan (ITP) with various assignments for members.
- Formalize commitments.

Step 3: Implement the transition goals through the sec-ondary program.
- Use a transdisciplinary approach.
- Obtain technical assistance related to sensory losses.
- Convene transition team follow-up meetings.
- Link family members to appropriate support re-sources.
- Invite feedback on team efforts.
- Discuss making connections with other people in community-based learning activities. Include input from participants in the ongoing relationships that will develop.

Step 4: Update the ITP through annual meetings.
- Phase-out involvement of school personnel while in-creasing involvement of adult service personnel.

Step 5: Ensure employment and community living outcomes.
- Explore "safety net" by examining employment and training options.
- Ensure recreation outcome.
- Ensure community living outcome.
- Ensure referrals to appropriate agencies and appro-priate support services (especially adult services related to deaf-blindness).

Step 6: Deliver follow-up services from state or multi-state deaf-blind program until age 22.
- Provide inservices to adult services agency workers.
- Maintain contact with young adult.

Adapted from Wehman, Moon, Everson, Wood, and Barcus (1988).

ning is revisited throughout the transition process; newcomers are approached at various stages; and the planning, implementation, and evaluation of strategies is often cyclical rather than linear. The steps are presented here to encourage at least one of the players—the participant observer—to keep a critical eye on the *process*, however these steps unfold. The reader should note that the literature sometimes portrays these steps in terms of systems change, the efficacy of which is now being studied and validated. Nevertheless, the following sections are written from the perspective not of changing what the system should look like, but rather of addressing the needs of the individual.

Finally, the transition from high school student to young adult is even reflected in the language of each young person's human environments. For example, in the educational milieu, we often refer to *students with deaf-blindness*. However, in the adult community, cultural advocates reinforce their positive self-identity by using the phrases *deaf-blind person, deaf-blind people*, and *deaf-blind community*.

Step 1: Organize an ITP Team When Student Is 14 Years Old

IDEA mandates the formation of the ITP team by the time the student with disabilities reaches the age of 16 years, 14 years if there is a significant need. Deaf-blindness is a significant need. In the previous case study, Tony's mother, Maria, was the primary team builder ready to address such a pressing need. Seeing that she could not support the growth of Tony's future alone, she surveyed the array of services and professionals and decided to work with whomever she believed would be the most effective. She then organized them into a team. This story is exceptional because it is not a case of a human services provider delving into the life of the individual, but one of the parent of an individual who is deaf-

blind becoming an active participant, and thereby less of an outsider, among a group of professionals (Benson & Turnbull, 1986; Dunst, Trivette, & Deal, 1988; Halvorsen, Doering, Farron-Davis, Usilton, & Sailor, 1989; Singer & Irvin, 1989; Thorin & Irvin, 1992).

Enlist Family Participation In a more responsive system, a service provider might see that Tony needed experiences in real-life settings; would respect the desires of the family, that is, for Tony to remain in the local community; and then organize an ITP team. Another way to achieve this step is for professionals to encourage family members to be the critical team builders. It is a truly empowering concept to allow families to drive the system, to support the many "Marias" who will make productive and cost-effective use of human services in the formation of transition teams.

Enlisting family participation involves spending time with the individual who is deaf-blind and his or her family and then facilitating their involvement by articulating their needs and defining their role in meeting these needs. This is done over time, and efforts may fail many times before they succeed. For example, a simple form letter may only begin this process, it rarely achieves the needed participation all by itself. Follow-up phone calls and personal contacts can be important strategies for getting critical players on board. People have to learn how their actions can make a difference.

Identify Individuals with Needed Expertise In many cases, looking for professionals skilled in the transition of youth who are deaf-blind is a search for people who do not exist; or if they do, they are too far away to be regular participants. Therefore, those individuals working toward creating new opportunities for people who are deaf-blind become the experts themselves because they have taken action. The consumers (e.g., the deaf-blind adolescent, his or her family, an employer, others) might need reassurance from other members of the team about the value of working together, recognizing that everyone on the team learns as they go along. Likewise the professional who finds her- or himself in this position should not be afraid to learn as part of the process. Seek help if it is available by being open to suggestions and by staying in touch with national efforts.[1]

Even experienced workers in transition do not go into new situations with prepared answers. Every situation is different. Begin by working with parents (they are usually the true experts on their children), the individual student, and his or her teachers to find the answers together as a team. Make use of vision specialists, consultants in the field of deaf-blindness, orientation and mobility specialists, and others with specialized skills whenever possible. Seek out nationally known experts if necessary, but do not let a lack of available local expertise translate into neglecting to take action.

Identify Resource People from Adult Services Although it may be difficult to gain the cooperation of skeptical professionals from adult services programs, plan strategies to establish contact, maintain ongoing communication, and enlist their participation in a systematic approach. Professionals in government or private vocational rehabilitation agencies, job developers, and supported-living providers are unlikely to have had experience working with many of the challenges faced by young people who are deaf-blind. However, with experience interacting with the team, adult services workers will also learn from the transition planning process as these steps uniquely unfold for each individual student.

Step 2: Hold Initial Transition Meeting

Hold the initial transition meeting as part of an annual IEP meeting, and raise the idea of meeting more frequently to plan for the individual's future. Do some "futuring" by expressing dreams and fears, mapping progress and choices, and so forth. Futures planning strategies are a new and exciting innovation in the area of transition planning (Mount & Zwernik, 1988; O'Brien, 1987). Teachers and others can use some proven ways to help individuals, families, and professionals (e.g., workers in education, adult rehabilitation, employment support, and employers) learn to dream and communicate together. Such "futuring" skills can be an important part of the team building process. (See chap. 6, this volume, for an in-depth discussion on futures planning.)

Gather, Generate, and Maintain Assessment Information Gather, generate, and maintain assessment information, including ecological inventories of learning settings and functional vocational assessments. People who know the young deaf-blind person well are best equipped to contribute assessment data for the team to use. Interviews such as those in the *COACH* planning guide (Giangreco, Cloninger, & Iverson, 1993) are valuable for recording family input. Professionals must use care when gathering information about how the individual functions in real settings. The team will collect more ecological information as future opportunities are refined to include specific environments for on-the-job work experiences, developing a social life, and changing living situations.

Enlist Input from Specialists in Sensory Impairments The transition plan will outline steps to begin involving the young person

---

[1]A good place to start is to subscribe to *Deaf-Blind Perspectives,* a tri-annual newsletter available through Teaching Research Division, Western Oregon State College, 345 N. Monmouth Avenue, Monmouth, Oregon 97361.

who is deaf-blind in new experiences. Interactions at school, in the community with family and friends, and with a variety of work experiences will reflect movement toward an expanding future. Specialists in sensory impairments will provide valuable input to assess what skills a student brings to a situation and how to support learning. For example, an orientation and mobility specialist might focus on improving the student's independent movement in new settings. A specialist in augmentative communication might provide important help to make interactions with others more meaningful, helping the deaf-blind person adapt to, and enjoy, new experiences.

Develop an ITP with Assigned Tasks for Team Members During the first attempts to build a team, people are really agreeing to "plan the plan." The ITP takes shape as a living document to be revisited over time. At this stage, team members might agree to stay in touch on a monthly basis, including those members who are in a position to support and expand learning experiences for the student who is deaf-blind. For example, specific team members may take on assignments and then report back to the team on their progress with such tasks as asking for ideas from friends, co-workers, and contacts in the community made by the young person who is deaf-blind. Team members may entrust one person with the activity of doing job market analysis and reporting back with new opportunities for after school work experiences.

Much has been learned about the career development process for young people with disabilities (Brolin, 1989; Brolin & D'Alonzo, 1979; Clark & Kolstoe, 1990; Pruitt, 1983; Sowers & Powers, 1991). Students who are deaf-blind lack many of the life experiences contributing to career awareness and exploration. There is almost no incidental learning

to contribute to the complex career development process. Therefore, experiences must be systematically developed and presented as important content of the ITP. Educators are beginning to develop learning sites off campus where it is possible to inventory skills and expectations required of work and social experiences (Browder, 1991). The transition team must "plan the plan" so as to systematically compensate for informal learning lost due to a lack of sensory information.

Formalize Commitments People's dreams must be greatly respected in any plan for the future; however, caution should always be exercised. There is plenty of room for disappointment, most often due to a lack of action. Even with the recent implementation of futures planning work, some parents have been frustrated by a lack of follow through. In the life of a transition-age deaf-blind youth there is no time to be wasted by inaction. Usually the student has already spent too much time cut off from life-building (i.e., career, social, self-care) experiences. A transition plan needs a written record to formally document team efforts and commitments to the student, including follow through by named participants on assigned responsibilities within specific time lines.

Step 3: Implement Transition Goals Through the Secondary Program

The entire construct of a transition team is built upon a transdisciplinary philosophy. The team comprises a variety of perspectives. Members have the opportunity to learn how other professionals view specific skills and environmental requirements. This approach demands intellectual flexibility and discipline among team members.

A carefully planned education program will create and increase access to the community (Falvey, 1989). School professionals must be flexible with their roles. It will take the help of more than just a single teacher or assistant to plan and implement regular learning activities away from the classroom. A meaningful part of school for a teenager who is deaf-blind will be to develop ongoing connections in the community through regular, planned excursions. Physical and occupational therapy, speech and communication, and other necessary support services can move from the traditional school setting and support learning activities in the community.

Obtain Technical Assistance Related to Sensory Losses Educators must establish goals that enable a student to reach maximum independence across a variety of settings (Ford & Davern, 1989). As stated in Step 2, specialists in sensory impairment are needed to assess the impact of deaf-blindness on new experiences. In keeping with the transdisciplinary approach, these specialists can also teach educators and support staff how to implement adaptive techniques. For example, specialists might support simulation experiences, such as using a blindfold on school staff to increase their skills at implementing systematic training steps that compensate for lack of vision or hearing.

Furthermore, the level of independence sought for a student who is deaf-blind must be examined with the aid of specialists. For example, the student who must rely on a sighted guide to walk across a street would be in danger if encouraged to make a crossing alone. At first glance this seems obvious, yet staff are often tempted to guess at a student's perceptual abilities. Such guessing by unqualified individuals puts individuals who are deaf-blind at risk.

Increasing independence includes supporting the student to develop relationships with individuals frequently encountered in the community. Specialists can model polite interactions and provide proper information about sensory loss. With such support, peo-

ple encountered in the community often become willing to offer an elbow and guide a student across an intersection on a frequently traveled route. Also, family members can work with specialists to make an inventory of their regular outings (for groceries, haircuts, to a place of worship, etc.) and specifically look for ways to support interactions between the young person who is deaf-blind and others in a variety of settings (Benson & Turnbull, 1986; Hamre-Nietupski, Nietupski, & Strathe, 1992). Specialists in deaf-blindness usually work for larger school districts, the state or regional educational services and vocational agencies, or can be found through contacting the regional representatives of the Helen Keller National Center for Deaf-Blind Youths and Adults.

Convene Transition Team Follow-Up Meetings How team members remain in touch will have been established during the planning process in Step 2. Team follow-up strategies can also be encouraged by building reporting systems into a transition plan and setting regular meeting dates. The ongoing discussion of accomplishments, reviewing of data, and troubleshooting of difficulties will establish accountability and build trust among team members. Periodic face-to-face contact is usually reinforcing when people come together to share accomplishments and hopes for further progress.

Link Family Members to Appropriate Support Resources The ongoing team effort will forge supportive relationships among family members and service providers. However, conditions of family life in the 1990s demand additional networking. Transition team members might respond to a family's economic or housing crisis by working with appropriate government and private agencies. Families might also be referred to agencies for vocational counseling, respite care needs, or evaluation of entitlements such as social security benefits.

Invite Feedback on Team Efforts Professionals are learning how much can be gained by inviting feedback from the friends and community contacts the student enjoys. Such contributions breathe life into the transition plan. The type of planning being described in this chapter requires input from many different sources and occurs over time. Developing a true multidisciplinary team requires gathering opinions from parents, support staff, and community members such as peers and employers.

The following case example illustrates the principles of ongoing support as a young deaf-blind adult interacts with complicated and unfamiliar social systems.

Marlena had little hope of staying with her family while she finished high school. One family member was jailed for exploiting her and some of her friends sexually and with drugs. Her only available parent was homeless, but did try to keep in contact with her. Marlena was far behind in school, hard-of-hearing, and was more frustrated than ever with her life. She was only vaguely aware that her vision problems were getting worse. Marlena usually thought of herself as clumsy or stupid, not realizing she needed to learn new ways to cope with her progressive loss of vision. She would rather pick fights, skip school, or run away than let anyone know that she was hurting.

The caseworker from social services found her a temporary opening in a group home for young adults with developmental disabilities. Marlena also tried going to a high school vocational training program but hated to use her sign language skills because that made her look even more like those other students who, she thought, were so retarded they could not even talk. Usually, she could not hear much of what was being said, pretended to understand, and then blew up when criticized. The staff at the home thought she had severe behavior problems and might not be able to stay. Life at the home became more difficult when she favored the staff over the other residents. The behaviors she had learned in the past about social relationships seemed too sexual and invasive to the residence staff. They told the case worker that Marlena was a high risk and had to go. But where?

The next place was a state mental hospital. The case worker was hoping it was only temporary, but told the vocational school personnel that it was hard to say because the region was in the midst of a recession and services were being cut back. Marlena needed someone to agitate and advocate, bringing her desperate situation to the public's attention. The case worker was brave enough to state the case honestly—encouraging others to go public with this injustice—but risked his job if he spoke out against the system. Marlena went to the state hospital.

Some of the vocational staff seemed relieved to hear that Marlena was too far away for the state hospital to transport her to their program. Other staff, however, were in touch with some specialists in deaf-blindness and a transition consultant. Someone found a way to contact a family member of Marlena's.

Marlena's benefactors at the school were taking action. No one person was able to do (or should have done) everything. A team formed with members including a school district transition specialist, two consultants in deaf-blindness from separate agencies, Marlena, a relative, and two workers at the state hospital who were upset with Marlena's misplacement. The team met with Marlena on a regular basis. Everyone knew that she had problems with anger, caring for herself, and staying out of trouble, but this was hardly surprising, considering her background and unmet needs for support.

Progress was made. Marlena turned 18 and was coached to call her caseworker's supervisor and her legislator from the hospital telephone. She could not hear their responses very well, but a benefactor stood beside her, listening in on the call, and mouthing their words for her to lipread. A legislator known for his work with minority populations was shocked at Marlena's predicament. He started making calls. The newspaper did a piece on the many people with deaf-blindness or others who did not need mental health treatment programs, but were nonetheless being warehoused in the state hospitals. The system was rattled, administrators responded with directives, and Marlena was released from the hospital.

Marlena moved into a house with a roommate who also needed support 24 hours a day. The nonprofit agency providing tenant support services asked some of Marlena's advocates for training on issues related to sensory impairment. Marlena went to a different high school and got a job, but she was soon fired for swearing at a boss who simply asked her to work a little faster. Today, she says she wants another job, but cannot figure out what she would like. She really has not yet had a chance to succeed at something long enough to decide.

Marlena's transitions in life were made more difficult by her significant disabilities: developmental delays and sensory impairments that included an untreatable, worsening vision condition. Her disabilities also included problems with anger and depression.

She had no reliable support or sense of security from her family of origin.

Marlena survived a string of ordeals during her transition years, yet she prevailed, and began to participate in the community as a young adult. She benefitted from the supports advocated for or invented by some interested professionals. Her benefactors knew that because of her age, the need for action was immediate. Transition was no longer purely a construct to be developed by outlining the responsibilities of various agency representatives and signing some collaborative agreements. Although such efforts can make a difference in the long run, in this situation, a team of individuals had to move quickly to make a difference for Marlena. They were persistent, they involved Marlena whenever possible, and, most importantly, they defined their role more by what action was needed than by a particular job title.

Marlena stays in touch with her benefactors, even when it is hard for her to admit that she is making some mistakes and probably should ask for more help. She may continue to move through life at risk of being very alone, or at the mercy of agencies ill-equipped to offer her support. Yet now she is able to tell anyone who asks that she feels very lucky to have found a way back into the community.

Step 4: Update the ITP
Through Annual Meetings

Phase-out involvement of school personnel while increasing involvement of adult services personnel. Clearly, transition planning for youths who are deaf-blind needs much more ongoing attention than what is given at an annual meeting. But formalized annual updates are an important component of the planning process. Certain team members, especially providers in adult services, come

from a culture that responds to formal meetings, agendas, and written reports. Sometimes these individuals, including administrators, need only be involved on an annual basis, leaving the dynamic and day-to-day transition strategies to workers close to the deaf-blind person's life.

The transition process described in the first case study in this chapter benefits both from the day-to-day interventions of the planning team and from the annual planning process. Administrators and new team members from adult services will be able to work with the team's style if introduced to it by the formal and familiar setting of an annual meeting. They too will then be able to learn about the unique and intensive need for adjustments required by the experience of deaf-blindness. Transition team members face the responsibility of analyzing their contribution to the plan and planning alternative supports for when they are no longer formally involved.

The second case study in this chapter realistically presents a youth struggling with transition without much family support. Ingredients of some of the transition steps were surely to be found in Marlena's efforts to better her situation. Her situation improved because her professional benefactors were experienced individuals who have implemented other step-by-step team planning efforts for young people. Their experience with the benefits of planning and follow-up over an extended time frame made it possible for them to be flexible and react quickly in a time of crisis. In the future, Marlena will benefit from ongoing interactions with some of her ITP team members. In her case, she thrived because her team was willing to ignore the lines drawn between school-related and adult-services personnel to maintain their relationship with her. The human connection overrode bureaucratic boundaries.

Step 5: Ensure Employment and Community Living Outcomes

Ensure Employment Outcome When facing questions of transition to a work situation, persons who are deaf-blind pose some of the most penetrating challenges to principles of economic democracy. This discussion must begin with the fair assumption that the American economy has conscientiously addressed diversity for less than 30 years. Yet the work world is a hundreds-years-old structure that was built with rules that favored able-bodied and clever white males. To change this structure requires much more than affirmative action policies or the passage of civil rights acts such as the Americans with Disabilities Act. Individuals who are deaf-blind most certainly "push the envelope." Costs and outcomes of special education are being challenged in the mainstream media and must be justified with outcomes consistent with majority values ("Review and Outlook," 1993). The authors' intent in addressing this issue is not to be strident or adversarial, but simply to clarify the challenge.

The development of equal access to the workplace for persons with disabilities represents a burgeoning movement in personnel policy and civil rights. In many cases, such as for individuals with physical disabilities and deafness or blindness, access may simply be a matter of developing the best mechanical accommodation. For example, equipment and furniture can be moved to wheelchair height or software that enlarges the image on a computer screen might be purchased. In the instances of persons with learning disabilities or mental retardation, systematic instruction, co-worker counseling, and natural supports have enabled persons with such disabilities to be gainfully employed (though perhaps disproportionately) in service positions or repetitive jobs that are otherwise difficult to fill.

In almost all of these cases, the employer enjoys the right of retaining the essential functions of a position in the job description. Furthermore, many employers whose organizations are thriving continue to hire people with disabilities. That is, the employment of persons with the above-described disabilities rarely presents undue hardships to the operation of the business. In fact, such hirings may come to be perceived by the employer as good business practice. When working with a family, school, or adult services agency, the employer is the party who ultimately has the greatest control of the situation. This arrangement is maintained and protected by the Americans with Disabilities Act, especially in terms of defining reasonable accommodation.

For many individuals who are deaf-blind who choose and seek opportunities to go to work, this might indeed be the case. For others, especially those with more severe disabilities, the challenge to find work is more difficult. Accommodations may not initially seem in any way reasonable to many businesses. It is less likely, at least in the foreseeable future, to hear employers make the by-now cliché remarks, such as, "They make really good employees," and "I treat her just like I treat everyone else around here."

The pursuit of employment for persons who are deaf-blind requires organization and planning even more intensive and comprehensive than planning for school and community activities. It requires very special outreach and use of systematic methods of support on the part of placement workers and employers. Collaboration among employers, training specialists, and the family will be necessary and possibly ongoing. Such interactions might be considered undue work and beyond what most currently believe is the limit of the employer's responsibility. Transition teams who implement the process of step-by-step exposure to work settings and encourage interactions with adaptive communication strategies are in a position to influence changing employment perceptions.

In order for team members to develop practical steps and reasonable methods for the integration of persons who are deaf-blind into the employment world, they must articulate a vision. The following is a brief consideration of work in the context of society as a whole. Clearly, full employment for individuals with disabilities is not about to become a reality in American society any time soon. In fact, full employment is not necessarily the goal at which the national will should be aimed. Full functioning and productivity in the American economy does not require full employment, and many individuals who do work are unsatisfied and alienated by their labor. A more vital and useful approach is to develop a vision of full *engagement*. American citizens should be able to find in their lives precisely what people satisfied in their work find—a meaningful role. If we begin to see the workplace as the setting where productivity and profit are necessary, but may produce insufficient results, and we then shape it and the community to become places where people are engaged in meaningful roles, then the employment of deaf-blind persons begins to assume its proper context.

Besides developing an approach based on the values articulated here and in the civil rights movement for persons with severe disabilities (Meyer, Peck, & Brown, 1991; Shapiro, 1993), the employment situations of persons who are deaf-blind will improve as the technology of job redesign, accommodation, and support develops (Gaylord-Ross et al., 1991; Warren, Horn, & Hill, 1987). Certainly, many if not all deaf-blind persons may be productively employed (and profit is

derived from their labor) as new technologies are developed. Such technology includes high and low technical communication devices; adaptations to the workplace such as *jigs* (extra aids or devices built into the steps of a task) and modifications of job requirements; and most importantly, the ongoing refinement of teaching strategies. But there is no reason to institutionalize some people in holding tanks while waiting for technological improvements. By creating places for them at work, deaf-blind persons can begin today to be part of the movement toward universal understanding of how individuals find and create meaning in their lives. To establish routines and jobs for persons who are deaf-blind is to create opportunities for them to make sense of their lives— to experience engagement. Equally important are the opportunities co-workers will gain from learning how to interact with such individuals, how to create social openings for them, how to support and be supported by others, and how to ponder the qualities of their own existence. From this philosophic perspective, the employer might consider a temporary forfeit of capital profit in the interest of the individual, the employees, and society at large.

Build Employment Support Network Explore building a "safety net" by examining employment and training options. As in other aspects in the individual's life up to this point, empowerment and caring will come from a network of carefully prepared supports. The individual may not qualify for an existing job position. Employment of persons who are deaf-blind should never be considered or implemented as an act of charity, but it may have to come from a commitment to their full participation in society that outweighs any prediction of their profit-generating capacity. If our intent as a society is to have a workplace that "looks like America," this should present no problem. The basic need of an organization to function, and of the individual to make an authentic contribution to the business, need not and should not be sacrificed.

Planning for work and living situations requires understanding of human nature and of individual experience. Some relationships feign caring, but foster learned helplessness. Services can masquerade as empowering, but in fact be negligent. Persons with severe disabilities, including deaf-blindness, will always be in need of supports at work, in the community, and at home. The challenge of developing appropriate services is to deliver supports that do not encourage or create dependency. In the case of young deaf-blind adults, service providers must strive for a balance between a huge need for connection/interactions with others and learning to be independent as much as is reasonable. Transition team members will no doubt find themselves inventing new ways for deaf-blind adults to receive ongoing, needed training.

Ensure Recreation Outcome The young person who is deaf-blind must be supported to develop autonomous as well as interactive recreational skills. She or he will not be able to sit in front of the television after work or go alone to the exercise club; social relationships will have to be deliberately encouraged. It will be important for the team to develop learning strategies and new recreational opportunities in the early stages of the futures planning process.

Young people who are deaf-blind must be taught acceptable ways to enjoy themselves. If they are not supported in this area, they often develop problem behaviors as a means of reducing frustration and increasing some form of stimulation to compensate for sensory deprivation (see chap. 12, this volume, for information on positive behavioral support). Team members may find themselves working with family members to encourage

the growth of meaningful relationships, including sexual ones.

Ensure Community Living Outcome When addressing the questions of transition to adult living situations, there will be a variety of choices and challenges facing the transition team. Families might find it difficult to discuss these in the early stages, but will usually appreciate fair warning about decisions and problems to be faced in the years to come. Transition team members must become aware of local resources and limitations. For example, there might be tenant support, group home, or independent living training programs available. There might also be waiting lists or lack of funding for programs that are not emphasized as priorities either by adult services professionals or by politicians.

Certain team members, especially some family members, the deaf-blind individual, and his or her friends, may need to join up with other advocacy groups to lobby for changes, develop more options, or establish more funding for group homes and supported living programs in order to shorten waiting lists. Such activities are more difficult during slow economic times, but must occur if acceptable living options are to remain available, especially for young adults with the complex needs related to deaf-blindness. Advocates not perceived as professionals often have more credibility and fewer constraints attached to such political efforts.

A final word about living options: choices will be individual, either because of the preferences of the young adult or his or her family. Sometimes these choices will be contrary to the philosophies of certain professionals, but the decisions must be left to the deaf-blind adult and/or those closest to the person. Some people might benefit best from individualized tenant support training. Some may choose to live with other deaf-blind people who have similar communication needs and methods. This arrangement is conducive to the sharing of competent staff who are skilled with sign language and familiar with deaf and deaf-blind culture and community. Such homogeneous groupings have become less politically popular in recent years. However, the deaf-blind young adult's desire to be with other deaf and deaf-blind people is his or her prerogative and choice.

Ensure Referrals to the Appropriate Agencies Deaf-blindness always poses the risk of isolation. Even with the best planning, circumstances can change. For example, an apartment building might close, or a company might downsize and lay off its workers. Such life challenges can be catastrophic for a person who is deaf-blind. Therefore, part of a transition plan should include education about and referral to appropriate support agencies (especially to adult services related to deaf-blindness). Whenever possible, the deaf-blind person should be supported to develop a strong relationship with individual workers who will remain in touch. If this is impossible, such workers as government agency case managers and the regional representative of Helen Keller National Center should become involved with individuals in the deaf-blind person's work and living settings.

Step 6: Deliver Follow-Up Services From State or Multi-State Deaf-Blind Program Until Age 22

With early planning and reliable implementation of transition strategies the young person who is deaf-blind will already be supported within the community upon graduating or exiting public school. A thorough transition plan will give team members some measure of confidence in the young deaf-blind person's future. Planning teams might continue their efforts beyond school by

agreeing that certain members will continue to meet periodically and provide further training in deaf-blindness to adult services providers.

Work situations and support agencies will have staff changes. The young adult who is deaf-blind will face new challenges and will always need to acquire more life skills. In most areas of the country there are state or regional deaf-blind projects that are allowed to provide direct services after an individual's exit from school until he or she reaches the age of 22 years. In addition, the Helen Keller National Center (HKNC) maintains a census of deaf-blind adults, and a regional representative may maintain contact with young adults in more remote settings. This deaf-blind census provides the federal government with important data used to establish funding levels.

Maintain Contacts with Young Adult and Family Adult service providers and employers might contract with specialists in deaf-blindness or arrange for technical assistance from HKNC. Families will be an important source of ongoing support and should be encouraged to work with any specialist who periodically becomes involved. Finally, the transition plan should incorporate strategies for the deaf-blind person and her or his family to stay connected with supportive resources. For some, the support may occur naturally in the community. For many, families and the individual will need to plan their own networks. These might include friendships with former workers and transition team members, parent and deaf-blind support groups, or other strategies uniquely designed for a particular individual.

Transition is a complex process with few short-term solutions or readily applied procedures that can be mandated within a service delivery system. Instead, team members are encouraged to become familiar with the needs of the young person who is deaf-blind and build a common understanding of mutually shared beliefs and goals. Such understanding takes effort and does not come easily (Varney, 1988). Like much that is valuable within strong communities, however, the shared commitment and sense of purpose brings benefits to team members as well as to the deaf-blind young person whom they serve. It is the team process that uses the best qualities of human community and becomes richly responsive to the ongoing changes in life.

REFERENCES

Barrett, S.S. (1992). Comprehensive community-based services for adults who are deaf-blind: Issues, trends, and services. *Journal of Visual Impairment and Blindness, 86*(9), 393–397.

Benson, H.A., & Turnbull, A.P. (1986). Approaching families from an individualized perspective. In R.H. Horner, L.H. Meyer, & H.D. Fredericks (Eds.), *Education of learners with severe handicaps: Exemplary service strategies* (pp. 127–157). Baltimore: Paul H. Brookes Publishing Co.

Brolin, D. (1989). *Life centered career education: A competency based approach* (3rd ed.). Reston, VA: The Council for Exceptional Children.

Brolin, D., & D'Alonzo, B. (1979). Critical issues in career education for handicapped students. *Exceptional Children, 45,* 246–253.

Browder, D.M. (1991). *Assessment of individuals with severe disabilities: An applied behavior approach to life skills assessment* (2nd ed.). Baltimore: Paul H. Brookes Publishing Co.

Clark, G.M., & Kolstoe, O.P. (1990). *Career development and transition education for adolescents with disabilities.* Boston: Allyn & Bacon.

Downing, J., & Eichinger, J. (1990). Instructional strategies for learners with dual sensory impairments in integrated settings. *Journal of The Association for Persons with Severe Handicaps, 15*(2), 98–105.

Dunst, C., Trivette, C., & Deal, A. (1988). *Enabling and empowering families: Principles and guidelines for practice.* Cambridge, MA: Brookline Books.

Edgerton, R.B. (1967). *The cloak of competence: Stigma in the lives of the retarded.* Berkeley: University of California.

Edgerton, R.B. (Ed.). (1984). *Lives in process: Mildly retarded adults in a large city.* Washington, DC: American Association on Mental Deficiency.

Everson, J.M., & Burwell, J. (1991). Transition to work: Addressing the challenges of deaf-blindness. *Journal of Vocational Rehabilitation, 1*(4), 39–45.

Everson, J.M., Rachal, P., & Michael, M.G. (1992). *Interagency collaboration for young adults with deaf-blindness: Toward a common transition goal.* Sands Point, NY: Technical Assistance Center, Helen Keller National Center.

Falvey, M.A. (1989). *Community-based curriculum: Instructional strategies for students with severe handicaps* (2nd ed.). Baltimore: Paul H. Brookes Publishing Co.

Ford, A., & Davern, L. (1989). Moving forward with school integration: Strategies for involving students with severe handicaps in the life of the school. In R. Gaylord-Ross (Ed.), *Integration strategies for students with handicaps* (pp. 11–31). Baltimore: Paul H. Brookes Publishing Co.

Gaylord-Ross, R., Lee, M., Johnson, S., Lynch, K., Rosenberg, B., & Goetz, L. (1991). Supported employment for youth who are deaf-blind and in transition. *Career Development of Exceptional Individuals, 14*(2), 77–89.

Giangreco, M.F., Cloninger, C.J., & Iverson, V.S. (1993). *Choosing options and accommodations for children (COACH): A guide to planning inclusive education.* Baltimore: Paul H. Brookes Publishing Co.

Halvorsen, A.T., Doering, K., Farron-Davis, F., Usilton, R., & Sailor, W. (1989). The role of parents and family members in planning severely disabled students' transitions from school. In G.H.S. Singer & L.K. Irvin (Eds.), *Support for caregiving families: Enabling positive adaptation to disability* (pp. 253–267). Baltimore: Paul H. Brookes Publishing Co.

Hamre-Nietupski, S., Nietupski, J., & Strathe, M. (1992). Functional life skills, academic skills, and friendship/social relationship development: What do parents of students with moderate/severe/profound disabilities value? *Journal of The Association for Persons with Severe Handicaps, 17*(1), 53–58.

Hardman, M., & McDonnell, J. (1987). Implementing federal transition initiatives for youths with severe handicaps: The Utah community-based transition project. *Exceptional Children, 53*(6), 493–498.

Individuals with Disabilities Education Act of 1990 (IDEA), PL 101-476. (October 30, 1990). Title 20, U.S.C. 1400 et seq. *U.S. Statutes at Large, 104,* 1103–1151.

Meyer, L., Peck, C.A., & Brown, L. (Eds.). (1991). *Critical issues in the lives of people with severe disabilities.* Baltimore: Paul H. Brookes Publishing Co.

Mount, B., & Zwernik, K. (1988). *It's never too early, It's never too late: A booklet about personal futures planning.* St. Paul, MN: Governor's Planning Council on Developmental Disabilities.

O'Brien, J. (1987). A guide to life-style planning. In B. Wilcox & G.T. Bellamy (Eds.), *A comprehensive guide to The Activities Catalog: An alternative curriculum for youth and adults with severe disabilities* (pp. 175–189). Baltimore: Paul H. Brookes Publishing Co.

Pruitt, W.A. (1983). *Work adjustment.* Menomonie, WI: Walt Pruitt Associates.

Review and outlook: Special ed's special costs. (1993, October 20). *The Wall Street Journal,* A-14.

Shapiro, J.P. (1993). *No pity: People with disabilities forging a new civil rights movement.* New York: Times Books.

Siegel, S., Robert, M., Greener, K., Meyer, G., Halloran, W., & Gaylord-Ross, R. (1993). *Career ladders for challenged youths in transition from school to adult life.* Austin, TX: PRO-ED.

Singer, G.H.S., & Irvin, L.K. (Eds.). (1989). *Support for caregiving families: Enabling positive adaptation to disability.* Baltimore: Paul H. Brookes Publishing Co.

Sowers, J., & Powers, L. (1991). *Vocational preparation and employment of students with physical and multiple disabilities.* Baltimore: Paul H. Brookes Publishing Co.

Thorin, E.J., & Irvin, L.K. (1992). Family stress associated with transition to adulthood of young people with severe disabilities. *Journal of The Association for Persons with Severe Handicaps, 17*(1), 31–39.

Varney, G. (1988). *Building productive teams: An action guide and resource book.* San Francisco: Jossey-Bass.

Warren, S.F., Horn, E.H., & Hill, E.W. (1987). Applications of advanced technologies. In L. Goetz, D. Guess, & K. Stremel-Campbell (Eds.), *Innovative program design for individuals with dual sensory impairments.* Baltimore: Paul H. Brookes Publishing Co.

Wehman, P. (1992). *Life beyond the classroom: Transition strategies for young people with disabilities.* Baltimore: Paul H. Brookes Publishing Co.

Wehman, P., Moon, M.S., Everson, J.M., Wood, W., & Barcus, J.M. (1988). *Transition from school to work: New challenges for youth with severe disabilities.* Baltimore: Paul H. Brookes Publishing Co.

Wolfensberger, W. (1972). *The principle of normalization in human services.* Toronto, Ontario, Canada: National Institute on Mental Retardation.

Chapter 18

Improving Educational Outcomes for Students with Deaf-Blindness

Rethinking Current Practices

Lyle T. Romer
and Norris G. Haring

Educational services to students with deaf-blindness have undergone significant and rapid changes since the 1970s. Applied behavior analysis was a major influence in changing our thinking about the capabilities of people with developmental disabilities. People who were formerly thought to have little or no ability to learn new skills were, in fact, capable of learning very complex chains of behavior. *The Journal of Applied Behavior Analysis*, from its inception in 1967, began publishing articles that demonstrated the learning capacities of people with developmental disabilities when instruction followed systematic use of behavioral principles, for example, the presentation of discriminative stimuli paired with differential consequences for correct and incorrect responses. As researchers, teachers, and family members, we began to realize as a result of those studies that we had seriously underestimated the learning potential of people with disabilities. This was a wrong that could now be righted by employing the new and powerful technology of applied behavior analysis.

As we became more sophisticated in our use of the new technology, we found that the skills people were acquiring were not being used to achieve functional outcomes. In the language of the new technology, the skills were under "restricted stimulus control." They were only being used in the artifical environments in which they were taught, and with the people who taught them. Students were not generalizing their new skills to the places where they would naturally use them. We learned that teaching skills in the environments in which they would ultimately be used (Brown, Nietupski, & Hamre-Nietupski, 1976) would enhance their usefulness to stu-

The activity that is the subject of this report was supported in whole or in part by the U.S. Department of Education (Award Nos. H086F9003 and H025F10007). However, the opinions expressed herein do not necessarily reflect the position or policy of the U.S. Department of Education, and no official endorsement by the Department should be inferred.

dents. We also learned there were other benefits that accrue when skills are taught in the context of the natural environments, where they had a functional impact on that environment (Stokes & Baer, 1977; Wilcox & Bellamy, 1987).

However, in our zeal to use the new technology in more natural environments we still missed something very important; we forgot to give the new technology a heart (Wolf, 1978). Without a heart, the new technology itself became the focus of our efforts. But what was the effect on the lives of people with deaf-blindness and other disabilities? This, at least at the beginning of the use of this technology, was not a question we asked often enough. After all, people were learning new skills; this should have been enough to live a more satisfying life. But later it was realized that we needed something more to go along with the new technology, lest we be accused, like the emperor, of wearing no clothes at all. What we needed was the wisdom to guide our use of the technology and a recognition that the new technology was not the only answer to all of the issues with which we were faced.

We needed to better understand the limits and the implications of our new technology. We still need to do this today. Certain questions are still relevant. Is technology valueless, or actually value neutral? Often we are told that the technology itself is not value laden, the values have to be supplied by the user of the technology. Technology can be used for good or for evil, it depends upon the user. But can the use of technology itself be a value judgment? Hughes (1992) rejects the argument that technology is value-free and asserts that indeed it is laden with values. Hughes refers to technology's tendency to reinforce controlling, systematizing, ordering behavior, even in the technology of self-instruction, self-monitoring, and problem solving.

Warnings about these issues of control were also issued by Skinner (1971), and more recently by Bannerman, Sheldon, Sherman, and Harchik (1990), who discuss the balance between the professional need to habilitate people and people's rights to have control over their own lives. Sidman (1989) also warns us about the negative implications of coercion in our society. Perhaps we were blinded to the controlling effect of technology. We wanted to right a wrong, and the technology was there for us to use. To some extent, we were seduced by the power of the new technology.

Fortunately, there were other voices telling us to look at other issues in the lives of the people we were trying to help. Foremost among those voices in the early 1970s was Wolf Wolfensberger. Wolfensberger (1972) talked about the principle of *normalization*, which originated in the Scandinavian countries. Normalization said that all people, regardless of their status or the labels affixed to them, deserved to live a life made up of the same patterns of activity as those enjoyed by people without disabilities. Normalization also said that people should not only have access to those normal patterns of living, but the means employed to make those patterns of living accessible also had to be normal in their appearance. Did our technology measure up to this standard? Not always, but it did help spur the development of the concept of *social validity* (Baer, Wolf, & Risley, 1987; Kazdin, 1977; Schwartz & Baer, 1991; Wolf, 1978), which in essence is focused on the same ideals as normalization. That is, are the outcomes of our efforts worthy, and are the methods used to achieve those outcomes acceptable?

What other kinds of efforts, besides our new technology, could we employ on behalf of people with deaf-blindness and other disabilities? First, we had to come to understand that acquiring new skills was not the only thing people with disabilities needed. Admittedly, we became very good at teaching new skills, but, unfortunately, we then turned everything into a skill-deficit problem (see chap. 6, this volume). We thought, if only we could teach enough skills, learners would be "fixed" and could then behave more like other people. We have been, and to a large extent still remain, heavily dependent on technology as the basis of most of our efforts to help people with disabilities. O'Brien (cited in Schwartz, 1992) likened the use of technology to a teeter-totter, one side of which is technology, with the other side way up in the air, as if a heavy adult were sitting on the technology side and a small child were sitting on the side up in the air. Perhaps, as suggested by Schwartz (1992), we need someone to jump onto the side of the child and bring some balance into our efforts to help people with disabilities. In this final chapter, the editors suggest that there are some critical aspects of our efforts to help that are missing or just developing, and that those elements are not related to technology. We also raise some questions about what inclusion of children with deaf-blindness means with regard to their quality of life.

THE MISSING ELEMENTS

Professionals in this field are all committed to helping people with deaf-blindness. But what are we helping them do? We believe that we are here to help them gain access to the same accomplishments that you and I associate with achieving quality in our lifestyles. Chapter 6 discusses in more detail those accomplishments. Essentially they have to do with something Sarason (1974) calls the "psychological sense of community." While we believe this concept of a psychological sense of community is still unfolding and defining itself, it currently means that people feel a psychological sense of commu-

nity when they are connected in a place to other people, and that those people respect each other because of the contributions they make to one another's well-being. We further believe that the psychological sense of community has elements of health, security, and safety in it as well. Well-being comes from believing that you are connected to people who care about you, who will provide help when you need it, and who will offer you companionship and support. Safety comes from knowing other people are concerned about your welfare and pay attention to the signs that say you are doing okay or notice that you are hurting and that something else needs to happen to bring you back to a state of health.

Asking What Kind of Help Is Needed

Lovett (1991) tells us the missing question in our efforts to manage the "inappropriate," "excessive," "socially unacceptable," "problem" behaviors that some people with disabilities engage in is: "How can I help?" We often proceed as if the answer to this question is somehow already known, as if through osmosis, by the person designing the program to be implemented. Perhaps this issue of behavior control really does come from the controlling value associated with technology by Hughes (1992) wherein special educators enforce behaviors by using behavioral technology. This type of control implies decisions made for, not with, other people.

Professionals working with individuals with deaf-blindness and other disabilities would do well to learn to ask about the kinds of help they offer, when help is needed and wanted, and what outcomes are being serviced. Fortunately, we are seeing the emergence of some ways in which professionals are learning to ask about how to help. The process of personal futures, or lifestyle planning, offers a method by which people with disabilities and their families can define a de-

sirable current and future lifestyle. But the
process will only work when professionals
recognize that this requires them to change
their roles. They are no longer the definers of
what help is needed, but rather the offerers
of help in service to the dreams and visions of
people with deaf-blindness and those who
care deeply for their future. Professionals
also need to accommodate to the fact that
their help is not always what is needed. In
fact, professional help often causes problems
for people with deaf-blindness. This realization can be devastating for professionals who
have seen themselves as helpers and then realize that their help is what frequently stands
between people and the outcomes that are
most important in their lives. This problem
occurs for two reasons, as follows.

First, when professionals provide all the
help, people are cut off from others in their
lives. No matter how good and how well-
intentioned the professionals are, they cannot meet all of a person's needs for a "psychological sense of community." People with
deaf-blindness need a variety of individuals
in their lives to achieve this psychological
sense of community. People have told us that
they need the strong emotional support of a
family; the companionship of friends, with
and without deaf-blindness; and connection
to the deaf-blind community and the perspective and empathy that is offered by that
community. Therefore, the first problem
when professionals do not ask how to help is
the tendency to see themselves as the answer
to all of the issues and problems that people
with deaf-blindness are facing.

Second, and this issue is directly tied to the
first, when professionals see themselves as
the sole answer, other individuals are less
likely to offer their assistance. Professionals,
in effect, operate as the conscience for the
rest of the community. As long as the professionals are taking care of things, no one else
feels compelled to get involved. When it is
apparent that help is needed and cannot be

provided by professionals, then the resources
of the community become available. We see
this scenario over and over in school communities. When students without disabilities
are told that they are the community and
that they can offer students with disabilities
their hospitality, they respond most gener-
ously. They sense that this is something real,
a chance to do something very meaningful
for another person (a feeling we could use a
great deal more of in education).

Asking for Help for Ourselves as Professionals

Once we figured out that asking how we can
help is the first crucial step, we needed to
then learn how to ask for help for ourselves.
We need help because we do not have all the
answers, nor do we have access to all the
things that people with deaf-blindness need
to achieve their goals. Schwartz (1992) describes how, at the turn of the century, children in orphanages were dying at alarming
rates. The orphanages tried to change their
procedures, their staffing patterns, all to no
avail. Why? Because the orphanages did not
have access to what the children needed
most—love. They could not create love.
Love already existed in great abundance, and
the orphanages needed to find ways for
those children to obtain the love that already
existed out there, somewhere else.

Our job, as professional educators, is to listen to people's needs for help, and then to act
as bridges to what they need. Sometimes this
means teaching a person with deaf-blindness
a new skill, communication perhaps. But it
might also entail, and this is what brings
meaning to our teaching, helping people
find someone to talk with about the things
that they both find important. Frequently
our job is facilitating connections with other
caring people who will offer opportunities
for people with deaf-blindness to achieve a
psychological sense of community.

Gretz (1992) and Hildebrand (1992) describe the problems they encountered when

they first realized that if they were truly going to respond to people's requests for help, they needed to ask others to become involved. They both admit this was difficult. They did not really know how to ask. They were also afraid that the people they asked would refuse. Perhaps one of the root causes of their fear was their training as professionals in just the opposite direction. They were taught that they were the experts and, therefore, were the people who should have the answers. Teachers are still predominantly trained in this mode. You are the teacher, here is your classroom, you're on your own, do your job. To ask others for help is to admit we are fallible. However, permit us to tell you right now that you are. We are not rendered perfect by our training. We, and more importantly, our students, will need other people to help students achieve their lifestyle outcomes. Realizing that we have to ask for the assistance of others is crucial to being able to help our students.

Collaborative Efforts

Over the past 3 years, the editors witnessed over 50 people form themselves into 12 collaborative teams to cooperatively plan for and carry out activities related to achieving worthy outcomes in the education of students with deaf-blindness (Romer, Haring, Graham, Mace, & Rado, 1992). We learned that none of these people ever wanted to work outside of a team again. We saw two groups benefit from the collaborative teams' efforts: 1) the students with deaf-blindness who received improved educational services and 2) the team members who felt empowered to make the decisions needed to offer these students meaningful educational opportunities.

We are not talking here about collaborative teams made up only of professionals. We are referring to teams that take in everyone who cares about and has something to offer to the education of the student with deaf-

blindness. Teams included the student, his or her family members (in many cases siblings and grandparents, not only parents), the student's friends and classmates from their school and neighborhood, members of the community (family friends, pastors, bus drivers) and, finally, professional educators and service providers. (See chap. 8 for a discussion of the issues related to collaborative teaming.) Suffice it for us to say here that if we truly see the need for our students to form associations with other students, with and without disabilities, then we must be able to form those associations ourselves among all of the people who can offer the caring for our students that we cannot create on our own.

Students with deaf-blindness are certainly not the only ones who need and benefit from another kind of collaborative team, that is, the friendship networks that were discussed in Chapter 11. True, those networks are almost always initially formed to offer opportunities for students without disabilities to learn the skills that allow them to engage in activities with students with deaf-blindness. However, we have also seen those networks become important sources of social support for the students without disabilities involved. Those students, without any instruction to do so, begin to find ways to offer each other support when they sense one of their members needs it. Not only can we not create this kind of caring, we also cannot, nor would we want to, limit it. If we want to find this kind of caring and acceptance for students with deaf-blindness then we better demonstrate our own caring for one another by collaborating with everyone who can offer something to our students.

INCLUSION OF STUDENTS WITH DEAF-BLINDNESS

Why did we decide to put this book together? Obviously we thought it was needed. A new book on this topic has not been published for several years. The teaching and support skills discussed in this book are not always familiar to teachers not specifically prepared to teach students with deaf-blindness. But even more importantly, we felt that there are enough notable differences in talking about inclusion for students with deaf-blindness to warrant a separate book, differences that are not always addressed, or even recognized, in books about inclusion for students with other severe disabilities. There always seems to be an implied, sometimes even explicit, feeling that whatever is good for and works with students with severe disabilities is also good for and will work with students with deaf-blindness. Over the past five years, we have come to realize that there are issues unique to children and youth with deaf-blindness that require careful thought on the part of professionals about how inclusion works for these students.

Recent developments in special education have brought about increased levels of commitment to the value of inclusion in the education of students with severe disabilities (Giangreco & Putnam, 1991; Stainback & Stainback, 1990; Villa, Thousand, Stainback, & Stainback, 1992). However, we are also beginning to realize that inclusion itself is only a contextual variable; there must be outcomes achieved that "enable all students to actively participate in their communities" (Ferguson, Meyer, Jeanchild, Juniper, & Zingo, 1992, p. 226). Merely being present with peers without disabilities in general education settings is not sufficient to bring about those outcomes (Billingsley, 1993; Romer & Haring, 1993). Plans to utilize the characteristics of inclusive environments (Stainback, Stainback, & Moravec, 1992) and employ effective and acceptable instructional methods (Billingsley & Kelly, 1994; Udavari-Solner, 1992) must also be part of any effort to support the inclusion of students with deaf-blindness.

We are becoming increasingly concerned with the fixation on inclusion itself. While we do believe inclusion of students with deaf-blindness with their peers without disabilities is good and valuable, we do not believe that inclusion in and of itself meets the need for a psychological sense of community for those students. We have seen too many students with deaf-blindness included with their peers for many hours a day, only to find that no meaningful relationships were developed with those peers, that no psychological sense of community was felt. We believe this is because, like behavioral technology, we have confused a process, or a behavior, with an outcome. Inclusion is a necessary, but by itself, insufficient element in the quest for all the accomplishments that make up a psychological sense of community. We are not retreating one inch from where we are, and where others have taken us, in our commitment to inclusion. However, we are afraid that if we continue to only talk about inclusion, we will be willing to judge it a success when we have only achieved inclusion, but left unfulfilled the promise of relationships and the support they bring to our students; a sense of self-determination in their lives; access to the status and dignity that comes from making contributions to other people; and increased competency in real, functional activities.

Focus must be placed on the valued outcomes in lifestyle that can only be achieved once students with deaf-blindness are included. True, we can only achieve those outcomes for our students if they spend time in all of the areas of our schools and communities and are thus able to meet significant numbers of people. But, have we also passed along an implied message that those relationships are only important when they are with people who do not have disabilities?

How much time do we spend providing support for two people with disabilities to form, develop, and maintain a relationship?

Do we really believe that those relationships somehow magically form without our support? The editors do not think so. In fact, with students with deaf-blindness, significant forces seem to be marshaled against such friendships forming. Most students with deaf-blindness go to school in settings where they encounter no other people who are deaf-blind or deaf, people whose culture has formed around a language substantially different from that of the dominant sighted-hearing world.

We believe that students with deaf-blindness should have opportunities to meet their needs for long-term, stable social relationships from at least three communities. First, they need the strong emotional and psychological support offered by a loving family. This is, sadly, not always available for all of our students with deaf-blindness. When it is available, we see no reason to break apart those relationships so that students, especially very young ones, can be removed to attend schools far distant from that family.

Second, we believe students with deaf-blindness should have opportunities to develop relationships with their peers without disabilities. This can only happen when they are in close proximity to those peers. But, it also requires the conscious support of others who are not afraid to ask how to help and to ask for the help of those peers.

Finally, we also believe that students with deaf-blindness should have opportunities to form relationships with other people with disabilities, especially other people with deaf-blindness. We feel strongly that this is a significant contribution to those students' psychological sense of community. No matter how many times you put on a blindfold and put ear plugs in your ears, you will not know what it is like to relate to the world through reduced, or absent, distance senses. You know those impairments to your senses will come off, you know what it is to see and to hear. Students with deaf-blindness should be able to enter into a community of other deaf-blind people to share in that sense of cultural identity with their deaf-blind peers and adults.

How does the latter happen without placing students with deaf-blindness in the same schools, which will often mean the removal of the support of their families as well as a reduction in opportunities to make friends with sighted-hearing children? The editors are fortunate to live in Seattle, a city with a rich and vibrant community of people with deaf-blindness. That community is a tremendous source of positive role models, social support, and affirmation to students with deaf-blindness. We are committed to supporting the access of students we work with in establishing ties to that community. This includes: 1) contacts among families of deaf-blind students and deaf-blind adults, 2) student participation in social events that occur among members of the deaf-blind community, 3) participation at a deaf-blind summer camp, and 4) involvement of deaf-blind community members in planning educational programs for students with deaf-blindness in conjunction with the student and his or her family members. For students outside of the Seattle area, we are committed to making every effort to either locate a deaf-blind community where they are or to find the resources to bring them into contact with the community in Seattle. This is something we are trying, and we do not yet know exactly how our goals can be accomplished. So we spend a lot of time asking the students, their families and friends, and the members of the deaf-blind community how to go about it. We are learning and benefiting from the contributions of the members of the deaf-blind community.

CLOSING REMARKS

Our technology is well developed. We can always learn more about stimulus control, competing behaviors, and the interrelationship of problem behaviors, communication, and other issues related to skill acquisition and maintenance. However, we truly feel that the most significant advances in our ability to help students with deaf-blindness lies not in refinements in our technology, but rather in increases in our ability to better understand what people want. We believe that what they want often means asking nonprofessional people to develop a relationship with our students and to support their entry into association with others. We think this will happen when we learn to listen to our students, their families, and the deaf-blind communities around the country; when we realize that we have limits in our ability to help our students; and when we are willing to ask for help from our communities. We believe that everything we need to do—listening, admitting our fallibility, and asking for the involvement of others—are the acts of people who are truly committed to creating caring communities. To bring about those changes in how we provide educational services to students with deaf-blindness, we have a responsibility, as educators, to demonstrate *every day* the ideals of tolerance, humility, and respect for others. We would do well to remember the words of author Wendell Berry, himself an eloquent spokesperson on the value of community, as spoken through the words of one of his fictional characters, Burley Coulter: "The way we are, we are members of each other. All of us. Everything. The difference ain't in who is a member and who is not, but in who knows it and who don't" (Berry, 1985, p. 136).

REFERENCES

Baer, D.M., Wolf, M.M., & Risley, T.R. (1987). Some still current dimensions of applied behavior analysis. *Journal of Applied Behavior Analysis, 20,* 313–327.

Bannerman, D.J., Sheldon, J.B., Sherman, J.A., & Harchik, A.E. (1990). Balancing the right to habilitation with the right to personal liberties: The rights of people with developmental disabilities to eat too many doughnuts and take a nap. *Journal of Applied Behavior Analysis, 23,* 79–89.

Berry, W. (1985). *The wild birds.* San Francisco: North Point Press.

Billingsley, F.F. (1993). Reader response: In my dreams. A response to some current trends in education. *Journal of The Association for Persons with Severe Handicaps, 18,* 61–63.

Billingsley, F.F., & Kelly, B. (1994). Acceptable instructional practices for students with severe disabilities in general education settings. *Journal of The Association for Persons with Severe Handicaps, 19,* 75–83.

Brown, L., Nietupski, J., & Hamre-Nietupski, S. (1976). *The criterion of ultimate functioning and public school services for severely handicapped students.* Madison: University of Wisconsin and Madison Public Schools.

Ferguson, D., Meyer, G., Jeanchild, L., Juniper, L., & Zingo, J. (1992). Figuring out what to do with the grownups: How teachers make inclusion work for students with severe disabilities. *Journal of The Association for Persons with Severe Handicaps, 17,* 218–226.

Giangreco, M.F., & Putnam, J.W. (1991). Supporting the education of persons with severe disabilities: Emerging findings, practices, and questions. In L.H. Meyer, C.A. Peck, & L. Brown (Eds.), *Critical issues in the lives of people with severe disabilities* (pp. 245–270). Baltimore: Paul H. Brookes Publishing Co.

Gretz, S. (1992). Citizen participation: Connecting people to associational life. In D.B. Schwartz (Ed.), *Crossing the river* (pp. 11–30). Cambridge, MA: Brookline Books.

Hildebrand, A.J. (1992). Citizen advocacy: Asking for citizens advocates in Beaver country. In D.B. Schwartz (Ed.), *Crossing the river* (pp. 31–44). Cambridge, MA: Brookline Books.

Hughes, C. (1992). Teaching self-instruction utilizing multiple examples to produce generalized problem solving among individuals with severe mental retardation. *American Journal on Mental Retardation, 97,* 302–314.

Kazdin, A.E. (1977). Assessing the clinical or applied importance of behavior change through social validation. *Behavior Modification, 1,* 427–452.

Lovett, H. (1991). Empowerment and choices. In L.H. Meyer, C.A. Peck, & L. Brown (Eds.), *Critical issues in the lives of people with severe disabilities* (pp. 625–626). Baltimore: Paul H. Brookes Publishing Co.

Romer, L.T., & Haring, N.G. (1993). The social participation of students with deaf-blindness in educational settings. *Education and Training in Mental Retardation and Developmental Disabilities, 29,* 134–144.

Romer, L.T., Haring, N.G., Graham, S., Mace, C., & Rado, E. (1993). *Innovations project final report.* (Grant No. H086F90003). Washington, DC: U.S. Department of Education.

Sarason, S.B. (1974). *The psychological sense of community: Prospects for a community psychology.* San Francisco: Jossey-Bass.

Schwartz, D.B. (1992). *Crossing the river.* Cambridge, MA: Brookline Books.

Schwartz, I.S., & Baer, D.M. (1991). Social validity assessments: Is current practice state of the art? *Journal of Applied Behavior Analysis, 24,* 189–204.

Sidman, M. (1989). *Coercion and its fallout.* Boston: Authors Cooperative.

Skinner, B.F. (1971). *Beyond freedom and dignity.* New York: Alfred A. Knopf.

Stainback, W., & Stainback, S. (Eds.). (1990). *Support networks for inclusive schooling: Interdependent integrated education.* Baltimore: Paul H. Brookes Publishing Co.

Stainback, W., Stainback, S., & Moravec, J. (1992). Using curriculum to build inclusive schools. In S. Stainback & W. Stainback (Eds.), *Curriculum considerations in inclusive classrooms: Facilitating learning for all students* (pp. 65–84). Baltimore: Paul H. Brookes Publishing Co.

Stokes, T.F., & Baer, D.M. (1977). An implicit technology of generalization. *Journal of Applied Behavior Analysis, 10,* 349–367.

Udavari-Solner, A. (1992, November). *Curricular adaptions: Practical tools to influence teaching practices in general education classrooms.* Paper presented at the Annual Meeting of the Association for Persons with Severe Handicaps, San Francisco.

Villa, R.A., Thousand, J.S., Stainback, W., & Stainback, S. (Eds.). (1992). *Restructuring for caring and effective education: An administrative guide to creating heterogeneous schools.* Baltimore: Paul H. Brookes Publishing Co.

Wilcox, B., & Bellamy, G.T. (1987). *Design of high school programs for severely handicapped students.* Baltimore: Paul H. Brookes Publishing Co.

Wolf, M.M. (1978). Social validity: The case for subjective measurement, or how applied behavior analysis is finding its heart. *Journal of Applied Behavior Analysis, 11,* 203–214.

Wolfensberger, W. (1972). *Normalization.* Toronto, Ontario, Canada: National Institute on Mental Retardation.

Index

Page numbers followed by "f" indicate figures; numbers followed by "t" indicate tables.